THE AMERICANS
AT NORMANDY

By John C. McManus

The Americans at D-Day:
The American Experience at the Normandy Invasion

The Americans at Normandy:
The Summer of 1944—The American War
from the Normandy Beaches to Falaise

The Deadly Brotherhood:
The American Combat Soldier in World War II

Deadly Sky:
The American Combat Airman in World War II

JOHN C. McMANUS

THE AMERICANS AT NORMANDY

THE SUMMER OF 1944—THE AMERICAN WAR FROM THE
NORMANDY BEACHES TO FALAISE

A TOM DOHERTY ASSOCIATES BOOK
NEW YORK

THE AMERICANS AT NORMANDY: THE SUMMER OF 1944—THE AMERICAN WAR
FROM THE NORMANDY BEACHES TO FALAISE

This book is printed on acid-free paper.

All photographs are courtesy of the National Archives and Records Administration unless otherwise noted.

A Forge Book
Published by Tom Doherty Associates, LLC
175 Fifth Avenue
New York, NY 10010

www.tor.com

Forge® is a registered trademark of Tom Doherty Associates, LLC.

Library of Congress Cataloging-in-Publication Data

McManus, John C., 1965-
    The Americans at Normandy : the summer of 1944—the American war from the Normandy
beaches to Falaise / John C. McManus.—1st ed.
        p. cm.
    "A Tom Doherty Associates book."
    Includes bibliographical references (p. 471) and index (p. 481).
    ISBN 0-765-31199-2 (alk. paper)
    EAN 978-0765-31199-3
    1. World War, 1939-1945—Campaigns—France. 2. World War, 1939-1945—Campaigns—
France—Normandy. 3. United States. Army—History—World War, 1939-1945. 4. World War,
1939-1945—United States. I. Title.

D761.M328 2004
940.54'2142—dc22

                                                                                2004052823

First Edition: October 2004

Printed in the United States of America

0 9 8 7 6 5 4 3 2 1

To those 9,387 Americans
who lie under crosses and Stars of David at St-Laurent . . .
and to their luckier comrades who made it home

CONTENTS

Part III: AUGUST

LIST OF MAPS

ACKNOWLEDGMENTS

This book, like its antecedent, *The Americans at D-Day*, would not have happened without the efforts of many good people, most of whom I thanked in the acknowledgments to that volume, but they deserve mention again. Doug Brinkley and his staff at the Eisenhower Center in New Orleans greatly expedited my use of their remarkable collection of World War II oral histories. This archive is among the very best sources of firsthand accounts from American veterans of that war. At the University of Illinois archives, Ellen Swain helped me navigate through an extensive collection of documentary material from the 3rd Armored Division. Ronald Marcello and Christopher Koontz at the University of North Texas were kind enough to send me transcripts of several interviews with Normandy veterans. Jay Graybeal at the United States Army Military History Institute helped find many good photographs that added much to this book.

The University of Missouri–Rolla interlibrary loan department ordered hundreds of books and articles for me. Scott Peterson and several other members of the library staff often went out of their way to find rare material. Without their efforts, this book would not have been possible.

The History Department at UMR provided me with financial support for my travels. I would like to thank, once again, my colleagues in the department for their advice, support, and friendship. Wayne Bledsoe, Jack Ridley, Tseggai Isaac, Lance Williams, Pat Huber, Jeff Schramm, Michael Meagher, Harry Eisenman, Diana Ahmad, and Larry Gragg all contributed perspectives on a range of issues. Special thanks go to my mentor, Russ Buhite, for his support and guidance. Larry and Russ read and commented on various portions of the manuscript, and I appreciate their time and expertise. Thanks also to Tom Fleming for being a daily inspiration.

My editors at Forge deserve my gratitude for their professionalism and good cheer. Before moving on to the Czech Republic, Brian Callaghan handled many of the onerous tasks of manuscript format, copying, and pre-production. Eric Raab came aboard in the middle of the project and promptly did a fantastic job at all of the above. Thanks for everything, Eric. Bob Gleason, executive editor at Forge, first came up with the idea of splitting my Normandy research into two volumes, and I believe this was fortunate. It reflects Bob's sage wisdom and his knowledge of the publishing world and history in general. Much appreciation goes to Ted Chichak, my literary agent for his counsel, advice, and sapience. Thanks, Ted. The excellent work of fellow Normandy authors such as Mark Bando, Stephen Ambrose, John Keegan, Max Hastings, Aaron Elson, George Koskimaki, Joseph Balkoski, Martin Blumenson, Mark Reardon, Glover Johns, James Carafano, Carlo D'Este, Robin Neillands, and a slew of others has added much to this book.

Friends and family have, knowingly or not, made special contributions. Ed Laughlin, a close friend who is a veteran of the 82nd Airborne Division, provided me with much good information on his division's experiences in Normandy. Many thanks to Mark Williams, Sean Roarty, Bob Kaemmerlen, Joe Carcagno, John Fowler, Mike Chopp, John Villier, Steve Kutheis, Ron Kurtz, and Dave Cohen—all good friends and good people.

My family deserves enormous appreciation. My in-laws, Ruth and Nelson Woody, Nancy and Charlie Swartwout, Doug, David, Angee, Tonya, and the kids are all very special people. My brother, Mike, is a fellow military history enthusiast (and a pretty darned good hockey linemate) who is often willing to tolerate my long discourses on my research. With such influences, it's almost inevitable that his son, little Mikey, will grow up to study military history. My sister, Nancy, her husband, John, and my nieces, Kelly and Erin, are awesome in every way. Michael and Mary Jane McManus, my parents, to whom I dedicated the preceding volume, merit all the appreciation I can possibly give them. They have done more for me than I can ever repay. As always, my wife, Nancy, deserves the most thanks. She found most of the photos in this book and is the embodiment of a loving wife and partner. Without her, I'd be nowhere. As with *The Americans at D-Day*, this book is hers as much as it is mine, although any errors are my sole responsibility.

My final word of appreciation goes to the Allied veterans of the Battle of Normandy. Long ago, in your youth, you laid your lives on the line, destroyed a monstrous tyranny, and bequeathed to successive generations the great gift of freedom. It is a gift we must still appreciate and fight for in the twenty-first century.

JOHN C. MCMANUS
St. Louis, Missouri
April 21, 2004

PREFACE

In the summer of 1944, the United States became a superpower and, in so doing, assumed leadership of the Allied war effort. On a diverse set of battlefields that spanned the globe—places as distant from one another as the Mariana Island chain, Italy, and France—that leadership came to fruition, but nowhere more significantly than at Normandy. The western Allied invasion of Normandy had not, as German Field Marshal Erwin Rommel hoped, been repulsed at the water's edge. But the success of the invasion in no way secured an eventual triumph for the Allies. Nonetheless, historians, in studying the Battle of Normandy, have largely concentrated on the invasion, as if merely getting ashore on D-Day somehow guaranteed victory for the Allies. In so doing, many historians have, at least implicitly, accepted Rommel's thesis that the battle would be decided on the day of the invasion. Rommel felt that Germany's only hope was to repel the Allies at the water's edge. If the Germans failed to do so, then the overwhelming might of Allied logistical superiority would inevitably defeat them. From this assumption came the viewpoint, espoused by some historians, that the U.S. Army fought badly at Normandy. In their view, American soldiers were outmatched in valor and expertise by the Germans, and the Yanks only won because of the sheer weight of numbers or matériel.[1]

These assertions are incorrect. Not only was Rommel wrong in his strategy to crush the invasion at the water's edge (his elaborate defenses held off the Allies for, at best, half a day), but the contention that American soldiers did not fight well is deeply flawed. The reality, as this book will show, was quite different. The United States Army came of age at Normandy. It became a tough, battle-hardened, thinking army whose soldiers routinely fought with great bravery. This does not mean that American leaders and soldiers did not make mistakes. Of course they did, but they generally learned from them.[2]

In the first volume of this series, I covered the American contribution to Operation Overlord. This book picks up where that one left off. Thus, *The Americans at Normandy* deals with the weeks after June 6, 1944, when the future of Europe was decided. The essence of compelling history is, I believe, the story of individuals who are shaped, defined, and affected by the events of their times. At Normandy, in the summer of 1944, at a key moment in the world's history, individual Americans, from the lowliest private to the grandest general, sacrificed and helped produce victory. This book will reflect their perspective. More than anything, I hope to convey, through new viewpoints, the American experience in, and the vital American contribution to, the outcome of one of the world's most important battles. In the end, only the reader can decide if I have succeeded.

In his brilliant book *D-Day*, the late Stephen Ambrose, in discussing the Normandy invasion, made the salient point that without the steady courage of thousands of Allied soldiers, sailors, and airmen "the most thoroughly planned offensive in military history, an offensive supported by incredible amounts of naval firepower, bombs, and rockets, would fail."[3] I would submit that the same argument applies to the Battle of Normandy as a whole. That is the essential focus of *The Americans at Normandy*.

PART I

JUNE

CHAPTER ONE

INLAND FROM OMAHA: THE WEEK AFTER D-DAY

As the sun slipped under the western horizon on the evening of June 6, Private First Class Karl Sulkis was wet, tired, and scared. He was also a member of the 1st Engineer Combat Battalion. The young engineer shivered in a foxhole that he had dug near one of the cliffs overlooking Easy Red beach. It had been a long day and Sulkis was exhausted, but he wondered, with considerable apprehension, what lay ahead. "We had only what we could carry, M-1, bazookas, grenades and machine guns. We were all soaked and pretty well done in."

Sulkis peered over the edge of his foxhole and, for a time, watched the silhouettes of the ships that dotted the waters just offshore. Overhead, tracers were whizzing here and there as naval gunners shot at enemy planes—real or imagined. He turned around and looked inland, all the while wondering when the Germans would counterattack the beachhead. When would Sulkis hear the dreaded sound of German tank engines and artillery? How could Sulkis and several thousand other Americans, disorganized and decimated by the assault on Omaha beach, possibly hold off a determined enemy attack? All night long, the young private remained awake, brooding, worrying, expecting the imminent arrival of strong German forces. Much to his relief, the counterattack never happened, but Sulkis believed that if it had, "we'd have been thrown back into the sea just before dawn."[1]

Actually, Sulkis need not have worried about that. The Germans were just as confused and disorganized as the Americans on that first night. The British had succeeded in driving a continuous five-mile wedge inland from their landing beaches at Gold, Juno, and Sword. German soldiers on the Cotentin Peninsula were operating in scattered pockets in reaction to the U.S.

paratroopers who had dropped (seemingly everywhere) in their midst. Even here at Omaha, the German beach defenses had not held.

As D-Day came to an end, the situation was fluid. There was no established front line. Instead there were clusters of Americans and Germans—dug in, patrolling, skirmishing, existing—in close proximity to one another all along the coastline. Some German soldiers were still bravely manning bypassed pillboxes or bunkers on the beach. German artillery could easily rake the entire beach. But, the Americans had carved out a 2,000-yard lodgment, with the deepest penetration being at the outskirts of Colleville. American troops held Vierville-sur-Mer but not St-Laurent, where neither side held sway. The coastal road behind the landing beaches was mostly under U.S. control. In sum, the soldiers of the German 352nd Infantry Division were in no position to launch any kind of coherent counterattack against the bloodied American force at Omaha.

Even if the Germans had been in a position to do so, they probably would not have succeeded in pushing the Americans into the sea. One of the enduring myths about the Normandy invasion is the notion that Hitler's sleeping habits, combined with a dysfunctional command setup, cost the Germans victory at Normandy. Hitler was a night owl. He routinely stayed up all night (quite often spending that time regaling his cronies with insufferably boring monologues) and slept until noon. He controlled the armored reserves in France, the most powerful weapon the Germans had to repel the Allied invasion.

On D-Day, Hitler characteristically slept late, no one dared wake him, and the result was that the panzer reserves remained frozen in place for most of the day. Powerful divisions like Panzer Lehr, 12th SS (Hitler Youth) Panzer, and 21st Panzer did not begin to move toward the beaches until late in the day. By that time, cloud cover that might have shielded them from Allied planes had lifted, forcing the tanks to proceed slowly and carefully. They made little headway and had little impact on that first day's fighting.

Certainly this did the German cause no good, but was it decisive? Could these German armored divisions have foiled the whole invasion? Certainly not. The belief that they could stems from Rommel's "Longest Day" supposition (Rommel himself was conspicuously absent on the very day he thought would be decisive—he was home celebrating his wife's birthday). The armored divisions, especially the 21st Panzer at Caen, were nearest to the British beaches. That proximity, combined with favorable terrain, would have allowed them to inflict plenty of damage on the British. That much is true. But even if they could have dodged Allied planes successfully enough to counterattack the Americans at Omaha, they would have achieved little success. The very bocage (hedgerow) terrain that would soon prove such a nuisance to maneuverable American tanks would have been a serious impediment to the heavier, more thickly armored, less mechanically reliable German tanks. Even had they made it through the maze of hedgerows leading to Omaha beach, the German tanks would have had no luck negotiating the craggy bluffs that over-looked Omaha (indeed, they would have gravitated toward the beach exits, which were still heavily mined, as the Americans were finding out).

The trump card, though, was Allied naval power. On three previous occa-sions in this war—Gela, Salerno, and Anzio—German tanks had counterat-tacked Allied amphibious forces only to be blasted by Allied naval gunfire. Why would Normandy have been any different, regardless of whether the ar-mored counterattack came in the American or British sector? The inescapable conclusion is that it would not have been different. German tanks roaming the invasion beaches would have made ideal targets for intrepid destroyers like the USS *Frankford*, the USS *Carmick*, or dozens of other powerful war-ships. Allied fighter-bombers would also have contributed to the destruction of any exposed German tank. Granted, all of this is supposition, but it is sup-position based on what happened in similar situations at other times in the war, along with a careful consideration of what an armored attack at Omaha would have entailed.[2]

In the end Rommel was wrong and Rundstedt was right. The Germans would have had a better chance of success if they had tried to defeat the inva-sion inland rather than at the waterfront. Even at Omaha, Rommel's elaborate beach defenses did not succeed in holding off the Allies for any significant amount of time. His was a wrongheaded strategy. Given Germany's strategic situation in 1943–1944, there was no way Rommel could have strongly forti-fied the entire coast of northern France in such a way that his defenses could have withstood the crushing weight of Allied firepower (especially naval fire-power). If an immortal Rommel were alive to defend his strategy, he might concede that point but argue that his panzer reserves were improperly used during the decisive hours of the campaign. Maybe so, but that still returns us to the issue of whether those tanks could have survived under the muzzles of Allied naval guns. Experience had already proven that they could not.

In hindsight, the Germans probably should have concentrated their im-pressive military engineering on enhancing the already formidable bocage terrain, in places that were out of the range of naval guns. Perhaps they should have built an extensive series of bunkers, pillboxes, "murder holes," observation posts, and the like into the hedgerows that were such an inher-ent asset to the defenders. One shudders at how difficult this kind of defen-sive line would have been to crack, especially if backed up by a powerful, mobile panzer reserve.

At Peleliu and Okinawa, the Japanese employed this "defend inland" strategy with great effect, but they eventually lost for three reasons: being cut off from their supply bases; lack of armored or mobile forces to go on the

Lagune

Bayeux

Port-en-Bessin

ENEMY RETIRING THIS AREA

St-Honorine

Colleville

St-Laurent

Formigny

Trévières

offensive; and sheer American valor. At Normandy, the Germans would have plenty of resupply capacity and plenty of armor. Quite possibly, only Allied valor would have stood between them and victory. Alas, we shall never know for certain.

At sunrise on June 7, the Americans at Omaha were preoccupied with one goal—drive inland. The day before, they had won the equivalent of a foot in the door. Now it was time to force that door open and enter the dwelling. The farther inland they could drive, the more ground they gained, the sooner the beach would be out of range of German artillery. The Americans badly needed space to maneuver tanks, trucks, half-tracks, artillery pieces, crates of supplies, and soldiers. In the long run, a constricted battlefield favored the Germans, since they were logistically inferior and possessed less mobility and manpower.

On the eastern flank, the 1st Division consolidated its hold on St-Laurent and Colleville. The 16th Regiment, wounded badly from the first-wave assault the day before, concentrated mostly on clearing out the remaining beach defenders and pushing east to Port-en-Bessin for a sturdy linkup with the British. The division's other two regiments, the 18th and the 26th, led the main drive south, along a three-mile front, against uneven resistance. In some areas the Germans stood and fought; in others they were in disarray. Operating in battalion-sized units, sometimes with vehicles, sometimes without, the troops of the Big Red One cautiously prodded forward.

At the extreme eastern edge of the entire beachhead, the men of Warren Coffman's C Company, 26th Infantry, crossed the coastal road that led out of Colleville. The son of a West Virginia coal town barber, Coffman had joined this unit in the spring as a replacement, and now he was a radioman. He lugged his radio on his back and a carbine in his hands and tried to keep plenty of space between himself and the next soldier. Coffman's entire company crossed the road on a run. "We went through a break in a hedgerow and started across a field parallel to the road. When we were about halfway across the field, an enemy machine gun opened up on us." The Americans dived for cover and started crawling through the field.

Luckily, the German gunner was firing high. Coffman saw his tracers angrily stabbing the air several feet above. At the end of the field, Coffman's platoon sergeant said, "I'll take care of that." He took two men with him. They worked their way around the machine gun "and tossed in a couple of grenades. That was the end of that machine gun crew. The field was covered with wires strung about head high to prevent gliders from landing."

All day they moved in this manner, in a southeasterly direction, encountering stray machine gunners or snipers. At dusk, as they dug in, something unsettling happened. Several Americans were resting in a ditch, immediately opposite a hedgerow (much of Normandy was honeycombed with sunken farm lanes that had ditches on the sides, bordered by hedgerows, creating a mazelike effect). All at once, a German stepped through an opening in a hedgerow and shot them up with his burp gun. The bullets tore into them, killing three and wounding several others. Before anyone had a chance to re-act, the German left.

Coffman was deeply disturbed by this incident—who knew when an-other German might pop up and kill him?—so he tried to dig the deepest foxhole possible. As he did so, "a bullet from my rear hit the base of the tree where I had been leaning just a few seconds before. I saw a German soldier coming over the hedgerow behind us. As I fired, it seemed as if the whole platoon saw him and fired about the same time. He was killed immediately. That's when I got really scared."

Coffman was so frightened that the next day he could not bring himself to leave his hole. His unit moved on without him, and sitting in the hole alone with only a green line of spooky-looking hedgerows around him, he quickly realized the error of his ways. "I got up my courage, got out of the hole and ran down the road where I found my platoon. We continued down the road. We had been told to bypass all resistance."

They moved steadily until the captain spotted a German artillery posi-tion. "A forward observer from the U.S. Navy showed up with a radioman to provide us with artillery support. The Captain showed him on the map where he wanted the fire placed. The Navy radio was too large to take any farther forward." To solve this problem, Coffman and the naval observer crawled forward through tall grass for a better look. They called in fire on the German position. "That big shell sounded like a freight train going by." Coffman did not think they hit the enemy gun, but his unit did succeed in getting around it. By June 8, the 1st Battalion had captured Etreham against little resistance. They even took three truckloads of German soldiers pris-oner. Exhausted from the events of the last several days, Coffman found a chicken coop and slept for twenty-four hours.[3]

A few hundred yards to the west, another battalion from the 26th was also moving quickly. The 3rd Battalion of the 26th had been held up north of Formigny (a town located about half a mile inland from St-Laurent) for a day or so. German troops holed up in the stone buildings of tiny Formigny. In many buildings they set up machine-gun positions that crisscrossed any north-ern approach to the town. The Americans made liberal use of air strikes and tanks before launching an uncoordinated attack on either end of the town. This liberated Formigny and allowed the 3rd Battalion of the 26th to side-step around the town and head east, straight down N-13, the main highway that led to Bayeux. They proceeded at a deliberate, steady pace for much of the afternoon on June 8. In the evening they reached the outskirts of Tour-en-Bessin, a village located about two miles west of Bayeux.

The day before, the Germans had been in Tour-en-Bessin. American reconnaissance aircraft detected their presence, and at 0900 on June 8 fighter-bombers blasted the place. Armored reconnaissance vehicles infiltrated the town shortly after the air strike and reported it "empty and flat," but as of 2040 on June 8 no sizable American force had moved into Tour-en-Bessin.

That soon changed when, at twilight, the 26th Regiment's 3rd Battalion, accompanied by six tanks from C Company, 745th Tank Battalion, plunged into the ravaged town. The tanks led the way, with the infantrymen strung out in two columns along the village street. One of those infantrymen, Private James Lingg of I Company, gaped at the smoldering ruins that had once been a small town. "There was nothing much left in the town." Slightly ahead of him he heard the staccato bursts of machine-gun fire belching forth from a couple of the tanks as they shot up possible sniper hideouts.

In a few hours they passed through the town, encountering only a few scattered snipers. In the darkness they pressed on to Ste-Anne, a smaller village that had not been bombed out. Orders came down to dig in for the night. Lingg took shelter in a ditch on the southern side of the highway. Beyond Lingg's field of vision, the 3rd Battalion was deployed in and around Ste-Anne. Company L was dug into shallow holes north of the town, and K Company was south of town. Lingg's I Company was spread out in the buildings and ditches of Ste-Anne. "A light rain began to fall and visibility got real bad."

Unbeknownst to Lingg and the other Big Red One soldiers, a German column was rumbling straight into Ste-Anne. These Germans, mostly mounted on bicycles or trucks, were retreating from the beach; they were hoping to make it across the N-13 and set up new defensive positions to the south. They blundered right into L Company and into the town itself. They were seemingly coming from everywhere. Private Lingg, confined to his wet ditch, hardly knew what was going on. "What happened was a wild fire fight at close range with both sides hampered by surprise and confusion. We had the enemy coming from behind us. They were coming across fields, through hedgerows . . . so we didn't have a front line per se. We had the enemy on all sides. It got so bad . . . that I decided there wasn't any sense in me shooting the other guy across the road or him shooting at me, so I sat down in the bottom of the ditch . . . and just let the war go along. I don't know if I was being smart or if I was scared."

Probably the latter. As Lingg lay in his ditch, he turned to a buddy and said, "Let's get the hell out of here and go back to the beach." Lingg's buddy talked him out of "this wild idea." In their hearts they both knew that high-tailing it for the beach would be considered desertion. They stayed put.

The Germans captured a significant chunk of L Company, but all night long forward observers called down deadly fire on the enemy. In total, six battalions of artillery, plus naval guns, pummeled the area, killing dozens of enemy soldiers but plenty of Americans, too. At one point, American shells hit two trucks crammed with L Company prisoners the Germans had taken. Many did not survive. By daylight, Ste-Anne was firmly back under American control, along with 125 enemy prisoners, but a substantial portion of the enemy force escaped east.[4]

Clearly the men of the 1st Division were learning that the Germans might just materialize anywhere. There were no front lines, only strong points, where retreating and advancing columns bumped into one another. Most of Lieutenant Franklyn Johnson's 18th Regiment was operating west of the 26th, almost directly due south from Easy Red Beach. A veteran of the North Africa and Sicily campaigns, Johnson had lost three of his platoon's four 57mm antitank guns, plus their accompanying vehicles, to the English Channel. On D-Day evening, he and several of his men had set up their one remaining gun near St-Laurent and waited tensely for the German armored counterattack that never came.

The next morning they hooked up their antitank gun to a half-track, joined up with the rest of the 3rd Battalion of the 18th Infantry, and steadily advanced south in the direction of N-13 and a town called Mandeville. "Ambling along a narrow sunken lane between hedgerows, we go through Surrain and Engranville with opposition only from scattered snipers," he later wrote in his diary. "Few civilians have remained, but those we encounter are friendly, handing us wine, flowers, and fruit. All around, the productive land shows little evidence of destruction; fat cattle roam the fields, and orchards bloom gloriously. We are surprised to hit none of the fixed German defenses which were predicted."

They crossed the Aure River against almost no resistance. Similar to the Merderet, the Germans had flooded the Aure as an impediment to Allied soldiers. "Peculiarly enough, the retreating Nazis have left standing the bridge across the inundated area. After a brief skirmish, we cross and march southward into Mandeville. Near a flaming barn at the edge of the village, we dig in during the long dusk."

That night, a German combat patrol attacked battalion headquarters in Mandeville. A confused fight ensued; for a short period of time the Germans captured several headquarters soldiers. The Germans smashed radios and telephone equipment and nearly killed the battalion commander. Someone flashed word to regiment (and eventually division and corps) of a "severe attack." Staff officers at V Corps spent much of the night organizing reinforcements for the 18th Infantry at Mandeville. They feared that, finally, the Germans were counterattacking in force. In the daylight, though, everything looked better. By then, the Americans in Mandeville understood that the German "attackers" were merely a platoon-sized patrol that had stumbled into town, right into battalion headquarters.

Lieutenant Johnson, who spent the night several streets away in a ditch-side foxhole, never even heard the shooting. In the morning, he heard about the attack when a breathless runner told him that battalion headquarters had been "overrun by tanks." Johnson found this hard to believe. He left his hole, went to investigate, and, in the process, found out the real story. He wondered why such a small group of Germans was wandering around an American-controlled town. "We have heard that the Nazis when in a bad spot frequently get a small group of their soldiers, usually boys fifteen to nineteen years old, drunk, and send them out as suicide squads to do as much damage as possible before being cut down."

A few hours later, a German half-track, full of troops, suddenly appeared in the town square. Johnson's flabbergasted antitank crew took one shot at the German vehicle, blew a piece off its rear, hurting no one, and promptly retreated back to the battalion command post (CP). Again several voices at headquarters called regiment for help. The Germans, meanwhile, sped through town and disappeared to points unknown. The whole charade made Johnson angry. "Any way you look at it, this is not the way a war should go: drunken kids, gunners who can't hit anything, enemy vehicles speeding through our position!" After a short rest, during which many soldiers washed up, shaved, and got haircuts, the battalion moved southeast, cross-country, using TNT charges to blast their way through undefended hedgerows.[5] In three days of fighting, the 1st Division made it off Omaha beach, linked up with the British to the east, and forged south of the N-13 highway at several points.

Back at the beach, the division's medics were busy as could be. Casualties from the assault were, of course, heavy, and now more men were getting wounded as the 1st Division fought its way inland. Sergeant Allen Towne's B Company, 1st Medical Battalion, had originally set up its aid station on a hillside overlooking Easy Red Beach. When their vehicles came ashore on D+1, they moved inland two miles and set up a more permanent aid station. They treated wounded Americans, wounded Germans, and even wounded French civilians. "One . . . French woman, had a shell fragment hit her in one arm." She had a severe compound fracture. "Her arm was so badly damaged we could not immobilize it properly. We did the best we could, gave her a shot of morphine and sent her to the clearing company. We also had an older man who had a large potbelly. He had a . . . fragment rip open the skin on his belly area and expose all his intestines." All they could do was cover up the intestines, make him comfortable, and send him back to England for surgery.[6]

Not far away from Towne, Dr. Richard Fahey and the 60th Medical Battalion succeeded in erecting several tents. The unit's job was to do life-saving surgery on those who were too critically injured to be sent back immediately. Once that was accomplished the unit sent most of their wounded back to LSTs for transportation to hospitals in England. Captain Fahey's job was to "prepare the wounded and try to bring them out of shock, readying them for the surgeons."

On one occasion, he treated a lieutenant with a bad head wound. "Shrapnel knocked a large flap into the front row of the steel helmet, bending it under his scalp in the frontal area of his head. He may have had a skull fracture hidden underneath. Blood was streaming down his face." Fahey gently wriggled the man's helmet off, in the process removing part of the man's scalp, too. "I cleaned the wound as best I could, and repaired the scalp with sutures, and more sutures." When Fahey finished, the lieutenant felt so good that he shouted, "My men need me!" and attempted to go back to the front. "I had to tell him he was going back to England . . . and that was final."[7]

LSTs carried most of the wounded back to England. The skipper of LST-133, Lieutenant (jg) Richard Willstatter, supervised the loading of eighty casualties on his craft. "The patients were all on stretchers in the small craft and 'ducks' that brought them alongside. A sling arrangement . . . was used to bring them up over the side, generally two stretchers at a time. Too much credit cannot be given to Captain Ely, the Army surgeon, who worked endlessly and with great skill on these badly shattered men."

Elsewhere along the expanse of Omaha beach, Pharmacist's Mate Frank Feduik's LST-338 also took plenty of wounded men aboard. Several times a day, the LST made runs to the beach. The doors would swing open and the crew would unload supplies onto the beach while litter bearers carried wounded men aboard. As a medical specialist, Feduik stayed on the LST and helped with the wounded. "We treated the wounded, mostly by applying tourniquets and giving morphine. Then we would mark the patients as to what time you had given the morphine to tell when they were due for the next shot. I remember one soldier. His leg was missing. He had stepped on a mine right on the beach. I gave him a morphine shot and told him he would be okay for a couple of hours. He jumped up and looked at the stump. I don't know where he got the strength."

Feduik tried to hold the soldier down, but he was too upset. "I'm a farmer. What am I going to do?"

Feduik hardly knew what to say. "You'll be okay." The navy man gently pushed the soldier back down to the deck. "He just screamed. He was only 20 years old."

They made repeated runs back to England, dropping off the casualties at ports of embarkation where the Navy administered more treatment. At one such naval hospital in Netley, Lieutenant Helen Pavlovsky supervised an operating room as casualties poured in for days after D-Day. She had been in the Navy since the year before and had been in England for only four months. Nothing could have prepared her for the awful sight of men who had been shattered in battle. "We . . . removed the bullets and shrapnel, did the debridement, cleaned them up, poured penicillin and sulfa into the wounds, wrapped them up, and sent them inland to the Army or to the British hospitals . . . or by air to the United States, especially if they were bad burn patients. We were busy and never thought of food or sleep or anything else. We did not sleep for the first 24 hours, and then finally sleep had to be rationed because no one would leave their work. We lived on sandwiches and coffee."[8]

The first several days after the invasion were extremely hectic for Pavlovsky and the other naval medics, but once the Army was able to set up field hospitals in Normandy, the load lessened. The field hospitals functioned in a similar role to that of the naval hospitals in England.

At Pointe-du-Hoc, the Rangers were still holding out. On D-Day morning, they had scaled six-story-high cliffs and neutralized dangerous German artillery pieces. Twice, during the daylight hours of D-Day, they fended off enemy counterattacks on their tiny perimeter near the cliffs. Farther inland, basically cut off from the main perimeter, other Rangers, like First Sergeant Len Lomell and Staff Sergeant Jack Kuhn (who had destroyed several German guns on D-Day morning), spent the day manning roadblocks, waiting to be attacked. In Lieutenant Colonel James Rudder's bomb crater CP, overlooking the sea, twenty wounded Rangers were struggling for life. Corporal Lou Lisko, Rudder's radioman, circulated among them trying to help any way he could. He gave some men a few mouthfuls of soup. Many others were too weak or groggy to open their mouths. One man, Captain Jonathan Harwood, an army forward observer, was lying on a stretcher; he looked unconscious.

Lisko bent over and examined Harwood, who was barely breathing. Lisko turned to Dr. Walter Block. "Should I give him some soup?"

Block shook his head and fought back tears. "No, he is not going to need it; he'll be dead in a couple of hours." Block and Harwood were both from Chicago and had known each other for years.

German shells were exploding uncomfortably close, showering the wounded with dirt and rocks. Block needed a better site for his aid station than an open bomb crater. Rudder knew the perfect place. Just over the lip of the crater, twenty or thirty yards ahead, was a concrete bunker. He told Lisko and Corporal Steve Liscinsky to use two German prisoners as shields,

29th DIVISION
7-8 JUNE

Axis of U.S. Movements on 7 June
Axis of U.S. Movements on 8 June
U.S. Night Positions 7 June
Enemy Resistance Areas
Tidal Flat

Contour Interval — 10 Meters

1000   0   MILE
YARDS

and leave the crater and make their way to the bunker. Lisko grabbed his carbine and got to his feet. One of the Germans was a freckle-faced kid who could not have been a day over eighteen. "We motioned for the young freckle-faced German soldier to come walking . . . out of this bomb crater. He started to walk up and the other German followed him . . . and they had their hands up over their heads. When the young German soldier reached the top of this bomb crater . . . he straightened up . . . and then we heard a burst of fire." From another crater somewhere a fellow German opened up on the freckle-faced prisoner. "The bullets hit him; he fell forward. The second German . . . rolled over on his back, and he had his hands clasped in a prayerlike motion, begging us not to send him up."

Everyone, including the second German, slid back down into the crater. Several feet away Rudder peered at the dead German "facedown with his hands still clasped on top of his head." Lisko crawled to the lip of the crater and examined him more closely. "You could see blood coming out of the back of his uniform where the bullets came out."

Within an hour, the Rangers managed to stifle enemy fire and move the wounded to the cold, dark bunker where Dr. Block monitored them all night long (Harwood finally died at 0200 on June 7). In the meantime, Rudder maintained a steely exterior for the benefit of his men, but, inside, he brooded over his unenviable situation. A 1932 Texas A&M graduate, Rudder was a rough-and-ready ex-football coach. He knew he had accomplished his mission, but at great cost. For all he knew, the invasion was a failure. His communications with the supporting ships offshore were rudimentary; his ammunition, food, and water were running low. He had even taken casualties from friendly naval gunfire. He knew that, farther inland, from the direction of Grandcamp, the Germans were massing for a night attack. Rudder worried that the coming attack might overwhelm his soldiers at the roadblocks. He wondered if he should pull them back to the Pointe. No, it was best to leave them in place. Maybe they would make contact with patrols from the 29th Division or the Ranger units that had landed at Omaha. The Texan wondered when, or if, relief would ever come for his beleaguered Rangers. If relief did not come tonight or even tomorrow, could his Rangers hold out? He was not sure.[9]

That night, the Germans repeatedly attacked the Rangers' advance positions, near the coastal road. Immediately south of this road, a force of about seventy-five Rangers (most from D and E Companies, plus a stray 5th Ranger platoon) was deployed in shallow holes and ditches along hedgerows that lined the grassy fields. As one historian described it, "the . . . Ranger position . . . formed a right angle, facing southwest, with equal sides about 300 yards long on two fields that ran back to the highway." A nearly full moon, often obscured by clouds, provided the only light.

At 2330 the first German attack hit the very point of the right angle, the effective middle of the Ranger position. The Americans heard shouts and whistles and then all hell broke loose. "They came out screaming with tracer bullets going off, flares in the air, and it sounded like thousands of them," First Sergeant Lomell remembered. About one hundred yards south of Lomell, the brunt of the attack focused on Lieutenant George Kerchner's position. All at once, their shouting and shooting shattered the dark silence. He realized they were not more than fifty or seventy-five yards away. "This was the most frightening moment of my entire life . . . grenades bursting, flares, men yelling, whistles blowing, and it just seemed like there were hundreds and hundreds of Germans running towards us."

The German fire was wild; their machine-gun bullets were too high to do much damage, and their mortars landed haphazardly, indicating that they did not know the precise location of the Ranger positions. The enemy attacked through an orchard and overran at least one outpost (no one was ever quite sure what happened to the BAR man and rifleman manning the outpost).

Private Salva Maimone, who had free-climbed the Pointe roughly seventeen hours earlier, was now in a shallow foxhole. The attack was taking place to his right, some fifty yards away. "We were shooting at the enemy tracers. Every time we'd shoot . . . they'd come back with another fire. Somehow, they'd know where to shoot. They had lots of mortar shells going in the position where they thought we were, but we weren't in there."

The enemy attack petered out, only to be followed by another, almost identical assault an hour later. "The more fire we'd put out, the more we'd get." The Americans had to conserve ammunition. BAR gunners were running low on clips for their voracious weapon. Some of the Rangers were fighting with captured enemy weapons, including grenades. The enemy was superior in numbers and firepower; only the tenacity of the Rangers, combined with the confusion of the darkness, kept them at bay. Most of the Ranger positions had not been overrun, but gradually the German fire was becoming more accurate, inflicting a growing number of casualties. Two lieutenants, Ted Lapres and Joseph Leagans, commanding a platoon-sized group near the eastern end of the line, contemplated withdrawal.

Just before daylight, the Germans attacked again. This time there was more whistling, a bizarre hollering of names that sounded like a roll call, and plenty more wild shooting. The ammo situation was now critical. Lapres and two other officers decided to lead a withdrawal to the Pointe. The situation was completely confused, though. Many of the Rangers, huddling under cover in positions strung out all along the two fields, had no idea what was going on twenty or thirty yards away. Some were unaffected by the third enemy attack (which occurred fifty yards to the east of the first two, right at

Private Maimone's position). Others had been overrun and had surrendered.

In the meantime, Maimone and six other men tried to hold out as best they could. "I was working on . . . my buddy, who was shot right through the shoulder, and the bullet ran all the way through his right shoulder and left a hole as big as my fist." Maimone gave him a shot of morphine, dumped sulfa powder on the gaping hole, and slapped a bandage on it. He and the others heard footsteps approaching. They all lay down and played dead. German soldiers burst into their midst. "They were right on top of us with bayonets. They all said . . . 'stand up; if not we're going to stick bayonets in [you].' So that's what we did." Maimone helped his buddy get to his feet. The squad of six German soldiers led them away. Maimone spent the rest of the war in a POW camp.

All told, about fifty Rangers made it back to Colonel Rudder's positions at the Pointe. Sergeants "L-Rod" Petty and Hayward Robey helped cover the withdrawal by laying down steady, accurate, measured BAR fire from their observation post (OP) in the orchards from whence the Germans came. About fourteen men from D Company (including Kerchner and Lomell) remained in place. They were hiding in a ditch along a hedgerow on the west side of the defensive position. For twenty-four hours they hid, sometimes coming under fire from destroyers lending support to Rudder's forces. A few others never got the word to pull back. They crawled to the bottom of their holes and hid as best they could. Most got caught. The Germans never followed up their attack with another push on the Pointe. Naval gunfire from the destroyers *Barton, Thompson, Harding,* and *O'Brien* helped keep them at bay.[10]

A bloody stalemate ensued. Rudder was down to only nineteen hold-outs, but his situation improved on June 7 when Major Jack Street, a Ranger serving on Admiral John Hall's staff, organized a relief party consisting of two landing craft full of food (mainly peanut butter sandwiches), ammunition, and thirty reinforcements. Block succeeded in evacuating some of the most seriously wounded on his landing craft. This helped replenish Rudder's ex-hausted Rangers, but it did not relieve them. All day long on June 7, as his men endured intermittent mortar and artillery attacks, mixed with long-range small-arms duels, Rudder rooted for American troops to break through to Pointe-du-Hoc.

Rudder did not know it, but several miles to the east a mixed force of Rangers, 29'ers, and tankers was trying to do just that. Major General Charles Gerhardt, commander of the 29th Division, originally planned to attempt a relief of Pointe-du-Hoc on the evening of D-Day. But the hellish beach as-sault, combined with German resistance at Vierville, slowed his forces down. He had to spend much of the first night consolidating his control of Vierville. Just after sunset on June 7, he cobbled together the following force and set them in motion west along the coastal road: A, B, and C Companies of the

2nd Rangers, C and D Companies of the 5th Rangers, the survivors of the 1st Battalion, 116th Regiment, plus ten Sherman tanks from the 743rd Tank Battalion.

At 0800 they shoved off. The tanks were in the lead. For three hours the column encountered only sniper resistance. The tanks used their machine guns to shoot up any suspicious trees, hedgerows, or buildings that might contain snipers. At this point, it seemed as if they would make it to the Pointe easily. But, when they got to St-Pierre-du-Mont, half a mile from the Pointe (quite close to the road intersection that led to the Pointe), the Germans stopped them cold. This was an entire enemy battalion, parts of which had unleashed the nocturnal attack on the Rangers. Sniper, machine-gun, and mortar fire scattered the American infantry into ditches and behind hedgerows. Enemy forward observers called down withering artillery fire. Lieutenant Gerald Heaney, a Minnesota lawyer in civilian life, spent most of the day under cover. "The going was slow, artillery was heavy and the small arms fire was intense. The tanks were unable to operate in the hedgerows and were confined to the road, where they were largely useless." Three separate times on June 7, the Americans tried to force their way through this resistance only to fail. "For eight hours, we received heavy artillery bombardment," Lieutenant Francis Dawson of the 5th Rangers, later said.

The tankers, worried about the accuracy of German artillery, called it a day. They turned around and rumbled back to safer positions. The infantry spread out in fields and along the road and dug in for the night. Rudder and company were consigned to another night without relief.[11]

Even so, there was contact that night between the embattled Rangers at the Pointe and their rescuers. Lieutenant John Reville, a platoon leader in F Company, 5th Rangers, had finished fighting a small battle at Omaha beach on the morning of June 7 when Major Street rounded up him, along with several members of his platoon, and sent them into Pointe-du-Hoc with one of the resupply landing craft. Lieutenant Reville reported to Rudder.

Rudder glanced at the lieutenant and immediately assigned him a mission. "You have to go tonight, through the German lines, and find your battalion."

"They're fighting up the road from Vierville," Reville replied.

"Well, go through the lines tonight, take a combat patrol, find your battalion, tell them what the situation is up here, and guide them back the next day," Rudder ordered.

That night, Reville's patrol experienced no problems linking up with the dug-in relief force half a mile away (the Germans at the Pointe were still sheltered in bunkers and tunnels). Reville reported to Lieutenant Colonel Max Schneider, C.O. of the 5th Rangers, at the stone barn he was using as his

CP. Reville filled him in on Rudder's situation and suggested he follow the same route his patrol had used to break out of the Pointe.[12]

Late the next morning, the relief force, augmented by the rest of the 116th Infantry, resumed the advance on Pointe-du-Hoc. The destroyer *Ellyson* blasted German positions near the cliff with 140 five-inch shells. The German battalion had pulled out during the night. At noon, Schneider's Rangers joined hands with Rudder's Rangers.

Sadly enough, the bloodshed wasn't over for the Rangers at Pointe-du-Hoc. The rest of the 116th, plus tanks from the 743rd, was closing in on the Pointe from the southwest. These Americans had no idea that the rest of the relief force had broken through to Rudder. Ahead of them all they could see was a cratered, devastated landscape. As they rumbled cautiously in the direction of the sea, they heard the sound of the captured German weapons Rudder's men had been using, in their desperation, to defend themselves during their forty-eight-hour ordeal. Rocco Russo, an F Company bazooka man who had had a bloody leg fall in his lap two days before on Omaha beach, was walking beside a tank, hoping to reach Rudder's Rangers. "When we neared the coast we heard German machine guns fire to our front. We started blazing away at the source of the fire."

They were shooting at the Rangers. Several men were hit and one was killed. Rudder's men—and Schneider's, too—could hardly believe this. Lieutenant James Eikner, the 2nd Rangers communications officer, was angry as could be. "After having fought off the enemy we now had to fight off our own troops." Eikner scrambled to his radio and tried to contact the tankers. "I told them that they had us under fire and I put up a signal of orange smoke and told them this was our HQ. They all zeroed in on the orange smoke."

Lieutenant Stan Askin of the 5th Rangers took cover in a crater and watched as several Rangers—clearly fed up with everything—took matters into their own hands. "Some of our men returned the fire in a burst of fury and killed a tanker." Only direct communication between the two American forces staved off further unnecessary bloodshed. "Finally we had to send two officers . . . under fire [to them], and more or less grab them by the throat and get them to let up on their firing," Eikner explained.[13]

At long last, the ordeal of the 2nd Rangers at Pointe-du-Hoc was over. Rudder's original complement of 225 had been whittled down to less than 90 men, many of whom were wounded. When they exited the point, they left behind a ghastly mess of dead, dismembered, decomposing bodies, as well as a torn landscape. "We left the area together," one of them later said, "but the sounds and smells of the battlefield still remain vivid in my mind. It's the smell of death . . . that really penetrates everything. It is a smell you'll never forget." These memories were left to the "lucky" ones, the survivors.[14] The rest of Rudder's men were dead, missing, or captured. Their sacrifice was not, as some have suggested, for naught. By destroying the guns and neutralizing the Pointe as an OP for the Germans, Rudder's Rangers contributed as much as any Allied soldiers to the success of the invasion.

Some of Rudder's survivors tagged along as the relief force immediately pushed westward to the coastal town of Grandcamp, roughly a mile away from the Pointe. Getting into the town proved to be quite a challenge. The eastern approaches, from which the Americans were coming, were flooded. The Germans had (for some unknown reason) failed to blow the only bridge over this inundated area. The terrain beyond the bridge was wide open, though, and it offered no concealment or cover to the American attackers. The ground sloped gently all the way to the eastern buildings of Grandcamp. The Germans, hiding in these buildings on high ground, could lay down accurate fire on anything, or anyone, crossing that bridge. The Germans were also dug into a trench system that snaked east of the town, along several knolls, offering a commanding view of the terrain the Americans hoped to cross.

The 5th Rangers tried to cross the bridge, but heavy German machine-gun, mortar, and rifle fire stopped them cold. The Rangers knew they had to pull back. Most made it off the bridge unscathed. A naval observer called for support. In response, the British cruiser HMS *Glasgow* poured shells into Grandcamp for one hour. In all, the cruiser expended 113 rounds, demolishing many of the buildings. The concussion from the shells practically lifted the Americans off the ground. The bombardment lasted until 1600.

When it finished, the 3rd Battalion of the 116th, accompanied by C Company of the 743rd Tank Battalion, renewed the attack. The tanks led the way across the bridge. One of them hit a mine. The rest made it across, followed by the infantrymen. Tank gunners and BAR men were blazing away at anything that looked suspicious. Once again, the German-held buildings erupted with deadly fire. Machine-gun positions, spread out somewhere north of the road, added to the enemy fire. Instead of flinging themselves to the ground (there was still no place to take cover), the 29'ers huddled behind the tanks and closed with the enemy. The volume of fire emanating from both sides was intense. The fighting was at close quarters. Whenever they could get close enough to the machine-gun positions, the Americans hurled grenades at them, hollering obscenities as they did so. The jarring blast of each Sherman's main 75mm gun only added to the cacophony.

The battle was threatening to stalemate. Two companies, K and L, had managed to push west of the bridge and were concentrating on killing off any enemy who still held positions north of the road. German fire from the town was still intense, and in the agony of the moment, when young Americans were being killed and horribly wounded, the very idea of entering Grandcamp seemed, to some, a distant hope. Ranger private Donald Nelson was lying still, trying to present as small a target as possible, even as German machine-gun fire grew more intense. "They kept getting lower and lower with that machine gun until we got down on our stomachs, and they weren't six inches above our hind end."

Company K of the 116th was pinned down in front of a knoll, not far from the first buildings of Grandcamp. Sergeant Felix Branham, a Virginian and squad leader who had been part of this company since 1938, was pinned down alongside everybody else. "There was a company of German infantry in an elaborate communications trench from which they directed heavy machine gun fire. Several attempts by our company and some Rangers failed to neutralize this fire." Sergeant Branham watched as a fellow Charlottesville native, Sergeant Frank Peregory, stood up. "[He] . . . began firing his rifle from his hip as he moved in the direction from whence the enemy fire came. Upon reaching the trench, he leaped in while firing his weapon, with fixed bayonet. Frank soon emerged from the trench with three German prisoners." Peregory handed over the prisoners to someone else and went back into the trench. "After what seemed an eternity, he again emerged from the trench, this time with thirty-two German prisoners."

Incredibly, Peregory had single-handedly neutralized the entire German position and opened the way into Grandcamp. Branham and many others felt that if not for Peregory, Grandcamp might not have been taken that day. He won the Medal of Honor for his exploits. The medal was awarded posthumously, because Peregory was killed six days later, near Couvains, "while attempting to capture a German machine-gun nest single-handedly," Branham said.

Thanks to Peregory's bravery, the Americans infiltrated Grandcamp. Tanks blasted away at buildings containing snipers or machine-gun nests. The infantry trailed along cautiously, pitching grenades through windows and watching out for snipers. A platoon-sized patrol from I Company, led by Lieutenant Norvin Nathan, pushed swiftly into the western end of town, capturing a pillbox that guarded an area overlooking the beach. By nightfall, Grandcamp belonged to the Americans. The sight of destruction and death was sobering to Private Nelson. "The town had been torn up. There were dead Germans all over the place. We had to wear a gas mask going through there—that's just how bad it was. You couldn't tell if you were stepping on dead Germans or logs or what. It was awful."

The 1st Battalion of the 116th had swung to the south and entered the demolished town of Maisy by nightfall. Naval fire had completely leveled the place. The 116th had tanks with them and the steel monsters shot up what small resistance the enemy posed along the road to Maisy. With these missions accomplished the 116th, a distinguished regiment that traced its heritage back to the Stonewall Brigade, went into reserve for several days. The men of this outfit had dealt with the worst of the Omaha beach assault. Now they needed two things: rest and replacements.[15]

The 29th Division still had one regiment on the water. The 175th Infantry was Major General Leonard "Gee" Gerow's V Corps reserve. The unit was supposed to land on D+1 and push south, lending support to the general advance off Omaha beach. The plan soon changed. General Gerow ordered General Gerhardt to capture Isigny as soon as possible. Located about seven miles southwest of Grandcamp, Isigny was a quaint fishing village that sat astride the Aure River. The capture of Isigny would lead the way across the Aure (which curled north all the way to the ocean) and also the Vire, a mile or so to the west. From there the Americans could then push west and link up with the VII Corps near Carentan. Gerow knew that it was imperative to link up the Utah and Omaha beachheads as quickly as possible.

Many of the 175th's officers had never even heard of Isigny. Now it was their objective. The men of this outfit had spent D-Day aboard their ships, impatiently waiting for the word to go ashore. At 1146 on June 7, Gerhardt issued the landing order to Colonel Paul "Pop" Goode, the venerable regimental commander. Each of the regiment's nine companies was aboard a separate ship. Goode could not possibly disseminate the landing order in any kind of unified, organized fashion. Instead, navy motorboats buzzed around the transport ships as crewmen on the motorboats shouted over loudspeakers, "All elements of the One-seventy-fifth Infantry urgently needed on the beach!" It took time for the soldiers to assemble aboard their LCVPs and LCAs (commonly known as "Higgins Boats"). Each company loaded onto its landing craft and proceeded to the beach at its own pace, so the regiment landed unevenly, with no real command and control.

The troops thought that their landing would be completely unopposed, but the beach was still under intermittent machine-gun and artillery fire, and there were plenty of mines around, too. Two landing craft hit mines on the way into the beach. Private Joseph Bria of H Company, riding uncomfortably in a Higgins boat, saw one of the craft get hit. "[It] was raised out of the water and was blown to bits. Parts of the craft sprinkled down on us." Bria glumly sat and thought to himself, "This could be my last day on earth."[16]

Most of the boats hit the beach safely, near Les Moulins draw, but mines were still a problem there, too. When the soldiers of Sergeant First Class Lester Zick's antitank company began disembarking from their LST, they erroneously believed that the beach had been swept. "We would not have been ordered off, unless the beach was clear of mines," Zick believed. "The ammunition vehicle went off first; then the three-quarter-ton vehicle with the 57mm gun moved down the ramp. The left rear wheel of the vehicle towing the gun caused a covered mine to explode." There were eleven men in the truck. "The explosion blew the vehicle apart. Six of them were killed, the others were injured . . . in a daze." Medics did what they could for the survivors while the rest of the vehicles unloaded without incident.[17]

The soldiers of the rifle companies debarked and quickly trotted to the seawall. They heard German machine-gun and artillery fire, but it was quite inaccurate. Far more disturbing was the detritus of the previous day's battle. "The scene was almost unimaginable," Captain Robert Miller, commander of F Company, recalled. "There were burning tanks. There were wrecked boats that were either sunk or broached in the surf and pounding themselves on the beach. Most noticeable of all, beginning at the water's edge, you could see the bodies of the assault elements." These bodies were "rolling back and forth in the wave surge at the high-water mark on the beach."

Harold Gordon, the son of a doctor, and the owner of a history degree from the University of Richmond, splashed ashore with H Company. He had always thought that the sight of dead bodies and blood would make him sick, but he managed to keep his composure. "You just couldn't visualize these torn and twisted bits of meat as anything human, and those who had died of bullet wounds mostly looked like wax mannequins dropped in haste by a window-dresser. Already they were beginning to turn purple (especially their faces and fingers)." Gordon tripped and fell and found himself "staring at the face of a dead sergeant." Gordon thanked God he had not been in the first wave and moved on.[18]

Gerhardt wanted the 175th to land at Dog Green, at the Vierville draw, but the Navy thought there were still too many mines at Dog Green. So, much to the general's chagrin, the unit landed at Les Moulins and had to move west for over a mile along the beach and up the Vierville draw. Private Bria was milling around the seawall with several other men when he heard "a loud voice, one of the high-ranking officers, shouting, 'Get away from the seawall! Keep moving! Get off the beach!'"

In spite of all the confusion, the soldiers of the 175th gradually walked west and filtered up the Vierville draw. Captain Miller was walking up the draw when runners told him to report to the regimental adjutant, Captain James Hayes. "Things are all screwed up," Hayes told him. "Colonel Goode was right. You can forget the invasion plan from here on." Hayes relayed the order to capture Isigny, a town Miller had never heard of (his original mission called for him to push south to the Cerisy Forest, a job later carried out by the 2nd Division). As Miller scrambled to familiarize himself with the route to Isigny, he thought of the wisdom of Goode's pre-invasion speech. As

Hayes alluded, the colonel had told his men that the elaborate plan would mean nothing once they were ashore. All that really counted now was getting off the beach and gaining ground.[19]

The draw was crammed with troops and vehicles. The place was under sporadic enemy shell fire, but the regiment was finally under some semblance of order. They went through Vierville and marched west along the coastal road. A mile ahead, at Gruchy, they left the coastal road and turned south, onto a smaller gravel road. The sun was setting now. Strung out in a column of twos, the men walked warily in the night; 1st Battalion was in the lead, followed by the 2nd and 3rd. Shermans from the 747th Tank Battalion were mixed together with the 1st Battalion, leading the way. The column stretched for two miles. The loud racket of the tank engines melded together with the steady tramp of boots on gravel.

Captain Miller was at the head of his F Company. "The night became miserable indeed because we were delayed by harassing fires and by enemy delaying detachments which endeavored to hold up our people." Farther back in the column, Corporal Gordon shuddered at the ominous sound of enemy machine guns, "a liquid rattle . . . like cloth ripping." He and his buddies hit the dirt. "It was our first baptism of fire and we had no idea what was happening, so there we lay on the hard roadway . . . head to heel, praying or cursing, according to our bent, while the tracers flashed above us in an ever-changing pattern." Small groups of enemy soldiers were trying to delay the Americans without getting drawn into a full-scale battle. The Americans drove them off.

For a few hours the 175th, and its armored partners, halted for a rest. The soldiers spread out into the fields, took shelter along hedgerows, and caught a few hours of sleep. At 0400 on June 8, the advance resumed. "We crawled forward with frequent halts, playing leapfrog with dimly seen tanks that constantly threatened to mow us down, and whose motor noise frightened us terribly," Gordon wrote.[20]

The column came upon a hard-surface road that ran east–west. This was the N-13 (the men of the 175th called it the Isigny–Bayeux Highway). Here they turned west. By now the sun had risen and Isigny was only six miles away. The soldiers of A Company were cautiously advancing behind four tanks. French farmers, working in their fields, paused and waved at the Americans. All seemed well until the troops reached the outskirts of La Cambe. Here the Germans had hidden an antitank gun and some infantry. The enemy opened fire, hitting several men while the rest dived into roadside ditches. The Shermans, still on the road, fired several volleys into houses in La Cambe. Suddenly, as if from out of nowhere, an 88 round pierced the armor of one of the tanks and exploded. The tank caught fire immediately, burning up any of the crewmen who could not get out. Several minutes went by and the Americans prepared to assault the town, but the German fire soon died down and the enemy disappeared. Clearly they had orders to delay the Americans, not hole up and fight them. The Yanks moved into La Cambe, and the infantry methodically checked the town, building by building, for any enemy presence.

Captain Miller's F Company had been lost much of the night, but in the daylight his scouts managed to find the N-13, make contact with some 1st Battalion troops, and move west until they came to La Cambe. There they joined the rest of the regiment as it entered the town. Miller heard the sound of aircraft overhead. He looked up and saw nine British Typhoon fighter-bombers, complete with invasion stripes. He watched them for a moment and saw that they were preparing to dive. Almost at the same time, he and his first sergeant realized that "their intentions toward us was hostile. I immediately blew the air alert on my whistle and the men then fled on either side of the road into open fields."

A quarter-mile outside of town, Corporal Gordon was sitting down to eat a K ration when he noticed the British planes making their descent. "They 'assumed the vertical' and tore down the earth to our front, smoke trailing from their wing guns. They dove while we cheered them on." Gordon and the others had no idea that they were strafing Americans.

Meanwhile, Captains Miller and Hayes (who had joined him shortly after spotting the planes himself) ran for their lives. They leaped over a stone wall and threw themselves flat beside a house for a few seconds until Miller "realized that the . . . old, heavy, stone house had a slate roof and that if the slates fell on us . . . we surely would be casualties. So I kicked Hayes and we both fled into the orchard behind the house." They found a little air-raid shelter that had been dug by the owners of the house. "The British fighter-bombers in line of stern dove on us one by one and strafed the center of the village, the main road, and the houses on either side of the road, and in turn dropped . . . bombs. The houses in the village, many of them, were simply blown apart."

At last the planes completed their ill-fated mission and flew away. It took Captain Miller fifteen minutes to reassemble his company and assess the damage. "I had lost five people . . . including a BAR man, the company mail clerk, two riflemen, and a member of the mortar section." He got his company on the move and out of La Cambe as quickly as possible "to get them away from the scene of the unpleasant happening and to reassure the men as much as possible." In total, the Americans lost six dead and eighteen wounded in this friendly fire incident. One of the wounded, Lieutenant Carl Hobbs, an intelligence officer on the 1st Battalion staff, had a live 20mm shell lodged in his shoulder. Luckily, it did not explode. Doctors at an aid station gingerly removed the shell.[21]

Colonel Goode set up his CP back in La Cambe. He was uneasy about his situation. His intelligence officers believed the Germans between here and Isigny would only fight a delaying action, as they had at La Cambe, but the colonel wasn't so sure. He was out here on his own. A new German division could appear at any time and cut him off from Omaha beach. He had very little artillery support, and his air support, as the painful events of the morning proved, was just as likely to hinder him as help him. Goode was inclined to lay low for the rest of the day and wait to be reinforced.

General Gerhardt would have none of this. Firmly in command now, the hard-charging Gerhardt was his usual aggressive, feisty self. Gerhardt was riding around the battle area in his jeep, the *Vixen Tor*. He encountered his second-in-command, Brigadier General Norman "Dutch" Cota, and told him to light a fire under Goode. Cota, whose ubiquitous bravery on D-Day at Omaha beach had perhaps saved the American beachhead, drove to La Cambe in his jeep. For much of the afternoon on June 8 he and Goode worked out a plan to advance the rest of the way to Isigny. However, as of 1900 the advance had not begun. Goode was still waiting for the artillerymen of the 224th Field Artillery Battalion to set up and provide support for his advance.

Suddenly Gerhardt's *Vixen Tor* drove into town and screeched to a halt outside Goode's CP. Oozing his customary impatience, Uncle Charlie hopped off his jeep and strode into the CP. "Has the attack on Isigny begun yet?"

Goode cringed. "No, sir, it hasn't."

Gerhardt blew his stack. "There's nothing in your way. Get into Isigny." When Goode expressed a desire to wait for the artillery, Gerhardt cut him off. "Never mind the artillery! Get those tanks moving and roll right in. I'll get in that jeep of mine right now and roll into Isigny. There's nothing there. Now get the hell in!" Without another word, he clambered into his jeep and left.

Goode now had no other choice but to set his men in motion. With the 3rd Battalion, plus tanks, in the lead, they set out west on the N-13. Their advance was successful, but they did run into three separate sources of resistance that night. The Germans had set up antitank guns, covered by infantry, at St-Germain-du-Pert to the south, Osmanville to the west, and a radar station in Cardonville to the north. The 747th lost six tanks to 88 fire, but eventually the Americans overwhelmed resistance in each area and the Germans retreated. The 3rd Battalion pushed the German defenders of St-Germain-du-Pert south, all the way across the flooded Aure River. At Osmanville, two companies from the 1st Battalion captured the town. Aided by fire from the *Glasgow*, the 2nd Battalion took Cardonville and the radar station.[22]

But the 88 fire there was especially heavy. With frightening alacrity, the dreaded projectiles came in with their telltale *zinggg-blam* report. Corporal Gordon took cover in a trench that the Germans had recently vacated. He and a sergeant "lay there together, and on the other side of me was a guy named McNeil, big and burly, and shivering like the rest of us. Now the shells were falling faster—and closer—and some were bursting in the hedgerow's trees, showering our trench with shrapnel. I just endured, shrinking, waiting for the next explosion to tear out my guts. Men were yelling and screaming with fear and pain and the red blossoms unfolded all about us, and the zinging of the hot metal through the air was clearly audible."[23]

In the early-morning hours of June 9, the Americans closed in on Isigny. The 3rd Battalion and their accompanying tankers were in the lead. They closed to within a mile and a half of Isigny and halted when a tank hit a mine that blew off its tread. The other tankers were worried that the road ahead was mined (and maybe the Aure River bridge into Isigny, too). The infantry took shelter in roadside ditches and catnapped. The tank crewmen remained in their tanks and waited.

Once again, Gerhardt arrived on the scene in his jeep. He drove up and down the column asking what was going on. Finally, near the lead tank, he found General Cota, as well as Lieutenant Colonels Alexander George (executive officer of the 175th) and Stuart Fries (commanding officer of the 747th). The four of them stood next to a tank and conferred, with Uncle Charlie as impatient as ever. He dismissed the possibility of mines. "Get those damn tanks going and follow them into Isigny. Now stop fooling around and get into that town." He got into his jeep and drove all the way back to his headquarters at Vierville.

Led by Cota, the column rumbled all the way to Isigny. Cota and two riflemen dashed across the Aure River bridge and into the town. Gerhardt was right. There were no mines. There was only destruction. Allied ships and planes had bombarded Isigny earlier in the day, and it seemed that hardly a building was left standing. "Rounding a bend in the road," Lieutenant Jack Shea, Cota's aide, remembered, "the burning heart of Isigny came into full view. Buildings on either side of the narrow main square were on fire. Heaped rubble had cascaded into the streets. It was a dead town."

In the rubble, a few snipers took potshots, only to be buried by 75mm shells from the tanks or bazooka shots from the infantry. First Sergeant Zick watched as one of the tanks zeroed in on a sniper. "A German shot at us from the church steeple. Finally, one of our tanks turned his turret around, raised his gun, leveled it, *bang* finis for the German in the steeple." The Americans took 200 prisoners at Isigny.

By late morning the entire regiment had filtered into the battered town. Corporal Gordon and his H Company got there shortly after daylight. Gordon was exhausted after a night of enduring shell fire and marching, all the

V CORPS ATTACK
9 – 11 JUNE

while carrying the receiver of a .30-caliber machine gun. A skinny young Frenchman came up to Gordon and offered him a drink from "a bottle of amber liquid." Gordon thought it was cider, so he took it and guzzled it down. "I was so tired I couldn't even choke. It burned all the way down, and half woke me from my lethargy. That was my first (and damned near my last) taste of calvados, the local firewater that runs something like 55 percent alcohol."[24]

Throughout the day on June 9, the 175th fended off an ineffective counterattack and fanned out west and south of Isigny. In the final analysis, Gerhardt was right to be aggressive and Goode was wrong to be cautious. Gerhardt behaved with just the right blend of intuition and aggressiveness on the evening of June 8. Without him, the 175th probably would not have taken Isigny for another day or two.

Other soldiers from the 29th Division were pushing south. The 115th Infantry, which had come ashore on the afternoon of D-Day, spent the next couple days eliminating German resistance along the coast, especially in St-Laurent. With the coastal areas secured, the regiment slowly advanced south, straight through thick hedgerow country. Late in the afternoon on June 8, they halted at the flooded Aure River. In this sector the river flowed west to east. The river was, of course, over its banks, and most of the area immediately north and south of it was under a muddy sheen of water. The regimental commander, Colonel Eugene Slappey, wanted to find out the depth of the water in this inundated area that lay ahead, so he sent a platoon-sized patrol from E Company to find out.

At 1730, Lieutenant Kermit Miller led this patrol, consisting of twenty-eight weary men, into the swamp. Miller's people had been fighting or on the move for close to seventy-two hours. At first, they found only shallow water. They waded, swam, and crawled in the stinky, muddy mess for several hours until they got to the river itself. Here the water was too deep to cross on foot. Miller splashed around looking for a suitable crossing area and saw a canoe on the opposite side. He took off most of his equipment, swam across the river, got in the canoe, and paddled it back to his waiting soldiers. They then used the canoe to ferry across the whole patrol, making several trips. Now they were back into the swamp, splashing their way forward as best they could. Several more hours passed. Every man was wet, tired, and muddy. Needless to say, they all stank terribly.

Twilight gave way to darkness at about 2300, and, finally, the men emerged from their watery purgatory. Firmly on dry ground now, they spread out and cautiously kept moving until they came upon the village of Colombières. Miller's patrol, moving with stealth, came upon three slumbering

German soldiers, who were supposed to be manning an outpost, and promptly took them prisoner. When the Americans entered the town they spoke to a Frenchwoman who told them the whereabouts of a German CP. Miller utilized the information well. He deployed his people around the building that served as the enemy CP and shouted for the enemy soldiers to surrender.

The Germans in this town never dreamed that the Americans might successfully negotiate the inundated Aure. They were taken by complete surprise, but they did not surrender. They responded to Miller's entreaties with rifle fire. Miller and his people scrambled for cover and shot at the enemy-held building with every weapon in their arsenal. Suddenly a German command car came barreling down the street. Several Americans turned their rifles on the command car and riddled it with bullets. The destroyed car and its dead occupants blocked the road for three more vehicles that followed. The Americans shot at them until they ground to a halt. The flashes from American rifle muzzles lit up the night. The noise of rifle and machine-gun fire was nearly deafening. Some Germans in the CP foolishly tried to escape. They made easy targets for Miller's riflemen, who cut them down mercilessly.

In a matter of minutes, the battle was over. The Americans killed nineteen Germans and took seventeen more prisoner. Three of Miller's men were wounded. The patrol and its prisoners took refuge in an abandoned stone barn. One of the POWs was a German medical officer. With only a flashlight for illumination, he removed two bullets from the abdomen of Private First Class Cleaverne Sharpe, the most badly wounded American.

The patrol members were near the brink of somnolent exhaustion. They were dearly hoping to rest here for the night and wait for their unit to catch up with them. Miller had brought along a radioman on this patrol, and he succeeded in making contact with E Company. The radioman told E Company that the patrol had captured Colombières and that the company could cross the inundated area. But there was no way that E Company, or the rest of 2nd Battalion, was going to attempt a crossing in the middle of the night. Miller's patrol was ordered to pack up and come back to the company. At dawn they left their barn and safely retraced their arduous route—prisoners in tow and wounded being carried—all the way back to E Company.[25]

Thanks to the intrepid work of Miller and his twenty-eight stalwarts, Colonel Slappey now knew the inundated area could be crossed. He also knew that German resistance to such a crossing would be minimal. Shortly after daylight his battalions plunged into the swamp. The experience was every bit as miserable as it had been for Miller's patrol. The 3rd Battalion was in the lead, and somewhere among this unit's wet masses of soldiery

First Lieutenant Colin McLaurin, executive officer of I Company, slogged his way along. "It was sloppy going. The entire area was covered with black, sticky mud and marsh grass sometimes a couple of feet high. Every hundred yards or so there were some kind of drainage ditches varying in width from three to seven or eight feet. Yes, they were filled with water. When we would come to one of these, we would try to get a running start and jump across." As an officer, McLaurin was carrying a lighter load than most of the men around him, but that did not always matter. "Every once in a while I would slip and with a loud splash, in I would go. After a few slips, all of us were muddy and wet from heads to our toes. The going was very rugged for the men who had to carry the heavy equipment. We passed through several areas which were completely covered with water at depths ranging from a couple of inches to a couple of feet."

With the help of engineers who brought up DUKWs and bridging equipment, McLaurin and the 3rd Battalion spent much of the day wading across the inundated area. When they got across, they entered Colombieres, site of Miller's battle the night before. There were no live Germans in the town, only dead ones. McLaurin found the remnants of the German vehicles that had blundered right into Miller's group. "Standing in the middle of the highway were three German staff cars, two of them occupied and one empty. There were three dead Germans in one and two dead enemy soldiers in the second, all still sitting but slumped in their seats. Ripped clothing and gaping bullet holes was ample evidence of sudden death. Three more corpses lay by the side of the road, no doubt killed as they tried to take cover. They were a grisly and gory lot, sitting and lying there cold and silent."[26]

By evening the 3rd Battalion had moved a mile south to La Folie. Slightly to the northeast, the 1st Battalion had crossed the swamp and fought its way into Bricqueville. To the west, the 2nd Battalion (including Kermit Miller and his men, who got almost no sleep after their patrol), crossed the swamp and fought all day to secure Calette Wood and a town called Vouilly. They accomplished all this by 1900, but their day was still not over. They had orders to keep moving inland. They spread out along a small road and tramped south for most of the evening. At one point, they took a wrong turn to the east and muddled around lost for a couple of hours, until they bumped into a reconnaissance group from the 110th Field Artillery Battalion, who helped them get their bearings. This, of course, only added to their fatigue. Some of the 2nd Battalion men could barely stand. "We were getting extremely exhausted," Private Maynard Marquis of H Company explained. "We couldn't figure out why we had to keep going." Maynard managed to stay awake, but others walked along in a kind of hypnotized state—half-awake and half-asleep. "Everyone was dead tired from the day's march," Staff Sergeant

Philip Hague, a medic, recalled, "and many of the boys fell asleep as soon as there was a moment's pause." One man, who had reached his limit, even shot himself in the foot.[27]

Not far ahead of the main column, Major Maurice Clift, the battalion's executive officer, was riding in a jeep, trying to find a good bivouac area in the inky darkness. He drove past a cluster of buildings, comprising a little village named Le Carrefour (his army map mistakenly referred to the place as "La Carretour"). A few hundred yards beyond the buildings he saw a pair of hedgerow-lined orchards on either side of the road. This, he thought, would make a perfect place to bivouac for the night. His superior, Lieutenant Colonel William Warfield, agreed.

At 0200, when the weary infantrymen at last made it to Le Carrefour, Clift and several staff officers directed them to take up positions in the orchards. The men were only too happy to comply. They were absolutely spent. They had been through the arduous experience of crossing a slimy, stinking swamp. They had spent much of the day fighting stubborn German strong points at Callette Wood and Vouilly. They had marched fifteen miles in twenty hours. Most of them had hardly eaten in that time. They had little strength left—officers included. Thus most of the troops simply flung themselves to the ground in the orchards and went to sleep. In so doing, they committed an egregious error (a cardinal sin, in the view of many). They failed to dig in and they failed to set up perimeter guards or OPs. If they had been lucky, they would have gotten away with this fatigue-induced mistake. But they were not lucky on this night.

Half an hour after the Americans collapsed into slumber in the orchards near Le Carrefour, many of them died. An entire German artillery battalion, reinforced with tanks and infantry from the 352nd Division, caught the 2nd Battalion by complete surprise. The enemy was in a perfect attack position, immediately to the rear of the vulnerable, exhausted battalion. The Germans had been retreating south all night, on secondary roads, and, by coincidence, their scouts had spotted the tail end of Warfield's column. Seeing the unsuspecting Americans bed down for the night at Le Carrefour, the Germans set up a carefully orchestrated ambush. Several Americans even heard the noise of the enemy vehicles to their rear but simply assumed the noises came from jeeps belonging to the 3rd Battalion (they had a vague notion that the 3rd Battalion was operating somewhere behind them).

Just after 0230, the Germans sprang their trap. The enemy pointed their weapons—everything from self-propelled artillery pieces to rifles—over a line of hedgerows and opened fire at nearly point-blank range into the orchards where the Americans were sleeping. Suddenly the dark night was lit up with German flares and tracer rounds. Their fire was intense. The orchards where the Americans had taken refuge were no larger than an acre apiece. They were bordered on every side by hedgerows. The enemy could scarcely have imagined better circumstances. They slaughtered the 2nd Battalion troops with impunity.

Private Marquis, the machine gunner from H Company, was in the center of one of the orchards, looking for a place to sit down, when the shooting started. "German machine guns and burp guns cut loose all around the field." He heard his captain yelling for a machine gun to be set up, but in the confusion Marguis could not tell where his commander wanted the gun placed. "You could not distinguish friend from enemy at ten feet. Mortars started to fall. The next four or five hours would be the most traumatic of my entire life." All around him men were getting hit, slumping to the ground or pitching backward against hedgerows. Some were killed in their sleep. In the darkness they looked like lumps. Marquis and his gunner managed to climb over a hedgerow, away from the Germans, and plop themselves down into a dirt lane that soon came under mortar fire.

Not far away, Lieutenant James Hogan, a platoon leader in F Company, was checking on one of his men who had called out to him. "All of a sudden firing broke out all around us. Shells landing and exploding, burp guns going off." Hogan turned around and saw one of the enemy self-propelled guns poking its barrel over the hedgerow. An awful instant later, "it fired into the field where we were. The man who was standing alongside me got hit, and fell on top of me and died. I could hear him sigh and then he laid perfectly still and was a complete deadweight." A brave, but unfortunately anonymous, group of men managed to set up a bazooka and destroy two of the self-propelled guns, but still the deadly fire continued.

Captain William Boykin was the commander of B Battery, 110th Field Artillery Battalion. He was attached to Warfield's battalion, observing for his guns, when he got caught in a crossfire in the orchard on the west side of the road. "Small-arms fire opened up on us from all four sides, and everyone ran to the edge of the fields to seek protection in the ditches along the side of each field, at the base of each hedgerow. This field, unfortunately, had no ditch on any side, and men just piled up as they threw themselves in the dark into what they hoped would be a ditch."

The surviving self-propelled gun rumbled to within several yards of his position and let loose a witheringly effective volley of shells, one of which exploded in the trees near Captain Boykin. "I felt something hit the back of my right shoulder. This knocked me down face forward." He could feel blood running down his back, but he had no idea of the extent of his injuries. For the moment, there was no time to find out.

Sergeant Hague, the medic, was in the other field, on the opposite side of the road, trying to set up an aid station with two other men, including his captain. "Jerry was firing everything he had at us point blank. The three of us quickly hit the dirt. Shells were falling directly behind us in the road where many had taken cover. Immediately there were heartrending calls for a medic but, realizing it was certain death to go to their aid, we stayed where we were. Everything around us seemed to have gone haywire."[28]

Indeed it had. In an instant, the embattled 29'ers had awakened to find their worst nightmare coming true. They fought back as best they could, but they were in deep trouble. The Germans would pop up at one point behind a hedgerow, fire several shots, and then disappear, only to shoot moments later from somewhere else. Warfield's men could not see the Germans well enough to shoot accurately. The best the 29'ers could do was point their weapons in the direction of the German fire and shoot.

Warfield himself was right in the middle of the Germans. He, his staff, and several officers were meeting in a two-story farmhouse at Le Carrefour when the shooting started. They dashed out of the house, right into the Germans. Everyone—Americans and Germans—scrambled in every direction, shooting indiscriminately. Lieutenant Edward Tucker, Warfield's supply officer, fell dead, right outside the front door of the house. The Germans, concealed now behind foliage along the road, hollered in English for Warfield's group to surrender. Warfield brandished a pistol, his only weapon, and screamed back, "Surrender, hell!" He and several others tried to run along the road, in the direction of the battalion's orchard positions. They had no chance. German machine-gun fire sliced into them. Their bodies lay in grotesque positions all over the road, blood seeping into the gravel.

In the orchards, the shooting had died down a bit, as the Germans ran low on targets. About fifty Americans had been killed in the first few furious minutes of the battle. Others lay wounded in bloody clumps all over the orchards. The rest were either captured or, like Lieutenant Hogan's men, scattered all over the place. He rounded up the survivors of his platoon and busted through a hedgerow to the south, away from the Germans. Hogan and his men set up a defensive position in a ditch. Not far away, they could hear Germans capturing another small group of Americans. The same Germans yelled at Hogan to surrender. He ordered his people to keep silent and stay still. "We were afraid to fire across the field, because we didn't know how many of our men were still there."

Private Marquis was in a nearby field, with several other men, doing the same thing—watching and waiting. "We . . . sat with our backs to the hedgerow." A few mortar shells came in but did not explode. Later, by the light of a flare, he saw a German in the distance. "I took aim and fired. A couple of other shots rang out at the same time. He went down."

The battle lasted little more than an hour or two. Then, still under cover of darkness, the Germans resumed their march south, right through the scattered, shattered, frightened survivors of the 2nd Battalion. Marquis, crouching in his cold ditch, heard the enemy troops pass by. "A group of screaming, hollering men went slowly up the road toward the German lines." The self-propelled gun stopped and fired two shots over the orchard where the slaughter had happened. "I can still see the streaks of fire from the gun to the explosion."

Captain Boykin had lost a lot of blood. He wandered the area, looking for the 3rd Battalion, a unit he believed was close enough to lend some help. He stumbled into a field with several bodies lying around. He thought they were dead bodies, but they weren't. They were none other than sleeping German soldiers. Boykin soon realized this and took shelter in a shallow depression. "I lay down there for a time, and shortly after I had been there . . . the first sergeant of this German bicycle infantry company aroused these guys, grabbed a bicycle, and moved out. I was right in the middle of this whole company. A short time later I moved out in the opposite direction!" He made it to an aid station where medics discovered a fragment that had entered behind his shoulder and lodged in his throat. They gave him morphine and sent him back to the beach for evacuation.

By the morning, after the sun rose, the Germans, like a nocturnal storm, were long gone. Only their dead remained behind. All day long on June 10, wounded and stunned survivors from Warfield's 2nd Battalion straggled back to the orchards at Le Carrefour, as well as many other 29th Division positions.

By this time, General Gerhardt knew what had happened. At 0400 he was visiting the 115th Infantry's CP near Colombieres when survivors began filtering in. They told him their tales of woe. One lieutenant even fell to the ground, pounding and sobbing uncontrollably that his men were dead and he had let them down. Only sedation quieted him. Gerhardt listened to the survivors and became angry. "No security! They just went into the field and went to bed!"

He decided to go to Le Carrefour immediately and collared one of his liaison officers, Major Glover Johns, to escort him in a jeep. "We would drive up the road to the next corner, stop, get out and creep up to look it over before going on," Johns recalled. "There could have been a couple of regiments of Krauts in that country anywhere." Luckily for them, they encountered no enemy. Finally, they made it to Le Carrefour—quiet by now—and surveyed the remnants of the awful slaughter. "We found dead Yanks and dead Krauts all over the roads and fields, with Colonel Warfield . . . dead at the head of his staff, pistol in hand." Gerhardt studied Warfield's body for a moment. "If you have to die, that's the way to do it," he asserted.

Private Marquis inspected many of the dead bodies that lay in the orchard from which he had escaped. He saw his captain, many of his friends, and several Germans. Among the dead was Lieutenant Kermit Miller, along with several members of his patrol. Marquis watched as one of his comrades looted an enemy body. "There was a GI pulling off [a] German's wedding ring and going through his pockets. I never could bring myself to do that." He was in the minority. Most men were too numb to care. "The frayed nerves were something else. Many were in a state of shell shock."

In a way, Warfield's battalion was fortunate. The Germans who ambushed them were only looking to inflict damage, punch a hole through the 2nd Battalion, and move on to defensive positions along the southern bank of the Elle River. They were not trying to annihilate the 2nd Battalion, only stun it sufficiently to allow their own escape. One can only imagine the damage that a well-supplied, resolute, well-coordinated counterattacking force might have inflicted upon the battalion.

As was often the case during the Normandy campaign, the Americans recovered fairly quickly and learned well from their mistakes. The new battalion commander, Lieutenant Colonel Arthur Sheppe, reorganized his decimated command well enough to keep pace with the 115th Regiment's other two battalions on a lightly opposed advance to the northern side of the Elle River on June 10 and 11. There they received 110 replacements and prepared to attack across the river. Needless to say, the 2nd Battalion never again bedded down for the night in combat without posting guards and observation positions.[29]

The Germans did what they could to interfere with the Allied navies and the enormous job of unloading supplies on the invasion beaches. In the week after the invasion, the Luftwaffe flew 1,683 sorties against Allied shipping. Almost all of these came at night. A formation of twenty or so night fighters and bombers would fly over the beaches, drop flares, and then drop bombs. The whole sky would light up with antiaircraft fire from the ships of the invasion fleet. Seldom did the antiaircraft fire hit anything. The air raids amounted to little more than frightening harassment. The Germans succeeded in sinking only one major ship, the destroyer USS *Meredith*, in these bombing raids.

Night after night, the Germans also sent their E-boats, manned by courageous crews, to gnaw at the fringes of the Allied fleet. In the American landing areas, Admiral Alan Kirk, commander of the Western Naval Task Force that covered Omaha and Utah beaches, set up an area screen consisting of destroyers, destroyer escorts, and patrol craft. Each ship patrolled an area about six hundred yards apart from another. Their prows cut through the water as they circled around like watchdogs. The E-boats sank a few small American ships, including a couple of LSTs, but comprised little more than a pinprick on the biceps of the mighty fleet.

Throughout June, the greatest danger for the ships was still mines. These floating weapons played a role in the sinking of several ships, including the

Susan B. Anthony, which was transporting a regiment of the 90th Division to Utah beach. Shortly after 0800 on June 8, the destroyer USS *Glennon* struck a mine as it prepared to lend fire support to 4th Division troops at Quinéville. "The effect was violent throughout the ship," the skipper, Commander C. A. Johnson, wrote. "The force of the explosion had been of such magnitude as to throw two men, who were standing on the fantail, 40 feet in the air, landing them in the water. One of these men was later recovered with both legs broken and possible internal injuries." The explosion also tore away a 600-pound depth charge from its rack and threw it fifty feet to a torpedo platform.

For nearly two hellish days the crew tried to save the ship. All the while, the *Glennon* was a stationary target for enemy shore batteries at Quinéville. At sunrise on June 10, the enemy guns finished off the damaged destroyer. The 267 surviving crewmen abandoned ship and sadly watched as it slipped beneath the waves in the early evening.

The *Glennon* wasn't alone in its misfortune. The destroyer escort USS *Rich* also set off several mines (one of which was fifty yards to starboard, another of which was directly underneath its keel, and the other at some close but undetermined point) while coming to the aid of the stricken *Glennon* on June 8. The results were not pretty. Much of the ship was torn apart. Depth charges flew everywhere; instrument glasses shattered; men were flung as much as fifty feet in the air. The ship's commanding officer, Lieutenant Commander E. A. Michel, was standing on the bridge when the third explosion flung him into the air and onto the main deck. He lost consciousness for a time and then awoke to the awful sight of devastation and bloodshed. "The force of the explosion and its effect on material and personnel were terrific. Not more than two or three of the men who were forward of the mast survived without . . . severe head, back, or leg injuries."

An officer on the nearby PT-502 saw the *Rich* sink within fifteen minutes of the third explosion. "With her back broken, with bodies and parts of bodies draped from her radar mast, her gun tubs and what remained of her funnel, the destroyer escort was a scene of holocaust. A lone figure bobbed by under the overhanging bow of the boat. The bow line was rapidly coiled to rescue this last living survivor, but before it could be tossed the man raised his face to the sailors . . . staring down at him, and in a firm, calm voice, said, 'Never mind; I have no arms to catch it.'" Before rescuers could be dispatched to snatch the maimed man from the *Rich*'s deck, he slipped beneath the waves. Perhaps he did not want to live with his disability. The *Rich* had a crew of 215; 27 of them were killed, 52 were missing (almost all of whom were drowned or incinerated), and 73 were wounded.

To counteract the silent threat of mines, minesweepers constantly patrolled the waters around Normandy. These unsung ships were like the navy's version of combat engineers—sweeping untold numbers of mines, only drawing attention to themselves when they failed. Their work was never done. There were always more mines to worry about. "The strain on officers and men of daily sweeping followed by nights on the patrol line or mine watching was undoubtedly severe," Admiral Bertram Ramsay later wrote, "and in bad weather ships' complements at times must have been near the limits of endurance."

The efforts of support ships like minesweepers, destroyer escorts, patrol craft, and PT boats allowed the destroyers, cruisers, and battleships to concentrate on lending fire support to the troops ashore (a job they performed magnificently). It also allowed the transport ships to move supplies to the shore unmolested. One of the major reasons the Germans believed the invasion had to come at Calais was because that region bristled with wonderful ports that the Allies would presumably need to keep their burgeoning armies supplied. To some extent, that was true. Ports were important, especially the longer the campaign continued. But the Allies at Normandy demonstrated an amazing capacity to land such vital things as food, ammunition, equipment, reinforcements, and vehicles right on the beach, from LSTs, LCTs, and LCIs.

Much has been made of the role the artificial mulberry harbors played in supplying the Allied armies at Normandy. They were ingenious creations but, for the Americans, were not all that significant. The American mulberry was not fully operational until June 16. Three days later, it was destroyed by a powerful storm that rocked the invasion area. The vast majority of cargo was unloaded from landing craft, moved inland on beach exits that the engineers quickly improved into fully functioning roads and from there to the fighting front.

To make this possible at Omaha beach, army engineers and navy demolition teams did an excellent job under adverse circumstances. The chaotic landing, combined with mines, obstacles, and the general clutter on the beach, presented them with quite a challenge. Nonetheless, in two days they cleared most of the beach, built an emergency air strip near St-Laurent (close to the present-day U.S. cemetery), and built the roads that would supply the U.S. Army in France for several months to come. By June 11, support troops working at Omaha beach were handling nearly 7,000 tons of supplies per day. By June 18, less than two weeks after D-Day, close to 200,000 troops, 27,000 vehicles, and 69,000 tons of supplies had been unloaded (at Utah the numbers were 110,000, 15,000, and 42,000, respectively).

All day long every day, landing craft made runs to the beach disgorging cargo—crates of ammo and food, along with artillery, vehicles, and other items. The support troops, many of whom were African-American, quickly established an efficient system of unloading and transporting supplies. Some units, like the predominantly black 83rd Quartermaster Trucking Company, drove their vehicles right up to the waterline so that cargo could be off-loaded as quickly as possible. Cranes maneuvered the supplies onto the waiting trucks. "We would take [the supplies] out to what we called 'dumps,' in the area for storing whatever kind of supplies they were," Sergeant James Hudson recalled. "If it was gasoline, they had an area for that. They had an area for food and clothing too. We even had some poison gas. They had an area for that. They had an area for the parts for the trucks. They had an area for the ammunition. Everything had an area. We ran a twenty-four-hour shift to get that stuff out of the water. I worked twelve hours and was off twenty-four."

It was not unusual for LST crewmen to make as many as thirty or forty trips back and forth between England and the beach. They would land supplies, take on prisoners or wounded, return to ports in England, reload, and repeat the process. They and the quartermaster troops kept the combat troops supplied and the Allied hopes of victory at Normandy alive.[30]

The first follow-up division to land at Omaha was the U.S. 2nd Infantry Division. Known as the Indian Head Division for its distinctive shoulder patch, the unit was new to combat. The division's 9th and 38th Infantry Regiments landed on June 7 while the beach was still under artillery and sniper fire. Within forty-eight hours, General Gerow had a job for them. They were to advance south, capture Trevieres, and push all the way to the Cerisy Forest (original objective of the 29th Division's 175th Infantry). This forest was located on high ground immediately astride N-172, the main road between St-Lô and Bayeux.

At noon on June 9, the 2nd Division's attack began. At this point, the two assaulting regiments still did not have most of their heavy weapons, vehicles, and artillery support. In the starkest terms, this meant that the soldiers of the rifle companies went forward into danger with almost no fire support of any kind, a tricky proposition to say the least. The 9th Infantry skirted east of Trévières but soon came under fire from Germans in prepared positions just outside the town. This fire, and a lack of immediate tank support, pinned down the 2nd Battalion for most of the day. Company E lost twenty men in this fight. At 2200 when the battalion received orders to resume its attack under cover of darkness, more problems ensued. Supporting artillery was finally in place, but someone made a terrible error. The American artillery shells screamed into the battalion CP. The shelling only lasted a few moments, but it inflicted seventeen American casualties. In spite of this screwup, the battalion managed to march a mile south to Rubercy by midnight.

A few hundred yards to the east, the 9th Infantry's 3rd Battalion made more progress on June 9, probably because this unit had more of its heavy weapons and equipment. In the early evening, they ran into tough German resistance at the little village of Haut-Hameau. The infantrymen took shelter in fields as observers called in a preliminary bombardment from mortars, artillery, self-propelled guns, and several destroyers. Once the barrage ended, soldiers like Private First Class Placido Patrick Munnia spent the whole night fighting in the village, eliminating the Germans any way they could. "Any method we could think of we had to use. We . . . had to go in there and flush them out, one by one, house to house. You'd crack open a door, throw a pineapple [grenade] in, or throw a concussion grenade in there and run, moving swiftly. You'd fire, walking and firing at the same time. You did all kind of stunts."

At one point, Munnia's squad came to a little farmhouse. The sergeant was worried about the possibility that an enemy sniper might be holed up inside. Cautiously the Americans approached the farmhouse. Then, when the sergeant signaled, they sprang into action. "One fellow was running before me. I ran for the door; he pitched a grenade through the window; I blasted open the door. It just blew." Two other men kicked in the door. "There were two Germans, with noses bleeding, hands high in the air, yelling, 'Comrade!' We immediately took them away and dashed them off quickly. They were startled. One German . . . lieutenant, blond-haired, blue-eyed . . . looked at us in amazement. He had the look of bewilderment."

They cleared out Haut-Hameau and moved on to a lonely cluster of fields southeast of Rubercy. In its first full day in combat, the 9th Infantry had lost ten killed and eighty wounded.[31]

In the meantime, the 38th Infantry was fighting its way into Trévières. Resolute German defenders had held up the 1st Division in front of Trévières for a day or two. Now, as the 1st Division moved on to other missions, the men of the 38th Infantry took on the job of driving the enemy out of Trévières for good. It took them more than a day to clear out the town. In the memory of one 2nd Division soldier, the Germans "fought with great tenacity, doggedly defending the town house by house. Many had to be literally dug up from the cellars before they would surrender."

During the battle, two entire battalions of U.S. artillery, the 15th and 38th, became available. The artillerymen fired 3,652 rounds in support of the assault troops in Trévières. This helped tip the balance of victory to the Americans. The fierce fighting in and around Trévières broke German resistance in that area. The Germans no longer had any effective forces to hinder the 2nd Division's movement to the Cerisy Forest. Between June 10 and June 12, the division advanced, against almost no resistance all the way through the forest, cutting the St-Lô–Bayeux road. Along the way, they witnessed the grisly aftermath of Allied fighter-bomber missions. The roads and fields were dotted with dead, bloated, rotting Germans. Many were freshly killed. Major Ralph Steele, the regiment's intelligence officer, found the decomposing remains of one group in a farmhouse the Germans had been using for a headquarters. "The German officers . . . had been killed as they were eating a meal. Some of the soup was still warm and their hard bread and dirty dishes . . . were still on the table." The noxious-smelling carcasses of cows and horses only added to the carnage. Some of the horses were still tied to their wagons or caissons. Broken, shattered enemy equipment was everywhere.

For a brief, tantalizing moment the road to St-Lô—the great objective of the whole American campaign—seemed open. But along the southern edges of the Cerisy Forest the 2nd Division began to run into determined, organized resistance, mainly from the elite troopers of the enemy 3rd Parachute Division. The Indian Head Division's advance came to a grinding halt along the approaches to the highest ground in Normandy—a notorious place called Hill 192.[32]

At the same time that the 2nd Division was capturing the Cerisy Forest, the 1st Division was on the move as well. By June 11, the Big Red One had progressed several miles south of its D+3 positions along the N-13 highway. Now the division was at the extreme eastern flank of the American armies in Normandy, with orders to advance steadily south to Caumont. On the morning of June 12, General Huebner lined up the 18th Infantry on his right flank and the 26th on the left and ordered them to get moving.

Throughout the day, they encountered little, if any, resistance. In just one day, the two regiments covered the entire distance of four miles to Caumont. The 18th Infantry cut D-11, the road that connected Caumont with St-Lô to the west. Only in Caumont itself did the Americans run into protracted fighting. At dusk, reconnaissance patrols from the 2nd Battalion, 26th Infantry, skulked their way into the northern fringes of the town. These brave men, prowling cautiously in staggered groups along the streets of Caumont, quickly saw that the enemy was here in force. They retreated back to their battalion CP, reporting that the Germans probably had as many as two companies, plus several self-propelled guns, in Caumont.

Around midnight, the battalion tried attacking the town. The Germans hurled them back. Their machine guns laid down withering fire on the roads into town. For a short time F Company captured a few buildings, but the Americans soon withdrew. At dawn they came back, this time with tanks from the 743rd. The tanks blasted suspected machine-gun positions and searched eagerly for the enemy self-propelled guns.

The infantry surged forward and concentrated on assaulting enemy-held houses. The fighting was eyeball-to-eyeball. Monfrey Wilson, a platoon sergeant, was attacking one such house with several other men when he heard

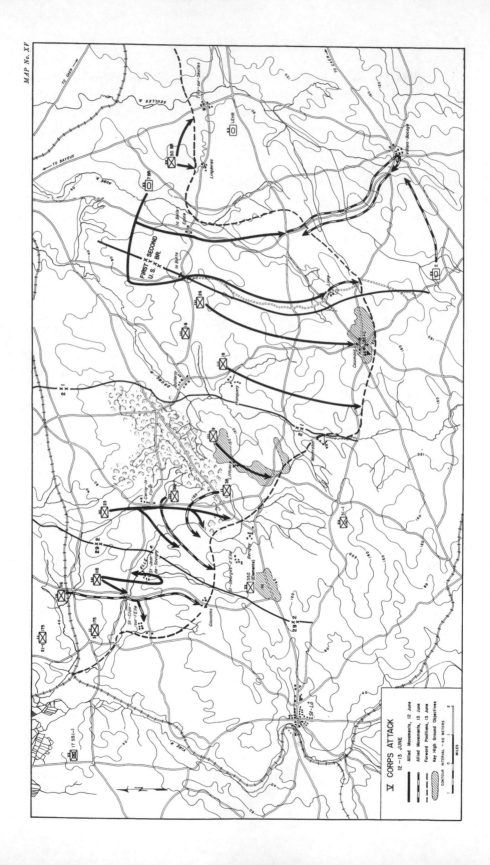

V CORPS ATTACK

12 – 13 JUNE

Allied Movements, 12 June

Allied Movements, 13 June

Forward Positions, 13 June

Key High Ground Objectives

CONTOUR INTERVAL — 40 METERS

MILES

a thud close by. "A German sergeant threw a grenade at us that landed between my corporal and me. It was a dud. We both shot him and he was hit twice, once below the heart and once above." The enemy soldier pitched over and into the street. "He lay there praying and crying. The medics picked him up and gave him blood. I later saw the doctor and he told me that he lived."

By 0900 the Americans had liberated Caumont. Many of the buildings were on fire (probably a result of the Sherman tanks' 75mm shells). The Americans extinguished what fires they could, rummaged around in the ruins, and found large vats of wine. One platoon from Captain Charles Murphy's combat engineer company was trying to put out a fire. They ran out of water and instead "used a vat of wine to put the damn fire out." Perhaps they had sampled a bit too much of the vino!

The 26th Infantry spread out south and east of the town. They prepared positions along a magnificent stretch of high ground that afforded a terrific view of miles of surrounding terrain. "From our position we could see several thousand yards to our front and observe anything moving," Warren Coffman, the C Company radioman, later wrote. Throughout the day on June 13, Coffman's company, and several others from the 26th Infantry, warded off patrol-sized counterattacks. "We observed four long columns of enemy soldiers moving toward us. The entire Company was put on alert. We sat there waiting while the enemy came closer, and closer. When they got within about a hundred yards, we were given the order to fire and the whole company began firing at once with rifles, machine guns and mortars. It made quite a noise, and caught the enemy by surprise. Many of them were killed but others kept coming. Some [enemy] soldiers were shot trying to get over the hedgerow into our position. After a short while, the enemy began to retreat."

The Germans did not get anywhere near Caumont. The resistance posed by units like Coffman's, plus thousands of rounds of artillery, negated any chance of the Germans regaining the town or its surrounding high ground. For the Americans, possession of Caumont meant that German artillery could no longer reach Omaha beach. The 1st Division now occupied the deepest Allied penetration along the Calvados coast (Caumont was about twenty miles from the beaches). In one week, Gerow's V Corps had fought its way through heavily defended Omaha beach and inland, capturing enough ground to accommodate the thousands of soldiers and vehicles pouring ashore as a result of the Navy's impressive logistical effort.[33]

However, the enemy was far from beaten. After taking Caumont on June 13, the 1st Division barely moved anywhere for an entire month. German reinforcements were pouring into the area. These were men from elite divisions like the 2nd Panzer, 17th SS Panzer Grenadiers, 3rd Parachute, and Panzer Lehr. Their arrival in Normandy had been seriously delayed by Allied aircraft, but now they were deploying along the hedgerow-honeycombed high ground between St-Lô and Caen. They had hoped to arrive in Normandy quickly enough to fulfill Rommel's vision of repulsing the Allied invasion at the waterline. Instead, they now found themselves fulfilling Rundstedt's vision of an inland battle to destroy Allied ambitions in western Europe. Their presence dashed Allied hopes of a quick, enveloping push for St-Lô in the west and Caen in the east.

The most evil harbinger of the stalemate that lay ahead occurred three miles east of the Big Red One at Villers-Bocage. On June 12–13, the British 7th Armored Division (the famed Desert Rats) boldly maneuvered around the front lines and plunged into Villers-Bocage, briefly liberating the town. But the British tankers ran head-on into German tanks, including one commanded by the famous tank ace Michael Wittman, who single-handedly destroyed several tanks and vehicles of the 4th County of London Yeomanry. In fact, German resistance at Villers-Bocage was so fierce that the division commander, Major General "Bobby" Erskine, and his immediate superior, XXX Corps commander Lieutenant General G. C. Bucknall, elected to withdraw. This was a controversial decision (debated for many years afterward) that effectively doomed the British to weeks of stalemate in front of Caen.[34]

They were not alone. For one week after D-Day the Americans had advanced steadily, closing to within five miles of St-Lô. But by June 13 the Germans had stymied them. For now, St-Lô remained a distant dream.

CHAPTER TWO

INLAND FROM UTAH: THE WEEK AFTER D-DAY

At Ste-Mère-Eglise, the crisp Norman night gave way to the fresh specter of daylight shortly after 0500 on June 7. The embattled American paratroopers in and around the town welcomed the sight of the sunrise. All night long, they had been under enemy artillery fire. German patrols had roamed around the fringes of town, bumping into U.S. roadblocks, exchanging bursts of automatic weapons fire that tore through the night. The paratroopers were weary. They knew that according to the original invasion plan, they were supposed to have been relieved by the 4th Division sometime on June 6. That had not happened. Colonel Edson Raff's task force of glider infantry-men and tanks could not pierce German defenses at Hill 20 (Fauville) south of Ste-Mère-Eglise. Raff had attacked three separate times but had gotten nowhere while losing three tanks and an armored car. Raff was stalled for the night, some twenty-five hundred yards south of Ste-Mère-Eglise.

Now, on the morning of the second day of Operation Overlord, the para-troopers remained alert for any sign of the enemy or their relief force, whichever came first. Sergeant Bill Dunfee, I Company, 505th Parachute In-fantry, had only been in combat for one day, but it had been quite an educa-tion. "We learned in a hurry to cut laterally into the side of your foxhole for a safe place to hide the family jewels. We also found that the safest place to re-lieve one's bladder was in the bottom of your foxhole. If Mother Nature re-quired further relief, you were in serious trouble."

That was because the Germans had been lobbing artillery and mortars into the American positions all night long; nor did that change after day-break. "The enemy really socked it to us with 88s and screaming meemies." Some of the 88s burst in the air, scattering fragments in deadly cones. The screaming meemies hurled rockets that exploded in random patterns all over

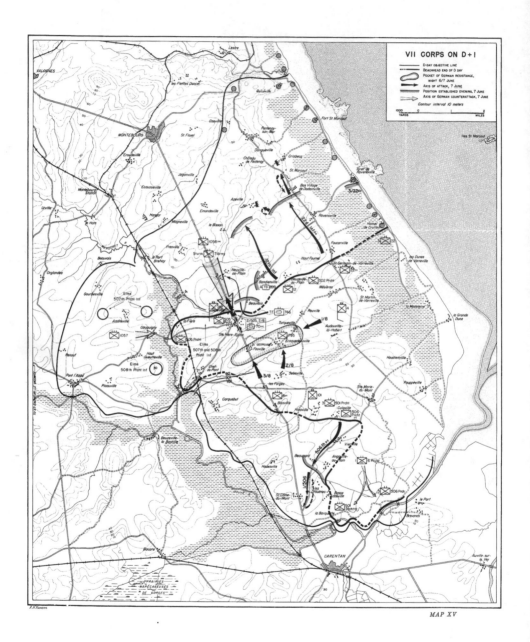

MAP XV

the battered town, sending rubble, dirt, and gravel flying in every direction. Dunfee saw one rocket score a direct hit on a mortar squad. "They were all killed, the explosion must have detonated a gammon grenade in the leg pocket of one man. [It] blew him to bits. His head, chest and right arm were all that remained intact." In the course of several hours of shelling, shrapnel destroyed Sergeant Dunfee's bazooka and his musette bag, not to mention his gammon grenade—luckily, it exploded too far away from him to do any damage.

Sometimes there were lulls in the shelling. During one such quiet moment, Dunfee called out to Louis DiGiralamo, a buddy in an adjacent foxhole, "Are you okay, Dee Gee?"

DiGiralamo had just finished relieving himself in the bottom of his stinking hole. "If blood smells like shit, I'm bleeding to death."

In spite of the circumstances, Dunfee smiled and chuckled. But in the back of his mind he wondered if he would live through the day.[1]

As Dunfee pondered his fate, the Germans prepared to attack Ste-Mère-Eglise. They came from Neuville, south along the N-13, which, in this section of Normandy, stretched from Carentan in the south, through Ste-Mère-Eglise, all the way to Cherbourg at the northern tip of the peninsula. By the morning of June 7, the Germans had amassed an attacking force of 6,000 troops. These soldiers, hailing from a variety of units, including the 1058th Regiment and the Sturm Battalion, were supported by ten self-propelled assault guns, plus armored cars and three battalions of artillery. During the night they had slowly worked their way through the network of hedgerows that bordered either side of the N-13.

There were 600 lightly armed American paratroopers defending Ste-Mère-Eglise. Lieutenant Colonel Benjamin Vandervoort, with his leg in a cast because of a D Day ankle break, knew that the Germans were coming, and his instincts told him to launch an attack of his own, on the flanks of the approaching enemy. For several hours now he had been receiving reports of German troop movements north of town. The most notable report came from the executive officer of D Company, Lieutenant Waverly Wray. Wray was an avid woodsman and Baptist from Mississippi. "He didn't use profanities," one of his men recalled, "the strongest expletive he used when provoked was 'John Brown,' an old Southern curse word. If he said, 'John Brown,' then he was mad." An experienced hunter, Wray was blessed with a keen sense of direction and an innate understanding of terrain. In the foggy dawn Wray could sense the German presence. He knew they were coming.

When Lieutenant Wray reported this to Vandervoort, the colonel ordered him to attack. Wray went back to his company and immediately set out on a one-man reconnaissance patrol to determine the path of his attack. Moving with incredible stealth, Lieutenant Wray prowled the area, noting several

German troop concentrations and the location of enemy artillery. He crouched behind a hedgerow and rested for a moment. All at once, he heard guttural German voices on the other side of the hedgerow. Wray listened for a few seconds. He knew enough German to ascertain that the voices belonged to enemy officers, who were conferring, probably planning their attack.

Wray hoisted his M-1, burst through an opening in the hedgerow, and found himself face-to-face with eight German officers, who were standing around a radio. "*Hande hoch!*" Wray commanded.

Seven of the Germans raised their hands, but one reached for a pistol. Wray immediately shot him between the eyes. This set off a free-for-all. The surviving officers scrambled for cover as two enemy soldiers, shooting from a trench to Wray's rear, fired a couple of bursts. Bullets ripped his field jacket and tore away half of his right ear. He dropped to a knee and, in coldly deliberate fashion, shot each enemy officer and then, after inserting a fresh clip into his Garand, the two gunners to his rear.

Lieutenant Wray made it back to his CP. He was an awful-looking bloody mess. Half of his ear was gone and there were holes in his clothes, but he refused medical help. "Who's got more grenades?" he wondered. Wray then helped place 60mm mortar fire on many of the enemy positions he had seen. As it turned out, Wray had killed the commander of the 1058th Regiment's 1st Battalion, along with several members of his staff. This enemy unit was supposed to lead the attack, but it was now confused and leaderless.[2]

Consequently, the German attack got off to a bad, uncoordinated start. A quarter-mile north of Ste-Mère-Eglise, enemy troops collided with American roadblocks and outpost positions. German self-propelled guns rumbled down the road, firing into buildings, as German infantry dashed from hedgerow to hedgerow. The German attack may have been confused and poorly coordinated, but enemy numbers soon took their toll. Swarms of German soldiers put intense pressure on the Americans north of town.

In one U.S. position, located just east of the N-13, about a block away from Ste-Mère-Eglise's hospital, First Lieutenant Charles Sammon and his platoon were having a difficult time fending off the enemy attack. The day before, Sammon had seen heavy combat near Neuville, protecting the flank of Lieutenant Turnbull's platoon that had held off the German's main D-Day counterattack at Neuville. Today Vandervoort had ordered Sammon to this spot with orders to blunt the enemy attack. So once again he found himself at the center of the action. The lieutenant and his men were settling into foxholes to the right of the road.

Sammon peeked over the edge of his foxhole and saw a German armored car, moving slowly, hosing down the buildings around the Ste-Mère-Eglise hospital. Two soldiers—strangers to Sammon—were trying to load and fire a bazooka at the armored car, but they couldn't get the bazooka to work. Sammon scowled. He wanted no part of such bravado. "I placed my men in position but told them not to fire at tanks or armored cars as our light machine guns would do nothing but attract their fire. I told them to wait for the infantry."

They did not have to wait long. The German infantrymen soon came straight at them. "They ran right into our position and I knew that we would have to retreat if we were going to fight another day. I hollered at the men to fall back." Firing and sprinting, they fell back to a new position around the hospital. Sammon was in such a hurry that he left his pack behind. Three of his men were hit during the retreat to the hospital. The lieutenant helped them into the hospital and saw something he never forgot. "Here were a couple of German Doctors working alongside a couple of American Airborne Doctors on what had once been a dining room table. They were sawing off arms, legs, etc. and throwing discarded limbs into a pile. The whole place was a mess of blood and bandages and I felt considerably better when I got back outside."

In the meantime, a German self-propelled gun (SP) worked its way up to the building containing Vandervoort's CP. From there the enemy gunners could see an unattended 57mm gun that was supposed to be covering the approaches to the CP. They opened fire at the gun and missed. Suddenly an American soldier ran out of a building, took control of the antitank gun, and fired two rounds at the enemy SP. The rounds hit home; the SP exploded, incinerating the German crew. This stunned the enemy and blunted their advance. Other German vehicles retreated or halted, and enemy infantry took cover behind hedgerows.

This allowed Lieutenant Sammon's platoon to reoccupy its original position. "We did this and in most cases jumped back into holes just as the Germans were jumping out. Needless to say, many of them failed to get out in time. I managed to get back into the same hole I had vacated." His pack was still there, but minus his K rations and his favorite pipe.[3]

Sammon did not know it, but the enemy attack had peaked. The Germans were stunned by the ferocity of American resistance. Many of them—especially those who came from the 1058th regiment—were demoralized from the previous day's bloody fighting. They were now content to hover on the fringes of Ste-Mère-Eglise, shooting when the opportunity offered but mostly just taking shelter. Hours passed. It was now well past noon.

Many of the Americans were also taking shelter, including Private Chuck Miller, a rifleman in D Company, and his buddy whom he only knew by the nickname Big Red. Somewhere to the left of the road, just outside of town, they were hiding behind a hedgerow. Mortar shells were exploding all over the place. After one explosion, Miller heard a trickling noise.

"What a time for Big Red to take a piss," Miller thought. Miller glanced at his friend. "Instead of [taking a piss] his blood was coming out of his stomach, just like urine, just pouring out of him." A fragment had pierced an artery in his abdomen. "It just burst open and he was dead in three or four minutes. There was nothing we could do. It was awful . . . to watch him die, but there was nothing we could do, except hold his hand, and try to make it a little bit easier for him."[4]

Private Miller grieved for his buddy and wondered when the amphibious forces would arrive. The paratroopers had been alone here in Ste-Mère-Eglise for better than a day. Rumors had been sweeping around the airborne ranks all morning that the 4th Division would arrive soon. In his CP in the middle of town, Major General Matthew Ridgway, commander of the 82nd, also wondered when he could expect relief. The son of an army colonel, Ridgway graduated from West Point in 1917. A solid professional and fine leader, Ridgway was destined to become one of the premier American generals of the twentieth century. Right now, the general was worried that the Germans would regroup and send armor at his embattled troopers north of Ste-Mère-Eglise. The night before, Ridgway had dispatched Lieutenant Walter Winton, his assistant G-3, to go through German lines and establish contact with Major General Raymond Barton's 4th Division. "By that time I'd been on my feet for about forty-eight hours and I didn't know if I could move my frame," Winton said. A doctor gave him some Benzedrine and "off I floated." In spite of his fatigue, Winton and his small patrol succeeded in contacting General Barton. Barton assured him that Raff's task force, along with Colonel Van Fleet's entire 8th Infantry Regiment, would reach Ste-Mère-Eglise during the morning hours of June 7. They were to advance from the south, crush German resistance at Fauville, Ecoqueneauville, and Turqueville, and enter Ste-Mère-Eglise.[5]

All morning long, they fought to achieve this objective. A predominantly Georgian battalion was defending Turqueville. Thanks to the efforts of Russian-speaking Sergeant John Svonchek, the Americans took Turqueville. Svonchek was captured that morning and moved to Turqueville under the supervision of the Georgians. In Russian he persuaded them to surrender. In total, 174 of them, including their German officer, surrendered to the 1st Battalion of the 8th Infantry.

The regiment's other two battalions were several hundred yards to the west, moving north along the fringes of the N-13. They encountered mostly straggling groups of Germans. The enemy parachute battalion that had stymied the American advance on Fauville the day before had pulled out during the night. Even so, the stragglers made things very difficult for the GIs.

The 3rd Battalion advanced along the fields and lanes that paralleled the highway. Private First Class William Jones, a sniper from Tennessee who had painted the name of his home state on the back of his field jacket, was advancing north with I Company. He and the others gravitated toward gaps in the hedgerows. But each time they did so, they came under fire. "As we went by the gaps, the bullets were whizzing right through the openings. You'd wait until one went by and then you'd run across the gap."

One time, after barely making it alive through one gap, he spotted a sniper. "I saw what looked like a knot way up in . . . a big tall tree. Well, I fired and it kind of gave a jerk. The second shot I fired he rolled off."[6]

The 3rd Battalion captured Hill 20 but lost contact with the 2nd Battalion, which had swung around the right flank in order to bypass German defenders and reach Ste-Mère-Eglise as soon as possible. The 2nd Battalion quickly took Ecoqueneauville and approached Ste-Mère-Eglise from the northeast. As they neared the buildings on the edge of town, they ran into trouble. "We were getting along fairly well until we ran into a complex of dairy farms, each separated by a road and a big stone wall around its house, barn, silos," Captain George Mabry, the battalion operations officer, wrote. The day before, he had successfully linked up with General Maxwell Taylor's 101st Airborne troopers in Pouppeville. Now he was trying to hook up with 82nd Airborne soldiers in Ste-Mère-Eglise. "We began getting a terrific amount of small-arms fire. We were shooting mortars at these houses and artillery had been brought in."

Captain Mabry crawled along a small hedgerow with several members of F Company. They peeked over the hedgerow, saw a German running, and shot him. All at once, an enemy grenade flew over the hedgerow and exploded near Mickey Donahue, one of the regiment's star boxers. Mabry took a shot at the German who threw the grenade, killed him, and then crawled to Donahue. "He was bleeding and looked as though he was going to die pretty soon. I dragged him up the little road, turned him over on his back, put his helmet under his head, took out his canteen and put [it] by his right hand." Mabry and two other men called for medics and resumed their attack on the dairy complex.

Nearby, Private First Class John Pfister of E Company hoisted a bazooka and pointed it at the window of a German-occupied building. "I fired my first rocket . . . and made a direct hit. It went right in the window. It exploded. The fire stopped . . . and we just moved on. We came on . . . a farmhouse and a barn and we heard something in the barn." Pfister and his buddies took no chances. "We fired [a] bazooka rocket into the barn. It went off. There were no soldiers. It was a horse. It came out and just took off."

Slowly and steadily, the 2nd Battalion filtered into Ste-Mère-Eglise from the east. As they did so, they saw the remnants of the bitter fighting that had taken place in the area on D-Day. Captain Mabry led the way. "We . . . saw many German vehicles on the paved road leading into Ste-Mère-Eglise. There must have been twenty to twenty-five trucks, strafed and riddled with .50 caliber MG bullets." The trucks had been destroyed by Allied fighter-bombers. "We saw a paratrooper hanging from a telephone line, his feet about a foot off the ground. His throat had been cut. It angered us." Some of the enlisted men threatened reprisal, but Mabry quashed that sort of eye-for-an-eye mentality . "I told them we will never do this, that's what we're fighting against." Minutes later, Mabry and the other 4th Division soldiers met up with live paratroopers, who were naturally thrilled to see them. Mabry and his superior, Lieutenant Colonel Carlton McNeely, found Van-dervoort and, in hopes of knocking the Germans off-balance before they could attack, began planning an attack of their own, to the north out of Ste-Mère-Eglise.[7]

As this was happening, General Ridgway was sending word to General Barton (once again through the able voice of Lieutenant Winton) of his need for tanks. Ridgway was still deeply concerned about a German armored coun-terattack on Ste-Mère-Eglise. Winton no sooner got to General Barton's CP at Audoville-la-Hubert when Major General J. Lawton Collins, commander of the VII Corps, arrived. Collins had come ashore late in the morning on June 7 and immediately proceeded to Barton's CP. The general was impressed with the urgency of Ridgway's request. "He was expecting an imminent attack by a column of German armor moving down on Ste-Mère-Eglise via the main road from Cherbourg," Collins wrote. "Ridgway urgently requested help from tanks he knew were attached to the 4th Division."

These tanks belonged to B Company of the 746th Tank Battalion. Collins knew that Barton could spare them, so he ordered Winton to take the tanks and guide them to Ste-Mère-Eglise.[8] They sallied forth from Reuville (about a mile east of Ste-Mère-Eglise) and made it to Ste-Mère-Eglise by early afternoon. At Ste-Mère-Eglise they turned north, rumbling up the N-13 toward Neuville. A few hundred yards north of Ste-Mère-Eglise, Ger-man artillery and mortar shells began exploding uncomfortably close to the tanks.

In the lead Sherman, Lieutenant Houston Payne, peering from his com-mander's cupola, spotted the enemy first. Clearly visible in the distance, some three hundred yards away, were five medium tanks and five other ar-mored vehicles. Ridgway had been right. They were massing for an attack. Payne gave the order to open fire. His first round destroyed a self-propelled gun. In mere moments he blasted and set fire to two Mark IV tanks, but then an enemy armor-piercing shell hit his tank, injuring him. His driver moved the tank off the road while Payne ordered the rest of his platoon to engage the enemy column. They did so, and several of the German vehicles tried to flee north in the direction of Neuville.

The 746th Battalion's commander, Lieutenant Colonel C. G. Hupfer, tried to flank them and beat them to the town at the same time. Hupfer succeeded in finding a sunken dirt road that led all the way to Neuville. In just a few minutes he led several tanks into the town. Payne's tank, back in the fight now, soon followed with two others. As he approached Neuville, Payne spotted a German tank, right next to the town church. His loader and gunner fired three rounds at the German tank, setting it afire. At close quarters, the other American tanks traded shots with the German vehicles. The Americans lost two tanks but destroyed all of the enemy vehicles. When they finished, they cruised through Neuville shooting up hedgerows, prompting the surrender of sixty German soldiers and the reclamation of nineteen American paratroopers who had spent the last twenty-four hours as POWs. The sickly sweet stench of burning flesh, hair, and steel permeated the air. Having fought this furious engagement at such close quarters, the tankers were not quite sure what to do next. They took up positions around the town and wondered where the infantry was.[9]

Unbeknownst to the American tank crews, McNeely and Vandervoort's infantrymen were energized by the sight of the tank battle. Quite literally, the armor arrived at the most opportune moment, just as the infantrymen were enduring enemy mortar fire and preparing to move forward. Lieutenant Sammon had been worrying for hours about the presence of a German armored car and a German tank just up the road from his position. Just as he was wondering when friendly armor would arrive, "I heard the unmistakable sound of a Sherman tank firing and looked up to see the German Armored car go up in flames. Two more well placed shots disposed of the German tank." Sammon scanned the area in an effort to see where the Shermans were. "When I did, I was greeted by the wonderful sight of three or four American tanks with a good friend of mine . . . riding on the lead one."[10]

Soldiers from E Company, 505th Parachute Infantry, with two tanks in tow, led the attack. These men, under the command of Lieutenant James Coyle, had watched in jubilant amazement as Hupfer's tanks roared by on their right flank. Now they edged their way north along hedges that shielded them from the view of anyone on the road. Coyle led his men along a series of sunken roads that flanked the N-13. He knew that the Germans, stunned though they may have been, would be ready for any frontal infantry attack up the highway. "I got permission to take [my men] north up a dirt road on the left . . . which provided better cover and concealment." Coyle had only been in combat for a day, but he already knew that the terrain of Normandy demanded this sort of tactical movement. Infantry moving through open fields or along open roads in the presence of the enemy would not survive long.

Coyle's sensible leadership paid great dividends. His company snuck up on the flank of an entire German infantry battalion. The Germans had only recently arrived at their roadside position and had not had time to set up outposts or interlocking machine-gun positions. The Americans had them cornered and opened up with everything they had. The tanks hosed the enemy soldiers with their 75mm guns and machine guns. Infantry troopers blazed away with their rifles and machine guns. The withering fire tore many of the German soldiers to pieces.

Sergeant Otis Sampson, who played such a prominent role at Ste-Mère-Eglise on D-Day, worked today with expert precision. He dropped mortar shells on the enemy and then, out of ammo, picked up a BAR and shot anyone who moved. "I was that close I couldn't miss. That road was their death trap. It was so easy I felt ashamed of myself and quit firing. I felt I had bagged my quota."

Some of the Germans tried, in their desperation, to get away. By now several 8th Infantrymen had joined in the slaughter, including Captain Mabry. "They came running across and reached the sunken road." The Americans shot them down. "German bodies were piled up in the road—a sight hard to believe."

Lieutenant Coyle stood up and commanded his men to cease fire, but he could hardly be heard above the din. He ran up and down the line making himself heard. The shooting died down. Two German potato masher grenades landed near his feet. He dived to the side and the grenades exploded harmlessly. The shooting started up again but soon died down once more. The Americans moved among the remains of what moments before had been a well-equipped, intact battalion of German soldiers but was now little more than a slaughter pen. Dead bodies were everywhere, "two or three deep" in Mabry's recollection. Joe Stanger, a radioman in the 505th, moved among the dead, looking for wounded enemy. "Dead Jerries lay strewn over the ground, their faces a series of grotesque masks." The live and unwounded Germans had their hands held high in surrender. "The Heinies started streaming themselves out under a white flag to give themselves up." The GIs took 200 prisoners.

Reinforcements followed up on the victory. More paratroopers and 8th Infantry troops, operating with newly arrived Shermans from the 70th Tank Battalion, spent the rest of the day pushing north into and beyond Neuville, finally ending up some three hundred yards north of that town. The remnants of the 6,000 German attackers fled north. Their commander, General Karl-Wilhelm von Schlieben, abandoned any hope of renewing the attack. Instead he concentrated his energies on rallying his survivors to establish a new defensive line to hold Cherbourg. Ste-Mère-Eglise was forever liberated. Thus ended the only serious German attempt in the Cotentin to fulfill Rommel's hope of driving the Utah beach invaders into the sea.[11]

On D-Day and in the week after, the experiences of American soldiers at Omaha and Utah beaches were exactly opposite. At Omaha beach, the toughest task was getting ashore. Once the strong German waterline defenses had been pierced, the advance inland was comparatively smooth, at least until German reinforcements stymied the Americans north of St-Lô. At Utah, getting ashore was the easy part. Advancing inland proved to be a much more difficult proposition. "We got off the beach well enough," a 4th Division veteran aptly commented, "but then we hit a wall."[12]

Even after his failed counterattack, General von Schlieben could call on parts of four infantry divisions in his defense of the Cotentin. He still controlled most everything west of the Merderet. East of the Merderet and north of Neuville he established strong defensive positions, anchored at key points by extensive fortifications. Roughly speaking, this line extended from Le Ham through Montebourg, all the way to Quinéville on the coast. It was the 4th Division's job to punch through this defensive line and clear the way for an advance to Cherbourg.

The division's 22nd Infantry Regiment, on the eastern flank, had the job of fighting its way up the coast. On June 7 and 8, the soldiers of this regiment attacked north, attempting to capture the German headland fortresses of Azeville and Crisbecq. These positions were a veritable maze of death. Each position contained a row of four massive concrete blockhouses. The blockhouses were supplied with underground ammunition storage dumps. Communications trenches connected the blockhouses with one another. The Azeville blockhouses contained four 150mm guns; Crisbecq had three 210mm monsters. Barbed wire and mines protected the approaches to the blockhouses, but that wasn't all. "An arc of concrete sniper pillboxes outposted the southern approaches to Azeville," the official history recorded. "Crisbecq . . . occupied a . . . commanding position on the headland overlooking the beaches."

The heavy guns in these fortifications, plus several more at similar strong points north of Utah beach, laid down a steady succession of harassing fire that hindered the unloading of supplies and reinforcements at the beach. There was no way to bypass or flank either position. They had been expertly located to impede the entire northerly advance of the invaders.

Starting at 0700 on June 7, the 2nd Battalion of the 22nd tried to capture Azeville. The battalion had no luck. German machine gunners, holed up in their pillboxes, poured lethal fire on the Americans. The GIs could not get anywhere near the blockhouses. Seeing the vulnerability of the Americans, the German commander launched a counterattack that drove the 2nd Battalion survivors all the way back to their starting point.

The 1st Battalion, aiming for Crisbecq, had an even more miserable time. These men passed through the town of St-Marcouf (not to be confused with a nearby fortification by the same name) and wended their way north up a pair of tree-lined trails that led to the Crisbecq defenses. The battalion's C Company was in the lead. This company was organized into special assault sections, similar to the boat teams used to storm the beach the day before. Each man had his own special job. Mortar crews were to lay down suppressing 60mm fire. Light machine gunners were to aim for the apertures of the blockhouses, as were the fire teams led by BAR men. The toughest job belonged to the flamethrower and demolition men who were supposed to sneak up to the blockhouses and roast or blast the enemy defenders.

To the west, German observers at Azeville saw C Company and the battalion's two trailing companies. Soon a deadly volume of large-caliber shells began exploding around the 1st Battalion troops. Up and down the trail men were hit as they hunched over and trotted forward. The fragments tore flesh from bone. The men could hear the terrible zinging sound the fragments made as they flew in every direction. The wounded, streaming blood from multiple wounds, lay prone and screamed for medics. The unwounded kept inching north, getting closer to Crisbecq. Suddenly they received German small-arms and tank fire from the left. The Germans were counterattacking.

The battalion commander was down. No one was going to get anywhere near Crisbecq on this day. At 1600, the acting commander, Captain Tom Shields, passed along orders to withdraw. His men had been in this meat grinder all day. Now it was time to get out. The retreat was a disorganized, panicked rout. Shields and his survivors retreated south, through St-Marcouf, back to the original jump-off point for this ill-fated attack. Nineteen men from A Company got left behind and, presumably, captured (no one knew for sure what happened to them). Another platoon wandered east, all the way to the beach. Along the way, they captured 113 prisoners before making it to the American lines under the cover of darkness.

At the beach, there were still plenty of enemy soldiers making trouble for the Americans. These brave German soldiers were holed up in blockhouses and pillboxes built into the seawall along a narrow strip of Utah beach north of the landing areas. To the west was a water-inundated area; to the east, the sea. Most of these reinforced concrete blockhouses contained artillery pieces. Ditches, tank traps, machine-gun pillboxes, barbed wire, and mines surrounded these imposing artifices. Inside the blockhouses, German artillery observers watched the American unloading operations and called down fire from the inland fortifications at Crisbecq and Azeville. The only way for the Americans to eliminate these enemy beach positions was to move along the seawall.

Lieutenant Colonel Arthur Teague's 3rd Battalion, 22nd Infantry, received a simple directive from General Barton—go in and destroy those fortifications. The directive may have been simple, but the implementation of it certainly was not. Teague drew on an incredible range of supporting firepower: Naval gunfire, ranging from destroyers to battleships, blasted the pillboxes. Next, tanks and 57mm antitank guns closed to within seventy-five yards of them and fired away. As they did so, mortar teams laid down even more fire. Riflemen, machine gunners, and flamethrower and demolition men waded through the inundated areas behind the German defenses, closing to within ten or twenty yards of the forts.

The whole thing seemed terrific in theory, but it was not. The supporting fire usually did little more than chip away at the concrete of these steel-reinforced emplacements. Enemy soldiers would lie in wait while the tanks, mortars, and naval gunners did their thing. Then, when the American infantry prepared to assault, the Germans would fire at them with everything they had, including artillery fire from the inland batteries. The result was bloodshed and carnage for the assaulting infantry. Many of them were caught in the open, right in the middle of the water, where they made easy targets for German machine gunners or riflemen. The dead bodies of many slipped below the waterline. Others lay bleeding to death in the dunes. The rest retreated as best they could. The battalion regrouped and tried again. Such was the pace of its advance.

It took the battalion the entire day on June 7 to go 2,000 yards and capture two blockhouses. Later that night, most of the battalion moved inland to thwart a possible German counterattack from Azeville and Crisbecq. The counterattack never came, but Teague succeeded in recrossing the inundated area and, during the early-morning hours of June 8, forcing the surrender of the German garrison at Taret de Ravenoville, a previously contentious fort. The last of the coastal forts, St-Marcouf, did not fall until more than one week after D-Day.[13]

The 12th Infantry, wedged in between the 8th on the left and the 22nd on the right, was making equally slow progress. The regiment's objective was the high ground northeast of Montebourg, but first it needed to capture Edmondeville, a town located slightly east of N-13. American artillery and naval fire had pounded Edmondeville throughout the day on June 7, but on the morning of June 8 the barrage increased in intensity.

Crouched in a muddy ditch south of Edmondeville, First Lieutenant Paul Massa, a naval gunfire spotter, carefully peered through his binoculars, looking for likely targets in the stone buildings that comprised Edmondeville. A few days earlier, at Plymouth, Massa had been moved by the British civilians who had collected near the docks to bid good-bye to the soldiers. Now there was no time for such sentiments. He spotted a church steeple. "What could serve as a better observation post?" he thought. Massa had his target.

He told Corporal Fishman, his radio operator, to turn his equipment on. Massa called Lieutenant (jg) Bob Turner, his naval counterpart in the Navy's fire direction center, and told him he had a target. In a matter of seconds, Turner assigned the cruiser USS *Tuscaloosa* to Massa. The *Tuscaloosa* was a powerful weapon, "about the equivalent of three divisions of field artillery," in Lieutenant Massa's estimation. He established communication with the ship's gunnery officer and gave him the proper coordinates.

"Fire when ready," Massa said.

"Salvo," the *Tuscaloosa*'s radio operator replied.

Massa picked up his binoculars and trained them on the steeple. "This first shell got everyone's attention as it came screaming in. The explosion was loud and spoke with authority." Smoke and debris rose from the far side of the church. Massa smiled. The shell had landed right where he wanted. He picked up the radio: "Fire for effect."

Salvo after salvo of flat trajectory shells slammed into the church. This was in addition to the fire from several other ships, along with supporting field artillery. The barrage lasted an hour, and then the entire regiment closed on Edmondeville. The 12th Infantry experienced varying resistance. Some groups were pinned down by accurate artillery fire originating from Azeville, a mere 1,000 yards to the east. Others fought house-to-house, along the fringes and in the heart of Edmondeville.

Massa's group from the 1st Battalion made it into the town against no resistance at all. The lieutenant now turned his former target into his greatest asset. The church steeple was still standing, so he and Fishman climbed up and into it. "There was a wood stairway part of the way up, and then a ladder the rest of the way up to the belfry." Massa was taken aback by the view. "The steeple was the best observation post I ever had. I got busy and directed naval gunfire at everything that looked like a worthwhile target. That included crossroads, bridges, and wooded areas." Massa had only one problem in the steeple. "Rifle squads from other units following the 1st Battalion were moving into the village. I saw the lead scout . . . stop in the middle of the road and point up to the steeple. Then every man in the squad began firing at the window in the steeple." This happened repeatedly. Each time, the leather-lunged Fishman succeeded in telling them to cease fire. "Fishman cussed them, never saying the same thing twice and using insults I had never heard before."

The fighting in and around Edmondeville was fierce. The enemy launched several counterattacks and even briefly threatened Colonel Russell

"Red" Reeder's regimental CP south of town. One of these counterattacks was executed by a bicycle battalion of infantry, most of whom were armed with burp guns. Massa called in fire from the *Tuscaloosa* on them. This fire, combined with artillery fire and 81mm mortar fire from D Company, 1st Battalion, smashed the enemy attack in a matter of ten minutes. All that was left was destroyed bicycles and mangled bodies. Later that night, Massa surveyed the scene of destruction. Dead Germans were everywhere. "I looked at one dead German soldier who was lying in the middle of the road. His helmet had come off and I was surprised at how young he looked. The thought occurred to me that his mother in Germany was probably praying that he was safe, and here I was looking at his body."

The capture of Edmondeville cost the 12th Infantry a staggering 300 casualties, but the Germans withdrew north to Joganville.[14]

That same day, the 22nd Infantry tried again to capture Azeville and Crisbecq. The 2nd Battalion at Azeville suffered nearly the identical fate as the day before. The 1st Battalion at Crisbecq came excruciatingly close to success. They drove the enemy out of St-Marcouf and advanced north, along the same trails, but this time under cover of a powerful blanket of naval, mortar, and artillery fire that bombarded the blockhouses of Crisbecq. This gave way to a rolling barrage 200 yards ahead of the infantry. Once again, C Company was the main assault group. As the two other rifle companies covered their flanks, the C Company troops pressed forward. Using pole charges, they blew up several pillboxes, but not the main blockhouses containing the 210mm guns. Soon they ran out of explosives and found themselves involved in a close-quarters fight with German soldiers in the trench system that zigzagged through Crisbecq. Screaming meemies poured in. The shrill shriek they made as they were fired tested the resolve of even the bravest Americans. As had happened the previous day, the Germans counterattacked from the left. Finally, the 1st Battalion men could take no more. They retreated, as fast as their legs could carry them. The unit was badly disorganized. All night long, stragglers filtered back to the American lines. Crisbecq remained under German control.

The regimental commander, Colonel Hervey Tribolet, decided to forget about taking Crisbecq. Why not just outflank it? With the 12th Regiment's capture of Edmondeville this was now possible, but the only way to do it was by capturing Azeville (located roughly a kilometer southwest of Crisbecq). On June 9, Tribolet threw most of his 3rd Battalion, plus tanks, into a flanking attack on Azeville. The Americans approached from the west and the north. Azeville's four blockhouses were cleverly camouflaged as buildings. In spite of the two previous attacks, the complex was practically unscathed. Small pillboxes, minefields, and barbed wire still protected every approach to the blockhouses.

All morning, the assault force worked its way forward as the 44th Field Artillery Battalion fired 1,500 rounds at Azeville. When the attack began, mines held up most of the tanks, but the infantry, mostly from I Company, made it close enough to several pillboxes to destroy them with rifle fire and satchel charges. The soldiers now had a path to the blockhouses. One tank and a bazooka fired at the nearest blockhouse but did little more than chip its concrete.

If Azeville was going to be neutralized, only the infantry could get it done. The demolition, fire, and flamethrower teams worked their way forward, under intermittent small-arms fire. They made it to the rear entrance of the first blockhouse and repeatedly tried to destroy the fortification with satchel charges and flamethrowers. None of this had any effect. I Company's commander, Captain Joseph Samuels, now played his last card. He sent Private Ralph Riley forward with the company's last flamethrower. Riley showed incredible courage. Knowing that at any moment a well-placed round could ignite the tanks of jellied gasoline that he was carrying on his back, Riley ran for seventy-five yards under enemy fire. Exhausted, he plopped into a shell hole behind the blockhouse and tried to squeeze off a flaming burst. But the flamethrower would not work! Riley fought off despair. He had to think fast. He opened the valve, held a lighted match to the nozzle, and shot a stream of fire at the door of the blockhouse. To his delight, a whoosh of flame shot from the nozzle. Somehow, the flames penetrated the door and began cooking off ammunition from within the blockhouse. A minute later, he saw a white flag protrude from within the blockhouse. "The rear door of the blockhouse swung open to let out an American parachute officer followed by two Germans," the official historian of the campaign later wrote. "The German commander surrendered all 4 forts with their garrison of 169 men." There is no telling how many lives Private Riley and the other men of I Company saved that day.[15]

With Azeville in his pocket, General Barton diverted his main effort to the northeast, in an effort to cut off Crisbecq and reach the coast at Quinéville. German resistance, if anything, got even tougher. Rainy weather made it difficult for Allied planes to lend support. The 22nd Regiment continued a slow, bloody advance along the coast—the regiment struggled for three days to overrun a fortified castle known as Château de Fontenay—while Colonel Red Reeder's 12th Infantry attempted to push to their objectives east of Montebourg.

This was bitter, horrible, grind-it-out, hedgerow-to-hedgerow fighting. For several days the men of the 12th steeled themselves for a dizzying series of attacks. On a typical day, they gained 1,000 or 2,000 yards. "The strain of combat was beginning to show in the gaunt, tired faces of the men," one officer recalled. The regiment lost two-thirds of its strength "fighting day and night, watching ... comrades fall." They learned how to survive. "They avoided digging foxholes in the hedgerows for they had learned by hard experience that the 88mm airbursts of the enemy inflicted more casualties by splintering the trees overhead."

Still the unit kept attacking. Colonel Reeder, was a down-to-earth, West Point–trained officer well known for his ability to connect with troops. He hated to see his men suffering so, but he could not afford to let up. Any reprieve in the attack simply gave the Germans more time to regroup and strengthen their defenses. "On the sixth straight day of our organized attack the German resistance increased," Reeder wrote. "They were on high ground near Montebourg and tanks failed to help us budge them." Reeder called for air support. The planes responded quickly, but they accidentally dropped several sticks of bombs short, killing one man.

Reeder went from company to company, checking on the status of his men. With him were his aide, Lieutenant Bill Mills, and nine riflemen. General Barton called Reeder over the radio and asked to see him at his CP. On the way there, the colonel came upon a scared group of brand-new replacements and stopped to talk with them for a moment: "Great to have you fellows with us. You're joining a winning outfit. The 12th Infantry has been beating the Germans for six days."

Reeder turned to go, walked with his group across an open field, and came under German artillery fire. An enemy observer had spotted them and called in fire. An instant later, an 88 shell cracked over Reeder's head. "I went down. My left leg was on fire. I sat up and looked at it. It was horribly mangled above the ankle." The shell "shattered my ankle and cut off my leg above the knee and hit me in three other places. My left elbow was torn open. I screamed and could not help it. Bill Mills, who was wounded and stunned in the same explosion, recovered quickly and placed a tourniquet on my leg." A shell fragment had pierced Mills's helmet. "His blood dripped on my face and uniform. He gave me a shot of morphine."

Reeder lay there for about fifteen minutes before a jeep, carrying six wounded men on stretchers, arrived. Reeder saw the medics removing one of the stretchers and assumed he was being given preferential treatment. "Oh no you don't," he ordered. "Take those men to the aid station, then come back for me."

The medic looked at Reeder. "Sir, this is a German."

Reeder's attitude changed in an instant. "Lay that son of a bitch in the shade."

The jeep took Reeder to the rear, where he saw General Barton long enough to give him a report. The general shook his hand. "I am so sorry, Red."

After the brief conversation, medics took the colonel to a field hospital for treatment. He fell asleep. When he awoke, Reeder saw General Collins in the dim light of the medical tent. "I am pinning on you the Distinguished Service Cross. Brad—General [Omar] Bradley—said to tell you he was sorry that he could not come himself. This is the first DSC to be awarded in Normandy."

Reeder told the general to tell his soldiers that he would be back. But Collins knew that Reeder's days as a combat leader were over. "I hope so, Red. But you have to get well."

Reeder was transported to an LST that took him to England. A plane flew him to the United States and Walter Reed Hospital, where he spent the next several months recuperating and getting used to an artificial leg. During his long, painful recovery a slew of distinguished visitors, including General George Marshall, came to see him. Eventually, the loss of his leg forced Reeder to retire, but his wisdom, strength of character, warm command style, and involvement with West Point sports made him a legend in the Army.

By June 14, when the Americans finally took Quinéville (partially thanks to timely reinforcement by the 9th Division's 39th Infantry Regiment), the 4th Division's line stretched from Le Ham at the Merderet, to the southern outskirts of Montebourg, to Quinéville and the sea.[16]

The drive inland from Utah was also different from Omaha because the Americans were pushing in three different directions, not just north to Cherbourg but also west to cut the peninsula (and south to Carentan, the subject of the next chapter).

At La Fière, Lieutenant John "Red Dog" Dolan and his mixed group of paratroopers were still holding out on June 7. The previous day, at substantial cost, his A Company, 505th, had taken the town and the west bank of the Merderet causeway. In an effort to escape German machine-gun and mortar fire, Dolan had pulled most of his men about 150 yards back from the La Fière bridge that had been so hotly contested the day before. Both sides needed the bridge—the Germans to attack Utah beach, the Americans to cut the Cotentin Peninsula. In the afternoon, Dolan noticed the volume of fire increasing. Several soldiers from his 3rd Platoon were hit, including the platoon sergeant, who was fatally wounded. Dolan could sense that another attack was coming.

Lieutenant Colonel Mark Alexander, a combat-experienced staff officer who would soon take over command of the 1st Battalion of the 505th, sensed the same thing. Not far away from Dolan's foxhole, Alexander was surveying the situation at La Fière and supervising the deployment of about forty paratroopers he had rounded up earlier that morning and sent here to reinforce Dolan. "On the bridge was a disabled Renault tank from earlier fighting [this was the tank Privates Lenold Peterson and Marcus Heim destroyed on D-Day]. The whole position was receiving heavy fire from the west bank around Cauquigny. I spotted two German tanks screened behind the buildings in the village of Cauquigny across the river."

Alexander found an abandoned American antitank gun and six rounds of ammunition. He put three men on the gun and instructed them to use it on the enemy tanks when they attacked.

Before long, the mortar and artillery fire slackened. Dolan slowly raised his head over the edge of his foxhole and intently studied the causeway. "The . . . attack was with . . . tanks and infantry. I was unable to estimate the size." Dolan hoped his bazooka crews and mines could take care of the tanks. He did not know that Alexander had salvaged the antitank gun.

The Renault tanks rumbled along the causeway. They were much more cautious than the day before. Today they tried to hang back, out of effective bazooka range. In one of the forward foxholes, Sergeant William Owens, one of Dolan's squad leaders, waited for the right moment to open fire. "We let them come on. When the lead tank got approximately forty feet from the mines, the tank stopped. Then our bazooka teams let loose and both got direct hits, disabling the first tank. This blocked the road . . . the other tanks could only retreat."

As they did so, Alexander's antitank gunners knocked out two of the tanks. At this point, the German infantry tried to surge forward and overwhelm the Americans. Owens and his people opened fire with every weapon at their disposal. "All we had was small arms and some 60mm mortars, but we succeeded in driving them back."

The Germans pulled back and poured down intense, accurate artillery and mortar fire. Their observers now knew the exact location of the American positions. An 88 shell scored a direct hit on an American radioman, sending flesh and radio parts everywhere. Owens's superior, Lieutenant William Oakley (who had led the successful attempt to take La Manoir buildings at La Fière the day before), got mortally wounded in the barrage. Owens was now the man of the moment. When the Germans came back, they used the hulks of their knocked-out tanks as cover. At a distance of not more than thirty-five yards they traded shots with Owens and his men, many of whom wanted nothing more of this fight.

The sergeant was in his late thirties. In civilian life, he had been a drill punch operator in Detroit. He glanced around and saw that at least half of his platoon's foxholes were empty. Horribly wounded men, with faces torn away or arms ripped open, were trying to crawl to the rear. S. L. A. Marshall later wrote: "The issue was being decided on the ground where Owens stood. If his platoon broke, the whole position was gone."

Owens led by example rather than words. He crawled from hole to hole, salvaging ammunition, resupplying his men, demonstrating a strangely calm demeanor. As if sensing the vulnerability of Owens's position, the German infantry ventured forward. "We gave them everything we had," Owens said. "The machine gun I had was so hot it quit firing." He picked up a BAR and fired it "until I ran out of ammunition. I then took a machine gun that belonged to a couple of men who . . . were killed. The gun had no tripod, so I rested it across a pile of dirt and used it."

For minute after awful minute the shooting continued. A supply sergeant, Edward Wuncio, kept braving the withering enemy fire to fetch more boxes of ammunition. Somehow, he made it to the forward positions and back several times. Owens was down to fourteen men. Some of them urged him to pull back, but Owens refused: "We will wait for orders. We haven't been told to go."

Moments later, Owens wondered if maybe his men were right, so he sent a runner to Dolan asking for orders. The lieutenant's reply was firm (although one can imagine not very comforting): "I don't know of a better spot than this to die."

Owens and his men held fast. "We stopped [the Germans] but they had gotten to within twenty-five yards of us." Owens estimated that there were about two hundred dead or wounded Germans scattered along the causeway. For a time both sides removed their wounded under a Red Cross flag, but there were plenty of Germans who did not receive help. Private Arthur "Dutch" Schultz and a buddy were policing the area near the bridge when they came across a live enemy soldier "lying on the ground crying for help, obviously in a great deal of pain. My friend went up to him and started prodding the man with his rifle asking for his pistol. The German was still crying when my friend put the muzzle of his rifle between the German's eyes and pulled the trigger. I watched and there was no movement in my friend's face. I was both appalled and awed by what I saw." Schultz, a combat rookie, wanted to be as tough and callous as his friend but could never quite suppress his inclination to look upon the enemy with mercy instead of hatred. "Fifty years later I saw him for the first time since the war at a reunion and brought up the incident—he broke down into tears." The Germans never again seriously contested American control of the east bank of the Merderet.[17]

On the west side of the river, American paratroopers were still holding out in isolated pockets as of June 8, hoping that the 82nd Airborne would soon establish a bridgehead west of the Merderet. A mile or two northwest of La Fière, in one of these pockets, Lieutenant Colonel Charles Timmes and his 507th Parachute Infantry troopers were confined to a small orchard where they had set up positions on D-Day. Whenever Timmes tried to probe beyond his shaky perimeter he met strong German opposition. He and his men continued to hang on as best they could. "On the morning of D-plus-Two, the Germans hit us at about seven or eight A.M., in an attempt to overrun the position," Lieutenant Gerard Dillon, a platoon leader in G Company, said.

Two days before, Dillon and two other men had crossed the inundated area with a message from General Ridgway to Timmes. Ridgway ordered Timmes to hold the orchard at all costs.

Dillon and the other troopers fought tenaciously to repel the German attacks. "They attacked three or four times with infantry supported by mortar and artillery fire, but were repulsed each time. On the night of D-plus-Two, we were running short of ammunition." They were also running low on food; they took to butchering dairy cows for meat. That night, Timmes ordered Lieutenant Johnny Marr to cross the inundated area and tell Ridgway of his need for more ammunition and supplies. Marr took one other man with him. They crossed the flooded Merderet (in the process finding, with the help of a friendly Frenchman, a ford) and made contact with the general. As it turned out, Ridgway was already planning an attack across the Merderet.[18]

Four miles to the south of Timmes, another group of Americans would have been thrilled to find that out, but they were not in communication with the general. Since D-Day, a force, consisting mostly of troopers from the 508th Parachute Infantry Regiment, had held Hill 30, a mass of high ground overlooking the Merderet River and Chef-du-Pont (a town Captain Roy Creek and his men had successfully defended on D-Day). Lieutenant Colonel John Shanley was in command of the Americans at Hill 30. His only contact with the American forces in Chef-du-Pont was by patrol.

Shanley dispatched fifty men to man a roadblock south of Hill 30. The roadblock covered the northern and western approaches to the Chef-du-Pont causeway. Someone found German mines and sowed them around the block. The Germans tried hard to eliminate Shanley's enclave at Hill 30, attacking several times. One of the worst attacks hit the roadblock on June 8, just as Shanley was reorganizing its defenses. He had practically blown a gasket when he found out that an American patrol had passed through the block unchallenged. Clearly, the roadblock positions had been set up carelessly and ineffectively.

Before Shanley could repair the situation, a company of German infantry attacked from the west. Some of the Germans got close enough to overrun American positions. The rest of the paratroopers hurriedly got into position and opened fire. One of them was Lieutenant Ralph DeWeese, who had come close to drowning in the Merderet on D-Day. Now DeWeese watched the Germans through his binoculars and ordered his men to open fire. "We had a terrific battle with them and were firing point blank at about 200 yards. We battled back and forth for about 2 hours. Colonel Shanley came up and said he'd send a platoon around the right flank."

Shanley had rallied this platoon on the top of Hill 30 and was using it to keep the German attackers off-balance. Lieutenant DeWeese watched Shanley take off in the direction of Hill 30. The lieutenant and his men lay prone against a hedgerow, firing over its top. "I was looking over and a mortar shell hit just in front of the position and I felt pieces of dirt hit my lips." The mortar fire increased in intensity. "They kept working on the road and placed a lot of mortar fire on the road block we had. We lost 5 men killed." Enemy rifle fire soon splattered against the top of the hedgerow, causing the Americans to duck, but another man was killed. The Germans were getting closer. Shanley bowed to the inevitable and ordered DeWeese and the other surviving Americans to abandon their roadblock and return to Hill 30. The Germans had the place practically besieged.[19]

As evening set in on June 8, Shanley's force was running dangerously low on ammunition, food, and blood plasma. The colonel sent out patrols to retrieve supply bundles in the Merderet along with whatever wounded had been left behind during the day's fighting. Private Ed Boccafogli, a young B Company, 508th, trooper who had slipped on vomit while exiting his C-47 on D-Day, participated in a patrol to find equipment bundles. They made it to the swampy Merderet and saw parachutes in the water. "Some of the parachutes had different colors, and the colors represented what would be in that bundle. But half the parachutes were already sunk. We'd see part of it standing up. We spread out along the edge and waded into the swamp." Boccafogli waded through chest-high water to a parachute. "Me and this other kid are pulling the parachute. And as we're pulling, bullets start ricocheting off the water from the other side. The Germans spotted us. I go under water, helmet and everything. I come up, get some air, pull." They made it to the bank. As they were pulling the parachute up, a bullet slammed into the other man's chest, killing him instantly. "We had to leave the body there." They dragged the bundle back to Hill 30, hoping it contained mortar or rifle ammunition. "I forget what was in there, but there was very little of what we needed."[20]

Private Tom Porcella, a twenty-year-old Long Islander, left the perimeter with a patrol of fellow H Company soldiers in search of wounded Americans. "We entered this field and saw two troopers lying on the ground." One of the troopers had his head blown completely apart. Porcella found his dog tag and saw that he was a friend of his from H Company. "It was a terrible shock for me to see what happened to him. I hope he died fast." A few feet away Porcella saw another ghastly-looking paratrooper. "He was just butchered meat. There was blood all over the place. One leg was mangled and the other was sort of grotesquely underneath his body." Porcella looked for his dog tag and heard a terrible groan. "I thought he was dead for sure. I was glad to see the guy was still alive, but I didn't know if he would ever make it." Porcella and three other men put the gravely wounded soldier on a stretcher and started to carry him back to Hill 30.

They were all weakened from a lack of food and sleep, so they stopped several times to rest. During one such break, Porcella spotted two dead

Germans lying against a hedgerow. "One German . . . had both hands together like he was praying and begging for his life, and his eyes were wide open. His expression seemed to be frozen right on his face. It looked like fear." The other German "had a different look on his face. He looked like he had a sneer on his face."

They moved on, got the wounded man to Hill 30, and went out searching for more. During the search, Porcella heard a voice call out, "Hey, trooper, come over here." Porcella saw a wounded paratrooper lying in a ditch. "He wanted to know how badly he was hit. Looking down at him, I saw all the flesh was blown away from the right side of his face. He started to cry and he was reaching for his face with a hand that was black with dirt. Quickly, I grabbed his wrist and told him not to touch his face and that he would be all right." The man begged for a cigarette and water. Porcella did not have any water, but he gave him a cigarette and moved on.[21]

That night, Shanley received a radio communication from Lieutenant Colonel LeRoy Lindquist in Chef-du-Pont. Lindquist informed Shanley that he planned to cross the Merderet and relieve Hill 30 in the morning, but only if the road was open. At 0230 on June 9, Shanley dispatched a twenty-three-man patrol under Lieutenant Woodrow Millsaps to open the road, cross the causeway to Chef-du-Pont, make contact with Lindquist, and guide his convoy to Hill 30. This was a big job. Down on the road, Millsaps and his men ran into fierce German resistance. Through superhuman effort, the patrol fought its way to the Chef-du-Pont causeway. Many of the soldiers were badly wounded. Millsaps had to beg, threaten, and cajole his able-bodied men to keep going.

When it came time to cross into Chef-du-Pont, Millsaps could only get one man, Sergeant William Kleinfelter, to go with him. During the crossing, they ran into German guards and fought them at point-blank range. Millsaps killed three of them (at least one by bayonet). This was the most soul-searing kind of combat—face-to-face, man-to-man, a desperate struggle for survival by slashing and killing your adversary.

As Millsaps grappled with the German sentries, Kleinfelter lagged behind and the lieutenant was not pleased. "What's wrong with you? Can't keep up?" he bellowed angrily at his sergeant.

"I don't know, but I think I'm shot," Sergeant Kleinfelter replied.

Millsaps checked and found out that Kleinfelter was right. He had six bullet holes in his left arm and shoulder, was losing blood, and was too weak to continue. Millsaps could not drag him or carry him, so he left Kleinfelter and made it to Chef-du-Pont. Lindquist and his command group had been listening to the sounds of fighting coming from the other side of the river, and hearing Millsaps's story, Lindquist decided that the road was not secure. He radioed to Shanley that the relief effort was canceled.

When Millsaps heard him, he got angry. He could not believe that, after all his men had sacrificed, Lindquist would not even risk an attempt to relieve Hill 30. The lieutenant begged Lindquist and his staff to reconsider. He was anything but diplomatic in his efforts at persuasion. In essence he was challenging the manhood of his fellow paratroopers. Lindquist relented and decided to send a relief force, but it was too late. He radioed Shanley, told him of his intentions, and found out that Shanley had withdrawn all of his men back to Hill 30. For the moment, the isolated troopers of Hill 30 were out of luck. Small patrols got blood plasma to them, but they were still cut off.[22]

Lindquist's decision meant, in effect, that only a strong push across the Merderet at La Fière could relieve the Americans west of the Merderet. As previously mentioned, General Ridgway on the evening of June 8 was already planning such a push. The establishment of a bridgehead over the Merderet was one of the 82nd Airborne's main missions, and it still had not been accomplished. The general was determined that this mission would, and must, be accomplished on June 9.

The plan called for the 1st Battalion of the 325th Glider Infantry to set out just after midnight on June 9. These men, who had arrived in Normandy two days before, were supposed to follow Lieutenant Marr across the ford he had found. The ford was, in actuality a road that the floods had not completely engulfed. Once they made it across the Merderet, the glider men were to link up with Timmes and another group of stranded 507th troopers under the regimental commander, Colonel George Millett. They were then to push south and attack the western end of the La Fière causeway. "It was a great deal to ask of a battalion that had not been in combat," Brigadier General Jim Gavin, Ridgway's second-in-command, later commented.

Gavin was right. The plan was far too ambitious. The 1st Battalion made it across the Merderet and hooked up with Timmes without any substantial problems. But Millett's 507th troopers got ambushed and cut to pieces by deadly fire originating from a building the Americans called the Gray Castle. Millett and many others got separated and captured. The rest of the survivors scattered into the night.

Enemy fire from the Gray Castle also harassed the glider troops as they pushed south, but it did not do the same kind of damage to them as it had to Millett and his soldiers. Steadily the glider soldiers kept moving in a skirmish line through the cool night. Clinton Riddle, a battalion messenger and draftee from Sweetwater, Tennessee, was moving with the headquarters group of B Company. He watched as the men ahead crossed an open meadow that led to an apple orchard. "We ran into a trap set by the Germans." German machine guns chattered from seemingly everywhere. "The whole company was caught in the crossfire. My foxhole buddy from Ohio was killed in the ambush." When Riddle saw him die, he could not help but think of his friend's family. He left behind a wife and a brand-new baby boy.

Company C got the worst of the ambush. This unit was pinned down along a sunken road. The Germans fired over their hedgerow cover, and into the road, with lethal effectiveness. First Lieutenant Wayne Pierce, the executive officer of B Company, was hugging the ground in one of the orchard's ditches, about thirty yards away from the road. He gazed through the darkness, trying to figure out what was happening to C Company. "Tracer fire was heavy from both sides. The firefight died down to just an occasional shot and became quiet." Pierce heard the sound of a vehicle on the road and figured it had to be a German tank.

The battalion commander, Major Teddy Sandford, sent Pierce word that "Company C is wiped out, we had better move back." Everyone around Pierce started retreating, and eventually he did the same, once he rounded up a couple dozen stragglers.

The 1st Battalion quickly retreated all the way back to Timmes's orchard position. Riddle, the messenger, crawled and ran his way back. "I found a little gully to crawl back far enough to get under a cover of some bushes. Then I . . . [ran] as hard as I could. We . . . dug in. While I was digging, a shell almost dropped to my foxhole."

The retreat was a rout. Like Riddle, most of the survivors fell back as quickly as they could until they were out of range of the deadly enemy fire. The unit stayed in the orchard and made no further attempt to capture the western edge of La Fière causeway. But later the next day Riddle had a chance to revisit the site of the ambush. What he saw never left him. "You could almost step on the bodies from one to the others. They were all in a line just as they had entered the orchard." Riddle's eyes settled on one particular dead man, a friend of his who was wearing a pair of black gloves his parents had recently sent him. One of the gloved hands extended up in the air "as though he was reaching for someone or something." Riddle turned away and fought tears. "I could not bring myself to wear gloves in combat for a long time after that . . . even during the Battle of the Bulge. Even now, I never pull a pair of gloves on but when I think of him."[23]

At 0530, just after sunrise, Timmes and company passed the word to Colonel Harry Lewis, commander of the 325th, that the attack had failed. Lewis dutifully informed General Ridgway. The general knew there was only one option left—he had to order a frontal attack across La Fière causeway. It was the only way his division could get across the Merderet in strength and finally accomplish its vital mission. He ordered Lewis to take his 3rd Battalion, plus some tanks from the 746th, and attack later that morning, after a preparatory artillery barrage. A company of troopers from the

507th would lend fire support and then follow the attackers if they needed help. General Gavin would be in overall command.

This was a good choice. The thirty-five-year-old Gavin was a living legend in the airborne. He had commanded the 505th Parachute Infantry during its perilous combat jump in Sicily and then, three months later, Salerno. On both of these jumps, the West Point–educated Gavin had jumped with his men into battle. His brilliant performance in these operations had earned him a promotion to brigadier general. He was a down-to-earth, energetic officer with movie-star good looks, forceful integrity, and a hands-on leadership style that prompted many in the 82nd Airborne to refer to him as the highest-ranking platoon leader in the Army.

At 0800, with the attack scheduled to begin within the hour, General Ridgway discovered that he had a problem. He met with his artillery commander and told him that he needed supporting fire in fifteen minutes. "Sorry, sir, but I have no shells left," the officer replied.

As Ridgway pondered what to do, deliverance arrived in the form of an old West Point classmate. Brigadier General John Devine, artillery commander for the newly landed 90th Division, had a hunch that the 82nd might need some artillery support for its push across the Merderet. This was pure instinct and preparation on Devine's part. No one ordered him to look out for the 82nd or proceed to La Fière on his own initiative, which he and Lieutenant Colonel Frank Norris, commander of the division's 345th Field Artillery Battalion, did on the morning of June 9. Devine was one of the few original senior officers in his division who was well suited to combat command. He showed superb judgment and anticipation that day.

Devine and Norris got to Ridgway's CP at La Fière, close to the causeway. The two generals greeted each other warmly. Norris stood by as the two old friends conferred. "Matt, what's going on around here, and how can we help?" General Devine asked.

"We have to force a crossing of that causeway over the Merderet. That's about eight hundred yards of busted-up road with a deep swamp on both sides, and the Krauts have perfect fields of fire to stop us. We plan to jump off at eight-thirty."

Ridgway told Devine that he had no artillery support. With that, Devine turned to Norris. "Frank, you have the nearest battalion of the Ninetieth. Can you shoot for this attack?"

Norris said yes, but with a caveat. "We can shoot, but not by eight-thirty. Only four of my howitzers are in our area now, but we should have a whole battalion ready to fire by ten-thirty."

Ridgway thought for a moment and then fixed Lieutenant Colonel Norris with a pointed stare. "Can you shoot a battalion of one-fifty-fives in support of our attack by ten-thirty?"

The young artillery officer, a West Pointer himself, returned the general's gaze. "Yes, sir, we can," he replied confidently. "General Ridgway drilled me for about ten seconds with his piercing brown eyes, and said nothing. He then turned calmly to his staff and General Gavin, and said, 'The attack is delayed until ten-thirty.' When he said that, I *knew* I had better be able to shoot by ten-thirty!"

Ridgway ordered Gavin to show Norris and Major Bob Salisbury, Norris's gunnery officer, the enemy positions he wanted hit. Gavin led them to a hole about seventy-five yards from the causeway. They crawled up to a slight rise "where we had a direct view of the causeway and the buildings on the far side. There were a number of old stone dwellings, houses and barns, that were occupied by the Germans [this was Cauquigny]. I pointed out the areas where we assumed the Germans to be and from which we had been receiving fire."

As Gavin spoke, enemy fire peppered the OP. Salisbury and Norris had to fight to suppress their fear. "This . . . was no picnic," Norris said, "especially for two greenhorns under their first hostile fire. The Krauts were sparing nothing, so we got mortars, 88s and long range machine gun fire as our introduction. Bob . . . conducted a brilliant adjustment of fire on Gavin's preferred targets. It was a textbook performance by a superb gunnery officer."[24]

The 3rd Battalion of the 325th was marching west from the direction of Ste-Mère-Eglise. They had to move quickly to make it to La Fière in time to attack at 10:45. Gavin knew that he had to follow up the 90th Division's artillery barrage with a quick attack, so he told Captain Robert Rae, commander of a mixed company of 507th Parachute Infantry troopers near the waterline, to be prepared to make the assault if the 325th did not make it to La Fière in time. All morning long, Rae and his men crouched in their fighting holes and hoped the 325th would soon arrive.

Gavin spent that same time making final preparations. He summoned the 3rd Battalion commander, Lieutenant Colonel Charles Carrell, to give him his orders and was disappointed at his response. Carrell, a fellow West Pointer who had been injured two days before in the glider landing, regarded the attack as tantamount to suicide. That very morning he had told one of his officers, Lieutenant Lee Travelstead, that he did not agree with the attack order.

Now he faced General Gavin and said, "I don't think I can do it."

Gavin was taken aback. "Why?"

"I'm sick," Carrell responded. His motivation for claiming illness is still somewhat unclear. He could have been using his own physical problems to save his men from oblivion (in the vain hope that Gavin would call off the attack), or he could have been skulking.

Whatever Carrell's motivation, Gavin was completely unmoved. "OK, you're through." The general relieved him on the spot, replacing him with Major Charles Moore, Carrell's executive officer.

General Gavin took no pleasure in firing Carrell. "But I had to do it. The whole battle was hanging by a thread," the general said years later.

Naturally, Carrell felt he got a raw deal. "This incident was . . . very painful to me. The way it was done. No chain of command and no consideration. I was treated very badly. It was unfair to all of us." Carrell later told Lieutenant Travelstead that "although he knew it would end his lifetime career, he could not in good conscience order such a suicidal attack."

That may be, but Gavin did not have time, on that morning of June 9, for the luxuries of careful deliberation or consultations with the chain of command (in any case, General Ridgway completely agreed with Gavin's decision). Gavin was absolutely correct that the battle at La Fière hung in the balance. If Carrell was not prepared to lead the vital attack (whatever the reason), then he had to go.

The incident with Carrell, plus the inexperience of many of the glider men, made Gavin quite apprehensive. He felt sure that, with all the supporting fire he had, the troops could make it across the causeway, but could they stay on the opposite side? Could they exploit the bridgehead? He was not sure. He went over to Captain Rae and told him to be ready, if the 325th faltered, to immediately attack. Gavin figured this would salvage the situation and rally the 325th.

True to Norris's promises, the artillery barrage began by 1030. Norris was proud of his artillerymen. "All twelve howitzers came into position. We put 180 rounds of 96-lb. . . . high explosive shells into the most dangerous areas of the causeway."

Tanks and self-propelled guns from the 746th added to the volume of fire, as did small-arms fire from Captain Rae's paratroopers. Gavin watched the barrage intently. "Everything we had opened up with a tremendous explosion. Dust and smoke and flames seemed to cover the far shore. Soon Germans, in a bad state of shock, their faces covered with dust, and blood trickling from their mouths, began coming across the causeway with their hands up."[25]

In this case, looks were deceiving. A few Germans were surrendering, but most were unscathed by the barrage. In fact, German fire on the causeway, its approaches, and La Fière was growing more intense by the moment. The German small-arms fire, coming from Cauquigny, was so thick that, in the memory of one American, it "beat like hail" on the American side of the river. Clearly anyone who tried to cross the causeway would come under devastating fire.

The men of G Company, 325th, could see this as they entered La Fière. Their job today was to lead the La Fière attack. They had gotten to the town in time to do so. They heard the sounds of battle from up ahead and understood the danger they would soon face. In columns, they were walking along the road, heading for the causeway. About two hundred yards from the causeway, the road straightened out, putting them in full view of German machine gunners in Cauquigny. Immediately the ripping sound of German MG-42s permeated the air. The glider soldiers dived for the shallow cover of ditches on either side of the road. Their commander, a Captain Sauls, understood immediately that to go forward on this road meant certain disaster. His men would be chopped into bloody hamburger. Better, for the moment, to take shelter in these ditches. He and his men were mixed together with dead and live 507th troopers.

Sauls figured there had to be a better approach to the causeway. He bumped into a 507th officer and asked if him if he knew a safer route to the causeway. "All I can tell you is we've taken a hell of a beating here for two days and there's a million Germans over there." Determining that this officer was useless, Sauls left the shelter of the ditch and began reconnoitering to the left. He circled around several of La Fière's buildings and found a side road that featured a shoulder-high stone wall that, except for a hole some seven yards in length, would offer cover all the way to the causeway. The only problem was that several dead Americans from Rae's company cluttered the road along the expanse of the wall. Rae's troops were deployed in holes along the riverbank, just beyond the wall. Sauls persuaded one of Rae's sergeants to help him move these bodies. With this accomplished the captain went back to his company, got his men out of the ditches, and led them to the wall.

A German machine gun had the seven-yard hole covered, so each man simply took his turn making the one-second dash across to safety. When they finished, G Company's two forward platoons were scrunched together over a distance of about fifty yards nearly where the wall met the road. Enemy artillery was exploding on the other side of the wall. Enemy machine-gun bullets were slapping into the wall. Each American soldier crouched as low as he could get, listening to the hellish symphony of death that awaited on the other side of the wall.

Sauls nudged his way to the front and peeked around the wall. On the causeway he saw the detritus of the battles Lieutenant Dolan's men had fought there on D-Day and June 7. A ruined tank and burned vehicles clogged the narrow causeway. Sauls saw several American mines scattered around the tank. Enemy fire was still kicking up dust and splashing water everywhere. Colonel Lewis had promised him that the artillery would lay down a smoke screen to shield his advance, but the smoke was nowhere to be seen. From somewhere behind him Sauls heard a few soldiers bitching, "What about that goddamned smoke?" It never came. They would have to go forward in the open. Lewis should never have promised the smoke, because he was in no position to deliver it. Only Norris's artillerymen could have done so, and they did not have the necessary white phosphorous rounds.

Sauls eased back under cover and checked his watch. Five minutes to go. He glanced at the line of men hugging the wall. These soldiers—his men—looked calm and determined. He caught the eye of a couple of his lieutenants and winked. They winked back. Above the din, somebody yelled, "Let's get to the other side; *beaucoup* mademoiselles over there, none over here." Laughter echoed up and down the line.

Sauls looked at his watch again. It was time to go. He waited an extra thirty seconds, just in case the smoke rounds were on the way. No such luck. Time had run out. He and his men now had to go forward into the maelstrom. "Go!!" Sauls yelled. With Sauls in the lead, the Americans got up and sprang forward. The enemy fire was all around them, coming from in front and both flanks. In jumbled groups they surged onto the causeway and ran forward as best they could.

Private Ed Jeziorski, one of Rae's 507th troopers, was in a foxhole, firing a machine gun in support, watching them go. "As the 325th glidermen moved past our positions along the causeway to start their attack the German fire began increasing." Many men were hit. "They were dropping on both sides of the roadway. They kept as low as they could so [as] not to make good targets, but as they were moving they were just being knocked down left and right. There was no place to hide on the open causeway. A lot of men were getting killed. The jerry small armes [*sic*] . . . intensified to the degree that it was purely an unbroken whine. Sounded almost like a million mosquitoes in a very confined space."[26]

To the attacking glider men every step seemed like an eternity. It seemed impossible that anyone could live through this insane assault. As they ran, they heard the buzzing sound of enemy bullets and the angry cracking of explosions from every direction. Sometimes they heard the telltale sickening splattering sounds that meant bullets or shrapnel had struck flesh.

Captain Sauls and the equivalent of about three squads made it across in this first rush. Those who kept running tended to make it. Those who faltered or looked for cover along the causeway got hit. American artillery was still dropping about twenty-five to fifty yards beyond the western edge of the causeway. This kept Sauls and his men from advancing through Cauquigny, but it also helped shield them from enemy reprisals. Sauls's men destroyed a couple of enemy machine-gun nests. The captain looked to the other side of the Merderet and wondered where the rest of his company was. Because of a bend in the causeway, he could not see the wall that served as the jump-off point for his company's attack.

One of Sauls's medics, Corporal Chester Walker, was running back and forth along the causeway, doing whatever he could for the many wounded. At one point, he saw two badly wounded men. "One of them had a bullet wound in his right chest and the other had a compound fracture in his leg and was in much pain. I gave him morphine and made contact with the aid station to get litter bearers to remove them from the field." Walker also treated Sauls, who had taken a bullet in the hand. "He had a bad wound in his hand and had lost a lot of blood." Still, the captain kept going.[27]

Back at the wall, the rest of G Company was moving up. The hole in the wall had the effect of splitting the company into two halves—the first half that assaulted with Sauls and the second that was now preparing to move past the hole and onto the causeway. The lead man, Private Melvin Johnson, approached the hole and said, "Here I go!" Halfway across the gap, a machine-gun bullet hit him in the head, shattering his skull, spraying shards and brain in a gory mix as Johnson collapsed to the ground. Blood trickled from the remnants of his lifeless head. This ghastly, tragic sight froze the rest of G Company, plus the two follow-up companies, E and F, into inertia.

Lieutenant Frank Amino tried to rally the shaken soldiers. "Let's go kill the sons of bitches!" he yelled. In one motion he bounded onto the causeway, followed by, at most, a dozen men. Many of the other G Company soldiers simply would not get up and go. They were too terrified of the danger of imminent death. But some from the weapons platoon tried to get going. They were heavily burdened by their machine guns and mortars, and that prevented them from running as fast as the riflemen. Consequently, several of the weapons platoon men trotted forward in short rushes and then looked for nonexistent cover on the causeway. Already this narrow roadway was beginning to clog up with the bodies of the dead, the wounded, and the cowering.

To make matters worse, a Sherman tank now tried to get across the crowded causeway. The Sherman (probably from the 746th) promptly set off one of the mines. This disabled the tank and wounded several of the nearby infantrymen. American soldiers littered both slopes of the causeway. Some tried to hide behind the dead bodies of their comrades. German machine gun and mortar fire continued to sweep through the whole 500-yard expanse of the causeway.

The clogging problem got even worse when E and F Companies recovered from their shock over Private Johnson's ugly death and got moving. "We would run a few yards, hit the ground, catch our breath and make another dash," Lewis Strandburg, a radioman in E Company, recalled. The fire was so intense, and the situation so chaotic, that he tossed aside his radio set and fought as a rifleman. "This went on for what seemed like an eternity, every minute of which I was expecting to feel the piercing of an enemy bullet or a piece of shrapnel."

Some of the soldiers from these two units got across the Merderet and fanned out in many directions on the west side of the river. Others got hit on the causeway or straggled. Officers—including Ridgway, Gavin, and Lewis—strode around, rallying the stragglers, shaming them, threatening them, ordering them, persuading them. "The fire was so intense," Ridgway said, "that the men were physically recoiling. We just grabbed our men and walked them out. The physical force of that firepower was such that they just stopped and started back—not from cowardice at all. This is where your personal presence makes a hell of a lot of difference."

One E Company officer, Lieutenant Bruce Booker (the company executive officer), saw several of his company's men trying to retreat back to the west side of the Merderet. He drew his pistol, fired six shots, shouted, laughed, and yelled, "Keep coming toward me and you see what happens!" The men turned back. Some of them could not help but snicker at the crazy lieutenant.

Later Booker got shot in both calves while leading a group across the causeway and directing fire on German positions in Cauquigny. He sat down and waited for the medics, but as he did so, he pointed to the west and shouted at anyone who even came close to hesitating, "Come on, you bastards! Get up there! God damn it, get up there! That's where the fight is!" Later, after a medic bandaged Booker's legs, he tried to walk but couldn't, so instead he crawled everywhere he went, still prodding, pushing, and urging his soldiers to keep moving.

Company E had good officers. One of them, Lieutenant Richard Brigham Johnson, led his platoon along the right side of the causeway. The fire was so thick, and the situation so dangerous, that he could only get a few men to follow him. "I was running somewhat down the north side of the causeway, in the faint hope that it would at least shelter my legs from any fire coming from the south side, when I stepped in a hole and sprawled full length in the swamp."

Johnson got out of the swamp and kept going, only to get pinned down by a German machine-gun position somewhere up ahead and to the right. The lieutenant glanced back and saw most of his platoon lying prone along the muddy embankments of the causeway, trying to present as small of a target as possible. The enemy machine gunner had a clear shot at the cowering soldiers but not, ironically, at Johnson, who was lying too close, in a dead spot not covered by the gun. "I could feel the breeze of those bullets passing behind me. If I had been one step later, I think he would have sawed me in half."

Adrenaline surged through Johnson's system. He was on a high, experiencing the frenzied state that can sometimes come over soldiers in combat. "I began to believe I was untouchable, could lick any number of Germans, and go all the way to Berlin."

The enemy gunner threw a grenade at Johnson, but it landed in a slushy puddle of manure. That absorbed most of the blast, except for a piece of shrapnel that sliced into his arm. In response, Lieutenant Johnson pulled the pin of a grenade, flipped the handle, counted several seconds, and threw it into the enemy machine-gun position. The German picked up the grenade to throw it back, but it exploded in his hand. Next, the lieutenant captured another enemy machine-gun team. Several soldiers from his platoon then joined him, but they got pinned down by American machine-gun fire coming from Shanley's men on Hill 30. Johnson's platoon sergeant, Henry Howell, got hit badly. A bullet ripped through his right arm, hit a rib, and came out the middle of his back. Johnson got hit in both ankles. Still, he kept fighting and was even wounded again before being evacuated that night.

In some ways, these follow-up attackers had a more difficult time than Sauls and G Company. "The first files had had only to face the fire," S. L. A. Marshall later wrote, "for those who followed, there was the extra ordeal of having to run the gantlet [*sic*] of their own dead and wounded." The humidity of the swamp, combined with the difficult footing of the dusty, crowded causeway, made it even more difficult to get across. Many of the able-bodied could not resist the heartrending pleas of the wounded for water or treatment. They stopped to offer the contents of their canteens or first-aid kits to the wounded. Enemy fire was still quite heavy, so many of them became casualties as they tended to the wounded.

German prisoners made the crowding on the causeway even worse. Dusty, bleeding, and bewildered, many of them tried to get to the east side of the Merderet, only to be cut down in the crossfire, sometimes deliberately killed by their own side or the Americans. Their rotting bodies added to the clutter.

The attack had been going on for just over half an hour now. Its success still hung in the balance. Small groups of Americans, some from Sauls's G Company, others from a mixture of E and F Company, were fighting individual battles along the western banks of the Merderet as well as the hedgerow-lined roads that fanned out in every direction.

From the vantage point of the east bank of the Merderet in La Fière General Gavin could not see any of that. None of the fighting on the west bank was readily apparent to him. He could see small numbers of American soldiers make it across the causeway, but then they disappeared from sight. Right in front of him he saw the horribly crowded causeway. Gavin was standing near Captain Rae's foxhole, watching the attack unfold. His instincts, honed over the course of nearly two years of war, told him that the American soldiers on the other side of the river needed help if they were to hang on to their dearly won bridgehead.

Gavin arrived at a decision. He turned to Captain Rae. "All right, go ahead, Rae! You've got to go and keep going."

Rae and approximately ninety other paratroopers left their positions and ran for the causeway. "We came out shouting, forcing our way through the log jam of dead and dying soldiers, and some soldiers refusing to continue the attack."

The enemy fire was withering. Artillery shells were exploding along the embankments of the causeway. Machine guns swept the whole area. A shell exploded perilously close to Private Richard Keeler, Rae's runner. Keeler and many others hit the dirt, looking for protection of some sort. Rae urged them to keep going: "If you're going to get it, you're going to get it, and you might as well start walking down the road with me." Private Keeler got up and urged many others to do the same. They made their way past the disabled Sherman, zigzagging through the dead, the wounded, and the stragglers who choked the causeway.

As Lieutenant John Wisner, Rae's intelligence officer, ran forward, the surreal scene reminded him of an escalator. "Two streams of men on the inside trying to run forward and on the outer side, streams of wounded trickling back, [many of them] still mobile enough to walk back or crawl back." He also found it impossible "to distinguish between the corpses and the litter cases as one passed them by." Many times he almost bumped into medics who were scrambling everywhere, helping wounded men.

Several yards behind Lieutenant Wisner, Private Jeziorski was struggling to make it across the causeway. He and his machine-gun team were spread out, five yards between each man. Jeziorski was carrying the machine gun on his right shoulder, a heavy burden even under the best of circumstances. He stumbled on an embankment when an enemy shell exploded near him. "After running several yards, the whole side of the road came up . . . in a heck of a mass of dirt and right on top of me and knocked me down. I had to scramble to . . . get out from under the thing." For a moment he lost his bearings, but he soon got going again. "Captain Rae kept telling us to 'keep moving, keep moving, keep moving!' The fire was very, very severe. It was a continuous hum, a buzz of the rounds going by you. Guys were dropping . . . how many of us got through, I don't know. There was no yelling or screaming. That's just hyperbole." Jeziorski made it across and set up his machine gun to rake over enemy positions near Cauquigny. His assistant gunner got hit, but then another man came up and brought Jeziorski more ammo.

"After we knocked out the German positions," Rae said, "I split my force sending half down a dirt road to the south where the 325th was having trouble. I took the other half of my men and attacked west. We remained actively engaged until we made our way into Le Motey [a mile due west of Cauquigny], spending the night there."

The paratroopers of the 507th and the glider men of the 325th fought bitterly all day and deep into the night to maintain their hold on the west bank of the Merderet. In the end, they succeeded in doing so. In retrospect, General Gavin committed Rae's company at the right time, just when the battle could have gone either way. Rae's people helped reinforce the courageous glider soldiers who had made the initial assault but also gave them confidence to hang on to their hard-won positions west of the Merderet in the face of intense German opposition.

Gavin's excellent leadership was also a factor. He crossed the river and helped shore up the American positions throughout the whole day and night (at one point, he prevented, during a German counterattack, what would have been a disastrous retreat back across the Merderet). As he did so, he inspected the remnants of many German positions and came away impressed with the strength of the enemy positions opposite La Fière. "I had not realized the extent of the German strength on the far side [of the Merderet]. In a field a hundred yards from the bridge were a dozen mortars dug in huge square holes in the earth. There was a great deal of artillery, half tracks, self-propelled guns. All along the road were litter, dead Germans, and abandoned vehicles. I came on a German 81 mm. mortar squad. They were all killed or wounded, lying in a ditch, head to foot." Gavin took a map from a dead enemy lieutenant whose hand was still warm. The general hoped that the map would reveal information about German troop dispositions, but it yielded nothing of value. Gavin consoled himself by taking the dead German's wristwatch. He had lost his own on the jump into Normandy.

Troops from the 3rd Battalion, 325th, linked up with Timmes, and later a battalion from the 508th Parachute Infantry Regiment forged across the causeway and made contact with Lieutenant Colonel Shanley's embattled force at Hill 30.

By the time the clock struck midnight on June 10, the mission of the 82nd Airborne Division had finally been fulfilled: American forces were across the Merderet in strength and were now in a position to start a westward push to cut the Cotentin Peninsula. The assault at La Fière was one of the boldest, toughest, and most epic American attacks of the entire war. Years later, many veteran troopers of the 82nd, such as Michael Pontrelli, agreed that the heaviest enemy fire they ever faced was at La Fière. "This was in my opinion the worst assault I was involved in of the entire war. The enemy caught us naked on the causeway, water on both sides and no cover. There were so many sights that day that I still remember and will never forget till the day I die. I lost a lot of good buddies that day. Real good friends. I pray for them every day to this day."[28]

The newest American unit in Normandy was the 90th Division. Once the All-Americans established a foothold on the western side of the Merderet, the 90th received the job of expanding on it. The division was to attack in a westerly direction and capture such towns as Amfreville, Gourbesville, and Pont l'Abbé. For the men of the 90th these orders stemmed from a change of plan General Bradley and General Collins had decided upon by June 9. The pre-invasion blueprint called for an immediate push on Cherbourg after D-Day, but the 4th Division's troubles north of Utah, combined with the 82nd's difficulty in seizing the western side of the Merderet, changed the plans. Bradley now wanted the Cotentin cut before Collins's VII Corps made any kind of serious push north to Cherbourg. Plus, the 82nd Airborne, after its three days of fierce fighting, needed to be reinforced. Collins sent the 90th to the Merderet to start the westward push across the Cotentin.

In the original invasion plans, the 90th was supposed to support the 4th Division's advance north to Cherbourg. In fact, one of the division's infantry regiments, the 359th, had been landed late on D-Day and had fought in support of the 4th Division for three days. But now Collins ordered the soldiers of this regiment to leave the 4th and return to their own division. In the meantime, the other two regiments, the 357th and the 358th, were supposed to launch an attack west of the Merderet at 0400 on June 10. These two units had been in Normandy for all of a day. They were, at this point, green, jittery, and unprepared for what they were about to experience.

The whole operation unraveled rather quickly. The two untested regiments had a difficult time finding their way during a night march to the Merderet. The crossings at Chef-du-Pont (358th) and La Fière (357th) were still under heavy German artillery fire. The night was pitch-black. "It took nearly all night to make the march because of the number of troops moving and the distance," Warrant Officer (jg) Oliver Wilbanks, the assistant adjutant of the 358th, recalled. "We marched on roads, some sunken and narrow. At times it was quite difficult to see even a few feet ahead." They crossed the Merderet at Chef-du-Pont. "Along the road were German dead, and the 'battlefield odor' was quite nauseating and unpleasant. The sight of human dead rings the horribleness of war straight to the heart more forcibly than a million words could do."

Lieutenant John Colby was a platoon leader in E Company, 357th Infantry. In the early-morning hours of June 10, he and his men finally made it to La Fière causeway. Shivering from the tense apprehension of what lay ahead (not to mention the chilly Norman air), Colby and the others tramped forward. "It is dark. We are walking across the stone bridge over the Merderet River." Shells were exploding just ahead. Colby figured they came from naval guns, but he was not sure. "They sound like trains flying through the air. There is an enormous flash and explosion, accompanied by clanging sounds. A shell has hit the bridge." The round, whether German or American, wounded several men. He could hear them crying for the medics. Colby tried to help, but there was little he could do. "I have realized that a casualty is much more than a military statistic . . . it is a real, bleeding, hurting human being." They crossed to Cauquigny, passed through it, and dug in just beyond. There they waited for the order to attack.[29]

The order came with the rising of the sun. The two regiments spread their battalions out and carefully marched west. Private Don Foye was a scout with H Company of the 357th Infantry. His job required him to walk, in tandem with another scout, about seventy-five yards ahead of the main body of troops. Foye was a teenage New Englander who traced his roots back to those who had come over on the *Mayflower.*

The morning was silent. He could only hear the gentle scrunching of his boots against the earth. He came to a hedgerow and was surprised at its height and thickness. The thing was a solid mass of earthen embankment, probably at least ten feet high. The top of the hedgerow was anchored with vegetation of all kinds. "The tree roots went down the whole 10 . . . feet, all through that, so it was not a mound of dirt . . . it was solid roots." He peered around the hedgerow and looked ahead. "Every 300 feet there was another one."

Foye made it through the first hedgerow, but just ahead the Germans were dug in and waiting. The chattering of their machine guns, rifles, and mortars shattered the morning stillness. The Americans scrambled for the cover of hedgerows, sunken lanes, and ditches. The whole scene was one of chaos. Men became separated from one another. Officers could not exercise much command and control—they could only see as far as the next hedgerow. It was like fighting in a maze.

Several fields away from Foye's H Company, Elvir Magnuson and G Company were also caught in the murderous crossfire. "Three mortar shells landed in front of me. I got to the next hedgerow." He and a buddy named Frankie were the only ones to make it that far. Everyone else in Magnuson's squad was killed or wounded. Elvir and his friend looked back and saw no live Americans. They had been cut off. They left the cover of the hedgerow and wandered around, looking for the remnants of their company. "A German machine-gun opened up on us. There was no hole in the hedgerow but we sure made one. We got a lot of scratches. We were both scared. Frankie got out his New Testament but was shaking so much I told him to give it to me. I turned to the 23rd Psalm. After I read it aloud, we calmed down." They eventually found their way back to the company.

Lieutenant Colby and E Company were in reserve, waiting in an assembly area, listening to the sounds of battle. Around midday they received orders to go up. "We begin to move up. Mortar rounds start falling in. Machine-gun fire breaks out. This goes on for several hours. We never see the enemy. At last, a number of dirty, weary paratroopers begin walking toward us along the road. They, it turned out, were the 'enemy.' There were about a hundred of them, and they had held off our whole battalion all afternoon, thinking we were Germans. There is no record of this battle, because military historians do not record minor blunders."

By the time the awful day of June 10 was over, the 90th Division had gotten, basically, nowhere. The 358th pushed about five hundred yards west of Picauville, well short of Pont l'Abbé, and suffered ninety-nine casualties. The 357th was stymied just beyond Le Motey. Dr. William McConahey was in command of a battalion aid station in the 357th. All day long he worked to save lives. "The casualties poured in at an alarming rate, and many of them were bad ones, too. Our litter bearers were having a real workout bringing in the wounded, and the aid station was working at top speed. When the wounded were carried in, I looked them over carefully, dressed the wounds and cleaned them out the best way I could, because they were so often dirty with debris from the field, grass and torn uniforms."

McConahey figured things couldn't get worse than on that first day, but the next two days saw more of the same. The 90th Division soldiers kept attacking and the Germans slaughtered them in droves. "It was brutal up there, and what a slaughter! The wounded poured back in dozens, and I've never seen such horrible wounds, before or since—legs off, arms off, faces shot away, eviscerations, chests ripped open and so on. We worked at top speed, hour after hour, until we were too tired to stand up—and then we kept going."

McConahey was a well-respected physician and officer. During the previous two years as the division trained for battle, he had made many friends. Soon they started showing up on his operating table. "I remember Major Jastre (executive officer of the second battalion), gasping for air and turning greenish from a huge sucking chest wound, while I struggled unsuccessfully to save his life. I remember Lieutenant Schiller, staggering into the station holding his bleeding, shattered shoulder. I remember Lieutenant Bowman, lying in a pool of blood in the station, after an 88-mm shell hit his jeep. I remember Captain Buck Shaw, when a litter squad carried him in after he had lain seriously wounded all night long in no-man's land. One of our aid men, Tschbrun, had found him about dark, and had voluntarily stayed all night with him until it was light enough to bring the wounded officer in.

"I remember the soldier who had watched with horror and terror as a lumbering tank rolled over his legs as he lay helplessly wounded on the ground. I remember the lad whose entire lower jaw was shot away. And I remember so many others . . ."

The 90th Division's commander, Brigadier General Jay MacKelvie, fed the 359th Infantry into the middle of his lines, but it made no difference. By the evening of June 13, his troops had barely reached their intermediate objectives—they got Pont l'Abbé but were battered by friendly planes just beyond the town—and he had suffered hundreds more casualties. "In its first four days of combat the 90th Division had made an inauspicious beginning," the Army's official historian wrote. "Unfortunately it had . . . run into a well-entrenched enemy in terrain favorable to the defender. On the other hand, the division was not making the progress expected of it by the corps commander."

Indeed it was not, and the reasons for that failure boiled down to two major problems: poor preparation and poor senior leadership. The soldiers of the 90th Division were well trained, well equipped, and more than willing to fight, but they had not been properly prepared for the challenging hedgerow terrain. This was the single greatest failing of the pre-invasion planning. The Allies, especially the Americans, thought too much about how to get ashore and not enough about how to deal with the unique Norman terrain. "We were rehearsed endlessly for attacking beach defenses, but not one day was given to the terrain behind the beaches, which was no less difficult and deadly," Charles Cawthon commented. He was in the 29th Division, but what he said applied to every American division at Normandy in June. None of them were ready for the hedgerows. "Although there had been some talk in the U.K. before D-Day about the hedgerows, none of us really appreciated how difficult they would turn out to be," General Gavin later wrote.

Actually, the planners did not even understand the nature of the Norman hedgerows. They figured these hedgerows were the same as the ones in England—little hedges that might provide a bit of concealment for the enemy but not much else. They were tragically wrong. Had they studied the history of Normandy or taken the trouble to glean information from French resistance groups operating in the area, they would have understood the true nature of the hedgerows, but they didn't. Instead they relied on aerial photographs that did not reveal the height, depth, or strength of the hedgerows. As a result, Allied soldiers were poorly prepared to fight amid the hedgerows. This especially affected the Americans because they fought in the thickest areas of the Norman bocage.[30]

But the problems of the 90th Division went deeper than that. Many of the division's senior officers were inept. The problems began at the top, with MacKelvie, who had previously served as the division's artillery officer. Once promoted, he was totally unsuited for command of a division. The soldiers who served under him found much to dislike. In a carefully considered evaluation, prepared long after the war, they ascribed to him many bad qualities: "no apparent knowledge of infantry tactics or battlefield leadership; unwillingness to accept sound advice from his knowledgeable subordinates [such as General Devine]; delayed all orders for nit-picking review; issued orders so late his subordinates had no time to coordinate essential details before the designated 'H-Hour,' which resulted in disastrous loss of life; was distant, cold, and remote in personality, even with his personal staff and major subordinate commanders."

MacKelvie was decidedly uninspirational. At one point during the three days his division attacked west of the Merderet, his assistant division commander, Brigadier General Sam Williams, an able and personally courageous man, found MacKelvie lying in a furrow, hugging a hedgerow for dear life. "Goddammit, General, you can't lead this division hiding in that goddamn hole," Williams exploded. "Get the hell out of that hole and go to your vehicle. Walk to it, or you'll have this goddamn division wading in the English Channel."

MacKelvie committed one of his worst gaffes when he relieved the respected commander of the 357th, Colonel John Sheehy, immediately before the invasion. MacKelvie thought that Sheehy was too old, so he replaced him with a younger but much less able colonel named P. D. Ginder. It is fair to say that Ginder's performance was abysmal. Lieutenant Max Kocour, a mortar forward observer with H Company, said of Ginder, "[He] was quite obtuse and almost constantly made the wrong decisions." Many others in the regiment agreed. Lieutenant Colby and many of his comrades found Ginder "full of boast and posturing . . . a classic loose cannon. Always in his jeep, always on the go somewhere, always issuing orders when he had no staff to transmit them (he sent his staff out of the HQ to get 'blooded' and learn about combat). He knew nothing about infantry organization or combat."

Captain William DePuy found Ginder to be the very epitome of a bad officer. "[He] was as close to being incompetent as it is possible to be. He knew nothing about an infantry regiment. He was erratic to the extreme. Three or four times [between June 10 and 13] he ordered the regiment straight ahead into a repeat performance of a failed attack. He will never be forgotten by the survivors." To make matters worse, one of Ginder's battalion commanders, Lieutenant Colonel LeRoy Lester, turned out to be a complete washout. He was potbellied, coarse, a blowhard. He made one combat reconnaissance on June 10 and turned himself into the aid station, claiming blindness. DePuy rated Lester a "despicable punk . . . he had given ample evidence of his character continuously during the two years before Normandy."

MacKelvie, Ginder, and Lester were only some of the poor leaders. Others (who will go nameless) throughout the division did plenty of damage. "The consequences of all this leadership failure could be predicted," DePuy said. The initial combat performance of the 90th Division was not good in spite of the "heroic efforts and tragic losses among the lower-ranking officers and the bewildered troops." The soldiers, NCOs, and junior officers paid the price for the failings of their superiors.

DePuy proved to be a solid combat commander. He eventually rose to battalion command and after the war became a high-ranking general. He made it his life's mission to ensure that American soldiers would never again be as poorly prepared and poorly led when they went into battle as the soldiers of the 90th Division were in the summer of 1944. DePuy was one of those responsible for reforming the Army after Vietnam and transforming it into the highly professional, effective force that won the Persian Gulf War.

General Collins was perceptive enough to understand the problems the 90th Division had at the senior level. The gravity of the situation hit home to him two days into the futile attack. A hands-on commander, General Collins went forward on foot to see what was holding up the attack. He could not find any battalion or regimental CPs, nor could he find any commanders, except for Lieutenant Colonel William Nave, an excellent battalion commanding officer in the 358th who would soon lose his life. Collins made his way to MacKelvie's headquarters. As he did so, he came upon several 90th Division men sitting around by the side of a road. "It was obvious they were malingering." Collins tried to appeal to their pride by citing the fine combat record the division had compiled in World War I. "They were not interested and said so." Most of them had not even been born at that time. At the moment, they cared little for anything but their own safety. "I ordered them back to the front, but could not stay to see if they complied."

When Collins got to MacKelvie's headquarters he told him about the malingerers and saw, very quickly, that MacKelvie seemed at a complete loss as to how to deal with such problems. At that point, General Collins knew it was time for a change at the top. He went back to his own CP, had a phone conversation with Bradley, and decided to remove MacKelvie. Collins relieved him on June 13, and this began a housecleaning throughout the division that did eventually enhance performance. Unfortunately, he replaced MacKelvie with Major General Eugene Landrum, his deputy at VII Corps but a man he barely knew. Landrum was not much of an upgrade. He had commanded the 7th Infantry Division in the Aleutian Islands in 1943. He was a classic lead-from-the-rear sort of general. His troops were not impressed with him. He "did not look or act like a combat leader. Short, fat, slow-moving, no demonstrated spark or drive. Sat in a wicker armchair in a cellar at Div. HQ from time to time. Unsympathetic and pessimistic in outlook, showed little confidence in his subordinates."

Landrum commanded the 90th until late July, when he, too, was relieved. For a brief time, after the 90th Division's initial failure and acute command problems, General Bradley's 1st Army staff recommended that the unit be disbanded and its soldiers parceled out to other units as replacements, but luckily that did not happen. In spite of the division's problems and in spite of Landrum's remote command style, the division steadily improved until it eventually (after Normandy) became one of the best, most reliable divisions in the U.S. Army. "In the end the 90th became one of the most outstanding in the European Theater," Bradley later wrote.[31]

Leadership and proper preparation made all the difference for the 90th, and the same was true for the entire U.S. Army in Normandy.

CHAPTER THREE

CARENTAN

General Omar Bradley knew he had to have Carentan. The crossroads town of some four thousand people was the key to the linkup of the Utah and Omaha beachheads. Carentan was situated astride the N-13 highway, as well as the Cherbourg–Paris railroad. It was on low ground amid a series of canals, rivers, and marshes that tied ribbons around the town. At one time Napoléon Bonaparte had flooded the area around Carentan in an effort to turn it into a fortified island. In 1944, the Germans also flooded much of the area surrounding the town. Any attackers approaching from the north, as the Americans were, had to reckon with the limited number of dry approaches to Carentan. They also had to reckon with the defenders of Carentan, Colonel Frederick von der Heydte and his excellent 6th Parachute Infantry Regiment. The colonel and his men had orders, straight from Rommel, to defend Carentan to the last man.

The capture of this town was one of the key missions of the 101st Airborne. From there, they were then supposed to link up with the 29th Division attacking west over the Vire River. This joining of hands among VII and V Corps soldiers would link up the two American beaches, making a concerted push for Cherbourg, and eventually St-Lô, feasible. So Bradley viewed the capture of Carentan just as a home builder would view the construction of a foundation—from it all else would flow.[1]

Anyone who wanted Carentan first had to take St-Côme-du-Mont, a small town located three miles north of Carentan on the N-13. Captain Sam Gibbons (the future congressman) and fifty other troopers had tried to take St-Côme-du-Mont on D-Day and they had failed. The Germans were in the town and they were there in strength. They foiled several other minor American attempts on the town. But in the twenty-four hours following the jump into Normandy hundreds of troopers of the 101st Airborne had been steadily moving south, toward their various unit objectives and Carentan. By the afternoon of June 7, many of them were fighting scattered battles east and south of St-Côme-du-Mont.

Private Donald Burgett, a nineteen-year-old Michigan native, and several other soldiers were fighting one of those battles at a crossroads a mile south of St-Côme-du-Mont. They were deployed east of the N-13, behind some hedges, taking mortar fire from Germans across the road. Burgett scanned the German-held area for any sign of the mortar crew. All at once, he spotted someone about one hundred yards away. It was a German soldier walking cautiously along, probably retrieving more ammunition. Burgett drew a bead on him and squeezed the trigger. "He went down hard and rolled over on a small pile of bricks, then, lying on his back, he dug his heels into the ground and twitched for several minutes. Finally, taking a deep breath, he arched his back up until only his shoulders and heels were touching the ground, then collapsed. I could have put another bullet into him, but somehow I was fascinated and watched him in his losing battle for life."

A few minutes later, Burgett noticed the dead man's long blond hair and became fixated on it. "GI's were never allowed to have hair that long, and it agitated me in a strange way that I can't explain. Deep inside, something primitive stirred within me." Caught up in the barbarity of combat, Burgett became obsessed with scalping the dead enemy soldier. He even thought of how he would salt and stretch the scalp on a willow limb. He attempted to crawl to the dead enemy soldier, but German fire snapped him back into reality.

As Burgett wrestled with his demons, an American M-5 Stuart light tank rumbled toward him from somewhere behind. Burgett looked back and saw the Stuart (from D Company, 70th Tank Battalion) crash through a small hedge and into his field. The presence of the tank gave the young paratrooper a sense of security. It shot up the German positions for a while but soon ran out of ammo. The commander popped his head out of his hatch and told Burgett that he was going to replenish his ammo but would be right back.

Burgett called out to him, "Hurry up . . . and for God's sake, don't forget us."

"I won't forget you," the tank commander replied.

Now Burgett watched as the commander made a very serious mistake that stemmed from haste. Instead of going back the way he came, he ordered his tank onto the road, where he could make better time than through the fields and hedges. Unfortunately, his spot on the road, right in front of a house that was serving as a German aid station, was also in full view of a German antitank gun crew. The enemy gunners needed only to fire once, and the results were terribly predictable. Burgett watched the whole tragedy unfold.

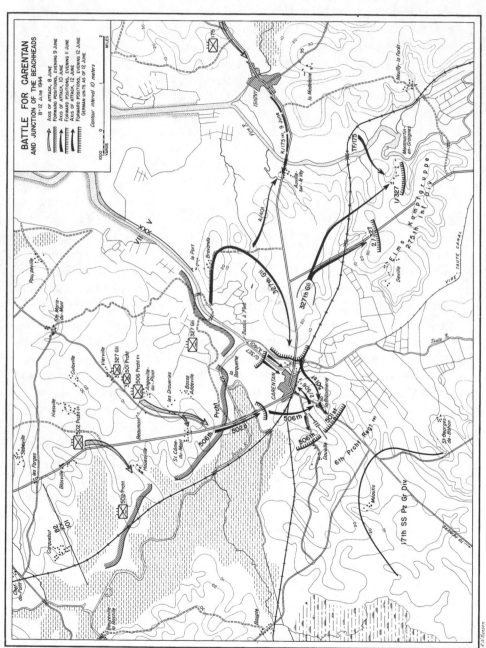

BATTLE FOR CARENTAN
AND JUNCTION OF THE BEACHHEADS
8–12 June 1944

Axis of attack, 8 June
Forward positions, evening 9 June
Axis of attack, 10 June
Forward positions, evening 11 June
Axis of attack, 12 June
Forward positions, evening 12 June
German units as of 12 June

Contour interval 10 meters

MAP XVI

R.A. Kasson

"They drilled an armor piercing shell clear through the turret. The small tank erupted in a violent explosion and started to burn. The whole crew died instantly. We could smell their flesh cooking in the flames, along with the heavy oily smoke. Seeing the tank crew die that way made me feel bad. That commander was a hell of a nice guy."

The tank commander's burned body was sticking out of the turret. He and his wrecked tank remained in that spot for several days, right at the road intersection, a place the locals and the American soldiers soon began calling Dead Man's Corner. The intersection is still known by that name.

Soon after witnessing the death of the tank crew, Burgett and his buddies received orders to retreat north to Beaumont. The brass was planning an all-out attack on St-Côme-du-Mont for the next morning.[2]

By this time, the paratroopers had been fighting, mostly without proper food or sleep, for nearly three days. Even though they were superbly conditioned, most of the troopers were nearing the brink of total exhaustion. "They were so beat that they could not understand words even if an order was clearly expressed." Captain Lloyd Patch, commander of the 1st Battalion, 506th, recalled. He had been pressed into service as battalion commander when his commanding officer, the revered Lieutenant Colonel William Turner, was killed by a sniper's shot through his skull. "I was too tired to talk straight. Nothing I heard made a firm impression on me. I spoke jerkily in phrases because I could not remember the thoughts which had preceded what I said." The division historian concurred with Patch. He later wrote that "much of what happened . . . made only vague impressions on the exhausted participants; later, trying to remember verbal orders, messages, and objectives, officers and men found many blanked-out periods."[3]

There was no time for a respite, though. General Taylor's attack on St-Côme-du-Mont began at 0445 on June 8. His plan called for two battalions of the 506th to pinch in from the north, while the 501st's 3rd Battalion and the newly arrived 1st Battalion, 401st Glider Infantry, closed in on the town from the east. The attack would be preceded by a rolling barrage from a mixture of 75mm and 105mm artillery support from the 65th Armored Field Artillery Battalion and the 101st Airborne's own 377th Parachute Field Artillery Battalion. There would also be tank and mortar support.

Given the condition of the men, it is not surprising that the operation was anything but textbook. In fact, the battle simply became known as "the Snafu Engagement." The five assault battalions did not follow the carefully drawn up plan. Instead, they mixed together in a confusing jumble of clumsy, uncoordinated attacks along the eastern and southern fringes of St-Côme-du-Mont. For most of the attackers, the day was a blur of random engagements with groups of Germans who were defending buildings, intersections, or hedgerows.

Private Bob Bowen's C Company, 401st Glider Infantry, was advancing near the 506th Infantry and got off to a late start when the 506th ran into stiff resistance early in the morning. Bowen's unit spent most of the day clearing out German resistance near the N-13, southeast of St-Côme-du-Mont. "I heard the loud outbreak of small arms fire and we waited. The scream of rockets sent us into the ditches." A mortar squad leader set up a 60mm mortar and bombarded the suspected enemy positions. The rocket fire ceased. "Once more the column began to move, almost snail like. The same thing happened again, with more small arms fire, met with an explosion of mortar fire and grenades. This time it took longer to proceed."

When the advance resumed, they crossed the N-13 and moved through a small hamlet "with row homes made of gray stone, marrow alleyways and U-shaped courtyards, with outbuildings for animals and crop harvest." They passed exhausted men from B Company of the 401st and dead Germans, too. Bowen gazed at the enemy bodies. "Their uniforms [were] stained with fresh blood that leaked into pools under their bodies. It was difficult to realize that just minutes before they had been living humans just like I was, probably with wives and children at home."

Bowen and the other Americans started taking machine-gun fire from a building just up ahead. They jumped into a ditch. The house had a hole in its slate roof. Someone fired a bazooka at the building. The bazooka fire rocked the enemy-held building, silencing the machine gun, and Bowen's platoon leader ordered his men forward. "He yelled to me to take a couple of men and cover the rear. I grabbed Shannon and Primas and we broke through the front door of the home, ran through to the rear and out the back door. Several Germans were running for a hedgerow. We fired. They vanished in the hedges."

Bowen and his buddies ran along the backs of the houses. "We could hear excited, heavy guttural voices in one house, tossed grenades through an open door and went on because [Lieutenant] Aspinwall was waving from the road. Company B was passing through. There was no time to clear all of the homes."

They moved on and advanced down the road, clearing out more buildings. Bowen ended up at Colonel Robert Sink's 506th Parachute Infantry regimental command post. The day before, Bowen had severely sprained his ankle. Today he was going on pure adrenaline. But all of the running and jumping had only made the ankle worse, tearing ligaments and tendons. Bowen's company commander insisted he report to the medics. The medics took one look at his swollen, discolored ankle and tagged him for evacuation. Only time could heal his ankle. For him the Battle of Normandy was over.[4]

As Bowen and the other glider infantrymen were working their way west, Captain Patch's 1st Battalion, 506th, was getting jumbled up in its attack. His

B and C Companies got caught up in a close-quarters fight with Germans on the eastern end of St-Côme-du-Mont. Private Burgett's Company A went in a significantly different direction. Jumping off at Beaumont, the company slugged its way south all day, through many of the same fields where Burgett's group had fought the day before. "We were heading across field after field," Burgett wrote, "screaming and yelling in wild charges that drove the enemy back." Whenever they ran into stubborn resistance, they called in withering, effective artillery fire. One such barrage convinced a group of Hungarians to surrender. "They came stumbling and crawling out of the hedges with tears streaming down their cheeks, crying like babies and begging us not to shoot them. They were a sickening bunch."

The company cut across the N-13, went right past Dead Man's Corner, passing the destroyed tank (which was still smoking), and dug in along some high ground that afforded a nice view of the terrain and the road that led south to Carentan. Burgett and several other men found the remnants of a German supply column. Dead, bloated cows and horses lay everywhere. The stench that emanated from them was nearly overwhelming. Shattered wagons and discarded equipment, including German paratrooper uniforms and weapons, littered the area. Burgett found a brand-new P-38 pistol. He also feasted on black bread and tubes of Limburger cheese.

From their positions the A Company men had a clear view of the four bridges that led into Carentan. Burgett and the others watched as German troops crossed the bridges. What began as small groups turned into streams of German soldiers making their way into Carentan. It was the better part of the German 6th Parachute Regiment. "The longer we watched, the greater their numbers became." For three and a half hours A Company watched in helpless frustration, hoping that Allied planes would materialize and attack the vulnerable Germans, but that never happened. Burgett and the others believed that the Germans were encountering no American opposition, but they were incorrect.[5]

At that very same time, Lieutenant Colonel Julian Ewell and his 3rd Battalion, 501st Parachute Infantry, were looking at the same sight. They had reached Dead Man's Corner. Once there, Ewell looked north in the direction of St-Côme-du-Mont and saw the German column, with many of its supply wagons, moving southwest. He correctly surmised that they were retreating from St-Côme-du-Mont, attempting to make it to Carentan. So he and his men turned south and tried to cut them off before they could make it to the bridges.

German machine-gun fire, coming from a collection of stone buildings near the first Carentan bridge, tore into Ewell's men. Seconds later, 88 fire from Carentan started pouring in. Ewell tried to call in friendly artillery, but to no avail. He and his soldiers withdrew to the east side of the N-13. As they did so, they started taking fire from the north. Another group of Germans, marching straight out of St-Côme-du-Mont, right down the N-13, attacked Ewell's outmanned unit. All day long, they fought for their lives, absorbing six different enemy attacks. Ewell's leadership was superb. At one point, he sensed that the Germans were close to overrunning his right flank (in hedgerows along the road) and led an attack that captured high ground on the west side of the road. From this hill the Americans poured effective fire into the left flank of those Germans who were working their way down the highway.

By late afternoon, the fighting died out. Ewell lost 40 of the 160 men he took into battle with him. The majority of the Germans got away into Carentan, where they would be heard from again. American patrols gingerly worked their way into St-Côme-du-Mont and found it empty. The town belonged to the Americans, but the 101st Airborne had failed to destroy its German defenders. The Snafu Engagement was a victory, but a hollow one.[6]

However, the first step toward the capture of Carentan had been taken. With St-Côme-du-Mont secure, General Taylor could now turn his whole division south to attack Carentan and establish contact with the 29th Division. On June 9, the 101st Airborne spent most of the day consolidating its positions north of Carentan and scouting the terrain around the town. Colonel Sink even personally led one reconnaissance patrol. He and nine men easily made it over the first bridge, but the second bridge, over the widest waterway, the Douve River, was out. The bridge had been destroyed either by the Germans or by Allied naval fire (this is still a point of contention and probably never will be resolved). Sink and the others found a rowboat and rowed across the Douve. They made it past the third bridge before taking heavy machine-gun fire. The patrol retreated back to the American lines.

By the time Colonel Sink reported his findings to division, Taylor was already formulating a plan for the capture of Carentan. Aerial reconnaissance indicated (erroneously) that only a battalion of enemy troops held Carentan. Taylor planned to take Carentan with a pincer movement. He ordered his men to cross the Douve in two places. In the east, the 327th Glider Infantry was supposed to cross the Douve at Brevands (where Captain Shettle and his men had held out on D-Day and thereafter) and push south. Part of the 327th would move southeast and link up with the 29th Division's 175th Infantry Regiment west of the Vire, near Isigny. The rest of the 327th would circle around Carentan from the southeast. The 502nd Parachute Infantry, led by Lieutenant Colonel Robert Cole's 3rd Battalion, was to cross the Douve at the four bridges, swing southwest of Carentan, and seize Hill 30, the commanding ground that controlled movement in and out of the town. At Hill 30, Cole's people were supposed to link up with the 327th. In the meantime, the rest of the 502nd and the entire 506th Parachute Infantry would cross the bridges in Cole's wake and circle around Carentan. The last phase of the operation entailed entering Carentan and clearing it out.

Taylor's concept was excellent. A pincer movement made great sense, but there was just one problem. There was only one northern approach to Carentan—the four bridges that spanned the N-13. Most of the area around the highway was flooded. The road, which eventually led to Carentan, was little more than a raised causeway (similar to La Fière and Chef-du-Pont), and the ground near and beyond the bridges was flat. This meant that Cole's attackers would be out in the open, on flat, marshy ground with practically no cover or concealment. This was disturbing, but it could not be helped. There was no other way to cross the water.[7]

Cole's attack was supposed to commence shortly after midnight on June 10, but the division's engineers had been unable to build a span over the destroyed Bridge Number Two. They had spent much of the night pinned down by 88 fire. Cole's battalion sat on the wet ground and waited while Lieutenant Ralph Gehauf took a patrol across the water on boats. Earlier that day, Gehauf had reconned Carentan in an observation plane. The place looked undefended, but he figured that was probably too good to be true. He understood that nothing trumped honest-to-goodness, on-the-ground, "see-it-yourself" intelligence.

Gehauf's patrol paddled across the Douve River and proceeded, single-file, down the causeway. At the fourth bridge, they discovered a Belgian gate obstacle. Only by arduously prying the gate could they force it open, but only one man at a time could get through it. Beyond the Belgian gate, they came under enemy mortar and machine-gun fire. Gehauf sent two runners back to Cole with a message to bring his mortars forward, but the runners passed along the wrong message. They told Cole not to go forward because the opposition was too heavy. At almost the same time, Cole got the word from regiment to postpone his attack. Disgusted, he and his men hiked to Les Quesnils and caught a couple of hours of sleep in wet fields. Gehauf and his men remained until after daylight, pinned down by enemy fire but still gathering good information on enemy positions. Finally, they managed to escape back to the American side of the Douve.[8]

All morning long, Cole and his men waited for the word to attack. He only heard that he was to receive artillery support for an attack some time in the afternoon. By noontime, he was quite impatient to get under way. He took Gehauf and returned to Bridge Number Two. To their disgust, Cole and Gehauf found that the engineers still had not done anything, so they took matters into their own hands. They rounded up a few men and built a rickety footbridge with planks and ropes the engineers had brought to the site.

The whole job took about three hours, but when it was finished, Cole's battalion began crossing the bridge. Gehauf's intelligence section led the way, followed by I Company, G Company, H Company, and the headquarters group. Slowly, and cautiously, each man negotiated his way across the bridge. The planks eventually gave way, so many of the soldiers crossed the Douve by hanging on to the ropes.

During the crossing the Americans were under intermittent enemy fire, mostly from 88s or mortars. But as they walked forward on the raised causeway and approached the fourth bridge, the fire grew thicker. It was coming from every flank and to the front as well. The Germans were throwing everything at them: 88 fire, mortars, machine-guns, and, perhaps most terrifying of all, accurate sniper fire. The ground was slick and steep. Many of the troopers sought cover along the embankments, but to no avail. Nor could they dig in along the embankments—the soil was too hard. The poplar trees that lined the road were no use, either. They were far too thin to provide cover and far too leafless to provide concealment. There was nowhere to go. Some tried to crawl forward; some hugged the ground; only a few shot back. Most could see little beyond their own slice of embankment or causeway.

Up and down the confused clumps of Americans that lined either side of the causeway, men were getting hit at a dizzying rate. Lieutenant John Larish was peeking around a tree when a sniper got him right between the eyes. He went slack, like a partly filled sack of potatoes. Another man felt a German machine-gun bullet crease both of his thighs. While lying on his back, he undid his trousers, pulled them down, and inspected the damage, "I thought that SOB got the family jewels!" he exclaimed with relief. Dead troopers were lying all along the causeway, many with bullet holes in their foreheads or between the eyes. Private First Class Theodore Benkowski got hit by an enemy sniper. He considered himself lucky—the bullet smashed into one of his eyes, costing him that eye but not his life.

This ghastly shooting gallery went on for several hours. All this time, Lieutenant Colonel Cole had been back at the second bridge, making sure none of his men ran away. At 1800, he turned that job over to his executive officer, Major John Stopka, and went forward, attempting to rally his men and get them moving forward. Cole walked around in plain sight of the enemy: "God damn it, start firing and keep firing! God damn you, listen, spread out; how many times must I tell you?!" Sniper bullets zinged by him, but he remained unhit. Cole was brave, but no amount of bravery was going to get this attack moving again. His battalion was stalled. Only a few men had been able to get across the fourth bridge, and they were pinned down, praying to themselves for survival, caught in a hellish crossfire.[9]

Only nightfall, and American artillery fire, offered any surcease. After darkness, the German fire slackened a bit, but Cole's 3rd Battalion was completely disorganized, strung out along the causeway. Many of the wounded could not be evacuated. The dead still lay where they had been killed.

Everyone else settled down for the night, knowing that in the morning they would have to attack again.

At midnight, they experienced something rare for American soldiers in Normandy. A German Stuka dive-bomber, and another unidentified enemy plane, strafed the battalion on the causeway. The Stuka came from the direction of Carentan. It flew at treetop level along the road and unloaded on the helpless GIs. Private Hans Brandt of G Company was half-submerged in the marsh, near Bridge Number Four, when he caught site of the enemy plane. The Stuka passed overhead and dropped a bomb, and in an instant, "the whole earth seemed to strike fire." The explosion lifted Brandt. For an awful second he was in the air. Then he splashed into the water, with a wrenched leg and deafened. For a few minutes he was unconscious, but when he awoke he got up and went to help several other men who had been hurt much worse.

With wing guns blazing, the Stuka flew north along the road. Tracer rounds splattered against the pavement "bouncing like ping pong balls" in the view of many Americans. Others noticed that the tracers kicked up sparks as they smashed into the paved surface of the road.

A little farther up the road, which the Americans soon nicknamed Purple Heart Lane, I Company took the brunt of the German strafing. The other enemy plane unloaded as many as eight bombs right on the company's position near Bridge Number Three. In a matter of seconds, thirty men were killed or wounded. In one day, the company had lost sixty-two of its eighty-five soldiers. Company I was finished as an effective fighting force.

Cole's men had had a taste of the horror and devastation of an aerial attack, something German soldiers in Normandy experienced routinely. Cole went back to regiment and received orders to continue his attack. That was just fine with him. For the rest of the night he prepared the remnants of his battalion for another push on Carentan. Company H, with eighty-four men, would be in the lead; G Company would follow with its sixty survivors while headquarters chipped in another 121. Cole was not the type to be easily dissuaded from an objective. He was a gentle but steely Texan who in battle turned short-tempered and irritable. A 1939 graduate of West Point, he was most afraid of letting his men down.

At 0400 on June 11 they moved out. In the darkness, they made it through the Belgian Gate on Bridge Number Four, over the Madeleine River, taking no casualties. The lead scouts veered to the right, across flat fields that led to a line of hedgerows and a cluster of four stone farm buildings belonging to the Ingouf family. The scouts were drawn to the farm buildings, one of their battalion's key objectives. The Germans were in the buildings and behind the hedges.

The lead scout, Private Albert Dieter, moved slowly in the morning mist, heading straight for the farmhouse. Like any good scout, he kept his weapon ready and his eyes constantly roving, looking for movement or other less obvious signs of the enemy. Behind him, the platoons of his H Company were strung out over a distance of some two hundred yards, almost all the way back to the bridge.

Dieter closed to within five yards of the hedgerow. All at once, the air exploded with the sound of German machine-gun, rifle and mortar fire. A burst of machine-gun fire shredded his arm from wrist to shoulder. Two other men behind him were killed instantly. Instead of hurling himself to the ground, Dieter calmly turned around and walked back in the direction he came, all the way to a ditch on the east side of the road, where much of H Company had taken cover.

Private Dieter spotted his commanding officer, Captain Cecil Simmons. "Captain, I'm hit pretty bad, ain't I?"

Simmons was honest with him: "You sure are."

"Will I make it?" Dieter asked.

The captain shrugged. "I'm not sure."

"Captain, they've always called me a fuckup in this company. I didn't let you down this time, did I?"

"No, you sure didn't."

"That's all I wanted to hear." Dieter got up and walked north along the road, looking for a medic. A few others followed him and got struck down by machine-gun fire. Dieter survived.

Back at the ditch where Captain Simmons was lying, the enemy fire intensified. Wounded soldiers were crawling back, plopping themselves next to the captain. For a few minutes Simmons turned into a medic, giving his men first aid. When the captain ran out of medical supplies, he took some from the pack of a stiffened, cold body of a dead German in the ditch.

Captain Simmons saw movement out of the corner of his eye. Private William Penden came running over and belly flopped next to Simmons. Penden was shaking violently.

"Are you hurt?" Simmons asked him.

"Hell, no, they haven't got me yet," Penden replied.

"Well, then, let's keep firing at the dirty devils," the captain ordered in his best command voice.

Penden crawled a few yards away, found a good firing position, and fired several rounds from his carbine. Simmons retrieved a clip for his own carbine and, with shaking hands of his own, shoved the clip into the breech. For some reason Penden had stopped firing.

"What's the matter, Penden?"

Penden did not answer and Simmons soon saw why. An enemy sniper had shot him in the left side, right through the heart.

Cole was close by, crawling in the ditch, looking for his forward artillery observer, Captain Julian Rosemund. When he found him, he barked, "Get some shell fire on the farmhouse and the hedges."

Rosemund called back with the request and reported to Cole that the guns could not fire until an absent artillery commander assented.

Cole, in the middle of a desperate fight for survival, had no patience for such command niceties. "God damn it! We need artillery, and we can't wait for any general."

He got what he wanted. For nearly half an hour the artillerymen, firing from positions near St-Come-du-Mont, dropped shells among the hedgerows and on the farm buildings. Cole watched the friendly artillery crashing in, but he was dismayed to hear no slackening in the enemy fire. If anything, it had gotten heavier.[10]

Cole slid back down into the ditch and wondered what to do next. Should he retreat? Should he sideslip these Germans and try to make it into Carentan? Should he attack? For a few minutes he was in a quandary. Then, like a thunderbolt, he made his decision. Three days before, at Houesville, Cole had ordered a successful bayonet charge. Now he was going to try his luck again.

Cole looked across the road and saw Major Stopka lying in a ditch. He got his executive officer's attention. "Hey, we're going to order smoke from the artillery and then make a bayonet charge on the house."

"OK!" Stopka replied. Cole should have expressly told the major that he wanted him to pass the order on to the rest of the scattered American force, but he merely assumed that Stopka would do so. Instead, Stopka only told the men immediately adjacent to him.

A few minutes later, smoke shells began exploding in front of the farm buildings and in a wide circle from the edges of Carentan (to Cole's left) and the Madeleine River (to Cole's right). At 0615, the smoke shells stopped and the U.S. artillerymen shot several fragmentation rounds at presumed German positions beyond the farm buildings.

Cole had a whistle in one hand and a pistol in the other. He put the whistle to his lips, blew, got up out of the ditch, and trotted forward. Only the men around him, numbering about twenty in all, followed. In this confused manner, one of the most storied episodes in the history of the 101st Airborne began.

In his own ditch, Stopka saw Cole and realized he had failed to adequately communicate his commander's orders. Frantically the major raced around rallying as many men as possible. "Come on! Let's go! Follow the colonel!" About forty men got up and followed.

Cole was considerably ahead of everyone else. When he got to the middle of the open field, he glanced behind and saw almost no one following. For a second, he thought his men had failed him. He took a knee, peered in the direction of the ditches, and took stock of the situation. Now he saw several men trying to make it across the field. Bullets and shrapnel filled the air. Cole could hear the whipping of bullets as they zipped through the grass around him.

The men of 3rd Battalion had not failed their commander. Instead, most of them had no idea what was going on. They either had not heard of the order to charge or had received stilted, confused commands. They were in the ditches talking in puzzled sentences like "I heard someone yell something about a fucking whistle!" or, "They say we should fix bayonets!" When they saw Cole, Stopka, and the others who carried out the initial charge, most of the confused soldiers began to understand that they were supposed to assault the German positions. In groups that usually numbered less than a squad, they rushed forward, into the storm of enemy fire.

Cole was striding all over the field, wildly firing his pistol, urging men to keep going. "God damn! I don't know what I'm shooting at, but I gotta keep on! These goose-stepping Heinies think they know how to fight a war. We're about to learn 'em a lesson!" Some of the men around him, in spite of the grim circumstances, laughed. Soldiers were falling like bowling pins, but Cole and the other survivors kept going. Stopka surged past them, screaming "Let's go! Let's go!"

The smoke was clearing now, and just ahead they could see the buildings. Cole tried to keep up with his subordinate. He jumped a low hedge and splashed into a ditch with water up to his neck. In a curious antithesis to the famous infantry slogan, he hollered to his radioman, "Don't follow me!"

Back at the ditch along the road, Captain Simmons was unconscious. An artillery shell had landed a few feet away, nearly killing him. He had an out-of-body experience. He was floating above the battlefield, looking at his body, watching his men charge the Germans. He saw one of his soldiers bayonet a German in the belly. The man actually lifted the enemy soldier off his feet.

Now Simmons felt someone shaking him, harder and harder. He snapped back into consciousness and saw Staff Sergeant John White looming over him, shaking him vigorously. Simmons cleared the cobwebs out of his brain, left the ditch, and trotted across the field with Sergeant White. The captain spotted a German and shot him. The enemy soldier involuntarily stuck his tongue out as he died, a gesture that struck Simmons as somehow humorous.

By now, Cole and the others at the vanguard of the charge had made it across the open area (roughly the length of two football fields), closed with the German defenders of the Ingouf farm, and either killed them or put them to flight. The Americans howled like demons as they charged. The whole thing was vulgar, like something out of a supposedly more primitive age. In short, it was warfare at its most elemental, at its ugliest.

Dead, dismembered Germans were lying everywhere—in foxholes, behind embankments, outside the farm buildings, and behind hedgerows. Very few of these soldiers had been bayoneted, although a few wounded Germans had been stabbed to death by H Company soldiers. Most, though, had been killed with rifle fire or grenades at close range. Their dead faces, with half-open eyelids, betrayed a mixture of fear, shock, and surprise. The rest were retreating west, in the direction of the Carentan–Cherbourg railroad. First Sergeant Kenneth Sprecher and Private George Roach shot the lock off the door of the main farmhouse and charged inside, only to find the place abandoned. Cole followed and used the building as his CP.

Lieutenant Edward Provost, a diminutive man whom Cole regarded as an ineffective runt, had led one of the few actual bayonet charges. He was tingling with a strange excitement, walking around saying, "They *squeal* when you stick 'em!" Private Bernard Sterno, who was wounded several times that day, watched Lieutenant Provost carry on. "He was kind of bloodthirsty." Clearly, Cole was dead wrong about Lieutenant Provost.

Private Sterno was going to help a sergeant who had been wounded in the chest when he discovered that his own finger was wounded. A medic bandaged the bloody finger and Sterno moved on to a line of hedgerows near an apple orchard that separated the newly won Ingouf farmhouse from the Germans. He and several other Americans traded shots with the Germans. Sterno noticed that his bandage was coming loose, so he got a medic to wrap it up. The medic ordered Sterno to the rear, via an access road that led east, past the farm buildings and to the N-13. As he was doing so, he came across three wounded Americans lying in a waterlogged ditch by the road. They begged him to flag down an ambulance that was just then driving along the road, but 88 shells blasted the ditches, forcing everyone to hug the ground.

Sterno saw shrapnel tear the eye of one American right out of its socket. The man now only had a bloody hole where his eye had once been. "Is my eye gone?" he asked Sterno.

Private Sterno could not bring himself to tell the man the truth. "Even if it is, you should be glad you have the other one."

Sterno bent over to put some sulfa powder on the man's awful wound. As he did so, another enemy shelled landed close by. Something impacted against his back, making him feel like he had been "kicked by a mule in the spine." A shell fragment had torn into his back and lodged itself in his groin.

Sterno shook off the effects of his new wound and looked around at the others. He saw the lifeless remnants of one of his H Company buddies, who had sported a handlebar mustache. The sight of the mustache prompted Sterno to think back to the evening before D-Day. General Dwight Eisenhower, the Supreme Commander, had visited Sterno's unit right before they boarded their planes. The general had stopped and asked the mustachioed man what he did in civilian life. "I was a waiter in a restaurant in Philadelphia, sir."

The general joked, "With that mustache, I thought you might have been a pirate."

Sterno stared at the mustache now. It was still well groomed, even though the man's head, from the nose up, was gone.

The man without an eye had been hit in the arm. Sterno saw that the arm was torn from its socket. The soldier was weakly crying, "My arm, oh, my arm, my arm."

Five feet away, another soldier was bleeding out of the ears, nose, and mouth, babbling unintelligibly—classic symptoms of concussion. Sterno felt blood running down his back . . . or was it sweat? He wasn't sure. Figuring that he couldn't do anything to help these badly wounded men, he left but had difficulty walking. He crawled toward the fourth bridge and dropped into a foxhole. A mortar shell exploded just outside the hole. Fragments ripped into his neck and killed a lieutenant lying next to him. Sterno lay there for a while, but later he got the strength to walk back to an aid station.[11]

With the exception of a brief truce (which both sides used to evacuate wounded and scout enemy positions), the fighting raged at the Ingouf farm for the rest of the day. Troopers from Lieutenant Colonel Patrick Cassidy's 1st Battalion, 502nd, reinforced Cole's force. Cassidy's soldiers occupied positions, near the road, at a spot called the Cabbage Patch. There they fought a bitter close-quarters battle with the Germans. "It was just like shooting at rabbits," Lieutenant Delmar Idol of A Company said, "and just as hard to hit them." The two sides fought hard to flank each other or force the other to quit. At one point, Idol was blasting away at the Germans with his tommy gun when some return fire smashed into the helmet of the man next to him. Lieutenant Idol expected to see the man fall dead, but, incredibly, he was unwounded. Idol picked up his helmet and saw that it had a hole through each side. "Damndest thing I ever saw. The bullets hit both sides of the helmet, but missed his head in-between!"

Cole and the rest of his 3rd Battalion soldiers spent the rest of the day in and around the farmhouse, fending off determined German counterattacks. The Germans were so intent on dislodging Cole because they knew that if the Americans succeeded in keeping this foothold across the Madeleine, it would be a major step toward the capture of Carentan. The worst counterattack came in the late afternoon, when German soldiers advanced to within one hedgerow of the Ingouf farmhouse. By then, Cole hardly had anyone left to man his firing line. From behind hedgerows that bordered the apple orchard a few survivors shot at the advancing enemy. Standing near a window in the farmhouse, Cole saw these men fighting as best they could. He was so very proud of them, but he knew they could not hold much longer. He contemplated a withdrawal.

But artillery changed everything. For much of the day Captain Rosemund was out of communication with the batteries near St-Côme-du-Mont. When he finally got through to them, he learned that the artillerymen were low on ammunition. "Then for God's sake, get some! Get it! Please get it! We must have some!" he pleaded.

Like something out of a movie, trucks laden with plenty of ammo arrived at the batteries just in time. Rosemund got all of the artillery support he could handle. He called the fire down on the Germans, who were now less than 100 yards away. The supporting artillery was so close that Cole and Rosemund could tell it was arcing over the roof of the house, landing just beyond in the apple orchard. The fire killed some Americans, but it stopped the Germans cold. "We lost some good men, but we had to have that fire," one American later said. In the words of another American survivor of the battle, the artillery rounds were "intense, devastating." Shrapnel from the artillery shells scythed through the exposed German infantrymen. In five minutes, their attack petered out. From his window, Cole exulted as he watched the artillery do its job: "Listen to it! Just listen to it!"

It was a successful end to a long, bloody, tragic day for Cole and his paratroopers. The water in the river was reddish-colored from the blood of so many Americans. The orchard, cabbage patch, open fields, and ditches around the Ingouf farm were littered with the bodies of wounded, or dead, soldiers. Once, Cole's battalion had had a strength of nearly 700 men. Now it was down to 132. That night, the 506th Parachute Infantry crossed the bridges and relieved Cole. He and his men marched north, away from the scene of their awful battle.

The price had been terrible, but the exhausted 502nd had done its job. They had opened the northern route into Carentan, paving the way for the 506th to swing southwest and execute that portion of Taylor's plan to envelop the town. In so doing, they had bested the German equivalent of themselves—most of von der Heydte's 6th Parachute Regiment was shattered trying to prevent the 502nd from crossing the four bridges. Cole won the Medal of Honor for his exploits on June 11, but he did not live to receive it. A German sniper killed him in Holland in September.[12]

The 327th Glider Infantry made good progress on June 10 and 11. The regiment crossed the Douve, seized Brevands, and established contact with reconnaissance troops from the 29th Division at Auville-sur-le-Vey on the west bank of the Vire River. Two days later, the regiment's 1st Battalion met up with two depleted, embattled companies from the 175th Infantry at Montmartin-en-Graignes (including the brave, ubiquitous General Cota, who insisted on leading this dangerous linkup mission). The rest of the 327th turned to the west and steadily advanced into the northeastern outskirts of Carentan by June 12. As the glider troops did this, the 101st Airborne's reserve unit, the 501st Parachute Infantry, crossed the Douve, skirted around the eastern edges of

Carentan, and made it to Hill 30, the key objective south of town. To get Hill 30, the 501st had to cross the Vire-Taut Canal, straight into enemy positions. Lieutenant Colonel Julian Ewell's 3rd Battalion led the way as the Germans raked them over with 20mm fire. "The strain of wading across a shallow pond with 20mm spraying the water was terrific. We were really shot—I was so damned exhausted emotionally that I just didn't care about anything. The people who did the real fighting were even worse. This attack . . . was the most trying one that I went through in all our fighting in Europe." Ewell's 3rd Battalion suffered 50 percent casualties, but it got the job done.[13]

On the evening of June 11–12, Allied naval guns, artillery, mortars, and tank destroyers blasted much of Carentan into rubble. In the meantime, the 506th Parachute Infantry traversed Cole's hard-won bridgehead and swung southwest in a disorganized, disorienting night march around Carentan that began at 0200 on June 12.

The fourth bridge had been repaired, but it was still shaky, plus the area was under enemy fire. Private Burgett and his comrades in A Company, 506th, cautiously made their way across the footbridge in pitch-darkness. "In single file and about twenty feet apart, we moved . . . across the flimsy construction . . . holding onto the rope while sliding our feet step by step across the wobbly planks. Mortar and 88 shells were landing around the bridge and machine-gun fire was harassing us. Looking down, I could see the dark swirling water below. If a man were wounded and fell in here he wouldn't stand a chance. The moon wasn't out and the night was very dark."

The enemy fire hit several troopers, including one close to Burgett. "He lay doubled up, a geyser of blood shooting from his mouth and running back underneath him in a puddle." The unwounded had to keep moving, past the Belgian gate obstacle. "One by one we had to squeeze through a small opening in its center while machine-gun fire sprayed it, sending sparks flying as bullets struck the pavement and metal."

Once they were south of the Madeleine River, they veered to the right (west), making their way through swamps. "Most of us put our cigarettes in our helmets to keep them dry as some of the water was up to our armpits. We moved silently, slowly and carefully through the water until we came out on high ground."

The column halted for a few moments while someone far up ahead cut the throat of a German sentry. "The Kraut's body lay across the opening [to a hedgerow], and one by one, the men stepped over it."[14]

Each man held on to the belt of the man in front of him, so as not to become separated. Even so, many of the companies lost contact with one another. Many officers spent the entire night trying to keep up with, or find, the unit ahead of them. Somewhere near the front of the column, Company E kept losing touch with Company F, and that worried Sergeant Carwood Lipton. "I knew we would not be able to find our way to our objective over the strange terrain on our own . . . and that we were strung out in a defenseless formation."

Lipton and the other E Company men made their way down a small footpath. A dead German along the path scared the hell out of many of the men, including Corporal Gordon Carson. "There was a German there with a rifle pointed right at you. He must have scared half the company. I said to myself, 'Why the hell doesn't he shoot and get it over with?' But he was dead and rigor mortis had set in. He was just like a statue there."

For the rest of the night the 506th worked its way south along the railroad line, all the way to Hill 30 and into position for an attack on Carentan by daylight. The night movement had been anything but smooth. Lieutenant Dick Winters, the mastermind of a brilliant D-Day attack on the guns at Brecourt near Utah beach, was disgusted. He felt that the difficulties were the result of the laziness of regimental staff officers who had blown off their night-problem training. This, he believed, turned a fairly easy night march into a complex fiasco. "It shouldn't have been. It wasn't that difficult. We . . . screwed away the night, just getting into position."

At 0600 the attack on Carentan began. Unbeknownst to the Americans, Colonel von der Heydte, low on ammunition, had retreated to the southwest with most of the remnants of his regiment. He left only stragglers behind (about a company-sized force) to impede the American attackers.

The Germans did not do much to hold up F Company as it entered the town, but they had a brief, sharp engagement with E Company. Winters and his men were moving along a road that led into Carentan from the south when they began taking enemy machine-gun fire. Several men went down and the company took shelter in ditches on either side of the road. "We were pinned down in the ditch," Private Wayne "Skinny" Sisk remembered. Machine-gun fire was "kicking up gravel in on us." Sisk pulled out a bottle of booze and passed it around. "I always carried a bottle. I wouldn't go into battle without it."

For the moment, the company was pinned down, paralyzed with inertia, not knowing what to do. Winters—a born leader if ever there was one—soon changed that. In a frenzy, Winters jumped into the middle of the road and hollered at his men, "Move out! Move out!" No one moved a muscle. Somewhere behind him, Winters heard his commanding officer, Lieutenant Colonel Robert Strayer, urging him to get his company out of the ditches and into Carentan. Winters dropped all of his equipment except for his rifle and ran all over the place, kicking butts, ordering his men to get going. "I was possessed. Nobody'd ever seen me like that. I will never forget the surprise and fear on those faces looking up at me."

Machine-gun bullets were zipping everywhere around him, kicking up dust on the road, zinging like bees. Somewhere in the back of his mind Winters thought about the dangers he was facing. "My God, I'm leading a blessed life. I'm charmed," he thought. After what seemed like hours but probably was only a couple of minutes, many of the paratroopers got up, fired their weapons, and ran into Carentan. Lieutenant Harry Welsh and several of his men destroyed the machine-gun position with grenades.

The company poured into the town, and cleared out German resistance building to building. Sergeant Leo Boyle, in a follow-up platoon, ran past the dead bodies of several German paratroopers. "Some of them had been piled like cordwood alongside the road. We got in the . . . residential area, a lot of apartments, two and three story apartments. We were getting fire from artillery on the streets especially on the intersections as we moved in so we were dodging, running across from one street to the other trying to move down and force the Germans ahead of us."

Sergeant Lipton got wounded by a mortar shell that sprayed fragments into his cheek, right wrist, and right leg at the crotch (barely missing his "family jewels"). Sergeant Floyd Talbert got to him, gave him first aid, assured him that nothing vital had been hit, and carried him to an aid station. Nearby, Sergeant Donald Malarkey was taking cover from the German fire when he heard praying from someone nearby. "I glanced up and saw Father John Maloney holding his rosary and walking down the center of the road to administer last rites to the dying."

By 0700 on June 12 enemy resistance petered out. Twenty minutes later, F Company linked up with the 327th Glider Infantry, which was entering the town from the north. Carentan belonged to the Americans.[15]

Of course, the Germans wanted it back. As June 13 dawned, General Taylor had placed the 506th and the 501st amid the hedgerows and on the high ground southwest of Carentan. He planned to keep pushing south. As the Americans advanced that morning, the Germans hit them with a major counterattack. The day before, they had launched a weak counterattack that the Americans easily parried. Today the Germans attacked in force, with tanks and infantry from the newly arrived 17th SS Panzer Grenadier Division, along with the remnants of von der Heydte's 6th Parachute Regiment. Their attack was a double thrust: they hit the 501st along the Périers–Carentan road south of Hill 30. An even more powerful spearpoint plunged into the 506th along the Carentan–Baupte road west of Hill 30, a couple hundred yards south of the railroad line.

Many of the 506th troopers were in the process of carrying out their own attack, advancing from hedgerow to hedgerow, when they ran point-blank into the German attackers. One of these troopers was Private Burgett. His unit had just climbed over a hedgerow and was swiftly moving through a field when they ran into the Germans. "The enemy opened up on us with rifle, machine-gun, mortar and 88 shells. We had to take the shortest route, straight into the enemy fire, to try and reach the safety of the hedge in front of us. Men were being killed and wounded in large numbers, some of them horribly maimed, with limbs and parts of their bodies being shredded or shot away. I could feel the muzzle blasts of the men behind me as they fired from the hip. Mortar shells blanketed the field. At least six machine guns were cross firing on us and that terrible 88 was shredding everything in sight. Bounding Bettys [mines] leaped into the air to sow their seeds of death on the ones who disturbed them. The explosion would send steel balls rocketing out in all directions. They were very effective. Men were being torn almost in half by them. We kept running right at the enemy. It was like a dream—no, more like a nightmare."

They did the only thing they could do—keep going. They ran as fast as they could, but to Burgett it almost seemed as if they were running in place. The nineteen-year-old private glanced to the right and saw an 88 shell score a direct hit on the chest of another trooper. "His body disappeared from the waist up, his legs and hips with belt, canteen and entrenching tool still on taking three more steps, then falling." Yelling and screaming, "like animals," they made it to the hedge and pitched grenades at the Germans. This forced the enemy back a bit, but not far. Burgett's group fought from field to field and hedge to hedge. A German grenade exploded a few feet away from him, disorienting him and temporarily deafening him, too. He lost touch with his unit and wandered around looking for them. A mortar shell landed close to him. "It felt as though a sledge hammer had struck me in the right arm and a shock like that of grabbing an electric wire flashed through my entire body."

Burgett fell down into a ditch and took stock of his wounds. He was worried that fragments had torn open his belly, but the real damage was to his right arm. "I took my knife and cut the right sleeve open. I was shocked to see that a chunk of flesh was missing from my arm. I could lay four fingers against the bone. A severed end of an artery hung about four inches out of the wound like a rubber tube, but no blood was coming from the wound at all." Burgett poured sulfa powder on the wound, swallowed sulfa tablets, and bandaged his wound. Then a medic found him, gave him more first aid, and helped him get to the rear. For him, the Normandy campaign was over, but he returned to his unit in time to jump in Holland and fought with the 506th for the rest of the war.[16]

The situation outside of Carentan was so confusing that American units were mixed up with one another and sometimes shot at one another. Private First Class Len Goodgall, of I Company, went out, at his captain's behest, and started searching for a missing machine-gun section. Goodgall had already experienced something unique for an airborne trooper in Normandy. He had fought with the Rangers at Pointe-du-Hoc. His transport plane had gone so far off-course that it dropped him and a few others from his stick into the ocean near the Pointe. Goodgall was lucky to avoid drowning. He made it to the base of the cliffs just as the Rangers came in, and joined them in their three-day fight.

Today, west of Carentan, he was in the middle of a terribly chaotic situation. He spotted movement in a ditch ahead. "Jesus Christ, these guys are popping up and down in a ditch, in the hedgerow." Goodgall thought they were Germans. "*Raus, schnell!*" he hollered. "Come out of there!" He got no answer. For a moment, Goodgall considered taking off, but he was worried about getting shot in the back. "So I jumped in the ditch firing my . . . tommy gun." To his horror, the men in the ditch were Americans. They were busy digging in, because they were under sniper fire.

"Did anybody get hurt?" Private First Class Goodgall asked.

A first sergeant from H Company, Gordon Bolles, was moaning and holding his back. "Shit, I killed this poor bastard," Goodgall thought. "I pulled up his shirt. I'd just grazed him, and I saw that. I couldn't believe it. Was I lucky!"

Later in the day, he got wounded by shrapnel in the knee. "It's frightening when you first know you're hit. Then you realize you're not gonna die, it's okay. But when you first get hit . . . to see the blood squirting . . . you're just frightened."[17]

Company E was on the extreme right flank of the American lines. They had only railroad tracks and swamps to their right. Just as Lieutenant Winters was giving the order to go forward, the Germans attacked with tanks and infantry. The antagonists shot at each other with everything they had. Just as it was elsewhere along the line of the 506th, the situation was chaotic and confusing. Winters was stalking up and down his line of soldiers, many of whom were in foxholes or nestled behind hedgerows. He urged everyone to hold fast, keep shooting. Lieutenant Welsh collared Private John McGrath to deal with a German tank that threatened to break through a hedgerow on the left. The two of them dashed into the open, loaded a bazooka, and fired. The rocket hit off the turret of the German tank but did no damage. The tank returned fire, whistling a shell just a few feet over their heads.

Welsh reloaded the bazooka and told McGrath to try again. "Lieutenant, you're gonna get me killed," McGrath kept saying over and over. Nonetheless, McGrath took aim and fired, scoring a hit on the vulnerable underbelly of the enemy tank. It burst into flames and stopped, dead in its tracks.

Farther to the right, Private "Skinny" Sisk was helping fire a machine gun at approaching enemy troops. He and Walter Gordon had rigged the gun to fire through a gate. They waited until the enemy got within range. "We opened fire," Sisk said. "I don't know how many we got, but I'm sure we got some of them. Anyhow, we broke up the firing for a while there." The enemy regrouped. "They dropped some mortar [shells] right in behind us and every one of us out. I got . . . some shrapnel in the hind end. Of course, that was embarrassing. They had to evacuate me then. I was numb from my hip down my right leg."[18]

Company E's situation was critical, but the unit managed to hold fast. To the left of E Company, F Company was having a terrible time trying to hold off the powerful German attack, especially the tanks. The company was directly in the path of much of the German armor. Bill True, a machine-gun crewman, at first had trouble determining if the vehicles and figures in the distance were friendly or enemy. He and his gunner, Ray Aebischer, were crouched behind a hedgerow. "You sure those are Germans and not *our* guys?" True asked.

"Damn right they're German," Aebischer replied. "I can see their helmets. Look where they are. We don't have anybody out that far!"

Aebischer squeezed off several bursts, stitching the ground ahead. A tank turned its turret in their direction and fired. The shell exploded close by, showering them with dirt, making their ears ring. They saw the tank's muzzle flash. Once again, dirt and wood shards flew everywhere around them. Someone screamed as he got hit. The tank did not quit. The enemy gunner put a round into the trees above the F Company machine gunners, inundating them with more shrapnel of both wood and metal. Several yards up the hedgerow, concussion from the explosion killed two men. To all the world, they looked like they were sleeping—no blood, no marks, nothing—but they were quite dead.

About 150 yards away, a hatch on the turret of one of the enemy tanks popped open. The enemy tanker emerged and started blazing away with a machine gun. Several Americans were hit. Company F's commander, Captain Thomas Mulvey, crawled over to his best rifle grenadier. "Why don't you fire at it?"

"The tank's too far away, sir, and I've only got a few rounds left," the man replied.

The captain promised to get him more ammunition. The soldier, a Private Ostrander, fastened the grenade to the end of his rifle and fired. The grenade hit the tank but did no damage. He loaded again and fired. They watched as the grenade arced in the direction of the enemy tank. Like a basketball that scores from half-court, the grenade dropped perfectly into the open hatch, dragging the enemy crewman down and exploding inside of the tank, a "one in a million shot,"in the view of one historian.

A couple of other men took out enemy tanks with bazookas, but it was not enough. The enemy armor was overwhelming. Several German tanks broke through F Company's lines and began roving around in the rear, shooting the Americans from behind, even shooting an aid station until the enemy crewmen saw its Red Cross flags.

The situation was growing more desperate by the minute. Captain Mulvey was not sure his men could hold any longer. For a brief moment his spirits rose when six Stuart light tanks came from Carentan, but, in a veritable instant, fire from the heavier-gunned German tanks drove them away. The Stuarts quickly turned tail and disappeared in the direction of Carentan.

The company could not hold. A soldier appeared at True's machine-gun position: "Fall back to the next hedgerow!"

The retreat turned into a bit of a rout. A significant chunk of Lieutenant Colonel Robert Strayer's 2nd Battalion front, encompassing F and D Companies, gave way. They retreated to within 500 yards of Carentan and left E Company's left flank wide open (something the E Company men deeply resented). Mulvey paid a steep price for this retreat. Strayer relieved him, much to the disgust of many F Company soldiers who had served under Mulvey since their intense training days at Toccoa, Georgia.

Strayer requested help and Taylor sent him some air support, in the form of strafing P-47s, some antitank guns, and parts of the 2nd Battalion, 502nd Parachute Infantry. At the leading edge of this relief force was F Company, 502nd, under none other than Lieutenant LeGrand "Legs" Johnson, who had bumped his head when Eisenhower unexpectedly entered his tent the night before D-Day. "When we jumped off, F Company was jumping, hollering, shooting and we got too far in advance. It was pretty hot action."

Johnson heard the loud rumbling of tanks coming from somewhere behind him. He went looking for the source of the sounds and, much to his delight, found that they were emanating from Sherman tanks, driving along the Carentan–Baupte road. As Johnson watched, a Sherman drew a bead on an enemy light tank and fired. The turret of the German tank flew off, sending the tank commander sprawling. He landed in the dust and writhed in agony. "He was still alive and his guts were wriggling—it was the first time I had ever seen anything like that."

The American tanks were the vanguard of a major relief effort staged by the 2nd Armored Division, which had arrived in Normandy a couple days before. They rebuffed the Germans along the two main roads and in the fields that surrounded them. It was almost like a stereotypical scene out of an old Hollywood Western, when the cavalry arrives just in time to save the day. The tanks, from the 2nd Armored Division's Combat Command A, attacked at about 1500 and turned the tide of battle.

"It was wonderful to watch them work," an F Company soldier recalled. "A tank would stop in a hole [in a hedgerow] made by a brother tankdozer, then turn a sharp right or left, wherever the Krauts were, and sweep every foot of the hedgerow. When and what they missed were mopped up and destroyed by the armored infantrymen. [It was] an awe-inspiring show of violence and destruction of the highest order." They shot up German infantry and scored enough hits on enemy tanks, self-propelled guns, and personnel carriers to thwart their counterattack.

In E Company's sector, Lieutenant Winters breathed a huge sigh of relief when he saw the tanks arrive. "What a wonderful sight it was to see those tanks pouring it to the Germans with those heavy 50-caliber machine-guns and just plowing straight from our lines into the German hedgerows with all those fresh infantry soldiers marching along the tanks."

The Germans were sent into headlong retreat and the threat to Carentan was over. Only dead enemy remained behind. "We . . . left hedgerow fields filled with stacks of German soldiers," Vincent Hooper, a crewman in A Company of the 66th Armored Regiment, recalled. "Our vehicles filled two fields by forming circles inside the hedgerows. We could occasionally hear the leaves in the trees overhead being spattered by burp gun bullets."[19]

Sergeant Mervin Haugh, a Stuart tank commander in B Company, 66th Armored, worked with another tank to clean out German infantrymen who had taken shelter behind hedgerows. "I pulled right up to where the Germans were—within twenty feet of where the end of them started. In the meantime, the tank behind me pulled up beside me. I didn't fire a shot." The other tank's commander pulled out his pistol. "He shot two Germans. They were near us, and they had their machine gun, and one of them killed him. He fell back down inside his tank. I got out."

Why the other commander elected to expose himself and shoot at the enemy with a pistol when he could have used his main gun or machine guns against them remains a mystery. Haugh and the accompanying infantry ended up capturing several Germans.[20]

The arrival of the 2nd Armored tanks and armored infantrymen at the key moment on June 13 was no accident. It resulted from the proper use of intelligence information. General Bradley was one of the select few Allied officers who was privy to information gleaned from Ultra, the code word for the top-secret cracking of German codes. This was one of the greatest secrets of the entire war (indeed it was still classified until the 1970s). On June 12, Bradley was entertaining a group of dignitaries, including General Hap Arnold (commander of the AAF), Admiral Ernest King (chief of naval operations), General Marshall, and Eisenhower. They had no sooner left Bradley's headquarters than he received an Ultra flash from Bletchley Park (home of the codebreakers) that revealed the German counterattack plans for June 13 at Carentan. "This was one of the rare times in the war when I unreservedly believed Ultra and reacted to it tactically." He wrote to General Gerow of V Corps and told him to divert half of the 2nd Armored to Carentan, a fortuitous and wise decision on Bradley's part.[21]

As a result, the Americans held Carentan. The Utah and Omaha beachheads were now joined. The first major American objective of the Normandy campaign had been achieved.

CHAPTER FOUR

STALLED BEFORE ST-LO

I n mid-June, the Americans were still hoping that St-Lô could soon be captured. North of this vital objective, German resistance was hardening, but
the Americans kept attacking. For three days, June 16 through June 18, two
American divisions, the 29th and the 2nd, plunged deeper into the bocage,
toward St-Lô.

The 2nd Division was still east of the 29th. The immediate objective for
the Indian Head soldiers was Hill 192, a dominating hill mass north of the St-
Lô–Bayeux road (N-13). Hill 192 commanded every approach to St-Lô. Anyone on top of the hill could see for miles, even all the way to Omaha beach on
a clear day. Hedgerows, brambles, and woods impeded the northerly avenues
of approach to Hill 192. So did one of the best units in the German Army—
the 3rd Parachute Division, which had traveled more or less unscathed from
Brittany to Normandy by the middle of June. The division was home to some
of the toughest, craftiest, and best-trained soldiers in the German Army. Almost all of them were armed with automatic weapons, either MG-42 machine
guns or MP-40 machine pistols (the GIs called them burp guns). These enemy paratroopers had not been in Normandy long, but they had used their
time well. They were dug into the hedgerows; their machine guns and mortars were perfectly sited; they were determined and ready to fight to the last.

At 0800 on June 16, Major General Walter Robertson lined up all three of
his regiments and attacked. On the left (east), the 9th Infantry got nowhere.
One platoon, while advancing through an open field, got caught in the crossfire of eight machine guns. The enemy gunners were concealed in
hedgerows that enfiladed most of the field. The guns made their characteristic ripping sounds, a sickening, terrifying noise to the American soldiers. The
fire swept through the platoon killing and wounding at least a third of the

men. The rest were lucky to escape with their lives. By day's end, the 9th Infantry had lost 140 men—20 killed—in exchange for a few hundred yards.

A mile to the west, the 38th Infantry's 3rd Battalion had more success. Soldiers from this unit made it all the way to within 700 yards of the crest of Hill 192, but the regiment's other units could barely make it past the start line. As a result, the 3rd Battalion almost got cut off. Reinforced by some of the division's engineers, the battalion dug foxholes and remained in place for several weeks. Their positions comprised a bulgelike salient in the German lines. Day after day, the men of the 3rd Battalion lived with the possibility of encirclement.

The 2nd Battalion of the 38th Infantry tried fighting its way to relieve the 3rd at Hill 192 but had great difficulty dislodging German defenders. Lieutenant Charles Curley was a twenty-two-year-old platoon leader in E Company, 2nd Battalion. Curley was a native of Richmond, Virginia. His father had fought in World War I. The younger Curley joined the Army in 1942 and graduated from Infantry Officer Candidate School in July 1943. The fight for Hill 192 was his first combat.

When his unit jumped off, they advanced to a farmyard that had been worked over by American artillery in the hours leading up to the attack. Dead animals were lying everywhere. The place stank of death. Curley and his men rushed an adjacent house and found no enemy inside, only a small dog. The dog, a black-and-white fox terrier, was lying in the middle of a bed, "shaking himself to pieces. He would jump at the slightest noise. [He] was in shock from all the shellfire. He calmed down . . . when one of the men gave him a drink of water."

Curley's men searched the house and made a nauseating discovery in one of the rooms. "Lieutenant, come and look at this mess," one of them called out.

Lieutenant Curley entered the room and saw an open dresser drawer. "I looked in the top drawer and saw that it had been used as an indoor toilet and was quite full." The other drawers were just as full. Curley's platoon beat a hasty retreat. "I can assure you, no one used this area for a headquarters for quite a while."

The company resumed its advance but soon got held up by withering accurate German fire that pinned down the entire lead platoon. Curley's men and others helped them escape by laying down covering fire. At the same time, the lieutenant took four of his men and tried to outflank, along a sunken road, an enemy machine gun that was causing much of the trouble. "Without problems, we made it into the sunken road and began moving towards where the gun was suspected to be." The sunken road was dark and confining. Curley heard one of his men yell, "Look out!"

"All hell broke loose. There was a pile of brush blocking the road ahead of us. A German located behind the brush fired a Burp Gun in our direction and kept firing until one of the men tossed a grenade behind the brush."

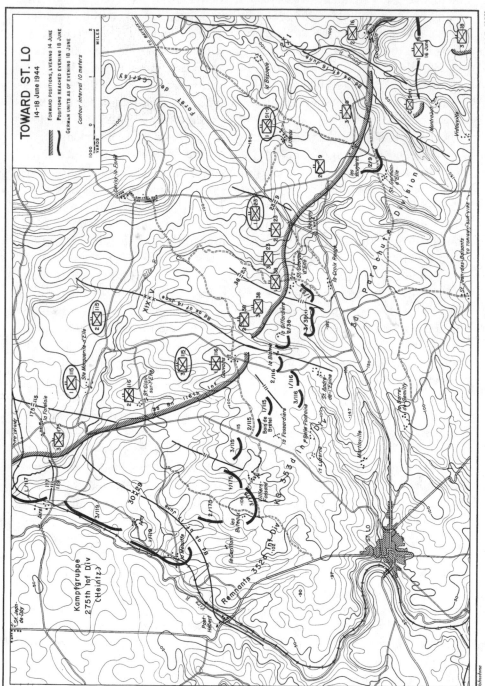

TOWARD ST. LO
14-18 June 1944

FORWARD POSITIONS, EVENING 14 JUNE
POSITIONS REACHED EVENING 18 JUNE
GERMAN UNITS AS OF EVENING 18 JUNE

Contour interval 10 meters

MAP XIX

R. Johnstone

The enemy fire stopped. Curley and the others beat a hasty retreat.

They sat down behind a hedgerow and rested. "Lieutenant, look at your pants," one of the men said.

Curley looked down and saw that his trousers were ripped at the crotch. "Obviously, a bullet had come very close. According to the men, after I looked at my pants I turned dead white and got sick. They just laughed and kidded about the family jewels."

Before the day was over, they took a few more hedgerows but could move no farther. The 2nd Battalion and the rest of the 38th were stymied.[1]

The 23rd Infantry, sandwiched between the 38th on its right and the 9th on its left, had perhaps the toughest time of all. This unit was dealing with some of the tallest, thickest hedgerows, along with streams and thick woods. "These were small farming lots of an acre or so, surrounded by stone walls, held thick with overgrown vegetation," Private Clem Turpin of the 23rd Infantry later wrote. "All the Germans had to do was poke their weapons through and let you have it. You couldn't see them behind these walls. They were gunning us down. If you were exposed, bang, you got hit."

When his company stopped for the night, Turpin's commanding officer assigned him and another soldier to outpost duty, 50 or 100 yards in front of the main American line. Exhausted from a stressful, active day, they dug in near a wall. "The next thing I knew it was dawn and the Germans were right there. One of them hung over our hole and fired about 50 rounds with his machine gun [probably a burp gun] straight down at us. Dust flew up all around and we jumped out and ran towards our line."

Much to Private Turpin's horror, a German tank now joined the enemy burp gunner. "As I was running for a break in the hedgerow, their tank fired low and the shell made a ridge as it skidded across the ground before it exploded into a tree." At that very same moment, Turpin was lifting his leg to jump over some barbed wire. "I could feel the projectile swoosh right between my legs. How lucky can you get?" Turpin was lucky, but many others were not. In the first twenty-four hours of its attack, the 23rd Infantry gained almost no ground but lost eleven officers and 162 men.[2]

General Gerow was not pleased. The 2nd Division was part of his V Corps and it was not doing well. On the evening of June 16, he visited the division's CP. Gerow was one of Eisenhower's closest friends but did not share his optimistic nature or his upbeat tone with subordinates. General Gerow could be an ass kicker if the situation called for it, and tonight, after a bloody, wasteful day, he was in no mood for excuses. At the division CP, he stood in front of a ten-foot-tall operations map and scowled. Gerow was tall, almost resplendent, in the uniform of a two-star general. Over and over, he tapped the map board with his riding crop.

A few feet away, Major Henry Spencer, the thirty-three-year-old commander of the 23rd Infantry's 1st Battalion, watched Gerow convey his displeasure. "As he would tap each position of each unit on the large map-board, he would be constantly asking questions. He would seldom wait for answers or comments to his questions, seeming to intimate that he already knew the answer. Suddenly, he started to beat the mapboard with his whip as though he was trying to punish it, as he barked, raising his voice a decibel or two, 'Who is commanding this regiment?' "

General Robertson was standing right next to Gerow. "That is the Twenty-third Infantry and the CO is Colonel Hurley E. Fuller."

"Get him here," Gerow snapped. "I want to talk to him."

Colonel Fuller strode to the map board. Overage and short, he was no match for the tall, imposing corps commander. The two men eyed each other for a moment, until the general asked Fuller to explain why his unit was in disarray and why it had not accomplished any of its objectives.

Major Spencer watched uncomfortably as Fuller froze, like the prover-bial deer in the headlights. "[He] . . . was just standing there, reminding me for all the world of an animal about to be slaughtered at the packing house."

General Gerow grew more impatient by the second. "Colonel, is there something wrong with your hearing?" he shouted. The colonel still just stood there mute. "God damn it, Colonel, I'm talking to you. Now you answer me!" Still Colonel Fuller said nothing.

For an awkward moment, silence reigned. Finally, Gerow had had enough. "In apparent disgust, the general gave the mapboard a mighty wallop with his whip, and turning to [Robertson], he rasped, "Robbie, have you got anybody here who can take that regiment?"

"Yes, sir, I do," General Robertson replied. "My G-3, Colonel Lovless."

"Relieve Fuller and put Lovless in command of the Twenty-third at once. That's all."

Gerow turned on his heel and left. The mood at the CP was hushed. "No one spoke to the relieved colonel at first; ignoring him as though he were not there," Major Spencer wrote.

Finally, one of the colonel's junior officers put an arm around him and led him away. Spencer drove Lovless, his new boss, to the house that served as headquarters for the 23rd Infantry.

Within twenty-four hours, Spencer was the one who was under pressure from senior officers. The division was going to make one more big push for Hill 192, and Spencer's 1st Battalion, 23rd Infantry, was to lead the attack. Robertson's second in command, Brigadier General George Hays, the divi-sion artillery officer, told Spencer that he would receive a rolling barrage from twenty battalions of artillery (three divisions' worth).

Major Spencer did not like, nor did he trust, this general or his plan. The major knew that several other battalions in the division had already failed with similar artillery support. Their attacks had broken down, partially because the artillery support had been inaccurate. Spencer knew he should keep his mouth shut, but he could not resist voicing his objections. He suggested a night attack, but Hays dismissed this out of hand: "Dammit, Spencer, that's insane."

Spencer explained how it could be done, but the general had no patience with his ideas. They argued back and forth for a few moments, until the general finally said, "That's about enough out of you, Spencer. You listen clearly and you listen good. You obey these orders and follow that rolling barrage. Do you understand me? Or do I have to get someone else to take that battalion in that walk up that hill?"

Spencer understood that it was time to shut up. He could not prevent this attack. If he voiced any more doubts, Hays would relieve him and put someone else in his command and his men would be just as dead. No, that was not what he wanted. "Yes, sir, General Hays, we'll give it our best shot."

Spencer returned to his battalion, told his men about the attack, and tried to explain the plan with as much enthusiasm as he could feign. He, of course, did not tell his subordinates about his sharp disagreement with the general. After the briefing, Spencer could not shake a keen sense of guilt over the lives that would soon be squandered. "It was not so much the price they were to pay—and that was paramount—but it was the cheap way in which they were to be expended. If we must give our lives, let us exact equal and fair compensation under conditions that would spell success."

Tense hour after tense hour passed. The attack was scheduled for 0700 on June 18. At 0630, Spencer and his command group were behind a hedgerow, sitting together in silence. "It was like the last minutes before the kick-off at a football game: tension, not much talk, and people doing useless things to kill time (like whittling on a stick). My mouth felt like it was jammed with cotton, and I kept trying to satisfy an insatiable thirst with swigs at my canteen." Spencer had a knot in his stomach, but he calmed down a bit when he thought of the riflemen in his lead companies. "What must they be thinking right now?" he wondered. They were the ones who would face the most danger.

The barrage began. "The earth actually was moving like a California earthquake. You could not hear what was being said by the man standing alongside. The very trees in front of us were bending from the concussions of the explosions." The American shells gradually exploded farther and farther away. Company B, in the lead, was supposed to have advanced one or two hedgerows by now, but they had not moved. Major Spencer saw them standing around, watching the shells explode, enjoying the fireworks. He went forward to get them moving.

Thanks to the major's prodding, B Company, with Spencer among them, hurled themselves over the first hedgerow. They ran across an open field and made it to a creek bed before coming under intense German fire. Enemy mortar and artillery shells were falling everywhere. Spencer caught site of his executive officer and asked him what he was doing up there. Before he could explain, a shell exploded a few feet away. "I felt something hit me in the back of my steel helmet that felt like a sledgehammer."

Spencer was stunned, but he took stock of his surroundings. His executive officer was missing his little finger, but that was the least of his problems. "His helmeted head was bending forward as though he were asleep. I reached down to check the pulse." There was none. Concussion had killed him.

A nearby sergeant "appeared to me as a ghost; seemingly without body or substance, yet blood was leaking and oozing from both his ears, his nose, his mouth, and even his eyes seemed to be weeping blood." Another man had been cut in two; only the remnants of his intestines connected the two pieces.

Spencer had shrapnel in his skull. A medic got to him and bandaged his head wounds. "I vaguely recall him working on me . . . making me feel like a mummy. I knew I was lying on a stretcher. I was drifting in and out of consciousness." Badly hurt, Major Spencer nonetheless got up from his stretcher and roamed around, trying to keep his troops moving forward. The major hardly knew what was going on, nor could he see clearly. He finally collapsed. Medics found him and dragged him back to the aid station. Just as Spencer had foreseen, the attack failed. The 2nd Division was stalled at the foot of Hill 192.[3]

For a few enticing hours on June 16, the 29th Infantry Division seemed to be making progress. The division had fought a bitter battle to cross the Elle River only a couple days before, and now they were once again on the move. All along the 29th Division front during the morning hours of June 16, the Americans were advancing, making gains of a mile or more. But by the afternoon the advance had slowed to a crawl as the lead units ran head-on into enemy reinforcements from the 3rd Parachute Division and the newly arrived 353rd Infantry Division.

The combat took place at close quarters, as the thick hedgerows or sunken lanes prevented either side from seeing one another until they were within shouting distance. The two sides engaged one another in sharp, costly firefights, contesting small fields and hedgerows. Captain Charles Cawthon's 2nd Battalion, 116th, made a push through wooded terrain for Villiers-Fossard and found itself in the middle of an intimate battle outside the town. "The fight flared and crashed at intervals all afternoon. The discovery that this was a key German position cost a staff officer and thirty-four men—the equivalent of one of our rifle platoons at full strength or, more nearly, two platoons at actual battle strength."

Cawthon had the misfortune of seeing the staff officer die. The dead man was a captain who served as the battalion operations officer, and he died under the weight of American bullets. "He was in the garret of a cottage looking over the terrain, and I, on the ground floor, was trying to locate our position on a mud-smudged map. A blast of rifle fire smashed into the attic, and three riflemen dashed in announcing they had shot a German directly above me. At the same moment, blood began to drip through the ceiling, and on the upper floor we found him, his life already leached away. The riflemen left with stark faces." The battalion did not take Villiers-Fossard. Cawthon and the others spent most of the day fending off German counterattacks, fighting to hang on to the mile of Norman soil they had gained.[4]

The regiment's 1st Battalion succeeded in driving a bit farther south, almost to St-André-de-l'Elpine. Sergeant Bob Slaughter had survived the hell of Omaha beach ten days earlier. Now, on June 16, he and his D Company comrades became enmeshed in the hedgerows before St-André-de-l'Elpine. Overhead, he heard the sound of fighter planes. A flight of P-47 Thunderbolts was strafing the area just ahead. One of them got hit and started losing altitude. The pilot brought it in for a crash landing on a road about half a mile in front of Slaughter's group. He and several others moved quickly, maneuvering along the sunken lanes, to get to the pilot. "There he was with his nose dug in the road and he was up in the cockpit, some of the medics were trying to get him out of the cockpit, and his back was broken, but as far as I know he was still living and the plane, thank goodness, didn't burn."[5]

In spite of the gains made that day, Colonel Charles Canham, the regimental commander, was not pleased with how his unit had performed. On the evening of the sixteenth, he told his battalion commanders that the attack would resume the next day. He remonstrated with them, urging them to light a fire under their men: "Get around the sniper and machine gunner and wipe him out. If you allow your unit to bunch up behind a hedgerow and wait for hours you are only playing into Jerry's hand. He will move around where he can enfilade you or drop artillery or mortar fire on you . . . It is time to get over the jitters and fight like hell."

Canham's exhortations came to nothing. The attack the next day went nowhere. General Gerhardt even threw two reinforcing battalions from the 115th Infantry into the fray, including Private Maynard Marquis's H Company. Marquis had survived the terrible ambush at Carrefour several days before. On June 17, his unit managed to link up with the 116th Infantry, but their joint attack came to nothing. At one point, H Company, along with its tank support, had to retreat. Private Marquis looked up and saw "one of our tanks [run] over seven or eight dead Germans. Their ribs and intestines were sticking up. That didn't bother me, but it was a hot sunny day and they started to smell. That awful smell did get to me."

Nothing significant was accomplished in this renewed attack; it only led to more Americans being killed or maimed. Another attack on June 18 ended up the same way, in spite of a massive artillery barrage before jump-off. The front north of Villiers-Fossard stalemated. German resistance was too strong, the terrain was too difficult, and there was not enough air, artillery, or tank support. The failure also stemmed from one other problem, though. The 116th Infantry had lost too many good men on D-Day. "The 116th Infantry was not the same regiment on June 16 that it was on D-Day," Major Thomas Howie, the regiment's operations officer, wrote several days after the ill-fated attack. "The new men are green. They need time to know the old men and officers and learn to work with them. This can't be accomplished simply by putting the regiment into a defensive position. They must be pulled out of the line and given a chance to effect a real reorganization." The 1st Battalion had, according to its commander, "hardly anyone left." Another officer reported that "everyone is done out physically. No leaders left. No reorganization is possible." Only a reprieve from the line would yield the kind of reorganization Major Howie envisioned.[6]

It is no accident that, of the division's three regiments, the 175th experienced the most success in this mid-June push for St-Lô. The 175th had not gone ashore on D-Day. It had landed two days later and fought westward to Isigny and across the Vire. In so doing, it had been bloodied but not decimated like the 116th had been at Omaha beach. The 175th was on the extreme western flank of the division when it attacked on the morning of June 16. Led by the 1st Battalion, the regiment advanced several miles, capturing slivers of high ground north of St-Lô. Soldiers from the 1st Battalion even made it as far as Le Mesnil-Rouxelin, a mere two miles north of St-Lô. They surprised a German CP and prompted the commanding general of the enemy 352nd Infantry Division, Major General Dietrich Kraiss, to flee to St-Lô. A mile northeast of Le Mesnil-Rouxelin, the battalion also captured Hill 108, the high ground that was the key to control of the whole area northwest of St-Lô.

The gains of the 175th pleased General Gerhardt. In a heady, optimistic moment, he called his superior, General Charles "Pete" Corlett, and told him, "I feel we'll be getting to St-Lô before long." Uncle Charlie's optimism was premature, though. The 175th was making excellent gains, against light resistance, but the regiment could not hope to capture and hold St-Lô if the rest of the division made no progress. Nor would the 175th be immune to the most important unknown factor of all—German counterattacks.

Sure enough, the enemy diverted two battalions from the newly arrived 353rd Division to counterattack Hill 108. The American positions on Hill 108 were like a belligerent finger pointed at the German lines. Starting at 0830 on June 18, the Germans pounded the hill with a variety of mortar and artillery shells. The intensity of the barrage stunned the GIs, who had thought the

Germans were in full retreat. "When these German 88's open up it is the nearest thing to hell on earth imaginable," Captain "Rod" Taggart, the regimental chaplain, wrote in his diary that day. Taggart, a Catholic priest, had been with the regiment for many months, saying mass, hearing confessions, dispensing advice, helping the wounded, and writing letters to families. "The enemy is entrenched behind strongly fortified machine gun nests, artillery batteries, etc. Our boys are doing magnificently, but it is so hard to hit what you cannot see."

The barrage tapered off and, within minutes, German infantry attacked from both flanks and the center. The Americans lost communication with their supporting artillery, from the 224th Field Artillery Battalion (most likely the wires had been disrupted by enemy shelling and the radios were being jammed by the enemy). This helped the enemy infantry to infiltrate the American positions. The two sides were so close to each other that anytime the shooting died down, the German taunted the Americans, probably in an effort to get them to reveal their positions. Lieutenant Colonel Roger Whiteford, the battalion commanding officer, responded with plenty of profanity as he roved from hole to hole, encouraging his men to stay put.

The fighting was sickening and desperate. Germans and Americans traded shots from either side of hedgerows. As so often happens in modern combat, small groups battled small groups, usually oblivious to all but their immediate surroundings. At an A Company position, a German shell exploded in the middle of one rifle squad, killing three men in an instant. A fourth man, whose dark complexion earned him the nickname Ali Baba in that politically incorrect time, had his feet blown off by fragments. Ali Baba writhed in terrible pain. He raised himself up and surveyed the bloody stumps where his feet had once been. Finally, he could take it no more. He pulled out his pistol and blew his brains out.

Company B of the 175th had it the worst. This unit was deployed in the most forward positions near the foot of the hill. As a result, B Company absorbed the brunt of the enemy attack. Several Americans retreated under the cover fire of a D Company machine gunner, Private Russell Woodward, who kept up his fire until he was mortally wounded. Other B Company soldiers got cut off. They fought in small pockets against swarms of Germans who were trying to get to the crest of Hill 108.

Sergeant Henry Hill's platoon was one of those isolated units. He was down to ten men. They were pinned down, enduring fire from enemy mortars, artillery, and tanks. "We had dug in at 2 hedgerows . . . 6' to 7' high on both sides. The . . . tanks were firing direct into [the] hedgerows" from a range of 300 yards. They were lucky. The tank fire was ineffective, and the weight of the German attack passed them by. Hill and his men spent much of the day maneuvering closer to the tank that had shot at them. They hopscotched from hedgerow to hedgerow and crawled, on their bellies, to within fifty yards of the enemy tank. A bazooka man got off two shots at the tank. "The first . . . round hit the tank tracks, the second hit above [the] tracks."

The Americans retreated to a nearby hedgerow and dug into it as deeply as they could. In the meantime, another enemy tank materialized and blasted them with devastating fire. Shell after shell slammed into the hedgerow, killing and wounding everyone. "My whole platoon & I was out of action. My heart was broken. I could not stand up." Shrapnel tore into the upper part of Sergeant Hill's left leg. Blood seeped everywhere. Hill tied a tourniquet on the leg. He heard awful moans and groans from his men and crawled around to do what he could for them. One of them had a broken hip and a broken leg. Hill gave him morphine but could do little else. Other men had shrapnel wounds, so he poured sulfa powder on their wounds. "I did the most I could do, by crawling from man to man. We were isolated."

Dispirited, in pain, and fading from loss of blood, Hill sat with his back resting on the hedgerow and gave himself a shot of morphine. "I started smelling awful odors, from dead Germans, cows & horses." He loosened his tourniquet so as not to cut off circulation too badly to his leg and tried to remain alert. Hours went by. He saw the outline of an American helmet approaching along the other side of the hedgerow. Hill was elated to see that it was one of his unit's artillery observers.

"Boy, am I glad to see you," the officer said. "How many of you are hurt?"

"My whole platoon," Hill replied.

"Hang in there, Hill," the forward observer said. "The Good Lord willing, I will be back with stretchers and jeeps by sunset."

He gave Hill his canteen, full of cognac, and told him to sip from it while he waited. All night long, Hill and his people hung on, waiting for the medics to find them. There were too many Germans in the area for the medics to get to them by sunset, but the observer (a Captain Williams) organized a group to go get Hill in the morning, after the German counterattack had been blunted (partially by artillery that came on-line at 1800 on June 18).

Back at the regimental CP, Father Taggart heard about the plight of Hill's platoon. Taggart felt terribly helpless and frustrated over his inability to lend any immediate help. He tried to alleviate that frustration by scribbling in his diary. "What drives me frantic is something like this. How I long to get to them. The only thing that deters me is the fact that going up would be suicide, while remaining here about 1/2 mile behind the front gives me the chance to do a greater good. I'm not afraid to go ahead. I have prayed to fear no physical ill but only to fear offending God by sin. My prayers have been answered—bullets and bombs do not upset me anymore."

The German attack was strong, but not strong enough. They could not dislodge the Americans from Hill 108. However, they did succeed in blunting the forward movement of the 175th. On the morning of June 19, a full twenty-four hours after the battle started, Captain Williams was finally able to lead the medics to Hill's stranded platoon. By then, Sergeant Hill and the other wounded were nearly delirious. The medics put them on stretchers and drove them on jeeps back to the rear. Hill had come very close to bleeding to death. He passed out and did not wake up until he reached a field hospital near Omaha beach.

The 1st Battalion had held Hill 108, but at terrible cost. The battalion suffered 250 casualties, including 60 killed. The bodies of the dead were strewn everywhere, rotting in the June sun. The regiment as a whole lost 334 men on June 18 alone. For its determined stand at Hill 108 the 1st Battalion won a Presidential Unit Citation. Among the survivors of this terrible battle, Hill 108, simply became known as "Purple Heart Hill."[7]

The orders came down before the fighting for Purple Heart Hill even ended. General Bradley was pulling the plug on the St-Lô offensive. Logistical problems—especially ammunition shortages—forced him now to concentrate all of his resources on one major attack at a time. He still needed to capture Cherbourg, a vital objective because it was the largest port in Normandy. Control of Cherbourg would, he believed, improve his logistical situation and go a long way toward destroying German combat power in Normandy. Quite simply, Bradley could not afford to push for St-Lô and Cherbourg at the same time.

Obviously, he was not having much success in getting St-Lô. In three days of bocage fighting, the 29th Division had nearly been destroyed, and the 2nd Division was not much better off. Bradley knew about the German reinforcements around St-Lô. He understood now that any serious St-Lô offensive would require much more in terms of supplies, reinforcements, firepower and planning. So he chose Cherbourg. "Cherbourg remained our . . . principal objective and I had no intention of pinning down forces at St-Lô until Cherbourg was safely in hand." This meant that his armies would now head northwest, in the opposite direction from Germany, but that could not be helped. Given the circumstances, Bradley really had no other choice.

He passed the word to Major General Corlett at XIX Corps. "Faced with the need for conserving U.S. strength, I held Corlett back and ordered him to stand his ground," Bradley wrote. The news filtered down the chain of command. Corlett's operations officer phoned General Gerhardt and told him to halt and dig in: "There has just been a big conference. The line is to be held and prepared for defense; active patrolling."[8]

For the soldiers of the 29th and 2nd Divisions the halt order came as a welcome reprieve. But several weeks of uncomfortable stalemate in the hedgerows lay in store for them. For the Americans in Normandy, everything now depended on whether General Joe Collins and his VII Corps could take Cherbourg and take it quickly.

CHAPTER FIVE

THE STRUGGLE FOR CHERBOURG

The first step in taking Cherbourg was to cut the Cotentin. General Collins assigned two divisions to do this job—the 82nd Airborne and the newly arrived 9th Infantry Division. He gave a support role to the 101st Airborne, which remained in defensive positions south of Carentan, protecting the southern flank of the 82nd and the 9th. Collins, as discussed in a previous chapter, had lost confidence in the leadership and combat readiness of the troubled 90th Division, so he ordered the division to protect the northern flank of the advance. He hoped that this supporting role would allow the 90th to work through its problems without imperiling VII Corps's mission of cutting the Cotentin and capturing Cherbourg.[1]

In this new role, the 90th turned slightly to the north and continued slugging its way through thick, heavily defended bocage in the vicinity of Gourbesville. The 2nd Battalion of the 357th was deployed just east of Gourbesville, and the 3rd had worked its way to a point about one thousand yards northeast of the town.

Private Richard Grondin had just joined A Company of the 357th Infantry Regiment, one of the units that was dug in near Gourbesville on June 14. Grondin was a nearsighted native of Medina, Ohio. Because of his eyesight, the Air Force, Navy, and Marines had no interest in him. Only the Army wanted him. He was drafted in March 1943 and had more than a year of training under his belt by the time he joined A Company as a replacement. The unit had been decimated during the previous day's fighting. Only one officer and one NCO remained. The situation was so bad that Grondin's company commander (the lone officer) offered him a squad and a promotion to sergeant because he had more training time than most of the other newcomers. Grondin refused. He was not even sure why he was here or what he was fighting for; the last thing he wanted was a leadership role. "I went overseas a private and I came home as a private."

The bespectacled Private Grondin sat morosely in his foxhole and waited for the word to move out, all the while thinking of the futility of war. "Is this really my war?" he wondered. "For whose benefit do I suffer? Did the wealthy get wealthier selling the rifle that I am cleaning? Are the career officers getting . . . faster promotions because of what I am doing? Who in the hell wants this piece of ground I am trying to capture? I sure don't. Is that poor bastard in the gray uniform . . . any different from me? Why are we shooting at each other?" Try as he might, Grondin could not think of any satisfying answers. He simply kept waiting in his foxhole.

Several fields away, Lieutenant Max Kocour, a mortar forward observer for H Company, was looking for targets. He had been in combat with the unit from the beginning, and he had already come to terms with many of the questions that were tormenting Private Grondin. "After a few days in combat, most of us came to grips with ourselves in varying degrees," Lieutenant Kocour wrote. Prayer comforted him. "I personally made an Act of Contrition several times a day or more, and decided that God was on my side, and decided that I would rather die than be a coward. Most of us . . . were afraid—but without being cowards. We could not stop for analyses and lectures" on the big picture.[2]

Men like Grondin and Kocour spent most of the day waiting for the attack order. A supporting air strike was canceled for lack of proper marking smoke. In lieu of this, staff officers and artillery commanders spent several hours arranging for a preliminary artillery barrage. The time was not well spent. "The circumstances under which the plan was drawn up were not conducive to good planning," Lieutenant Colonel Ken Reimers, commander of the supporting 343rd Field Artillery Battalion, commented. "We sat on the slope of a slight rise with no cover or shelter. We couldn't see anything." Reimers had no time to properly coordinate his supporting fire. Nor did he have any chance to speak with the commanders of the rifle companies that were to make the attack.

The push for Gourbesville did not start until late in the day on June 14. When it did, it began with avoidable tragedy. The artillery marking rounds landed among the troops who were preparing to attack. The explanation for this disaster bordered on the stupefying. Colonel Ginder, the incompetent commanding officer of the 357th, had been relieved, but he was still making trouble. Instead of going to the rear, Colonel Ginder, after his relief, went to the 3rd Battalion. According to Reimer, Ginder bullied the 3rd Battalion commander "to advance his men 150 yards beyond the . . . front lines. This caused the first rounds . . . to fall right on top of our troops."

The short rounds were an evil harbinger. In an entire night of fighting,

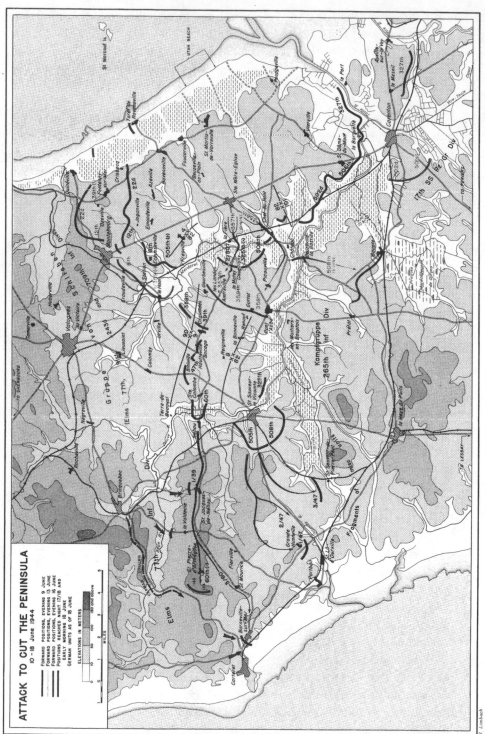

ATTACK TO CUT THE PENINSULA
10 - 18 June 1944

Forward positions, evening 9 June
Forward positions, evening 13 June
Forward positions, evening 16 June
Positions reached night 17/18 and
early morning 18 June
German units as of 18 June

ELEVATIONS IN METERS

MILES

MAP XXI

R. Limbach

the 357th failed to capture Gourbesville. Soldiers from the 3rd Battalion did infiltrate the town during the early-morning hours of June 15, but there were not enough of them to clear the many enemy-held buildings.

Meanwhile, east of Gourbesville, Lieutenant John Colby's E Company was moving cautiously, trying to find the road that led west, into the town. A couple days before, Colby had taken over command of the company when his captain got wounded. Colby was in the lead, somewhere out in the darkness ahead of his men. "Battalion said there were no Germans along the route, so, like an idiot, I took the lead instead of sending our scouts out ahead. It was black as ink."

Through the inky blackness Colby made out the silhouette of a small hedgerow. Just as he pushed through it, "a submachine gun emitted a long burst right in front of my face." The burp gun "sounded like a piece of cloth being ripped loudly. I fell backward and passed out cold from fright." Lieutenant Colby was lucky. The natural tendency of the MP-40 to kick upward sprayed the bullets above his head as he fell over. One of his men roused him and told him he had not been hit. Colby got up, shook off his fear, and ordered his scouts to resume the advance. "They found the road and started along it. A jeep came along with its blue lights showing faintly and went right past us."

It was Colonel John Sheehy, Ginder's predecessor and successor. Sheehy had commanded the 357th in the years leading up to D-Day but had been relieved (by the now deposed General MacKelvie) in favor of Ginder. When Ginder was fired, Sheehy was the logical choice to replace him.

Sheehy, his aide, and a jeep driver were looking for the lead units. The colonel wanted to know why Gourbesville had not been taken, so he piled into his jeep and went driving through the night to find out. Sheehy was a courageous man, perhaps to a fault. "I don't believe [he] has any fear," one of his officers commented at the time.

Colby and his men watched the jeep disappear into the night. Moments later, they heard German machine-gun fire. "We began moving towards the shooting, and here came a figure on foot, running towards us. We grabbed the man. It was the jeep driver." He was the only survivor. Sheehy and his aide had been killed.

Colby's company fought a brief skirmish with the Germans manning the roadblock that had felled the colonel. Company E spent the rest of the night waiting for orders to move into Gourbesville. The orders never came. Frustrated and confused, Colby took his people back to their starting point. They got there as the sun rose.

The 357th Infantry seemed cursed. In just four days of combat it had lost two commanders—one from incompetence and the other from excessive bravery. "We all felt very badly about Sheehy's death," Colby wrote. "He was a fine, courtly gentleman. The real tragedy is that this fine soldier, who had lived and worked with his regiment for two years, was arbitrarily replaced by an incompetent Ginder, and then was returned to command his now exhausted, depleted regiment. Many of his subordinates believed his heart was broken and he almost invited ambush."

The leaderless 357th resumed, on June 15, its attempt to take Gourbesville. Once again, the 3rd Battalion attacked from the northeast and the 2nd Battalion from the east. The day was clear and warm. Visibility was excellent. Companies F and G were to lead the 2nd Battalion's advance. The word had spread about the botched fire missions of the day before. Consequently, the soldiers of these two units got spooked by the supporting U.S. artillery. Lieutenant Colby's E Company was in reserve, a few hundred yards behind the lead companies. He watched in fascinated horror as panic developed among the assault troops. "Shells began falling between the forward companies and the edge of the village, nearer the forward companies than the village. To my astonishment, men of Fox and George companies began running toward the rear . . . toward me. Many men threw down their weapons." The panic spread. Some of Colby's men attempted to flee, but he and his sergeants kept them under control. Still, the 2nd Battalion was no factor in the eventual capture of Gourbesville. The 3rd Battalion finally secured this objective late in the afternoon on June 15. "I'm sure it could have fallen sooner if proper coordination had been made between the artillery and the infantry," Lieutenant Colonel Reimers commented.

For the next few days, the 90th Division continued its inconclusive fighting in the hedgerows from Orglandes to Le Ham. The unit continued to learn the hard way in combat, but it did, at least, protect the northern flank of the advance to the west coast.[3]

In all honesty, the Germans had more important things to worry about than the muddling of the 90th Division. The 9th Division and the 82nd Airborne were moving quickly, thus putting pressure on the Germans to hold them, evacuate their troops from the Cotentin, or suffer the consequences of being cut off. The 9th attacked west from Orglandes to Ste-Colombe, home to a key bridge over the Douve River. A couple miles to the south, the 82nd Airborne also pushed west, jumping off from Pont l'Abbé with the goal of seizing St-Sauveur-le-Vicompte, home to another major Douve crossing route. Quite simply, the flooded Douve River was the last natural barrier between the Americans and the west coast. If U.S. troops could cross the Douve, then it would be almost impossible to keep them from sealing off the peninsula. On June 15, both divisions fought along the westerly roads.

The 9th, a veteran unit with extensive combat experience in North

Africa and Sicily, spent the day warding off German counterattacks. Late in the morning, an enemy armored counterattack hit the lead units of the division's 60th Infantry. The German tanks came from the north. The Americans fought back with bazookas and 57mm antitank guns, knocking out three light tanks against the loss of two of the 57mm guns. The Germans turned around and retreated north.

The advance resumed, but the counterattacks continued. All day long the 60th Infantry and the 47th, alongside, brawled with German infantry and tanks. Heavy and accurate American artillery fire helped ward off these attacks, especially the 155mm fire of the division's 34th Field Artillery Battalion. At one of the guns belonging to A Battery, a couple miles behind the lead troops, Corporal Robert Baldridge was doing his part, helping his crew fire their 155 "Long Tom" in support of the infantrymen. Baldridge was a thoughtful, educated young man with a deep sense of the merits of service to his country. He had left Yale to go on active duty. His father had served as an artilleryman in World War I and in 1942 returned to active service, this time in the Air Force. Robert Baldridge's brother was a forward observer in the 27th Infantry Division in the Pacific. Even his mother was heavily involved in the war effort, serving almost full-time as a Red Cross volunteer. Baldridge could probably have parlayed his education and social advantages into something safe, but he wanted to do his part for the war effort and he believed doing his part meant serving in combat.

He and his crew fired round after round. One of the hardest things to do was hoist the ninety-five-pound shells into the breech, but they were well trained. "[We] started firing in earnest, at preselected targets which were roads and known troop assembly areas. Gun elevations were gradually raised, hurling a rolling barrage that enabled our infantry to start advancing. After two hours of steady firing we heard the results were good. We packed up and moved out, following the infantry who were mopping up dazed German soldiers." By nightfall, the division had captured Reigneville, one of the key objectives east of Ste-Colombe.[4]

The 82nd enjoyed a similar advance. General Ridgway attacked with two regiments, the 325th and the 507th. David Waters, a 507th code clerk turned rifleman who had destroyed a German tank on D-Day, volunteered to be a lead scout. He had just received a "Dear John" letter from his fiancée. "It said she was sorry, but she had married a Lieutenant J.G. in the Navy. Of course I was upset. If I was to have a future, she was a very big part of it but, more than that, it changed my whole outlook. I didn't care anymore." The carnage around him only worsened his mood. "The countryside was littered with dead cows, victims of stray bullets, bombs, grenades, etc. In three or four days their carcasses would bloat up to the point of bursting." He led his unit in combat that day, and they advanced several hundred yards against mostly snipers and roadblocks.

Lieutenant Gerard Dillon and G Company, 2nd Battalion, were leading the whole 507th. "We went into a sunken road between two hedgerows." His company commander, Captain Ben Schwartzwalder, spotted a German troop concentration on a hill up ahead and ordered his 60mm mortar teams to plaster it. In the meantime, Dillon's platoon worked its way up to good attack positions behind a hedgerow along the road. "I told all of the men . . . that once they got over the hedgerow to start firing as fast as they could and run as quickly as possible down into [a] valley between the hills and up the other hill to the next hedgerow. We did this and arrived at the next hedgerow to find that the Germans had started to retreat from our advance."

They took the hill, dug in, and stopped for the night when the 505th Parachute Infantry came up to relieve them. That night, Dillon got wounded when an enemy mortar shell dropped a few feet behind his foxhole. He and his platoon sergeant were sitting on the edge of the foxhole when the round came in, "knocking both him and me into the hole. Fortunately, I had my helmet on. [He] did not. [He] was killed instantly. I fell into the hole with shrapnel in my back, just to the left of my spine, and another shard went through the back of my helmet and caught me behind the right ear. The helmet is what saved me." Medics evacuated him to an aid station and then to England. He rejoined his unit in time for the Market-Garden jump into Holland.[5]

The tough fighting on June 15 broke most of the German resistance east of the Douve, opening the way for the 9th and the 82nd to capture their bridges the next day. Lieutenant Colonel Michael Kauffman's 2nd Battalion, 60th Infantry, plus tanks from the 746th Tank Battalion, made it to Ste-Colombe by lunchtime in what General Collins called "one of the most brilliant actions . . . in the entire war." Kauffman's battalion, led by E Company, succeeded in crossing the flooded Douve. As at other places in Normandy, this crossing consisted of a causeway, buttressed by several bridges. The last bridge was out, and that meant the tanks had to turn back. The infantry went on alone. On the west bank of the Douve, just outside of a river town called Nehou, they spent the day under intense artillery fire. They were low on ammunition but high on resolve. Kauffman himself went to the rear, commandeered a deuce-and-a-half ammo truck, and drove it back to his men. This alleviated the ammunition shortage, and Kauffman's men, joined now by the 60th Regiment's 3rd Battalion, held on for the night.

As this was happening, the 82nd Airborne made it to the east bank of the Douve, overlooking St-Sauveur-le-Vicompte. The 325th had bivouacked about one thousand yards east of this point the night before. Now it combined with tankers from the 746th Tank Battalion, along with paratroopers from the 505th and the 508th, to make it this far. The Americans, including

General Ridgway himself, observed the town and clearly saw the Germans retreating west. Ridgway understood that the Germans had no intention of fighting for St-Sauveur-le-Vicompte, so he got in touch with Collins and asked for permission to enter the town. Collins eagerly granted permission and arranged for artillery fire to rain down upon the exiting Germans.

Led by the 1st Battalion, 325th, along with tanks from A Company of the 746th, the Americans rolled across the Douve River and into St-Sauveur-le-Vicompte. Troopers from the 505th, including Private William Tucker, an I Company machine gunner, soon followed. "[The bridge] was under constant fire and many dead bodies were floating in the water. It was a question of running like hell over the bridge." The bridge could support infantry but not tanks, so the engineers spent much of the day strengthening the bridge.

There were still a few German holdouts in some of the town's ruined buildings, but long-range tank or machine-gun fire took care of them. The 505th troopers now took the lead in Ridgway's advance. They passed through St-Sauveur-le-Vicompte and made it to the railroad tracks, and high ground, just outside of town. Here they fought the remnants of the German defenders of St-Sauveur-le-Vicompte.

The Germans were still dug in on the other side of the railroad embankment. "You couldn't go over it at all," Lieutenant Jack Isaacs recalled. Isaacs had jumped into Normandy as a platoon leader. One by one, his superiors got killed or wounded, making Isaacs the company commander. He and his men fought most of the day and night against the Germans at the railroad embankment. "We were chucking grenades back and forth. There was no way we could cross that railroad without being wiped out."

Late in the afternoon, they were hit with a German armored counterattack. "The tanks were coming from the area near the underpass. I positioned my guys to deal with them. We had only three bazooka rounds left and scored direct hits on one of the tanks and we knocked the treads off the other. The other three withdrew."

During the attack, a pair of P-51 Mustangs materialized. A couple hundred yards to the right of Isaacs's G Company position, Sergeant Bill Dunfee, who had survived the Ste-Mère-Eglise battle of a few days before, tried to signal the friendly fighters. Dunfee wanted to point out the position of one of the enemy tanks. "I got up on top of the railroad embankment and when they came down, I kept pointing at the tank with my BAR." The whole process seemed very clear to Dunfee. He was wearing his jumpsuit and pointing his American-made weapon at a stationary German tank. But this was not apparent to the fighter pilots speeding overhead at several hundred miles per hour. To them, Dunfee was only a blur, something or someone to be targeted. "Those dirty birds started shooting at me and dropped a bomb! The machine-gun fire looked like little twinkles on both of the wings." Dunfee cursed and dodged the fire. "Between the C-47 pilots' letting us out too high [on D-Day] and the P-51s strafing us, I didn't have too high an opinion of the Air Force right then."

The fighting continued to rage outside of St-Sauveur-le-Vicompte all night long. Lieutenant Isaacs lost many troopers—he was down to only seventeen men—but by dawn he was able to advance behind the enemy positions. "They started to withdraw. We were in an excellent position to deliver flanking fire, and I Company was delivering frontal fire, and we caused a great many casualties amongst the retreating Germans."

The juiciest target of the day was a towed 88 and several support vehicles that were rolling south down the road, right in the kill zone of G Company. Isaacs and his soldiers were lying behind hedgerows that paralleled the road. At just the right moment, they rose up and blistered the Germans with every weapon they had, achieving complete surprise. "The very rapid fire that we were able to deliver . . . wiped out everybody on the German side. We knocked out the towed vehicle, the eighty-eight, the two or three vehicles accompanying it."

When the shooting died down, all that remained was the battered carcasses of what had once been a German artillery column. The bodies of the enemy soldiers were torn to shreds from grenade shrapnel or pockmarked with holes made by American rifles or machine guns. Blood had spattered everywhere. Already flies were buzzing around the warm, rotting flesh of these Germans. The Americans were glad they had won, but they experienced no elation at the slaughter. "I entered Normandy as a twenty-one-year-old platoon leader," Isaacs said, "and in ten days was a forty-two-year-old company commander."[6]

The victories at St-Sauveur-le-Vicompte and Ste-Colombe opened the way for a dash through the western Cotentin. Collins ordered the 9th Division to take the lead in capturing the mere six miles that now stood between the Americans and the coast. General Eddy dispatched two of his regiments, the 60th and the 47th, to finish the job. "We're going all the way tonight," he told his regimental commanders on June 17.

In a spectacular twenty-four-hour running battle, the men of these units made it to the coast. For soldiers like Private Max Dach of the 47th Infantry, the advance was a dizzying, exhausting, stream-of-consciousness experience. "We had to cut the Cherbourg peninsula. No rest there, hardly any sleep. We were scared all the time. We had to dig holes at night no matter how tired we were and absolutely make no noise. We didn't eat good, we slept on the ground with . . . no more than our jacket or raincoat for cover. Not pleasant."[7]

Corporal Baldridge, the artilleryman, spent most of the advance hunting for and shooting at German Nebelwerfers, which were constantly harassing the Americans. "Fortunately, they were not very accurate, but their banshee wail was scary. Our FO's [forward observers] learned to counter-battery them by quickly adjusting fire on a point maybe two hundred yards away from the Nebelwerfers, whose firing produced a very high flash of flame. This adjusting fire would not unduly alarm the German rocket men, until suddenly they would be deluged with a full 'fire for effect' by our batteries when the final correction of two hundred yards was deemed ready to make. Fascinating, what tricks these pros could produce under hazardous conditions."[8]

True to Eddy's word, the Americans cut the peninsula by the time the sun rose on June 18. The 60th Infantry was in Barneville-sur-Mer on the west coast. The 47th had cut the road leading south out of Barneville and had captured St-Lô-d'Ourville, another coastal town.

This put the Germans in the Cotentin in a desperate situation. As early as June 13, both Rommel and Rundstedt had sniffed out the American intention to cut the peninsula. Two days later, they knew there was no way to prevent that from happening, so they hoped to salvage their best troops, most of whom were part of the 77th Infantry Division. But Adolf Hitler, true to form, forbade any southerly withdrawal. He still hoped to hang on to Cherbourg as long as possible; he also hoped to maintain control of the western Cotentin coast. The former objective was sound, but not the latter. By the time reality set in on June 17, it was too late to withdraw most of the 77th Division, much less the tattered remnants of the 91st, the second-best German formation in the peninsula.

During the daylight hours of June 18, soldiers from these two units launched desperate counterattacks against 9th Division roadblocks and positions along the coast. In one instance, some twelve to fourteen hundred Germans escaped to the south (and captured about one hundred U.S. prisoners) when they blasted through 47th Infantry positions at St-Lô-d'Ourville.

But most of the Germans did not escape. A major artillery column from the 77th Infantry Division attempted to roll right through Barneville but was decimated by the 9th Division's 60th Field Artillery Battalion. The powerful U.S. artillery destroyed the better part of the enemy column. Another major attack hit the GIs of the 1st Battalion, 39th Infantry, who were manning a roadblock farther to the west at St-Jacques-de-Nehou. The fighting here was bitter as at least a battalion of enemy troops (once again from the 77th Division) tried to escape. The two sides shot at each other from point-blank range, each side often close enough to hear the other talking.

The Americans had no artillery support, only their mortars and their rifles. They withdrew about six hundred yards but came back, under cover of mortar fire and air strikes. Some of the Germans had seeped through their roadblock, but the majority had not. The 39th Infantry soldiers took sixty prisoners and found 250 enemy dead, including the division commander,

Major General Rudolf Stegmann, who had apparently been killed in the air strike. The 1st Battalion suffered thirty-six casualties.

So now the noose was tightened around the German neck in the Cotentin. The enemy had the remnants of four divisions (plus irregular troops like naval personnel or military police) to defend Cherbourg—the inferior 243rd and 709th Divisions, whatever remained of the 91st, which had been badly mauled around Ste-Mère-Eglise, and the 77th, which was in the best shape of all of them. From a tactical point of view, the presence of the 77th strengthened the German defense of Cherbourg. But from a strategic point of view this fine unit was going to waste, because the Germans were cut off. With no possibility of escape, the demise of the Germans in the Cotentin was just a matter of time. The question now was just how long it would take the Americans to stamp out enemy resistance and capture Cherbourg. The longer the Germans could deprive the Americans of the use of Cherbourg's port facilities, the more pressure they would put on the shaky Allied logistical situation in Normandy.[9]

Nature exacerbated Allied logistical problems. By June 18, 314,514 troops, 41,000 vehicles, and 116,000 tons of supplies had been landed over the American beaches. But at the stroke of midnight on June 19 a powerful Channel storm, the worst in more than forty years, brought the unloading to a halt. For the next three days strong winds howled across the beaches. Heavy surf pounded beaches and ships alike. LCTs, LSTs, and other craft were swept ashore. They smashed against one another, and many were wrecked beyond repair. Many ships put to sea, escaping the worst of the storm, but others could not make it that far. These ended up with damaged propellers or anchors. Sometimes they slammed into nearby ships. The grinding noises of colliding metal could be heard above the noisy storm and the pounding surf. Anyone aboard any kind of craft, large or small, experienced the abject misery of being jostled mercilessly by the wind and surf. Rain poured down in torrents.

The newly opened mulberry port was having a tough time standing up to the storm. The caissons and pontoon runways were buckling in the swell. On June 20, a salvage barge and five LCTs, sloshing out of control in the choppy seas, collided with the center pontoon runway of the mulberry. Seabees had already been working hard, in dangerous conditions, to stabilize the mulberry, but when this happened, it made their task nearly impossible. In automobile terms, the mulberry was "totaled." The caissons and steel bombardons so necessary to the existence of this ingenious artificial port continued to break loose. By June 22, when the storm finally abated, the mulberry was nothing more than a jumbled collection of steel and concrete chunks floating together with wrecked ships. In light of this severe damage, Admiral Kirk decided to make no attempt to repair the mulberry.

The worst consequence of the storm was not the destruction of the mulberry harbor (which contributed little to the Allied supply effort in Normandy) but the fact that it halted unloading operations. For obvious reasons, almost nothing came ashore during the storm. For instance, on June 18 the Allies had unloaded about 73 percent of their projected supply tonnage for this point in the campaign. Four days later, the percentage had plummeted to 57 percent.

After the storm, General Eisenhower hopped in a plane and "flew from one end of our beach line to the other and counted more than 300 wrecked vessels above small boat size, some so badly damaged they could not be salvaged." When he landed, he met soldiers from the 83rd Infantry Division, a unit whose arrival in Normandy was delayed by the storm. Instead, the soldiers had spent several days bouncing around their ships, miserable and seasick. "The day they finally got ashore," Ike wrote, "a number of them [were] still seasick and . . . exhausted." Captain James Shonak, commander of the antitank company of the division's 331st Infantry Regiment, could attest to the hell he and the other soldiers experienced aboard ship during the storm: "Most of the men were sick as dogs . . . they couldn't or wouldn't eat. We were becoming physically worse. Losing weight, and strength . . . tossing out food. What a mess . . . and we had not even landed yet!"

General Bradley also walked the beach and was "appalled by the desolation, for it vastly exceeded that of D-Day. Operations on Omaha had been brought to a standstill. Even the beach engineers had crawled into their damp burrows to escape the wind and the rain. In four days the Channel storm had threatened OVERLORD with greater danger than had all the enemy's guns in 14 days ashore. Hundreds of craft had piled up on the shingle where they lay mangled beyond the reach of the surf."

As Bradley surveyed the damage, he knew that it meant big trouble for his already difficult supply situation. "Nothing pained us more than the enormous losses we had sustained in tonnage with this shutdown on the beaches. Each day the deficit mounted until we fell thousands of tons in arrears, especially in ammunition." Bradley's army was down to three days' supply of ammunition. The shortage was so acute that the general had to postpone plans to exploit a push out of the Cotentin to the south. Even Bradley's first priority, the impending drive for Cherbourg, would suffer from the rationing of ammunition.

Bradley wiped sea spray from his glasses and kicked at the sand in frustration. Nature was proving to be an even greater enemy than the Germans. A naval lieutenant, wearing a Ranger jacket, ambled over to him. The general smiled wryly. "Hard to believe a storm could do all this."

The lieutenant looked carefully at Bradley's three stars. "General, we would much sooner have had the whole damned Luftwaffe come down on our heads."

It was as if the young officer had read the general's mind. In their wildest dreams, the Germans could not have hoped to do this much damage to Allied logistical efforts. Bradley sighed. Maybe capturing Cherbourg would help solve this damnable supply situation.[10]

On June 18, while the storm was still brewing, Bradley and Collins agreed to the following plan to win Cherbourg: Collins would line up three divisions, the 9th on the left, the newly arrived 79th in the middle, and the 4th on the right. Starting in the early-morning hours of June 19, all three divisions would begin a northerly advance up the peninsula. Every step of the way the advance would be supported by artillery, naval gunfire (especially for the 4th Division), and, weather permitting, air attacks. In a pincers move, the 9th and 4th would bust into Cherbourg from the west and east, respectively, while the 79th fought its way into the town along the ubiquitous N-13 highway.

In truth, Collins was the author of this plan. He was a dynamic and experienced commander, whose record of success was impressive. In the Pacific theater he had commanded the 25th Infantry Division through the difficult campaigns at Guadalcanal and New Georgia. In the process he won a slew of medals and a golden reputation. Command of the "Tropic Lightning" division, in addition to his energetic manner, earned him the nickname Lightning Joe.

One of his greatest strengths was an intuitive understanding of terrain and its importance in dictating the pace of battle. He saw many parallels between the jungles of the Pacific and the bocage of Normandy. In planning the push for Cherbourg, he worked closely with Mason Young, his corps engineer, who prepared excellent maps for the general's perusal. Collins saw that the Divette and Douve Rivers divided the Cotentin into two halves. "The eastern compartment, in which the 4th Division had been fighting, contained two small cities, Montebourg and Valognes, whose solid stone houses could become strong enemy redoubts. The compartment west of the Douve was more open country, with fewer natural obstacles, and was not held in strength. Ground rose steadily in both compartments to the hills ringing Cherbourg, broken only by the narrow Trotebec and Divette streams, both of which flowed into Cherbourg harbor. We knew from aerial photographs that the Germans had organized this ring of hills, cresting to four or five miles from the city, with a formidable series of mutually supporting strongpoints consisting of concrete machine-gun, antitank, and 88-mm gun emplacements, and tank barriers."[11]

Collins's intelligence people told him that the Germans would probably fight a delaying action before withdrawing into their inner ring of defenses just outside of Cherbourg. That is exactly what happened. In the west, the 9th Division, moving along the open coastal terrain, encountered very little resistance. In nearly two days the division covered seven or eight miles before slowing down before the western ring of the German Cherbourg defenses. In the center, the 79th Division made excellent progress but endured several enemy counterattacks. In spite of this resistance, the 79th also reached the inner ring of defenses by June 21.[12]

The 4th Division, in the east, dealt with the toughest opposition. The 4th was still fighting through hedgerow country. Plus, it was nearest to the Channel storm, so it experienced high winds, clouds, and rain. "The rain and wind made conditions unbearable for the men in the field," one soldier wrote. In a tough, hedgerow-to-hedgerow fight, the 4th Division enveloped Montebourg. The 8th Infantry closed the ring from the west and the 12th Infantry from the east. Private Harper Coleman, the II Company, 8th Infantry, machine gunner who had come ashore on D-Day, slogged forward with the rest of his unit. "This was the way it was for most of the time, one hedgerow to the next on your stomach, or lower, if you could. Many incoming shells to all sides, and Burp . . . guns all the time. We would advance some distance and bog down when no one could go forward. After some time there would always be the next order to start another attack. This went on day and night."

In I Company, not far from Coleman, Private William Jones, the Tennessean, helped root out Germans who were fighting a delaying action west of Montebourg. The enemy was dug into the hedgerows. "They would lay there and fire at you until they ran out of ammunition and they would jump up and surrender. They were real dedicated people."

Some of the most stubborn German defenders were dug into positions along the western edges of Montebourg. Companies C and F of the 8th Infantry, supported by B Company of the 70th Tank Battalion, circled behind these Germans, attacked them from the rear, and spent much of June 19 fighting them. Enemy antitank guns were concealed cleverly along the lanes leading into town. Even as the infantry was methodically destroying enemy resistance, the German antitank guns were menacing the B Company Shermans. Bob Knoebel, a gunner in the lead Sherman, was manning his post, looking for targets. "We were going from one side of the road to the other, and our tank was instantly on fire. In fact, I glanced in back of me and the flames were already up in the air, just that quick."

In no time, Knoebel bailed out, jumping from his seat and sliding down the front slope of the tank. He and his platoon leader landed on the road, right next to each other, in front of their burning tank. Just ahead, German soldiers were pointing their weapons at them, waving for them to come forward and surrender. Knoebel and the lieutenant had no desire to become prisoners. They ran away, all the while dodging enemy fire. Knoebel came to another tank whose commander urged him to join his crew. He had no sooner settled into his familiar gunner's slot when the tank commander ordered the driver to get going. This lieutenant wanted to flank the antitank gun that had destroyed Knoebel's original tank. "We started across this field and got hit with five *Panzerfaust* shells. So the second tank I was in got knocked out, and now I'm wounded. We bailed out." Knoebel had been hit in the legs. He and the commander took shelter in a nearby ditch, but the Germans soon came along and captured them.

In spite of this resistance, the 8th Infantry cut the Montebourg–Valognes highway by late afternoon. To the east, the 12th Infantry fought its way across the Montebourg railroad, capturing the high ground north of town in an all-day battle. With this accomplished, General Barton knew the time had come to move into the town itself. He ordered his reserve unit, the 3rd Battalion, 22nd Infantry, to enter Montebourg. Advancing from the south along the N-13, they entered Montebourg against virtually no opposition. Only ruins and refugees remained. Montebourg had been the target of U.S. artillery for about a week, and it had been almost completely destroyed. The surviving townspeople emerged from cellars. They were dirty, frightened, and bewildered. "[They] are living in the most extreme poverty," Lieutenant John Ausland, an artillery officer, wrote to his family. "Clothing as such is unknown. All they have are rags. Dirty berets are the most common head dress for men. Women's dresses are torn and dirty."

The streets of Montebourg were so choked with rubble that it impeded the advance of the 22nd Infantry. Engineers like Sam Ricker had to come up with bulldozers to clear the streets. "When we entered Montebourg, there wasn't anything there but rubble. It was our job to clean the roadways out. Most of the time we took a bulldozer and they moved all this debris to the sides where trucks and jeeps and different vehicles could advance."

The following day, June 20, troops from the 8th Infantry entered Valognes and found it empty, except for the usual rubble and abject destruction. But Valognes was even worse than Montebourg. Here Allied aircraft had done much of the damage. Once again, bulldozers had to clear the rubble for traffic, but it took them several days to do so. Most of the 4th Infantry Division bypassed the town and kept pressing north. By June 21, soldiers from the division had run into the main German defensive ring on the eastern fringes of Cherbourg.[13]

The stage was now set for the final push to Cherbourg. Before it commenced, General Collins gave his opposite, General von Schlieben, the chance to surrender. Everyone on both sides of the lines knew that the German position was hopeless. The enemy was penned into a small perimeter, cut off by land and sea. Collins knew it was a long shot, but a small part of him hoped that the Germans might come to their senses, recognize the inevitable, and lay down their arms. On the evening of June 21, he broadcast a surrender ultimatum (the broadcast was translated not just into German but also into Polish, French, and Russian because of all the auxiliary troops who were part of von Schlieben's army). Collins also sent the ultimatum to von Schlieben by messenger. He gave the Germans until 0900 on June 22 to lay down their arms. After that, they would be annihilated. General von Schlieben never even replied. His orders, straight from Hitler, were to hold out at Cherbourg as long as he could. This would give his naval engineers time to demolish the port facilities and would indefinitely deny the use of the seaport to the Americans, worsening their supply situation.[14]

More than ever, Allied aircraft were having a major impact on the Battle of Normandy. They did so in two ways: isolating the battlefield and providing direct support for the ground troops.

In order to isolate Normandy, the fighters and bombers flew deeper into France, attacking railroads, bridges, fuel depots, troop concentrations, choke points, tunnels, and the like. They made it very difficult for German reinforcements to get to the battle area. Most German units had to get there the old-fashioned way—on foot. Allied aircraft, particularly fighters under the command of General Pete Quesada, severely impeded one major formation, Kampfgruppe Heinz. This brigade-sized unit needed the better part of a week to get from its original base in Brittany to the Cotentin. The Germans in Kampfgruppe Heinz loaded aboard trains but found themselves continually harassed by U.S. fighters, so much so that most could not safely remain aboard the trains. By the time the survivors reached Normandy they were tired, hungry, and demoralized. Nor was this the exception. Soldiers from the 265th Infantry Division, also coming from Brittany, had a virtually identical experience. Panzer Lehr, one of the most powerful units in the German Army, trekked from central France, and was plagued by Allied fighters (plus French resistance saboteurs). By the time Panzer Lehr reached Normandy it had lost 130 trucks, half a dozen tanks, eighty-four half-tracks, and plenty of soldiers, too.

In an eight-day period in mid-June, the 8th Air Force flew 5,900 sorties and dropped over 14,000 tons of bombs in support of the ground forces at Normandy. The 8th destroyed or severely damaged fifty-eight marshaling yards, thirty-eight bridges, twenty-two trains, and nine supply convoys.

This was impressive, but the medium bombers and fighters (better suited for this kind of thing) were even more effective. In just one mission against the marshaling yards at Rennes, B-26 Marauders and their fighter escorts destroyed 75 percent of the railroad stations, twelve locomotives out of a possible twenty-six, and 150 cars out of 400. Through June 18, fighters had severed northern French railroad lines in twenty-three places and had blown up sixty-two locomotives, along with another 600 cars. "Railway transportation is impossible because the trains are observed and attacked in short order," a German staff officer wrote in his unit's official war diary. "Troop movements and all supply traffic by rail to the army and within the army sector must be considered as completely cut off."[15]

Fighter pilots like Lieutenant Alvin Siegel made this happen. His unit, the 358th Fighter Group, took full advantage of the long summer Norman days. One evening, they took off at 2030 from their base in High Halden, England, while it was still light and hit marshaling yards at St-Quentin. The sun was setting by the time they reached the target. "We really had no equipment for night flying on our planes except our eyes." It was a clear evening and they could see the target well. "We did a fair amount of damage that night, some trains, and good wagons, trucks, and so forth." Flying home was difficult, though. "It was pretty frightening in a way to think that you couldn't see. You couldn't see if any German fighters were around. You had to sit on the edge of your seat . . . until you got home over the field." He and everyone else made it back.[16]

Lieutenant William Hess's 364th Fighter Group flew many freewheeling "target of opportunity" missions designed to prevent German troop movement in northern France. "You are flying down real low, maybe under 500 feet, and going like hell. You pick out a target that needs to be hit or knocked out, and you turn your bomb loose and hit your throttles and go, get out of the way. If you were dive-bombing, you might come across a target at 10,000 feet and roll the airplane over and come straight down . . . vertical and drop or turn your bomb loose then pull out. Sometimes you would be maybe a thousand feet high, and maybe you would be at treetop level and going like the wind."[17]

These missions were exhilarating, but they were also quite dangerous. Lieutenant Leonard Schallehn found that out the hard way when his 405th Fighter Group ran into withering fire during a June 16 raid near LaVelle. That day, Lieutenant Schallehn was not even supposed to fly. He was planning to go to London "for a little party with the guys." But somebody got sick, so Schallehn filled in. He did not even have time to change out of his dress uniform. "The only thing I did was change my shoes."

They overflew the target and prepared to dive-bomb. Schallehn watched the plane ahead of him go vertical, and a few seconds later he followed. The G-forces (emblematic of the crushing weight of gravity) were nearly overwhelming. He felt as if a giant was pinning him back into his cockpit seat. All at once, Schallehn heard something hit his P-47. "Whatever hit me, I don't know. I started losing oil." He asked his flight leader to assess the damage. "I had a couple of minutes to chat with him, and then finally my engine went dead completely and he told me to get out of the airplane. I bailed out."

Schallehn was luckier than most. He landed in a cornfield and wandered on his own for three days before hooking up with friendly French farmers who put him in touch with the resistance. They hid him for several weeks, until late July, when an American reconnaissance group liberated him.[18]

Close support missions were doing just as much damage. There were still too many friendly fire incidents, but General Quesada's IX Fighter Command pilots were gradually perfecting effective ways to support the ground troops. The 9th Air Force was divided into the IX Bomber Command (medium bombers), the IX Troop Carrier Command (the C-47s and gliders that had carried the airborne units into Normandy), and the IX Fighter Command, under Quesada's control. Quesada, the youthful, imaginative fighter general, enjoyed a close relationship with General Bradley. The two men liked and trusted each other. By the middle of June, Quesada had moved to France full-time. He set up his headquarters right next door to Bradley's near Grandcamp. "The only thing that separated us was a hedgerow," Quesada said, "so a single bomb could not kill both of us. I liked him right off. Brad did not tell me how to run the air war, and I did not interfere with the alignment of divisions along his front."

Bradley especially liked that Quesada, unlike the vast majority of senior air officers, understood the vital importance of close air support. "[He] helped more than anyone else to develop the air-ground support. He succeeded brilliantly in a task where so many airmen before him had failed, partly because he was willing to dare anything once. Unlike most airmen who viewed ground support as a bothersome diversion to the war in the sky, Quesada approached it as a vast new frontier waiting to be explored."

This attitude marked Quesada as something of an outcast among his air force peers, most of whom were fixated on the possibilities of strategic bombing as a war-winning weapon (not to mention the vehicle by which an independent air force could be achieved after the war). Quesada was right, though. Strategic bombing in World War II, on the one hand, did terrific damage to the Axis, but it fell far short of winning the war. Close air support, on the other hand, was of inestimable value to Allied armies in their march to victory.[19]

Each night, staff officers from 1st Army and IX Fighter Command met to coordinate their efforts the next day. The ground officers presented requests for air support, and Quesada's operations officer, Colonel Lorry Tindal, assigned groups to provide that support for each sector of the front.

By morning these orders would be disseminated among the twenty fighter groups under the control of IX Fighter Command (most of which were still operating from bases in England). For fighter pilots like Captain Bill Dunn, an ace in the 406th Fighter Group—Dunn served with the Eagle Squadron before U.S. entry into the war—these support missions entailed taking up station above the battle areas. "A system was employed that we called 'cab ranks.' Four of our Jugs [P-47s] . . . would be assigned to cover a portion of the front lines. If the ground commander in that sector required an air strike on an enemy position that was tough to crack, he could call the cab rank in the air by radio . . . to make the strike. The enemy target was identified for us—sometimes by terrain features, sometimes by colored smoke shells—and down we'd dive to bomb, rocket, or strafe, depending on the type of target. As a safety factor, so we didn't mistakenly hit our own troops, the infantry guys laid out panels of fluorescent orange cloth on the ground to indicate our front lines."[20]

Fighter pilots like Dunn did tremendous damage to the Germans. Between June 7 and June 18, American fighter-bombers, flying these "cab rank" missions, destroyed nearly 1,000 vehicles, including fourteen tanks. The number of German soldiers they killed can only be imagined. Unlike most of the air war, this kind of fighting was not impersonal. The fighter pilots, on their strafing runs, flew so low that they could see their targets, both man and machine. Their guns and bombs were so devastating that they could hardly miss. "It was during one of [these] missions that I first knew I had killed men," Quentin Aanenson, a pilot in the 366th Fighter Group, later wrote. "Four of us were at low level . . . when suddenly we caught a column of German soldiers on a road. We caught them before they could hide in the fields. We killed a lot of them on the road and then strafed the ditches to catch as many as we could." The twenty-two-year-old Minnesota native knew that this was his job, but it nauseated him nonetheless. "I will always remember the feeling I had when my bullets smashed into them. Some just crumpled to the ground, but the tremendous impact of .50 caliber bullets at 120 rounds a second threw most of the bodies several yards. I got sick when I landed, and that night . . . I had to keep reminding myself that I had to do it—that I had probably saved some American boys' lives by killing Germans that day."

Most of the fighter pilots did not struggle with the killing the way Aanenson did. Quite the contrary. They relished these close support missions as a tangible way to aid the ground combat soldiers, a group they collectively admired and respected. Captain John Marshall, a squadron leader in the 404th Fighter Group, loved the excitement and adrenaline of flying close support for the infantry in the middle of June in the Cotentin. "This dive-bombing I'm a fiend about," he wrote to his father. He described it as "deliberate, hell-raising destruction. Like vultures we go out just looking for trouble. An even temper and good judgement is all you need, with reasonable luck. Now and then some poor fool gets caught walking down a road or bailing out of a car—my Quaker background goes all to hell. When these guns bark, it has a faint resemblance to smashing a tomato with a ball bat." One time, Marshall blazed away so furiously, and intently, at a column of enemy soldiers that his gun barrels melted. When he landed his P-47, his crew chief took one look at the guns, "pushed his hat to one side and said, 'Jesus, Captain Marshall' with a broad grin."[21]

Men like Marshall were supporting General Collins's VII Corps, so the general fully comprehended how effective airpower could be. Collins, by his own admission, was a "tremendous believer in doing everything we could in the combined arms." His experiences in the Pacific had taught him that attacks only succeeded with proper coordination, and that meant "infantry, artillery, air and engineers." Thus it is not surprising that as his soldiers prepared to assault the main German defensive line around Cherbourg, Collins requested as much air support as possible.

Bradley did, too. At one of his nightly meetings with Quesada, Bradley asked him if his IX Fighter Command could lay down a powerful bombardment that would blast a hole through the German defensive line of pillboxes, bunkers, barbed wire, and tank traps. For about twenty minutes Quesada pored over maps, charts, and reconnaissance photos. When he was finished he told Bradley he would do whatever he could to support the offensive, but that his fighters would need support from heavier aircraft. He flew back to England and consulted with General Lewis Brereton, his superior, who commanded the entire 9th Air Force, along with several other senior officers.

Between June 18 and June 21, as the storm raged along the invasion beaches, Quesada and Collins crafted a final plan. Collins wanted "air pulverization" across twenty miles of front. He wished to demoralize the enemy, disrupt his communications, and stun him, all in the confined space of the upper Cotentin. Collins and Quesada agreed that the heavies were not well suited for this task. They were not accurate enough. To do this job, Collins wanted as many fighters and medium bombers as he could get. He also wanted the bomb line to be as close to his front-line troops as possible; this way the bombs would certainly do great damage to the Germans. But they also might kill some Americans. For this reason, Colonel Harold Holt, an experienced fighter group commander who was present while the two senior officers planned the aerial bombardment, suggested a buffer zone of at least 500 yards. "Joe, you had better listen to these men," Quesada urged. "They've been doing it successfully for many weeks." Collins listened and agreed.[22]

At 1240 hours on June 22, with the last vestiges of the storm gone and the ultimatum unanswered, the air attack commenced. The weather was perfect—clear, high ceiling, crisp, an airman's dream. British fighters came in

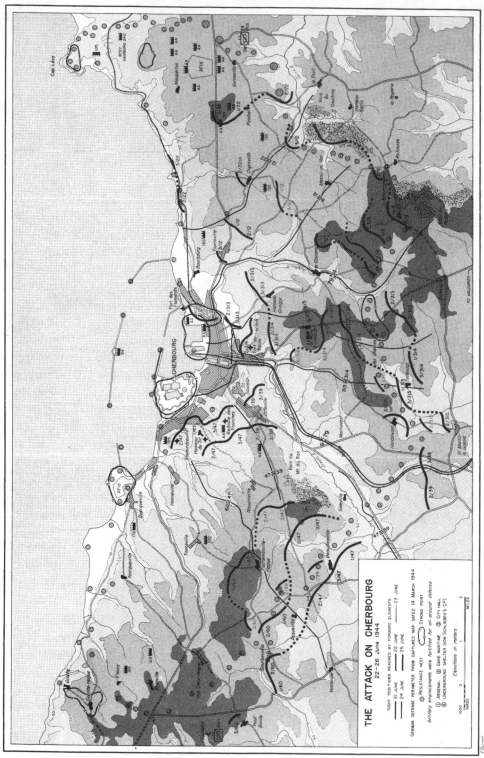

MAP XXIII

THE ATTACK ON CHERBOURG
22-26 June 1944

Night positions reached by forward elements

——— 21 June   ——— 23 June
——— 22 June   ——— 25 June
——— 24 June

GERMAN DEFENSE PERIMETER FROM CAPTURED MAP DATED 14 MARCH 1944

⊗ Resistance nest   ⌒ Strong point

Artillery emplacements were fortified for all-around defense

⊙ Arsenal   ② Gare Maritime   ④ City Hall
③ Underground shelter (von Schlieben's CP)

Elevations in meters

1000   0   1   2
        YARDS   MILES

first. A combination of rocket-firing Typhoons and Mustangs blasted the enemy positions. In their wake they left explosions and screams that could be heard even above the din. The British attack, flawlessly executed, lasted about twenty minutes.

The Germans had been stunned, but more than that, they had been alerted. Seconds after the British planes disappeared over the horizon, an armada of 562 American fighters screamed in. For nearly an hour, group by group, they overflew the German lines. A mighty sheet of German flak rose to meet them. The volume of fire was almost unbelievable—small-arms, 20mm, 88mm, heavier stuff, basically anything that would shoot. Tracer rounds zigzagged crazily; smoke puffs were everywhere. The ground twinkled with muzzle flashes. Lieutenant Gabriel Greenwood, a twenty-seven-year-old fighter jock from the 405th Fighter Group, was in the cockpit of his P-47, right in the middle of the barrage. "It was as though the earth had erupted and spread . . . up into the sky through our planes. [I] never saw so much flak, tracers, flares, or felt so many concussions before." In spite of the danger, he and his flight dived for the deck and commenced their dive-bombing runs. "It was really a hellhole. A battlefield in all its awful magnificence."[23]

The American fighter pilots could hardly see any targets, because the British attack had created great clumps of smoke and dust. Rather than carry out a systematic bombing or strafing pattern, the Americans simply attacked whatever targets happened to present themselves. To Lieutenant Edward Michelson, buzzing along the deck at better than 300 miles per hour in his P-38 Lightning, the whole scene was one of chaos. "The ground fire was so intense it seemed the only safe place to be was below treetop level." Not far away from Michelson, several pilots from his 367th Fighter Group ran straight into a deadly crossfire of flak. "We were on the deck in a ravine when all hell broke loose," Captain Jake Reed remembered. Just ahead, two P-38s, in a matter of seconds, turned into nothing more than boiling fireballs. Several other planes got hit and went down. The 405th lost five pilots killed in this strafing run. Captain Reed's plane was peppered with shrapnel. He dropped his bombs on a flak battery and managed to escape.[24]

Lieutenant Siegel of the 358th was about a mile away. His unit did not run into quite as much opposition. He and his squadron mates dropped their bombs on gun emplacements and climbed a couple hundred feet to get a better look at the area around Cherbourg. Suddenly Siegel spotted a truck on a highway. "I peeled off and dove. At that altitude I just barely had enough time to line up on the truck, squirt a short burst of fire and pull up immediately. I had to pull up right away to keep from going into the ground. I looked around and the truck was burning mightily and black smoke was curling up into the air. There must have been some type of munitions on that truck that made it burn so black."[25]

The biggest downside to this aerial barrage was the possibility that the American planes would mistakenly attack their own troops. The confusion caused by German fire, drifting marker smoke, and simple disorientation led to several friendly fire incidents. The 22nd, 47th, and 60th Infantry Regiments all reported getting attacked by the American fighters. These units took several casualties. By 1330, they were calling their division headquarters to request that the air attacks be stopped. At this point, though, little could be done.

In any case, the fighters were all gone by 1400, when the ground troops went forward. But the aerial bombardment was not yet finished. Now the medium bombers came in. Their mission was to provide a rolling barrage ahead of the ground troops. For one hour, the mediums bombed blind through the smoke, dust, and some clouds that blew in from the sea. They were flying higher than the fighters, but they also had to fly through the intense flak. In the tail gunner's seat of one B-26, Sergeant Leroy McFarland watched as a plane directly below and behind him took several hits. The plane was flown by Lieutenant Robert Saltzman. His bomb bay doors were jammed open. "He was pouring smoke out of one engine; he dropped out of formation. I kept an eye on him as long as I possibly could. Finally, he disappeared from view altogether." McFarland never saw an explosion, so he still held out hope that Saltzman's plane could make it back to England. Sure enough, when McFarland's plane returned to base, there was Saltzman. "He . . . dragged that aircraft back to England with the bomb bay doors jammed open, no hydraulic fluid, a smoking engine . . . ground looped, and ran off the runway and finally destroyed the aircraft."

Losses among the medium bombers were minimal—one aircraft lost, another (Saltzman's) damaged beyond repair. Just like the fighters before them, they inflicted casualties on friendly troops. Bombers attacked the 9th Division, killing and wounding several men and making that division suspicious of close air support for the rest of the war.

Perhaps the worst thing about the bombing mission is that it did not do much good. It succeeded in disrupting German communications, killed some enemy soldiers, blew up a few gun positions, and demoralized some of the defenders, but it did not come even close to the kind of battle-winning "pulverization" that Collins had requested. The bomb strikes were just not coordinated well enough, nor were they accurate enough (some medium bombers even dropped their loads *behind* the American lines). In the final analysis, the bombing did more good than harm, but it was nowhere near the kind of decisive punch Collins and Quesada had envisioned.[26]

All of this meant that the ground troops experienced a major fight in attempting to puncture the enemy defensive line. All three divisions encountered serious resistance, and gains were minimal on June 22 and June 23. In the west, the 9th Division tried to cut Cap-de-la-Hague, a finger of land that jutted into the sea west of Cherbourg. The division fought methodically against Germans who were dug into high ground. "It was necessary to reduce these prepared positions one-by-one," the division historian wrote, "and the day's battles followed a pattern: meeting strongpoint, reducing by artillery and tank-destroyer fire, assault and then on to the next emplacement."[27]

Some units, like twenty-year-old Private First Class Dominic Dilberto's L Company, 39th Infantry, found evidence of damage inflicted by the air raids. As his company cautiously advanced, they found several dead Germans. "Their bodies were bloated, black and emitted a sickening stench. This area was dotted with huge coastal gun emplacements. In one such pillbox emplacement we found a dazed German officer just sitting there waiting for us. He was our first prisoner."[28]

Dilberto and his comrades were lucky. Most of the 9th Division's opposition was tougher. Cleverly placed machine guns, antitank guns, mortars, and entrenchments held up the advance all along the 9th Division's front. Snipers were a problem too. Private First Class Lloyd Guerin, like so many others in the division, joined in Normandy as a replacement. He was thirty-four, a rather advanced age to be an infantryman. In fact, he had volunteered for the paratroopers but had been rejected because of his age. During the fighting on June 22–23, his squad leader picked Guerin and another man to deal with a sniper that a tank had flushed out: "Hey, you two, go up and get that sniper."

Guerin was rather bewildered by the assignment. "He might as well have told me to build a stairway to Heaven. I didn't know what to do. We crawled about 100 yards up a ditch. I looked back and the other guy wasn't there. When I got a little further the sniper stopped firing. I don't know what happened—either someone shot him or he left. But the tankers said it was OK so I went back. The squad leader asked me what happened and I said, 'Job completed,' or something like that." It took the division three days of fighting to dislodge the enemy from their high ground and pierce the defensive line.[29]

The story was much the same in the center, where the 79th Division continued its previous advance along the N-13 highway. German defenses were formidable. Lee McCardell, a correspondent for the *Baltimore Sun*, was with the 79th Division as it slowly advanced. "So-called pillboxes in the first line of German defenses . . . were actually inland forts with steel and reinforced concrete walls four or five feet thick. Built into the hills of Normandy so their parapets were level with surrounding ground, the forts were heavily armed with mortars, machine guns, and 88-mm. rifles. Around the forts lay a pattern of smaller defenses, pillboxes, redoubts, rifle pits, sunken . . . mortar emplacements permitting 360-degree traverse, observation posts and other works. Approaches were further protected by mine fields, barbed wire and anti-tank ditches at least 20 feet wide at the top and 20 feet deep. Each strongpoint was connected to the other . . . by a system of deep, camouflaged trenches and underground tunnels."

The commanding officer of the 79th Division, Major General Ira Wyche, lined up his three regiments and sent them forward to penetrate these stout defenses. Artillery supported the advance but could only do so much good. The shells disrupted German communications, exploded some of the mines, disrupted the barbed wire, and blasted some of the smaller positions. However, the larger forts were impervious to even large-caliber shells.

Lieutenant Byron Nelson, an artillery forward observer, found this out firsthand. He and the other two members of his observation team found a favorable spot and began calling in fire. "We had an . . . Observation Post . . . on the high ground above the city and harbor with a great panoramic view. There were four large concrete rounded 'pill boxes' . . . heavily armed and manned, that were giving our infantry a bad time. We brought fire on them with our 155's. The . . . projectiles literally bounced off the pill boxes."

Wyche's commanders had to attack these heavy fortifications with small groups of infantry or engineers, supported by tanks and mortars. In deadly, terrifying fashion they crawled close enough to the pillboxes to kill the defenders with grenades, satchel charges, or flamethrowers. The division's 313th Infantry attacked on the left and the 315th Infantry on the right. Within a day or so they began making headway, and this allowed some of the pillboxes to be attacked from the rear. By the evening of June 24, the 314th Infantry, which had carried the weight of the center of the attack, had made it to within sight of Fort du Roule, a formidable concrete structure built on a ridge that commanded access to the southern entrances to Cherbourg.

The survivors of this bloody advance were filthy and exhausted, "with beards . . . like burlesque tramps," McCardell commented. They had thrown away anything nonessential. The typical soldier "hadn't had his shoes off for a week. His feet were killing him. He would have given ten bucks for a clean pair of 10-cent socks. Aside from canned rations and hand grenades which filled all the pockets of his grimy, mud-stained fatigues, he carried only what he wore plus his canteen, a shovel, an ammunition belt, an extra bandolier, a knife, bayonet and his rifle."[30]

Of Collins's three attacking divisions, the 4th Division had the toughest time. While the 22nd Infantry pushed northeast, to reach the sea and seal off the tip of the peninsula at Cape Levy, the 12th and 8th Regiments pushed northwest toward Cherbourg, straight through wooded, hedgerow-infested terrain. The 22nd Infantry spent most of June 22 trying to keep from being surrounded. The 8th, still commanded by Colonel Van Fleet, got almost nowhere. Many soldiers from the unit got caught in a devastating artillery barrage in the Bois de Roudou. Tree bursts tore many of these men apart. In one day, the 8th lost thirty-one killed and ninety-two wounded.

When the 8th renewed its attack on June 23 and 24, it focused on capturing La Glacerie, home to the kind of strong emplacements so typical of von Schlieben's ring of defenses. Lieutenant John Ausland suggested calling in fighter support. "As a result, on June 24 twelve P-47s dropped twenty-four hundred pound bombs, all but one of which hit the target area. Nevertheless, the 2d Battalion attack failed, with heavy casualties. The Germans simply came out of their dugouts after the bombardment was over and started firing. Later in the day, with the help of tanks, the battalion captured the stronghold and took over sixty prisoners. While some of the guns had been destroyed by the air bombardment, most of them were intact."

That victory cost the lives of several 8th Infantry soldiers. The sight of their bodies deeply affected Lieutenant Colonel Carlton McNeely, commander of the 2nd Battalion. One of his subordinates, Captain George Mabry, found him sitting behind a tree, with his head in his hands, crying. Mabry sat down next to McNeely and asked him what was wrong.

"George, it tears me up to see so many of our fine young men being killed like that."

Mabry agreed, but for the good of those who were still alive he urged McNeely to set his feelings aside. "Colonel McNeely, only by the grace of God there lie you and I. It's tough to steel one's feelings in a situation like this, but you must establish some attitude that would preclude [death] . . . from affecting you so much. My attitude is, you German SOBs, you killed my buddies, I'm going to get ten more of you for that. We cannot afford to let the death of our friends affect us so much because it will affect our ability to fight" and lead.

McNeely knew that Mabry was right. Awful as it seemed, he had to put the dead out of his mind and focus on his job. "After talking a while he regained his composure," Mabry recalled.

To the east, the 12th, making the main effort, found itself fighting in hedgerow country similar to the southern Cotentin. "You couldn't see more than 50 yards," Lieutenant Ralph Hampton, a forward observer, recalled. "You had to use a map to know where you were. The map had lines on it for each hedgerow—looked like a spider's web. Those hedgerow battles were very severe, with 'screaming meemies' and poor observation."

As was true elsewhere, it was difficult for tanks and infantry to coordinate in this thick terrain. Well-concealed enemy antitank guns or *Panzerfaust* grenadiers often blew up Sherman tanks before the crews knew what hit them. During the attack, Clarence McNamee, a tank crewman in B Company, 70th Tank Battalion, saw one of his company's tanks take a direct hit from an antitank gun. In the wake of the explosion, one of McNamee's best friends jumped out of the stricken tank. "He ran around behind it, which was the wrong thing to do, because if they hit it once, they sure as hell could hit it again, plus the risk of gasoline exploding and burning." McNamee heard the supersonic, cracking sound of the German antitank gun. "An 88 [shell] came in on the tracks and took his head right off his shoulders. It was sickening. While killing became second nature, this was a friend. He had played accordion for us just the night before."

The 12th gained only a couple hundred yards on the first day but got about halfway to one of its key objectives, Tourlaville, on the second day. Vulnerable though they were, this slow advance would have been scarcely possible without the help of tanks. Lieutenant Paul Massa, another forward observer, was still operating with the 12th Infantry's 1st Battalion. He had been with this unit ever since D-Day. On the morning of June 23, he and his team were advancing about hundred feet behind armor from the 70th Tank Battalion. "We had tank support . . . that was great. The tanks sprayed the trees and hedgerows with their machine guns and the battalion really began to move. Suddenly there was an explosion. At first, I thought that the tank's 75mm gun had fired. The tank stopped, his motor roared like it had slipped out of gear, and then the lid of the turret flew open and the crew scrambled out. All except one man. He was trapped inside, and I listened to his screams as he burned to death. After that, the other tanks pulled out. Otherwise, they would have been sitting ducks for the German gun that got the first tank."

Somehow the German gun was knocked out, the advance continued, and the day wore on. German mortar and artillery shells hindered the advance. Massa got separated from his radioman, Corporal Fishman. As Massa was lying in the ditch, hoping the shelling would stop, he found a newspaper clipping. He picked it up and read it. There was a picture of an attractive young woman and her daughter working in a garden. "The caption told how Mrs. Natalie Pugash and her daughter of Tampa, Florida, were making a victory garden while First Lieutenant Joseph Pugash was serving overseas with the Army."

Massa's mood brightened. Pugash was a good friend of his from Artillery Officer Candidate School. He folded the clipping and put it in his pocket. As he did so, he wondered how Pugash could have lost this prized piece of home. "I promised myself that I would see to it that he got it back."

Just then, Fishman came crawling along the ditch. Without any preamble, Fishman said, "Lieutenant Pugash is dead. His body is on the other side of this hedgerow."

Massa felt like he had been hit over the head by a sledgehammer. "If

Fishman had said that my own brother was dead, it would not have hit me any harder. By this time, I had seen too many dead friends. I couldn't bring myself to go look at Joe's body." Massa almost felt as if he would lose his mind.

The push for Tourlaville resumed. For Massa and the other soldiers, the whole experience was a blur. "I prayed a lot in Normandy. I didn't pray that my life would be saved, because there were times that I was sure that I was going to be killed. I prayed that my soul would go to heaven."

The fighting was so bitter, so terrifying, so methodical, that, for some, crippling wounds seemed like a good alternative to staying in the combat zone. "I remember one young fellow holding up the bloody stump of his left arm and saying, 'Hey, Lieutenant, this ought to be worth a drink in any bar, don't you think?' And I agreed with him."

Later in the day, Massa encountered an NCO buddy who had lost his right leg below the knee. The sergeant was lying on his back while a medic applied a tourniquet. Massa sat down next to him, gave him a cigarette, and commented, "Tough luck, old buddy."

He said, "No, Lieutenant, I should say 'tough luck' to you. I got my ticket to the States now. You've got to stay in this hell until you get killed or wounded." In his heart, Massa knew the sergeant was right.

The 12th Infantry's 3rd Battalion finally captured Tourlaville on the evening of June 24. From the streets of Tourlaville the soldiers could actually look down on Cherbourg. In three days they had captured 800 Germans and killed hundreds more. The advance had been a bloodbath, though.

Lieutenant Massa walked away from the other survivors and surveyed the route of advance. The lanes, fields, hills, and hedgerows were the very embodiment of the human tragedy and waste of war. "Fragments from large-caliber shells mutilated and mangled human bodies. Dead men had huge holes through their bodies, and arms or legs torn off. One man was in a sitting position, with the top of his head neatly removed. The inside of his head was empty, as though everything had been scooped out."

Three miles away, in the battered, confined subterranean shelter in southern Cherbourg that comprised General von Schlieben's CP, the general was writing in his diary: "Concentrated enemy fire and bombing attacks have split the front. Numerous batteries have been put out of action or have worn out. Combat efficiency has fallen off considerably. The troops squeezed into a small area will hardly be able to withstand an attack on the 25th."

Just outside the city, at VII Corps headquarters, General Collins sensed the same thing. His three divisions, over the course of three days of terrible fighting, had overwhelmed von Schlieben's defensive ring around Cherbourg. The Americans were literally at the edges of the city now. They had the Germans penned in from every side. Collins knew they could not take much more of this. The moment for the final assault on Cherbourg had, at long last, arrived.[31]

Lightning Joe kept his troops on the move. He wanted to put maximum pressure on the disorganized, crumbling German defenses. Instead of one continuous line of defenses, he was now facing isolated pockets of enemy soldiers who were holed up in buildings, cellars, and well-built concrete fortifications along the coast or the southern approaches to Cherbourg. Collins ordered all three of his divisions to push into the city's suburbs on June 25.

The approach to the western environs of Cherbourg was dominated by Equeurdreville, an imposing-looking concrete fortress. The fort was built on high ground and surrounded by a dry moat with only one, mined bridge. The road leading to Equeurdreville was also mined. Engineers dealt with the mines. Tank destroyers, artillery, mortars, and P-47s blasted the place for much of the morning on June 25. After this, Major Woodrow Bailey's 2nd Battalion, 47th Infantry, assaulted the fortress in the early afternoon. Bailey's mortar men did terrific work. They dropped their shells on the fort just as the riflemen and machine gunners were nearing the walls. This enabled them to get across the bridge, chuck grenades over the walls, and get into the fortress. As it turned out, the Germans were primarily using Equeurdreville as an artillery OP. In fifteen minutes the American infantrymen cleared the place and captured eighty-nine prisoners. This helped open the way into Cherbourg. From here, the 9th Division fought street by street, clearing out stubborn defenders, snipers, artillery positions, and the like. In one day, they captured over 1,000 enemy soldiers. They also besieged the naval arsenal, where some of the most die-hard Germans were holding out.[32]

In the east, the 12th Infantry of the 4th Division fought along a direct line from Tourlaville to the eastern suburbs of Cherbourg. This forced them to deal with stubborn artillery and antiaircraft positions, many of which were situated along cliffs overlooking the sea or the city. Major Gerden Johnson's 1st Battalion was in the lead. At one point, they came upon an enemy hilltop position. Johnson's troops could only see the top of the grassy hill. The day was warm and sunny. The grass blew gently in the breeze. "From behind the hill two white flags suddenly appeared," Johnson later wrote. The white flags, combined with the warm day, made the whole scene seem peaceful, almost serene. "The leading companies continued to advance without firing, Co. B on the left disappearing down into [a] wooded draw. Suddenly Co. B came under a barrage of mortar and 20 mm anti-aircraft fire from the hill where the white flags were observed to still be waving. The barrage lasted for approximately fifteen minutes."

Major Johnson's command group was right behind B Company. He and his officers took the brunt of the fire. Lieutenant Ralph Hampton, the forward observer, was with them. "The enemy turned round their antiaircraft guns and wiped out the whole . . . battalion headquarters except the colonel, S-4, and myself."

Johnson managed to get up and find several Shermans (from the 70th Tank Battalion) that were supporting his battalion. He told the tank commanders to open up on the hill with everything in their arsenal. "After a hot fire fight which lasted until 1330, the garrison surrendered." In view of what had happened, the Americans showed amazing restraint. They took 400 enemy soldiers prisoner. "The 'hill' turned out to be an underground fortification and contained a hospital and an officer's club, as well as three eight inch guns, several 88mm guns, 20mm anti-aircraft guns and mortars."

Like the 9th Division in the west, the 4th Division now forced its way into the eastern outskirts of Cherbourg, fighting close-up, personal battles with enemy stalwarts, many of whom were holed up in bunkers equipped with antiaircraft or antitank guns.[33]

On June 25, the most dramatic fighting of all was going on in the center, where the 79th Division was attempting to take Fort du Roule. The place looked like something out of the medieval period. The French had built it before the war and the Germans had improved upon it. Fort du Roule was situated on the highest hill immediately to the south of Cherbourg. The fort had solid four-foot-thick concrete walls. Its lower levels featured heavy guns that pointed seaward. The upper terraces bristled with blockhouses, pillboxes, and portholes that housed all manner of automatic weapons and mortars. The landward side of Fort du Roule was built on a sheer drop and surrounded by an antitank ditch, so there was no easy way to approach the fort.

At 0800 on June 25, P-47s attacked Fort du Roule. One after the other they dived and unloosed their bombs, most of which overshot the mark. The air strike did almost nothing to soften up the fort. Artillery helped a bit more by battering the walls and stunning many of the defenders, but as always, the real job of taking the place fell to the infantry, in this case the 2nd and 3rd Battalions of the 314th Infantry Regiment.

The soldiers of these two battalions spent the entire day fighting for Fort du Roule. The seemingly simple act of making it to the fort's walls was difficult. Many of the Americans were pinned down by withering small-arms fire in the draws and antitank ditches that protected the southern approaches. With the help of well-coordinated artillery support, the Americans fought their way to the walls. But here the Germans shot at them from close range. They would fire from portholes or straight down from positions atop the walls. The Americans had to deal with not only this fire but also artillery fire coming from concealed German positions elsewhere in Cherbourg. There was pretty much no time when the GIs were shielded from fire. The terrain was difficult because the ground was steeply sloped and open. The Americans could do little else besides hunt for enemy strong points and eliminate them with demolitions, grenades, bangalore torpedoes, or aimed fire.

Two acts of incredible bravery helped the 314th Infantry prevail at Fort du Roule. Corporal John Kelly's platoon in E Company was pinned down on a slope by accurate machine-gun fire originating from a pillbox in the upper section of the fort. Kelly grabbed a pole charge (roughly ten feet long and containing fifteen pounds of TNT) and inched his way up the slope, all the while under heavy small-arms fire. Bullets were kicking up dust and chunks of ground all around him. In spite of this, Kelly placed the charge at the base of the strong point, right below the pillbox. The charge exploded, but it was ineffective. The fire continued.

In crawling through the fire this first time, Kelly probably had to muster more courage and resolve than most people ever demonstrate in a lifetime. But he went back, got another pole charge, and did it all over again. This explosion did some damage but did not finish off the enemy. So Kelly went back a third time. Following the explosion, he hurled numerous grenades into the pillbox. The surviving enemy soldiers had had enough. They surrendered and the advance into Fort du Roule proceeded.

On the other end of the fort, First Lieutenant Carlos Ogden, who had just taken over K Company from his wounded commander, was pinned down by terrifying machine-gun and 88 fire. He and his men were lying along the slopes, trying to make small targets. Ogden knew this could not continue for any length of time. If he and his men kept on this way, they would all be hit. They were sitting ducks. "I knew we were going to get killed if we stayed down there," Ogden later said. So, he armed himself to the teeth, with an M-1 rifle, a modified rifle grenade launcher, plus plenty of ammo. He stood up and, all alone, advanced up the slope, toward the fort's walls. The 88 and machine-gun fire intensified. A machine-gun bullet slammed into his head but somehow did not kill him. Blood was streaming down his face. But Ogden kept going until he was within range of the German 88. He pointed the grenade launcher and fired, destroying the 88. Now he turned his attention to the machine-gun nests, firing everything at his disposal at them. The enemy fire slackened. Ogden turned around, went back down the slope, got his company, and led it into the fort.

These two acts of heroism helped the Americans blast their way into the fort. They also helped persuade many of the Germans to surrender. The 314th spent the rest of the afternoon, and part of the evening, clearing out the upper part of Fort du Roule, section by section, position by position. They had the place under control by 2200 on June 25. They flamed out the rest of the defenders on the lower level the next day. Both Kelly and Ogden won the Medal of Honor.[34]

The push into Cherbourg on June 25 would have been even tougher for the ground troops if not for the assistance of the U.S. Navy. A day or two before, even as Collins's VII Corps troops were approaching the city, General Bradley met with Admiral Kirk. "Unwilling to waste time on a siege . . . I asked Kirk to attack the fort's coastal guns from the sea. Had Kirk told me to go soak my head in the Channel, I could not have held his prudence against him. For Cherbourg had been porcupined with guns that outranged and outnumbered those of his biggest ships."

Kirk, of course, knew this and had no great wish to expose his ships to such dangers. He knew he might lose many of them. "Is it worth that much to you?" he asked Bradley.

"It is. We must take Cherbourg just as soon as we can," Bradley replied.[35]

Hearing this, Kirk readily agreed. He assembled a bombardment fleet, placed it under the command of Admiral Deyo, and set his ships in motion from their English ports on June 25. Deyo divided his fleet into two groups. Group 1 consisted of the USS *Nevada*, *Tuscaloosa*, and *Quincy* and the HMS *Glasgow* and *Enterprise*, screened by six destroyers. Group 2 had two battleships, the USS *Texas* and *Arkansas*, plus five more destroyers. Minesweepers patrolled the waters ahead of the bombardment ships, and several planes flew antisubmarine patrols. By noon, the fleet was in place just outside of Cherbourg Harbor.

This was perhaps the most unusual bombardment the U.S. Navy unleashed in the European theater. Most of the time when the Navy lent fire support, it shot at defended coastlines or ahead of American troops. If navy gunners fired too long, they might miss the target, but otherwise there was no harm done. Firing short was normally the biggest danger; short rounds meant friendly casualties. But this time, American troops would actually be advancing *toward* their own navy. Long rounds would hit American soldiers. Short rounds would merely upset Channel water. So, in this rare case, the Navy preferred to fire short rather than long. "This situation posed an interesting gunnery problem," Lieutenant Massa, the forward observer, said. "The navy guns would be firing in the direction of our troops. A mistake in range would be a catastrophe."

For that reason, Collins made sure that the Navy was very conservative in its bombardment. Only confirmed targets, radioed to the ships by observers like Massa, could be shot at in Cherbourg. Such fire missions were rare. "As it turned out, there was never an opportunity to direct naval gunfire on [the city itself]. Units from the three American divisions . . . were entering the city at various points, faster than I could plot their positions on my map."[36]

On this day, the Navy shot most of its ordnance at German coastal batteries outside the city. In so doing, the fleet kept these guns from concentrating on the soldiers who were pouring into the city. Water Tender Second

Class Bernard Hydo was aboard the USS *Rodman*, a destroyer that drew the unenviable duty of acting as a decoy to flush out the location of German gun positions. His battle station was midship damage control, topside, on the superstructure between two smokestacks. He wore a headset and had access to a phone, in order to communicate with the bridge. As the action unfolded, he recorded everything in his diary: "The ship is running at top speed now (about 34 knots) moving in close to draw plenty of fire. We are zig-zagging crazily, laying a smoke screen at maximum speed. Shells are bursting all around us and luckily, mostly in our wake. Other destroyers have now moved in near us and are also zig-zagging, and each laying a heavy smoke screen. Each time the Germans [fire] at the Rodman, their gun flashes [give] away their hidden positions which was the purpose of the maneuver."[37]

The gun duel began. Several ships got into a fight with German gunners at Querqueville, some three miles west of Cherbourg. The mighty guns hurled salvos at one another. Aboard the heavy cruiser *Quincy*, in his sky control battle station, high above the deck, Lieutenant James Blackburn, a naval academy graduate and gunnery officer, excitedly spotted targets for his gunners. He could see the coast and make out enemy shells headed in the ship's general vicinity. "The next ten or twelve salvos were at us. We knew it, but there were so many shore batteries blazing away that it was impossible to tell who was doing the shooting. Our five-inch opened up at one of them and we kept a few 5-inch smoke shells between ourselves and the shore."

Minute by minute, the enemy shots were getting more accurate. "They started straddling us. The shells whistling overhead made everybody hug the deck. Shells were falling ahead, astern, and on both sides. The 20mm on the forecastle [was] deluged with spray and the stern 40mm quad mount got wet. There were between six and eight hits less than fifty yards from the ship. Quite a lot of hot shrapnel fell about the ship."

A destroyer sailed past and disgorged smoke, helping obscure the *Quincy* for a few moments. "We were performing exaggerated maneuvers at 25 knots and blasting away with the main battery." With Blackburn spotting, his gunners shot about 70 five-inch shells "where I thought they would be the most helpful. We were scared and feeling helpless. So many places were shooting, that target identification was difficult to establish." Spotter planes were having trouble seeing the enemy guns, and shore party observers "could not tell our burst from the army artillery." In the midst of this melee, Lieutenant Blackburn marveled at the fact this his sailors "were munching away on sandwiches and drinking coffee."

For about three hours the *Quincy* and the other ships dueled with Querqueville and its environs. The engagement was inconclusive. The Allied ships scored several hits on various batteries while sustaining almost no damage to themselves. There were plenty of close calls, though. The *Nevada* dodged twenty-five near misses from large-caliber shells. "We were straddled several times . . . and one salvo was so close that the skipper ordered full speed ahead and a hard turn to starboard," Ross Olsen, an electrician's mate on the ship, recalled. "The next salvo from the beach was right on target as it hit astern and right in our wake." A couple enemy shells even whizzed right through her superstructure without hitting anything. In the end, the battleship suffered no casualties and only a few nicks from shrapnel.[38]

Six miles east of Cherbourg, Group 2 inflicted more damage but, in turn, suffered casualties. The target here was "Battery Hamburg," a cluster of casemated guns located on a hill near Cape Levy, which flanked the city. There were all manner of guns at Battery Hamburg, including 88s, antiaircraft guns, and eleven-inch guns manned by enemy naval personnel. The naval guns had a range of 40,000 yards, twice as much as the two American battleships, the *Texas* and *Arkansas*, assigned to bombard them.

In a chaotic battle that lasted more than two hours, the two sides fired at each other through clouds of smoke and dust. On the Allied side, the *Texas* was in the thick of the action. This venerable battleship, which had done such fine work supporting the Rangers at Pointe-du-Hoc, dueled with the enemy eleven-inch guns of Battery Hamburg. Aboard the *Texas*, Martin Somers, a *Saturday Evening Post* correspondent, stood on the bridge, right next to the skipper, Captain Charles Baker. "A destroyer begins to lay a smoke screen. The destroyer just ahead of us gets four near misses. Water spouts high around her. An 11-inch shell misses us by 300 yards, but the enemy's shooting improves rapidly. Four near misses . . . bracket us. We're hit below the water line on the port side twice, but the 6-inch shells bounce off the heavy armor." The shells ricocheted and exploded, sending geysers of water eighty feet high.

The *Texas* was firing back with its fourteen-inch guns. "The fierce blast of our own guns mingles with the explosion of near misses from the batteries." One of the American shells hit home, piercing the casemate of one of the enemy eleven-inch guns, destroying the gun, killing the crew. Captain Baker, meanwhile, was darting around the bridge, watching where the near misses hit, shouting evasion orders to the helmsman. For over half an hour Baker's hunches were perfect, but this soon changed. Winds blew smoke away from the *Texas*, exposing her to German spotters who could not have asked for a larger, juicier target.

At 1316, an enemy eleven-inch shell screamed in, skidded across the top of the conning tower, hit a supporting column of the pilothouse, and exploded. The men on the bridge took the brunt of the explosion. Somers was one of them. "Crash, shriek, and the sky has fallen, it seems. The enclosed bridge is suddenly dark, as glass, shrapnel and debris of all sorts fly around us. Clouds of yellow brown smoke obscure everything, and we simply do not know what has happened."

Captain Baker, a genteel Virginian and naval academy graduate, was unhurt. He shouted, "All hands below!" and supervised an evacuation from the bridge. He also made sure the gunners kept firing. Somers regained his senses and took stock of what had happened. "The forward half of the enclosed bridge deck beneath our feet was blown out and rolled back, so that it cut up and pinned down some of those who were forward near the wheel and other instruments. They were mowed down by shrapnel in addition to being mangled by the edge of our rolled back deck. Only those of us aft on the enclosed bridge escaped injury." The helmsman was dead, "his legs torn off as he stood at the wheel." He had bled to death quickly. Eleven other men were wounded.

The ship was hit again, but this time the German shell was a dud. The shell "tore a hole through the portside above the water line, passed cleanly into the cabin of Warrant Officer M.A. Clark . . . the ship's clerk, where it came to rest. It never exploded, even during the last hour of action while our fourteen-inch guns were shaking the ship with their fire and the enemy was placing more of their shells near us."

As this went on, Somers went down to sick bay to check on the wounded. The seriously injured "had broken and torn legs and arms, causing great loss of blood. All were suffering from intense shock. Without transfusions they would not have had a chance to survive."

At 1501, the fleet disengaged and headed out to sea. The *Texas* had fired 206 shells from its main batteries and the *Arkansas* another 58 from its. The destroyers had hurled 552 five-inch shells at Battery Hamburg. One of the destroyers, the USS *O'Brien*, had absorbed a direct hit that killed thirteen men and wounded nineteen others.

On the heights that overlooked Cherbourg, General Collins stood, watching the whole spectacle. "It was a thrilling and . . . an awe-inspiring sight. I knew definitely then that Cherbourg was ours." The naval fire had not actually knocked out many of the German guns, but it had kept the crews busy, diverting them from dealing with the greatest threat—the enemy army behind them. Collins was so grateful for the Navy's courageous support that he wrote to Admiral Deyo and told him that the bombardment "did much to engage the enemy's fire while our troops stormed into Cherbourg from the rear."[39]

As Collins suspected, enemy resistance in Cherbourg was on the verge of collapse. On the evening of June 25, von Schlieben sent a message to Rommel reporting that "loss of the city is unavoidable. Is the destruction of the remaining troops necessary?" Rommel relayed Hitler's order to fight to the end. "You will continue to fight until the last cartridge in accordance with the order from the Fuehrer."

The next day, troops from the 39th Infantry, supported by tank destroyers, captured von Schlieben, his staff, and 800 others by blasting them out of their underground stronghold in southern Cherbourg. "The tank-destroyer's projectiles had caused so much dust and fumes . . . that the German soldiers, once finding that the white flag had been raised, began to pour out," Major General Manton Eddy, the 9th Division commander, wrote in his diary. "These Germans were in such a rush that they denied the General his wish for a more formal surrender. The avalanche of soldiers carried him and his party with it."

Von Schlieben and Eddy met and discussed terms. The German commander declined to order a general surrender of all German forces in the Cotentin. Truthfully, he did not have much choice, since he could not communicate with many of the isolated pockets of Germans in and around Cherbourg. But the fighting went on for another day as the Americans dealt with the last holdouts, particularly those holed up in the naval arsenal near the docks. This group did not surrender until 1000 on June 27, when the last organized resistance in Cherbourg finally came to an end (some Germans outside the city held on for a few more days).[40]

Lieutenant Byron Nelson, the forward observer in the 79th Division, now entered the town. He walked through the shattered streets of Cherbourg until he found a tavern called Emil Ludwigs, right on the beach. "I was with . . . General Green, 79th Assistant Division Commander, a Bird Colonel, and three Lt. Colonels. Don't ask me what I was doing in such exalted company; I . . . a lowly shave-tail, a ninety-day wonder. There was a picture of Hitler hanging on the wall. The Colonel took it down, threw it on the floor and ground his heel, 'right in Der Fuhrer's face.'" Nelson had no illusions about who had won this battle for the United States. "The real hero of the Battle of Cherbourg . . . was the lowly Infantryman."[41]

The Americans captured nearly 20,000 prisoners. The enemy POWs walked along the streets of Cherbourg, sometimes four abreast, hands held high or on their heads. Sergeant Hank Henderson, a medic in the 4th Infantry Division, watched them go by. "One little German corporal stepped out of ranks and said, 'I would like to see that automatic artillery in action before you shoot me.' He thought it was automatic because our batteries fired [so rapidly]." Henderson was almost speechless. He told the German soldier that the artillery was not automatic; nor would he be shot.[42]

The capture of Cherbourg eliminated the German presence in the Cotentin, but the victory was, at best, incomplete, at worst, flawed. Bradley's greatest reason for investing so much of his combat power in taking Cherbourg was the capture of the port facilities. No sooner had the Americans gained control of the city than they realized that the Germans had demolished the port of Cherbourg, thoroughly and professionally. Colonel Alvin Viney, an engineer, took one look at the harbor facilities and knew it would take a long time to repair them. He reported to his superiors: "The demolition of the port of Cherbourg is a masterful job, beyond a doubt the most complete, intensive, and best planned demolition in history."

The Germans had strewn the harbor with hundreds of mines, of all types, but that was only the beginning of their handiwork. For the entire month of June their naval demolition teams had been busy. They blew up the electrical control system and the heating plant. They filled the docks with 20,000 cubic yards of masonry. They blocked the entrance to the harbor with two sunken ships. They destroyed every quay and every crane. They opened up the harbor's breakwater barrier so that seawater could flow freely everywhere.

The Americans had hoped to have Cherbourg operating in three days. Instead, it took nearly three months. When American engineers and port battalions arrived, they had an enormous job on their hands. It took them over two weeks just to clear the mines. The port could not take any cargo until July 16. It took the Americans until late September to clear all the obstructions out of the harbor and get Cherbourg into full operating status. Before that time, the Americans could only off-load small amounts of supplies (close to 4,000 tons by the end of July). In that time, Cherbourg barely had one-quarter of the capacity of Omaha beach. Only the railroad and petroleum off-loading facilities could be repaired and put into operation quickly. It is fair to say that Cherbourg contributed very little to the Allied supplied effort during the Battle of Normandy. The food, ammunition, and other supplies that kept the average American, Canadian, or British soldier going mostly came from the invasion beaches.[43]

So June came to an end and with it the exploitation phase of the Normandy invasion. It was at this point that the battle transformed from an amphibious assault to a bona fide land campaign. The Allies were ashore; they would not be thrown back into the sea. They had captured major slices of Normandy but had not achieved any semblance of a mobile advance deep into France, and that was, in essence, the point of this whole operation. Ike's directive, after all, was to "enter the continent of Europe and . . . undertake operations aimed at the heart of Germany and the destruction of her armed forces." As June ended, the Allies were nowhere near the fulfillment of that goal. Instead, the battle was stalemating and this was Germany's best remaining hope—to pen the Allied armies into Normandy and bleed them to death. The Americans had already suffered over 37,000 casualties; the British and Canadians, nearly 25,000. The Germans had lost over 80,000 men, but the enemy was fighting harder than ever. Some of the Allied commanders were worried that they had blundered into a static situation reminiscent of World War I.[44] In sum, the strategic situation in the west was still in the balance at the end of June. Only an Allied breakout in Normandy, led by the U.S. Army, could tilt that balance in favor of the Allies.

PART II

JULY

CHAPTER SIX

THE HEDGEROW MAZE

From Portbail on the western coast of the Cotentin all the way to Merville, northeast of Caen, Allied and German soldiers faced each other along a stalemated 130-mile-long series of holes, OPs, and trenches. The Germans wondered how long they could hold this line. The Allies wondered if they could ever break this deadlock.

By early July, there was plenty of fighting and dying going on along this front but precious little movement. The British and Canadians were still stuck in the environs of Caen. The Americans, in spite of the liberation of Cherbourg and the Cotentin, were stymied in the thick bocage terrain that shrouded Normandy from Caumont to Montgardon. The British and Canadians were fighting as hard as they could, but they were dealing with the best and toughest German resistance, not to mention the challenges of combat in an urban landscape.

Several factors combined to stalemate the Americans. The weather was constantly wet and rainy. Day after day, storms blew in from the sea, across the Cotentin Peninsula and all along the American lines, pelting the soldiers, making them wet, miserable, and muddy. More important, the bad weather reduced the number of sorties Allied planes could fly. This allowed the Germans to reinforce and resupply their front-line positions. The American supply situation still was not very good. In the troubled aftermath of the Channel storm, Bradley could not promise his commanders adequate amounts of ammunition, especially artillery shells. Nor had he been able to build his army up to top strength. The arrival of reinforcing divisions, like the 83rd, had been delayed by the storm.

More than any of this, the terrain, and the enemy's clever use of it, stopped the Americans cold. The typical Norman hedgerow was centuries

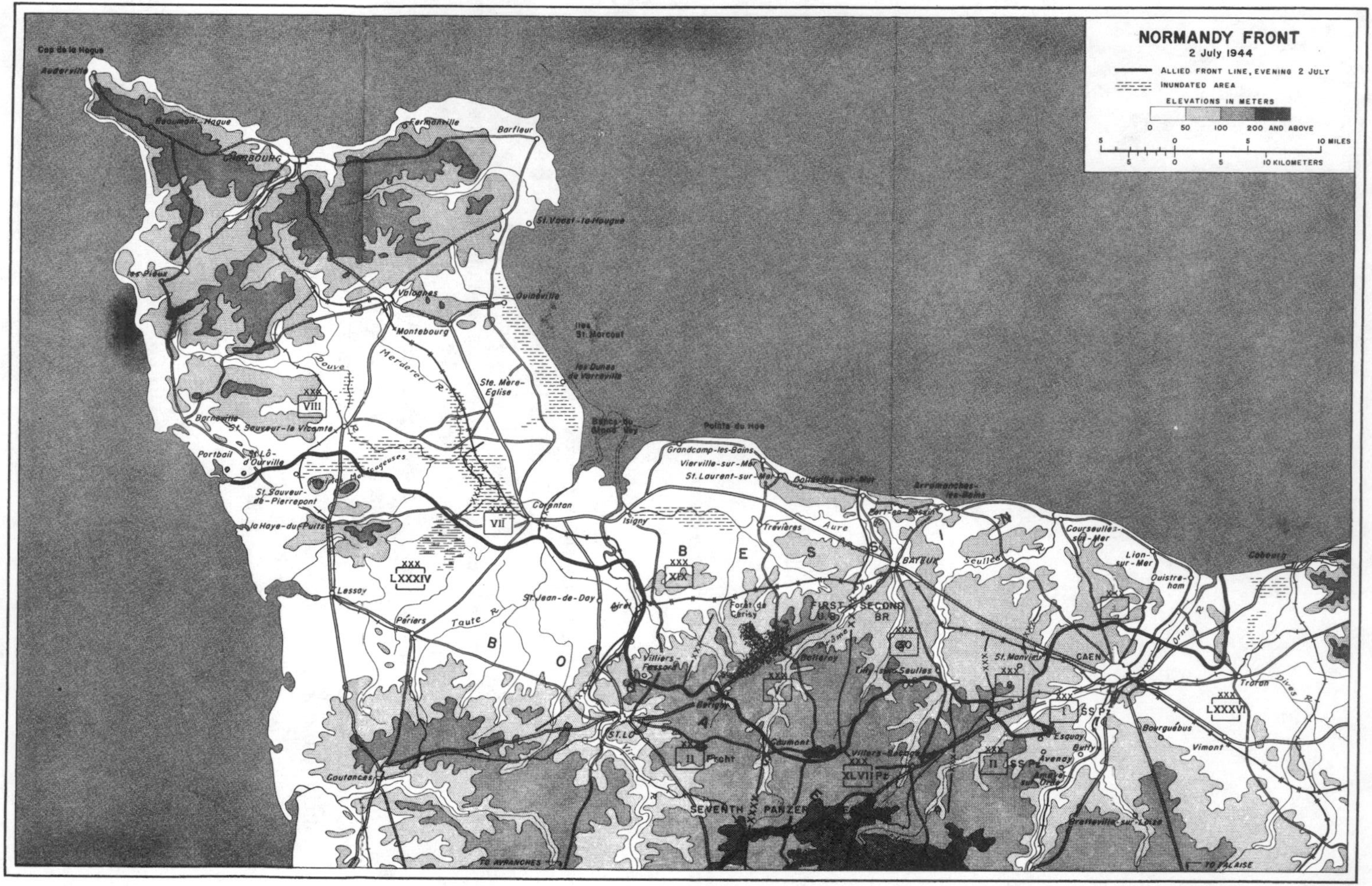
NORMANDY FRONT
2 July 1944
ALLIED FRONT LINE, EVENING 2 JULY
INUNDATED AREA
ELEVATIONS IN METERS
0 50 100 200 AND ABOVE
10 MILES
10 KILOMETERS
Cap de la Hague
Auderville
Beaumont-Hague
CHERBOURG
Fermanville
Barfleur
St. Vaast-la-Hougue
les Pieux
Valognes
Quinéville
Iles St. Marcouf
Montebourg
les Dunes de Varreville
Ste. Mère-Eglise
Douve
Merderet R.
VIII
Barneville
St. Sauveur-le Vicomte
Portbail
St. Lô-d'Ourville
St. Sauveur-de-Pierrepont
la Haye-du-Puits
VII
Carentan
Isigny
Pointe du Hoe
Grandcamp-les-Bains
Vierville-sur-Mer
St. Laurent-sur-Mer
Arromanches-les-Bains
Trévières
Aure
BAYEUX
Seulles
Courseulles-sur-Mer
Lion-sur-Mer
Ouistre-ham
Cabourg
LXXXIV
Lessay
Périers
Taute R.
St. Jean-de-Day
Airel
XIX
Forêt de Cerisy
FIRST U.S.
SECOND BR
Villiers-Fossard
Tilly-sur-Seulles
St. Manvieu
CAEN
Orne R.
Troarn
Dives R.
LXXXVI
Bourguébus
Vimont
Esquay
Avenay
Bully
ST. LÔ
Vire
II
Caumont
Villers-Bocage
XLVII Pz
II SS Pz
I SS Pz
Coutances
SEVENTH
PANZER
Bretteville-sur-Laize
TO AVRANCHES
TO FALAISE

MAP II

old and proved to be a formidable defensive weapon. As far back as Roman times, Norman farmers had used the hedgerows as earthen boundaries. "They varied in height," Don Foye, a scout in the 357th Infantry, said, "but the dirt itself may be 12 feet, 10 feet high. Then in that they planted some kind of vegetation that grew into short trees. The tree roots went down the whole 10 or 12 feet, so that was not a mound of dirt anymore, it was solid roots. You couldn't shoot through it. And every 300 feet there was another one. The roads would be lower than the fields on either side of them, and on either side of any road . . . was this enormous 12-foot hedgerow. On top of that there might be another 10 feet of [vegetation] growth. Trees, or thorny things you couldn't crawl through. You couldn't see anywhere."[1]

The Germans could not have asked for terrain better suited to their objective of stalemating the Allies. They made resourceful, and clever, use of the hedgerows. They constructed their defenses in successive belts. The forward lines consisted of interconnected, mutually supporting fields manned by infantrymen who were dug into the hedgerows themselves. The main forces were dug in behind these front outposts, in a belt of successive hedgerows that bristled with machine guns, mortars, rifle pits, and artillery positions, supported by tanks or self-propelled guns.

The enemy defended a typical field in the following manner: They dug heavy machine guns into each corner of the hedgerow that bordered the field. These machine guns could crisscross their fire and cover most of the field. In between these two heavy guns, they placed riflemen, burp gunners, and light-machine-gun teams who only added to the volume of fire. If there were hedgerows that bordered either flank of the field, they dug light-machine-gun teams in there, too. Once these small arms had pinned down American attackers, the Germans called in artillery and mortar fire, which was normally quite accurate because German observers had presighted the entire field. German soldiers with handheld *Panzerfaust* antitank weapons lay in deep fighting holes in or along the forward hedgerows. If American tanks punched through the hedgerows or rolled through the small openings that led into each field, the *Panzerfaust* soldiers hit them at close range. Booby traps and mines, sown into the vegetation at the top of the hedgerow or in ditches along them, only added to the dangers.

Nor were the Americans prepared for the hedgerows. As mentioned in a previous chapter, most of the pre-invasion training concentrated on getting ashore, not fighting in the bocage country. No one understood, or knew, the true nature of the hedgerows or what it would be like to fight in them. An army survey of 100 junior officers found that all of them were surprised by the realities of the hedgerows. Not one of the officers had any knowledge of the hedgerows before going into Normandy. One captain in the 83rd Division said that his unit's training had "not taken the hedgerows into consideration."[2]

The result was dreary stalemate along the American line by the end of June and the beginning of July. The troops dealt with all manner of hardships—inertia, weather, filth, boredom, and the constant danger of close proximity to the enemy. Life at the front was a constant struggle for survival. Enemy observers were all over the place, well concealed in the confining hedgerows or the steeples of small-town churches. They called down mortar and artillery fire on anyone who moved on the American side of the line.

Charles Cawthon, now a major and the executive officer of the 2nd Battalion, 116th Infantry, 29th Division, especially hated German mortar fire. "Mortars . . . were particularly dreaded because the shells approached with a whisper, in contrast to the warning banshee screech of incoming artillery." One clear, warm day he saw a youthful battalion runner get killed by a lone mortar shell. With great sadness in his heart Cawthon examined the body, "lifeless in the grass. He was slightly built and looked in death like a boy dressed in a soldier suit who, tired of playing at war, had fallen asleep in the meadow, face serene and hair stirring in the breeze." Seemingly out of nowhere, a graves registration team materialized. "The two-wheeled death cart came, pulled by its attendants who of a necessity appeared ghoulish, and took him away. Thus casually did death arrive and life depart."[3]

The enemy ordnance was a danger, night and day, round-the-clock. Any place that was within range could be a target. The American combat soldiers lived with this gnawing uncertainty, and it ate away at their morale, not to mention their sanity. Lieutenant William Maher was a platoon leader in the 330th Infantry of the 83rd Infantry Division. In late June, his unit relieved troopers from the 101st Airborne in their front-line outposts a mile south of Carentan. To Maher, each day seemed to last an eternity. The tension and stress of mortal danger, combined with the responsibility of command, quickly pushed him to the breaking point. "There is only one word which will amply describe this experience, and that is just plain hell," he wrote to his parents. The living conditions were awful. "These damn holes are infested with rats and vermin of every kind."

Nighttime was the worst. Maher peered into the darkness imagining what kind of danger might be out there. Noises startled him. His mind played tricks on him. Under his breath, he asked God for help. "I prayed consistently and still do. No matter how skilled and experienced you are in this game, it all depends on the mercy of God in the final analysis. I have witnessed it and I know. I rarely sleep at night. I don't dare. At times, from lack of sleep and tension, where you're on the verge of exhaustion, you wonder if you can go on. During the black hours . . . a man thinks hard and long about life and war. It is hard to maintain the Christian attitude toward war—that is, to wage war without hatred—but if you want to survive you have to become violently mad, and after witnessing the experience of a few comrades, that becomes easy. I will never be at ease in the dark again."[4]

Added to the fear of imminent death was the misery of the elements. That meant dealing with wet weather and chilly nights. It also meant not being able to wash. The soldiers lived in filth, and the filth attracted pesky insects. John Aller, a mortar man in F Company, 331st Infantry, 83rd Infantry Division, especially hated the fleas that populated the Norman mud holes in which he and the other soldiers lived. "I always thought fleas lived on dogs, but in these hedgerows it just wasn't the case. They thrived on the gas-impregnated clothing and they were everywhere on our body, especially around our waists. We were issued flea powder to get rid of them but to no avail, they thrived on the powder. It would be many months before we would even get a shower."[5]

One officer in the 29th Division wrote that the days on the line "were hot and dusty, and the nights were cold, and . . . there was everywhere the sickly smell of dead men and animals. Puffed-up, swelling carcasses of cattle and horses, sprawled in ridiculously awkward shapes in the fields, and both our own and enemy dead lay against the hedgerows, sometimes for days before they could be removed. No man . . . who lived through those days will ever forget the smell."[6]

American soldiers dug deep holes, covered them with planks or sheets of metal, stayed under cover, and prayed to avoid a direct hit. This subterranean existence was stifling. They could not, of course, stay in the holes all the time. Whenever things got quiet, some men crawled out of their holes, soaked up sunshine, and tried to catch a breath of clean, Norman air. This could be very dangerous, though. Lieutenant Lyle Groundwater, a platoon leader in G Company, 359th, was in charge of a small slice of territory on the eastern edge of the 90th Division's zone at the base of the Cotentin. On a quiet, sunny day, when the war seemed far away, he and a fellow platoon leader were sitting, talking, in the grass of an open field. An enemy artillery shell landed almost right on top of them. Lieutenant Groundwater was blown six feet into the air before falling on his face. "I looked around, and there was an arm laying there right in front of my head." At first he thought the arm belonged to the other lieutenant. "I began to push myself backwards . . . on my stomach . . . and that darn hand came with me." Groundwater was stunned at the realization that the arm belonged to him. "My God . . . it must just be hanging by a shred," he thought.

The shock of this horrible wound blinded the lieutenant (psychiatrists call this hysterical blindness; it is a symptom of combat fatigue). Even though he could not see, Lieutenant Groundwater soon discovered that he had been hit in the windpipe. "I could hold my hand out in front of my face and feel blood squirt out of it." The other lieutenant was calling his name, but "I couldn't answer him because my throat had been shot, and I couldn't see him."

All at once, Groundwater heard the sound of bolt-action rifles. German soldiers were nearby. He started to throw a grenade in their direction but then thought better of it. The next thing he knew, the enemy soldiers were gone and a team of medics had moved him to a gravel road. He heard a doctor performing triage. He hovered over Groundwater: "He's too far gone." When Groundwater heard that he summoned all of his remaining energy and wiggled his fingers. This got the attention of one of the medics, and he gave Groundwater a blood transfusion. The chaplain came along and gave him the last rites, but still Groundwater hung on. Eventually he made it as far back as a hospital in Britain, but several times he came close to dying. "Just before I finally went over the edge, I started to loosen my bowels, which I guess is one of the last things you do." Only the thought of prayer brought him back. Groundwater spent five months in the hospital, but he survived.[7]

Of course, American artillery observers made sure that the Germans suffered plenty of casualties. Not far away from where Groundwater was wounded, in the sector covered by the 357th Infantry of the 90th Division, Lieutenant John Colby spent much of his time lying on wet ground, observing the German-controlled hedgerows, looking for targets. He held a sound-powered field phone to his ear. When he saw something, he called for fire. Colby and a fellow observer would try to determine where the first round hit. "We watched for the round. With luck, we saw the burst. The first burst was usually off target . . . so our procedure was to 'correct' for the next round. If the second round did not hit the target, the procedure was repeated until the desired effect was achieved."

To the infantrymen, the "desired effect" meant total obliteration of whatever was being shot at. That could be German troops, machine-gun emplacements, mortar emplacements, church steeples, a tank, a truck, or anything that Colby thought might conceal Germans. The artillerymen, always on the lookout to conserve ammunition (thanks to the supply problems), would shoot off three rounds at a time. Colby often cajoled them into firing more by providing "graphic details, real or imaginary," of the kind of damage they were doing to the enemy. That was normally good for another dozen rounds.[8]

The most dangerous activity was patrolling. The American generals did not want their soldiers to become complacent; nor did the generals want them to get used to sitting around in defensive positions. A typical rifle company on the front line sent out reconnaissance or "combat" patrols every night. The reconnaissance patrol was designed to find out where the enemy was; the combat patrol had the objective of capturing an enemy prisoner, who could then be interrogated for useful information. Neither activity was especially popular with the soldiers, but combat patrols were particularly dreaded. "The combat patrols, led by lieutenants until expended, and then by sergeants, reduced to near nothing the life expectancy of all who took part," Major Cawthon commented. "The patrols did little more than demonstrate the 'aggressive posture' desired by [the generals] and proved that the German outposts were still no more than a hedgerow or so beyond our lines, which we knew in any event."[9]

Somewhere in the vicinity of Villiers-Fossard, a few miles north of St-Lô, Lieutenant Brayton Danner led a squad-sized group on one such patrol. Danner, Illinois-born and OCS-trained, was new to his unit. He joined G Company, 115th Infantry, 29th Division, in late June. He spent a few days getting used to the horrors of the front until finally it was his turn to lead a combat patrol. Now, in the fog of dawn, he and several other men were supposed to check out a tree line some six hundred yards in front of their positions.

One by one, they stood up and moved forward in patrol formation. The first scout was about fifteen yards ahead, with Danner behind him and each man separated by several yards—close enough to maintain contact with one another but far enough apart to minimize casualties in the event they were ambushed or shelled. They made it to the tree line and realized it was different than they expected. "[It] turned out to be a hedgerow with an apple orchard behind." Danner was inspecting the hedgerow, peering into the apple orchard, when a German machine gun opened up. "Hundreds of bullets were mowing the seed heads from the timothy plants at my side."

One man was hit and killed (Danner did not know this until later). The whole patrol hit the dirt, until Lieutenant Danner ordered his scout to deal with the machine gun. "GO, MAN—GO!!" The scout sprang to his feet and raced to the hedgerow. "I saw him raise his rifle above the hedgerow, point downward, and fire a clip of eight into the gun crew. An instant later I was on the hedge a few yards to his right, seeing an orchard full of men erupt, racing in all directions, heading for holes and dugouts. I dropped one that was running away, and another, running across my front."

Lieutenant Danner saw a pile of antitank mines and wondered whether he should shoot into it. As he pondered what to do, he noticed movement to his front. "A soldier rose up in front of me with his finger on the trigger and let fly a burst of bullets past my head. Before I could point my carbine, he dived into a dugout to his left."

Everything was chaos now. Danner's men were running all over the place. He was not sure what to do next. He unhooked a grenade, pulled the pin, let fly the handle, waited a few seconds, and threw it into the enemy dugout where his would-be killer had taken shelter. A second later Danner heard a muffled explosion. Running to his right, he found an opening in the hedgerow. "There . . . I saw my enemy—a big man, on his back, head and shoulders toward me. He was ripping open the fly of his trousers. Fragments of my grenade had torn into his belly and groin."

Mindful of his order to capture a prisoner, Lieutenant Danner ran over to the wounded German. "I reached in and grabbed him at the shoulders—and nearly got my arms blown off. A Landser to my left with submachine-gun had seared the sleeves of my jacket without so much as scratching my arm. I tried again—ever so quickly this time. Same result." Out of his peripheral vision Danner saw another German take up a firing position to his left. For several moments the two traded shots. To Danner's front, German soldiers were trying to work their way toward him. At the same time, the wounded German in the dugout was crying for help in his language, "HEL-FE!"

Suddenly a German officer rose up and rushed toward Danner, "a superb specimen of man, binoculars flapping, Schmeisser at the ready. At the moment he saw me I shot him in the forehead, and again in the chest as he fell. Strangely, as he pitched forward I noticed his blue eyes and blonde hair."

Lieutenant Danner's platoon sergeant made it over to him, slid down beside him, and gasped, "Gotta get the hell out! ARTILLERY!" Danner and the sergeant ripped the shoulder patch off the wounded German, dived over the hedge, and made it back to the American lines. The lieutenant told his company commander that they had killed seven Germans but captured no prisoners. He could not resist adding, tongue in cheek, "SOMEBODY COULD GET HURT OUT THERE!" Indeed, they could and did. When Danner found out about the man on his patrol who had been killed, he threw up. "For . . . many years I could not tell this story."[10]

Reconnaissance patrols were not much safer. One night, near Mont Castre (soon to be a major objective of the 90th Division), twenty-two-year-old Lieutenant J. Q. Lynd of the 359th Infantry took three of his best men out on patrol in an effort to locate enemy strong points. They darkened their faces with charcoal and carried only rifles and ammo. Before they left, they studied reconnaissance photographs and a map, memorizing the terrain and the planned route of their patrol. Making their way to the very forward American positions, they lay down and waited for full darkness. A light rain began to fall.

Finally, it was time to go. All four of them belly-crawled as quietly as they could, "through the fields, sneaking through small hedgerow openings. It was slow, uneasy, tense progress as we oozed southward through three of the 'no man's land' fields. We had just started down one of the deeper drainage furrows within the fourth field when we heard a click-knock sound somewhat like two wooden blocks tapping together. We froze, slowly crouched, and listened intently."

The sound had come from their left, but what was it? They listened for several moments but heard nothing else. "So we started to ease forward again. Within minutes [we heard] another wood-block sound on our *right* side. Trouble!" They eased back down the ditch a few paces and stopped to listen. The night was pitch-black, so they could not see anything. In an instant, they heard three shots ring out, "right into our previous stopping place." They backtracked a few more paces. Three more shots buzzed right into the spot they just left. Lieutenant Lynd knew it was time to get out of there. "We ran full speed down the ditch, through the small hedgerow opening." Again, three shots rang out, so close that the bullets splattered mud on them. The four men ran all the way back to regimental headquarters.[11]

In essence, the members of a reconnaissance patrol were part scout and part decoy. In a best-case scenario, they saw and located enemy positions without being seen (a tall order at night, when most patrols occurred). In reality, they ventured into no-man's-land until they blundered into something. If all went well, they escaped and reported what they had seen in the confusion of a firefight. If all did not go well, soldiers were killed or wounded.

The latter fate awaited Lieutenant Franklyn Johnson when he joined a squad-sized patrol to check out a disabled German tank near the Vidouville road in the 1st Infantry Division's sector. Johnson, the antitank platoon leader in the 18th Infantry, had been fighting since North Africa. In spite of his experience, another newly arrived officer was leading the patrol. "[He] explained in a Midwestern drawl that his overall objective was to see if any Germans were left in or near Vidouville." So they now had two objectives—check out the tank and check out Vidouville. "Two scouts led the patrol down the gentle, forested slope to a meandering creek." Johnson was at the back of the patrol, just in front of the two riflemen who were pulling rear security. "No sound could be heard except chirping crickets and cawing songbirds, and booming heavy artillery miles to the east. Waist-deep in muddy water, we crossed the stream, two at a time, rifles held high overhead." They exited the stream and cautiously moved along a hedgerow. As they did so, they found several empty sniper hideouts.

Johnson knew the area well enough to realize that they were within three fields of the tank. "Suddenly a volley of sniper fire crashed out. I heard a heavy thud in the underbrush ahead. A shout, another thud, a glint of metal in a tree ahead." The two scouts were dead. Lieutenant Johnson ran forward, past the prone forms of the rest of the patrol. They were confused and scared, looking for targets, rifles ready but not firing. In a millisecond, everything changed. "A searing slash of pain under my left shoulder blade." The enemy rifleman's bullet tore through Johnson's body. "I found myself lying flat on my back on the ground, stunned." The other lieutenant was crouching over him. "His fingers were stained with my life's blood, now seeping . . . into the Normandy soil."

Johnson felt light-headed and weak. "I'm dying—take the men back," he told the other officer. He obliged Johnson. As the American soldiers left, Johnson lay there and waited to die. He thought of his parents, whom he never expected to see again. He doubted his body would ever be found and felt sad that his parents would ever know what had happened to him. Then he heard voices coming closer. "Guttural shouts in German and rough hands carrying me penetrated the film of nightmarish fantasy. My captors carried me through the woods." As he was being carried, Johnson saw the bodies of the two scouts. The enemy soldiers took him to a headquarters where an intelligence officer questioned him.

Only then did the Germans treat his wounds. "After a night of pain and misery, the doctors operated. As their sharp blades cut relentlessly through my back flesh and bone into my left lung cavity, the local anaesthesia could not hold. Shock took over . . . Air rushed through my back . . . The surgeons put in a crinkly cellophane-like material . . . They sewed me up . . . I blacked out again." Lieutenant Johnson spent the rest of the war in a German POW camp. After the war, he earned a Ph.D. and served as president of Jacksonville and California State universities, in addition to heading up President Lyndon Johnson's Job Corps.[12]

The stalemate, and everything it meant, could not go on forever. The Americans had to figure out a way to break the hedgerow deadlock. This meant devising new tactics that would succeed in the maze of the bocage. Officers, NCOs, and privates all devoted considerable thought to how best to defeat the German hedgerow defenses.

The biggest challenge was coordination. Terrain and German resistance made it difficult for the Americans to utilize all of the powerful weapons in their arsenal. The fighting was at such close quarters that artillerymen often could not lend much support, for fear of killing fellow Americans. Infantry squads and platoons had trouble maintaining contact with one another in the dizzying array of fields and hedgerows. They could be 50 or 100 yards away from one another and never know it because of the stifling mass of green around them. Tankers at first tried to attack along main roads, until German antitank fire savaged them. This drove them from the main roads and severely hindered their mobility. There was no way to spread out and maneuver among the sunken lanes and tall hedgerows.

To have any chance of success, soldiers from every combat branch had to work closely with one another. Every implement of American firepower had to be brought to bear on German defenders at the moment of attack (when the Americans were exposed and vulnerable). Combat commanders reorganized their units into combined assault teams. The typical assault team consisted of one infantry squad, an engineer team, plus mortar men, a light-machine-gun team, and one Sherman tank. Sometimes entire tank platoons operated with entire rifle companies, but the basic principle was the same—each group was to do what it did best in an effort to destroy German resistance.

The trouble was that the hedgerows presented all sorts of problems for the tanks. The Shermans could easily rumble over smaller hedgerows, but there were not many of those along the German defensive line. Most hedgerows were at least eight feet high. Even if a Sherman could negotiate its way over such tall hedgerows without flipping over, their lightly armored underbelly would be exposed to German *Panzerfaust* fire. Some way had to be devised for tanks to bust through hedgerows so that they could provide necessary supporting fire for attacking infantrymen.

All over Normandy, American soldiers of various units pondered solutions to this problem. Special Shermans, fitted with bulldozer blades, could punch through even the thickest hedgerows, but they were in short supply (four per division). General Bradley contemplated ordering hundreds of dozer blades for his tanks, but that would probably take weeks and the general did not have time to wait.

The 747th Tank Battalion did not have any dozer tanks, so this unit's crewmen experimented with demolitions as a way to bust through hedgerows. They found that fifty-pound explosives would do the trick. But there were two problems with this approach. First, engineering officers found that each tank company would need as much as seventeen tons of explosives in an attack. The U.S. Army in Normandy did not have this much ordnance; nor could the explosives be transported to where they needed to be. Second, the Americans who tried this method found out the hard way that blowing a hole in a hedgerow merely alerted the Germans to the location of the attack. The enemy zeroed in on the newly created hole with machine guns, antitank fire, *Panzerfausts*, and mortars. In effect, this demolitions approach was little different from attacking through the small openings that already existed in most of the hedgerows—such openings were the obvious route of any attack, and that turned them into kill zones.

But what if the tanks could create an opening without alerting the Germans? The dozer tanks had already shown that the hedgerows could be punctured. Since there were not enough dozers, American tank crewmen improvised other ways to punch holes in hedgerows. First Lieutenant Charles Green of the 747th salvaged discarded railroad tracks and welded them to the front of his company's tanks. Green's men found that this worked quite well. The railroad tracks ripped gaping holes in the hedgerows, allowing the tanks to lay down suppressive fire on German defenders.

This concept spread rapidly throughout Bradley's army by July. American soldiers scavenged for anything sharp and metallic that could be welded to the front of a tank. Sergeant Curtis Culin of the 2nd Armored Division devised the most ingenious, effective, and famous hedgerow-cutting device. Using scrap iron from a German roadblock, Culin and his men welded several pieces of iron onto the front of their tanks. The jagged saw-toothed cutters worked magnificently. Soon tanks with such cutters proliferated throughout Normandy. By late July, more than 60 percent of American tanks in Normandy had these cutters. Their bizarre appearance earned them the nickname rhino tanks, but they contributed as much as any weapon to breaking the deadlock.

Yet another problem needed to be overcome. There was no effective way for infantrymen and tankers to communicate with one another amid the din of battle. Their radios were mostly incompatible. If the infantry soldiers wanted to talk to the tank crewmen, they had to bang on the tank to get their attention, hardly an effective way to stay in touch. The Americans established communication by jury-rigging two-way telephones or intercom systems. These solutions were not without some glitches, though. To speak on the phone, infantrymen sometimes had to climb onto the back of the tank, behind the turret, thus exposing themselves to enemy fire. If infantrymen wanted to avoid doing this, they strung more wire, allowing themselves to talk on the phone as they lay under cover behind the tank. But these long telephone wires sometimes got caught on branches or in treads. The best way to communicate was by fitting an interphone box to the back of the tank. This allowed infantrymen to plug into the tank's interphone system and talk with the tank crew. But by the end of the Battle of Normandy many tanks still did not have this capability. The issue of infantry-tank communication was not completely resolved until after the war.

By July, many American soldiers had been retrained to breach the hedgerows. The new tactics and modifications were in place. The typical attack now unfolded in this way: A Sherman tank punched through a hedgerow and fired white phosphorous shells at German machine-gun positions that were concealed in either corner of the opposite hedgerow (usually across a field spanning about fifty to seventy-five yards). Next, the tankers sprayed the entire expanse of the enemy-held hedgerow with machine-gun fire. As they did so, 60mm mortar crews laid down fire into fields behind the German hedgerow. Meanwhile, the infantrymen stayed close to the tank, protecting it from *Panzerfaust* fire. One by one the infantry soldiers moved through the opening in their hedgerow and advanced into the field, firing and maneuvering as they went. They took pains to avoid the flanking hedgerows to their right and left. Instead they concentrated on destroying the enemy positions in front of them. If they could do that, they would pierce the German defenses and could then clean up anyone left behind on the flanks.

"What we finally learned . . . [was to] find a hole, get through that hole and get in their rear, and then the whole bloody thing would collapse," Captain William DePuy of the 90th Infantry Division later said. As infantrymen like DePuy got closer to the Germans, they pitched grenades into their holes. The Sherman now came forward and helped the infantry finish off the enemy.

"You ALWAYS tried to protect your flank and rear with reserve squads or a platoon including machine guns, to keep the Germans from sneaking up on you from behind . . . which they tried over and over," Captain James Shonak, a company commander in the 83rd Division, recalled. "If we suspected Germans to be in the trenches or behind a wall, we would send airbursts and/or artillery fire would be called. The riflemen would go first (quicker), with support from machine gunners. Then the grenade launchers would go next. Anti-tank would go if they suspected any tanks or vehicles with armor." Sometimes they concealed their movements with smoke.

Colonel John A. Smith, chief of staff of the newly arrived 3rd Armored Division, outlined the tanker's point of view: "In general, the tanks would advance to a hedgerow, covering a small field to its front with fire, while the supporting infantry squad or squads moved up to the two flank hedges. In the meantime, a tank dozer [punched] a hole through the hedges from which the supporting tank was firing. As the infantry progressed along the two lateral hedges, it cleaned out any enemy infantry and proceeded to take the hedge across the field to clean out any infantry that had been neutralized by the tank fire. The tank would then go through the opening made by the bull dozer and proceed to the next hedge, where the operation would be repeated."

At times, tanks were not available, so the infantry had to blast holes in the hedgerows and move forward by themselves. This could only be done with some kind of flanking attack. Sergeant O. T. Grimes, a platoon sergeant in F Company, 116th Infantry, 29th Division, participated in many such assaults. "This attacking force keeps close to the two perpendicular hedgerows leading up to the vertical hedgerow, held by the German enemy. The second platoon of the Company is then committed, using the same procedure. While these two attacking platoons are more or less crawling their way forward; the third platoon of the company keeps a base of fire on top of the enemy hedgerow, [pinning] down the enemy troops. The fourth platoon of the company, which is the weapons platoon, consisting of two machine guns and three mortars, have been consistently punishing the enemy, while the attack has been in progress. Hand grenades really come into play in this kind of battle, as they are thrown over the enemy-held hedgerow and blow out the enemy on the reverse side of the hedgerow. This procedure in hedgerow combat proved to be highly effective."

This was the American approach in July. It was effective, but it was not perfect. The Yanks had to advance hedgerow to hedgerow, field to field, taking casualties all the way. But it had to be done this way. Captain DePuy wished that he and his comrades had learned these new tactics "during the two years we were in training in the United States and during the three months we were training in England." Instead, the Americans had to learn all of this on the job, in combat, opposite a tough, determined enemy. In the judgment of Michael Doubler, author of an influential book on how the U.S. Army fought in Europe, the Army and its soldiers showed remarkable ingenuity, flexibility, and resourcefulness in dealing with the hedgerow problem. "In its search for solutions to the difficulties of hedgerow combat, the American army encouraged the free flow of ideas and the entrepreneurial spirit. Coming from a wide variety of sources, ideas generally flowed upward from the men actually engaged in battle and were then either approved or rejected by higher commanders. Within the bottom ranks of the army, individual soldiers suggested ways that enabled their units to move against the enemy."[13]

Doubler had it exactly right. The U.S. Army was poorly prepared to fight in the Norman terrain, but it adapted quickly and effectively. An American spirit of individuality and imagination helped solve the deadly problems that confronted the Army. Moreover, all of this happened none too soon, because in early July, General Bradley ordered a major southward push. The new tactics and methods, combined with every bit of resolve and bravery each American soldier could muster, would be necessary to break the deadlock.

CHAPTER SEVEN

LA HAYE-DU-PUITS

On July 3, the American front got moving again. Two of Bradley's corps, the VIII and the VII, attacked along the western flank of the American line. Bradley hoped to pierce the German defensive line in the west, in the vicinity of La Haye-du-Puits—a crossroads village located several miles south of and just down the road from St-Sauveur-le-Vicompte—turn the enemy's flank and force him to retreat as far as Coutances.

The three divisions of VIII Corps, the 79th, the 82nd Airborne, and the 90th, took the leading role. The corps commander, Major General Troy Middleton, was a consummate professional. He had enlisted in the Army in 1910, earned a commission, and commanded a regiment in combat in World War I. In this war, he had done a fine job as commander of the 45th Infantry Division in the Mediterranean. This performance earned him a promotion to corps commander.

Middleton planned to take a series of key high points around La Haye-du-Puits and envelop the town. On the extreme west flank, the 79th Division would overwhelm the German defensive positions known as the Mahlmann Line (after General Paul Mahlmann, whose 353rd Division defended the line) along the Montgardon Ridge. To the east, the 90th Division drew the mission of seizing the crossroads of Beau Coudray, along with Hill 122 (also called Mont Castre). Middleton wanted these two divisions to keep pushing south, beyond La Haye-du-Puits, and join hands somewhere around Lessay. In the center, the 82nd Airborne, now reduced to half-strength after a month of continuous combat, was to capture Hills 131 and 95 north of La Haye-du-Puits.

Bradley relaxed the rationing of artillery ammunition for this attack. More than a dozen battalions of artillery supported Middleton's men. For the

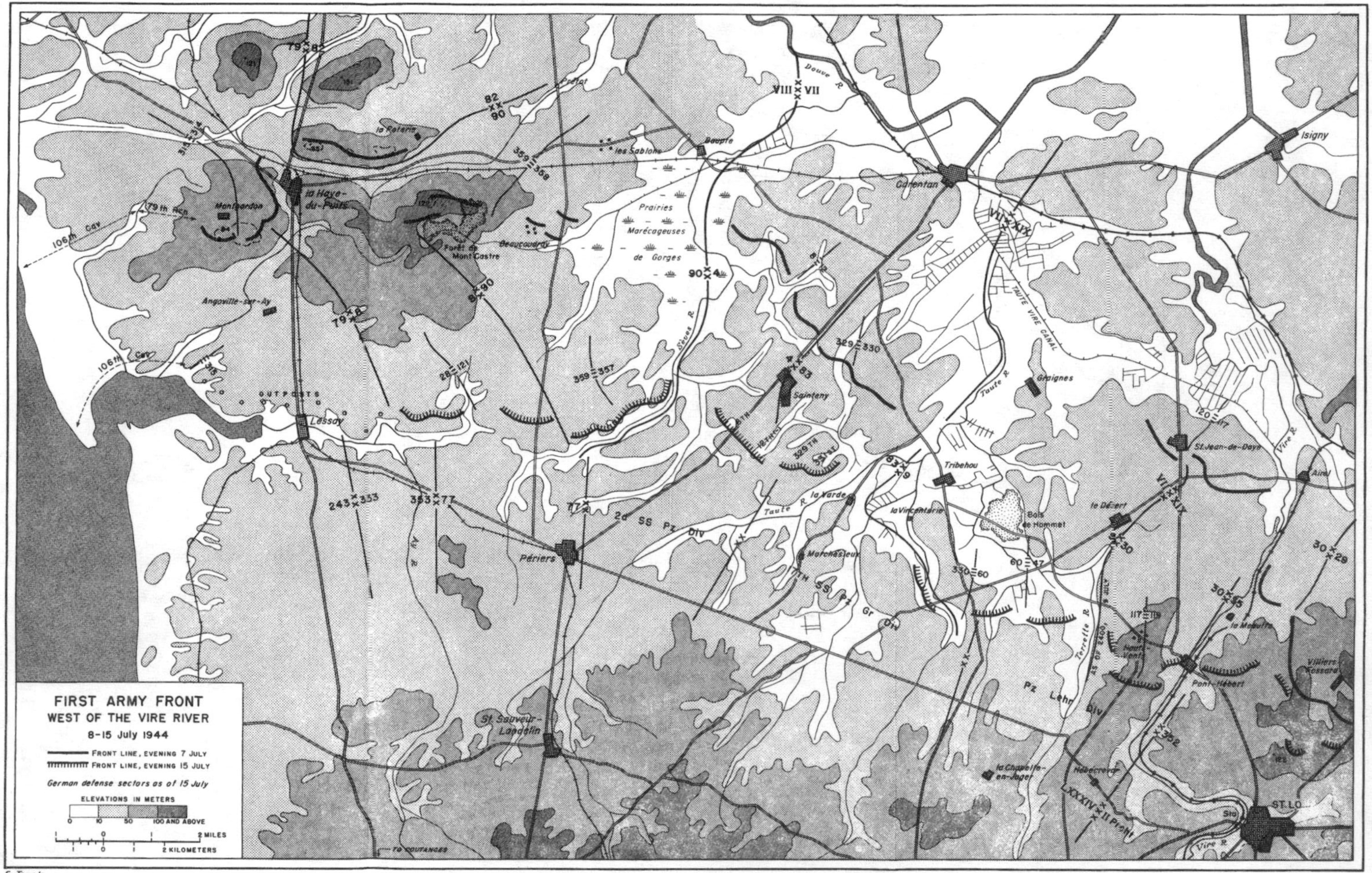

FIRST ARMY FRONT
WEST OF THE VIRE RIVER
8-15 JULY 1944

FRONT LINE, EVENING 7 JULY
FRONT LINE, EVENING 15 JULY
German defense sectors as of 15 July

ELEVATIONS IN METERS

| 0 | 50 | 100 AND ABOVE |

0   1   2 MILES
0   1   2 KILOMETERS

MAP III

F. Temple

first two days of July these artillerymen shot hundreds of rounds, some of which were heavy 240mm shells, into the German lines. On the afternoon before the attack, Middleton received a call from Bradley's 1st Army headquarters, assuring him that he could have all the air support he desired. Thrilled, Middleton quickly compiled an extensive list of targets for the airmen. As darkness approached on July 2, everything seemed to be proceeding smoothly. But, almost as if on cue, at the stroke of midnight, trouble started.

At first there were only a few raindrops. Then a steady drizzle. By 0300, the drizzle had turned into a steady downpour. Hour after hour, the rain kept coming down, even picking up in intensity. The ground troops knew exactly what this meant. Nothing was going to fly on this day. No bombers, no fighters, not even the cub-sized artillery reconnaissance planes that were so effective at spotting enemy positions. The dogfaces were on their own.

At the forward positions of I Company, 505th Parachute Infantry, 82nd Airborne Division, Private Bill Tucker and a few other men were on an ammo detail, stumbling through the mud. Tucker was soaking wet, cursing, and mightily sick of combat altogether. He had jumped on D-Day, and that seemed like years ago. Tucker and many others in the 82nd felt they had done their part in this campaign. Platoons were down to about fourteen men apiece. Tucker was irritated that he and his buddies were being asked to carry out yet another attack. "Why can't the paratroopers fight like the infantry?" Tucker thought. "At least they have hot meals in their stomachs . . . with replacements coming in every day." He had little patience for the mud and the darkness. "It was pitch dark, pouring with rain," and they were lost.

Finally, the sun rose and they discovered they were close to their own holes, in an outpost position just ahead of the main American line. Each man lowered himself into the watery, muddy foxhole that he called home. Tucker and his buddy Sergeant Larry Leonard plopped into the hole where they had set up their .30-caliber machine gun. At 0745, the last pre-attack artillery barrage began. "The Germans started as well and it fast became a nightmare. The Krauts did a lot of firing and the shells landed around the outpost." The barrage was deafening. Tucker and Leonard busied themselves with shooting at hedgerows in the distance.

At 0830, the veteran troopers of the 82nd left their holes and went forward. They were a sorry sight. The men in Tucker's platoon had "ten days growth of beard, faces black and greasy, pants torn, and raincoats hanging down around their ankles." The rain only added to their bedraggled appearance. Under cover of the barrage, they snuck up to the hedgerow they had previously shot up. At the appointed moment, they vaulted over the hedgerow and ran forward, firing all the way. The Germans fired back, but they seemed confused and lethargic. The Americans quickly got to the enemy positions. "Let's get the bastards out of their holes!" Tucker hollered.

They shot enemy soldiers at point-blank range. Several others, including many Ossies, surrendered. The whole area stank of decomposing men and animals. Enemy artillery and mortar shells were landing nearby, but the Americans kept moving out of range. There were mines, though. The rain exposed many of them, but not enough. Tucker saw Mike Caruso, a buddy who loved to jitterbug, run down a road to the right. "There was an explosion and Mike screamed for help. A Medic came running up." Tucker told him to go get Caruso. "A few seconds later the Medic was blown to kingdom come by a trip wire [Teller] mine." When they found Caruso, he was badly wounded, "with one of his legs hanging off." Somebody patched Caruso up and he survived.

Tucker and the others moved on. They slogged up Hill 131, hedgerow by hedgerow. During the ascent, Tucker had a close call with a sniper. "It seemed to me that I was getting picked on because I was carrying the machine gun receiver, and after about three or four cracks of bullets right near my head from sniper fire. I actually squawked to the rest of the squad about it. I had the crazy idea that I was the main target of some madman sniper following us."

By noon, they and much of the rest of the 505th made it to the northern slope of Hill 131. In addition, they pushed west and cut the St-Sauveur-le-Vicompte–La Haye-du-Puits road, one of the division's key objectives. At the cost of four dead, twenty-five wounded, and five missing, the 505th captured 146 enemy soldiers.[1]

Meanwhile, a few hundred yards to the east, troopers from the 508th left their forward positions and fought toward another slope of Hill 131. A few minutes before H-Hour, in a wet, muddy culvert, Private John Delury, a scout in H Company, was lying motionless, waiting for the word to move out. He and several other H Company men heard the rip of an enemy MG-42. "Machine gun fire was cutting the leaves on the hedges above us and it was green confetti wafting down on us." All of the men were wet, tired, and hungry, but more than anything, they were frightened. The idea of getting up and braving that scythelike machine-gun fire was almost too much to imagine. "It was during times like these that men would give their all to be someplace else, drinking a hot cup of coffee. But our fate was sealed; we were there and in moments we would have to stand up and charge the enemy."

Delury felt sick with fright. The only thing that kept him functioning was his belief that, when the dreaded moment came, everyone would share the same dangers. "There's an underlying motivation in the combat foot soldier and that is: what he's doing he's not doing alone." But to Delury's shock and consternation, orders soon came down for the scouts to go first, all alone.

"We were to go over the top first and onto the open field ahead of everyone else. Some cowardly leader had decided to test the amount of enemy fire still in front of us."

One of the awful realities of war is that every soldier is expendable. Delury always knew that, but now it sank home to him in a way that few others could ever understand. His officers were using him as a guinea pig. He glanced at his friend Tom Porcella, the Long Islander who, weeks before, had helped so many wounded troopers on Hill 30. Porcella looked inexplicably calm. He gazed at Delury: "Well, maybe I'm going to die in this battle." Delury admired his friend's quiet courage. "Well, Tom, you'll soon find out." They shook hands and wished each other luck.

There was only about a minute to go now. Private Delury was so sure he was about to die that in the last moments before he ran forward he felt like he was going before a firing squad. He heard the dreaded signal to move out. He ran out of the culvert and into an open field, firing away with his Thompson. When he emptied his clip, he hit the ground, rolled over a few times, reloaded, and resumed his fast pace. He was aware of the rain pelting down on him but little else. To his immense relief, German resistance was fairly light and his comrades soon came forward to join him. He never understood what happened to the enemy machine gun that had poured out such withering fire in the moments before the attack.

Delury slowed down and Porcella forged ahead of him. "Over the top went all the troopers shouting, cursing, and shooting. I was going so damn fast and without realizing it I was leading the attack. When I turned around to see where everybody was, to my surprise . . . the entire body of men were following me, hedgerow after hedgerow."[2]

Porcella and the others made excellent progress, but there were some casualties. A machine gun killed one man in H Company and wounded another. Private Robert Salander got hit by mortar fragments minutes after the attack began. "I was kneeling when the mortar shell hit about ten yards away from me. I felt something hit me in the back. It felt like a Mack truck, knocking me flat on my face. I asked a guy next to me to see if I was hit in the back. He said no." The other soldier must not have looked very closely. Salander had a hole in his back, but it was covered up by an ammunition bandolier. "All that day, I went without being able to bend from the waist." Not until the next morning, when Salander felt blood running down his back, did he understand the extent of his injuries. "I put my hand there and felt the hole and the blood, and was happy because I knew that I would be off the lines."[3]

The 508th soon reached the foot of Hill 131. "It was raining hard as we assaulted the hill," Private Dwayne Burns recalled, "but this seemed to help because the Germans were trying to stay dry and were not as alert as they should have been." American artillery and mortar fire had disrupted enemy communications. Troopers like Burns were on the Germans before they knew what was going on. "As we drove deeper into German territory their resistance weakened and large numbers of prisoners were taken."

After taking Hill 131, Burns and the other 508th troopers kept going. Burns's F Company had captured an enemy machine-gun crew. He and another man were ordered to escort them to the rear. They marched the four POWs to the rear and turned them over to another group of paratroopers. "We were glad to get rid of the Germans and get back to our own company." Burns caught a few hours of sleep but then went on another errand to the rear "and took the same road. There in the ditch were the four Germans that we had turned over that morning. They were dead." Burns fought the urge to throw up. "Someone used a machete on their heads." As Burns looked at the sickening remnants of these enemy soldiers, a wave of anger came over him. "Why them? These poor slobs were just pawns in the game of war, the low man on the totem pole. Just like me they had dreams, desires, ambitions and maybe a wife or a sweetheart back home. Now they lay there in the ditch with their brains oozing out into the mud."

Burns was on the verge of total despair. He could not understand why anyone would do that to another human being. He asked around and found the men who had done the grisly deed. "They explained that it was the same machine gun crew who had shot down their medic while he was trying to help our wounded. They had demanded an eye for an eye."[4]

One of the reasons the 508th's attack succeeded so mightily was the leadership of Lieutenant Colonel Mark Alexander, the officer who had helped supervise the antitank defenses at La Fière in the days following the invasion. Soon after that, Alexander was promoted to the executive officer position in the 508th. On July 3, Lieutenant Colonel John Shanley, commander of the 2nd Battalion, and the same man who had commanded the troops at Hill 30, got wounded by a mine. Alexander knew that an inexperienced captain was next in line to take over the battalion, so he persuaded his commanding officer, Colonel Lindquist, to let him temporarily take over Shanley's battalion.

Alexander held the battalion together and led the attack on Hill 131. When the fighting was over, he deployed his men in defensive positions and reported, by phone, his success to Lindquist. Alexander was sitting under a tree. As he hung up the phone he heard the sound of an incoming round. "The Germans lucked out. They put a round of 81mm mortar into the top of the tree. I was hit in the back by two shell fragments. It felt like someone had stuck a fence post in my back."

Medics got to him and taped his chest tight, so that his lung would not collapse. They got Alexander to a field hospital where doctors operated on him. "When I came to after surgery, Major General Ridgway was sitting on a stool by my cot holding my hand. He was talking to me but I do not remember what he said as I was only semi-conscious." Alexander had tubes running in and out of nearly every orifice. He needed months to recover.[5]

The 325th Glider Infantry, slightly to the east of the 508th, ran into the toughest resistance on this first day. General Ridgway soon figured out that the 325th was dealing with the main German defenses. They were anchored along Hill 95 and a few other hills, collectively known as La Poterie Ridge. All night long the glider men attacked, but they could not seem to crack the enemy line. They gained ground but could not dislodge the Germans from the key hills.

The next day, July 4, Ridgway ordered the two paratrooper regiments to turn southeast and help the glider regiment execute a frontal attack on the high ground. A tremendous artillery barrage preceded the attack. "About 4:00 a.m. our artillery barrage began, and the like I hope to never hear again," Richard Mote, a gun mechanic in A Battery, 456th Parachute Field Artillery Battalion, 82nd Airborne, wrote in his diary. He and the other artillerymen poured it on. "Everything from small mortars to 240 . . . mm. guns, including tanks and self propelled jobs. The noise was so great that the ground trembled as in an earthquake."[6]

Infantrymen like Lieutenant Ralph DeWeese of H Company, 508th, spent the morning watching the artillery and waiting to go forward. "Man! What a terrific barrage that turned out to be. We started to advance and had to cross an open field." The artillery lifted too soon, allowing the Germans to open fire on the advancing paratroopers. "The Germans opened up with machine guns and mowed the men down like flies. We kept going."

Men were dying all around Lieutenant DeWeese. Soldiers were yelling at others to keep moving; others were prone, screaming in pain from horrible wounds. The Americans were in a presighted kill zone. About twenty yards away from DeWeese, Private Delury was running straight ahead, trying to keep the German-controlled hills in sight. "There was no protection for us. The artillery coordinator [forward observer] who was carrying a large . . . radio on his back . . . was killed." This meant that there would be no U.S. artillery response. "We couldn't outrun the bullets and there was no cover to get behind. I hit the ground and made the smallest target I possibly could by putting my head toward the path of enemy fire." He had lost his helmet. Needless to say, his wool knit cap offered no protection. "I was in weeds about three feet high and I could hear the bullets cutting them and making thudding sounds entering the ground around me."

With every fiber of his being, Delury wanted to flee, but his training "overruled that instinct." He knew that if he stood, he would be killed. He felt like a Christian in Roman times, being sacrificed in the Coliseum with "the enemy seated in the left spectator seats with machine guns and the paratroopers in the arena." Somewhere in the distance he heard a familiar voice yelling his name.

Several yards away, Private Porcella was hiding in a small hedgerow, looking back at Delury, calling to him. "I asked him if he had contact with anybody in front of him," Porcella said. Delury couldn't see Porcella at first. He looked around in confusion but eventually recognized his friend's voice. "I've heard welcome voices in my life," Delury related, "but I think that was the sweetest." Yelling back and forth, the two ascertained that most of their squad was decimated. Porcella told Delury to crawl over to him. "The grass was high and Delury started to crawl towards me. I kept talking so he could follow the direction of my voice. Finally, he arrived and I was darn glad to see him." For a short time they believed that they were the only survivors from H Company, but by working their way through an adjacent hedgerow they found other survivors from the company. A sergeant and a lieutenant came up and passed along orders to counterattack, but the small group spent the rest of the day pinned down by German artillery fire.[7]

The 82nd Airborne's attack was in disarray. General Ridgway now showed a ruthless side. He ordered his commanders to keep attacking. They were not to stop until they had captured Hill 95 and the rest of La Poterie Ridge. In the general's view, there was no time for his commanders to retreat and regroup. Every man was to go forward and maintain the momentum of the attack.

Lieutenant Colonel Louis Mendez, whose 3rd Battalion soldiers (including H Company) had been shattered by the day's attack, could hardly believe his ears when Ridgway called him on a field radio and told him to keep going. Mendez was a rarity—a Mexican-American alumnus of West Point. He was an excellent commander—courageous, dedicated, resourceful, and intelligent. He also enjoyed a deep bond with his men. "I loved those men. I felt like they were my sons." Just days before, Mendez had gone to the aid of one of his men who had been wounded by an enemy shell. "I was trying to take care of him as best I could when" another shell hit and "blew his head off, and his brains were all over me. It affected me terribly. I cried many times to do something for him as he died in my arms."

Today Mendez had seen many more of his men die. When Ridgway gave him the order, Mendez sat in the grass and stared at his radio, wondering if the general had lost his mind. The very idea of sending them forward again seemed unthinkable. "I knew it was suicide; we had hardly any men left." Mendez snapped: "You come down here and give me that order here, General!"

Ridgway did not relent. "You are a West Point officer. Do your duty and execute the attack."

Mendez understood that he had little choice in the matter. His men were going forward, with or without him. He said, "Yes sir," broke the connection, and, for the first time in his life, swore. "I was very upset and knew many of my men would be killed."[8]

The attack continued. Several hundred yards south of Mendez, Lieutenant DeWeese and thirty-three other men, mostly from H Company, were in the very front of the advance. In reality, they were isolated by intense German machine-gun fire coming from the vicinity of the ridge. "We couldn't go to the rear or the left because that was also covered by machine guns." Then German artillery started coming in. "It was a terrific barrage and started pulverizing the ground."

DeWeese knew he had to do something fast. The other men were looking at him with expectant expressions on their faces as if to say, "You're in command; what are you going to do to get us out?" DeWeese saw only one way out—a line of inundated hedgerows that led south. He and the others plunged into the water and, hunched over, sloshed ahead. Along the way, they saw a "solid line of dead and wounded of the 2nd Battalion that had gone through there." The wounded warned them to stay down, so DeWeese's men crawled on their stomachs. They were all soaked, but better to be soaked than dead. They kept going, found an opening in the German defenses and made it to a road, where they established contact with two tank destroyers.

Meanwhile, Lieutenant Colonel Mendez was leading several men on a charge. One of his officers was running toward him, trying to give him a message. "I don't recall what the message was about, but . . . he got in the line of enemy machine gun fire." The officer went down in a heap. "I picked him up . . . and the enemy was firing at us. I was trying to weave back and forth so the machine gun would miss us. I was carrying him over my shoulders—he was a 195-pounder." A machine-gun bullet slammed home. "I can still hear the thud and I thought I had been hit. It didn't hurt me though." Instead it hit the officer and killed him instantly. "So I was taking a dead man off" the battlefield. "That was the biggest cry I've ever had. The day we charged the hill has affected me for fifty-five years."

The fighting raged into the night. Mendez's battalion captured part of Hill 95 but then had to withdraw or risk annihilation from the inevitable enemy counterattack. During the night, units from the 325th, 507th, and 508th assaulted the ridge and Hill 95. Private Burns and several other F Company, 508th, survivors went up the ridge that night and made it to the top, "killing more than 150 Germans in some of the hardest fighting we had ever seen. We also took 80 prisoners, while we had four troopers killed and three wounded."

By daybreak, La Poterie Ridge and Hill 95 were firmly under American control. In three days of fighting, the All-American Division advanced four miles, killed 500 enemy troops, took 772 prisoners, and destroyed or captured numerous enemy guns. The troopers spent a few more days on the line, mostly in static positions, before the welcome word came down that they were going back to England. No division contributed more to the American victory at Normandy.[9]

The 82nd Airborne had run into tough resistance in the push for the high ground north of La Haye-du-Puits, but Middleton's other two divisions, the 79th and the 90th, encountered much more difficult opposition. He had assigned the main job in this offensive to those two divisions. They were heavier and better supported, and their soldiers were fresh compared with the exhausted, embittered airborne survivors. All of that soon changed.

On the western flank, the 79th, just a week removed from its victory at Cherbourg, moved forward during the early-morning hours of July 3. In five days of fighting, the division pierced the enemy's forward Mahlmann Line positions, located almost within sight of the coast, and advanced south. On July 4, Independence Day, they captured Hill 121. From this point on, the going got tougher. The division spent several days fighting, hedgerow by hedgerow, and seized most of the Montgardon Ridge. Patrols from the division linked up with the 82nd and pushed into La Haye-du-Puits, but the Germans were there in force and the patrols had to retreat.

On Montgardon Ridge, the Germans were hunkered down in well-sited bunkers, protected by barbed wire and mines. Whenever the 79th Division soldiers made any headway, the enemy counterattacked. In one instance, they surrounded two companies from the 314th Infantry as they were resting along a sunken road. German infantry, supported by armor, popped out of the hedgerows that bordered the sunken road. The fighting was harrowing and intimate. The Americans were taken by complete surprise, but they had one thing going for them—they had communication with their artillery. The regiment's artillery batteries provided accurate, effective fire. The artillery, combined with the fighting resolve of about sixty soldiers who fought ferociously at several points along the road, broke up the German attack. But the enemy still got away with sixty-four prisoners. They also bought precious time to strengthen the main defenses on Montgardon Ridge. In six days of fighting, the 79th, assisted by the newly arrived 8th Infantry Division, gained the crest of the ridge and La Haye-du-Puits itself (by the evening of July 8), all at the cost of more than 2,000 casualties, half of whom were hit on July 7 in horrible fighting for the crest.[10]

The 90th, the bad luck bird of the U.S. Army in Normandy, had an even worse experience around La Haye-du-Puits. To the men of this troubled division, the very name Mont Castre soon equated with blood, horror, and exhaustion. Mont Castre, the unit objective, was a 300-foot-high ridge, crowned by Hill 122. The western half of Mont Castre was bare, with only two ruined stone houses along the slopes. The eastern half was densely wooded with bramble, vines, and small trees (somewhat similar to the Wilderness of Civil War fame). The division's two assaulting regiments, the 359th and the 358th, were to advance through a narrow corridor of hedgerows, with swamps on their left and hills on their right. There was no good way to approach Mont Castre because it was so elevated in relation to the surrounding terrain. On a clear day, it was possible to see the beaches from the heights of Mont Castre. If the 90th wished to advance up the barren west side, the soldiers would be out in the open; if they attacked from the east, they would be concealed in the brush, but this would impede movement and it would conceal German defenders as well.

Early in the morning on July 3 (while 82nd Airborne troopers and 79th Division soldiers attacked to the west), the 90th Division soldiers pushed forward in the driving rain. They fought their way through enemy outpost positions in the hedgerows. Major William Falvey, a staff officer in the 358th, stayed close to the lead elements of the rifle companies, helping supervise supporting artillery fire. "Because of information we had obtained from intelligence sources, including our patrol activity, we were able to place heavy artillery fire on enemy front-line locations."

Falvey found an unexpected source of information. "We captured a German captain and determined from his pay book that he was a staff officer. The pay book showed . . . that he had a wife and four children, and it gave his home address." Major Falvey also found something else in the enemy captain's pay book—a picture of the German officer and four Parisian prostitutes all sitting nude together at a table. Falvey and his interrogator, Sergeant Walter Midener, told the captain that they would have to send the picture to the man's family if he did not provide details "of all the defenses in the area." In exchange for the incriminating picture the enemy captain sang like the proverbial canary. He even told them the location of several OPs atop Hill 122. American artillery knocked them out of action.

Unfortunately, the frisky captain's knowledge only went so far. Plenty of other Germans in the area went undetected until it was too late. The Americans spent the day rushing from hedgerow to hedgerow, dodging enemy shells (no doubt directed by observers atop Mont Castre), fighting small groups of Germans in the driving rain. Private Claude Gilley, a rifleman in G Company, 358th, constantly flirted with death as he and his buddies moved south. "I was going from one hedgerow to another when two Germans raised up from a machine gun. I was looking down the barrel. The machine gun was jammed." Gilley took them prisoner and walked them back to the regimental military police. "On the way back to the company I found a German cradling his rifle with his back to me. I put the peep sight on him, pulled the trigger, and the bolt jammed. Instead of shooting me, he ran into a field of rye or wheat." Gilley worked the bolt on his rifle until it was operating properly and fired a few errant shots at the fleeing enemy. The men in his company heard his shots and mistook him for a German. "My company didn't know it was me, so they started shooting back. I jumped in a ditch and started yelling. It took a while to get them to stop."[11]

On this first day, the division had breached the ring of enemy outposts but little else. The 90th advanced through about a mile of hedgerows, suffering 600 casualties, one of whom was Captain Harvey Safford, a forward observer in the 915th Field Artillery Battalion, a unit that was supporting the 359th Infantry. Late in the afternoon, Captain Safford and one of the men on his observer team were lugging their radio equipment, trailing behind a column of infantrymen, on a blacktop road. All at once, enemy mortar shells started exploding in a field just ahead. As each second passed, they got closer. "There was no place to get into, there was no ditch along the road, so I started running to the right. The next thing I knew, I was lying on the side of the road. A mortar shell fragment had hit my leg and broken it, so I stayed there. A couple of infantrymen wrapped my leg in my jacket and used a disassembled rifle as a splint. They gave me some morphine and stayed with me for two or three hours."

Captain Safford was lapsing in and out of consciousness, but he finally heard one of them say, "He's not going to last very long; we might as well go." They left. Sometime after dark, stretcher bearers found him and took him to the battalion aid station. Safford spent nearly a year in a succession of hospitals before he was eventually discharged with a disability.[12]

The division was still plagued by inefficiency and low morale. During the first day's attack, one battalion from the 358th was pinned down all day by flanking fire from a few German self-propelled guns. Another battalion blundered into the tiny village of Les Sablons, a collection of six stone houses, and lost its entire communications section to German machine-gun and artillery fire. The regimental commander, Colonel Richard Partridge (Major Falvey's boss), ordered his troops out of the town while his artillery plastered the place. When the Americans came back they were attacked by two half-tracks and one assault gun. The enemy fire was accurate enough to make the Americans think that they were being hit by a major armored counterattack. Some of the soldiers panicked and ran. Others took shelter in the stone houses of Les Sablons. The three enemy vehicles held up the regiment's advance for the entire day and into the night.[13]

On Independence Day, the fighting got even worse as the 90th began to bump into the main Mahlmann Line defenses near the base of Mont Castre. The 90th was dealing with the best German troops and the toughest part of the Mahlmann Line. The Germans had sown much of the area with mines. Private Henry Williams knew all about enemy mines. Back at Camp Barkley, Texas, he had taken a course in mine detection. Today, as his unit cautiously advanced along a sunken road, he glanced to his right and saw several mines protruding from ditches and embankments bordering the road. "It was clear that mines were here. I called to the man ahead of me and the one behind me to look out for mines and the word spread rapidly."

Actually, it spread like wildfire and slowed the column down to a crawl. The officers were not pleased. One of them strode up and down the column and asked, "Who passed the word about the mines?"

Williams stepped forward. "I did, sir."

"How do you know there are mines?"

Private Williams pointed at a mine. "I don't, sir, but if you will step on this spot we'll find out."

The officer, impatient with Williams's smart-aleck response, threatened a court-martial. They argued until they heard a muffled explosion from somewhere up the sunken lane. Soon after, they saw a group of men carrying a soldier with his legs almost blown off. Both of them knew that only a mine could have done that. "Go on, do your job," the officer quietly told Private Williams.

Williams got in the lead and marked any mines he found. Slowly, arduously, they advanced. "The men had learned by now to take advantage of every ounce of protection. Mother Earth was the best protection we had, although camouflage was second best." They came to an open field, with knee-high grass, and started to cross. The Germans saw them and opened up. Bullets were snapping all around Williams. "I fell to the ground but the bullets kept coming. The grass was falling over me as it was being mowed. I lay so flat on the ground that I must have made a dent in it." The unit was pinned down. Williams and many others grabbed their entrenching tools (e-tools) and dug makeshift holes.[14]

Throughout the day, the fighting raged between the 90th and its adversaries as both sides attacked and counterattacked. Armor from the 712th Tank Battalion was now supporting the 90th Division. The tankers and the infantrymen were still learning how to coordinate with one another to implement the bocage-busting tactics that the U.S. Army had improvised in the previous weeks. The 712th's armor ran into problems in the disorienting bramble at the foot of Mont Castre.

Sergeant Mike Anderson of the 712th was sitting in the driver's seat of a 105mm self-propelled assault gun as it advanced on a paved road. This assault gun was nicknamed the priest because of the pulpit-style parabola that housed the gunner. Anderson's priest was in the lead, with two others in tow. The three assault guns rumbled past a farmhouse.

Anderson heard an explosion behind him. The second priest had been hit by an unseen enemy tank and was in flames. "After we passed the farmhouse, we got into [an] orchard, and we were weaving back and forth around the trees. There was a German tank in the corner. He shot at us a couple times. The first one hit the ground, and the second one knocked our track off. We fired back, and our first round went over it. The gunner dropped the barrel as far as he could and let the next round go and it caught that German tank right under the big gun, right above where the driver was sitting."

The enemy tank was finished. Anderson saw the German crew bug out and run away—except for the driver. "We walked over and looked at his tank. The driver was still in there . . . dead." There was still a shell in the breech of the enemy tank. "If they'd have closed it, I think that's the one that would have gotten us before we got them." Instead, Anderson and his crew lived to fight again.

Many others who fought in the attack on July 4 did not. The 90th Division gained two miles and lost nearly 550 men. In spite of the terrible losses of these first two days, the Americans had only made it to the foot of Mont Castre; more bitter fighting remained to be done.[15]

General Eugene Landrum, the divisional commander, now threw in the 357th Infantry, his reserve regiment. Over the course of several days, the struggle for Mont Castre focused, more and more, on Hill 122. The battle was a step-by-step wicked brawl. "The fighting in the thick undergrowth of the forest will never be forgotten by those of us who went through it," Major John Cochran of the 359th later wrote. "How any of us survived the intense, concentrated artillery fire will never be understood." Cochran's unit was fighting its way up Hill 122 when one of his sergeants could no longer endure the barrage. "Sgt. Lutz panicked. He jumped up and started running to the rear. As some of us screamed at him to get down, an artillery round exploded near him and he fell dead. The death of Sgt. Lutz became indelibly written in the minds and memories of those who saw him die."

On another part of the hill, Private Gilley led the way as his G Company, 358th, slowly advanced. Gilley warily trudged up the slope of the hill. Just ahead he saw a hedgerow. In a split second, a German popped up behind the hedgerow and fired a clip from his burp gun. "I jumped, but he got me in the right hip." Mortar rounds screamed in, as did artillery. Gilley's buddies were falling all around him. Wounded men were crying for help.

In spite of his own wound, Private Gilley kept moving (in what direction, he had no idea). "I captured a prisoner. He said, '*Ich nicht Boche. Ich bin Polska.*'" Gilley disarmed the man and headed back down the hill. As he did so, he heard someone begging for help. "I saw it was a GI laying face down, arms stretched out. His right leg was laying over his right arm. I told him I wished I could do something for him." Gilley made it back to an aid station and was eventually evacuated to England.

The Germans were reinforcing their embattled defenders of Hill 122, and that made the fighting even more ferocious. As the Americans pushed to the top of the hill, the Germans succeeded in surrounding the better part of two American battalions. Major Cochran's 1st Battalion, 359th, was one of them. "It soon became obvious we were in a bad situation. Dangerously low on ammunition, we had little or no rations and water, and badly needed fresh batteries to power our radios. There was no way the medics could evacuate our wounded."

Cochran's commanding officer, twenty-seven-year-old Lieutenant Colonel Leroy "Fireball" Pond, was one of the best officers in the entire division. A quiet but intense schoolteacher from Arkansas, Pond had earned his commission through ROTC. Courageous and resolute, Pond made sure that his men were spread out in positions formerly held by the Germans. He knew that his soldiers had to stay alert; the Germans would try to probe their perimeter, looking for a way to overwhelm them. The Germans cut his telephone wires, so his only communication with other Americans was by radio.

Help was on the way, though. Lieutenant Jim Flowers, a platoon leader in C Company, 712th Tank Battalion, was fighting his way to Pond. Flowers had five tanks, laden down with supplies. "They needed rations. They needed water. They needed medical supplies. They needed ammunition. Plus they needed batteries for the radio."

Flowers and his platoon clanked up a crude road that slashed across the hill. "There was a heavy mist. I couldn't see very far anyhow, so I got inside the tank, closed the turret hatches, and tried to see out the damn periscope. Only there's no good way to get the water off of the front glass of the periscope." Flowers had only been in combat for a few days, but he sensed trouble ahead. He scanned the trees and brush of the surrounding terrain. Something did not look right. There was movement where there shouldn't have been. A German *Panzerfaust* team was only yards away, drawing a bead on Flowers's tank. "Up close, it looked like a 16-inch coastal artillery piece, although it was really a little over three inches around. Whew, I saw that damn thing pointing at me, and fortunately we were able to get a shot off before he could get us in his sights and squeeze one off."

Flowers tried several times, even after sunset, to get through to Pond on the evening of July 6, but he could not make it. Each time the American tanks rolled forward, the Germans menaced them with antitank weapons. They did not destroy any tanks, but their fire was accurate enough to deter the American advance.

The next morning, Flowers and his people tried again. Their tanks made an awful racket as they rumbled up the muddy road. They flushed two enemy soldiers out of the bushes. These men were Poles in German uniforms. Since Lieutenant Flowers had no idea where the German antitank defenses were, he forced the two captured soldiers to march ahead of his tank. He figured that they knew and that they would seek cover when the column approached danger. Flowers proceeded this way for about a hundred yards but then thought better of it. "Uh-uh, Flowers, you can't do this," he thought. This had to be a violation of the Geneva Convention. The men had surrendered. They were not to be put into danger. Flowers told his driver to stop. The POWs looked back at him. Flowers waved them to the rear.

The advance resumed at the same deliberate pace that had prevailed all morning. Flowers, like any good tank commander, kept a sharp eye on the terrain ahead, searching for enemy tanks, antitank guns, or *Panzerfaust* gunners. Then, on the left, he saw a muzzle, pointed right at his tank. It was a German 88mm antitank gun, a deadly weapon whose shells could puncture his Sherman's armor much the same way a pencil could puncture a sheet of paper. "The Lord was on my side." Flowers saw the gun before the crew saw him. "I swung the turret around and had Jim Rothschadl, my gunner, pick him up in his sight and lay one round of high-explosive on that gun, and we knocked him out before he could fire a shot at us."

The tanks moved on and, within an hour, found Pond's battalion. "I dispersed my tanks behind his infantry. They took the supplies that I'd brought, and if I'd have been a 20-year-old beautiful blonde he'd probably have kissed me."

By the end of the day on July 7, the Americans had a tenuous hold on Mont Castre and Hill 122. This was deceptive, though. Staff officers could not tell where friendly and enemy lines were. The weather was rainy and the ground muddy. Bypassed pockets of Germans still held out all over Mont Castre. German reinforcements were still counterattacking all over the area. Landrum had already taken terrible casualties, and his manpower reserves were stretched to the limit. He even threw his engineers into the line as infantry.[16]

He also sent his last reserves, from the 357th Infantry, into the extreme left flank of his division, at a forlorn crossroads called Beau Coudray. Beau Coudray offered little room to maneuver. It was a cluster of buildings nestled along a road between grassy meadows at the foot of Mont Castre in the west and swampland in the east. Following two days of fighting, Barth had, by July 6, three rifle companies south of the town, two north of it, and one astride the crossroads, close to the ruins of a medieval fortress that hinted at the area's strategic importance to bygone generations of warriors.

Barth also had plenty of artillery and self-propelled guns bunched up north of Beau Coudray. For instance, Lieutenant Colonel Ken Reimers, commanding officer of the 343rd Field Artillery Battalion, had all of his batteries, plus "a battery of self propelled 75mm guns, a company of tank destroyers, and the 969th F.A. Bn., another 155mm howitzer unit."

Reimers, sitting in his headquarters tent, opened up his diary and wrote: "Even if I don't need it at this time, I don't mind having so much artillery around. At least I know it is here if I need it." The problem was that Reimers did not have any good OPs. The Germans still controlled the most desirable high ground overlooking Beau Coudray.

The Germans understood that if the Americans remained in Beau Coudray, they could use it as a springboard to encircle the entire German defensive system along Mont Castre. The enemy commanders paired their infantry reinforcements, many of whom were paratroopers from the 15th Parachute Infantry Regiment, with tanks to counterattack Beau Coudray. This attack hit Barth's men with violent fury on the evening of July 6–7.

The shelling was intense, blasting men out of their holes, shattering buildings, blowing up lines of communication. Behind a hedgerow wall at the southern edge of town, Private Leonard Lutjen heard the explosions and the confused shouts that indicated an enemy attack. He was a machine gunner in L Company of the 357th, a unit that had fought its way into town over the previous twelve hours. Now he leaned over the wall, kept a firm grip on his .30-caliber Browning machine gun, and waited for targets to materialize. "A sniper moved behind me and fired. The bullet hit me in the left cheek, passed through my mouth, fractured my right jaw, and came out under my ear but missed my tongue. I had my mouth open at the instant it hit. I fell off the wall." The Germans were very close, threatening to overrun his whole squad. The squad took his gun, left a rifleman to guard him, and left. "They said they would take me to the aid station later."

Lutjen was in shock and groggy. He lay still and waited. Two soldiers came back to get him. They carried him to a three-story house and told him litter bearers would come along and take him to the aid station. They never had the chance. The attacking Germans surrounded Private Lutjen's L Company and another one that was positioned south of Beau Coudray. During the night, the enemy attacked the building where Lutjen, and now another wounded soldier, had taken shelter. "We were both lying under a large window. A German machine-gun zeroed in on the window and glass and tracer bullets were flying everywhere. It seemed like they fired two thousand rounds. For a while I heard American voices, then I heard German orders and curses."

Private Lutjen wanted to do something—anything—to get away from the approaching enemy. He crawled behind a liquor cabinet and pulled a blanket over himself. But the Germans burst into the room and found him. "They . . . took the blanket off me. I expected a bayonet in the heart, but they put the blanket back over me." This first group of Germans went into the next room and found six of their dead comrades, who were also using this house as an aid station. German medics came in and offered Lutjen morphine, but he refused it because he did not trust them. "I was in Beau Coudray for five days with practically no food, water, or medical care. A mortar fired through the second floor of the house while I was there. A German soldier came in and threatened to shoot me."

At last, a German ambulance came for him. He was reunited with his company commander, his squad leader, and the rifleman who had stood guard over him moments after he was wounded. Lutjen ended up in a POW ward in Rennes with other wounded Allied prisoners and was liberated by early September when American forces took the city.

For a day or so artillery support from Lieutenant Colonel Reimers's battalion and others helped stave off disaster for the two companies trapped in and around Beau Coudray. Much of the rest of 357th retreated north of Beau Coudray. On July 7, even as Private Lutjen was lying wounded, hoping to be rescued, Colonel Barth counterattacked Beau Coudray with a rifle company and two Shermans. Devastating mortar fire harassed them as they moved south. The survivors made it as far as the northernmost hedgerows of the village before running into a German attack against their right flank. In minutes all of the officers and NCOs were dead or wounded. The leaderless remnants of this relief force wanted no more fighting on this day. In small groups they made their way back through the muddy fields to the safety of American positions north of Beau Coudray.

That night Barth organized yet another relief effort. He placed this force, composed of one company of infantry and two platoons of tanks, under the commander of his 3rd Battalion, Lieutenant Colonel Tom Kilday. "I [told him] that the attack of his entire force . . . was to jump off at daylight" on July 8. When the sun rose and the sounds of battle from the vicinity of Beau Coudray diminished to nothing, Barth realized that Kilday's attack had not happened. Kilday had done nothing. To Barth, this was the last straw. For several days he had doubted Kilday's competence, especially when he heard from one of his officers that Kilday had been spending a lot of time sitting around "taking no interest in anything." Now the colonel had had enough. "I relieved Lt. Col. Kilday, realizing that his mental and physical condition was such as to make further command on his part impossible."

Barth replaced him with Major Edward Hamilton, a superb commander and a 1939 graduate of West Point. Hamilton had relieved another battalion commander in the regiment a couple weeks before. Now he took over the 3rd Battalion. As he and his men approached Beau Coudray, they made contact at 1000 with an L Company sergeant and a few other men. The sergeant told Hamilton that, the night before, their officers decided to break

the company up into small groups so that they could break out in the darkness. The company had only enough ammunition left for a bold breakout
move. Each group was to follow another on a carefully selected escape route.
The first group, led by this sergeant, made it through and inflicted ten casualties on the enemy, but this alerted others to what the Americans were doing. They captured the rest of L Company, in addition to I Company, which
had surrendered after German armor overran its CP. When Barth heard this
report, he knew there was no further point to any relief expedition. Two of
his rifle companies were gone.

The 357th paused, licked its wounds, and received replacements for the
next day or so. Then Barth put his head down and bulled his way back into
Beau Coudray. In three days, Barth's soldiers, in more horrendous, costly
fighting, cracked the shell of German resistance in the area. They pushed
through Beau Coudray and on to Le Plessis, another clump of buildings a
few hundred yards to the south. But by now, July 12, the division had lost
more than 2,000 soldiers dead, wounded, captured, or missing.

Lieutenant Flowers and his crew were among these casualties. After
helping Pond and his stranded battalion atop Hill 122, Flowers and his platoon moved on to help another hard-pressed unit, the 3rd Battalion of the
358th, under Lieutenant Colonel Jack Bealke. With help from Flowers's
tanks, Pond's men had pushed south from Hill 122 to seize a smaller hill
mass. In the meantime, Bealke's battalion was still back on the forward slope
of Hill 122, but Bealke was surrounded by German paratroopers. Flowers
heard about their plight and decided to go help them.

Early on the morning of July 10, Flowers, an iron-willed southerner,
hopped into a jeep and reconnoitered the route himself. "I saw enough to
know that the going was not going to be real easy but it's not going to be disastrous. So I went back . . . and I got my tank commanders together." He
briefed them on the route and told them to move out (one driver refused and
was quickly replaced, something Flowers did not know about until many
years later). The column, numbering four tanks, along with a couple of
trucks full of supplies, easily broke through to Bealke. Only a few German
infantrymen opposed them, and the American tanks used their machine
guns to shoot them down.

Bealke's infantry soldiers heard the machine guns in the distance. These
men had spent a frightening night in a scraggly and forbidding forest, out of
touch with any other unit. They had dug themselves slit trenches or foxholes
and alternated watch with one another until the welcome dawn arrived.
There were dead Germans in the area. Their bloated bodies raised a terrible
stench. As the morning sun rose, Private Bob Levine, a mortar man in K
Company, was learning to look past such ugly sights. "You could . . . com-
partmentalize . . . actually . . . just see what you want to see." He was lying in

a slit trench when he heard the sound of the rescuing Shermans. "Nobody could believe it. Tanks? That was the last thing anybody expected. But we heard them, and then suddenly" they came into view.

Thirty-two-year-old Jack Bealke watched the tanks approach. He was the epitome of a citizen soldier. In civilian life back in Booneville, Missouri, before the war, he had owned a service station. Now, in wartime, he was in command of several hundred combat infantrymen. When he saw the tanks he was thrilled. Bealke watched as the commander of this armored force, a kid who looked to be about twenty-one, jumped down from his tank and strode over to him. He and the kid—Flowers—introduced themselves to each other. "[Bealke] was glad to see me," Flowers recalled, "to say the least, he was glad to see me."[17]

The two officers knew they had to get out of here. "Some of that brush . . . was kind of like a thicket," Flowers explained, "you couldn't see through it much less walk through it, and they had been catching hell." They decided to push south, off Hill 122, until they made it to a paved road that led to Pond's battalion. "Bealke and I made a plan on how to get out of there. I'd take my tanks and knock this underbrush and thicket down so his infantry could get out. That's one of the reasons they were trapped in there [the terrain]."

Once the tanks knocked the underbrush down, the infantrymen were to take the lead, so as to protect the tanks from *Panzerfaust* fire. This was easier said than done. "At first, this infantry was walking in front of me, but that didn't last long. We hadn't gone but a short distance and they fell back in line with my tanks. And that didn't last but a few yards. They just couldn't get through" the thick underbrush. The infantrymen fell back and the tanks were on their own as they rumbled to the bottom of the hill and started up the road.

In a few minutes a dangerous gap of almost 500 yards had opened up between the tanks and the infantry. Flowers did not know it, but the Germans were counterattacking Bealke's infantry soldiers back at the foot of Hill 122. Private Levine was in the lead group of infantry, hacking their way through the bramble, when he and his buddies lost sight of the tanks. It was as if they had vanished into thin air. "We just found a hedgerow and crouched in behind there, and that's when we suddenly looked around and heard fire coming from behind us . . . we were out there all by ourselves."

German soldiers were on the other side of the hedgerow, shouting and shooting. They pitched grenades right into the middle of the cluster of Americans. One of them exploded near Levine, and a piece of shrapnel tore into his right thigh. Private Levine was looking at his leg, trying to figure out the extent of his wounds, when he glanced up and saw something very frightening. A German paratrooper, who had camouflaged his helmet with underbrush, was hovering over him, pointing a tommy gun at him. "He looked . . . 20 feet tall. I was fascinated with the gun, because it was polished. I would assume he had taken it from one of our guys."

Other Germans followed in the wake of this lead soldier. They hollered for the Americans to stand up and get rid of their weapons. Levine complied, but another American did not. "The guy to my left broke and ran, and immediately they just shot him. The kid had panicked." Levine was a Jewish kid from the Bronx, but it did not dawn on him that the Germans might single him out for poor treatment. "At that point it didn't occur to me that I'm walking around with an H [Hebrew] on my dogtag." He was fortunate. The Germans seemed not to notice that he was Jewish. They herded the other prisoners and him to the rear, where Levine received medical attention (the shrapnel had broken his leg). He ended up in the POW hospital at Rennes and was liberated by September.

As Bealke's battalion was fighting at close quarters with enemy paratroopers, Flowers and his tankers kept moving, off the road and into the surrounding fields in the shadow of Hill 122. They covered about 150 yards before entering the kill zone of German antitank guns. "I recall seeing a blinding flash of light and hearing this big bell ringing," Flowers later said. An enemy armor-piercing shell, firing from somewhere to the left, hit the left side of his turret, just below where Flowers was standing, and bounced off. Flowers roared at his driver to back up. The radio was alive with excited voices calling to each other for information on the location of the enemy gun.

Flowers and his crew had not pulled back far when they heard the crack of another gun. This time the enemy shell pierced his Sherman's armor right through the "right sponson, where a bunch of ammunition is stored, and ignited the propelling charge in this 75-millimeter ammunition and clipped off my right forefoot. Instantaneously, the tank is a ball of fire."

In quick succession, the Germans picked off each tank, including the one commanded by Sergeant Kenneth Titman, a Nebraska native. About fifty yards behind Flowers's stricken Sherman, Titman's tank went up in flames. "They hit my tank and it exploded, and I hollered, 'Abandon tank!' The tank was on fire." As he was scrambling out of his Sherman, Titman saw Flowers's tank on fire as well as another tank just next to his. "I jumped out of the turret and hit the back deck. Blood was coming out of the top of my combat boot, and I knew I was hit." When Sergeant Titman jumped to the ground, he looked up in time to see his loader on fire, coming out of the turret. He hit the ground, rolled around, and extinguished the fire. Two other crewmen got out, but not the gunner, who had absorbed a direct hit from the antitank shell. Titman had some of the gunner's flesh on his helmet. The sergeant crawled to a nearby ditch and was taken prisoner by two Germans.

Just ahead of Titman's roasting Sherman, Flowers and his crew were engaged in a struggle to exit their flaming tank. The lieutenant pushed his badly burned gunner, Corporal Jim Rothschadl, through his hatch and to the ground. Flowers still had no idea that his foot had been sheared off. When he tried to hoist himself out of his turret, he collapsed down into the blazing tank. Only with a superhuman effort could he raise himself up and out of the turret, but in the process the flames burned his hands and face. His other three crewmen, T/4 Horace Gary, the driver, Private First Class Gerald Kiballa, the bow gunner, and Private First Class Edward Dzienis, the loader, all made it out of the bottom hatch. Dzienis was the last of them to make it out and, as a result, suffered some burns to his hands and face. "I didn't even feel [it] as I was burning," he later wrote.

Flowers and his crew were lying stunned in the field, mere yards away from German soldiers. The enemy was taking shelter behind a hedgerow several yards in front of the tank. Corporal Rothschadl was lying in a small hole, wondering what to do. "My hands were all burned, and my face. I stuck my hands into the dirt." Rothschadl also had a severely wounded foot. "The tendon on my right foot was cut. I don't know if it was a gunshot or a shrapnel wound. I could take my foot and pull it up until my toe touched the leg. Meanwhile, the goddamn devils were firing at us. I could see tracers going over the top of the hole. After awhile the firing stopped, to almost nothing."

Dusk was setting in. Flowers was lying close to his tank. He knew that if he and his men did not move toward the hedgerow, the Germans would eventually pick them off at will. He called to Rothschadl to come over to him. "Jim . . . please come over here. Please come over HERE. Corporal Rothschadl!" He must have said this a dozen times. Finally, Rothschadl summoned enough energy and obeyed by crawling to his lieutenant. Flowers, the rest of the crew, and a few infantrymen were huddling near the hedgerow.

Flowers ordered them to attack the Germans on the other side of the hedgerow. "I gathered up whatever we had, and we attacked that hedgerow, and got over on the other side. It was messy, but it didn't last long." It was war at its most gruesome—wounded, desperate men fighting for their very lives, within spitting distance of the enemy. In spite of their wounds they ran the Germans off and kept moving along a hedgerow until they found a good resting place.

By now, Flowers was a bloody mess. "The blood is squirting out of my foot, and my face and hands are burned, all the skin is falling off my hands. So I had Gary . . . help me get my belt off. I had coveralls over my o.d. [olive drab] uniform. I got my belt off and put it around my right leg above my knee, and picked up a stick, and we twisted the stick to make an improvised tourniquet."

Gary gave a shot of morphine to each wounded man, including an infantryman who had been hit badly in both legs and the stomach. Flowers ordered Gary to take anyone who could still walk and go for help. The Germans were all over the place, though. They ambushed this group as it worked its way toward Bealke's embattled battalion. During the ambush, Private First Class Dzienis saw his buddy Private First Class Kiballa get killed. "Gerald was shot. I was next, and [a bullet] missed my head. I said my prayers." A medic had bandaged Dzienis's burned hands and given him some morphine. Dzienis was lying alone in the field, feeling woozy and light-headed. He heard German voices approaching him. "My mouth is open. I breathe without moving. Eyes shut. They look at the others as they pass me. One German soldier kicks my face and some dirt falls in my mouth. Then I was out." He woke later, in darkness, and could tell by the smell of his burned hands that they were infected. German soldiers came along and captured him.

Back where Flowers and the two other wounded men were waiting for help, the lieutenant heard movement on the other side of the hedgerow (in the same field where his tank was still burning). For a moment Flowers thought it was a rescue crew, but reality soon set in. It was an enemy patrol. He grabbed a tommy gun and sprayed a couple of clips in the direction of the noises. "I don't know whether I hit any of them or whether they knew where the firing was coming from." Nothing happened. The patrol melted away.

Later that night, though, the Germans came back. "They were in file, and they just walked around us. I don't know whether they thought we were dead or what." They obviously saw the three Americans, but they walked right by. Their last man was a medic with a red cross on his arm. "That boy came over and he looked at us, and he checked my tourniquet. The bleeding had long since stopped. He checked it to be sure that I had released the tension on it." The German medic opened his aid kit and took out a roll of gauze bandages. He slid Flowers's watch and ID bracelet higher on his wrists. "He went to work bandaging each finger individually, and then my whole hand up to a point above where the burns were. He looked at my burned face. Of course there was nothing he could do about that." Flowers asked him for water, but he said nothing in return.

He went over to Corporal Rothschadl, whose face was badly swollen, almost grotesquely so, by now. "I could see if I pulled the skin down below my right eye. I was so goddamn thirsty. I said, 'Wasser.'" The German took out his canteen, and for a brief moment Rothschadl thought he was going to give him some water. "He took the cap off and tipped the canteen upside down. He didn't have any water. But he bandaged my hands." The infantry soldier was moaning for help, but there was little the German medic could do for him.

Morning came and still the three men were waiting to be rescued.

Amazingly, a German platoon came along and dug into the same field, completely ignoring the three Americans. An American artillery observer must have spotted them, because U.S. artillery shells began raining down among the Germans. The shelling was accurate and devastating. Flowers tried to curl himself into a ball and avoid getting hit. "Our artillery . . . ended the war for some of the German kids because I could hear them screaming." The explosions were deafening. Flowers was paralyzed with fear. "A shell landed between the infantryman and me." The lieutenant screamed at the top of his lungs. "One shell fragment hit my left leg, knocking it off about seven inches below the knee. This wound was peculiar. The lower part of my left leg ended up lying across my chest."

Flowers was bleeding badly from this new stump that was once the lower part of his left leg. With shaking, swollen, bandaged, burned hands he took the belt off his right leg and tried to fashion it as a tourniquet for his freshly wounded left. "I . . . pulled it up as tightly as I could, twisted the stick, and slowed the blood down." He checked Rothschadl and found that he had not been hit. Then Flowers checked the infantryman. He had been shredded by the shell. Blood was spurting out of his right leg, and in Flowers's view, he was "a bloody damn mess." Flowers did the best he could to save the man's life. "With whatever mobility I had left in my bandaged hands, I managed to tear some of his clothing off of him and get it ripped up into strips to put some compresses over the places where he's bleeding badly." The infantryman clung to life and Flowers kept a close watch on him.

The three of them lay there in a stupor for the rest of the day. Sometime after noon the next day, the infantry soldier summoned the energy to speak to Flowers, who was lying near him: "I'm not gonna make it. Can you give me the last rites?"

Flowers was a Baptist, not a Catholic. He did not know anything about how to administer Extreme Unction, the last rites of the Catholic Church. Instead, he crawled to the soldier and prayed over him. When Flowers finished, he admonished him, "Don't even think about dying. Hang in there. They're eventually going to find us." Later in the morning, the infantryman once again said he was dying. Flowers prayed over him again. "He seemed satisfied and quietly died."

Not long after the soldier died, Flowers inspected his own legs and saw that they were getting gangrenous. He turned to Corporal Rothschadl. "Jesus Christ, Jim, you'd better go get some help." Rothschadl pulled the skin down from his swollen eyes, saw the gangrene, and knew that Flowers needed help soon or he would die.

Rothschadl hoisted himself to his feet, went through an opening in the hedgerow, past the still smoldering tanks, and walked in the direction where he believed the American lines to be. At one point, he blundered right in front of a German machine-gun position. The enemy gunners did not shoot him. They merely laughed at him. "There were three guys behind it. They were looking at me. I thought, 'Well, okay, shoot me. Go ahead.'" Rothschadl was in so much pain, he did not even care. "They must have thought I looked awful. My clothes were burned . . . and I was all puffed up."

Rothschadl moved on and eventually found some American medics. They gave him some water—although nowhere near as much as he wanted—put him on a stretcher, and started to evacuate him. He told them about Flowers and begged them to go back and get him. They left, came back, and told Rothschadl that the lieutenant was dead (they must have found someone else's body). Rothschadl knew they were wrong. He made them go back again.

This time they found Lieutenant Flowers, badly wounded but still very much alive. When they got to him, Flowers was fighting to remain conscious. "Wait; here's another one," he heard. Flowers rose up slightly and faced his rescuers. A litter team evacuated him to Dr. William McConahey's battalion aid station. McConahey was amazed at the lieutenant's quiet courage. "He was calm, cheerful and not in shock. In fact, he was in excellent general condition, although both feet hung in tatters and would have to be amputated." McConahey looked at Flowers and said, "You're in surprisingly good condition."

Flowers smiled. "Well, Doc, I just had the will to live!"

His forty-eight-hour ordeal was over, but his long recovery was just beginning. In this small unit action that helped consolidate American control of Hill 122, nine out of twenty of the tank crewmen in Flowers's platoon were killed. His 1st Platoon, C Company, 712th Tank Battalion, won a Presidential Unit Citation, and he himself won the Distinguished Service Cross.[18]

In ten days of fighting, the 90th Infantry Division attained some but not all of its objectives. The 90th captured Mont Castre and Hill 122 but still needed to join hands with the 79th Division south of La Haye-du-Puits. It took several more days for that to happen. The fiasco at Beau Coudray, combined with the generally slow pace of the 90th's advance, did nothing to enhance its reputation with senior commanders like Bradley. This was not entirely fair. To be sure, the division still had problems, but it also, as previously mentioned, was dealing with the toughest enemy resistance (probably about fifty-six hundred top-quality German troops). Weak commanders like Kilday were being weeded out. Slowly, but surely, the 90th was getting better.[19]

The fighting around La Haye-du-Puits probably would have been even worse if not for a supporting attack by General Joe Collins and his VII Corps.

Collins's corps was deployed two kilometers to the east of Beau Coudray, just across the Prairies Marecageuses de Gorges swamp. The American front line in this marshy terrain was a few miles south of Carentan. Bradley's staff was still a bit worried about the possibility that the Germans could retake that town and cut the Allied beachhead in two. So when Collins attacked on July 4 he had three objectives: take the heat off Carentan, support the major push to the west by Middleton's VIII Corps, and, if possible make it to the main east–west highway (the D-900) that led to St-Lô. Collins had three infantry divisions under his command, but he could only use parts of two of them, the 4th and the 83rd, in the constricted corridor in front of him. Hedgerows dominated the whole area. Most of the roads were little more than sunken wagon trails. There was almost no room for vehicles to maneuver. The survivors of Colonel von der Heydte's 6th Parachute Regiment, plus troops from the 17th SS Panzer Grenadier Division and the 2nd SS Panzer Division, defended this area.[20]

General Collins knew the going would be difficult. "When I studied the terrain on the Corps front I knew we were in for tough sledding. Any commander worth his salt hates to make frontal attacks, but there was no alternative here."[21]

Collins was filled with trepidation, but many others were not. On Independence Day morning, at the forward positions of the 83rd Division, there was almost a festive mood. This was the first major attack for the soldiers of this outfit. They watched as several battalions of artillery pounded enemy positions. Benjamin Johnson, a medic in the 2nd Battalion, 330th Infantry, stood and marveled at the U.S. artillery barrage. "How in hell can any live Germans be over there, after such a long and heavy bombardment?" Johnson, like many other green troops in the division, was naive. The bombardment looked much more effective than it was. It did little damage to the enemy defenders.[22]

When the division went forward, it immediately encountered problems. Supporting tanks from the 746th Tank Battalion chewed up the infantry's communication wires so the division commander, General Robert Macon, could not talk with his forward units. Macon had commanded the 7th Infantry Regiment in North Africa before his promotion to divisional command. He was a competent, experienced soldier, but this assignment was too much of a challenge for a rookie division commander.

The ground was soaked from previous rains. The Germans, as usual, were dug into nearly every hedgerow and along the sunken lanes. They had laid out minefields that impeded the progress of the Americans. German snipers picked off U.S. engineers as they tried to clear mines. One of the American regimental commanders got killed by a sniper. The soldiers of the forward rifle companies were mostly strung out in pinned-down clumps a few hundred yards ahead of the jump-off point.

Corporal John Aller, the mortar man assigned to F Company, 331st Infantry, was in one such pinned-down group. His unit's objective was a farmhouse located across a swamp from their original positions. They made it easily across the swamp and were advancing on the house when the enemy let loose on them. The Americans had walked right past concealed Germans, into an ambush. "We realized now that we was surrounded. We were in clear view for them to take pot shots at us, which they surely did."

The Americans could not call for artillery support for fear that it would fall right on top of them. Nor could they spot the Germans who were plaguing them. One of Aller's buddies plopped down beside him and said, "This is hell." Aller, lying facedown in an indentation, did not disagree. "We were laying head to head, when he raised his head to say something more, when I heard a crack, like a cap pistol going off. Off flew his helmet from the impact as we never fastened our chin straps for fear of the concussion." All he said was 'Oh! My head.' I looked at his forehead, I could see a black indentation in the center with a little blood oozing from it. As I raised his head to render first aid, my hand came in contact with his brains that had been blown out in the back. I knew it was no use, as he was beyond help." Horrified and terrified, Aller rolled over several times, until he was as far away from that spot as possible. Later in the day, the remnants of Aller's platoon made a dash across the swamp and back to the jump-off point. "I heard rifles blasting away at us, and projectiles slamming into the swamp with a thud near me, which made me run all the faster."

The attack was going nowhere. Collins was on the phone with Macon, cajoling, advising, and threatening, but it was no use. Enemy resistance was too stiff, the terrain was too challenging, and the 83rd was too green. In just one day of fighting, the division lost 1,400 men, most of whom were captured, straggling, or wounded.[23]

Slightly behind the lines, at the Norman farmhouse that served as a battalion aid station, Johnson the medic spent the whole day up to his armpits in blood and gore, dealing with the detritus of this offensive. "A sergeant from E company was carried in . . . stepped on a land mine . . . both legs gone. He asked me to take his boots off! A Pfc from G company walked in . . . lower half of his face was gone. He died! Another one was carried in with the end of his ring finger shot off. He was in complete shock. My sergeant was over in a corner suffering from shock . . . nerves."[24]

In spite of the terrible debacle that had taken place on this first day, General Collins ordered the 83rd to attack again on July 5. He wanted Macon's men to capture Sainteny, a small town located a couple kilometers south of the forward positions. More than anything, Collins wanted the 83rd to drive a wedge in the German lines. This would allow him to feed the 4th Division into the battle and, he hoped, rupture the German defenses. But the July 5 attack was, in essence, a carbon copy of the day before—more terror, more hopelessness, more gruesome bloodshed, more young men shattered beyond repair or maimed forever. "Our progress for the day was very slow," Corporal Aller recalled, "with the gains measured in yards or hedgerows, with casualties very high, but we . . . killed just as many as they inflicted on us. When I held my rifle to my shoulder and went to fire at a human, it made me shaky and so nervous . . . but you had to kill or be killed."

At VII Corps headquarters, General Collins was fuming. He was at the point of total exasperation with General Macon and his 83rd Division. Collins called Macon and asked him, "What has been the trouble? You haven't moved an inch." When Macon tried to explain, Collins told him to get moving "or else." This prompted Macon to call his subordinates, with whom he was in touch today, and roar at them all day long. He mercilessly told them to take their objectives with no excuses. When one of his battalion commanders complained that he was being counterattacked, Macon told him, "Do not pay any attention to it; you must go on down [in attack]." Another battalion commanding officer told Macon he had no reserves left, only a couple hundred men. "You go on down there and [the enemy] will have to get out of your way. To hell with the [enemy] fire, to hell with what's on your flank, get down there and take the area. You don't need any recon. You have got to go ahead. You have got to take that objective if you have to go all night."

These "kick-ass" exhortations were easy to make from the safety of a headquarters behind the lines. They were quite another matter for the combat soldiers who had to risk their lives to make it happen. The soldiers of the 83rd were doing the best they could. Their commanders were not all that skilled at coordinating their attacks with artillery, tanks, and air, but the average soldier was doing his part. Even the most crack unit would not have been able to make much headway in this morass of a battlefield that negated the U.S. advantages of maneuver and firepower. "There were no gigantic charges, no sensational advances," one NCO later wrote, "just slow, costly movement, creeping and crawling from hedgerow to hedgerow, movement that always drew additional mortar, artillery and machine gun fire. We became acquainted as never before with blood, death, fear, and courage." By nightfall on July 5, the 83rd Division had made it halfway to Sainteny, but at the cost of 750 more casualties.[25]

Collins decided that he could not wait any longer for the 83rd to open up room for the 4th, so he sent the 4th into the battle on July 6, straight through the forward companies of the 83rd. The 83rd was still pushing for Sainteny, but Collins's decision assigned the 4th Division the lead role in the offensive. He hoped that the Ivy Division, as a veteran unit, would have more luck than the inexperienced 83rd Division. Of course, casualties had turned over the composition of the 4th Division's front-line rifle companies since D-Day, so the division's "veteran" status was debatable. In combat, rifle companies routinely suffered casualties in excess of 75 percent, and the 4th Division, having fought its way ashore at Utah beach, then up the Cotentin Peninsula and into Cherbourg, had, by this time, lost most of its D-Day veterans.[26]

Spearheaded by the 12th Infantry Regiment, the 4th Division attempted to push southwest towards Périers, a key town situated a few miles to the south. "[We] experienced hedgerow fighting at its worst," one regimental officer late wrote. "A hundred yard gain on a three hundred yard front often meant a whole day's work for a battalion. Enemy lurked behind every hedgerow. German gunners were dug in every few yards. Forward movement brought certain fire."

General Barton threw his whole division into the fray. The fighting was intense, with both sides attacking and counterattacking each other repeatedly. Private Harper Coleman, an H Company, 8th Infantry Regiment, machine gunner and one of the few remaining veterans of D-Day, survived many close calls during this fighting. Hour after hour he saw his buddies get hit. "We lost quite a few people. How anyone made it I still do not know. I saw one of the [battalion] commanders killed by a sniper as he was standing near our machine gun position." Next, a sniper bullet killed a member of Coleman's squad. The enemy rifleman fired at Coleman. The bullet creased his shoulder and the top of his hand, "nothing serious but too close."

During one attack, Coleman's company advanced through the remnants of a German column that had been decimated by American artillery. The rotting, swollen bodies of men and horses were sprawled everywhere. Entrails of horses and men mixed together. Flies buzzed everywhere. A column of Sherman tanks ran right over the enemy dead, flattening their remains against the pavement and the ditches. Somewhere close by, a wounded German was moving. "I saw one of our Lt's shoot [him] in the head as he was begging for water. The man just seemed to have lost all control. He just looked at him and said, 'Water, hell.' Nothing we could do about it then, just keep moving on."[27]

The battle area was so muddy, so marshy, so constricted with hedgerows, that tanks could hardly maneuver at all. "Rain kept pouring down from the constantly clouded skies above, soaking the earth, filling our foxholes, and drenching our already muddy fatigues," an NCO remembered. "The mud was getting deeper, threatening to prevent the movement of our tanks, half-tracks, jeeps and trucks which were often mired in the swampy fields of Normandy."

When the rain slackened and the weather warmed up, armor from the

70th Tank Battalion supported the attack, but the tanks ran into the usual problem of puncturing the hedgerows. Sergeant Carl Rambo was a tank commander in the 70th. During the offensive, his platoon, plus a dozer tank, received orders to hook up with some infantrymen and destroy a German defensive position. The dozer tank punched a hole in the hedgerow opposite the German position and then backed out. Rambo could see straight through the hole, across the adjacent field and the German-controlled hedgerow. His tank and the others shot up the German hedgerow with their main guns and their machine guns.

Sergeant Rambo's platoon was under the command of a new officer, riding in the lead tank (Tank Number One), who was eager to attack. Against Rambo's wishes, he gave the order to go and led the way himself. "I said hold up a minute until we get some more ammo up ready to fire, but he said no, we have to go—follow me. He stuck his nose through that hole and the Germans zeroed in on him. Hit, the whole crew bailed out. The Germans were just across the field in the next hedgerow, so close we could see them." Rambo's tank and the others shot up the German hedgerow again, hoping to keep the enemy at bay while the stricken crew escaped.

Several feet away, in another Sherman, Private Carl Hallstrom was sitting in the loader's seat, ramming shells into the breech of his tank's 75mm gun, watching through his periscope as the lieutenant's crew tried to escape. Outside it was warm, but here inside the tank the heat was stifling, almost unbearable. "Our own infantry was about four hedgerows behind. Jerry was shooting at the five men from over the top of the hedgerow, so we sprayed the hedge with our machine gun."

Hallstrom heard his tank commander issue an order over the intercom system: "Pull up behind Number One so that those five men can use us for cover."

The driver protested, "If we go up there, we'll get knocked off."

"Let's go anyway," the commander replied.

The driver gunned the engine and the Sherman surged through the opening and into the field. Grateful for cover, the lieutenant and his four crewmen clustered behind Hallstrom's tank. For a moment it seemed like all was well, but then Hallstrom saw a muzzle flash from within the enemy hedgerow. "It seemed like a ball of fire was hurtling toward us. Then the flames were roaring all about my body, licking at my face. I pushed the hatch open and dove out. I reached the ground ten feet below in one leap and started running." The Germans, only thirty yards away, fired at Hallstrom and the other exiting crewmen. "I don't know how they missed us. Bullets were kicking up dust all around us." Private Hallstrom glanced back and saw flames emanating from all the tank hatches. He also heard the ammo cooking off. He ran as fast as he could and hurled himself into a swamp. "As I lay there, dirt from machine-gun bullets sifted down from the ground above my head and went down my neck." He escaped further danger by crawling to safety through a drainage pipe.

Back at the attack position, more U.S. tanks were getting hit. Confused, terrified, angry voices collided with one another over the radio. Frank Ciaravella, Sergeant Rambo's loader, heard a loud noise. Their tank had been clipped in one corner, on the assistant driver's side, by an enemy shell. Miraculously, no one was hurt. "There was a lot of noise, a lot of fumes. The radio kept squawking. Sergeant Rambo . . . was ordering move here, move there. People were excited. Four of our tanks were burning. We got hit twice on the turret but the shells bounced off." Another shell hit their slope plate and went straight through, leaving a small hole but doing no other damage.

Sergeant Rambo was barking orders to retreat. As his tank backed up, his gunner fired at the Germans. Rambo saw that the dozer tank was also retreating. "They caught him on the right side and fire came out the top. The tank commander tried to get out but dropped back in. No one else got out." In ten minutes, four tanks were knocked out. Five men had been killed and another five wounded. The Americans retreated. Someone called in an air strike. The pilots discovered that there was a German tank dug into the hedgerow (accounting for the muzzle flash Hallstrom had seen). Later in the day, another group of Americans went back in and overwhelmed the position, but behind it was another, and another, and so on.

The Americans finally captured Sainteny on July 9 and the slow, deliberate, bloody fighting went on a few more days after that. The Germans were steadily pushed back, but Collins did not even come close to achieving any kind of breakthrough. It was his low point, and his most ignominious moment, in the Normandy battle. But he would soon redeem himself. For now, the only tangible result of all this terrible fighting was that it relieved pressure on the VIII Corps at La Haye-du-Puits. Martin Blumenson, the Army's official historian of the Normandy campaign, wrote: "The VII Corps attack . . . prevented the Germans from employing all their available armor at La Haye-du-Puits; it . . . also weakened the St-Lô sector just to the east."[28]

General Bradley was having no luck piercing the enemy defensive line in western Normandy. Indeed, his July offensive was shaping up as little more than a World War I–style bloodbath with hundreds of men being sacrificed for minimal gains. He now turned his attention a few miles to the east, where General Corlett and his XIX Corps were poised to attack.

CHAPTER EIGHT

PRELUDE TO ST-LO

Bradley had good corps commanders. In spite of his recent reversals, Joe Collins was one of the best generals in the U.S. Army (in my view he would have made a better army commander than Bradley). Generals Middleton and Gerow were both solid, dependable professionals. So was General Corlett, whose expertise in amphibious warfare should have been put to better use in the planning for Overlord. Corlett was not loud, nor was he flashy. He was the kind of senior officer who inspired his subordinates through his character, demeanor, and expertise.

By early July, Corlett had two quality divisions under his command—the 29th and the 30th. The latter unit had arrived in mid-June and had been manning stalemated front-line positions for several weeks. The 30th was a combination of national guard units from Tennessee, North Carolina, South Carolina, and Georgia. Major General Leland Hobbs, an excitable but effective general, was in command of the 30th. The soldiers of the division had become accustomed to the fear and desperation of the front line, but they had not, as of yet, participated in an attack. That changed on July 7 when Corlett attempted to buttress Bradley's floundering offensive by ordering the 30th to cross the Vire River (east to west, curiously enough) and capture the northwest approaches to St-Lô.

Early in the morning on July 7, two companies from the division's 117th Infantry Regiment, a unit well trained for river crossings, boarded boats and crossed the Vire. The river was sixty feet wide and about ten feet deep, but the biggest obstacle for the infantrymen was the steep banks on the far shore. Engineers equipped the assaulting infantry with scaling ladders, and these worked well. Throughout the day, several more companies followed and fanned out along the roads and lanes west of the river. The 117th encountered sporadic resistance. The Germans were not well prepared to defend the crossing, but they had troops all over the area. So, instead of dealing with a prepared defensive line, the 30th was fighting against groups of Germans who popped up seemingly everywhere and fought with varying degrees of effectiveness.

All day long, the 30th Division's engineers worked to build bridges across the Vire. Enemy artillery fire made this a dangerous undertaking, but the engineers built several temporary bridges adequate for infantry, if not heavy vehicles. The most important crossing route was a damaged stone bridge that connected the villages of Airel, east of the Vire, and St-Fromond-Eglise, west of it. In order to move vehicles to the west side of the Vire, in support of Hobbs's infantrymen, this bridge had to be operational. Division engineers cleared a wrecked truck off the bridge and strengthened it with treadways. By early afternoon on July 7, their work was done. Several tanks from the 743rd Tank Battalion crossed the repaired bridge, rolled west, and ended up battling elements of the 2nd SS Panzer Division north of St-Jean-de-Daye.[1]

The 117th Infantry led the way for the 30th Division, but the division's other two infantry regiments, the 119th and the 120th, also crossed the Vire on July 7. The 120th pushed through low country and hedgerows, enveloped St-Jean-de-Daye, and took the town by nightfall. In this rapid advance, wounded men often got left behind, and that, oddly enough, was the way it was supposed to be. Combat soldiers were trained to keep moving and accomplish their mission. They were not supposed to slow down and take care of the wounded. That was the job of medics, like T/5 Robert Bradley, who trailed along and dealt with the wounded.

Bradley was a native of Washington, D.C., and a former medical student at the University of Maryland. After Pearl Harbor, he neglected his medical studies because he thought he should be doing something for the war effort. Finally, at the end of 1942, he could take it no more. He left college, enlisted in the Army, and requested to be assigned as a combat medic.

For Bradley, the job of searching for wounded men was lonely and scary, but one thing consoled him. "That was the incredible, unspeakable, light of hope in the eyes of the wounded as we popped over a hedgerow." That day he found a group of six wounded men behind one hedgerow. He tracked down several other medics to lend a hand, and they went to work. "We had to use our judgment quickly and work on only those men whose lives we might save. One or two [were] dying with the gray-green color of death appearing beneath their eyes and finger nails. These we could only comfort." Another two, making the most noise, had superficial wounds that the aidmen helped them bandage. "The remaining . . . two were those for which the aid men were really trained. These were . . . men with severe wounds with excessive bleeding or those nearly in shock who needed immediate care."

Bradley and the other medics counted themselves lucky to save four of the six wounded men.[2]

Late in the day, at his headquarters at Grandcamp, General Bradley (no relation to medic Bradley) took stock of the day's fighting. He saw that the 30th Division was making good progress. It had not captured all of its objectives, but it was on the move and German resistance was light compared to the way they were fighting around La Haye-du-Puits. Maybe there might be an opening to St-Lô here, Bradley thought. The general had just the weapon to exploit that opening—the 3rd Armored Division. For several days he had thought about attaching this powerful unit to Corlett's XIX Corps. All that time the armored division had been in limbo, and Corlett, who certainly wanted control of it, did not know if he would get it. Now the time was right to give it to him. Bradley talked to his staff and issued the necessary orders.

Several miles away, General Corlett was feeling sick as a dog. He had contracted malaria in the Pacific, and the disease had never really gone away. He was at his CP, lying in bed, shivering from a flare-up of the malaria, when he found out that the 3rd Armored Division was now his. In spite of his illness, he wasted no time in taking action. He called Major General Leroy Watson and told him to cross the Vire at the Airel bridge and "power drive" south with the purpose of reaching the corps objective—the high ground a couple of miles northwest of St-Lô.

This concept was fine, but Corlett's illness, combined with the uncertainty over the final disposition of the 3rd Armored, led to a lack of coordination among Corlett's headquarters, 30th Division headquarters, and the brain trust of the 3rd Armored. The officers had no time to plan routes of advance, artillery support, air strikes, supply routes, or traffic patterns. Moreover, most of them were inexperienced. To borrow a World War II slang term, all of this led to a serious "fubar" situation as the 3rd Armored Division converged on the Airel bridge.

The 3rd Armored was one of only two "heavy" armored divisions in the U.S. Army. In September 1943, the Army had scaled down the size of its armored divisions to enhance their maneuverability. Only the 2nd and 3rd Armored escaped this reform, because they had already been constituted the old way and any sort of change would have impaired their battle readiness. Thus these two divisions possessed 232 medium tanks, where the typical, sleeker divisions had 168, and had 16,000 soldiers, as opposed to 12,000 in the lighter outfits. While the other armored divisions were triangular (divided into three combat commands), the 2nd and 3rd were divided into two large combat commands. One of the 3rd Armored's combat commands (A) had seen action for a few days in late June at Villiers-Fossard. The other, Combat Command B (CCB) under Brigadier General John Bohn, was new to combat. This was the outfit that began crossing the Airel bridge as the sun set on July 7.

Bohn's CCB was massive. It consisted of 800 vehicles, 300 trailers, and 6,000 men in a convoy that stretched twenty miles. General Hobbs ordered his division to clear the road and make way for the tanks, but this was impractical. The Airel bridge was a bottleneck, attracting a critical mass of troops and vehicles from both divisions. Bohn's vehicles soon mixed uncomfortably with 30th Division soldiers at the bridge and all along the muddy road. The half-tracks and tanks splashed cold water and mud on the infantry troops. In some cases, they came so close to running the infantrymen over that they had to scramble into the slimy ditches that paralleled the road. The 3rd Armored vehicles also tore up the infantry's communication wires. In response, the 30th Division troops hollered, cursed, and threatened the armored soldiers.

Stories of the callousness of the 3rd Armored spread like wildfire among Hobbs's men. "[The stories] may have been exagerrated [*sic*], but it is a fundamental law of physics that two objects cannot occupy the same space at the same time," Colonel Ralph Rogers, the operations officer for CCB, later wrote. Major Haynes Dugan, an intelligence officer in CCB, added: "The Vire river crossing was really our first major commitment and it was a mess from the word go. There was a feeling on high that we just *had* to get into the action fast and there was not proper coordination with the 30th Infantry Division on road use and our tanks were crowding their infantry off the narrow road leading to the bridge at Airel, creating ill feelings between the two headquarters."

As Dugan indicated, when General Hobbs found out about the snarl at the Airel bridge he became quite upset. In his view, the presence of CCB in his bridgehead was now slowing his advance to a crawl. He could not get supplies or reinforcements forward. Hobbs also believed that the green tankers were inflicting casualties on his men by their "promiscuous . . . fire" as they went into action west of the Vire. Hobbs got so angry at the 3rd Armored that he ordered his artillery chief to give 30th Division soldiers any requested fire "wherever they are, irrespective of armor or anything else."

The bridge and its environs was a scene of chaos. Traffic was halted everywhere. Soldiers cursed at one another. Tanks, jeeps, half-tracks, trucks, and other vehicles were lined up bumper-to-bumper or stuck in glutinous mud along ditches. To top it all off, the bridgehead was still under enemy small-arms and artillery fire. The artillery was especially deadly, inflicting many casualties. First Lieutenant Albert Bowman, a medical officer in the 30th Division, helped treat several of those casualties when an engineer friend of his asked him for help. Bowman wrote about it later in a stilted diary entry: "He had been occupying small space between two buildings, with rear closed by another, and open end facing enemy. Shells were dropping in this trap like hail; his own jeep was burning and there wasn't a whole man in the place. [We] evacuated the living (about 6) as fast as we could slap dressings on them and [get them] cleared out, leaving several dead, some with half their bodies burned up already." Bowman found the body of another friend, "lying between [a] burned out jeep and [a] wall."

All night long, the traffic jam continued, and Hobbs grew angrier by the minute. He believed that the terrain between his units and the corps objective, the high ground near St-Lô, was lightly defended. He was convinced that shorn of CCB, his division could reach this objective easily. Beyond that, he was disgusted with General Watson and General Bohn, who he believed were no help in resolving the jam. Nor was he shy about voicing these complaints to Corlett in a slew of angry phone calls. Regardless of who was at fault, the traffic jam slowed the American advance to a crawl for the better part of a day.

On the evening of July 8, Corlett attempted to resolve the situation. He called Hobbs and gave him operational control of CCB. But by now Hobbs did not even want Bohn's tanks. He told Corlett that the 743rd Tank Battalion, plus some attached tank destroyers, provided him all the armor he needed to make his advance. Corlett did not relent. He told his subordinate that he would have to keep CCB, if for no other reason than because it "could not go anyplace else." Hobbs had no choice but to agree, albeit with the suggestion that CCB could "just trail along." But Corlett told Hobbs to put CCB in the lead, so as to make a quick dash for Hill 91, located about two miles north of St-Lô. This hill, aptly called Hauts Vents (High winds) by the French, dominated the road into St-Lô.[3]

The unhappy result of Corlett's maneuvering was more tension between Hobbs and the 3rd Armored. The 3rd Armored had been trained to avoid the major roads as too dangerous. The unit's commanders had the mind-set of fighting hedgerow to hedgerow or along sunken lanes. This only exacerbated the 3rd Armored's reputation as a heavy, ponderous formation not suitable to flexible, fast-paced warfare. During the night of July 8–9 Bohn's tanks were cautiously edging their way south, in a driving rain, through muddy trails and fields. Believing that enemy opposition north of Hauts Vents was negligible, Hobbs ordered General Bohn on July 9 to get his tanks onto the main road (N-174) and cover the three miles to Hauts Vents as quickly as possible.

Bohn tried to comply with this order, but he encountered great difficulties. Most of the roads that led to N-174 were nothing more than tiny trails. Many were blocked by fallen trees or overhanging hedges. Even N-174 itself was slick, muddy, and crowded. Any kind of impediment—a tree, a roadblock, a wrecked vehicle—could freeze Bohn's whole CCB in place. In effect, the traffic jam that had engulfed the Airel bridge twenty-four to thirty-six hours earlier was merely moving south.

Bohn mounted his jeep and rode along the column, trying to get the jam unsnarled. Colonel Rogers, his operations officer, was with him. "Progress to the forward elements was slow and painful along a muddy, sunken trail jam-packed with both armored and infantry vehicles and the red placque [*sic*] with a single star denoting Brigadier General's rank on the bumper . . . had little effect in easing his way. He talked with several of our commanders and exhorted them to cease attempting to clear the fields along the flanks of the trail, to mount up the infantry on the tanks, and to proceed at full speed along the trail to its junction with the main road . . . and thence . . . south-west to seize and hold Hauts Vents."

Bohn's CCB was divided into two task forces. When Bohn found his lead task force commander and ordered him to get on the main road to Hauts Vents, the officer resisted. In his training, he had been ordered to avoid ma-jor roads like the plague. Now Bohn was telling him to do just the opposite. The task force commander heatedly asked Bohn if he realized that his orders were contrary "to General Corlett's directives, General Watson's directives, and the rehearsals . . . of the tank-infantry teams." Bohn responded by tak-ing charge of the task force himself, while the commander predicted that "it was fatal to get on the roads." Bohn got the column moving toward N-174, but valuable time had seeped away. It was well past noon now, and CCB had only covered 600 yards in the last eight hours.

Miles to the north, at 30th Division headquarters, General Hobbs heard about the glacial progress of CCB and decided that it was time to issue an ul-timatum to Bohn. Hobbs sent his assistant division commander to Bohn with word to take Hauts Vents by 1700 or relinquish command. With his job now on the line, Bohn knew he had to produce fast results. So he detached eight tanks from I Company, 33rd Armored Regiment, and ordered them to dash for Hauts Vents.

Hobbs was antsy for good reason. He kept receiving intelligence reports that reinforcements from the 2nd SS Panzer Division and Panzer Lehr were on the move and positioning themselves to counterattack his 30th Division and the 3rd Armored. Even as the drama between Hobbs and Bohn was play-ing out—and the I Company tanks were driving south—advance elements of these powerful enemy divisions were hitting the 30th Division in several places. Some of the 30th's soldiers were withdrawing (Hobbs even had re-ports that the CP of the 2nd Battalion of the 120th, located a couple miles west of CCB, had been overrun), but most succeeded in halting these prob-ing attacks. Even so, rumors were flying everywhere among the Americans that enemy tanks were about to launch a major counterattack.[4]

Thus it was in this tense environment that Captain William Redmond led his I Company tanks south in search of Hauts Vents. They were operating under radio silence, to prevent the Germans from getting a fix on their position. Redmond's tanks made it to N-174 with no problem. At this main highway, they were supposed to turn *left* (south) and go for several hundred yards before turning right on a secondary road that led to Hauts Vents.

Redmond's tank was in the lead, perpendicular to the road. In the tank behind Redmond's, Lieutenant Henry Earl, a platoon leader, stood in his turret and watched his leader. "Redmond stopped his tank, seemed to hesitate, swinging his turret, first to the right, then to the left. He then . . . [made] a right turn." An expression of surprise and consternation swept over Earl's face. "The other way, Bill!" he muttered to himself beneath the deafening roar of his Sherman's engine.

He knew that Captain Redmond was making a wrong turn, but he did not have the confidence to tell him. The noise of the tank engines negated the possibility of calling to Redmond. What's more, this was Lieutenant Earl's first day of combat, and he knew he had a lot to learn. Maybe there was something he did not know. The standing order was radio silence. What if he violated that order, calling Redmond on the radio, only to find out that Redmond had simply changed directions? Nor did Earl wish to halt the whole column, run over to Redmond's tank, and risk the scorn that would be heaped upon him if, somehow, he was wrong. So he shut his mouth and followed his captain. In so doing, he made a big mistake.

Trailing one by one behind him, all of Redmond's tanks followed him up the highway at full speed. They were heading north now, away from Hauts Vents, back in the direction of the American lines. The terrain on either side of the road was marshy with tall grass. The day was misty and overcast, almost foggy. Visibility was poor.

About one thousand yards up the road, the soldiers of C Company, 823rd Tank Destroyer Battalion (attached to the 30th Division), were waiting in defensive positions astride the highway, peering south into the mist. The 823rd was equipped with three-inch (76mm) towed antitank guns designed to kill tanks. Moments before, these men had encountered stragglers from the 117th Infantry who walked by and warned them that German armor was right behind them. Soon after, enemy artillery rounds started exploding in the area, and that seemed to confirm the reports of the retreating soldiers. The tank destroyer crewmen tensely waited, checking their three-inch guns and watching for any sign of enemy armor.

Meanwhile, Captain Redmond's tanks were still moving north, right into the muzzles of the tank destroyer unit. There were some Germans in between, though. Lieutenant Earl heard the report of an enemy antitank gun on the right "and at a right angle to the highway. He missed the rear of Redmond's tank by a couple of feet." The shock waves from the enemy gun stunned Lieutenant Earl. "The intensity and length of those waves were beyond belief."

Redmond's tanks ground to a halt, a few yards away from the enemy gun, and his turret traversed right. Redmond took a shot but missed. In the meantime, Earl had ordered his driver to halt while he got a fix on the gun. Earl traversed his turret to the right and told his gunner to fire. His crew took three shots. On the third shot, they saw "the gun flipping through the air."

With the enemy antitank gun destroyed, Redmond's company resumed its advance, but not for long. At almost the same moment, they ran into another German gun on their right in addition to the American tank destroyers up the road. Earl saw that the enemy gun crew had placed their weapon behind a low wall "that encompassed the property of a small French farmhouse. The crew was manhandling the gun to meet the new threat from the rear." One of the American tanks slid to the right, shot up the enemy crew, and got stuck in a gulley.

As this was happening, Redmond's tanks and the tank destroyer men from the 823rd spotted each other. Having just encountered enemy antitank guns, Redmond and his people assumed that the guns in front of them were more of the same. At the same time, the tank destroyer troops were unable to see clearly in the fog. They saw armored vehicles shooting in the distance and made what seemed like a reasonable assumption—these must be the enemy tanks they were expecting. Lieutenant Ellis McInnis, one of the tank destroyer officers, even called his company commander to confirm that the tanks he saw were German. "What you are looking for is in front of you," his commanding officer replied.

McInnis hesitated a moment longer, just to be sure. Finally, when the "enemy" tanks fired their machine guns and main guns into McInnis's positions, he no longer had any doubt. He told his platoon to open fire. In seconds, one of his crews scored a direct hit on the lead tank. The tank skidded to a halt, and smoke billowed from it. McInnis's crewmen had just destroyed Captain Redmond's tank.

Lieutenant Earl saw this happen, but from a very different vantage point. He was right behind Redmond and saw his tank "sitting dead on the highway." Earl ordered his driver, Sergeant Fred Nulle, to edge forward to the left side of Redmond's smoking tank. Inside the tank, the captain was badly wounded. The crash of the shell had activated his radio. He cried, "I am in dreadful agony," and somehow wriggled free of the tank. Earl's Sherman had to brake to keep from running over the injured captain, who was "lying on the ground, seriously wounded, trying to roll off the highway."

The rest of I Company's tanks kept moving closer to the tank destroyer unit, firing all the way. Lieutenant Earl saw the antitank gunners score another direct hit on a Sherman, "striking the turret just below the periscope, ripping a 14/18 inch [hole], killing the gunner and the tank commander."

The Shermans were inflicting plenty of damage, too. As they got closer to the antitank guns, the crewmen took cover in ditches along the road. The tanks machine-gunned them. One of the tank destroyer soldiers, Sergeant Malery Nunn, who had already been grazed in the cheek by a machine-gun bullet, recognized the silhouette of the Shermans. He courageously left the cover of the ditch and tried to signal them to cease fire, but to no avail. Disgusted, Nunn dived back into the ditch.

Not far away, a bazooka team from the 823rd left their ditch and tried to retreat behind a hedgerow. As they ran, a Sherman drew a bead on them and fired its main gun. The 75mm shell hit one of the retreating soldiers, Private First Class Ernie Jacobs, right in the head. In a millisecond, his head disintegrated in a macabre flash of pinkish-grayish brain and skull. Fragments from Jacobs's skull hit Sergeant Carl Hanna in the back of the head.

Back on the road, an I Company Sherman pumped a round into one of the tank destroyer units' half-tracks from the incomprehensibly close range of fifteen yards. "How could they have mistaken the half-track for anything but an American vehicle?" the soldiers of the 823rd wondered. Amazingly, no one was killed, but the driver of the half-track suffered a serious chest wound.

This sickening, amicidal battle raged for twenty-five minutes before the two sides realized they were shooting at friendly troops. Two I Company tanks were destroyed, and one three-inch antitank gun was damaged. More important, ten Americans were dead or wounded (four from the 823rd and six from I Company). The troops of the 823rd were especially peeved because they had been the first to recognize what was happening. They had made repeated attempts to identify themselves, but the I Company Shermans rebuffed them. One of the tank destroyer officers, in reporting the morale of the command that night, said the mood was "satisfactory but mad as hell."

Certainly the I Company tankers should have been more aware of who they were shooting at, but their encounter with the two German antitank guns probably had much to do with their case of tunnel vision. The tragedy was the product of bad weather, bad luck, inexperience, and, more than anything, a bad decision on the part of Captain Redmond (and to a lesser extent Lieutenant Earl) in making the wrong turn.[5]

Be that as it may, the six remaining tanks of I Company, 33rd Armor, turned around and resumed their mission. When they reached the N-174, they made the correct turn this time (left) and proceeded by road all the way to Hauts Vents. The six tanks, now under the command of Lieutenant Earl, spread out and formed defensive positions on the hill. They spent the rest of the afternoon and the evening fighting brief skirmishes with groups of

Germans who seemed to be heading north, right past them. "We ran into soldiers, some in pairs, others in groups of three or four, some with steel helmets, others with . . . caps—some were armed, others were not. We could tell . . . we were deep in German lines." Earl and his tankers nervously waited to be reinforced. At one point, they even got strafed by American fighters. Luckily, no one was hurt. "Glances to the rear became . . . frequent."

No reinforcements were on the way. Lieutenant Earl sent back word of his position, but his radios would only transmit, not receive. Thus he had no idea what was taking place a mile to the north. By the time American planes strafed Earl's tanks in the fading light of early evening, Bohn's CCB task force was rolling south on the N-174, unimpeded, heading straight for Hauts Vents. Bohn passed the word to 30th Division headquarters that his I Company had taken Hauts Vents, but Hobbs and his staff dismissed the report. Here they fell prey to their own snap judgments about Bohn and CCB. After two days of frustration and misadventure, Hobbs simply could not believe that tanks from CCB had made it to Hauts Vents.

His skepticism was regrettable, (although perhaps a bit understandable), but now that skepticism led Hobbs to make two poor decisions. Bohn wanted to keep going, all the way to Hauts Vents, and relieve Lieutenant Earl, but Hobbs told him to halt, set up defensive positions, and give his tankers "a good night's rest." They didn't need a good night's rest as much as they needed to get to Hauts Vents. Hobbs, after all, had ordered Bohn earlier in the day to capture Hauts Vents by 1700. Not only did General Hobbs refuse to believe Bohn when he told him he did capture it by 1700; he was now preventing Bohn from carrying out the order! Hobbs ordered Bohn to halt because the 30th Division had been absorbing German counterattacks all day. The division had taken 300 casualties; the Germans were on the move all over the area, and General Hobbs was concerned that CCB might end up too far forward, vulnerable to German flanking attacks. Bohn tried to call Lieutenant Earl back from Hauts Vents, but of course Earl's radios were not receiving any transmissions.

Basically, General Hobbs was flip-flopping on his earlier intention to capture Hauts Vents, and yet the general held Bohn accountable for his own change of heart. This was where he made his second bad decision. At about midnight on July 10, he relieved Bohn. Major William Walker was sitting with General Bohn on the side of the N-174 highway when the radio in Bohn's jeep crackled to life. A voice, calling from 30th Division headquarters, ordered Bohn to report there immediately.

Bohn listened for a moment and said, "Well, Walker, this is it." The general hung his head and cried. Walker wanted to console him. For a few minutes they reminisced about old times with the division. Then Bohn stood up, got in his jeep, and said, "I am leaving you in command of this area."

Colonel Rogers was with Bohn. On the drive to the 30th Division CP, Bohn muttered a few comments about dreading the impending confrontation with General Hobbs, but mostly they rode in silence. The headquarters was located in a small underground room. The brightness, neat sense of order, and cleanliness of the room was a bit of a culture shock to Colonel Rogers. "General Hobbs was surrounded by a covey of clerks and staff officers busying themselves around neatly posted large scale situation maps. It appeared to me that some of the locations of major 30th Div. units shown on the maps were rather fanciful, to be charitable about it. In sharp contrast to General Hobbs's neat, clean uniform complete with shirt and tie, General Bohn's field uniform was wet, muddy, and disheveled and he sported several days growth of beard."

Hobbs launched into a soliloquy. He castigated Bohn for lack of aggressiveness and blamed his own division's lack of progress on Bohn. General Bohn's response was "low-keyed and factual," according to Colonel Rogers. Hobbs would have none of it. "I know what you did personally," he told him, "but you're a victim of circumstances." He fired Bohn and replaced him with Colonel Dorrance Roysdon, Bohn's executive officer.[6]

Six hours later, at Hauts Vents, the rising sun burned away the thin fog that had shrouded Earl's tanks during the lonely, frightening vigil in this windy no-man's-land. All night long Lieutenant Earl had waited for relief, but it never came. He could not hold out much longer here. With no orders and literally no idea what was happening anywhere around him, Earl decided to withdraw. He ran to each tank, hollering withdrawal orders. "We high-tailed it out of there before we could be boxed in. We went back through the 30th Infantry Division."

Earl did not know it, but the Americans had just lost a great opportunity. Had General Hobbs allowed General Bohn to keep moving on the previous evening, he would have made it to Earl's positions and consolidated American control of Hauts Vents. Instead, the Americans, because of confusion and poor command decisions, had relinquished control of this vital piece of high ground. This negated any chance of a quick push for St-Lô.

On July 10, when Colonel Roysdon resumed CCB's advance toward Hauts Vents, it was too late to capture it easily. German armored reinforcements, preparing to launch a major counterattack, were pouring into the area. Consequently, Roysdon's column ran into stiff resistance as it approached Hauts Vents during the daylight hours of July 10. All day long, the Americans fought for the hill.

By late afternoon, some of Roysdon's tanks were ascending Hauts Vents. Riding atop one of those Sherman tanks, Lieutenant Ralph Balestrieri looked at the terrain ahead. His tank was about three hundred meters from the top. Actually, it wasn't quite "his" tank. He was a forward observer from the 58th Armored Field Artillery Battalion. Like any good observer, he placed himself at the very front, so that he enjoyed a good sense of where to place artillery fire. As the tanks rolled upward, American artillery was supposed to support them. Balestrieri wondered when the shell fire would begin. The thought had no sooner flashed through his mind than he heard streaking sounds from behind. Here came the U.S. artillery. But the explosions were too close. "The concentration fell short causing the tanks to fall back about 50 yards while I called for a cease fire to give a correction. The original concentration was fired from the map on orders, from someone in command."

The botched fire mission, in addition to German resistance, foiled American attempts to take Hauts Vents on July 10. The next day, Roysdon tried again. Scout cars and half-tracks led the way as the column rumbled south. Behind them were the Shermans. The column was just about to turn right on the road that led to Hauts Vents when they started taking devastating anti-tank fire from somewhere on the left (east) in the vicinity of Belle Lande. One after the other, the Germans picked off six Sherman tanks, most of which caught fire. The crews scrambled out as best they could, but some did not make it. The sickly sweet odor of their burning flesh mixed with the smell of early-morning dew.

The Americans returned fire and this silenced the enemy antitank guns. Colonel Roysdon strode up and down the column, getting everything organized and restoring morale. The advance resumed but then slowed down when (once again) short U.S. artillery rounds landed among the vehicles of CCB. With this straightened out, they started climbing the hill, just like the day before. The Germans were at the top, raining fire down on the American tanks and half-tracks. The American tanks and artillery responded in kind. For about an hour the battle seesawed. Finally, Roysdon ordered a dismounted assault on the crest of Hauts Vents. "[He] formed the GI's in a line of skirmishers and went up it like taking San Juan hill," one officer recalled. A line of tanks followed the skirmishers. Roysdon was perched in the turret of his tank, Thompson in hand, "shouting orders over his radio and out to an infantry CO who was walking alongside the tank." The colonel directed fire at any pocket of resistance in the numerous clumps of trees and bushes that dotted the hill.

At 1736, the hill was theirs, this time to keep. Roysdon gave his men all the credit, describing their actions as "amazing . . . enough cannot be said." German troops counterattacked throughout the next day and night, but they made no headway. One of the reasons they failed was Lieutenant Balestrieri's fire missions. He worked closely with an aerial artillery observer to call down accurate fire on German troop movements around the hill. "[It] was . . . an old fashioned, forward observer's dream . . . [a] 14 hour turkey shoot. In each fire for effect [the aerial observer] gave a full description of effect on target much in the manner of a sportscaster, interspersed with comments like 'It hit the breech,' or 'The whole crew on one gun wiped out,' or 'Geez! Right down the tube.' Very few rounds were wasted on adjustments."

With Hauts Vents in his pocket, General Hobbs now regretted relieving General Bohn. "If he had had a little more of a chance," Hobbs told General Corlett, "he probably would have" captured Hauts Vents just like Roysdon. Hobbs was a good division commander, but this had not been his finest moment. He knew he had acted rashly in firing Bohn and learned from it.[7]

The capture of Hauts Vents absorbed German troops and resources when they could least afford it. The rumors of an impending enemy attack were true. The American intelligence officers were right about the whereabouts and disposition of Panzer Lehr. This powerful unit, one of the best in the German Army, had indeed traveled west from the Caen front to launch a counterattack on XIX Corps. Parts of that attack were already under way on July 9 and 10, but the main offensive began during the early-morning hours of July 11. The Germans hoped to break through the forward positions of the 30th Division and the 9th Division (newly arrived in the sector) and drive a wedge in the American lines.

Under cover of darkness, dozens of Mark IV and Mark V tanks, augmented by self-propelled guns and mechanized infantry, penetrated thinly held outpost positions of the 9th Division at Le Désert and la Charlemanerie (both located southwest of St-Jean-de-Daye). In some cases, American troops saw the silhouettes of the enemy vehicles and infantry but believed them to be American. Only when they heard German being spoken did they realize what was happening. In most cases, the Germans rolled right by before anyone could even shoot at them.

The enemy attack relied on American confusion. As long as there was darkness the Germans made headway. They gained as much as 2,000 yards in some places. But as the sun rose German fortunes sank. In the light of day the Americans could now see what they were dealing with. Plus, they had had a few hours to figure out what was happening and respond. In the 9th Division sector, for instance, the German gains turned into a liability for them. American tanks and troops swung behind the attacking Panzer Lehr battalions and blasted them at ranges of 300 to 700 yards. Fighter-bombers joined in the fray. Many of these planes had been slated for other missions but were diverted in response to the German attack. In droves they hit Panzer Lehr's attacking vehicles. The fighter jocks could hardly miss. Enemy tanks and half-tracks, packed together on the narrow roads that led to Le Désert and La Charlemanerie, made ideal targets. American

P-47 and P-51 pilots unleashed 500-pound bombs on them and made repeated strafing runs. In all, they destroyed twenty-two tanks.

Tank destroyers, mainly from the 9th Division's 899th Tank Destroyer Battalion, did almost as much damage. Companies A and C of the 899th were equipped with M-10 Wolverines, a tracked vehicle whose main gun could, from certain angles, penetrate German armor. The tank destroyer crews at first tried to hold fast along the roads and trade shots with the Germans. However, when they realized that their shots were not penetrating the thick frontal armor of the enemy Panther (Mark V) tanks they maneuvered behind them and destroyed them from the rear. The tank destroyers destroyed twelve Panthers and one Mark IV. American artillery, antitank guns, and bazooka teams added to the carnage. The 9th Division had blunted the attack in their sector by midafternoon. "Enemy tanks clogged the roads and highway hedgerows showed signs of action," one soldier recalled, "the French countryside was snipped and churned . . . marred as only war can disfigure."

The story was much the same to the southeast, where one battalion of Panzer Lehr tanks and two battalions of mechanized infantry hit the 30th Division. The strongest enemy push was against the 3rd Battalion, 120th Infantry, at the village of Le Rocher, located at the northern foot of Hauts Vents. The German armor nearly overran the battalion CP. By daybreak, the two sides were so close to each other that they could make out the facial features of their enemies. American infantrymen fought the German tanks off with rifle grenades, bazookas, and small arms.

Sergeant Thomas Kattar of Massachusetts was a member of K Company, 120th Infantry. Near le Rocher his unit was pinned down along a hedgerow by enemy tank and mortar fire. Periodically Kattar's captain peeked through the foliage and saw a German tank in an adjacent field, tormenting them with steady fire. Somewhere down the line of pinned-down men, a company bazooka team was down. Both men were wounded and their weapon was destroyed. The tank had to be stopped before it could do any more damage.

The captain turned to Kattar. "See what you can do about that tank."

Kattar's eyes widened. "Me, Captain?"

"Yes, you, Kattar."

Another sergeant volunteered to go with Kattar. The two of them got up and, under fire, began searching for a bazooka. At last they found one. Kattar carried the bazooka, and the other man trailed slightly behind. They dived behind the shelter of the hedgerow and set up very close to where the first bazooka team had been wounded. Slowly and cautiously Sergeant Kattar lifted his head and snatched a quick look into the field. "I looked up over the hedgerow . . . and there I saw that big" tank. He lowered himself and nodded to his loader. The other sergeant inserted the bazooka's 2.36-inch rocket, attached the arming wire, and tapped Kattar on the shoulder.

Sergeant Kattar steadily raised himself up into a shooting position—no easy feat with the awkward, heavy five-foot-long bazooka tube in his hands. "I took aim and let it go. We hit the tank and blew it up."

The other man was excited: "You did it, Sergeant! You did it, Sergeant!"

Kattar was not as elated, because he knew the enemy would respond. "Get down!" he snapped.

Sure enough, German fire poured in on them. "All at once bullets from the enemy were coming around, over the hedgerow, all around, on top of the hedgerow."

The two men hugged the ground and, when the fire abated, crawled back to the captain. The captain took one look at Kattar, smiled, and said, "You did a good job, Kattar."

One by one, bazooka teams like Kattar's hit enemy tanks or drove them off. They destroyed five German tanks and four armored cars, two of which mounted flamethrowers. They also captured sixty prisoners. The enemy could not replace these losses because, by afternoon and evening on July 11, CCB's presence on Hauts Vents prevented them from reinforcing their attack. So instead they retreated. The Panzer Lehr attack was over. It was a miserable failure. The division lost 25 percent of its combat strength and gained nothing. The Germans had found out that, in Normandy, attacking was far more difficult than defending.[8]

Still, the presence of Panzer Lehr meant that the northwest approach to St-Lô was a dead end. Panzer Lehr was battered, but it was still quite formidable and it stood directly between Corlett and St-Lô. His divisions no longer had the opening that had been in front of them four days earlier. The Americans, because of poor coordination between the 30th Division and CCB, had squandered their opportunity for a quick dash into St-Lô from this direction. Instead, the 30th, the 9th, and the 3rd Armored spent the next several days steadily slugging their way south against the kind of entrenched, hedgerow-dominated defenses at which the Germans excelled. They sapped German strength, but they were not in a position to capture St-Lô anytime soon. Clearly now the best entryway to St-Lô was from the east where the 29th and 2nd Divisions were poised to strike. The final battle for this vital objective was about to begin.

CHAPTER NINE

AGONY AND BLOODSHED: ST-LO

In the sixth century, a Christian bishop named Lo (or Lauto) lived a life of kindness and devotion in the Norman town of Briovera. After Bishop Lo's death, the Catholic Church recognized his life of good works by conferring sainthood upon him. The townspeople were so proud of this favorite son that they changed the name of their city from Briovera to St-Lô. With only a few thousand residents, the town of St-Lô was not big, but it was located at the confluence of every major road in Normandy (some of which had been built by the Romans). Basically, St-Lô was a crossroads to everywhere in Normandy. This made it a desirable target for invaders, and there were many of them over the centuries—Vikings interested in plunder, Plantagenet English kings interested in the French crown or the local crops, even French Catholics interested in hunting down heretics during the Reformation. None of these invaders had the slightest intention of "liberating" the population of St-Lô. They wanted what invading armies had usually wanted throughout history—power, loot, plunder, or women.

As the U.S. Army approached venerable St-Lô in July 1944, it was only the latest in a long line of invaders, but its agenda was quite different. The Americans did not want war booty; they wanted to liberate the people of St-Lô from the Germans, whose conquest of St-Lô in 1940 had been bloodless. So it was supremely ironic that the American liberators of St-Lô inflicted more damage on the town, more death and destruction on the populace, than any other single invader, including the Germans. Since D-Day, American bombers and artillery had reduced St-Lô from a prosperous market town of 12,000 to a smoking ghost town of ruined masonry. In the first day of bombing alone, 800 civilians died. Many more lost their lives over the following weeks. By the middle of July, more than 60 percent of the buildings in St-Lô had been destroyed.

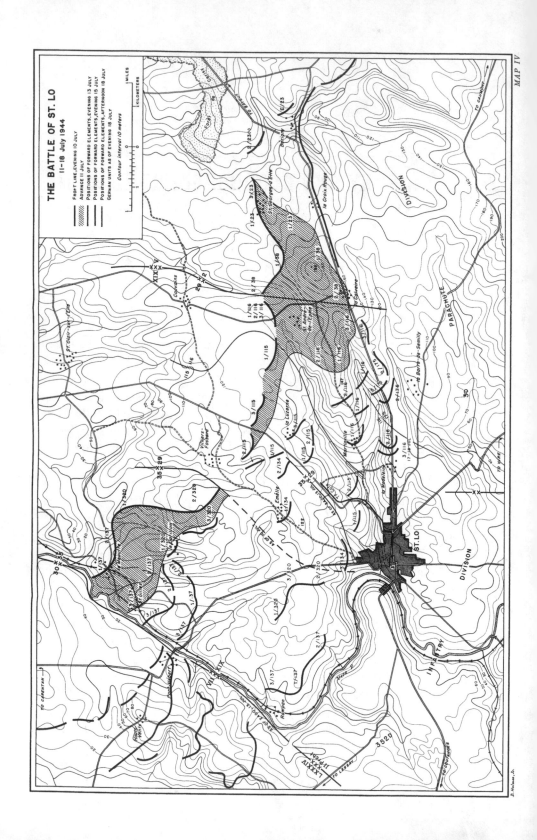

THE BATTLE OF ST. LO
11–18 July 1944

FRONT LINE, EVENING 10 JULY
ADVANCE 11 JULY
POSITIONS OF FORWARD ELEMENTS, EVENING 13 JULY
POSITIONS OF FORWARD ELEMENTS, EVENING 15 JULY
POSITIONS OF FORWARD ELEMENTS, AFTERNOON 18 JULY
GERMAN UNITS AS OF EVENING 18 JULY

Contour interval 10 meters

MAP IV

D. Holmes, Jr.

All of this was tragic, but it had to be done. St-Lô was the epicenter of movement for German reinforcements in Normandy. It was also a vital enemy CP and nerve center. Anyone hoping to eliminate the German presence in Normandy had to destroy the German Army's ability to utilize St-Lô. In a way, the destruction of this previously serene city was an extension of the transportation plan that had been implemented in the spring of 1944. This plan recognized one regrettable but inescapable fact—some of France would have to be destroyed in order to liberate it.

Thus St-Lô was a rubble-choked, ghostly wasteland by the second week of July, but the destruction had not diminished its vital importance. General Bradley knew by now that his 1st Army would achieve no breakthrough in Normandy without controlling St-Lô. At one time he had hoped to bypass the city, envelop it, while Middleton's VIII Corps broke the German lines at La Haye-du-Puits. But that, obviously, was no longer possible. Hundreds of Americans were getting killed or wounded every day. This plodding, stolid, hedgerow-to-hedgerow campaign had to end soon. He longed to punch through the German lines and turn this into a fluid, maneuver-oriented campaign. To make this happen, the general was pondering a major breakthrough plan (called Operation Cobra) that would include the use of heavy bombers. But he knew that the plan could not be implemented unless he had St-Lô. Eight major roads led south from St-Lô's city center. Without those roads, his armored divisions would have little chance of exploiting any breakthrough in the remaining German defenses. There was no getting around the fact that St-Lô had to be taken.[1]

The leading role in the final push for St-Lô went to the 29th and 2nd Divisions. Both of these outfits had spent the last month in static positions three miles northeast of St-Lô. This was the thickest of the bocage country. The two armies were dug into the hedgerows; they sat facing each other in a prolonged stalemate. American aerial photographs revealed, in one sector alone, close to 4,000 hedged enclosures in an area that spanned eight square miles. The 29th Division was to smash into St-Lô from the east, advancing directly along the Martinville Ridge, a finger of high ground that snaked east from the town all the way through the American lines. In this way the 29'ers would outflank Hill 122 (different from the Hill 122 known as Mont Castre), which dominated the northern roads into St-Lô. The 2nd Division was supposed to protect the 29th's left flank by capturing Hill 192, the highest ground in Normandy. The U.S. Army named these hills for their height in meters.

General Charles Gerhardt, the 29th's commander, planned to line up two of his regiments, the 115th and 116th, and tear through the defenses of the elite German 3rd Parachute Division east of St-Lô. The 116th would assume the lead, advancing into St-Lô along one of the main roads. If all went as planned, the 116th would fight its way into St-Lô and German defenses on Hill 122 would come unhinged. The attack was supposed to begin on July 9, but rain postponed it for two days.

Instead of an attack on July 9, a curious incident happened near La Fossardière. A group of American soldiers, manning the outpost positions of B Company, 115th Infantry, 29th Division, saw movement to their front, from a German-controlled hedgerow. A German medic, waving a white flag, nonchalantly climbed over the hedgerow and walked toward them. The German wore a white smock bearing a large red cross. He walked to within a couple paces of the outpost, saluted stiffly, and handed the Americans a note. It identified him as a captain and requested a two-hour truce so that both sides could retrieve their dead and wounded from no-man's-land.

The American sergeant at the outpost knew that a decision for such a truce had to be made by someone of higher rank than he, so he sent the message up the chain of command. The battalion commander, Major Glover Johns, was sound asleep. He had left strict instructions not be disturbed. The highest-ranking officer that could be found was Lieutenant George Grimsehl, his intelligence officer. Lieutenant Grimsehl saw no harm in a truce, so he agreed to it. Medics spent the next couple of hours removing the swollen, maggot-ridden dead from the orchard that comprised no-man's-land. The Americans found one man who was badly wounded, dehydrated, but still alive, and they evacuated him. When the allotted time for the truce elapsed, the two sides went their separate ways and the war resumed. A little later, Major Johns woke up and found out about the truce. He was "annoyed with Grimsehl for taking so much on himself" but did not say anything because he knew he had left instructions not to be disturbed while he was sleeping. He merely made a "mental note not to indulge . . . in such luxuries again." The incident passed into seeming insignificance.

The next night, July 10, General Gerhardt visited the forward positions of his two assaulting regiments and told his commanders that the attack would begin the following morning at 0600. In the cramped hole that comprised the 1st Battalion, 115th Infantry, CP, Major Johns and his staff finalized their plans, ate a C-ration meal in thoughtful silence, and waited for the morning. The night was clear, starry, and silent. Johns was thinking about how his attack would proceed in the morning when the world exploded. "Suddenly a terrific firing broke out. Every German cannon, mortar, rifle and machine gun . . . cut loose simultaneously. The sound of mortars coughing on the German side blended with the scream of incoming shells. The sharp roar of artillery shells overrode the flatter crunching of mortars, while the vicious, snarling, still sharper crack of 88's stood out above both, and the ripping of German machine guns filled in the tiny intervals between explosions."

The phone in Johns's hole started ringing. His rifle company commanders, one after the other, reported being vigorously attacked by German paratroopers. Lieutenant Stoen, at B Company's forward positions, begged for as much artillery support at possible. "The bastards are all over us," Stoen cried, and hung up. Johns tried to call regiment, but the lines were out. He could hardly hear himself think because of the volume of noise from the shelling and shooting. His artillery officer tried to call for fire, but the lines were dead. Johns tried calling the fire direction center by radio, but he could not get through and would not be able to for at least twenty more minutes.

Johns felt helpless and impotent, unable to exert any control over the situation. He needed information and he needed it badly. Finally, he got out of his hole and listened to the sounds of the battle. "Although the fire was concentrated chiefly on the edges of the gap between the two companies at the orchard, it was hitting all along the front. Some rounds tore into the field and hedgerow near the command post while others rushed overhead to burst in the trees." Johns correctly deduced that his battalion was being hit by a major counterattack.

Some four hundred German paratroopers were in the process of breaching the 1st Battalion's lines. In so doing, they were probably utilizing information from the German "medic" who had asked for the truce two days earlier, because they seemed to know the location of every position. The enemy soldiers swept past the American outpost holes in the orchard and ran along the hedgerows, pitching grenades, firing their burp guns at point-blank range. One officer in B Company, Lieutenant Fletcher Harris, heard one of the grenades land next to his foxhole. Harris picked up the grenade and started to throw it back, but it exploded, severing his right hand. The dark night prevented either side from seeing each other very well. The fighting took place at close quarters, with German and American mortar rounds exploding randomly.

Lieutenant Stoen managed to pull most of his B Company back a few hedgerows and hold fast. Company C remained in place and fought the Germans off. But A Company, holding the most forward positions in the orchard, had no such luck. The German attack hit the men of this company particularly hard. The company was cut off, totally out of communication with Johns or anyone else. Some members of A Company found an escape route along a sunken road and ran for their lives. Breathless and frightened out of their minds, they sowed panic in the rear areas of the 115th Regiment, prompting a 4.2-inch mortar unit, and part of an antitank company, to take flight.

The Germans infiltrated A Company's whole perimeter, cutting the scared Americans off from one another. These little groups resisted as best they could, "with rifle butts, grenades and anything else that could be found," one soldier remembered. They had no choice. For these men, there was nowhere to go.

Others, like Lieutenant Robert Davis, got captured. "Before I knew what was going on, the Krauts were in there with us. They killed two . . . boys—right in front of me. I held up my hands and my radioman did too. They took my pistol belt . . . then the others went on and one Kraut pushed us toward the rear. We walked a long time. Some of our own mortars came in close. We . . . found some old German fox holes." The holes were covered with sheet metal. The German guard turned his back on the two Americans and investigated one of the holes. "My radioman jumped him. My man jerked off his helmet, hit the Kraut in the back of the neck with it." At that moment, Lieutenant Davis remembered that he still had a hunting knife stashed in his leggings. The Germans had only taken his cartridge belt; they had made no attempt to thoroughly search him. Davis reached down, grabbed the knife, and strode toward the dazed German guard. "I jumped him. I hit him with the knife and it went into him. Then I hit him again and again and again. I couldn't stop hitting him even after . . . I knew he was dead. My radioman pulled me off him." The two men made it back to Johns's CP, but they had to be evacuated with combat fatigue.

In all, the German attack lasted three hours. By 0200 Major Johns and his artillery observers established contact with the artillery fire direction center. They called down plenty of rounds on the suspected locations of enemy infiltrators. They also plastered the likely routes of enemy reinforcement and resupply. Gradually, the enemy paratroopers drifted back to their own lines. By the time the sun rose, the battle was over. Johns sent a patrol to make contact with the beleaguered survivors of A Company. "We found their platoons that morning, right in their original positions, with dead Krauts all around them." The 1st Battalion had suffered 150 casualties, the Germans a like number. American graves registration teams removed eighty-seven enemy bodies from the area.[2]

The German attack had been blunted, but the 115th was in no shape to go forward at the planned time on July 11. Major Johns needed several hours to reorganize his battalion and get it ready to go. The 115th did not move out until late in the morning. Meanwhile, 500 yards to the left of Johns's battalion, the 116th Infantry attacked, as planned, at 0600. Colonel Canham, the regimental commander, ordered his battalions to line up in columns, one behind the other. Utilizing the new tank-infantry tactics, Major Sidney Bingham's 2nd Battalion led the way. Bingham had led his unit ashore on D-Day. Today he would lead them in the fight for St-Lô. "Our plan was to move south astride the road through St. Andre de L'Epine with F Company on the left, E on the right and G in reserve. About 2,000 yards south we were to make a 90 degree right turn on the high ground and move west along the ridge to the village of Martinsville [*sic*]."

An hour-long artillery barrage preceded the advance. Among the F Company soldiers who were watching the bombardment, waiting for the word to move out, Rocco Russo watched the American shelling and felt a sense of awe. "The artillery barrage that day was . . . frightening. Even hearing friendly artillery coming over was terrifying. We were so close to the German lines that shells meant for them could easily hit us." Russo was a rare bird—a front-line 29'er who was with the unit on D-Day. Casualties had turned the ranks of the 29th Division's rifle companies over many times by now. Only a few D-Day veterans like Russo remained.

The artillery tapered off, and Russo watched as dozer tanks rumbled forward. "The tanks . . . cut holes in the hedgerows for us to move through. Some of us would go through the holes, others would climb over the hedgerow. Either way, we were very vulnerable to enemy fire."

A couple hundred yards to the rear of Russo, Major Charles Cawthon, another D-Day veteran, watched the soldiers go forward into the unknown. "Bending as under tremendous burdens, the files moved forward through the ground mist toward the hedgerows from which they would jump off." Cawthon and the rest of the headquarters personnel followed. Artillery fire, both American and German, intensified. "Salvo after salvo crashed along the front. Under cover of this noise, the tanks moved up and . . . tore up the telephone lines as they went. The ear-shattering blast of high-velocity tank guns and the beat of machine guns joined in, until it seemed that sound alone would destroy everything."

At the appointed time, two companies of American infantry soldiers pressed forward. Many took shelter behind tanks as they advanced. In no time, they all ran into a terrible wall of deadly fire. The first German-held hedgerow shielded a sunken lane that the Germans were using as a trench. Machine-gun fire ripped into the attacking American troops, shattering bones, tearing internal organs, here and there killing men instantly. Mines were everywhere. Several unfortunate soldiers tripped mines, blowing off feet or legs.

Enemy mortar fire added to the casualties, as did short rounds from U.S. artillery. Private John Robertson of F Company was hunched over, clutching his rifle, trotting behind a tank, when an American artillery shell landed right in the middle of his squad. "My squad . . . was really butchered up. Some of us were blown forward, some backward. It was a big mess." Private Robertson was knocked down. It took him a few moments to regain his senses and realize that he was wounded. "I got up and started limping back. As I was slopping along thinking about why my shoe was full of 'water,' I felt my leg and my hand went all the way to the bone. It was blood that I was slopping in. I practically passed out, but vaguely remember being patched up by a medic."

The fighting went on this way for several hours that morning. Major Cawthon spent most of his time going back and forth between the forward positions and the CP, compiling information—Colonel Canham was constantly on the phone haranguing him for reports—and coordinating the fire of a 4.2-inch-mortar unit on German positions along the Martinville Ridge. Dead Americans were lying all over the place. "The attack had progressed only two or three fields. Marking the limit of advance was a tank, and while I watched, a soldier climbed up behind the turret, apparently trying to see what lay ahead. As he raised up, a burst of bullets swept the turret, knocking him backward as though jerked with a rope."

The whole area stank of cordite and death. Thin wisps of smoke blanketed the fields and hedgerows. The surviving infantrymen were lying at the base of those hedgerows, trying to find rudimentary shelter from all the fire. Cawthon screwed up his courage and made a dash for the CP. As he ran, he kept thinking that this attack was every bit as bad as Omaha beach. He made it safely to the CP, but with plenty of bad news about casualties. Half of the platoon leaders and sergeants had been hit. Three out of the battalion's four company commanders were down. The three attacking rifle companies were down to about sixty men apiece. A mere 500 yards had been gained.

At first glance, the attack seemed to have failed, but the Germans were even worse off. The morning's worth of ferocious fighting destroyed their forward defenses. In the early afternoon, the survivors of the 116th discovered, to their surprised delight, that enemy resistance was crumbling. The Germans were in retreat. They were now setting up a new defensive line about a mile and a half east of St-Lô. Major Bingham's battalion made a right turn at St-André-de-l'Epine and followed the spine of the Martinville Ridge west for two miles.

As they advanced, they saw the remnants of their enemies. "All was devastation, blasted and burned," Major Cawthon wrote. "German paratroopers, whole and in parts, lay about. It was difficult to reconcile these diminished, inert figures in round helmets and blood-soaked camouflage smocks with those who had been, that same morning, among the most dangerous fighting men of the war."

Cawthon and a few others in the command group paused and studied the grisly scene. Everything stank of burned gunpowder or burned flesh. A German self-propelled assault gun was listing to one side, emanating smoke from a blasted chassis. Here and there lumps of flesh dotted the ground. The whole scene was nauseating. Standing next to Cawthon, Major Bingham's orderly shook his head and said, "I don't understand it. I just don't understand what it's all about." Cawthon nodded in agreement. "There could be no elation in a sight at once so brutal and pitiful."

Bingham's depleted battalion made it all the way to within sight of Martinville. They dug in about a mile east of the town. This 3,000-yard gain was the greatest American advance on this first day of the offensive, and it brought the 29th to within two miles of St-Lô. For a brief time on July 11 General Gerhardt even entertained hopes of taking St-Lô that day, but that was not realistic. The 2nd Battalion's flanks were wide open. The 115th, after parrying the German nocturnal attack, had advanced only a few hundred yards. The other two battalions of the 116th did get into the fight at 1400, against little resistance, and that helped the 2nd Battalion's situation. Later General Gerhardt threw in a couple battalions from the 175th to further protect Bingham's southern flank. But, there was no way his men were going to take St-Lô on the first day. The German defenders were just too strong and too well prepared for that kind of dramatic ending to the story of St-Lô.[3]

Bingham's people would not have had as much success as they did on July 11 without the support of the 2nd Division. The division had a straightforward mission: capture Hill 192 and the road just beyond it. On a clear day, a man standing atop Hill 192 could see all the way to the invasion beaches. Of course most days in the summer of 1944 were not clear, but Hill 192 was still an excellent OP. On a typical cloudy, hazy Norman day, a man on top of the hill could see most of the eastern approaches to St-Lô. This meant that German artillerymen on the hill were in a position to harass the whole 29th Division, every step of the way to St-Lô—unless the 2nd Division could take the hill.

The men of the 2nd Division had been living in the shadow of Hill 192 for nearly a month. Thanks to patrolling and aerial reconnaissance, the officers were familiar with practically every inch of the hill and its environs. The slopes of the hill rose gently to a flat top. These slopes consisted mostly of hedgerows, fields, scattered woods, and the odd farmhouse. The leeward, or southern, side of the hill was blanketed with a diamond-shaped patch of woods.

The Americans had been bombarding Hill 192 for weeks prior to the attack, until the place looked like a "moth-eaten white blanket," in the estimation of one U.S. officer. The Germans on the hill lived in dugouts, tunnels, and bunkers. To further soften up these positions, the plan called for air strikes on the morning of the attack, but cloudy skies, fog, and rain forced the commanders to call off the strikes. Only a twenty-minute artillery preparation preceded the 2nd Division's attack, but the artillery was formidable. Some of the shells had a proximity fuse lodged into their nose. The fuse contained a tiny radio transmitter that detonated the shell at a predetermined distance from a target rather than upon simple contact with the ground. This maximized the killing power of the shell's shrapnel.

When the shelling began on that misty July morning, U.S. infantrymen watched from their forward positions. Captain George Duckworth, the commanding officer of F Company, 23rd Infantry, sat transfixed, watching explosion after explosion, wondering how anything or anyone could live in the targeted area. His unit was about to attack the eastern slope of Hill 192. "The noise was deafening as we watched the fiery explosions. Dust, smoke, brush, rocks, and debris of all kinds erupted over the entire surface of the hill and the surrounding area."

At nearly the stroke of 0600 the barrage petered out, and for the briefest few moments an eerie silence pervaded the battlefield. Then Shermans from the 741st Tank Battalion gunned their engines, staggered forward, and punched holes in the most forward hedgerows. The air was soon alive with the sound of their .50-caliber machine guns and 75mm main guns. Captain Duckworth stood up, moved forward, and gestured everyone else to follow. His company, along with many unseen hundreds of U.S. soldiers (including Bingham's troops several hundred yards to the northwest in the 29th Division sector), spread out into attack formation and walked toward the hill.

Duckworth's men clustered behind the tanks and advanced "with ferocity and grim determination. The tanks, with their plowshare attachments [prongs], were awesome and a complete surprise to the enemy." Duckworth saw several tanks battering their way through hedgerows. "When a tank hit a hedgerow at full speed, the plowshares threw dirt, rocks, brush, and other debris into the air. The tanks then roared on into the next field . . . and opened fire with the cannon and machine guns on the next hedgerow to the front."

Duckworth and his F Company soldiers trailed along and shot up any enemy positions. "As we charged into the enemy front line positions, we found many still in foxholes, dugouts, and hedgerow positions. Even though they were somewhat dazed and deafened by the artillery bombardment, they were able to bring a heavy volume of small-arms fire down on us." The enemy soldiers were young, tough, and dedicated, almost fanatical. They were from the 3rd Parachute Division, one of the best units in the German Army. Quite often, they held fast and died in their holes as Duckworth's men "closed in and overran them with our tanks and infantry. It was a fierce, no-quarter-asked and no-quarter-given battle, often man-to-man with rifle butts, bayonets, and trench knives. There were no enemy offers of surrender and I do not recall that we took any prisoners in the initial penetration of their defenses. Some may have surrendered or been taken prisoner after we moved forward."

Even many of those prisoners had a difficult time surviving long enough to make it to a POW camp. Clem Turpin had come to Normandy as a private, but attrition had turned him into a sergeant. A month before, in the 2nd Division's initial push for Hill 192, he had nearly been eviscerated by a shell from an enemy tank (it passed right between his legs). Now, as the morning of July 11 unfolded and Turpin's squad methodically pushed its way up the hill, it became enmeshed in bitter close-quarters fighting with the German paratroopers. "A machine-gun fired at us from a few feet away. I hit the ground and could feel the bullets going between me and the dirt and shattering my cartridge belt. We got up and charged the hill again. I looked around and saw an enemy anti-tank gun and a hole nearby. I fired into it and heard screams. The crew . . . crawled out and surrendered. I captured their anti-tank gun and took them prisoner."

Turpin turned the gun around and fired five shots at German positions farther up the hill. Next he began to escort his three prisoners to the rear. Along the way, he caught the prisoners trying to crunch American communication wire under their boots. Turpin fired several warning shots at their feet and they stopped. One of Sergeant Turpin's men came along and he told him to escort his three captives to the battalion CP. "He was gone only about five minutes." This was nowhere near enough time to make it to the battalion CP. "Who knows what he did with those prisoners." Most likely, the prisoners had resumed their sabotage efforts and the man killed them for it.

The 23rd's attack continued to progress, in spite of fierce enemy resistance. Company A got pinned down in an ambush near St-Georges-d'Elle, in a valley that was appropriately named Purple Heart Draw. Only the resolve of A Company's soldiers, plus some timely help from C Company, broke German resistance.

The advance resumed. Whenever the American tanks saw houses, they poured fire into them, knocking out many enemy machine guns and even a few antitank positions. Some of the tanks buried enemy soldiers alive in their dugouts. One Sherman entombed an entire German heavy-machine-gun team when the tank punched through a hedgerow. Riflemen fastened grenades to the muzzles of their weapons and placed scores of well-aimed shots over hedgerows, right into enemy-occupied holes. The Americans filtered behind the Germans whenever they could. Duckworth's F Company, for instance, maneuvered, undetected, behind a platoon of enemy soldiers at the extreme eastern slope of Hill 192. "One of my BAR men braced his gun on top of a downed tree stump and mowed down a line of enemy troops before they knew we had penetrated behind them."[4]

Some six hundred yards to the west of Duckworth and his C Company, 23rd Infantry, other 2nd Division soldiers were also fighting their way up the hill. Colonel Ralph Zwicker, commander of the 38th Infantry, sent his first two battalions straight at Hill 192. The night before the attack, Zwicker had taken the precaution of withdrawing his units several hundred yards while the pre-attack barrage went on. This negated friendly fire casualties, but the wily German defenders figured out what was happening. Under cover of darkness they had pressed forward and had occupied the former American positions. In so doing, they protected themselves from the pre-attack barrage. They were also lying in ambush for the lead units of the 38th Infantry as they picked their way through the early-morning mist. In the first half hour of the attack, enemy *Panzerfaust* fire knocked six tanks of the 741st out of action. With the help of a rolling artillery barrage—division artillery fired 20,000 rounds on this one day—the Americans fought for several minutes just to make it to the line of departure.

From there, they worked their way up the hill. German resistance was determined, well organized, and bitter, especially on the western flank where E Company of the 38th Infantry ran into a nest of German resistance, quickly dubbed Kraut Corner, near the tiny hillside village of Cloville. There was half a company of German paratroopers at Kraut Corner, but they fought with the effectiveness of a unit two or three times that size. Lieutenant Charles Curley's 1st Platoon found itself on the opposite side of a hedgerow from the forward positions of Kraut Corner. The Richmond native had joined his unit several weeks before as a replacement. By now he was experienced and confident, and it showed in his performance on this challenging day.

Curley and his men were taking cover behind the hedgerow, preparing to move into the next field with their accompanying tank, when a group of Germans threw several egg-shaped concussion grenades at them from the other side of the hedgerow. The Americans dived as far away as they could from the detonating grenades. The only casualty was a man wounded by his own knife as he hit the ground. Before Curley could issue any orders, one of his squad leaders tried to take matters into his own hands. "Sergeant Kuhlow . . . in haste climbed up on the hedge and was firing down on the other side when he was shot and killed. One of the men dropped a fragmentation grenade over the hedge, but it was thrown back up in the air and damn near got a few men."

Curley ordered everyone to settle down while he tried to figure out what to do. He and his sergeants realized that the Germans were dug in under the hedge. If Curley's platoon tried to climb over the hedge, the enemy could shoot straight up into them. "We had to get them out of their holes before we could move on." The whole of E Company was now depending upon Curley's platoon, because in adjacent fields the bulk of two other E Company platoons were pinned down by withering small-arms and mortar fire.

Lieutenant Curley looked to the rear and signaled his supporting tank to come forward. When it closed to within twenty feet of the hedgerow, Curley halted it, ran behind the tank, and grabbed the phone that had been rigged on the back. He and the tank commander decided to fire a few 75mm rounds along the top of the German-controlled hedge. The tank fired twice, to no avail. Next the tank tried to ram the hedgerow with its prongs. Even this did not work. Once again, Curley and the tank commander spoke. The tank commander told Curley that there was a dozer tank a couple fields away. "I didn't know [that] so I told him to rush that tank up."

Moments later the dozer tank appeared. Curley told the dozer's commander to punch low holes in the hedgerow. "No problem," the dozer commander replied.

His tank rumbled up to the hedgerow and proceeded to punch a gaping hole right through it. "Instantly, Germans began flying over the hedge as if launched by springs," Curley wrote. "About ten men . . . hit the ground on our side and started running back across the field towards our rear with arms held high as if the devil himself was right behind them." The Americans hollered for them to halt, but they kept going, all the way to the company command group, who were, of course, quite startled to see them.

Curley's men shrugged and resumed their advance, right through a field to another hedgerow. They were now about 150 yards northwest of Cloville. The men could see the village in the distance. They knew that the remaining German defenders of Kraut Corner were hidden in and around the demolished, roofless buildings of this tiny village. Warily the Americans looked to and fro as they took shelter behind this hedgerow. Curley was standing in front of one of the tanks, looking over the hedge, pointing toward the buildings, trying to tell the tank commander to lay down covering fire for the platoon's impending assault on Cloville. The tank's main gun was just a few feet behind Curley's head. Suddenly someone to Curley's right screamed, "There's a German tank!"

Lieutenant Curley turned to his right "to see who was hollering when the 75mm gun over my head started moving to the right, then fired. I was thrown up against the hedge and thought that the world had come to an end. I tried to get up but there was another explosion and all colors of red and white smoke rolled around me." Curley thought that the tank had been hit, but he was wrong. It, and another American tank, had destroyed a German self-propelled gun that was hidden slightly to their right on a sunken road that led away from Cloville. Curley was standing so close to the Sherman's gun that the concussion knocked him out. His runner revived him with some water to the face. The lieutenant's ears were ringing and he had lost his helmet, but he was OK. "I learned a lesson that day that lasted a long time. From that day forward, I don't believe that I ever walked in front of a tank in combat."

In the next hour and a half, the Americans fought their way into Cloville. An 88mm self-propelled gun, plus a Mark IV tank, anchored the German defenses. One Sherman took out both of the enemy armored vehicles. When this happened, the American infantry poured into the rubble of Cloville and systematically cleared the Germans out. They either surrendered or died.

Throughout the afternoon, Colonel Zwicker's two battalions steadily overwhelmed the Germans on or near Hill 192. The 1st Battalion's B Company passed the crest of the hill by 1330 and made it all the way through the diamond-shaped woods. Most of the trees of these woods were gone or burning. American white phosphorous shells had set the place on fire. Only the smoking husks of the trees remained.

In spite of persistent danger, the 2nd Battalion, including Lieutenant Curley's E Company, secured the western slopes of Hill 192 and reached the road by late afternoon. "A sniper fired a lone shot, hitting one of my men in the head." The man's lifeless body fell to the ground. Curley and several others heard the dull crump of U.S. artillery up ahead. They kept moving and found the sniper lying in the middle of a sunken road "where the artillery had hit him. Although wounded badly, he seemed to be trying to roll over and reach behind his back. We rolled him on his side to see what was bothering him. Believe it or not, there was a Luger in a holster on his belt. We would never know if he was trying to reach it or not. He died just as the medics got to him."

Later, as Curley's platoon was crossing a wheat field, they came under U.S. artillery fire. His platoon guide got hit and died instantly. Lieutenant Curley got on his radio and screamed, "We are getting hit by short rounds from our rear." It took several minutes to straighten out the confusion. It turned out that the 2nd Battalion was being shelled by the 116th Infantry's cannon company.

By late afternoon, Curley's platoon, along with much of his battalion, controlled the western slopes of Hill 192. They also cut the N-172 highway that led west to St-Lô. To the east, the 23rd Infantry had reached the road as well. There were still a few German holdouts on the south slopes of the hill, but for all intents and purposes they had lost Hill 192. They tried a few weak counterattacks, but U.S. artillery decimated them. By the next morning, they were all gone. In capturing Hill 192 (and 147 prisoners) General Walter Robertson's 2nd Division lost 69 killed, 328 wounded, and 8 missing. These were tragic losses, but the unit had seized one of the key pieces of terrain on the St-Lô battlefield. Hill 192 was, in the estimation of the Army's official historian, "the best observation point in the St. Lô sector, a point from which the Americans could look down the Martinville ridge" toward St-Lô.[5]

The capture of Hill 192, combined with the substantial advance of Major Bingham's 2nd Battalion, 116th Infantry, on July 11 convinced General

Gerhardt that his soldiers could make it into St-Lô with one more big push the next day. "We are going to get on that objective or else," he told General Corlett in a phone conversation.

Uncle Charlie's optimism was misplaced. The Germans had been bloodied on July 11, but they were still quite potent. They retreated and set up a new defensive line a mile and a half east of St-Lô. Gerhardt planned to advance along the spine of the Martinville Ridge and the N-172. He figured that American control of Hill 192 provided a clear flank to the south, while a speedy advance would shield his men from German harassment from the area's prominent patch of high ground in the other direction—Hill 122 to the north of St-Lô. From the start, Gerhardt planned to outflank and envelop Hill 122. He believed that now was the right moment to do so. In reality, Gerhardt was sending his troops into a constricted kill zone. When the 29'ers resumed their attack on July 12, they were right under the eyes of enemy observers atop Hill 122 in the north as well as various smaller hills to the south of the Martinville Ridge. That meant flanking artillery and mortar fire from both sides.

Battalions from all three of the division's regiments participated in this renewed push for St-Lô. None gained any more than a few hundred yards. All took terrible casualties. Major Johns and his 1st Battalion, 115th Infantry, participated in this attack in spite of their hellish experiences of the previous day. Not only had they absorbed the German counterattack; they had also lost sixty men, including an entire platoon, in an afternoon attack that had netted them nothing more than a few hedgerows. In the space of one day, Johns's battalion had lost one-third of its strength.

When he and his men pushed forward again on July 12, their luck, at first, seemed to change. "The scouts darted forward cautiously, slipping from cover to cover, expecting to draw fire at any moment. They made the first hedgerow, where the Germans had been the night before. No fire. They peeped over the hedgerow, still expecting a trap. No trap. No Germans."

At least not yet. Johns and his men advanced at a deliberate, wary pace through a few orchards until their first objective, Belle Fontaine, was in sight. Johns chanced a look through his field glasses. Everything ahead seemed peaceful, but that soon changed. "The German artillery, silent until now, opened up." Major Johns no sooner took cover when a runner slid next to him, panting all the way. He reported that Lieutenant Stoen, the B Company commander, was down with a shrapnel wound. Johns inwardly cursed. "Stoen out! That was a bitter blow. He'd made a fine company commander."

Johns was pondering what to do next when he heard the telltale ripping sounds of German machine guns. The lead scouts had finally flushed out the leading enemy defenses of Belle Fontaine. The forward platoons halted and waited for supporting fire. "The company commanders were inclined to hold their men under cover and use their mortars, both 60-mm and 81-mm, to blast out the Germans before trying to continue the advance. This method took longer, but it saved a lot of men, and the battalion was woefully short of men just then."

There was still plenty of danger, though. This methodical approach shielded Johns's infantrymen from enemy machine-gun fire, but it exposed them even more to German mortar and artillery fire, so much so that Johns considered it a "toss up whether men saved by not assaulting machine gun positions would be sacrificed later to the enemy artillery fire."

He nearly found out the answer to this vexing question firsthand. He was sitting down, resting for a few moments, with his back against a hedgerow, when a mortar shell burst atop the hedgerow, a mere foot away from his helmet. Johns was dazed but otherwise unhurt. Realizing that his position had been spotted, he and his command group moved along a sunken road to another spot. Along the way, they found a dead enemy soldier. "It was a German paratrooper, his little helmet still fast on his head as he lay with his back against the side of the road, his hands clenched tightly at his sides, his eyes staring up at the sky, and his teeth showing as he still bit down hard on his lower lip. Both his legs were cut cleanly off just below the hips. He was quite dead." Thirty yards away, in a nearby field, Johns found one of the missing legs, but he never found the other. The enemy paratrooper had been killed by American 4.2-inch mortars. Johns and his 1st Battalion captured Belle Fontaine but went no farther that day.[6]

To the right of Johns, the 2nd Battalion of the 115th tried to take the ominously named village of Bourg d'Enfer (Market town of hell). The battalion made it to the southeastern edge of the village against no resistance. They were moving through an orchard that was bisected by a small dirt road. Unbeknownst to the Americans, the road marked the beginning of the German defensive line south of Bourg d'Enfer. When the Americans neared the road, German paratroopers ambushed them.

Lieutenant Brayton Danner, a platoon leader in G Company, 115th, was down to about fifteen reliable men now. The others had been killed or wounded or had drifted to the rear at the first opportunity. He and his small group approached the road and ran into a wall of small-arms fire. "Suddenly a LOT of fire came from the next hedgerow. To our left front was a cluster of farm buildings [Bourg d'Enfer], but between them and us were hedgerows, apparently enclosures for farm animals."

Danner wanted to lead his men forward, but he needed authorization to do so, because his unit might get cut off. He and his men took cover behind a small hedge and traded shots with the Germans. Danner's lone remaining squad leader was engaged in a personal duel with a German rifleman, "each man trying to outwit his enemy on the opposite hedge. Both rose up and fired, and a moment later the sergeant was by my side, dragging his M1. Where his Adam's apple had been there was a terrible hole. A part of his trachea was gone, and blood was spurting from a torn vessel. He brought up the muzzle of his weapon to show me that the front sight had been knocked off."

Lieutenant Danner knew that he had to act quickly to save the squad leader's life. "I reached into my jacket, brought out an OD colored cloth, wadded it, and pushed it into the opening." He told the man to run for the rear while he laid down cover fire with his carbine. "As I glanced back . . . I saw that he was running as if his life depended on it—which I reckon it was." The man was still dragging his broken rifle.

The firefight continued inconclusively for several minutes. Somewhere to the right Lieutenant Danner heard his lone machine gunner calling for him. The lieutenant crawled over to him. "I think I've got a fever," he told Danner. The man's face was flushed and the whites of his eyes were streaked. Danner felt his forehead. Sure enough, he was burning up with fever. Still, Danner could not afford to send a sick man back in the middle of a fight.

Seconds later, the issue was moot. Danner heard the crack of a bullet and heard it whoosh by him and into the machine gunner. "He continued to look at me, a small round hole in the center of his forehead." The machine gunner keeled over. Enraged and terrified, Lieutenant Danner whirled and saw where the shot had come from. "I . . . emptied my carbine into the cloud of smoke from the rifle, which had fired the shot. I remember the anger, which tore through me. It was an M1 rifle in the hands of an enemy soldier, which had killed the boy."

Somewhere off to the left, the Germans launched a counterattack. In a matter of a few minutes, a rumor spread among the Americans that a retreat had been ordered. The 2nd Battalion withdrew in haste and chaos all the way to its jump-off positions. By the time it got there, it was a confused, disorganized, frightened rabble.

When Lieutenant Danner got the order, his depleted platoon left behind the body of the machine gunner but not the gun itself. In quick rushes, they ran back from the same direction they had come earlier that morning. Danner and his runner Buzz were the last ones out. An enemy artillery shell exploded between them. Danner felt himself flying through the air. "The backwash catapulted me into the air, tore my carbine from me, and I found myself facedown in a hole on top of a dead German soldier. I just lay there, stomach churning, my face against his face, and I talked to him. I told him how lucky he was to be dead with no more pain, or fear, or hunger, or sleepless nights, or homesickness." Danner and Buzz both survived the blast and made it back to the battalion.[7]

In one day of fighting, the 115th Infantry's 1st and 3rd Battalions had gained 500 yards apiece, the 2nd Battalion nothing. Twenty-one more Americans were dead and another eighty-seven wounded. When General Gerhardt found out about the 2nd Battalion's debacle, he blew his stack and told Colonel Godwin Ordway, the regimental commander, to relieve Major Maurice Clift, commander of the 2nd Battalion. "I think a change is indicated in the 2nd." Ordway complied. He fired Clift and replaced him with Major Asbury Jackson, the former S-2 officer of the 116th.

On July 13, Gerhardt tried again to push into St-Lô from the east. This time there was supposed to be plenty of support from air strikes, tanks, and artillery. Only the artillery came through. Bad weather canceled the air strikes. Logistical problems plagued the tanks. The artillery provided good fire support, but it was not enough. Once more, the 29'ers were taking devastating fire from well-sited German artillery and mortars, plus plenty of machine-gun and rifle fire from whatever hedgerow happened to lie in front of them. Once again, advances were measured in yards instead of miles.

Two battalions of the 175th moved, with great confusion and clumsiness, through the 116th and attacked west on either side of the N-172 near a village named la Boulaye. Before the attack, Uncle Charlie called Colonel Ollie Reed, the 175th commanding officer, and told him to push his men ruthlessly: "What it takes is driving. You are the guy that has to do it. We've got to get on those final objectives. Time is wasting, but I think your gang is in good shape, so get them rolling."

Compared to the other two regiments, they were in good shape, but not for long. Their communications were out and they had little tank support. The attack went, almost literally, nowhere. Both battalions of the 175th ran into a wall of fire. Casualties were heavy. At one of the battalion aid stations, Father Rod Taggart, the regimental chaplain, did what he could for the wounded. He put on a good face for these stricken men, but inside he was tired, pensive, and depressed. "I suppose it is natural for me to become saddened at the sight of so many boys I had grown to know and admire," he wrote in his diary, "fine admirable mother's sons who have gone before us. I wonder how long a man can go on like this surrounded by ever mounting tragedies. Dear God give me the grace to persevere. It's just so awful. Even as I write a barrage of German artillery is landing in the next field!"

Officers tried everything to keep their men moving, but to no avail. At the edge of one anonymous hedgerow not far from the N-172, Corporal Harold Gordon, the doctor's son who was serving in H Company, 175th, was bending under the weight of several boxes of machine-gun ammunition. He and several others had braved shell fire to get this ammo to the forward positions. Along the way they passed the remnants of those who were not so fortunate, including "headless boys from the 116th, crumpled on top of one another. One head was missing, the other lay some yards away. They were beginning to get ripe." They also passed a burned-out Sherman whose dead crew was still burning inside.

Gordon dumped the ammo boxes at the feet of a heavy-machine-gun team at one end of the hedgerow. Not far away, the seven remaining riflemen of F Company were sitting against the hedgerow, with blank looks on their faces. Gordon watched as the battalion commander tried to motivate them to keep attacking. "[He was] literally frothing with rage, threatening them alternately with his .45 and with court martial, calling them 'yellow dogs' and other choice epithets. They just sat there, unmoved and unmoving. Twice [he] made as though to go over the hedgerow himself. Once he picked up a light machine gun tripod, but set it down again and harangued the riflemen again. Then he picked up the receiver and started to climb over, once again changing his mind. The riflemen just sat there as he raved on. They'd had it. That was all."

They had reached the point when orders were no longer to be followed because they meant instant death or dismemberment—and for nothing. The battalion commander's authority meant nothing to them. His threats of a court-martial were laughable. A court-martial was preferable to being ripped into shreds by a German machine gun. Nor was force an option. The commanding officer's puny pistol did not compare to their M-1 rifles. The riflemen knew they were being asked to do the impossible. They knew they were being asked to squander their lives for nothing more than the robotic ruthlessness of higher commanders. They would have none of it.

As he watched the battalion commander strut around, Gordon grew increasingly angry. "I was very unhappy about the whole thing and picked up a mud-encrusted M1 rifle." Gordon sat in a foxhole and cleaned the rifle, all the while wondering whether he should turn it on his battalion commander. One of Gordon's buddies plopped down next to him, fingered the trigger of his carbine, and asked, "Should I shoot the bastard now or wait a while?"

Both of them waited and watched. In the meantime, a fresh-faced new lieutenant from the regimental staff strutted up and down the hedgerow. Periodically he stuck his head up over the hedgerow and said to the riflemen, "Look, they can't shoot; they can't hit me! What are you afraid of? You're all yellow."

The riflemen still sat and did nothing. Disgusted with the whole scene, Gordon went back for more ammo. When he returned, he saw the lieutenant's dead body sprawled out on a stretcher. "That son of a bitch from regiment finally got what he asked for!" Gordon's buddy told him.

Gordon nodded. "Damned swine!"

The 175th took a few hedgerows but little else on July 13. Overall, the division was now a few hundred yards closer to St-Lô, but little else had been accomplished. At least 200 more Americans had been added to the casualty lists.

As Gordon's story indicated, the soldiers were growing weary of the callous, hard-driving attitude of some of their officers, especially General Gerhardt. From his first day in command back in England to now, the men were of two minds about him. They knew that Gerhardt was competent and somewhat courageous, but he was, in their view, too bullying, too aggressive, and reckless, perhaps even a little too ambitious for a promotion to corps command at their expense. Many of the veteran 29'ers (even some of the officers) sarcastically asserted that Gerhardt already was a corps commander of sorts. "He has a division in the field, a division in the hospital, and a division in the cemetery."

He won no love from his soldiers when, after the two nightmarish days of fighting on July 12 and July 13, he visited the front and ordered his troops to clear the area of dead animal carcasses and discarded equipment. The men were exhausted. They were doing well to dig in (a backbreaking task under even the best of conditions). Now, thanks to Gerhardt's exacting, fastidious personality, they had to expend precious energy cleaning up the battlefield. They especially hated the odious task of burying the dead, bloated, stinking, hard-to-maneuver cows that were lying everywhere. But they did it.[8]

Even Gerhardt had to face the fact that his division needed rest and replacements. His hopes for a quick dash into St-Lô were gone by July 14. So were his hopes of enveloping Hill 122 from the south. So he ordered his unit to rest for twenty-four hours while General Corlett turned over responsibility for Hill 122 to one of the newest American units in Normandy, the 35th Division. For several days General Corlett had suspected that, at some point, the hill would have to be assaulted. Gerhadt's hope of outflanking it was worth pursuing, but the 29th Division's two bloody days at Martinville Ridge on July 12 and 13 convinced Corlett that St-Lô could not be taken without possession of Hill 122. Gerhardt's 29th had lost more than 1,000 men in only a few days. It was not strong enough, at this moment, to take Hill 122, but the 35th, even though it had been fighting for several days north of St-Lô, still had a fresh regiment to throw into the fight.

The 35th was a national guard division. It was a well-trained and-equipped unit, but like every other American division in Normandy, it was not well prepared to deal with the hedgerows. Two regiments from the 35th, the 137th and the 320th, had fought for the better part of three days to secure the northern approaches to Hill 122. The division's other regiment, the 134th Infantry, remained in reserve. When Corlett decided to assault the hill, he ordered the 134th to do the job. In so doing, the soldiers of the 134th were taking over a sector previously assigned to two battalions of the 115th Infantry. Throughout July 14, the 134th took over for the exhausted 115th, whose survivors were more than happy to head for a reserve area.

Major General Paul Baade, commander of the 35th Division, kept the 137th and 320th in the line. Their job now was to siphon off German strength while the 134th made the main effort to seize Hill 122. The hill was little more than a gentle incline that overlooked the northern outskirts of St-Lô. But, of course, a dizzying network of hedgerows and sunken lanes honeycombed Hill 122. The commander of the 134th, Colonel Butler Miltonberger, chose a narrow dirt road as his axis of advance. The road was located a mile east of the main highway (N-174) that led north out of St-Lô and all the way to Isigny. Mitonberger's dirt road stretched from Villiers-Fossard in the north, through the tiny village of Emelie at the foot of Hill 122, up the hill's gradual plateaus, over the hill's flat crest, and down an incline into St-Lô's northern suburbs.

Hard-core survivors from the enemy 352nd Division defended Hill 122. This was the same unit that had opposed the American landing at Omaha beach on D-Day. The soldiers of this outfit, most of whom came from Hannover, had been fighting and dying ever since. In the last three days they had absorbed forty American attacks and had lost 840 men. They settled into their dugouts and holes along Hill 122 and prepared to oppose yet another attack.

For more than three days now Miltonberger's men had been anxiously awaiting word to go into action. When the word finally came on the night of July 14, the reactions were varied. "Some had conditioned themselves strongly not to be affected by the death and pain which they knew they would see," Captain James Huston, an intelligence officer in the 3rd Battalion, wrote. "Then suddenly, perhaps after several hours . . . of such conditioned nonchalance, the terrifying fact might seize upon them—the next one might be me! Some were horrified at the thought of being mangled. To others, it was not so much death itself that they feared, it was the thought of the effect on loved ones at home. They wanted so much to live; there were so many things they wanted to do, if only they could be at home again!"

At 0515 on July 15, even as the morning sun burned away the last foggy layers of evening, Miltonberger's 1st and 2nd Battalions began their advance on either side of the dirt road. As they cautiously picked their way forward to their line of departure, a rolling barrage from American artillery tore pathways for them. From the vantage point of a supporting position Captain Huston watched them go. "Perhaps there was a trace of cold sweat at the temples and in the palms of the hands, and a tenseness in the stomach and dryness in the throat, but they pressed on with an increasing momentum toward the hedgerow which would be their last barrier to the bullets of enemy fire."

At a no-man's-land hedgerow located parallel to the dirt road, the leading men of A Company prepared to push into enemy-held territory. They were hiding behind the base of the hedgerow. It was a solid earthen wall and formed an embankment that gave them shelter. Bullets and tracers were whizzing overhead. These men knew that everything in front of them was enemy. Yet it was their job to go straight ahead, right into danger.

One of the soldiers, Private Bob Goldstein, stole a quick look at the other members of his rifle squad. During the days of waiting they had talked about how scared they would be when they entered combat, but no one looked scared. Goldstein thought for a moment and realized he was not scared, either, "much to my surprise."

Nineteen-year-old Goldstein and the others were as ready as they were ever going to be. Earlier that morning, they had turned in their packs, blankets, and other nonessentials for combat. They were wearing their OD tops and bottoms. Their cartridge belts were packed with ammunition—eight round clips for those with M-1 Garands, fifteen round clips for those with carbines, and twenty round clips for the BAR man. Their sleeves were adorned with the divisional patch, but they had blackened any white portions of the patch, so they could not be easily spotted. For the same reason, they were wearing their field jackets inside out "to prevent any possible shine on any smooth surface of the jacket." This was a common practice among American soldiers in Normandy.

Private Goldstein only had the essentials hooked onto his cartridge belt: "First aid packet, canteen, entrenching tool (pick) and bayonet. Also draped over the back of the cartridge belt was a folded raincoat. Slung over one side was an ammunition bag in which I carried hand grenades, rations (K), extra socks, a few toilet articles. And lastly were two bandoliers of ammunition." Each bandolier contained more than half a dozen clips for his M-1 Garand.

His squad leader, Sergeant Lou Mattes, looked over the hedgerow, grabbed hold of a thorny bush, and pulled himself over to the other side. Goldstein followed, and then the rest of the squad. "The next few minutes were just like maneuvers—except that live ammunition was flying all around us. We would make short dashes, hit the ground, wait until the others moved up. We were deployed in a skirmish line, that is, the squad moved forward into an extended but irregular line."

German mortar shells began dropping among them. "They were just small mortars (50mm) but extremely accurate and the Germans had the range on every hedgerow. Although they burst just a few feet in front of our faces they did absolutely no harm to us." They hopped over a hedgerow and "moved quickly through . . . knee-high grass in the next field."

Along an 800-yard front, Miltonberger's two lead battalions, plus two companies of supporting Shermans from the 737th Tank Battalion, were advancing in like fashion, against varying degrees of firepower. A few men lost their nerve and ran for the rear. One platoon leader, whose unit was under intense machine-gun and mortar fire, broke down completely. He stood up and ran away, only to be severed by machine-gun bullets.

Most kept going forward as best they could, even as casualties mounted. "It was not always a picture of thin lines of advancing men growing thinner as men fell while the others continued marching," one officer wrote. "One did not really see very many men fall. Many of them were caught as they lay in foxholes or behind hedgerows. Others, of course, were caught as they moved forward, but few really saw it happen because their view was hidden—again the hedgerows—from those a safe distance away, and those who were close were themselves dropping to the ground in an effort to find protection." In one instance, an unlucky platoon leader and two other men took shelter in a foxhole during a particularly heavy enemy artillery barrage. An instant later, a shell exploded in the foxhole and the bodies of the three men disintegrated, almost as if they had never existed.

Other officers and NCOs were showing incredible courage, leading their men from field to field, hedgerow to hedgerow, through withering enemy fire. At each hedgerow there was a natural tendency among the survivors to take cover and rest. After all, they had beaten the law of averages to come this far, so most were in no hurry to chance it again. "It was hard going. There were probably no men who were unafraid," Major Huston wrote. He was a thoughtful, perceptive man who was working on a doctorate in the history program at NYU when the war began. He had a reserve commission in the Army because of his ROTC training in his undergraduate days at Indiana University. Two months after Pearl Harbor he was called to active duty, and he had spent most of the last two years with the 35th Division.

During the attack, his duties as intelligence officer took him all over the battlefield. His training as a historian had taught him to observe and keep records of everything he saw. "There were strong men who had the courage to go on in spite of fear, and there were some weaker men who could not go on. Many felt an overpowering desire to get back—back away from those bursting shells and crackling bullets; a few yielded, and became stragglers. It took discipline of the highest order to keep going in the face of that machine gun and artillery fire."

The job of the leaders was to get the men off their butts and keep them moving, so that the momentum of the advance could be maintained. At one hedgerow, Private First Class Lloyd "Lem" Crumbling, a BAR man, watched as his company commander tried to get his troops up and moving. Crumbling and the others were lying behind a hedgerow, taking cover from German artillery fire. The captain ran around like a man possessed, screaming at his men. "Get up! Get up! Get up and shoot! Be like me! Stand up! Get up!" the captain shouted.

As Crumbling and the others wearily got to their feet, a mortar shell whooshed in and wounded the captain. "It blew him up. Two GI medics put him on a stretcher, and they were taking him back through the field, and here a shell hit them and blew all three of them up."

The valorous captain's death robbed Crumbling and the others of initiative for a time, but they eventually resumed their advance. They crept up to the hedgerow; Private First Class Crumbling poked his BAR over the top and fired. The other soldiers followed suit. "You'd never know if you hit anything. The way everybody else was shooting, you don't know whether you . . . really killed a German or not."[9]

By early afternoon, the 1st Battalion was in Emelie, fighting building to building, and the 2nd Battalion, slightly to the east, was nearing the village of Les Romains. Roughly two thousand yards of territory had been gained. Company C had absorbed 60 percent casualties. The other rifle companies had not suffered quite this much, but they were losing plenty of men. Private Goldstein of A Company got hit as his squad was trying to find a safe way through a hedgerow near Emelie. "[A] mortar shell hit the hedgerow about waist high. The blast threw me forward and up and in that split second, I saw a medic going through a break in the hedgerow and I screamed for him and then fell back. I was never totally unconscious but I was dazed to the extent that I remained perfectly immobile." He had been hit in the back by a large piece of shrapnel.

The medic did not respond to Goldstein's call, nor did the other soldiers going forward and beyond the hedgerow. "They may have seen me but . . . they must have thought that I was dead. And I gave myself up for dead. That's no lie, I was completely resigned. I never felt more calm and at ease as I did then or during the whole day."

After lying there stunned for a while, he realized he was still alive. He knew he had been hit in the back. Blood was all over his cartridge belt. He tried to take all eight of the sulfa pills he was carrying in his shirt pocket, but he dropped his canteen, spilling most of its contents on the ground. He recovered the canteen and took what pills he could. Later two GIs came along, laid him on his stomach, and put a bandage over his gaping wound. Mortar rounds were still coming in, so the two men moved on quickly. He wanted to tell them to stay, but he could hardly speak. "I tried yelling several times for help but my efforts were too feeble. I just couldn't get any power."

Not until well into the next day did help arrive in the form of medics with stretchers. As they maneuvered him onto a stretcher, he was in excruciating pain and he could hear air being sucked into and out of the hole in his back. At the battalion aid station, he started to get a sense of just how badly he had been wounded. "When I looked at the persons who were looking at my wound, I guessed from the 'Oh, my God!' expressions on their faces that I must have been seriously wounded. The wound was bandaged quickly, and I was taken back a little further to the rear to a field hospital."

Eventually, Goldstein realized the severity of his wounds. He had suffered a torn diaphragm, a badly lacerated spleen (which had to be removed), and a punctured lung. Doctors operated on him several times, removing four inches of his ribs and numerous small pieces of shrapnel. It took him months to recuperate. After the war, he attended college on the GI Bill, married, had children, and became a pioneer in the field of audiology.[10]

A couple miles north of Emelie, at the 35th Division's CP, General Baade sensed, at midafternoon, that the moment was right to go for broke. Miltonberger's attacking battalions had clearly pierced the forward German defenses. Miltonberger was even now throwing his reserve battalion, the 3rd, into the battle. The summit of Hill 122 beckoned from 600 yards beyond Emelie. Baade ordered his assistant division commander, Brigadier General Edmund Sebree, to organize a task force for a final push up the hill. The task force consisted of the 134th Regiment's A and B Companies, in addition to its 3rd Battalion. For support and mobility Sebree added two platoons of engineers, a platoon of tank destroyers, and some tanks from the 737th, plus vehicles from the 35th Division's reconnaissance troops. They were to attack at twilight, following a brief P-47 strike and an artillery barrage.

For three hours they fought their way along the dirt road, up the northern slope of Hill 122. For a relatively inexperienced unit they coordinated with their artillery, tanks, and mortars quite well. "The tank-infantry combinations struck at machine gun nests and other strongpoints of enemy opposition," the division historian wrote. "Each use of the infantry-tank teams required close coordination and amounted to separate small actions in themselves. In many cases the infantry commanders rode on, or walked by the tanks, directing them personally. Tank destroyers overrode and smashed dugouts and strongpoints after the infantry had passed through."

The advance of foot troops with artillery support worked quite well on this night. The task force made it to the crest of Hill 122 by midnight on July 16. However, the Germans were still hunkered down on the leeward side of the hill and they were sure to counterattack. The American tanks and tank destroyers spread out into defensive formations while the infantrymen, exhausted though they were, dug fighting holes. The engineers spent much of the night stringing barbed wire, sowing mines, and filling up sandbags for the infantry positions.

Even before sunrise on July 16, the enemy attacked. Seesaw fighting raged on Hill 122 for much of the day. The worst peril for the Americans was not necessarily the attacking enemy infantry or tanks. They could be suppressed by American artillery and often were. The biggest danger was accurate artillery and mortar fire that seemed to thicken with every renewed enemy attack. Private First Class Crumbling crouched in a fighting hole and hoped he would not be hit. A mortar round exploded a few yards away, close to a hole occupied by a new man. Crumbling was not hurt, but he wondered about the new man. He peeked over the edge of his hole and asked, "Are you all right?"

There was no answer and Crumbling soon saw why. "He was all gone. His head and arms and everything were blown off. The rest of him was laying there. I didn't even know the guy. He was a replacement."

Crumbling's turn to get hit came several minutes later. He got out of his hole briefly. As he did so, a mortar round exploded nearby and he felt shrapnel tear into his knee. "I looked down and blood was running out." Crumbling fell down and another soldier tended to his wound. "[He] looked at me and said, 'A million dollar wound!' I said, 'I hope so.'" A million-dollar wound excused a soldier from combat but without crippling him.

Crumbling hobbled down the hill and back to an aid station at Emelie. At one point, he unknowingly walked through a minefield. By the time he got to the aid station, his pants were soaked with blood. "They cut my pant leg off and bandaged [me] up, and they put a compress [on the wound]." Crumbling was evacuated to a hospital in England where he spent three months recovering from his leg wound. He never saw combat again.

Meanwhile, on July 16 groups of American infantrymen, in the face of German counterattacks, retreated down the northern face of the hill. Some even fell back as far as Emelie, but German successes were short-lived. Each time American control of the hill wavered, 134th Infantry officers rallied their soldiers and pushed the Germans off Hill 122. By late afternoon the hill belonged to the Americans. The 35th Division was now only a mile and a half away from St-Lô. From atop Hill 122 the soldiers could even see the damaged spires of churches. German defenses around St-Lô were finally giving way, if only a little. The 35th Division kept pushing south to the outskirts of St-Lô, but it went no farther. The honor of taking St-Lô would go to the 29th Division.[11]

Even as the 35th Division fought and bled at Hill 122, the 29th Division resumed its push for St-Lô. The division received some replacements on July 14, bringing most of the rifle battalions to about half-strength, and on July 15 resumed the attack. At the CP of the 2nd Battalion, 116th Infantry Regiment, Major Charles Cawthon watched as his battalion commander, Major

Sidney Bingham, briefed his officers. "The weather was notably clear and bright, in contrast to the clouds and rain that had hung over the battlefield for days. The company commanders, all lieutenants, were assembled along a hedgerow, and Major Bingham told them what we were to do; unit boundaries were fixed and maps marked. Within the hour, the artillery preparation began and the fighter-bombers roared and dove in over the objective."

The better part of the 116th Infantry, plus the 115th Infantry to the north, went forward and tried to make headway throughout the daylight hours of July 15. Mostly they went nowhere. German antitank guns, hidden somewhere to the south, picked off seven tanks that were supporting the 116th's attack. That regiment's advance stalled.

On the division's right, Major Johns and his 1st Battalion, 115th Infantry, led the way. The major watched the dogfaces of his rifle companies trot toward the enemy-controlled gullies, marshes, and hedgerows that lay in front of them. "Baker and Charlie [companies] moved out. Charlie was lucky. They made it across the marshy ground before the Germans woke up to what was going on. The first hedgerow on the far side, for some reason best known to the enemy, was only outposted." The C Company soldiers "drove in the outposts and seized the hedgerow in a matter of minutes. But there they stuck."

The wet, marshy ground prevented tanks from getting forward to support the infantry. One tank was already stuck and abandoned. The infantrymen were on their own. Company B had gone practically nowhere. They were "lined up behind a low hedgerow facing the Germans across 150 yards of a deep ravine. They were methodically pounding the opposite hedgerow with 60- and 81-millimeter mortars while the artillery and more mortars smoked the right flank. A determined little group of men crawled around in the shallow folds of [a] field that gave them their only cover."

As the battle ebbed and flowed, Johns experienced brief moments of elation when he received reports of hedgerows cleared or machine-gun nests knocked out. For instance, at one point, C Company, led by a bold squad of riflemen and supported by white phosphorous rounds from 81mm mortars, took a hedgerow, along with twenty-eight prisoners. This was good, but it was not enough. The battalion gained no more than a few hundred yards in a full day's fighting. "The terrain . . . was exceptionally rough. The Germans had honeycombed the whole area with foxholes and gun emplacements that covered each inch of open space without ever letting the attacking forces see where the fire was coming from. It was not a constant hack-and-slash thing. War is made up of countless individual actions which do not necessarily take place simultaneously. Riflemen take cover when fired on, and seek a target. Artillery and mortar observers choose places from which they can get the best observation of enemy lines. Squad and platoon leaders move about, sizing up the situation . . . company commanders do the same. All these actions take time." When all was said and done, Johns's 1st Battalion gained only about five hundred yards.[12]

All day long, General Gerhardt talked on the phone at his CP, prodding his commanders for results. Much of his fury was directed at Colonel Ordway, in whom he was losing confidence. When Gerhardt called him to find out how the 115th Infantry's attack was going, Ordway told him not much progress had been made. "The answer to that is keep moving . . . so keep them going now," Uncle Charlie snapped. By dusk it was clear that the 29th Division would not get into St-Lô on that day and Gerhardt's mood, at times optimistic in spite of the problems of the day, soured. "We did all right today, but did not make the grade," he told General Robertson of the 2nd Division.

Indeed, the 29th seemed to be stymied, but at about dusk on July 15 a small glimmer of hope presented itself. Somehow, Bingham's battalion punched through German defenses on the Martinville Ridge. "We attacked astride a road, F Company on the left, G Company on the right and E Company in reserve," Bingham remembered. The major and 200 of his men made it as far as La Madeleine, a patch of high ground at an intersection about half a mile east of St-Lô. "Though we were completely cut off I decided to stay put. Fortunately, the radio of the Artillery Liaison Officer was working and we got word of our situation to Regiment."

When General Gerhardt heard about Bingham's dramatic advance, he was ebullient. "There's no stopping this Bingham!" But then the gravity of Bingham's situation sank in to the general. The major's battalion had penetrated a previously impregnable screen of enemy strong points, but it was now cut off. Should Gerhardt order Bingham to retreat, thus giving up half a mile of precious real estate, or should he keep Bingham in place and risk the annihilation of his best battalion? "We don't want him to be pulled back, but we don't want him chewed up either," Gerhardt told Colonel Philip Dwyer, who had just taken over command of the 116th (Canham had been promoted and transferred to another division).

Generals get paid to make these kinds of tough decisions. Gerhardt opted to keep Bingham in place and rescue him in the morning. The general called Colonel Ordway and told him to fight his way to Bingham's "lost battalion." Ordway thought this was a tall order. His regiment had gotten nowhere in the last twenty-four hours. How could it now fight its way a mile and a half through enemy territory to rescue Bingham? Gerhardt would have none of this. He told Ordway to carry out the rescue order. Ordway assented and chose his 2nd Battalion for this job.

The 2nd Battalion, like many others, was short of riflemen. The colonel sent cooks, drivers, wiremen, and other rear area personnel to the front as combat soldiers, but it did no good. The attack failed miserably. "Each little group . . . ran for the hedgerow ahead with bullets ripping in from the right—from the area we'd gotten into position to bypass the evening before," Lieutenant Danner of G Company recalled. "For each GI alive . . . there seemed to be a couple lying in grotesque positions where they had fallen. It was a day of running, yelling and shooting—accent the yelling." Danner was once a fair tenor in his hometown choir, but a whole day of screaming orders damaged his voice forever. "My vocal cords simply gave out. They say a soldier has only so much bravery, and when it's used up, he's not worth shit. I reckon I was nearing that point." By the time the attack petered out, he was down to eight men in his platoon. They found a farmhouse with a barrel of wine and helped themselves, drowning their collective sorrows. The battalion lost sixty-six men. German counterattacks pinned down the other two battalions of the 116th. There would be no relief for Bingham and his outfit today.

At La Madeleine, Bingham's surrounded group spent the day digging deep holes and waiting for a major German attack. They had four 81mm mortars and four .30-caliber light machine guns. Bingham deployed them effectively into a perimeter defense. Small groups of Germans at the fringes of the 2nd Battalion bumped into them throughout the day. One small enemy unit appeared in front of Rocco Russo's F Company position at midday. "We saw some Krauts coming towards us and prepared to drop a mortar shell in one of their pockets . . . when Major . . . Bingham appeared and asked to use my M-1 rifle." Russo enjoyed a special bond with his battalion commander, with whom he had fought on D-Day. He handed the officer his rifle, concentrated on dropping shells down his mortar tube, and was pleased with the results. "We all were very pleased that we wiped out that group. We congratulated each other on a fine performance." Bingham gave Russo his rifle back and told him that help was on the way.

The day as a whole was fairly quiet for the 2nd Battalion, because no concerted enemy attack came. The Germans did not seem to have a full appreciation of the presence of these Americans in their midst. Bingham's men dealt mainly with the symptoms of being cut off. "All we did was dig in," Sergeant Ronald Cole of E Company explained. "We got pretty hungry and thirsty because . . . we had only two rations apiece. Most of us had eaten both [the day before]. Everyone's canteen was dry. We didn't do much talking. When we did talk we talked about food and something to drink and when they would relieve us. Some of the men sneaked halfway down the hill behind us to a couple of abandoned houses and found water."

One of those men was Russo. The water well was under German machine-gun fire, but the job had to be done. There were many wounded Americans who desperately needed the water. The unwounded were just as thirsty. Russo crept up to the house and surveyed the water well. "To get water, it was necessary to go into the well on a wooden ladder that reached into the water." Russo had two other men with him. "[They] did not want to go into the well so I told them I would go. Seemed to me it was safer in the event of German machine gun fire to be in the well." Russo steeled himself and began climbing the ladder. "The machine gunners did start firing and the other two joined me on the ladder very quickly. After brushing off the cigar butts and other scum from the water, we filled all of the canteens that we had carried down and fired our way back to our location and distributed the canteens to the others."

As night fell the men heard the sounds of German tanks moving somewhere in the distance. Behind them, enemy artillery fire plastered the valley that led back to the rest of the 29th Division. At division headquarters, General Gerhardt ordered a new series of attacks for the next day. The majority of his rifle battalions were at less than one-quarter strength, but there would be no respite. Uncle Charlie knew that the Germans were hurting just as badly, perhaps even worse.

The most important assignment belonged to the 116th Infantry's 3rd Battalion, under the kind, mild Major Thomas Howie. Throughout most of the Normandy campaign Howie had served as the regimental operations officer, but on July 13 he had taken over command of the 3rd Battalion. His personality did not mesh with Gerhardt's. The general was hard-charging, gruff, and energetic. Before the war Howie had taught English literature and coached football at Staunton Military Academy in Virginia. He was circumspect, scholarly, and polite. Back in England, when Gerhardt had turned up the pressure on his officers, Howie was often in his crosshairs. But he had weathered the general's imprecations with dignity and humor. Now he was the man of the moment.

Just before sunrise, Howie and his men moved out. Howie felt that his greatest weapon was stealth. There was no pre-attack barrage or any other supporting fire that might betray their intentions. "Only two men in each platoon were permitted to fire, and then only in the event of an emergency," Colonel Dwyer said. "The others were to rely on their bayonets and hand grenades."

In this manner, they seeped through the German lines and made it to Bingham's battalion by sunrise. Howie's 3rd Battalion troops shared what rations they had, but they were traveling light. They had not brought much in the way of supplies with them. Their orders were to make contact with the 2nd Battalion and then join together in a westward assault on St-Lô. But Bingham's men were in no condition for any such attack. Their ammo was low, they had dozens of wounded men (being treated by one U.S. medic and a captured German medic), and they had had little sleep or food over the course of two days. Howie got on the radio and reported this to Colonel Dwyer. The colonel ordered Howie to leave the 2nd in place and attack with his own battalion. "Will do," Howie replied.

He called his officers together and gave them their attack orders. Just as the meeting broke up, accurate German mortar fire started coming in. "Before taking cover in one of the two foxholes we were using," Captain William Puntenney, Howie's executive officer, recalled, "Major Howie turned to take a last look to be sure all his men had their heads down. Without warning a shell hit a few yards away."

A fragment sliced through Howie's back and into his lungs. "My God, I'm hit," he gasped. Blood was oozing out of his mouth.

He keeled over and into Puntenney's arms. "I caught him. I called a medic, but nothing could be done. He was dead in two minutes."

Captain Puntenney covered Howie's body and prepared to launch his attack. Before he could do so, the Germans unleashed an attack of their own that lasted the entire day. The Americans held them off, with artillery, mortars, and judicious use of small arms, but now there were two isolated battalions instead of one. The 1st Battalion of the 116th, plus soldiers from the 175th, made repeated attempts to relieve them but failed.

In the early evening, shortly before sunset, the enemy sent several tanks against the American position at La Madeleine. The frightening sound of the tank engines got louder and louder as the tanks got closer to the Americans. In one foxhole, Rocco Russo's heartbeat quickened with every passing moment. "Once the tanks got close enough to fire, it would be curtains for us since we had no tanks of our own and we were so close together that artillery fire was useless." He turned to his foxhole buddy and suggested that he start saying his prayers.

Russo did not know it, but some serious help was on the way. Division headquarters had called the Air Force for support. Somewhere up in the sky, P-47 fighters from the 404th Fighter Group were nearing the area. The fighter pilots were looking for the St-Lô road and for red panels that the infantry soldiers had laid out in front of their positions. In spite of the fact that the setting sun was casting shadows everywhere, the pilots spotted the panels and the road.

Russo heard the buzzing sound of the planes and glanced up in surprise at the sky. "All of a sudden . . . P-47 fighter planes came down and attacked the tanks. They knocked out three of the tanks and the others turned and headed back into St. Lô. It was like a miracle! I made a promise that the first opportunity that I would get, I would buy some Air Corps Pilot a bottle of Scotch." Other American planes dropped blood plasma. Later that evening, a forty-man carrying party got through with food and more medical supplies.

The next morning a rifle company made it to La Madeleine and finally ended the ordeal of the two battalions.[13]

Meanwhile, on July 17, Gerhardt kept pushing for St-Lô. The strong enemy counterattacks at La Madeleine convinced him that the time was right to turn up the pressure on the Germans north of the Martinville Ridge. He figured that their attacks against La Madeleine meant that they had weakened their defenses northeast of St-Lô. Perhaps this route might represent the opening into St-Lô that he had been waiting for. He picked up the phone, called Ordway of the 115th, and told him to send his 2nd Battalion on an end run to La Planche, a crossroads hamlet located about a mile east of St-Lô and a mile north of La Madeleine. If the 2nd Battalion could make it to La Planche, it could turn west and sail down the main highway into St-Lô. At least that was what Gerhardt hoped.

When the soldiers of the 2nd Battalion moved out on the afternoon of July 17, their progress was slow as they dealt with enemy snipers, artillery, and mortars. Gerhardt was incensed. He called Ordway's CP, got his operations officer, and roared, "The key to this thing is your Second Battalion. Expend the whole battalion if necessary, but it's got to get there."

In the wake of this grim command, the battalion kept moving. By early evening, they were close to Martinville, moving west along a small blacktop road that led to La Planche. The remnants of Lieutenant Danner's platoon were at the vanguard. Danner's lead scout was forty feet ahead. Another man trailed twenty feet behind him. Danner was next. As he watched his two lead men pick their way forward, Danner's chest felt tight. The tightness was a symptom of fear. Danner had been in combat for nearly three weeks. He knew when danger lurked nearby.

A machine gun opened up. "My lead scout crumpled to the blacktop. The second let go of his rifle, his knees buckled and he fell short of the left-hand ditch. I was hugging the earth on the right-hand shoulder." A runner came along and told Danner that the company commander wanted him to get that gun.

Danner sighed and rounded up what few men he had left. He told them to drop everything except weapons and ammo and follow him. They climbed a hill to the left of the road and attempted to flank the gun. Danner thought he spotted a likely hiding place for the enemy machine gun and fired a whole clip in that direction. He yanked out the empty clip, shoved in another, and turned to locate his men. "In that instant a searing, white-hot fire tore through my chest." Lieutenant Danner's carbine spun in the air and fell to the ground. He emitted an involuntary bloodcurdling scream and pitched facedown onto the ground. "Bullets were raining down, smoke from . . . rifles was drifting over me, I wasn't breathing. I COULDN'T breathe."

Danner mustered all of his strength just to breathe again. "I heard a huffing, wheezing noise from a spot in my back. Still alive—I was STILL ALIVE! I rolled onto my side and discovered that my left arm was useless. MY LEFT ARM AND LEG WERE PARALYZED!" With his right hand he unhooked his cartridge belt, found his sulfa pills, and started them toward his mouth. "I felt a hard slap on my hand and the pills were gone. A bullet had passed through near the base of my thumb. Bullets were striking all about me."

Lieutenant Danner saw a plank-covered culvert in a ditch and crawled into it. One of his men was calling to him, asking him if he was OK. As he did so, Danner heard him groan and cry, "I'VE BEEN HIT!" The lieutenant told him to run for it.

Danner's lifeblood was seeping out of his terrible chest wound. All around him, the battle raged. From time to time bullets smashed into the wooden plank that sheltered him. Danner whispered the Twenty-third Psalm to himself and thought of how difficult his death would be for his parents. He was in despair, so much so that he almost did not want to survive. "How would I reconcile that I had LIVED when so many good [men] had DIED?"

Minute by minute, the pain in his chest grew worse and his wheezing even louder. He decided that he wanted to die in the open, in the fresh air, so he crawled out of the culvert and lay against the hillside. A bird flew out of the bushes, hovered above him, and sang. Danner focused his attention on the bird.

A little dog trotted over to him "with tail wagging to lick my face. He licked my cheek and my lips and then, before I could push him away, he lay dead—a quivering, bloody mass. In a mere second the Landser above me had riddled him with bullets." Danner pushed the dog's carcass away and resumed his praying. The bird came back and sang again.

After what seemed like hours, American armored vehicles came down the road. A battle ensued and, minutes later, surrendering German soldiers walked by. Medics got to Danner, bandaged him up, and drove him to a field hospital. The doctor took one look at Danner's wound and said, "Soldier—YOUR war is over. You're going home!"

At nearly the same moment, at his parents' farm in Illinois, Danner's mother was working in the kitchen. All of a sudden a little bird appeared "out of nowhere" in the kitchen and flew wildly back and forth. Danner's mother ran to the shed where his father was working and told him about the bird. When they came back to the kitchen, the bird was gone. They took it as a sign that something had happened to their son Brayton. Later, when Lieutenant

Danner compared notes with his mother, he found that the bird she had seen fit the exact same description as the one that sang above him as he lay wounded outside of La Planche.

He needed months of painful recovery, but he eventually healed and regained the use of his left side. He even met his wife, an army nurse, in the hospital.

The remnants of Ordway's 2nd Battalion made it into La Planche by 0230 on July 18, but that was not good enough for General Gerhardt. Six hours later he relieved Ordway and replaced him with Colonel Alfred Ednie.

Gerhardt did not know it, but the Germans were nearly finished. During the night, their commanders had decided that they could no longer hold St-Lô. Their lines were cracking, and they had no more reinforcements. Plus, Field Marshal Rommel had been badly wounded on July 17 by strafing British fighter planes. Most of the enemy soldiers retreated to the south, leaving behind only strong outpost positions north of the city.

Late in the morning, when Gerhardt received reports of feeble resistance, particularly from Major Johns and his 1st Battalion, 115th, he decided to go for the kill. The general had an ace up his sleeve for just this moment. A couple days before, he had organized a highly mobile battle group whose mission was to roll into St-Lô whenever the enemy's main defenses crumbled. The task force consisted of the 29th Division reconnaissance troops, a platoon of Shermans from the 747th Tank Battalion, a platoon from Cannon Company of the 175th, a platoon of engineers, a company of tank destroyers, plus military policemen and artillery observer teams. He called this special unit Task Force C because it was under the command of General Norman Cota, his courageous assistant division commander. They were at Couvains, several miles behind the lines, waiting for the word to drive for St-Lô.

Gerhardt alerted them at noon on July 18, and they moved out three hours later. Lieutenant Edward Jones, commander of the reconnaissance troop, was in his M-8 armored car, near the head of the column. "Recon troop took the lead with one quarter-ton jeep as point, one quarter-ton jeep to cover, and one armored car to overwatch. We moved . . . from Couvains to the St-Lô–St-Clair Road, passing . . . division headquarters on the way."

When they reached the St-Lô–St-Clair Road, which would be their route into the city, they picked up speed. Opposition consisted of random mines and sniper fire but little else. They soon linked up with Major Johns and his 1st Battalion. The infantrymen hopped aboard tanks or spread out in staggered columns behind the vehicles. Late in the afternoon, they reached a knoll that overlooked the city from a distance of some one thousand yards. The Americans could hardly believe the destruction before their eyes. During the push for St-Lô, most of the men had not been able to see any part of the city, except a spire here and there. Now they were looking at the full ruination of this ancient town. The roofs of houses were caved in, the streets were choked with rubble, telephone poles were down, trees were scattered everywhere, and masonry was heaped in ugly piles all over the place.

They kept going even though they were now under artillery fire—especially now that they were under artillery fire. The faster they moved, the quicker they could get away from it. A shell exploded near Major Johns, but he was unhurt. He was running up and down the road, rallying his men. He saw a man rolling in and out of a ditch, grabbed him by the arm, and pulled him upward. "Come on, boy, let's go."

The man could no longer walk. "[He] tried to get up but stumbled awkwardly forward. The soldier had no feet. He was trying valiantly to stand on the stumps of his two legs, where his feet had been sliced cleanly off just at the ankles." Johns saw that the new amputee was a medic. He gently lowered him back into the ditch, told him to stay put, and assured him that his buddies would be along any minute. He patted him on the back. "See you later, bud."

The major kept running along the road. Now and again, he made eye contact with his men and told them to keep going. Some cheered and waved as they moved forward. As Johns was running, his eyes were drawn to a lumplike object lying along the road. "By the side of the road lay a headless, legless torso, clad in a light blue blouse and darker blue garment that covered the lower portion. It looked as though it had been there for a long time." This was one of the first dead civilians Johns had seen. He wondered if the person had been a man or a woman.

The head of the column was entering the northern portion of St-Lô, close to an eerie-looking cemetery. "German troops were entrenched in the cemetery," Lieutenant Jones said. "We received small arms, MG, mortar, and a few rounds of artillery. I pulled out and around the lead vehicles to add more firepower." The Americans raked them over with everything in their arsenal—from rifles to 75mm main guns on the Shermans. One of Jones's men shot a German in the head as he was preparing to fire a *Panzerfaust* at one of the U.S. vehicles. "German were dropping all over. It seemed as if everyone in this part of the country was shooting at us."

The Germans soon retreated and took to sniping at the Americans from the remnants of two- and three-story buildings. The tanks and armored cars blasted away at any window that might contain a sniper. During the cemetery firefight the American vehicles had bunched up, so Lieutenant Jones tried to unsnarl this traffic jam. He was directing traffic, dodging enemy artillery fire, when General Cota came up to him. "I gave him a quick report and kept waving vehicles to move ahead. While standing near me, General Cota was hit by a shell fragment in his arm. I can remember the blood running from his sleeve and dripping off his fingers. It was not a bad wound, but he just stood there talking; it didn't bother him in the least." Seemingly nothing frightened Cota.

Johns had two rifle companies left—A and B. He ordered A Company to clear the western half of the city and B Company the eastern half. The soldiers worked in small teams, with tanks and tank destroyers.

There was still some German resistance, but the main peril now was enemy artillery. The Germans realized they were about to lose St-Lô and, in their fury, sent in every round of artillery and mortars they could muster. They even tried a few weak counterattacks that U.S. artillery easily blunted. The artillerymen found good OPs. Lieutenant Colonel John Cooper, commander of the 110th Field Artillery Battalion, and a captain climbed the rickety 225-foot-high spires of the heavily damaged Notre Dame Cathedral. From this vantage point they could see every German move south of St-Lô. They descended and ordered other observers to utilize this great OP, but before they could oblige, the spires collapsed.

Throughout the day on July 18, the enemy artillery fire was so intense that Major Johns took shelter in a mausoleum near the cemetery. The mausoleum contained a sturdy underground crypt and a sarcophagus where Johns set up his maps. Lieutenant Jones took shelter in his armored car, close to the mausoleum (which, according to the inscription, belonged to the Blanchet family).

The city remained under fire for the next couple of days, but it was finally, after nearly six weeks of bitter struggle, under American control. Gerhardt sent the word out at 1830 on July 18. In barely a week of combat, the 35th Division had suffered 2,000 casualties and the 29th Division 3,000 in the push for St-Lô. Many thousands of others, belonging to units like the 2nd Division, the 30th, the 9th, and the 3rd Armored, had become casualties, either in this final push or in the weeks of frustration amid the hedgerows. At St-Lô, it took the Americans one week to travel a distance that in peacetime could be covered in one hour—on foot.

Sometime after dark on July 18, Lieutenant Jones heard an ambulance jeep arrive in the street near his position. Curious, he watched medics remove a stretcher from the jeep and lay it on the ground. There was a dead body, covered with an olive drab blanket, on the stretcher. "The next morning, in a lull, the stretcher was carried and placed on top of rubble that had been knocked down from the . . . wall of the [Ste-Croix] church located on the south side of the square in St-Lô [a block west of the cemetery]. An American flag was draped over the body."

The body was Major Howie's. General Gerhardt, in spite of all the differences he had had with this cerebral man, ordered his body to be honored at a good viewing point in St-Lô. He believed that the popular Howie was the ideal representative of all those who had died to capture the city. He was right. Somehow, Howie was the perfect embodiment of the 29th Division and its indomitable spirit. He was the manifestation of a generation of American youth that had come to liberate France, at tremendous cost. The major, like all the other dead men, had so much to live for and probably not as much to die for. As one 29th Division officer said, "life and laughter ended at St-Lô" for Howie and the other dead men.

All day long on July 19, American soldiers and French civilians paid their respects to the flag-draped body that was nestled into the ruins. Lieutenant Jones, greatly moved, watched them leave flowers or say a short prayer. "I did observe it all. It was simple and direct, no fanfare or otherwise. It was a little too dangerous [for] anything else."

The next day, the 35th Division relieved the battered remains of the 29th in St-Lô. At the Blanchet mausoleum, Major Johns turned over his CP to a battalion commander from the 134th Infantry Regiment. "The wiremen took out the phone, [I] shook hands and said goodbye and good luck to the new arrivals." He left St-Lô, but not without thinking of so many others who never made it this far.

At the same time, half a mile to the east, near the N-172, Major Cawthon surveyed the ruins of the city. "I took a last look around the now quiet battlefield. Salvage crews were at work, and much of the wrecked equipment and weapons had been removed. But the deep wounds in the land were undressed and gave the appearance of a verdant desolation. The base of every hedgerow was scalloped with holes, for no man had stopped even momentarily without digging in. Practically every hedgerow had been fought for, plowed by shells and gaped with raw passages for tanks. Whole trees were blasted down, shattered limbs hung from others. The sweet, sickening smell of high explosive persisted in the heavy air."

Cawthon, in a subdued mood, ruminated on the wasteful tragedy of all this. He and the rest of the battalion CP had been separated from Bingham and the others and had not shared their vigil of isolation of La Madeleine. For that Cawthon never quite forgave himself. Cawthon's reverie was pierced by the sight of a ragged group of men, in columns of twos, marching down the road. It was the 2nd Battalion, 116th, and Major Bingham was at their head. "The column was pitifully short; at first I thought it was only one company and that the other would follow. Then I realized that this was all there was, and the memory still dries the throat and stings the eyes." Bingham and his survivors were "bowed with a mortal weariness" and the weight of all they had endured. Cawthon felt tears welling up in his eyes. He turned away. This was the greatest and the worst sight he had ever seen.[14]

CHAPTER TEN

———

COBRA

By the time the St-Lô battle finally came to an end, Bradley's 1st Army had suffered 40,000 battle casualties in only seventeen days of combat. Combat fatigue accounted for the loss of another 10,000 men. Infantrymen suffered 90 percent of the 1st Army's casualties. "Over a stretch [of combat] you became so dulled by fatigue that the names of the killed and wounded . . . might have come out of a telephone book for all you knew," one dogface later wrote. "All the old values were gone, and if there was a world beyond this tangle of hedgerows . . . you never expected to live to see it."

The killed and wounded were not just names out of a telephone book. They were Americans, most of them quite young, with families, hometowns, strengths, weaknesses, talents, vices, hopes, dreams, and plans for the future. For every dead soldier there was a life of unfulfilled potential, perhaps even unfulfilled achievements or generations of unborn children and grandchildren. Every wounded man suffered pain, in varying degrees. Some recovered from their wounds; some did not. Some were grazed; some were crippled. The victims of combat fatigue battled demons that, for some, would never go away. In short, the extensive casualty list of July represented a monumental amount of tragedy.

In exchange for these staggering losses, the Americans had captured St-Lô and had moved the front line some twelve to fifteen miles farther south. At this rate, the bloodletting in Normandy would soon be comparable to that of the Argonne Forest in World War I or Grant's offensive in the summer of 1864, two of the bloodiest campaigns in the history of the U.S. Army.[1]

The horrible losses haunted General Bradley as July unfolded. He knew that this carnage had to stop, but how to do it? From the first, he had wanted to fight a fast-moving battle of maneuver, but to this point he had been unable to make that happen in the confining hedgerows that dominated Normandy. The general was a pensive man. He liked to sit in isolated silence in his trailer and study maps of the battle area. The only problem was that the maps were starting to overrun one wall in the trailer. To oblige him, his staff pilfered a mess tent, complete with floorboards (so that Bradley would not have to walk in mud), and crammed a huge eight-foot-high acetate map board of Normandy into the tent.

As the bloody July days unfolded, Bradley spent more and more time in the tent, studying his maps, trying to figure some way for a breakthrough. "I paced the dry planking of that floor, scribbling boundaries, penciling roads, coloring the river lines" with an assortment of crayons. As he worked, he consulted with members of his staff, picking their brains for insight or for flaws in his own thinking. The first task was to find the right terrain, the kind of place where a breakthrough could be exploited. "You had to look for a place where you would not be hung up by swamps or river crossings. You wanted . . . terrain where there was a good road net so that you could use maximum troops and one from which you could break out on the other side and have a good road net to go in different directions after you had broken through the crust of German resistance."

Possession of St-Lô would give Bradley the roads he needed, but what about terrain? The more he and his staff studied the map, the more their eyes settled on the area just west of St-Lô, specifically the St-Lô–Périers–Lessay road (N-800). "On the near side of that road the Carentan marshes gave way to dry ground and beyond it the hedgerows thinned toward the corner of Brittany, 25 miles farther south." This was the terrain that Bradley believed could be the focus of an advance, all the way to Coutances, near the southwest coast of the Cotentin.

To get there, Bradley would make use of every weapon at his disposal, including heavy bombers. Even as Bradley stood in his tent, poring over his maps, General Montgomery, his nominal superior, was using the heavies to take Caen. Moreover, Monty planned to use them again in Operation Goodwood, his plan to push beyond Caen, into the good tank country of eastern Normandy. At Caen, the bombers had not been as much help as Montgomery hoped (nor would they be for Goodwood), but maybe they were still useful nonetheless.

Maybe, Bradley thought, the heavy bombers could help him punch a hole through the German line, right at the St-Lô–Périers highway. He knew the perfect spot for the punch. He picked up a crayon and began drawing on the map. "A few miles outside of St. Lô I marked a rectangular carpet on the Périers road, three and a half miles wide, one and a half deep. The enemy was first to be paralyzed by saturation bombing of that carpet." The road would be a perfect marker for the airmen, "a long straight line that would

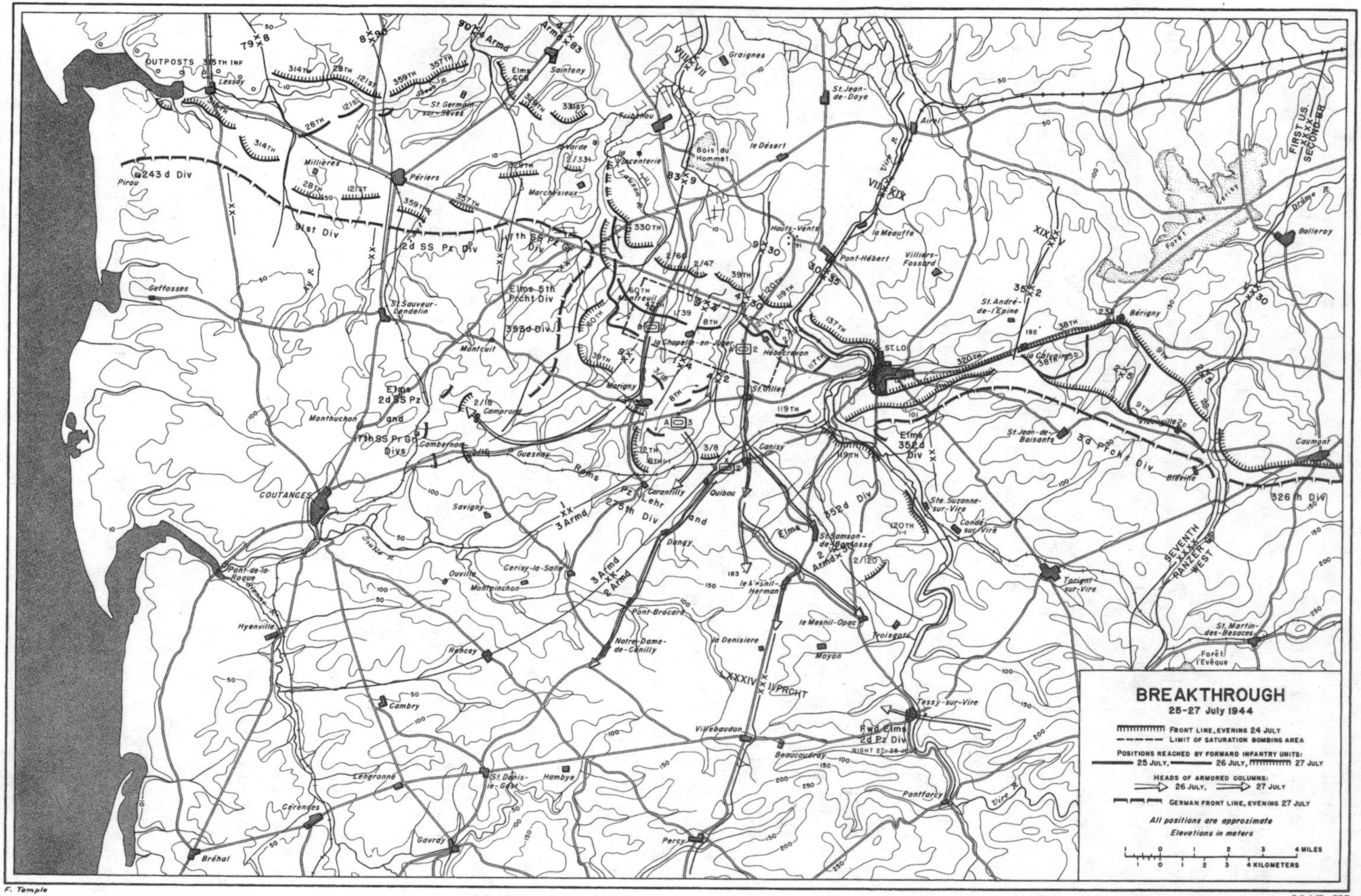

MAP VI

BREAKTHROUGH
25-27 July 1944

FRONT LINE, EVENING 24 JULY
LIMIT OF SATURATION BOMBING AREA
POSITIONS REACHED BY FORWARD INFANTRY UNITS:
25 JULY, ———— 26 JULY, ———— 27 JULY
HEADS OF ARMORED COLUMNS:
———→ 26 JULY, ———→ 27 JULY
GERMAN FRONT LINE, EVENING 27 JULY
All positions are approximate
Elevations in meters

0   1   2   3   4 MILES
0   1   2   3   4 KILOMETERS

F. Temple

separate our positions from that of the Germans. *The bombers, I reasoned, could fly parallel to it without danger of mistaking our front line* [italics in original]."

Some difficulties had to be worked out, though. When the heavy bombers had been used at Caen (and earlier in the year at Monte Cassino in Italy) two problems had emerged. First, their heavy ordnance had left massive craters that made it hard for vehicles to advance. Second, ground troops had to be moved back a long way to avoid being bombed by their own planes. This made it difficult for them to attack the Germans quickly, while they were still stunned by the bombing. Bradley and his staff worked through these issues with their air force counterparts. The planes would use 100- and 260-pound antipersonnel bombs that did not leave large craters. To maximize the possibility of a quick attack after the bombing, the ground troops would only be moved back 1,500 yards from the bomb line. This was farther away than what Bradley wanted but closer than what the Air Force wanted.

When the bombers were done, the ground troops would strike swiftly, leaving the Germans no time to recover. "We would crash through with two infantry divisions; one on the right [the 9th Division] to hold open that shoulder [of the penetration], another on the left [the 30th Division] with its flank on the Vire south of St.-Lô. Just as soon as those shoulders were secured, a motorized infantry [1st Division] and two armored divisions [2nd and 3rd] would lunge through that hole in the line. The motorized infantry would push on to Coutances, 15 miles to the southwest, in hopes of bagging the remnants of seven German divisions blocking Middleton on his front." Eventually, Bradley envisioned sending the armored divisions into Brittany to capture supply ports that the logisticians coveted.

By July 12, the breakthrough plan was solidified. For good measure, Bradley added another infantry division, the 4th, to help the 9th and the 30th make the initial assault in the carpet-bombed area. Bradley's operations officer, Brigadier General Truman "Tubby" Thorson, code-named the plan Cobra. In the succeeding days, Bradley and his staff met with the corps commanders and briefed them on Cobra. Bradley assigned the lead role to Collins and his VII Corps, a smart move, since Collins was his best commander. VII Corps would be a veritable army during the attack—it would consist of four infantry divisions and two armored. Collins also took the lead in modifying the plan (although just how much he did so remains a matter of controversy among historians), turning his corps into a sleek force well suited to exploitation and a possible breakout from Normandy.

Bradley originally planned to launch Cobra on July 18, concurrently with Montgomery's Goodwood, in a kind of one-two punch that would put maximum pressure on the Germans. However, bad weather in the St-Lô area forced Bradley to continually postpone Cobra. In the meantime, Goodwood proved to be a disappointment. The British gained several miles of hard-won ground, but at prohibitive cost (several hundred tanks and thousands of casualties). The operation was not quite a failure, but it did not produce the kind of breakthrough Monty would have hoped for.[2]

Even as Goodwood raged, Bradley finalized his plans. He spent July 19 in England, conferring with the airmen on the pre-attack carpet bombing mission. They met at Stanmere, North London, at a shabby old mansion that served as the headquarters of the Allied Expeditionary Air Forces. As Air Marshal Trafford Leigh-Mallory (Ike's air commander), Air Marshal Arthur Harris (commander of Britain's Bomber Command), General Carl "Tooey" Spaatz (commander of all U.S. strategic air forces in Europe), and the other airmen listened, Bradley stood and explained his concept of a saturation bombing. His ideas were not new. They had been discussed in the Allied command as early as June (and had led to the carpet bombings that presaged the Caen and Goodwood operations). With the exception of Leigh-Mallory, most of the airmen around the table had generally been opposed to the use of heavy bombers in close support for ground troops. The bombers, in their view, should be hitting strategic targets deep in Germany, winning the war by themselves.

Spaatz, who had bitterly opposed the transportation plan back in the spring, was one of the most strident advocates of the use of heavy bombers for exclusively strategic purposes. To him, the use of heavy bombers against tactical targets amounted to nothing more than the Air Force doing the Army's job. The tremendous potential of airpower, Spaatz believed, should not be squandered "in plowing up several square miles of terrain in front of ground forces to obtain a few miles of advance."

Spaatz was a fighter pilot by trade. He had never experienced a day of ground combat in his life, yet he felt qualified to pass a damning judgment on the Allied ground armies in Normandy. Back in June, as he sat in the safe comfort of his headquarters in England, he had written in his diary: "Our forces are now superior to the Germans opposing us, both in men and matériel. The only thing necessary to move forward is sufficient guts on the part of the ground commanders. All the power of the British and Americans is being contained in a narrow beachhead by fourteen half-baked German divisions." Spaatz had no idea what he was talking about when it came to ground combat. After all, this was the same man who back in the spring, had advocated invading Norway rather than France.

Surprisingly, in light of the views of generals like Spaatz, the airmen at today's meeting were, by and large, enthusiastic about Bradley's plan. But they did have reservations, one of which was an insistence on the aforementioned compromise on the proximity of the ground troops to the bomb line.

However, the main point of contention had to do with the approach the bombers would take to their targets. Bradley (and General Quesada, too) wanted them to bomb laterally, horizontally, right along the St-Lô–Périers highway. If they did this, there was almost no possibility that they could drop their bombs on their own men. The airmen acknowledged this but said it was not feasible. Bradley had said that he wanted them to drop their bombs in one hour. There was no way that 1,500 heavy bombers could horizontally traverse the rectangular target area in merely an hour, or even two or three. What's more, a horizontal bombing route would leave them quite vulnerable to heavy antiaircraft fire.

General Hoyt Vandenberg expressed the alternate view espoused by many of the airmen present at the meeting that day. The 8th Air Force, he said, "would desire to bomb perpendicular to the front." In essence he was arguing for a longitudinal approach. The bombers would fly over their own lines, perpendicular to the road, and subsequently release their loads in the allotted hour over the target area. In this way, on the one hand, they would be less vulnerable to antiaircraft fire and could overwhelm the Germans with the kind of concentrated saturation bombing Bradley envisioned. On the other hand, this perpendicular approach risked the possibility of short drops on the ground troops.

The assembled commanders spent much of the rest of the meeting debating this issue. Before long, the meeting began to break up when Leigh-Mallory had to leave and Bradley had to fly back to Normandy before the onset of darkness. By the time Bradley left, he believed that the airmen had agreed to the horizontal approach. In reality, they had done no such thing. No one at the meeting realized it, but the miscommunication was about to lead to tragedy.[3]

Although the main feature of Cobra was the carpet bombing and the anticipated breakthrough that would follow, there were other elements to the plan. When the breakthrough happened, Bradley wanted General Middleton's bogged-down VIII Corps (currently slipping and sliding in the swamps of the western Cotentin) to rapidly move south, toward Coutances. For this to happen, Middleton needed two pieces of key ground—La Varde causeway across the Taute River in the 83rd Division's area of operations and Seves Island in the 90th Division's sector.

Between July 17 and 19 the 83rd launched two attacks to take La Varde but failed. The troops were fighting in swamps. Their weapons jammed because they were so filled with silt and so rusted by brackish water. The causeway was located in flat country devoid of any covered approaches. This allowed German machine gunners and artillerymen to fire at the Americans as though they were "shooting across a billiard table," as one U.S. officer put it. They inflicted 50 percent casualties on the attacking Yanks. On July 19, Middleton called off any further attacks.[4]

The story was much the same at Seves Island for the 90th Division. The island was about five miles south of Carentan and a mile or two north of Périers. It was two miles long and a half mile wide, and it was wedged between the swollen, swampy expanse of the Seves River. There was a village, St-Germainsur-Seves on the island, plus a blacktop road that led to Périers. This was the very heart of the Norman low country. There was, really, no dry approach to Seves Island, only swampy, muddy, inundated areas devoid of any foliage.

The most logical way to capture such an objective was at night, but General Eugene Landrum, commander of the 90th, did not think his unit could handle the nuances of nocturnal combat. The division had been chewed up in the last several weeks, especially in the fight for Hill 122. Replacements dominated his rifle companies. Landrum did not think they could pull off a night attack, so he decided to take Seves Island during the day.

On the morning of July 22, he sent one full regiment, the 358th, into a frontal attack. A battalion from Colonel von der Heydte's 6th Parachute Regiment defended the island from well-prepared positions. The preliminary bombardment from U.S. artillery landed too far behind the Germans to do much good. When the infantrymen went forward, they had to wade through waist-deep water, in plain sight of the Germans on the island. Along the entire Normandy front that morning, they were the only attacking American troops. "When we jumped off," Major William Falvey, an operations officer in the 358th, recalled, "all the German guns on this 25-mile front could be aimed and fired at us on our narrow front. When we attacked, the enemy machine-gun and artillery fire was the thickest we had ever seen. The artillery was like hail."

The fighting raged all day on July 22, as the Americans tried desperately to establish a foothold on Seves Island. The GIs of the 358th made repeated attacks. In one of them, a battalion commander ordered Captain Arnold Brown to take his G Company and attack all alone across the swamp. The battalion commanding officer promised artillery support that never came. From the first, Brown did not feel good about this. He was a Kentucky native who, years earlier, had run away from home, joined the Army, worked his way up through the ranks, and earned a commission. He was new to combat, but he had enough training to understand that this was a hopeless mission. When he voiced his doubts, they were squelched. "He ordered us to go anyhow, so what am I gonna do? Take a chance of being court-martialed for disobeying an order? I couldn't do that."

Captain Brown deployed his men and gave them the signal to move out. He stood up and shouted, "Follow me!"

He sloshed forward as fast as he could. The long marshy grass that permeated this part of the swamp whipped at his trousers as he ran. "I got out about 50 yards, and the Germans opened up with guns, even some tanks firing. I look back, and there are three men following me. So I hit the ground. Now what the heck are three men gonna do? So I lay in a prone position, and one machine gun was cutting grass over my legs and I believe if he had searched up any higher he'd have cut the cheeks of my butt off."

The enemy machine gunner kept shooting. The tearing sound of the gun was terrifying. The captain heard bullets tear into one of the men behind him, killing him instantly. He hugged the ground all the harder. Out of his peripheral vision he could see the bullets hitting about three feet away. "The bullets were bouncing. I could see them. I was holding my carbine, and I felt something roll across my hand, I caught three of those bullets." They were spent bullets that bounced off the ground and plopped on top of him.

Several minutes passed and the enemy machine gun stopped shooting. Captain Brown told the surviving two men to make a run for it. "So they dashed back. I should have got up and went with them . . . but I lay there until they reached cover. Then I got up, and these Germans were ready for me. I had three machine guns firing at me, like you see in a movie. They ripped up the dirt on the right side, the left side, the bullets I could hear like hornets around me. And I didn't zigzag. I just took off as fast as I could dash. It was fifty yards, and I didn't get a scratch."

In an entire day of this kind of stop-and-start fighting, parts of two battalions managed to ford the swamp and establish a foothold on Seves Island. They were in close proximity to the enemy, fighting off counterattacks from within small perimeters on the confining island. By nightfall, they were still holding out, but they were cut off. Enemy artillery and machine-gun fire was so thick around Seves Island that the engineers could not build the bridges necessary for reinforcing tanks and other vehicles to move onto the island. As the night unfolded and the desperation of the situation began to sink into the Americans on Seves Island, they steadily withdrew to a perimeter on the northern edge of the island. Stragglers drifted back across the swamp to the American-held side of the Seves River.

On the morning of July 23, the Germans attacked the U.S. perimeter with three tanks. Some of the Americans got away, but at least 300 threw down their weapons and surrendered. From the vantage point of the northern side of the Seves River, American staff officers watched as U.S. soldiers on the island shouted, "Cease fire," waved white flags, and walked toward the Germans.

There were dead and wounded men lying all over the area. Three American chaplains organized a cease-fire with the Germans, and for three hours the two sides worked together to evacuate the wounded. In the late-afternoon hours on July 23, following the truce, American patrols prowled the area, hunting for stragglers. Dozens of Americans had bolted from the island rather than surrender. Some had even escaped from the Germans after surrendering. The patrols were ordered to find them and bring them back.

Sergeant Don Foye participated in one of those patrols. For weeks he had been serving as a first scout and a squad leader. This afternoon, as he and the other patrolling Americans searched for stragglers, German paratroopers ambushed them and took them prisoner. For some reason that Foye never understood, the Germans decided to execute all of their prisoners. They lined the Americans up against a hedgerow, walked down their ranks, and shot them one by one. Foye stood with his arms against the hedgerow, heard the shots, and prepared to die. "Everybody else . . . was shot." Finally, it was Foye's turn. He heard a German soldier approach him from behind. "He shot me in the back of the head with something. I guess it was a pistol." The bullet tore through the lower part of Foye's face and he collapsed into a ditch. The Germans were working their way up and down the ditch, finishing off anyone who might still be alive. Foye, bleeding and struggling to remain conscious, heard a German hovering over him. "He kicked me in the side and rolled me over, and I thought he'd probably shoot me again, but he didn't. He checked my watch. I remember him checking my watch." He did not take the watch, though.

Foye lay there dying until a medic named Wally Ansardi found him. "I couldn't talk, but I tried to pull him down" because the area was still under sniper fire. "[A piece of] my tongue got cut off when a bullet went through. And I had no chin." Ansardi saw that Foye had no jaw left and did the best he could to administer first aid. He wrapped Sergeant Foye's head in towels and helped him to the aid station, where doctors gave him multiple units of plasma. Over the course of many months and years, they rebuilt the lower part of his face and Foye learned to talk again. Eventually, he recovered so well that the only vestige of his wound was that he had no feeling on the right side of his face.

The 90th Division's failure to take Seves Island, and the surrender of 300 of its soldiers, convinced Bradley and Eisenhower to once again make changes at the top of the division's command structure. They relieved Landrum (without prejudice) and replaced him with General Raymond McLain, who turned out to be a fine commander.[5]

The failed attacks of the 83rd and 90th Divisions were disappointing, but they had little impact on Bradley's plans. La Varde and Seves Island both ended up as a forgotten prelude to the Cobra offensive. Even as the 83rd and the 90th fought in the swamps of the western Cotentin, Bradley fretted over the weather. Day after day, the weather forced postponement of Cobra. On Sunday morning, July 23, in the nicely furnished trailer that served as his living quarters, he woke up, poked his head outside, looked skyward, and shook his head in disgust. For three straight days the weather had been lousy, and today was more of the same. Overhead, there were solid clouds and mist. He wondered how much longer he could keep Cobra a secret from the Germans. Every day of postponement enhanced their chances of sniffing it out. Bradley's chief of staff, Brigadier General Bill Kean, walked by and greeted him. "Dammit," Bradley grumbled, "I'm going to have to court-martial the chaplain if we have any more days like this." Kean chuckled.

Eisenhower was just as antsy. A couple days before, he had flown over from England to visit Bradley. That day, as the two generals watched the rain pour down in torrents, Eisenhower said, "When I die, they ought to hold my body for a rainy day and then bury me out in the middle of a storm. This damned weather is going to be the death of me yet." Bradley felt the same way.

The weather report was more encouraging for July 24. Forecasters predicted suitable skies for the Cobra bombing. Bradley sent the word to his army that the attack would proceed that day. Soldiers of the lead units left their forward positions, as unobtrusively as they could, and fell back several hundred yards to create the agreed-upon safety zone.

In its final form, the Cobra bombing plan called for the use of the entire 8th and 9th Air Forces. The fighter-bombers would be the first to go in. Some eighty minutes before the ground troops were supposed to move, 350 fighters would hit strong points on either side of the St-Lô–Périers road. About five minutes after the fighters were finished, close to 1,600 8th Air Force heavy bombers would begin their bomb runs. They were to bomb from an altitude of 15,000 feet, in tight box formations, and in three major waves that would each spend about fifteen minutes over the target area. More fighters would follow up and strafe targets of opportunity. Right behind them, a fleet of nearly 400 medium bombers of the 9th Air Force would bomb south of the road, along the anticipated route of advance for the ground troops. In all, Cobra would employ more than 2,500 planes to tear a hole in the German lines. They would unleash 5,000 tons of high explosives, napalm, and white phosphorous on a target area of six square miles.

At 1300, after the Air Force finished its bombing, the ground troops were to move forward immediately. In the west, the 9th Division, supported by one regiment of the 83rd, would capture Marigny, a couple miles south of the road. The 4th Division would cover the center, pushing all the way to the crossroads east of Marigny. To the east of the 4th Division, the 30th was to bull its way to St-Gilles, turn east, and set up blocking positions. Once the three attacking infantry divisions had opened up holes in the enemy lines, tanks from the 2nd Armored and 3rd Armored, plus mechanized infantry from the 1st and 4th Divisions, were supposed to slash through the opening, turn west, and head for Coutances. The ground plan was rather like a football running play. The 9th, 4th, and 30th Divisions were like linemen opening holes in the opposing defensive line. The armor and mechanized infantry were, collectively, like a running back dashing through the largest hole to gain as much yardage as possible.[6]

Late in the morning on July 24, General Bradley and several other high-ranking officers gathered in an abandoned war-damaged stone house near Pont Hébert to watch the bombing. The house was a mess. An artillery shell had made a hole in the roof. Torn-up furniture was scattered everywhere. Curtains were in tatters. Rats and other rodents skittered around the floor and in the rafters. Bradley and his generals did not care about the mess. They kept looking at the skies and seeing an unwelcome sight—clouds, lots of them. As the minutes ticked by, the clouds showed no sign of abating. The generals shuffled their feet nervously and hoped that their forecasters' predictions of clear weather would soon materialize.

They did not. The thick clouds meant that the bombing missions would have to be canceled and Cobra postponed another day. Air Marshal Leigh-Mallory was also in Normandy to watch the big attack. He was back at Bradley's headquarters, closer to the beach, scanning the skies, receiving weather reports from his meteorologists. He vacillated all morning over what to do. Finally, he sent word to the 8th and 9th Air Forces to cancel the bombing. The only trouble was that he sent that word too late. Only the medium bombers were still at their bases. The fighters and heavy bombers were already in the air, and many of them never got the word to abort the mission. On and on they flew, struggling with the clouds, trying to avoid midair collisions and find their targets.

Shortly before noon, at Pont Hébert, Bradley and his group heard the sounds of fighter planes approaching from behind them. Dozens of P-47s buzzed overhead and shot up unseen targets a mile or two to the front. As the fighters strafed, they unloosed their bombs. A steady stream of explosions caused the earth to rumble. Standing near Bradley, Major Chester Hansen, his aide, began to feel uneasy. The explosions seemed too close. He had seen the same thing in North Africa, and he knew it meant trouble.

Hansen's instincts were correct. Even as the uneasiness settled into his gut, some of the American fighter pilots were becoming disoriented; they were shooting and bombing on the wrong side of the bomb line. They strafed the 197th Field Artillery near Hauts Vents. They bombed the 743rd Tank Battalion in its bivouac at Hebecrevon. They hit two companies, plus some artillery and a headquarters detachment from the 120th Infantry, 30th Division, inflicting casualties.

At Pont Hébert, Hansen watched in horror as eight fighters headed right at them. "One flight went off to the left of us. The other came straight for us and let their bombs go." Hansen, Bradley, and the whole assembly of generals and staff members hurriedly sought shelter. "There was a wild scramble for cover," Major Bill Sylvan recalled. "But few reached farther then the rear of the house before the bombs hit, crunch, wham, thud, some 500 yards to the southwest of us." One of the bombs scored a direct hit on an ammunition truck a few hundred yards away, sending flames shooting into the sky and killing five soldiers. Bradley and the others were fine. A few minutes later, the fighters left and silence settled over the area.[7]

This was deceptive, because the situation was about to get worse. High overhead, hundred of heavy bombers were now over the target area. German antiaircraft fire greeted them. From as far away as the front-line positions of the 358th Infantry the soldiers could see the bombers. Warrant Officer (jg) Oliver Wilbanks and several other soldiers watched the procession. They saw the flak score a direct hit on a B-24. "We saw it start straight down and explode in many pieces high in mid-air. It was a dreadful sight." The plane was piloted by Lieutenant Ed Florcyk of the 489th Bomb Group. Only one of his crewmen got out of the plane. Florcyk and the others perished.[8]

American artillery had fired red smoke shells to mark the location of the St-Lô–Périers road, but the smoke was hard to pinpoint through the cloud cover. In the noses of the heavy bombers, bombardiers squinted over their bomb sites, vainly hoping for a break in the clouds. Most of them could not see anything. That morning, in briefing, they had been told not to drop their bombs unless they were absolutely sure they were over hostile territory.

Most, like Lieutenant Frank Dimit of the 95th Bomb Group, obeyed. Dimit's crew was flying its seventh mission. In the bombardier's compartment in the nose of his B-17, he hunched over his Norden bomb site. Outside he could hear the menacing pinging of flak, like pebbles on a tin roof. He alternately scanned for a break in the clouds and peered at the lead plane in his group, looking for guidance from the lead bombardier. There was no way to bomb through this cloud cover. He called his pilot, Lieutenant Eugene Fletcher, on the intercom and told him it was no use. He and the other bombardiers could not find the target. "[It] was clouded over so we didn't drop the bombs."[9]

Farther ahead in the bomber stream, the story was the same for Lieutenant Richard Baynes and his 466th Bomb Group. Baynes, a pilot, was struggling with his B-24, trying to keep it in formation. A few minutes before, his number four engine had quit, "but we wanted to complete the mission, so we flew continually hitting the feathering button on that prop to prevent it from running away. There was cloud cover over the target when we arrived. Since visual contact and accuracy were critical," they held on to their bombs.

Elsewhere in the formation, the same was true for the aviators of the 448th Bomb Group. Lieutenant John White's crew held on to their bombs. This was the right thing to do, but it left White frustrated that he was not able to help the ground troops. "It seems a damn shame to do it when those guys need them so badly but in a case like this it's all we could do," he wrote in his diary. "We can't take a chance on dropping them on our own boys."[10]

Some mistakes happened, though, and they led to tragedy. Over Chippelle, the new home base of the 404th Fighter Group, a packet of chaff—aluminum strips designed to jam the radar on German flak guns—smacked against the Plexiglas window of a B-24 bombardier's compartment. The bombardier, perhaps a little flak-happy, flinched and hit the toggle switch at his right hand. This jettisoned his bombs right over the airfield. The bombs destroyed two fighters, but more important, they also killed four men and wounded fourteen others. Luckily, the other bombardiers in that formation had the discipline and good sense to hold on to their bombs, or the loss of life would have been more extensive.

Something even worse happened next, though. Colonel Dale Smith, commander of the 384th Bomb Group, was flying in the lead plane for his unit. He glanced down and saw nothing but a series of low, unbroken clouds. "As we approached the drop zone I found it difficult, because of . . . clouds, to make out the road, even though it was supposed to be marked with red smoke." Smith could not see the target, but he knew that the formation was still over American positions. He looked ahead in the formation, where the 379th Bomb Group was flying, and watched, to his horror, as the lead bombardier of that group unleashed his bombs. "I saw them fall and knew what would happen next. Other bombardiers . . . would see the bombs drop and . . . would toggle off their own bombs. The error would snowball until the whole group had dropped its bombs [north] of the road."

Sure enough, several other aircraft from the 379th dropped their bombs. Colonel Smith scowled and gritted his teeth. Knowing that fellow Americans were about to die, he grabbed his mike and yelled, "Don't bomb! Don't bomb! Don't bomb!" Smith's words came too late for the planes ahead. Their bombs were already gone, but his crews held on to their ordnance while he searched for a secondary target. His bombardier found a road junction well south of the St-Lô–Périers road; they bombed it and headed home to their base at Grafton Underwood.

Many of the short bombs fell on the 30th Division. A concentration of bombs fell right onto the soldiers of the 2nd Battalion, 120th Infantry, as they waited for the word to move out. Many of them were out of their foxholes or in transit, and the ensuing lack of cover made them vulnerable to the bombs.

Some were killed by concussion, others by large pieces of shrapnel. The unit lost 24 men killed and another 128 wounded. The neighboring 119th Infantry lost 5 killed and 28 wounded. Dozens of other men had to be evacuated because of shock or combat fatigue.

Another unfortunate by-product of the bombing was that it alerted the Germans that a ground attack was imminent. In response, many German front-line soldiers occupied the positions that VII Corps infantrymen had vacated in order to create the safety zone. This meant that after the horror of the short bombings many of the infantry soldiers (particularly those from the 4th and 9th Divisions) had to fight their way back to their original positions, at the substantial cost of 174 more casualties.[11]

The bombing had done some damage to the Germans, too, but that was beside the point. Americans had mistakenly killed Americans, and that was all that mattered on this day. Back at Pont Hébert, Bradley heard about the friendly casualties and knew that he had to postpone Cobra for another day. The general was dismayed and incensed. When the postponement order had been dispensed, he turned to General Pete Quesada and asked, "How the hell could this have happened?" Quesada shrugged. He had no idea.

When Bradley returned to his headquarters, he found out that the planes had taken a perpendicular approach to their targets. Obviously, he was displeased to hear this. The question now was whether this was intentional or not. He voiced his concerns to Leigh-Mallory, and the latter promised to go back to England and check it out. That night, at 2330, he phoned Bradley, who was impatiently sitting in his trailer, waiting for his call.

"I've checked this thing with the Eighth," Leigh-Mallory said. "They tell me the course they flew today was not accidental."

Bradley was a mild-mannered person, but he felt anger welling up inside of him. "But why, when they specifically promised us they would fly parallel to the Périers road?"

They had not made this promise, and that was at the core of this tragedy. Bradley had left the July 19 Stanmere meeting believing that the airmen had promised to fly parallel to the road. The airmen left the meeting believing that Bradley understood that they intended to fly perpendicular to the road, over the heads of friendly soldiers. Leigh-Mallory seemed to have no idea what had been decided. Basically, the whole thing had stemmed from a miscommunication, a foolish and preventable error on the part of senior commanders. "The human truth is that people heard what they wanted to hear" at the Stanmere meeting, Quesada later said. Their mistake cost the lives of more than two dozen young Americans.

Nonetheless, Bradley did not own up to his share of the blame. "I was shocked and angered." He accused the Air Force of "a serious breach of good faith in planning. Had I known of air's intent to chance the perpendicular approach, I would never have consented to its plan. I have seldom been so angry. It was duplicity—a shocking breach of good faith." Bradley never really forgave them, nor did he ever publicly admit any culpability for the disaster.

During Bradley's phone conversation with Leigh-Mallory on the evening of July 24, the two men could not afford to dwell on what had happened. They had to make an immediate decision on what to do the next day. Leigh-Mallory told Bradley that the airmen could only bomb with a perpendicular approach. The one-hour parallel bombing that he had originally wanted was not an option. So Bradley could choose to have the planes, with the implicit risks, or he could not have them at all. Without the planes, Cobra would be just another hedgerow slugging match. Moreover, Bradley was worried that the day's bombing had alerted the Germans to his intentions. The longer he delayed launching his offensive, the more time they would have to reorganize and strengthen their defenses along the St-Lô–Périers road. Plus, the next day was supposed to bring good weather, and who knew how many more of those days there would be?

Leigh-Mallory asked the American general what he wanted to do. Bradley sighed. "We've got no choice; the Boche will build up out front if we don't get this thing off soon. But we're still taking an awful chance. Another short drop could ruin us." Even so, he told Leigh-Mallory to proceed. Cobra was on for July 25.[12]

Dawn came and so did anticipation. The day was bright, sunny, almost hot. The clouds of the previous morning were long gone. Given the vagaries of Norman weather, the airmen could not have hoped for better conditions. At air bases in Normandy and England, fighter pilots and bomber crews ate breakfast, sat through briefings, and prepared to take off. North of the St-Lô–Périers road, the ground troops sat in foxholes, dugouts, or ruined buildings and nervously chatted about what lay ahead. Among the Americans there was a palpable sense of excitement in the air, maybe even a sense of hope that today would put an end to the hedgerow nightmare. The soldiers had not had this much excitement or expectation since D-Day.

In a small apple orchard next to a battered stone farmhouse that served as the headquarters for the 8th Infantry Regiment, staff officers and commanders gathered together for one final briefing. The 8th was scheduled to lead the ground attack this afternoon, just as it had led the way on Utah beach nearly two months ago. Shell craters marred the orchard, as did shattered, splintered tree limbs, lying at crazy angles and every which way. A stone wall had once surrounded the orchard, but shell fire had reduced the wall to nothing more than a jumbled pile of rocks. The attic of the farmhouse had collapsed to the ground floor. Chickens and rabbits roamed the orchard.

The air carried the distinctive odor of Normandy in the summer of 1944—a mixture of rich black soil, manure, cider, gunpowder, moisture, and, of course, the stench of death from rotting cows and rotting human beings.

The officers stood or squatted in a circle around Colonel James Rodwell, the commanding officer of the 8th. Rodwell had replaced the beloved Colonel James Van Fleet just a few weeks before when Van Fleet got promoted. Everyone had a mimeographed sketch of the front lines, outlining targets to be bombed. They also had copies of the unit's orders. Colonel Rodwell went over them step-by-step. As he did so, many of the officers took notes with little pencils in pocket-sized notebooks.

Standing unobtrusively on the edge of the circle of officers, Ernie Pyle, the famous war correspondent, listened to the briefing and tried to blend in. By now, Pyle had seen a lot of war. He had been covering nearly every battle since North Africa. He had emerged as the primary advocate of the combat soldier, eating with them, chatting with them, drinking with them, sharing their misery and their dangers, telling their story to millions of Americans back home. It is fair to say that he was the best known, and probably the most beloved, war correspondent. Pyle had seen enough death and tragedy to last him a lifetime. Yet, somehow, there was nowhere else he would rather be than right here with these front-line soldiers of the 8th Infantry. He had spent the last several days with them, and he intended to accompany them on their attack today.

Colonel Rodwell wrapped up his briefing and glanced at Pyle. "Ernie Pyle is with the regiment for this attack and will be with one of the battalions, so you'll be seeing him." All heads turned and looked at Pyle. Everybody was smiling at him, but Pyle felt embarrassed. He hated to call attention to himself, but he had little time to dwell on his discomfort. General Barton, commander of the 4th Division, soon arrived. Everyone snapped to attention, but the general told them to carry on.

When Barton arrived, Pyle detected a keen sense of emotion among the gathered leaders. This was the general who had led them ashore on D-Day, through the Cotentin all the way to Cherbourg, through the swamps just northeast of here. Today he would lead them through the German lines—they hoped. "The general stepped into the center of the circle," Pyle reported. "He stood at a slouch on one foot with the other leg far out like a brace. He looked all around him."

A moment passed as Barton thought of what he wanted to say. When he spoke, his voice was tight, as though he was trying to stifle his emotions. "This is one of the finest regiments in the American Army. It was the last regiment out of France in the last war. It was the first regiment into France in this war. It has spearheaded every one of the division's attacks in Normandy. It will spearhead this one. For many years this was my regiment and I feel very close to you, and very proud." As he said this, his voice almost broke. His face was lined with deep wrinkles, products of the responsibilities of command. "That's all. God bless you and good luck." He quickly strode away, to deal privately with the emotions that were churning inside of him. Pyle felt a lump rising in his own throat. A minute later, Colonel Rodwell dismissed the group, and they headed to their forward positions.[13]

All over VII Corps, the ground soldiers sat and waited in eager anticipation of the arrival of the planes. Almost all activity came to a halt as the troops settled in. It was as if they had taken their seats and were waiting for a show to begin. For nearly an hour, an eerie calm pervaded along the front. Then they began to hear the rumbling of aircraft engines.

The fighters were once again going in first. At exactly 0938 Colonel Harold Holt and his 366th Fighter Group led an armada of 350 fighters into the target area. Holt and his pilots marveled at the sight below them. "As we approached [the St-Lô–Périers road] we had to gasp." They saw hundreds of American tanks and vehicles on the north side of the road, lined up, bumper-to-bumper, waiting for the signal to move out. On the German side of the road they saw nothing. Enemy vehicles and troops were well concealed.

As Holt led the way, the fighters started their bomb runs. "Stretched before us was a veritable battlefield . . . exploding shells, colored smoke pots billowing red clouds to outline our bombing area, and panels providing a well-defined troop line." To avoid any possibility of short bombings, ground troops had laid down colored cloth. As Holt indicated, artillerymen fired red smoke to mark the dividing line. Each U.S. vehicle had an orange or pink recognition panel. Plus there was the St-Lô–Périers road. The fighter pilots were flying low and they could see all of this. They knew exactly where they were. One after the other, they unleashed their 500-pound high-explosive or incendiary bombs on the German side of the road. With their wing-mounted machine guns they shot up anything that looked suspicious. There were so many planes that the pilots had to take turns making their bomb runs.

Roughly one thousand yards north of where the fighters were bombing, Ernie Pyle and several 8th Infantry soldiers were standing in a farmyard, watching the spectacle. "We . . . watched them barrel nearly straight down out of the sky. They were bombing about half a mile ahead of where we stood. They came in groups, diving from every direction, perfectly timed, one right after another. Everywhere we looked separate groups of planes were on the way down, or on the way back up, or slanting over for a dive, or circling, circling, circling over our heads, waiting for their turn. The air was full of sharp and distinct sounds of cracking bombs and the heavy rips of the planes' machine guns and the splitting screams of diving wings. It was all fast and furious, yet distinct." In their wake the fighters left rising clouds of smoke and dust.

American howitzers shelling German forces as they retreated near Carentan.

American soldiers hanging out laundry in a captured German pillbox.

A German POW is marched to a holding area by an American tank crew in St-Lô.

German POWs in a trench on a Normandy beach, awaiting detainment.

Tens of thousands of German soldiers were made prisoners during the final phase of the battle of Normandy.

Bomb damage in Cherbourg after its liberation, summer 1944.

This dead soldier was one of the Germans who made a "last stand" to hold Cherbourg. Captain Earl Topley, who led one of the first outfits into the liberated port city, blamed him for killing three of his men.

Louis Lisko at Pointe-du-Hoc after the invasion. *U.S. Army Military History Institute*

An officer standing in front of a long-range naval gun near Toulon. The Allied forces in Operation Dragoon landed on the Mediterranean coast near this port on August 15, 1944, and a month later linked up with troops from Operation Overlord in northeastern France.

4th Infantry Division, 8th U.S. Infantry. *U.S. Army Military History Institute*

Norman D. Cota. *U.S. Army Military History Institute*

Matthew B. Ridgway. *U.S. Army Military History Institute*

Charles H. Gerhardt. *U.S. Army Military History Institute*

James M. Gavin. *U.S. Army Military History Institute*

Clarence Huebner. *U.S. Army Military History Institute*

Maxwell D. Taylor. *U.S Army Military History Institute*

J. Lawton Collins. *U.S. Army Military History Institute*

Russell P. Reeder *(right)*, with General George C. Marshall, U.S. Army Chief of Staff. *U.S. Army Military History Institute*

General Dwight D. Eisenhower, Supreme Allied Commander, in Paris, at the headquarters of the European theater of operations. He wears the five-star cluster of the newly created rank of General of the Army.

American generals, 1945. *Seated (left to right):* William H. Simpson, George S. Patton, Jr., Carl Spaatz, Dwight D. Eisenhower, Omar Bradley, Courtney H. Hodges, and Leonard T. Gerow. *Standing (left to right):* Ralph S. Stearley, Hoyt S. Vandenberg, Walter Bedell Smith, Otto P. Weyland, and Richard E. Nugent.

The fighter attack took twenty minutes, and the Germans did not shoot down even one of the attacking fighters. The mission was surgical, effective, and impressive. "My fighter-bombers came in with specific targets, a specific area," General Quesada later said. "We did not try to carpet-bomb, and it worked."[14]

Other fighter pilots were patrolling 20,000 feet above the deck, flying top cover for the massive aerial armada, making sure the Luftwaffe did not interfere. One of them, Lieutenant Raymond Conlin of the 357th Fighter Group, was sticking, like any good wingman, close to his leader. Every few seconds Conlin glanced down and caught a quick glimpse of the strafing fighters. Most of the time, though, he scanned the skies for enemy fighters. All of a sudden, Captain Kit Carsons, his leader, rolled over and dived. "I followed him down as he tacked on to the rear of an Fw 190. The game was on and I was in a wild ride earthward trying to stay in position on Capt. Carsons. At the time it seemed we were almost vertical chasing the 190, the pilot was doing his big barrel rolls downward trying to get us off his tail, but we were right with him. As Capt. Carsons closed into range he started to get strikes on the other ship." When they were 300 feet from the deck, the enemy plane finally crashed. "The pilot must have been dead because he did not bail out."[15]

It was just past 1000 hours now. From the north, behind the American lines, the GIs heard the throbbing, thunderous rumble of the approaching heavy bombers. There were close to 1,500 B-17s and B-24s, split up into three waves, flying in tight formations. "At first they were the merest dots in the sky," Pyle wrote. "We could see clots of them against the fat heavens, too tiny to count individually. They came on with a terrible slowness. They came in flights of twelve, three flights to a group and in groups stretched out across the sky. They came in a constant procession and I thought it would never end. I had the feeling that even had God appeared beseechingly before them in the sky, with palms outstretched to persuade them back, they would not have had within them the power to turn from their irresistible course."

Many of the ground troops stood with their necks craned, watching in awe as the fleet of bombers passed right overhead. The heavies were flying at altitudes ranging from 12,000 to 16,000 feet, but they looked even closer than that. "They looked close enough for me to get their license number. The line seemed endless," Lieutenant Chester Jordan, a platoon leader in K Company, 47th Infantry Regiment, 9th Division, recalled. A mile or two north of Jordan's forward position, the bombers looked just as daunting to the soldiers who were part of the great columns of armored vehicles. To Sergeant Ray Reeder, an M-8 armored car commander in the 3rd Armored Division, the bombers looked like "a swarm of house flies heading across the sky."[16]

High above Reeder, Lieutenant Richard Baynes was flying in one of the leading planes. Baynes's 466th Bomb Group was leading the whole 8th Air Force. "The target area [is] clear," Lieutenant Baynes heard from his bombardier. He was ready to salvo on the signal from the group's leader. "We dropped our bombs right in the designated spot, and the lead pilot, navigator and bombardier were awarded the French Croix de Guerre for their efforts. There was meager flak."

Now the air was full of descending bombs from the first wave of bombers. The bombs struck the earth and exploded in terrifying clusters. "The bombs cascaded down," Major Hansen wrote, "spewing earth skyward, erupting with a thunderclap that never seemed to subside as wave after wave picked up the terrible tympani of the movement."

Bradley and Collins were at a damaged café adjacent to the VII Corps CP at Goucherie. The two generals gazed at the skies, watching the bombers unloose their loads. "The roar of our incoming heavy bombers was terrific as, once again, they passed overhead," Collins wrote, "and the 'carumps' of the bombs shook the café as they exploded."

Waves of concussion swept over the whole area, producing the effect of an earthquake. "The ground was trembling and the trees were shaking with the shock," Sergeant Allen Towne, a 1st Infantry Division medic, wrote in his diary. At the 8th Infantry positions, the concussion bounced some of the soldiers around in their foxholes. At the farmyard where Pyle and his group were observing the bombing, they could feel the concussion in their chests even as curling waves of smoke floated toward them. "The bombs came . . . like the crackle of popcorn and almost instantly swelled into a monstrous fury of noise that seemed surely to destroy all the world ahead of us. A wall of smoke and dust . . . grew high in the sky. It filtered along the ground back through our orchards. It sifted around us and into our noses. The bright day grew slowly dark from it. Everything was an indescribable cauldron of sounds. The thundering of the motors in the sky and the roar of bombs ahead filled all the space for noise on earth. Our own heavy artillery was crashing all around us, yet we could hardly hear it."[17]

The first wave was flying through intense flak. In the copilot's seat of a B-24, Lieutenant John Crowe of the 491st Bomb Group flinched repeatedly at the numerous black oily, menacing flak bursts that crackled outside of his window. To him and his crewmates, it was "the most intense and accurate anti-aircraft fire that any of us ever experienced. One, two, three, just that fast, directly in front of the [plane's] nose, and then another salvo of three. The [enemy] gunner was leading us too much, just by a hair." Crowe could scarcely believe that his plane was able to fly through this wall of flak without a direct hit. He and his crew escaped with only minor damage to their plane.

Others were not so fortunate. Observing from the cupola of an M-7 priest in a position about two miles behind the bombing, John Symanski of the 12th Infantry saw the enemy flak score some fatal hits. "We could clearly see our planes getting hit, bursting into flames, parachutes opening as the crews abandoned their ships."

The massive waves of bombs from the heavies destroyed some of the enemy antiaircraft guns but not all. American artillery tried to knock out the surviving guns. The eyes and ears of the artillerymen were aerial observers who flew tiny Piper Cubs about five hundred feet over the lines, looking for enemy flak positions. All along the front, the little planes could be seen buzzing back and forth, in lazy, slow circles. One infantry medic thought the mite-sized planes made for a humorous sight amid the awesome power above and below them. "The funniest thing I ever saw was those Piper Cubs. They were spotting for the artillery so the 88s couldn't hit our bombers. Little bitsy Piper Cubs protecting these great big sons of bitches way up there with the bombs." In one of the spotter planes, First Lieutenant Allen Knisley, an observer pilot for the 3rd Armored Division, and another officer flew back and forth, looking for the muzzle flashes of enemy guns. As they called back the coordinates of enemy flak batteries, they saw them get obliterated by bombs and shells. "We cruised along at about 500 feet, watching the bombing. It was really awesome!" By and large, the artillery was successful in destroying enemy antiaircraft positions. In total, enemy flak brought down six bombers and damaged another fifty-nine.[18]

So far the operation was going well. The first and second waves had bombed on-target, amid thick flak, and had suffered minimal casualties. The third wave now soared over the area and prepared to unleash even more fury, but the bombardiers in these planes had serious trouble finding their targets through all the smoke, dust, and debris. Most could not even begin to see the St-Lô–Périers road or much else. The wind was blowing to the north, which meant that the thin wisps of red smoke were slowly working their way north of the St-Lô–Périers road and over the American lines.

In the majority of planes, the bombardiers worked their way through these problems and released their bombs over German territory, but some bombardiers were hopelessly confused. In one formation, the lead bombardier was having problems with his bomb sight. Despairing that his site would not work, he released his bombs visually—over American territory. Another mistook gun flashes, probably from U.S. artillery, for red smoke and toggled his bombs north of the St-Lô–Périers road. The rest of his group followed suit. Elsewhere in the formation, a command pilot saw his wing commander drop his bombs and blindly followed the lead, against the strenuous objections of his crew. Lieutenant Irwin Stovroff of the 44th Bomb Group was a bombardier in this part of the bomber stream. He saw the planes ahead letting their bombs go and did the same. "We did drop some bombs on the

Allies' position. We came in behind the lead group and followed to the smoke to let our bombs go." At least thirty-five heavies dropped their bombs over friendly troops. The mediums came in and made things even worse; forty-two of them used the smoke as an aiming point and thus bombed the American lines. The crews of these planes were totally unaware of what they had done.

In his Piper Cub, Lieutenant Knisley was painfully aware of the tragedy unfolding before his eyes. He got on his radio and called his headquarters, telling them what was going on, but it did no good. "There was no direct radio contact between the forces on the ground and the [strategic] air forces. Thus there was no way to stop the carnage. It was truly a helpless feeling." Knisley could do nothing but keep flying and watch the whole sickening scene.[19]

Meanwhile, on the ground the bombs were doing tremendous damage. All four assault companies of the 8th Infantry got bombed. Ernie Pyle and the men around him scattered for any cover they could find. The bombs were falling almost literally on top of them. "We dived for cover. Some got into a dugout. Others made foxholes and ditches and some got behind a garden wall—although which side would be 'behind' was anybody's guess. I was too late for the dugout. The nearest place was a wagon shed which formed one end of the stone house." Pyle hit the ground flat and squirmed under a wagon in the shed. An officer, whom Pyle did not know, soon joined him. "The bombs were . . . crashing around us. We lay with our heads slightly up—like two snakes—staring at each other. There is no description of the sound and fury of those bombs except to say it was chaos. The feeling of the blast was sensational. Our ears drummed and ran. We could feel quick little waves of concussion on the chest and in the eyes."

A few fields away from Pyle, the commander of B Company, 8th Infantry, was screaming at his men to pop as much colored smoke as they could. "We put on all the orange smoke we had but I don't think it did any good, they could not have seen through the dust. The shock was awful. A lot of the men were sitting around . . . in a complete daze."[20]

Some of the bombs were falling right into the laagers of the 8th Infantry's armored support, the 70th Tank Battalion. "A bomb exploded 30 feet from me," Captain Robert Crisson, the battalion's executive officer, recalled. "I was flat in a ditch. I can remember looking up after the explosion and seeing dirt and rocks raining down all around me. When I got up, I was half out of my senses." Crisson saw a fire burning a short distance away. He jumped from his ditch and extinguished the flames, lest they attract more bombs. "You're not rational. Many of the men were out of their heads the same way I was. We found them just wandering around and unable to understand clearly when you spoke to them." Nearby, at A Company's laager, a bomb set a Sherman on fire. Lieutenant Henry Bauer dismounted from his tank, ran to the flaming Sherman, and evacuated the crew. Considering the close proximity of the bombing, the battalion was fortunate to suffer few casualties.[21]

Half a mile to the west, Lieutenant Chester Jordan of the 9th Division was standing near a hedgerow, watching the bombing. He was a brand-new platoon leader in K Company, 47th Infantry, too new to understand the deadly peril that was developing around him, until he heard "a flubbering sound. I looked around and saw something that looked like a wooden dasher out of an old cream freezer." Jordan glanced at his experienced platoon sergeant and asked, "Sergeant, what in the hell is that?"

There was no time for an answer. "We were blown from the hedgerow." Stunned but unhurt, Lieutenant Jordan got to his feet and looked for shelter. "The nearest hole was ten feet away. It was a neat job, 3 to 4 ft. deep with a roof leaning against the hedgerow. I did not stop to ask the owner's permission. I became the meat in a three man sandwich."

When the bombing diminished, they emerged from the hole and searched neighboring hedgerows for casualties. Jordan's platoon was relatively unscathed except for one man who had been buried in his hole. "His friends were frantically excavating him. He suffered only fear and dirt." Jordan heard cries for a medic coming from a few fields away. He walked over there and saw a tank sliding into a huge impact crater. In front of the tank, two men were trying to bandage the head of a wounded soldier. "The severity of his head wounds looked as though they might be wasting their time. At the next tank we found an unbelievable scene. Bodies were ripped apart and flesh was strewn over hundreds of square feet. There were heads without bodies, bodies without heads, hands still clutching rifles but with no arm attached. Confusion reigned, it was impossible to tell the wounded from the dead."

Nearby, Lieutenant Jordan saw the remnants of both the 3rd Battalion and K Company CPs. His battalion and company commanders were alive, but that was about it. His captain was standing in a daze, staring at nothing. "I think the bastards got me," the captain said to Jordan, "look at my right leg." Jordan checked and saw that the captain was unwounded. A piece of shrapnel had pierced his canteen, making him think that blood was running down his leg.

When he finished his inspection of the captain, Lieutenant Jordan turned his attention to the executive officer, who was "on his knees next to the Captain with his head bowed as though in prayer. I couldn't see a wound or blood anywhere on him but he wasn't moving." A medic asked the executive officer if he needed help. "When the medic touched him [he] fell over—stone cold dead. The poor medic jumped back and looked as guilty as though he had killed him." Jordan's regiment had just sustained forty-seven casualties, the majority in his battalion.[22]

Two miles to the east, the bombing was hitting the 30th Division even harder. Lieutenant George Tuttle, a liaison officer, was in a dugout that served as the CP of the 119th Infantry Regiment. Yesterday he had been caught in the bombing, so he was quite attuned to the hair-raising sound of short bombs. "The ground was shaken and rocked as if by a great earthquake. The concussion, even underground, felt as if someone was beating you with a club. Whole hedgerows disappeared and entire platoons were struck. Huge geysers of earth erupted and subsided leaving gaping craters." All around the area, soldiers were being killed by U.S. bombs. "Some men, who received direct hits . . . were blown to bits and no evidence of their existence remained."

Not far away, the critical mass of the short bombs was dropping on the luckless 120th Infantry. Lieutenant Sidney Eichen, an antitank platoon leader, lunged for whatever cover he could find, all the while listening to titanic explosions that obliterated everything around him. "My outfit was decimated, our anti-tank guns blown apart. I saw one of our truck drivers, Jesse Ivy, lying split down the middle." Captain Ernest Bell, the operations officer of the 2nd Battalion, "was buried in a crater with only his head visible. He suffocated before we could get him out."

The situation was getting worse by the minute. A stick of bombs landed right on the 92nd Chemical Mortar Battalion, putting it completely out of action in only an instant. The battalion suffered twenty-eight casualties and lost half its ammunition and at least thirteen of its mortars.

The 120th Infantry's rifle companies were also getting hit hard. Many of the assault troops were lying in ditches or in fields, waiting for word to move forward. They were not dug in or well protected in any way. Lieutenant Murray Pulver, a platoon leader in B Company, was standing in a field with two of his sergeants watching the spectacle when bombs began exploding uncomfortably close. "My God, those bombs were going to hit us! We dove into our shallow slit trench, and I started to pray . . . I knew that we were all going to die. I began reciting the Twenty-third Psalm. We were covered with dirt, and the dust and the acrid smell of burnt powder choked us. The terror seemed to go on for hours, but actually it ended within a few minutes."

Close by, T/5 Robert Bradley, the E Company medic who had dropped out of medical school to join the Army, was busy treating two lightly wounded soldiers—they had accidentally stabbed each other with fixed bayonets—when he saw a general walking toward him. The only general whom Bradley had ever seen at the front was General Hobbs, his division commander, but this was not him. Instead it was Lieutenant General Leslie McNair. The blue-eyed general, a 1904 graduate of West Point, had commanded Army Ground Forces, the organization responsible for the building and training of the army ground combat divisions. Now he was in Europe, ready to take on a new, but mysterious, assignment.

Bradley knew none of this. He only knew that this wayward general was asking him about the two men he was treating. All of a sudden, Bradley heard the sound of planes releasing their bombs right overhead. Like many other soldiers in the 30th Division, he had experienced this gut-wrenching sound the previous day and he was finely attuned to sense it again. "Bombs . . . were soon bursting all around us and everyone ran desperately for cover. The general ran down the road to the right . . . and I ran to the left. There was great confusion." Bradley took cover in a slit trench left of the road while McNair found shelter in a small building with an air force observer. T/5 Bradley got lucky and General McNair did not. A bomb scored a direct hit on the general's OP. The ensuing explosion shredded McNair's body and threw him sixty feet into the air. The crimson, pulpy remains landed ignominiously in a small field. Only McNair's shoulder patch and stars betrayed any hint of what had once been a lieutenant general. The rest of McNair was little more than a bloody mess. He was the highest-ranking officer in the U.S. Army to be killed in action in World War II.

The bombing slackened. Seeing that there was nothing he could do for the general, Bradley went back to his original E Company positions. Men were scrambling all over the place, e-tools in hand, trying to dig out those who had been buried by the force of the explosions. "A fairly large number of men had been buried in their foxholes or deep slit trenches and no amount of digging could get them out in time. These were probably the most horrible casualties I ever saw in the war because their faces were still pink and they were unwounded, and yet they were dead!" To deal with the horrors his eyes were witnessing, T/5 Bradley kept humming melodies from a Dvořák symphony. He and several other men saved a few soldiers, but not many.

Many live soldiers had no visible wounds, but they were suffering from shock, combat fatigue, or the effects of concussion. Bradley saw two men walk right into a wall "and fall down, nearly unconscious." One officer tried to speak to a soldier who was suffering from shock. "His face was as yellow as the dead ones that lay near him, and his eyes seemed to be on fire. He tried to answer my questions but his vocal cords were uncontrollable and he couldn't utter a sound." In another company, the men were stumbling around "as if walking in their sleep," one officer recalled, "their hands and feet lacked coordination. They had the look of punch drunk fighters." Some soldiers went crazy under the weight of the bombs. They dropped their weapons, their equipment, and simply fled to the rear as fast as they could.[23]

By 1230, the bombing was finally over. Less than 3 percent of the Air Force's bombs had fallen within American lines, but they had killed 111 Americans and wounded another 490. Almost three-quarters of the casualties were members of the 30th Division. Hundreds more Americans, in a variety of units, were missing, concussed, or suffering from combat fatigue.

At the little café OP in Goucherie, General Thorson told Bradley and Collins about the friendly casualties. "Oh, Christ," General Bradley cried, "not another short drop?" Thorson nodded gravely. Bradley walked over to a chair in the corner, sat down, shook his head, and kept muttering, "Not again," to himself.

Throughout the ground forces, from privates to generals, a wave of anger simmered against the Air Force. "We're good soldiers," General Hobbs told one of Bradley's staff officers, "but there's absolutely no excuse, no excuse at all. I wish I could show some of those [fly]boys, decorated with everything a man can be decorated with, some of our clearing stations."

The criticism of the flyboys was understandable but not completely fair. For the most part, the aviators had done what was asked of them. By 8th Air Force standards, the bombing was quite accurate. The percentage of stray bombs was well below the usual average. The real problem was that the bombers had been earmarked for a mission that did not suit them. They were not accurate enough to hit precision targets, but they were asked to bomb with precision, and in dangerous proximity to friendly troops. In this instance, Spaatz and the other air barons were correct in their reservations. The heavies were designed to hit strategic targets—railroad marshaling yards, power plants, factories, cities, refineries, and the like—with massive amounts of bombs over an extensive area. Given the limitations of the technology of the time, short drops should not have come as a surprise. They were the price of employing heavy bombers to do a fighter-bomber's job. The medium bombers, of course, did much of the damage on July 25, but that was because they made the mistake of bombing as the heavies were bombing, on the smoke lines that were drifting over friendly lines.

In the end, everyone was at fault. The air and ground commanders had not communicated well with one another; nor had they coordinated their efforts very well. The air commanders ordered their crews to hold their bombs unless they knew they were over the target, but not all of the crews obeyed. The crewmen who made these terrible errors had to live with them the rest of their lives, but their superiors were ultimately responsible.

In postwar interviews and memoirs, Bradley consistently blamed the Air Force for the tragedies. But he, more than anyone else, was at fault. Cobra was his baby. He deliberately sought the help of the strategic air forces (a reasonable and wise concept) but failed to take proper precautions against the dangers their help would create. He could have agreed to withdraw his troops farther back from the bombing line (another 1,000 yards would have made all the difference). He could have, and should have, made sure his ground troops were well dug in, well spread out, and prepared for the possibility of short bombs. Basically, he should have done everything in his power to protect his troops from the very real possibility of inaccurate bombing.

On the first day of Cobra, he thought the Air Force would bomb parallel to the St-Lô–Périers road, but even if it had, there was always the possibility that planes could go off-course and bomb their own men. On the second day of the bombing, he knew the risks of a perpendicular approach and accepted them as a necessary by-product of war. More than anything, Bradley did not learn from the immediate past. On D-Day, he had placed great hopes on the ability of heavy bombers to disrupt German beach defenses, but they had not done so, mainly because they were not accurate enough. On that day, cloudy skies had prevented bombardiers from seeing their targets. The same thing happened on July 24. In effect, it happened again the next day, when smoke and dust, blowing in the direction of U.S. positions, caused some bombardiers to release their bombs over the heads of their own troops. On D-Day, at Omaha beach, the fruits of such inaccuracy were untouched enemy beach defenses; on July 24 and 25, during Cobra, the fruits of inaccuracy were friendly casualties. In both cases, Overlord and Cobra, Bradley failed to understand the limitations and perils of strategic bombers in support of ground troops.[24]

CHAPTER ELEVEN

BREAKTHROUGH

In spite of the short bombings, Cobra had to go forward. Bradley and Collins both agreed on that, and it was the right decision. Another postponement would have rendered the friendly fire casualties of both July 24 and 25 meaningless. The time had finally come for the assault companies—what was left of them—to attack. Collins did a fine job of reorganizing his front-line units and setting them in motion mere moments after the planned H-Hour. By early afternoon, the attack was well under way, even as another wave of medium bombers hit targets several miles to the south of the St-Lô–Périers road.

The question on the minds of many of the American soldiers was how much damage the Air Force had done to the Germans. Major General Fritz Bayerlein was the commander of Panzer Lehr, one of the major German units defending the area. The bombing knocked out his communications with his forward units, so he hopped on a motorcycle, visited his advance CP at Le Mesnil Amey, and eventually watched the bombing from a stone tower. According to him, all was chaos on the German side of the line. "It was hell. The planes kept coming overhead like a conveyor belt, and the bomb carpets came down, now ahead, now on the right, now on the left. The fields were burning and smoldering. My front lines looked like a landscape on the moon, and at least seventy percent of my personnel were out of action—dead, wounded, crazed or numbed. All my front line tanks were knocked out." As on the American side, bombs buried men alive, cut communications, turned vehicles over, and left large craters.

Even so, Bayerlein exaggerated the effects of the bombing. The experience of being carpet-bombed was by no means pleasant for the Germans, but by and large, most enemy front-line soldiers emerged unscathed. "We moved out after the bombing and found the enemy right where they had been before the bombing," one American tank commander commented. Many Germans in the most forward positions were hunkered down in tunnels or deep dugouts that only a direct hit could bury. The bombing did more damage in the German rear areas than at the front. By the best estimate, the bombing reduced German combat power by about one-third. The greatest effect of Cobra was on enemy communications, reinforcements, supply depots, and mobility. The hard crust of the German divisions in this sector remained in place, but they had little to back them up and their officers found it difficult to execute command and control. In sum, the bombing diminished the enemy capacity to resist but did not destroy it.[1]

The infantry set out for two major objectives: Marigny in the west and St Gilles in the east. Both of these towns were situated about three miles south of the St-Lô–Périers highway. The troops had orders to keep moving and bypass any strong enemy resistance. The soldiers were laden down with extra food and ammunition to minimize supply traffic on the southerly roads. The job of the leading units was to exploit the shock factor of the bombing, breach the German lines, keep advancing without regard to their flanks, and, as previously noted, open up holes for the follow-up armored and mechanized forces.

When the infantry soldiers went forward on July 25, they were surprised, and disappointed, to encounter tenacious enemy resistance. The fighting was generally hedgerow-to-hedgerow, not much different from what had been going on all over Normandy during the month of July.

Many of the Americans were especially surprised by the volume and accuracy of German artillery fire. Lieutenant Chester Jordan's platoon, like the rest of the 9th Division, was slowly pushing toward Marigny. His 3rd Battalion had been decimated by the short bombings, but General Eddy, Colonel George Smythe, commander of the 47th Infantry, and Lieutenant Colonel Donald Clayman, the battalion commanding officer, reorganized the unit well enough that it joined in the attack by early afternoon. Jordan and his men were moving along a series of hedgerows, looking for German resistance. The rookie lieutenant was scared stiff, and his greatest worry was that his men would sense that fear. The platoon came to a house next to a rectangular pond. Tall poplars shaded the pond.

Suddenly they heard a shrieking sound. "An artillery barrage began falling to our left rear. It was close enough to shake me up as I dove for the trees by the pond." Lieutenant Jordan considered jumping into the pond but soon thought better of it. The shells were exploding all over the place. He glanced upward and realized the dangers the trees might pose. If a shell exploded near one of the poplars, a tree burst could shower him with shrapnel, man-made or otherwise. He looked back across the yard and saw that many of his soldiers had taken refuge in a large shell hole, even as their sergeant yelled at them to stay away from the hole. "It looked better than the tree did to me so I joined them."

They lay in the hole and waited out the shelling. When it finally stopped, Lieutenant Jordan got them up on their feet. "We double-timed across a road intersection that had probably been the artillery's target all along. We found ourselves in a group of demolished houses but we didn't slow down or hesitate." They took cover along a hedgerow adjacent to the buildings. When the word came to move out, Jordan nudged the man next to him to get going, but the man did not move, because he was dead. "The helmet rolled off the dead G.I. I had been sharing a break with." The incident did nothing to quell Lieutenant Jordan's gnawing fear.

About five hundred yards to the west, First Lieutenant James Alford, a tank platoon leader in B Company, 746th Tank Battalion, was leading his five Shermans toward the St-Lô–Périers road. Alford hailed from Gonzales, Texas. A year and a half ago, he had graduated from the ROTC program at Texas A&M University. He had joined the 746th about a month before, while it supported the 9th Division in the hedgerows of the Cotentin. Now he stood in the turret of his Sherman, looking for any sign of the enemy. His Sherman was in the lead as his platoon crunched through a farmyard that was surrounded by stone buildings. "When we went around the farmhouse, there was a company of German infantry deploying in an open field." Alford traversed his turret in the direction of the enemy and ordered his gunner to open fire. "[He] refused, saying I was mistaken and they were American infantry." Lieutenant Alford could see the soldiers much better than his gunner. They had camouflage smocks and rounded helmets—the standard uniform of German paratroopers—so he repeated his order.

In the five seconds this exchange took, the Germans spotted Alford's platoon. "I watched a German soldier fall prone upon the ground and aim his rifle at me." Only the top of Alford's head was above the turret, far enough that he could see but without exposing most of his head. This gave him a false sense of security, almost detachment, as he watched the enemy rifleman. "I bet he's going to try to shoot me," Alford thought.

The German paratrooper took aim and fired. "The bullet struck the front of my helmet, and the only thing I can compare the feeling to is if someone hit you on the head with a 10-pound sledgehammer. I can't tell you what laws of ballistics or physics were at work, but that bullet went through the steel helmet, then followed the contour of the inner helmet liner across the top of my head and went out the back of the helmet at my neck. It knocked me into the turret. Then my gunner was willing to open fire."

The Sherman's main gun boomed and the coaxial machine gun opened up. Lieutenant Alford lay still for a few moments in the turret, trying to regain his senses. "I was stunned . . . but immediately felt my head expecting to find blood and brains. The bullet carved some skin from the top of my skull and burned up the stash of toilet paper I kept tucked in the webbing of the liner. I had a hell of a headache for a few days [but] I got off real light. Two of my tank commanders weren't so lucky. They were also hit by snipers in that farm complex."

Alford's unit was attached to the 60th Infantry, which, compared to the 47th, had not been hit very hard by the bombings. The 60th's 2nd Battalion pushed across the St-Lô–Périers road and made for high ground south of the highway, along the route to Marigny. They hit strong enemy resistance on the high ground. A combination of *Panzerfaust* and antitank gun fire took out a couple of Shermans while another one ground to a halt, seemingly immobilized. Enemy small-arms and mortar fire was intense. The Germans were shooting right down at the Americans. No one could move for fear of being shot to pieces.

In situations like this, the initiative of one individual could and sometimes did make all the difference. Captain Matt Urban, commander of F Company, was chafing at the lack of progress in capturing this German-held hill. A graduate of Cornell University, he was a veteran of many battles with his unit, dating all the way back to North Africa. A month before, he had been wounded with multiple shrapnel wounds, including a bad one in the leg. In the hospital Captain Urban became obsessed with getting back to his unit, especially when one of his soldiers, on a visit, told him about the terrible casualties they were taking in the hedgerows. Urban went AWOL from the hospital, hitchhiked rides, and hobbled back to his company on this very morning. "The sight of him limping up the road, all smiles, raring to lead the attack, once more brought the morale of the battle-weary men to the highest peak," an F Company sergeant recalled.

Urban still had bandages on his shrapnel wounds, but he thought little of such things. A leader to the core, he was full of fury, spoiling for a fight. "I was full of anger, remorse and despair. I'd seen my men mutilated, chopped up. I was seeking revenge. I was like a tiger. It was all bubbling up inside of me, and it exploded."

Urban spoke with a lieutenant in command of the tanks and coordinated a plan that, basically, hinged on the use of the immobile tank. At a collective signal, Urban, the lieutenant, and a sergeant dashed for the tank. German machine guns opened up and killed the other two men instantly. Urban kept running—hobbling really—toward the tank, even as bullets narrowly missed him. He heard the supersonic snapping of rounds as they whizzed past him.

Urban made it to the tank and climbed aboard. He checked the .50-caliber machine gun mounted on the turret and saw that it was still in working order. Then he poked his head into the turret and ordered the crew to get the tank moving, straight up the hill. They were scared, but they complied.

The tank was not immobilized after all. It started rolling forward. As it did so, the crew fired the main gun and Captain Urban let loose with the .50-caliber. Tears were streaming down his face. "I was crying as I went up that hill. I thought I was a goner, that I was headed for certain death." Instead, he and the crew made it to the top of the hill. They had destroyed the enemy machine-gun positions and prompted the Germans to flee. In so doing, they helped the 9th Division open one of the first major holes through the German lines south of the St-Lô–Périers road.[2]

Half a mile to the east, in the center of the American attack, the 8th Infantry, plus armor from the 70th Tank Battalion, fought along the northern approaches to the road. The main impediment to their advance was a well-dug-in company of German soldiers in an orchard. The battle here raged for two hours, until eighteen Shermans from the 70th came up and blasted the enemy foxholes. The Americans continued across the highway and proceeded 700 yards but soon ran into a nest of enemy troops along a sunken road. Two tanks anchored the German position. The American infantry and tanks had gotten separated from each other during the advance, so the infantry had to deal with the German tanks as best they could. T/5 Hank Henderson, a medic, watched as an NCO took a bazooka team and infiltrated behind the enemy tanks. "He knocked the first one out. [We] could hear the other one squeaking, and he went on up the road so they wouldn't discover what he'd done to that one, and he knocked [the] other one out. So we got two of them there with a bazooka." The 8th Infantry made it as far as la Chapelle-en-Juger.

On the eastern flank of the attack, the 30th Division fought all day against dug-in German tanks and self-propelled guns near Hebecrevon, a crossroads village astride the St-Lô–Périers road (N-800). Hebecrevon was also a foothold on the road to St-Gilles. At one point during the fighting outside Hebecrevon, a light tank from D Company, 743rd Tank Battalion, encountered three heavily armored Mark V Panthers. The crew knew they were badly outgunned, but they bravely opened fire on one of the Panthers. They scored three hits in quick succession, but each one ricocheted off the Panther's armor. "Good God, I fired three rounds and they all bounced off," the gunner bellowed over the battalion radio net. The crew backed up its Stuart tank and retreated. In fierce, bitter fighting, the 30th and the 743rd made it into Hebecrevon by midnight.

By nightfall, the leading edge of the VII Corps advance was a mile south of the St-Lô–Périers highway, well short of Marigny and St-Gilles. On the face of it, the day had been disappointing. German resistance had been significantly tougher than expected. The Cobra battle was shaping up as just another field-to-field, deliberate, slow-paced offensive, like every other American attack that July. "There was little reason to believe we stood at the brink of a breakthrough," General Bradley wrote. "Rather, the attack looked as though it might have failed." In fact, the reality was otherwise. "[Cobra] had struck a more deadly blow than any of us dared imagine."

Collins was the first to sense this. At his VII Corps CP, he soberly digested the reports of slow progress throughout the day but noticed the absence of German counterattacks. This seemed strange to him. He knew that German defensive doctrine mandated quick-hitting counterattacks while advancing Allied troops were off-balance and before they could dig into their newly won terrain. Today that was not happening. Nor were the Germans fighting a coordinated battle from a continuous defensive line. Instead, they were resisting at various strong points, along the strategic points of advance. Clearly, they had no communication with one another. Collins knew that his troops could probably have gained more ground today, but the hedgerow fighting of the last several weeks had made them cautious, not to mention the fact that many of them had been bombed by their own air force. Were the Germans holding back their reserves for a major counterattack or were they out of reserves? Perhaps they had simply withdrawn their main line of defense to avoid the bombing and were waiting to maul the Americans.

Collins had planned to throw in his mechanized forces only when the lead infantry divisions achieved major breakthroughs in the German line, but now he began to rethink that plan. Maybe now the moment was right to set his armor in motion. If he did so and the Germans were still out there in strength, his armored divisions would be bogged down along the small roads south of the St-Lô–Périers road. The traffic jam would be monumental, probably far worse than what the 3rd Armored Division had experienced several weeks before at the Airel bridge. However, if the attack today had smashed the main enemy defenses, then the time was now to exploit that, before the Germans could rally. If the German rear areas were in disarray from the bombing (as reports indicated), then an exploitation might just be possible.

Collins scanned his operations maps and thought some more. It was almost dinnertime now. The sun would set in a few hours. If he was going to set his armor in motion, he needed to do it soon. The more Collins thought about the situation, the more he sensed that things were better than they appeared. He picked up the phone and gave the necessary orders—the armored units were to attack in the morning.[3]

Under cover of darkness, the mechanized units rolled south. All night long, they snaked slowly along the roads. The columns stretched for several miles. Collins had set in motion two major strike forces. In the east, Combat Command A (CCA) of the 2nd Armored Division, with the 22nd Infantry Regiment of the 4th Division attached, was in position to drive for St-Gilles. In the west, the whole 1st Infantry Division, plus Combat Command B (CCB) of the 3rd Armored Division, was poised to assist the 9th Infantry Division in its push for Marigny. Colonel Truman Boudinot, the colorful commander of CCB, could hardly contain his excitement. "We're going to make a breakout of the damned beachhead," he told his officers during the night, "and it's got to be successful even if it means the annihilation of CCB."

South of the St-Lô–Périers road, and about a mile north of Marigny, in the forward positions of the 9th Division, Lieutenant Jordan of K Company, 47th Infantry, awoke from an exhausted slumber. The night before, his platoon had halfheartedly dug into an orchard. The soil was rocky and full of roots. The men were so tired from the day's fighting that they merely scraped out shallow depressions for themselves. Jordan gave orders for 50 percent alert (one man on guard, another asleep), but "I am sure it was a 0% alert in just a few minutes."

Luckily for his platoon, the night was quiet. Now Lieutenant Jordan shook the cobwebs of sleep out of his brain and took a look around. His eyes settled on a nearby hedgerow. "I saw the most artistically macabre sight of my war. A German soldier was kneeling against the hedgerow as though modeling for a sculptor. His head was bent gracefully over his helmet which lay in his hand and rested on his knees. The top of his head was in the helmet as was most of the resulting blood."

Jordan could not take his eyes off the dead German until he heard the buzzing sounds of P-47s overhead. They were flying low and close. This made Jordan nervous and he told his platoon guide to lay out the orange recognition panels. The planes dived at a target on the other side of a small village, not far from Jordan's position. "Their rockets, bombs and machine guns made unbelievable racket as they fired at something. I found, when we moved out, that they had absolutely creamed three German tanks. One had been flipped over and a rocket had blown out most of the bottom. It looked like an outsized bullet hole in a tomato can."

Jordan's unit had orders to stay off the roads (so as to make room for the soon-to-arrive mechanized columns of the 1st Division and CCB) and launch small, local attacks. He received word that K Company was supposed to tie in with the 60th Infantry, slightly to the west. This meant that Jordan's platoon had to make a flanking assault on a German-controlled wooded area. "Four of the battalion tanks [from the 746th] were to work with us. Our tanks made their usual dreadful noise as they joined us and I knew they would attract every kraut gun this side of Berlin. While we were waiting for the tanks one of my men decided to end his war by shooting himself in the foot."

Medics evacuated the SIW casualty and Jordan's platoon went to work. In front of them were several hedgerows that needed to be taken. A dozer tank plowed into the first hedgerow. "The tank's treads and/or weight did not provide enough traction for it to cut through those matted masses of roots and dirt and it had to do a lot of hauling and filling to make a hole. No matter, we were in no hurry to go anywhere."

At last, the dozer tank punched a hole in the hedgerow. The tank, and one of Jordan's squads, laid down a base of fire as the rest of the platoon poured through and over the hedgerow. Lieutenant Jordan was in the lead. "I stepped on a dead German as I went over the hedgerow. As we worked our way forward a burp gun let go but it didn't hit anything close to me. We went to the next field and on to our objective. We ran into nothing but dead Germans and discarded equipment. I counted thirty bicycles in one hole. We dug in at our objective.[4]

Immediately to the north, the mechanized column had crossed the St-Lô–Périers road and was making contact with Jordan and other infantrymen from the 9th Division. The 1st Division was spread out on the east side of the D-29, the main road to Marigny, while the CCB tanks and other vehicles flanked the west side of the road. "When we reached the front lines of the Ninth Division," Sergeant Christopher Cornazzani of the 18th Infantry recalled, "our medical aidmen were running off in all directions [because] there were wounded all around us." Sergeant Cornazzani and many others felt depressed at the sight of the 9th Division wounded. They were a sobering reminder of what lay ahead.

Slowly the column passed through the 9th Division and rolled south. The vehicles delicately weaved around bomb craters. Inside the tanks, halftracks, and trucks soldiers kept an eye out for the Germans, who resisted randomly from behind hedgerows or roadblocks. There were at least a dozen firefights as the vehicles pushed south. "We would either attack down [the] road," Private Robert Gravlin of B Company, 23rd Armored Engineer Battalion, wrote, "or through a field in an attempt to come from behind" and flank the enemy positions. "Periodically, we would pull off [the] road, and our self propelled artillery, 105 MM guns mounted on tank treads, would zero in on German positions and fire volleys based upon grid maps of the terrain. After each bombardment, we would push off again, our halftrack following right behind one of our Sherman tanks. We were constantly under small arms fire and the all purpose German long barrel 88 MM artillery guns." He and the other engineers also kept busy filling in the craters.[5]

By the afternoon, the Americans were at the northern edges of Marigny. Between the Yanks and the town, there were two companies of the 2nd SS Panzer Division, plus some holdouts from the 353rd Infantry Division. The German defenses included several Mark IV tanks and at least two self-propelled guns. If not for patrolling fighter-bombers, there would have been even more enemy armor around Marigny. The American planes had shot up several German tanks as they formed up for a counterattack that morning. Not only did this prevent a strong enemy response to CCB's advance; it also scattered many of the enemy tanks in the area, leaving only a few to defend Marigny. The planes were still patrolling as the American vehicles closed in on Marigny.

The ground troops still had not spotted the German defenses at Marigny. At the leading edge of CCB, Sergeant Ray Reeder stood in the turret of his M-8 "Greyhound" armored car and glanced upward in search of the planes. Not only could he hear them, but he also could see indications of their presence. "The metal links of their expended ammunition sometimes fell on our vehicles and the roadbed. Their support saved many lives because as we moved we would pass the dead men and the big guns which would have played hell with out light armor. We were moving down country type roads with low hedgerows lining the road."

Sergeant Reeder's car kept driving along the road. His driver kept an eye out for the numerous craters in front of him, even as he stayed close to the other reconnaissance vehicles (mostly armored cars, jeeps, and light tanks). "As we moved," Reeder recalled, "we passed one of the most gruesome sights imaginable. In the middle of the road sat the smallest of the German vehicles, in the driver's seat sat a German soldier with his hands clutching the steering wheel, but his head consisted only of his lower jaw and his ears. He had just recently been killed, apparently by one of the planes supporting us. That kind of a sight is a low blow to the gut regardless of whatever you have already seen."

Not long after this, the two sides opened fire on each other. The air was full of the sound of booming tank guns, artillery, mortars, and even machine guns. American fighters circled overhead, looking for targets. They had to be careful, because the friendly armor of CCB was in such close proximity to the decidedly unfriendly armor of the 2nd SS Panzer Division.

In one of the leading Shermans, churning through a field a few hundred yards north of Marigny, Sergeant E. A. Struble saw the muzzle of a Mark IV flash in the distance. A second later, his tank was on fire. "My tank was knocked out, all of us got out of it O.K. I was lying in the field, when I realized I was hit and bleeding." Struble saw that some of his fellow crew members were also wounded and pinned down in the field. The Germans were no more than fifty yards away. "[They] knew we were wounded, and had no weapons, and they tried all the harder to kill us. They would advance and try to finish us off, but each time they were killed by a machine gun" firing from somewhere behind Struble.

He lay still and prayed for deliverance. "I have never prayed so much in my whole life as I have in battle." The mysterious American machine gun kept pouring accurate fire into the Germans and they finally gave up trying to kill Struble and his cornered tank crew. The wounded men made it out of the field and to the rear for medical treatment. "I later learned that my own twin brother Elmer was firing that machine gun . . . sounds like a plot for a movie."

As the battle raged inconclusively, Colonel Boudinot abandoned the head-on approach into Marigny. Instead he hoped that a flanking maneuver might just work. He ordered his tanks and infantry to keep the Germans north of Marigny busy while another column looked for an infiltration route west of the town. Following an air strike, they veered west in the afternoon shadows on a small dirt road that was flanked by hedgerows. As usual, Sergeant Reeder's Greyhound was in the lead. His commanding officer, Lieutenant James Cleveland, ordered him to investigate a break in the hedgerows. "As we entered the break, I could see a barn surrounded by a stone fence at the other end of [a] long narrow field." There were enemy soldiers all around the stone fence. He told his gunner to open fire. "[We] started firing at the figures I could see at the stone fence and near the barn."

The German return fire was intense. Back on the road, several vehicles were hit. In response, some Sherman crews started firing blindly in the direction of the Germans. Reeder's armored car was not far away from the enemy and it got caught in this chaotic crossfire. "I remember a very loud clang and a flash of red fire. My car had been hit by an anti tank round." A 75mm round fired from a Sherman somewhere back on the road had torn through the left side of the Greyhound. Sergeant Reeder blacked out. When he awoke he was lying on the ground with several soldiers around him. "They told me that my driver . . . and the radioman . . . were killed, but my gunner and I were OK." Reeder and the other man were evacuated with shock and combat fatigue.

The flanking move was at a standstill, not just because of the Germans or friendly fire but also because of mines on the little road. John Kropilak, a jeep driver, and two other men were driving on the road when their vehicle tripped a buried mine. "There was a terrific explosion and we were thrown along the roadside. The [jeep] commander and I crawled into a gully past Nick [Cappabianca] who appeared injured and I feared dead. He nodded his head and I was relieved that he was alive. I was covered with mud, my gun barrel filled with mud and I suffered a broken ankle and numerous other injuries which rendered me defenseless." Cappabianca got up, ran over to them, handed each of them a rifle, and suggested they make a break for it. "I can't move; my ankle is broken," Kropilak replied.

They heard rustling sounds on the other side of the hedgerow. A German threw a grenade at them, and Cappabianca responded with one of his own. He turned back to Kropilak and said, "Stay here and protect your flanks; I'm going to get help." He took off but later came back with several vehicles and evacuated his two buddies.

The afternoon shadows were getting even longer now. Back at the command half-track of CCB, Colonel Boudinot was anxious to take Marigny by the time sun set. He issued orders to keep attacking on the western flank but soon thought better of them. In the dark, his tanks would be especially vulnerable to antitank fire. Reluctantly, but wisely, he ordered CCB to stop attacking, button up for the night, and renew the attack at first light.

They never got the chance. CCB was from the 3rd Armored Division, but for this operation it was under the command of General Clarence Huebner, the respected commander of the 1st Division. During the night, Huebner issued new marching orders to CCB: skirt past Marigny and head due west, along the N-172 (an excellent paved highway) for Coutances. In the meantime, Huebner's 18th Infantry would take care of Marigny. Huebner's change of plan was in reaction to orders he received from General Collins. On the evening of July 26, Collins believed that the Americans controlled Marigny, so he told Huebner to strike west and grab Coutances, one of the prime objectives of the Cobra plan. Huebner was not sure if his men really were in Marigny, but he took steps to follow Collins's orders. The plan worked. The 18th Infantry took Marigny by late morning on July 27 and CCB rolled west four miles to Camprond. The breakthrough on the western hinge of Cobra was now a reality.[6]

The same was true in the east, but there it came more easily. The commander of the 2nd Armored Division, Major General Edward Brooks, sent his CCA, under the command of Brigadier General Maurice Rose, across the St-Lô–Périers road early in the morning on July 26. Rose's CCA had the entire 22nd Infantry of the 4th Division attached to it. The day before, the 30th Division had cleared the way for this armored advance.

Today the column did not encounter any resistance until it crossed the St-Lô–Périers road. An enemy antitank gun opened up and destroyed a Sherman tank. The Americans responded with overwhelming firepower and soon were on the move again. Their biggest obstacle was craters. The U.S. vehicles deployed on either side of the main road to St-Gilles and worked their way south.

On the west side of the road, trailing in the wake of an advancing Sherman, Lieutenant George Wilson, a brand-new platoon leader in E Company, 22nd Infantry, was nervously dealing with his first day of combat. He was frightened out of his mind, but he managed to function by concentrating on putting one foot in front of the other. Wilson was revolted at his surroundings. The area showed the unmistakable signs of the Air Force's carpet bombing. "The dead from both sides lay twisted and torn, some half buried by overturned earth. Bloated cows with stiff legs thrust skyward in death lay everywhere, as did burned-out vehicles and blasted equipment. I've never been able to erase it from my mind."

As the tanks advanced, the crews shot up anything that looked suspicious, and this made Lieutenant Wilson feel a little better. Soon German prisoners began trickling in. Many of them looked dazed and disheveled. The tankers and infantrymen waved the enemy POWs to the rear and kept moving, veering around craters as they did so. "Bomb craters big enough to swallow a jeep were so close together . . . it was difficult for our tank drivers to zigzag through."

Several hundred yards north of St-Gilles, they ran into formidable resistance. The Germans had set up a roadblock complete with Mark IV tanks, self-propelled guns, and several machine-gun positions. The opposing tanks traded inconclusive shots while Rose's forward air controllers called for support. The U.S. Army, in the course of this Normandy campaign, was proving to be a remarkably flexible, innovative organization. The Americans had developed ways to breach the hedgerows. Maybe even more significantly, General Quesada's aviators had learned to coordinate brilliantly with their ground counterparts. Fighter pilots now had radios that could communicate directly with observers on the ground, many of whom were pilots themselves. The aviators had also perfected close support tactics, through daily repetition and command emphasis. When the war was stalemated in the hedgerows, this air-ground team did not have much effect on the fighting (mainly because the lines were so close and the Germans were so well dug in and hidden). However, the fighting was more fluid, more mobile, now. The fighter pilots found a target-rich environment.

Thus, as CCA rolled south, it had a bodyguard of American fighter planes flying overhead. Now the P-47s dived to the deck and blasted the German tanks. They unleashed their 500-pound bombs and shot up the road with their .50-caliber guns.

North of the target area, Lieutenant Wilson was feeling sick. "One of our tanks accidentally ran over a dead cow. It was bloated, and when it burst its entrails wound around the tank treads—and there was the terrible mouth filling stench to add to the gore. It was too much for me. I fell down on my hands and knees and was retching miserably when the sudden roar of a diving plane made me look up." Two P-47s released their bombs and Wilson thought they were headed straight for him. "I dove down flat in my own vomit—needlessly, for the bombs sailed on another two hundred yards ahead." By the time the planes finished their bomb runs and turned for home, they had destroyed four Mark IVs and a self-propelled gun.

The fighters had absorbed some serious flak, though. On the way back to his base at St-Pierre-du-Mont, Lieutenant Quentin Aanenson saw one of the most popular men in his 366th Fighter Group, Captain Jack Engman, struggle with flak damage. "At about 8,000 feet, he called us and said he was going over the side, and that he would see us later at the base. He jumped clear and we circled him as he was falling. But his chute wasn't opening as it should have by then. He just kept falling—and we kept screaming for him to pull the rip cord. He fell 8,000 feet, and we could see his body actually bounce several feet into the air when he hit the ground. We were almost crazy" with grief.

At 1530, the Americans rolled into St-Gilles. Wilson's group entered the town from the west. He and his men were spread out on either side of the road, behind the lead tank. To their left was a high stone wall. Wilson was near the front of his platoon, right with the tank. All of a sudden, a shell exploded in a building ten yards in front of him. The lieutenant and his men hit the dirt and the tank screeched to a halt. Wilson crawled into a gutter, looked ahead, and saw a terrifying sight. "A Jerry Mark IV . . . was cutting around the corner only a short block away and heading directly toward me." Lieutenant Wilson was caught in between the two opposing tanks. He could not climb the wall, nor could he get into any of the buildings. He had nowhere to go. He lay in the gutter and watched the two monsters fire at each other from point-blank range. "Each tank fired as rapidly as possible as the distance [between them] closed to less than one hundred yards. The muzzle blasts shattered windows in the houses and storefronts, and each explosion knocked my helmet halfway off my head. The concussion smashed at my ears."

For several long moments both tanks somehow missed each other. Then, in the blink of an eye, the German tank brewed up. "Two Krauts crawled out of the tank's belly escape hatch and ran back for the corner. Both were knocked down by machine gun fire from our tank." Seconds later, Wilson was stunned to see the German tank commander jump down from his turret and run right toward him. "I struggled to my feet but could not raise my M-1 rifle to my shoulder. As I shook with excitement and fright my rifle came up to my waist and fired three times—and was empty." The enemy tanker fell to the ground with a wound in his thigh and Wilson tried to reload. "I . . . was all thumbs. I just couldn't get that damned clip to fit into the breech. The Kraut sergeant had blood seeping from his ears and mouth due to the concussion of his tank being hit, and, with his eyes staring directly into mine, he grabbed his thigh where my bullet had struck and hobbled across the street into a doorway—all before I managed to get my rifle reloaded."

The German got away, but Wilson did not feel too bad about that. "The shooting of my first man, face-to-face, was not covered by the infantry school back at Fort Benning, and I was deeply shaken. I'm glad I didn't kill him." Lieutenant Wilson was trembling uncontrollably. He needed several minutes to compose himself.[7]

With St-Gilles in tow, the Americans had now achieved a breakthrough on the eastern shoulder of the offensive. Rose wanted to sustain the momentum, so he ordered the column to keep going. The objective now was Canisy, two miles south of St-Gilles. CCA resumed its movement. The Germans were throwing in artillery and mortars but little else. On the northern outskirts of Canisy, fighter-bombers had destroyed a railroad overpass. The remnants of the overpass had collapsed into the road. The Germans tried to use the rubble as a fortified position, but the American armor simply swung around either side of the overpass and raked the Germans with flanking fire. After that, fighter-bombers—still prowling the skies as sundown approached—devastated the town.

As this was happening, Lieutenant Wilson and his platoon were enjoying a much-needed rest. They plopped down in an apple orchard and catnapped. Many of them sat against a hedgerow that bordered the orchard. Wilson was half-asleep, trying not to dream about the German he had shot a few hours earlier, when he heard someone sit down next to him. He opened his eyes and saw that it was one of his sergeants. The sergeant told Wilson that he was having premonitions of death. "He . . . asked if I'd make sure his personal effects were sent home if he didn't make it. I tried to talk him out of his obvious depression but got nowhere." The man simply shook his head and slumped next to the hedgerow.

A few minutes later, Wilson and the others heard a tank approaching. "One of our tanks [was] making a big racket coming up the hedgerow behind us. We got out of there fast, except for the sergeant. We yelled at him to get moving, but he just sat in a daze as the tank plowed through and buried him alive. A bunch of us dug him out . . . but it was too late."

"What a needless, stupid death," Wilson thought. The sergeant was the second man to die in Wilson's platoon that day, and the lieutenant felt terrible. He realized that he could not dwell on it, though. "I knew then I'd never survive if I let myself get tied in with every case. It was vital for me to build some sort of protective shield within myself and concentrate only on what had to be done in the present."

In the wake of the air strike, they climbed onto the tanks and rolled into Canisy. Half the town was on fire. "It was a bit larger than Saint Gilles, up to maybe seven or eight hundred people. The drifting smoke screened the fires a little and made an eerie glow in the oncoming darkness. It was all very spooky."

General Rose now wanted a patch of high ground three miles south of Canisy. He split his force into two columns. The first one headed southeast to St-Samon-de-Bonfosse and got there within three hours. The other kept going due south with the intention of making it to Le Mesnil-Herman, a tiny village adjacent to a key piece of high ground called Hill 183.

In the darkness, two German tanks bumped into the latter column as it moved along the little road that led to Le Mesnil-Herman. The American tanks ganged up on the enemy armor at close range and quickly set them afire. The ammo began cooking off in one of the destroyed tanks, lighting up the night. The American column resumed its advance. Sitting atop a Sherman, Lieutenant Wilson watched one of the enemy tanks burn. "As the Nazi tank burned and its shells began to explode, we were forced to detour in the field around it." When they returned to the road, a German colonel drove up in a staff car. The Americans captured him immediately.

Other Germans were lurking in the area. Lieutenant Colonel Lindsay Herkness, the commanding officer of the 2nd Battalion, 66th Armored Regiment, was standing in the road, supervising a group of men who were trying to tow the destroyed enemy tanks off the road. He noticed movement at a nearby hedgerow, glanced up, and saw a German captain and his aide walk right onto the road a few yards away. The enemy captain pointed his Luger pistol at Herkness and fired. The bullet grazed his ribs and exited through his tanker's jacket. In the meantime, Herkness drew his .45 pistol, shot, and killed the German officer. The other enemy soldier fled. Lieutenant Colonel Herkness allowed the medics to bandage his wound, but he refused to be evacuated.

By 0200 on July 27, the column was at a road intersection 300 yards north of Le Mesnil-Herman. Lieutenant Wilson's platoon was in the lead. He and his men were spread out, riding on the decks of five Shermans. Wilson was riding on the third one in the column—the armor platoon leader's tank. The journey had been a blur: men nodded off but jolted awake lest they fall off the tanks they were riding. Their kidneys were numb from the bumpy ride; their ears were ringing from the deafening noise of the engines; their lungs were burning from the stale engine fumes they had been breathing for hours.

One hundred yards ahead of Wilson's position, the lead tank stopped and the rest of the column followed suit. The roar of the tank engines was loud, yet somewhere off to his right the lieutenant heard excited voices jabbering away in German. Alarmed, Wilson spun his head to the right and realized that the Germans were no more than ten feet away from his tank. "I threw a hand grenade and at the same time yelled at Sergeant Williams, just behind me on the tank, to shoot his rifle grenade."

A second later, a *Panzerfaust* shell rocketed through the night and exploded against the Sherman's frontal armor, three feet away from Lieutenant Wilson. Luckily, the shell did not penetrate the armor—the German's aim was probably upset by the grenades. "Nevertheless, it left huge catlike claw marks across the front of the tank, some almost two inches deep and very jagged." One of Lieutenant Wilson's hands was slightly burned, but otherwise he was unhurt. "The tank commander inside our buttoned-up tank evidently wanted no more of that spot, for suddenly we took off at full speed, jerking ahead so fast that some of us nearly lost what were at best very precarious seats."

At nearly the same moment, a *Panzerfaust* slammed into the tank behind them, setting it ablaze. Wilson glanced back and saw what amounted to a funeral pyre for the crewmen inside and also for his infantrymen riding on the tank. He never knew what happened to any of these men—he just never saw them again.

The burning tank lit up the night "as brilliantly as a high school football field on a Friday night." Wilson and his men jumped off their tanks and scrambled into ditches for cover. The lieutenant conferred with the armor platoon leader about what to do. They decided to radio their superiors for instruction. "We got word simply to turn around and rejoin the main body of the task force, now in a field about a quarter mile back. Great—but *how?*"

Wilson and the tank commander conferred again and devised a plan. In spite of the light of the fire, the tankers gingerly turned their vehicles around—they were now pointed north. Wilson crouched next to the commander's tank, picked up the interphone, and asked what to do next.

"Well, it looks like the only way out is to make a fast break for it," the armor officer replied.

"Then should I get my men mounted back on the tanks as fast as I can?"

"Hell, no, they'll shoot your men off like flies."

Lieutenant Wilson did not know it, but the conversation was over. Without any warning, the tanks took off, so quickly that the phone was jerked right out of Wilson's hand. The Germans fired *Panzerfausts* at each one of the retreating U.S. tanks but missed.

Wilson scrambled back into the ditch and wondered what to do. He was furious with the tankers for abandoning them, but he knew he had to let his anger go, because his men needed him. "Some of [them] were on the edge of panic. One was crying, and I noticed a few others were trembling. I didn't particularly blame them; we were surrounded by Germans who could see us plainly and soon should move in on us."

Lieutenant Wilson spoke with his sergeants and cobbled together an escape plan of sorts. The men were to form up in two columns with ten yards between each man. At Wilson's command, they all were to run down the road, while pitching grenades and firing their rifles at the roadside hedgerows that were sheltering the enemy.

At the appointed moment, Wilson stood and led the way. "Let's go!" In unison, all twenty-four men took off running. "The Jerries fired machine guns and tossed grenades into the road. One grenade landed about three feet from me, but I was long gone when it went off." They passed the burning tank and kept running north. "It was very hot and bright . . . and smelled of burned flesh. A couple of dead GI's lay by the road, but we couldn't help them, so we kept on pounding down the road like a bunch of berserk Indians, firing all the while."

They made it back to CCA's bivouac, dug small slit trenches, and collapsed into them. All twenty-four soldiers made it out, with only two slightly wounded. Wilson's men made sure that he received a Silver Star for his leadership that night outside of Le Mesnil-Herman.

The next morning, CCA renewed its attack on Le Mesnil-Herman. Lieutenant Wilson's platoon, much to his chagrin, was once again in the lead (since they knew the enemy's location better than anyone else). The day was sunny and warm and soon it was alive with the sound of gunfire. Wilson's men advanced behind the tanks. The Shermans fired with everything at their disposal. Surrendering Germans started pouring in; they waved white flags or walked with their hands on bare heads.

Wilson's platoon made it to the first buildings of the town. "We moved from house to house and found that most of the enemy had fled." Not all of them, though. Soon Wilson's platoon started taking sniper fire as they crossed a street. Wilson crossed, looked back, and saw his radioman bend over to pick up a K-ration box that he had dropped. "[He] was shot by a sniper hiding in the upper floor near a store. Our platoon medic rushed out to pick up the radioman but he was already dead. Before the medic could run back, the sniper shot him in the side—even though he wore on [his] chest and back the big red cross on white background that is supposed to give immunity." The medic made it to shelter, gave himself first aid, and refused to be evacuated.

The Americans captured the rest of Le Mesnil-Herman and pushed south. Tanks from the 2nd Battalion, 66th Armor, took Hill 183 while Wilson's 22nd Infantry, plus armor, cleared a series of apple orchards south of the town. The fighting was still intense, as German infantry battled tanks with *Panzerfausts*, destroying three of them in short order.

One of the tanks met its end while working with Wilson's platoon. The Sherman plowed through a hedgerow without waiting for Wilson's infantrymen to provide any support. "The waiting Germans hit it with a panzerfaust in the underbelly. The tank immediately burst into flames but continued to roll on for about thirty yards until it stopped against an apple tree." Wilson watched the tank commander emerge from the turret, pistol in hand, and charge back at the hole his tank had made in the hedgerow. Even though he was bleeding from the nose and ears, he captured the six Germans who had just put his tank out of action.

The sergeant asked Wilson to help him retrieve his wounded crewmen. "Several of us rushed right out and got two of the crew out." The other two men were dead. "After dragging the wounded tankers back to our side of the hedge, we yelled for a medic." Wilson's wounded medic came up and went to work. Mortar shells were exploding all over the place.

A captain, in command of the tank company, got on his radio and called for a vehicle to evacuate the wounded men. When the vehicle, a half-track, arrived, several men volunteered to help the medic load the wounded aboard the half-track. Everyone else watched from a distance. Near the half-track, four men bent over to hoist a stretcher that contained one of the wounded tankers. "A mortar shell . . . exploded with a bright flash and sharp crack right on the stretcher. The wounded man was blown to bits; he never knew a thing. Our medic was killed." The other men were badly wounded but made it aboard the half-track. Wilson and the tank captain exchanged glances. The captain was crying. Wilson shed no tears, but he felt the same sorrow. "To my mind, the medics were the unsung heroes of the war."

By 1500 on July 27, CCA had cleared out German resistance south of Le Mesnil-Herman and captured Hill 183.[8]

Lieutenant Wilson was right about the medics. They were the unsung heroes. All over Normandy during the breakthrough, the Army Medical Corps was saving the lives of hundreds of wounded Americans. By now there were plenty of evacuation hospitals, field hospitals, aid stations, and collection centers in Normandy. When the front was static, the process of evacuating wounded men to those facilities was not much of a problem. But now, with combat units moving quickly, the medics faced a formidable challenge in treating wounded men and transporting them to rear area hospitals. Medics like Captain Fred Smith of C Company, 45th Armored Medical Battalion, practically worked around-the-clock. Smith's company was attached to Colonel Boudinot's 3rd Armored Division CCB.

Captain Smith succeeded in getting wounded men fast treatment by making maximum use of his unit's vehicles. "One or two ambulances were attached to each aid station. These ambulances brought casualties to the treatment station, first passing the ambulance platoon CP at which point another ambulance would be sent to the aid station from which the loaded one was returning. The treatment station varied from two to five miles from the aid station at this stage of the game. So we would have one treatment section leap frog the other. No one had an easy job or was ever in a safe spot."

During the push, combat medics like Captain Smith treated the wounded and quickly sent them back to permanent facilities like the 77th Evacuation Hospital near Ste-Mère-Eglise. The 77th was a 750-bed hospital set up in a collection of large tents in which doctors and nurses operated day and night. The unit had been in operation for two weeks now. In one day alone in late July, they performed 200 operations in a twenty-four-hour period. The motto of the commanding officer, Colonel Dean Walker, drove this unit during these harried days: "The men at the front don't observe union hours, so why should we?"

A war correspondent named Virginia Irwin watched the doctors and nurses work feverishly to save as many lives as they could. A continuous stream of ambulances poured into the hospital. The drivers and orderlies unloaded the litters as fast as they could. Many of the wounded were in terrible shape and looked like they could not be saved. "Some of them had arms and legs missing, some were only a hopeless jumble of blown-to-bits humanity. I saw sights that I shall remember when younger generations are reading of this bloody war in books of history."

Several miles to the west at St-Sauveur-le-Vicompte, another tent hospital, the 101st Evacuation, also treated hundreds of casualties during the offensive. Lieutenant Mary Ferrell worked in the hospital's shock ward, where newly arrived patients were processed and readied for surgery. She had joined the Army one year before at Fort Knox, Kentucky. At first she had a tough time with homesickness. She missed her family so much that she could hardly eat, and she lost fifteen pounds. But gradually she got used to the demanding job of being an army nurse.

Now, in Normandy, she stood in a tent filled with wounded soldiers. "When patients arrived they were immediately checked by the nurse or corpsman and if condition required the Medical Officer was called to the patient. This ward was usually staffed with 1 medical officer, 2 nurses and 3 enlisted men for each 12 hour shift. As patients arrived in ones or twos, those in moderate degree of shock were placed on cots, those in severe shock had their litters or stretchers placed on carpenter horses because that was much easier for the medics. Each patient had their Field Medical Tag usually tied to a button on their jacket or to the tie on their shoe. This tag was checked for extent of injury, time of morphine and amount of plasma, and for record of tourniquet."

Lieutenant Ferrell and the other medics checked vital signs and dressings and made sure the patients were comfortable. "It was most important to note the bleeding and the time and amount of narcotics given because after the casualty became warm and the circulation increased hemorrhage could start and the effect of the narcotic could be lethal." The nurses also cleaned the wounded men up. "Faces were sponged to clean off dried blood and mud, and sips of water were given when improvement was noted and the nature of their injuries or the imminence of general anasthesia [sic] did not dictate otherwise."

Day after day, as she watched these young men fight for life, Ferrell's admiration for them grew. "Nursing in this ward was a very gratifying experience. The patients were very appreciative of their care, to have their hands and face washed, clean pajamas and their cigarette held for them was like a dream, after their hedgerow and foxhole experiences. The toughest sergeant when wounded was just another homesick American boy yearning for his home and loved ones, and [we] were the closest thing to his family."

Once badly wounded patients were operated on and stabilized at hospitals like the 77th or the 101st, they were loaded aboard planes or LSTs and sent to permanent hospitals in England. The care at such hospitals was more intricate. Medical personnel focused on rehabilitating patients, not just saving them from imminent death. Private Robert Kauffman, of D Company, 36th Armored Infantry Regiment, took a bullet in the abdomen, plus *Panzerfaust* fragments. He had a large hole in his gut. Doctors in Normandy operated on him and evacuated him to a facility in southwestern England. "The large, freshly painted ward was already filled to capacity and was always alive with the banter of unquenchable G.I. humor and ongoing teasing with the nurses. A special bond quickly developed among the men in the ward."

The horrible scars of war were more than evident in Kauffman's hospital ward. "In the bed beside me was a young soldier who still trembled with fear. After being seriously wounded, he had lain in his foxhole beneath the dead body of a fellow soldier for two days. There was another man across the aisle from me who filled only half his bed. He had been run over by a tank and had his legs amputated below the hips. He stared stoically at the ceiling for hours on end to avoid the painful downward glance at the flat, taut blanket where his legs and feet should have been. There were men in all manner of casts, some in body casts, others in leg casts that were elevated in traction, and still others in arm casts, with the arms locked forward . . . like mimes frozen in mid-performance."

The Medical Corps in June and July treated close to 100,000 patients. They returned 22,639 to duty and evacuated about 60,000 more to England. They saved almost everyone; 2,027 soldiers, a mere 2 percent, did not survive.[9]

Early in the evening on July 28, General Bradley sat down at a small table in his mahogany-paneled trailer and wrote a quick note to Eisenhower: "To say the personnel of the First Army Headquarters is riding high tonight is putting it mildly." Bradley paused briefly while he thought of what else to tell Ike. The trailer was small, but it was luxurious by wartime standards. It had electric lights and carpet. Next to Bradley there was a leather couch. Nearby there was a telephone mounted on a trolley so that he could stroll over to the map as he spoke on the phone. Bradley was a modest man—Ernie Pyle had dubbed him the "GI's general" because he dressed like an ordinary soldier—but liked his twenty-six-foot-long trailer. The place was a nice refuge from the chaotic war raging outside. Bradley resumed his writing: "Things on our front look really good. I can assure you that we are taking every calculated risk and we believe we have the Germans out of their ditches and in complete demoralization and expect to take full advantage of them." He went on to say that he was issuing orders to push for Avranches, a coveted town about thirty-five miles south of Coutances. Avranches was the key to Allied entry into Brittany, as well as a complete breakout from Normandy. "As you can see, we are feeling pretty cocky," Bradley concluded.

The situation was every bit as positive as Bradley described it, and better. In just three days of hard fighting, the Americans had ripped a gaping hole in the German defenses west of St-Lô. The three lead infantry divisions had done their jobs masterfully. Within the first twenty-four hours of the offensive, all of them had succeeded in punching gaps in the German defenses south of the St-Lô–Périers road. The armored divisions and mechanized infantry, unleashed by Collins on July 26, roared through the gaps and fanned out deep into the German rear areas. By now, Bradley had thrown everything at his disposal at the Germans. The entire 2nd and 3rd Armored Divisions were on the move. In the west, General Middleton's VIII Corps was pushing south. To the east, General Corlett's XIX Corps and General Gerow's V Corps were also attacking.

In response to all of this massive pressure the Germans west of St-Lô were retreating. Even now, as Bradley wrote, they were falling back from their previously impervious positions along the Ay River in the western Cotentin. Soldiers from the 79th, 8th, and 90th Infantry Divisions, plus the newly arrived 4th and 6th Armored Divisions, were chasing the Germans as they fell back to positions north of Coutances. The whole 3rd Armored Division, along with the 1st Infantry Division, was fighting farther south, hurriedly trying to swing west to Coutances and the sea, so that the retreating Germans would be cut off. The 2nd Armored Division's CCB was even farther to the south, trying to pull the noose ever tighter around the throats of the Germans. To the east the 30th Division was holding blocking positions along the Vire River, preventing German counterattacks against the rampaging Americans. The only real threat to Bradley's breakthrough was near Villebaudon, at the eastern edge of the battle area, where the enemy 2nd Panzer Division, plus tanks and self-propelled guns from the 116th Panzer Division, were in position to unleash major counterattacks on the 2nd Armored Division's CCA.

There really was no front now, just a battle area. There was plenty of vicious fighting going on but also plenty of mobility—the very thing the U.S. Army in World War II was designed for. The Americans, in mobile columns, were rolling south and west, trying to make it to the coast, gain as much ground as they could, or bag as many Germans as possible. In the process, there were a myriad of sharp, hard-hitting engagements as the two sides came into close contact with each other. These last few days of July were a blur for the soldiers. Time lost its meaning as everything seemed to be happening at the same time. "They slept—whenever they might grab an hour or so of rest, in slit trenches, and they kept their helmets on," one 3rd Armored Division officer wrote of his men. "Shelled, mortared, raked with machine gun fire, and terribly fatigued by the pace of the constant assault, these men . . . gave the enemy more steel than he could send. They rolled forward in blinding clouds of dust, eating cold rations while moving, and never letting up the pressure."[10]

By the evening of July 28, the 3rd Armored Division's CCB, under Brigadier General Doyle Hickey, was fighting hard at Cerisy la Salle and Montpinchon, some two miles east of Coutances. German soldiers conducted a fighting withdrawal all night long and even drew some support from the usually invisible Luftwaffe. When the Americans took these two towns, they denied the enemy a vital escape route.

At the same time, CCB of the 2nd Armored Division was pushing south and west in an attempt to seal off other avenues of escape. The unit had fought its way through Pont Brocard, Notre Dame de Cenilly, and Dangy (where they had nearly captured General Bayerlein), and they were still on the move as the sun set. The situation was so confused and chaotic that it was not unusual for Germans and Americans to come face-to-face with one another on the roads. Sergeant Charles Rost, an M-5 Stuart tank driver in the 67th Armored Regiment, was sitting at his controls when he saw a two-and-a-half-ton truck approach his tank head-on. Rost saw that the truck was crammed with at least seventy wounded, bandaged German soldiers, most of whom were standing up in the rear of the truck. Sergeant Rost watched in surprise—and amazement—as the German driver braked next to Rost's tank, backed up briefly, and then went forward, right along the long column of American vehicles. "With all the American vehicles . . . behind me, I'll never understand why he drove that way. I just figured the German driver was excited." Rost never knew what ended up happening to the German truck. Rost's tank and the rest of the CCB column kept moving.

Elsewhere in the column, Private Theodore Bocci and the rest of his squad from F Company, 41st Armored Infantry Regiment, were guarding about one hundred German prisoners who had been captured throughout the day. Many of the German POWs were SS men. Several French Maquis fighters, armed with discarded weapons, were assisting Bocci's squad. A German-speaking Maquis fighter eavesdropped on POW conversations and heard an SS medical officer outlining an escape plan. When the Frenchman told the Americans about this, several of Bocci's buddies, in matter-of-fact fashion, removed the SS officer, walked him down the road, and executed him with a .45-caliber pistol. "We never gave it a second thought," Private Bocci said.[11]

Several miles to the east, the other half of the 2nd Armored Division (CCA), plus the 22nd Infantry, helped hold the eastern flank of the whole breakthrough. General Rose's CCA had split up and fanned out in several directions. During the daylight hours of July 29, one of his columns was fighting its way along a ridge that paralleled a main road (D-13) near the town of Villebaudon. The column consisted of seventeen Sherman tanks, a platoon of tank destroyers, four self-propelled guns, plus artillery, mortars, and, of course, infantry. The Americans were attacking east, hoping to capture Tessy-sur-Vire. The Germans, mainly from the 2nd and 116th Panzer Divisions, were pushing west from the other direction.

The Americans were advancing along a ridge that paralleled the road. Suddenly they started taking devastating fire from their right flank. Lieutenant Wilson's platoon was trailing 100 yards to the rear and the right, behind the two leading rifle companies. "The Germans opened up on the forward rifle companies with rifles, machine guns, mortars and artillery. The

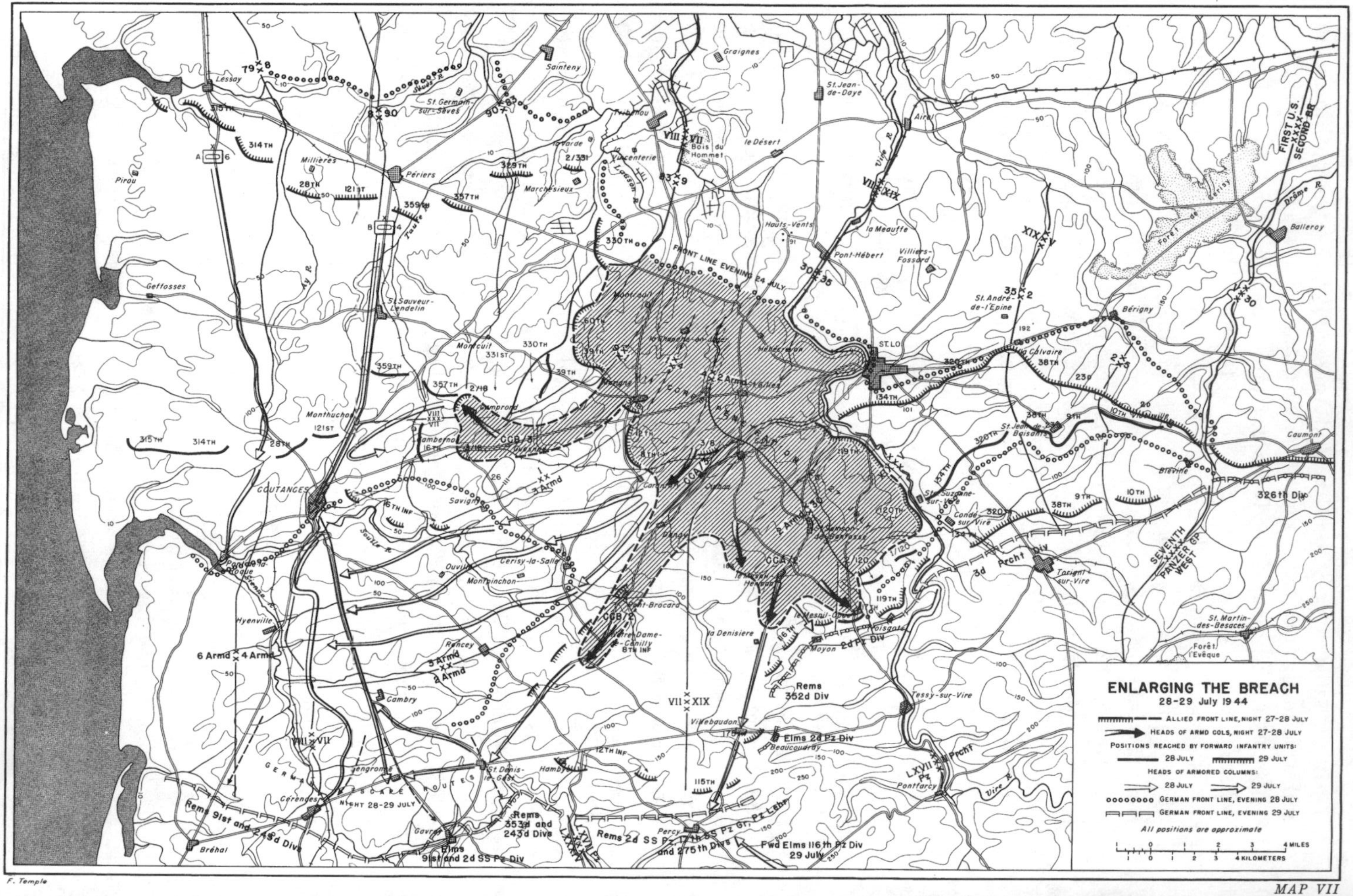

ENLARGING THE BREACH
28-29 July 1944

ALLIED FRONT LINE, NIGHT 27-28 July
HEADS OF ARMD COLS, NIGHT 27-28 July
POSITIONS REACHED BY FORWARD INFANTRY UNITS:
          28 JULY
          29 JULY
HEADS OF ARMORED COLUMNS:
          28 JULY
          29 JULY
GERMAN FRONT LINE, EVENING 28 JULY
GERMAN FRONT LINE, EVENING 29 JULY

All positions are approximate

0   1   2   3   4 MILES
0   1   2   3   4 KILOMETERS

MAP VII

F. Temple

exposed infantry instantly hit the ground and dove for any cover available, returning the fire as soon as they got in position." Lieutenant Wilson was hugging the ground. He heard U.S. artillery scream over his head and slam into the hillside. He chanced a look at the German-controlled ridge. "The calm hillside exploded into a full-scale battle. Quick pinpoint flashes of small-arms fire blinked along the bottom of the hedges. The sudden bright flashes of bursting shells flowered among the dark green helmeted shapes of the infantry."

Wilson moved his platoon behind a thick hedge. As he did so, five Shermans and two tank destroyers took up positions around his soldiers. The two sides poured fire at each other. As this happened, Wilson noticed a red smoke shell explode right in their position. The shell was a marker for U.S. artillery. In a matter of seconds, the friendly artillery shells started exploding near Wilson and the other Americans. "Few things are as terrifying as the target area of an artillery barrage. You cannot think, cannot talk, and there is no place to go. You must fight your instincts to get up and run."

Wilson and many of his men tried to wedge themselves under the hedges. A few tried to take shelter under the tanks. This was a bad, and fatal, idea. The tank crews buttoned up in response to the artillery and backed away. Looking through their slits, they could not begin to see the prone infantry. "Two of my men were crushed by the maneuvering tanks. I told myself they were already dead from the shelling."

The barrage intensified as mortar shells started dropping in. One of the shells scored a direct hit, ripping right through the back of a man who was lying next to Lieutenant Wilson. "His buddy and I were splattered with flesh and blood but were not touched by shrapnel. His body must have absorbed the shell. The survivor broke in panic and ran wildly past me." Wilson got up, ran after him, tackled him, and subdued him. "He . . . regained control and just about then the barrage ended."

As if the friendly artillery fire were not bad enough, German 88mm guns devastated the American armor. "[The 88's] power was awesome. A direct hit did not bounce off the sloping four-inch solid steel armor plate front of a Sherman tank; *it went clear through and out the back.* I saw smoking tanks ripped through from front to back by a single armor-piercing 88. Rarely did any of the crew survive, for along with the shell itself were the ricocheting chunks of metal it tore off, not to mention the inevitable concussion and internal bleeding. By nightfall, nine of our 17 tanks [were] demolished and the infantry . . . almost wiped out." Wilson only had six of his original forty men left. He was the only surviving officer in E Company.

CCA and a company from the 30th Division needed three more days to capture Tessy-sur-Vire. In the process, the 2nd Armored, the 30th Division, and soldiers from the 29th Division fought hard and prevented the two

German armored divisions from fighting their way west to rescue their re-treating comrades.[12]

The Germans west of St-Lô were in a trap and they were trying to fight their way out of it. American troops now controlled Coutances and nearly every other escape route along the southerly roads. July 29 was a clear, hot day, perfect hunting weather for American fighter-bombers. As the day un-folded, desperate groups of Germans clashed with American soldiers. The 2nd Armored Division's CCB was one of the main units responsible for seal-ing the Germans into a trap. On the afternoon of the twenty-ninth, Ameri-cans from A Company, 41st Armored Infantry Regiment, and C Company, 238th Engineer Combat Battalion, were manning outpost positions near Roncey, three miles southeast of Coutances. One of the engineers, Lieu-tenant Lawrence Cane, was sitting in a jeep observing. He spotted a mas-sive number of German vehicles on a parallel road, moving south. Sheltered by hedgerows that lined the road, Cane calmly drove his jeep south, shad-owing the enemy convoy. The Manhattan native knew an important target when he saw one. He was a veteran of the Abraham Lincoln Brigade, an American-dominated irregular unit that had seen extensive action against Franco's fascists in the Spanish Civil War. In fact, Cane had been the only veteran of the Lincoln Brigade to storm ashore on D-Day. Now he picked up his radio and told aerial observers, circling unseen somewhere up above, what he had just seen. At nearly the same time, the aerial observers spotted the convoy, too.

Within fifteen minutes, the fighters—the Germans called them *Jabos*, which meant hunter-bombers—descended on the German column, which stretched for three miles along the narrow road that led through Roncey. The enemy convoy was literally a fighter pilot's dream. Some five hundred vehi-cles were bottlenecked on the road. Squadron by squadron, the American fighters dived to the deck, dropped their bombs, and strafed the Germans, until their wing-mounted machine guns ran out of ammo.

In one of the P-47s Captain John Marshall, a squadron commander in the 404th Fighter Group, picked out a line of trucks, nosed his plane over, and dived to attack. His pilots followed him closely. Marshall could see their tracer rounds out of the corner of his eye. The captain squeezed off a four-second burst and saw his .50-caliber bullets hitting several vehicles. For months now, he had been wanting to shoot up a motorcycle. At this speed, so close to the ground, it was tough to pick out individual targets, but somehow he noticed a motorcycle buzzing past some trucks. "I had my motorcycle, but the S. of a B. pulled up alongside an ambulance before I could 'let go.'" Cap-tain Marshall grimaced, held his fire, but soon found a new target. "[I] . . . made up for it in tanks, trucks, anything you can name." His squadron ex-pended all of its ordnance and flew back to their base at Chippelle. "We've loaded as much lead into the invincible (hell) enemy's back as we have into his guts," he told his sister in a letter.

Some Germans fled their vehicles and took cover in ditches. Others tried to outrun the fighters or maneuver their machines into ditches or alongside hedgerows. A few enemy antiaircraft crews pointed their weapons skyward and shot at the hated *Jabos*. Lieutenant Quentin Aanenson and his wingman had strafed the convoy and climbed to 1,000 feet for the return trip home when "suddenly [my wingman] started into a shallow dive over a wooded area. I saw no tracers, but it was apparent he had been hit and was going in. I watched him frantically trying to disconnect everything and bail out—I was just a few feet away from him—but he was too low. He waved to me an instant before his plane crashed into the trees and exploded. Debris flew everywhere—I barely got through it. To this day I can still see the expression on his face as he looked directly at me before crashing. In that instant, he knew he was dead."

Most of the fighter pilots had little to fear from the Germans, though. The enemy soldiers were trapped, like animals being led to the slaughter. There was, for most of them, no place to hide. Private Anthony Blazus, a member of A Company, 41st Armored Infantry, saw the carnage firsthand. As the planes strafed, he was hugging the ground in a ditch by the side of the road. Hours earlier, Blazus had been captured by SS troops while he manned an outpost position south of Roncey. Not surprisingly, the Germans were now more concerned with survival than with guarding Private Blazus.

The Vestaburg, Pennsylvania, native watched as the Germans scurried everywhere. In the midst of the chaos, a German general was trying to direct traffic. Tanks, half-tracks, self-propelled guns, and trucks were all over the place. "[American] fighters . . . swooped low, bombed the self-propelled guns, and methodically blocked the road. Terrific blasts just ripped those big guns apart and tore bodies into a thousand pieces. The tanks on the flanks just took off across the fields. Merciless planes raced up and down the column, cannon blazing and bombs dropping, until the whole [area] was a red, blazing tangle of shattered bodies and wrecked vehicles."

The slaughter went on from 1510 to 2140, just before sunset—six hours of carnage and terror for the enemy. The American pilots were filled with excitement. They were like hunters who had finally cornered their quarry. "I have been to two church socials and a county fair," one of the fighter pilots gushed at debriefing, "but I never saw anything like this before." American tanks, artillery, and tank destroyers added to the enormous firepower. By nightfall, the better part of an enemy mechanized division had been destroyed and the road had been made impassable with smoking, burning junk. In all, the Americans destroyed fifty-six tanks, 204 vehicles (trucks, half-tracks, and the like), and eleven self-propelled guns. They damaged another fifty-six tanks and fifty-five vehicles and probably killed hundreds of enemy soldiers.

They also took the fight out of many others. When the shooting finally ended, Private Blazus stood up and got out of his ditch. "It looked as though everyone was dead or torn to pieces. But then about 80 Germans picked themselves up . . . and came over and asked me to take them prisoner. They'd had enough." Blazus, who had won a Distinguished Service Cross for his bravery six weeks before at Carentan, was happy to oblige them. He picked up a weapon and marched all eighty Germans south to the nearest American outpost.[13]

As darkness settled over Normandy on July 29, the 2nd Armored Division had set up a cordon of roadblocks along the likely German escape routes in the vicinity of Roncey. Various units from the 2nd Armored were deployed along a seven-mile expanse of road (D-38) from Notre Dame de Cenilly in the northeast to St-Denis-le-Gast to the south. Those Germans who were lucky enough to have survived the cauldron at Roncey were now caught between the rapidly moving VII Corps to their north and the 2nd Armored to their south. The only way for them to escape was to smash right through the 2nd Armored Division's roadblocks. Many of the Germans were experienced SS soldiers who were used to fighting out of encirclement from their days on the Eastern front. They were determined to escape south or die trying, and that determination made for violent face-to-face battles on the night of July 29–30. "It was like having a bag full of wildcats trapped and trying to prevent them from escaping from the bag," one American officer commented.

The 2nd Battalion, 41st Armored Infantry Regiment, and the 3rd Battalion, 67th Armored Regiment, were deployed at a crossroads and in fields north of St-Denis-le-Gast. The Americans were mostly hunkered down in their tanks and half-tracks, keeping watch but hoping for a quiet night. Shortly after midnight on July 30, in pitch-darkness, a mixed battalion of enemy infantry and armor from the 2nd SS Panzer Division clashed head-on with these two American units.

Private Lawrence "Chubby" Williams, a reconnaissance trooper in the 41st, was one of the first to hear them coming. Clutching his M-1 carbine, he crept up to a hedgerow and heard German voices on the road. He had four grenades. One by one, he tossed them over the hedgerow and onto the road. The exploding grenades tore the Germans apart, blowing some in half. With all of his grenades gone, Williams felt naked with only an M-1 carbine in his hands. He turned to a fellow soldier and tried to talk him out of his tommy gun. "He run and left me. He got up on a Sherman tank that was parked in the field. I could see his knees knocking. But he wouldn't let me have the Thompson."

Close by, Williams's commanding officer, Lieutenant Colonel Wilson Coleman, was dashing around the 2nd Battalion, 41st, positions, checking his outposts, trying to find out what was happening. Coleman peeked around a hedgerow and was rewarded with a clear view of a German tank that was leading a whole enemy column. The commanding officer grabbed a bazooka, found someone to load it for him, aimed it at the tank, and fired. The bazooka shell streaked through the night, scored a direct hit on the German tank, and set it afire. Coleman tossed the bazooka aside, found his jeep farther south on the road, and started to return to his headquarters. As he did so, the enemy column sprang to life with deadly fire. Some of it swept through Lieutenant Colonel Coleman and killed him on the spot.

The battle soon degenerated into dozens of small skirmishes, as the Germans fanned out in all directions in the fields that bordered the roads north of St-Denis-le-Gast. German vehicles kept rolling southwest along the road. Squads of enemy soldiers were steadily infiltrating the previously American-controlled fields. A steady cacophony of machine-gun, rifle, and tank fire echoed across the orchards and hedgerows.

Private Williams and another man were roaming around, looking for Germans. They heard guttural voices on the other side of a hedgerow and squatted down. Williams whipped out a Beretta pistol he had taken off an Italian soldier in Sicily. The foliage at the top of the hedgerow started moving. Williams pointed the Beretta at the foliage. When a German soldier's head popped through the foliage, Williams pointed the pistol against the underside of his jaw and fired. The enemy soldier pitched backward and fell dead. The rest of his squad, four men in all, surrendered to Williams and his buddy.

At another hedgerow, Staff Sergeant Joseph Barnes stood, like an assassin in the shadows, and cut the throats of three Germans as they attempted to run past him. Nearby, a private had his tommy gun shot out of his hands, became infuriated, and beat a German to death with his helmet.

To the west, Private Michael Gainey was manning a Browning .30-caliber machine gun at the edge of an access road. He and his assistant were in a perfect firing position, right on the flanks of the advancing German infantry. The two of them could see the silhouettes of the enemy soldiers as they skittered south, toward St-Denis-le-Gast. Gainey's machine-gun team opened fire at the silhouettes. Rows of enemy soldiers went down. The two Americans fired their Browning until they melted the barrel. A supply sergeant found them a water-cooled machine gun and they went back to work.

Their fire was so devastating that an SS sergeant assaulted their position by himself. He snuck up on Gainey and his assistant from behind and flung a potato masher grenade into their position just as someone spotted him and shot him. The ensuing explosion showered Gainey and the other man with shrapnel and blew them onto the road. Staff Sergeant Elza Tucker dragged Gainey and the other soldier to a medical half-track.

The German sergeant was lying in the field, badly wounded, screaming at the top of his lungs for help. Several minutes went by and still the screaming did not stop. Private Williams could hear it in his position and it was nearly driving him nuts. "SHUT UP, YOU SUNUVABITCH!" he yelled.

The screaming continued. Finally, Williams could stand it no more. He told the men around him to hold their fire. He was going to drag the wounded enemy sergeant to safety. Williams ventured out into the field and walked toward the SS sergeant. When he was within a few paces, the German rolled over, pointed a pistol at him, and squeezed off two shots that somehow missed. Williams was both terrified and infuriated. "Why, you sonofabitch!" He ran back to the American position, borrowed a BAR from someone, and emptied two full clips into the enemy noncom.

In the meantime, the battle was growing more hectic by the minute as the Germans pushed through the American positions. "All hell was breaking loose," Private Eugene "Breezy" Griffin recalled. He was holed up in a radio half-track somewhere along the road. "Artillery bursts were going off overhead, tracers of every size and color were lacing the sky, and our mortar half-track . . . burning, cast an eerie flickering light over the landscape punctured by explosions. Our own artillery was firing over our heads from some distance away, and the whining and screaming rounds were bursting on the ground or just above it, not too far in front of us. I knew our battalion headquarters was mostly surrounded by the enemy. They seemed to keep on coming and coming without end. We killed them by the scores and hundreds and still they came."

The Germans blasted the headquarters of 3rd Battalion, 67th Armor. One Panther tank maneuvered into a perfect firing position when it poked its gun barrel over a hedgerow and picked off vehicle after vehicle in an open field. The Americans fled as best they could. The Germans overran the headquarters and American outpost positions north of St-Denis-le-Gast and roared into the town itself. There they ran into the headquarters group from the 41st Armored Infantry. This was a unit made up mostly of specialists, staff officers, and support personnel, but they fought toe-to-toe with the Germans for much of the night, slowing their advance.

The same was true of A Company, 67th Armor, especially Sergeant Douglas Tanner, commander of an M-5 Stuart light tank. German soldiers were all over the town, running building to building, firing at the retreating Americans. Enemy tanks and self-propelled guns were on the D-38 road, rolling south through the town.

In the turret of his Stuart, Sergeant Tanner, a twenty-three-year-old Mississippian, ordered his driver, T/4 John Kapanowski, to maneuver their tank right into the middle of the road, between the advancing German armor and the retreating vehicles of A Company, 67th Armor. The leading enemy vehicle was an 88mm self-propelled gun. Tanner knew that the puny 37mm main gun on his Stuart was no match for the enemy gun, but he ordered his crew to open fire. They got off a shot or two before the enemy track returned fire. Two 88 shells tore through their Stuart and badly wounded Sergeant Tanner. "The tank was hit twice in succession and caught fire," T/4 Kapanowski later wrote.

Kapanowski and his assistant driver scrambled out of their hatches. The heat of the fire was getting intense, but they paused to drag Tanner away from the tank. "We got him out of the turret and laid him on the sidewalk, alongside the tank. He lived about a minute after we got him out, still cool and talking. Only two of us got out of that tank alive."

The actions of Tanner's crew allowed the bulk of A Company, plus other American vehicles and soldiers, to escape from St-Denis-le-Gast before it came under temporary German control. Tanner was posthumously awarded the Silver Star.

Another man who helped other Americans escape was Sergeant Howard Robinson, a half-track driver in B Company, 41st Armored Infantry. Robinson's half-track was somewhere along the southwestern edge of St-Denis-le-Gast. He parked the track in a wooded area and, along with five other men, radioed information about the fast-moving Germans to his regimental commander, Colonel Sidney Hinds. "We hid behind a hedgerow and watched them march through. What a sight! About five tanks and two half-tracks with at least 25 men walking behind each one. They all acted as if they were drunk, firing burp pistols and MG's and 88s at every step or turn of the wheel. They passed right through the town."

They and other Germans passed through St-Denis-le-Gast and kept moving. Some got away to the south, but others became disoriented and moved west, right into more 2nd Armored positions between Guehebert and Grimesnil. The French called this area La Lande des Morts (roughly translated as the Land of the Dead) because of a battle that had been fought there between the English and French in the Hundred Years' War. The fifteenth-century battlefield had been littered with the bodies of dead soldiers from both sides. Tonight this twentieth-century battle would only add to the area's troubled history as modern weapons created yet another killing ground on this Land of the Dead.

At 0100, a wandering column of Germans, estimated to number twenty-five hundred soldiers and at least ninety vehicles, ran right into the Americans at Grimesnil. There were American tanks and mechanized infantry here—F Company, 67th Armor, I Company, 41st Armored Infantry—along with engineers and headquarters vehicles.

Captain James McCartney, an officer whose combat service dated back to North Africa, was the commanding officer of F Company, 67th Armor. He and several other soldiers heard a clinking sound somewhere off in the darkness.

The sound was made by the banging of a steel chain on a German self-propelled gun. As the Americans peered intently down the road, a shell ripped into a jeep McCartney had parked by the side of the road earlier. Other enemy shells blew up American half-tracks that were parked along the road. McCartney scrambled into a ditch, watched the battle for a couple minutes, and then ran over to three Shermans that were deployed in a nearby field. Under his supervision, the Shermans slowly retreated while pouring harassing fire into the German convoy. At one point, McCartney was running through a hedgerow gap when he collided with another soldier. Both of them fell down. "Excuse me," Captain McCartney said. The other man did not respond. As they got up and brushed themselves off, McCartney saw that he was a German. They both took off in opposite directions.

The Germans overran McCartney's forward positions and kept moving west. As they did so, a platoon of engineers under the command of Lieutenant John Wong prepared to pour flanking fire into them from their rear. Wong loaded a clip of M-1 ammo with tracer rounds, slammed it into the chamber, and took aim. He could see a vehicle—camouflaged with shrubbery that gave it the appearance of a bush—moving up and down the road. "I quickly fired two clips of tracer into the 'bush' at point blank range." The rounds ricocheted off the armor of the camouflaged vehicle. "Tracers had hit the thick steel gun shield and were flying in all directions as if spewed from a Roman Candle." The rest of the platoon opened fire, stripping away the camouflage. "As the enemy's leading elements came into cannon range, we opened up. Then mortars and automatic weapons joined the battle. Shells crashed in on the unsuspecting Germans in an exploding hailstorm of steel. The firing was continuous and concentrated." Wong's platoon killed plenty of enemy soldiers but did not have sufficient weapons to deal with enemy armor. Instead, they hemmed the enemy in from behind. Most of the platoon gravitated away from the road as the German armor kept rolling west.

The battle climaxed when the Germans clashed with the main American defensive line near Grimesnil where there were tanks from B and E Companies of the 67th, plus half-tracks from various companies of the 41st, in addition to self-propelled artillery. The Germans tried a frontal attack against the American roadblocks. The whole scene was chaos—armored monsters shooting at one another from within 50 to 200 yards, machine-gun tracers streaking through the night, mortar shells exploding, rifles adding to the hellish noise.

The German armor kept getting closer and closer. They seemed on the verge of overrunning yet another American unit. In the midst of this teetering situation, Sergeant Hulon Whittington, a squad leader in I Company, 41st Armored Infantry, ran for the closest American tank. Whittington's platoon leader and platoon sergeant were both missing. He knew that he was, at least for the moment, the leader of his half-track platoon. Through the eerie half-light of the battle he could see the leading German vehicle crawling ever closer.

He climbed onto the turret of an E Company, 67th Armor, tank, commanded by Lieutenant Bill Dooley, and got the lieutenant's attention. Whittington suggested a perfect firing position, right behind a stone farmhouse, and pointed at the lead German vehicle (a 150mm Hummel self-propelled gun) as it approached them. Thanks to Whittington's help, Dooley's gunner put a 75mm round right into the Hummel. The self-propelled gun screeched to a halt, and that made it an even better target. Several other U.S. tanks shot at the Hummel, destroying it. This turned the Hummel into little more than a roadblock. Other German tanks and self-propelled guns tried to swing around the Hummel, but as they did so, American flanking fire devastated them.

When this happened, the enemy column was effectively trapped. Their only chance of survival tonight was to keep moving, shoot their way through stunned groups of Americans, and dodge their way around U.S. firepower. Now they were pinned down and that made them stationary targets for every weapon in the American ground arsenal. Tank fire, mortar fire, and especially artillery fire scythed through the enemy vehicles. "These concentrations, mixed with WP [White Phosphorous] mortar and reinforced by our tank and infantry fire, had a devastating effect on the enemy," Lieutenant Dooley wrote. "These fires were continued until dawn . . . on the enemy and almost annihilated him. Shortly after dawn, small enemy forces attempted to infiltrate into our position. Many of these were killed beneath and around our tanks."

Throughout the night, Sergeant Whittington fought like a man possessed. He led several infantry attacks on the enemy column, including at least one bayonet charge. When his platoon medic got hit, Whittington dragged him to safety and gave him first aid. Whittington earned the Medal of Honor for his actions that night.

The Americans lost fifty men killed and another sixty wounded in the nighttime battle, but the Germans suffered much more. When dawn finally came, the Americans at the Land of the Dead beheld a scene out of hell itself. Once again, as it had been 500 years earlier, the land was littered with the bodies of dead soldiers. The GIs found 600 dead Germans, including a general and three women in Wehrmacht uniform. They captured another 1,000 enemy and counted at least ninety wrecked vehicles. The carnage was ghastly, almost soul-searing. Major Jerome Smith of the 2nd Battalion, 67th Armor, described the aftermath of the battle as "the most godless sight I ever saw on any battlefield. A bloody mass of arms, legs, heads, and cremated corpses." Colonel Wheeler Merriam's 82nd Reconnaissance Battalion policed the area and captured several hundred prisoners. Death, misery, and destruction were everywhere. "There were sickening groans and feeble cries for 'wasser' from this horrible pile of burned and bloody flesh. The ditches on either side of the road were filled with dead and wounded German soldiers—some decapitated, others disemboweled. The air was filled with the sickening stench of death and cremation."

All along the expanse of roads where the battle had raged, the Americans picked through the detritus, looking for survivors, souvenirs, and intelligence. Captain Jack Hart, an operations officer in a 2nd Armored Division artillery unit, came upon a live German "virtually burned and blown to pieces. Somehow he pointed to my automatic and then to himself. He wanted me to kill him and put him out of his pain. To this day, I regret I did not. I didn't have the guts." Elsewhere Private Alvin Brooks walked among the remnants of the enemy attackers, and the sights appalled him. "So many Germans had been burned up in vehicles when artillery landed on them. You'd see half a man here, half a man there." Not far away, Private Owen Harrison, a member of Lieutenant Wong's engineer platoon, surveyed the carnage he and his comrades had inflicted on their enemies. "I saw Germans blown to bits all over the road, vehicles blown to smithereens—it was a terrible sight. Germans with brains blown out—no eyeballs in their head . . . limbs blown off— a leg lying here, an arm lying there."[14]

Cobra was over and with it the month of July. The Battle of Normandy had turned inexorably in favor of the Allies, but it was not over. The question now was whether or not the Allied armies could turn their success at Normandy into a war-winning defeat of the Germans. In planning Cobra, General Bradley had hoped for something more limited. He wanted to swing behind the German lines, all the way to Coutances, and trap the whole German Army in western Normandy. His commanders came close, but they did not quite do that. The Americans captured Coutances by July 28, Gavray by July 30, and Granville, on the coast, by July 31, but thousands of German soldiers escaped south. Still thousands more, at places like Roncey or St-Denis-le-Gast, did not escape. By any measure, General Bradley's Cobra plan had been a success. Finally, the Allies had achieved a breakthrough in Normandy. Now, at last, it was time to break out and end the fighting in Normandy for good.

PART III

AUGUST

CHAPTER TWELVE

BREAKOUT AND CHASE

The U.S. Army in World War II was designed to reflect, more than anything else, one dominant characteristic of American life—mobility. From the earliest days of the American nation, mobility had been a persistent theme—mobility by class (downward or upward), mobility by region, movement west to satisfy the dictates of social tensions, economics, or Manifest Destiny. Mobility—the freedom to go where you wanted, live where you wanted, be who you wanted to be—was at the core of American notions of individuality and freedom. There was a constant sense of movement in America, especially in the industrialized, automated age. By the beginning of the twentieth century, 193,000 miles of railroad track crisscrossed America. That was more than all of Europe combined. In the 1920s, Henry Ford made the automobile affordable for the average American. By the eve of World War II, the United States was among the most automated, mechanized nations in the world (although it would not have suitable roads for all those cars until after the passage of the Interstate Highway Act of 1957).

The Army reflected this automated society. In World War II, the U.S. Army was, by far, the most mechanized force in existence. A variety of vehicles served in every possible capacity, so that the Army could move and fight fast, so it could be mobile—from the Higgins boats that got soldiers ashore, to the DUKWs and deuce and a halves that moved supplies and soldiers, to the jeeps that served in every capacity, to the myriad combat vehicles such as tanks, tank destroyers, self-propelled guns, half-tracks, and mechanized antitank guns that were created for specific jobs on the battlefield. The preponderance of planes and ships that aided the armies only added to the transportation dominance of American arms by 1944. American soldiers were comfortable with vehicles—they knew how to tinker with them, nurture them, get the most out of them.

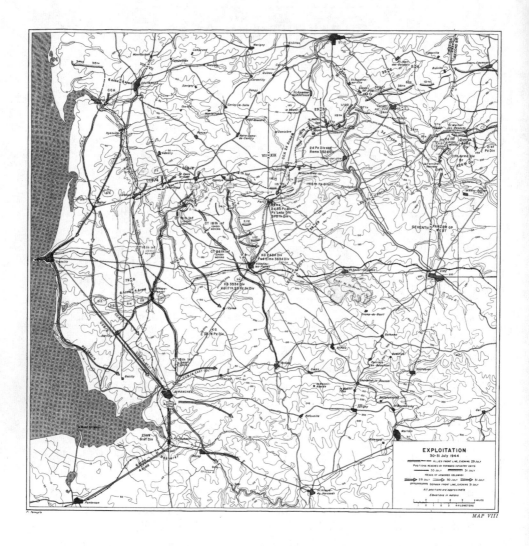

EXPLOITATION
30-31 July 1944

ALLIED FRONT LINE, EVENING 29 JULY
POSITIONS REACHED BY FORWARD INFANTRY UNITS:
30 JULY   31 JULY
HEADS OF ARMORED COLUMNS:
29 JULY   30 JULY   31 JULY
GERMAN FRONT LINE, EVENING 31 JULY

All positions are approximate

Elevations in meters

MAP VIII

Thus the United States in World War II combined its burgeoning technological prowess with its immense industrial capacity, along with the traditional American reverence for mobility, to create the fastest-moving, fastest-fighting, most overwhelming army on the planet. In Normandy, after Cobra, this mobile approach to warfare helped lead to one of the great victories in modern military history.

In the final hours of July, along a blacktopped road (D-9) that led south to a Norman town known as Villedieu-les-Poeles, American mobility was on full display. As late-afternoon shadows crept over the road, dozens of U.S. tanks, half-tracks, trucks, jeeps, and self-propelled guns of the 3rd Armored Division's Combat Command A sped south against no opposition. Near the head of the column, Lieutenant Colonel Leander Doan stood in the turret of his personal M-4 Sherman and scanned the road ahead. This operation could not be going any better. His orders were to proceed to a crossroads two kilometers west of Villedieu-les-Poeles and establish blocking positions. There were retreating Germans all over the area—some wanted to hold fast and fight; others wanted nothing more than to get away or surrender—and he hoped to bag any who were retreating southeast in the vicinity of Villedieu-les-Poeles.

The day was warm, the air was fresh, and the sun was still shining brightly. Finally, after all the weeks of rain and clouds, the weather was suitably summery. No more did he and his men breathe air heavy with the stench of hedgerows, mud, and dead cows. They were on the move, just as he and so many others had yearned to be for so many weeks now. Doan was a tall, loose-jointed Texan. He was also a fine commander. Two days before, at Gavray, he had left the safety of his tank and personally led a group of scared infantrymen across the Sienne River to capture a key objective for his 3rd Armored Division.

Now, on the evening of July 31, he was in command of Task Force X, one of three mobile strike forces that comprised CCA. More than anything, Doan had one word on his mind—*speed*. This task force and the others like it were designed to exploit the hard-won breakthrough the Americans had achieved a few days earlier. The goal now was to plunge deep into enemy territory, without regard to flanks, absorb counterattacks, destroy or capture as many enemy as possible, and unhinge the whole German position in Normandy.

Doan's vehicles zipped along at the unheard-of speed of twenty-five miles per hour. They encountered no opposition and made it to their objective by 1800. No sooner had they begun to settle in for the night than Doan's radio crackled to life with fresh orders: "Do not stop on initial objective. Proceed to the Sée River before halting for the night."

The Sée River was near Brécy, a town five miles to the south on a smaller road than the D-9. Doan was supposed to capture Brécy, cross the Sée River (immediately south of town), and set up blocking positions on a nearby hill mass known as Hill 242. Within a few minutes his task force was back on the move.

Once again, the engine noises of tanks, trucks, half-tracks, and other vehicles filled the air. Lieutenant Colonel Doan heard the smooth purring sound of another kind of engine overhead. He glanced up and took in the reassuring sight of several P-47s buzzing overhead. These fighter planes were his own private air force. As his column advanced south, deeper into what could be enemy territory, the planes covered them. The fighter pilots functioned as Doan's eyes and his mobile artillery.

Thanks to the tactical adjustments of General Pete Quesada, Lieutenant Colonel Doan could communicate directly with the fighter pilots on a VHF radio in his tank. Just ahead, there was a railroad crossing. Doan knew this was a likely ambush point for the Germans, so he asked the planes to check it out. Sure enough, the Germans were there. In twos and threes the planes strafed some Germans who were manning antitank guns behind the crossing. Each P-47 had eight .50-caliber guns mounted on its wings. A single .50-caliber round could blow a man's head off or tear out his chest cavity. The P-47s were shooting hundreds of these deadly rounds in a matter of only seconds. A few of the spent casings rained down on Doan and his men. Most clattered off the road. The staggering firepower of the planes drove the Germans away from their guns and their concealed positions. Doan's column rolled right through them, shot up the enemy guns, and kept moving.

They were about halfway to Brécy when the colonel noticed that the column was slowing down far too much for his tastes. Soon everyone ground to a halt. "What on earth is this all about?" Doan wondered. Doan radioed the lead half-tracks and found out that they were lost. He had no time for this. He told his driver to maneuver his tank to the head of the convoy and lead the way. The advance resumed.

When they were just outside of Brécy, the fighter pilots called and asked Doan, "Shall we bomb Brécy?" Doan's response was curt and to the point: "Yes." As the ground troops watched, the fighters unleashed their wrath on the little Norman town. The explosions of the 500-pound bombs were earsplitting. Stone buildings crumbled into rubble. Dust rose high in the air. Five separate flights of P-47 Thunderbolts pounded Brécy. After about fifteen minutes of this, Doan grabbed his binoculars and scanned Brécy, but he saw no evidence of the Germans, so he got on the radio and called off the air strike.

"Let's go," Doan ordered. The vehicles swept into action again. They were now only a short ride from the northern edges of Brécy. Within minutes, they were entering the town. Doan's tank was right behind the lead half-track as it turned and glided right down the main street of the town. Doan glanced to the right and saw something that could only be termed as surreal. There, strewn along the curbside of the road, were several German soldiers, lounging as if they had not a care in the world. "Didn't the air strike warn them of some sort of imminent danger?" Doan wondered. He supposed not.

The American tanks and half-tracks opened fire with machine guns. The bullets sparked off the concrete curbs and shattered shop windows. They also shattered German bodies. Doan's radioman was in his gunner's seat, so he could not immediately traverse his turret into a firing position. Frustrated, Doan whipped out his Colt .45 and blasted away at the scurrying enemy soldiers. The whole incident seemed like the product of a screenwriter's imagination, but it was all too real. Clearly, the Germans were shocked at the presence of U.S. tanks here in Brécy. Such was the pace of the U.S. advance.

When the Americans were satisfied that they had eliminated any vestiges of the enemy, they kept moving, all the way through the town. Immediately south of Brécy, they encountered another lazy group of Germans, sitting around in an orchard, swilling wine and eating "while their equipment was lying around unprepared for action," Doan said. Once again, the Americans cut the Germans up with well-aimed machine-gun fire. The fire killed many of the enemy soldiers and scattered the rest.

Shaking their heads at the foolish behavior of the enemy, the Yanks rumbled south to the northern bank of the Sée by 1930. All along, they had suspected that the bridges over the river were blown, and they were right. As an engineer platoon came up, Doan dismounted and prowled around the banks, looking for a good place to construct a ford.

The Germans were surprised by the presence of Doan's battle group but regrouped and soon created problems for the Americans. The advance of Task Force X had been so rapid that the unit was spread out all along the road, back in Brécy, and even on the northerly approaches to the town. In many cases, companies, or battalions, were out of touch with one another. While Doan's group, numbering about two hundred men, was building a ford—mainly with rocks scavenged from the area—other members of Task Force X were fighting in Brécy and its environs.

Throughout the night (once the American fighter planes were gone), confused battles raged as the Germans moved into Brécy and a patch of woods just northeast of town. At one point, the enemy infiltrated all the way to the center of Brécy, close to where Doan had shot at their lounging countrymen with his pistol only a few hours before. The Germans shot up several jeeps from the 3rd Battalion, 36th Armored Infantry, and drove several of the unit's soldiers into the surrounding buildings.

At nearly the same time, the battalion commander, Lieutenant Colonel

Carlton Russell, a thirty-four-year-old ROTC graduate of Mississippi State College, was wondering where in the world the bulk of his command was. He had made it to the Sée River with Doan and was helping to build the ford when he noticed that most of his vehicles were not with him. He and his driver, plus an artillery battery commander whose battery was missing, all hopped into a jeep and headed for Brécy. They drove for a mile, until they could see fires burning in the center of town. The driver slowed down and they studied the scene. "Looking down a long hill toward the center of the square, we could see vehicles on fire and of course shells exploding. We did not really know what to do or what was going on. We got out of the jeep and dodged our way down to the melee going on. There were several American jeeps on fire, particularly the camouflage nets that each one carried."

They saw a small group of men trying to extinguish the flames. In the flickering half-light they walked up to them. When they got to within spitting distance, Russell saw that one of the men was wearing a camouflage suit, more characteristic of German uniforms than American (among U.S. units in Normandy only the 2nd Armored Division's 41st Armored Infantry Regiment wore spotted camouflage uniforms).

For the life of him Lieutenant Colonel Russell could not figure out why one of his soldiers was wearing this camouflage outfit. "If you do not pull off that camouflage suit," he blurted, "someone is going to think that you are a German." With a startled look on his face, the man glanced at Russell. In that instant, it finally dawned on Russell that the man in the camouflage suit was indeed a German. "The enemy had taken over the center of town and they were wanting to save those vehicles for themselves."

The two adversaries were literally eyeball-to-eyeball. Lieutenant Colonel Russell was carrying a pistol, but before he could shoot, the German soldier knocked it from his hand. They grappled with each other against the burning jeep. The enemy soldier had a rifle slung over his shoulder, and Russell summoned all of his strength to grab it from him. "I proceeded to grab it from him, and being that close, I had to just knock him in the head with the rifle . . . [I] could not shoot him because we were so close."

The enemy soldier tumbled to the street, but his comrades were lying prone, taking shots at Russell. Somewhere in the colonel's peripheral vision he could see his driver and the captain blazing away with submachine guns. Russell ducked behind a jeep and opened fire with the German rifle. "While doing this, one of their shots hit and bursted the stock of the rifle." Clearly it was time to get out of there. The three Americans regrouped and ran back to where their jeep was parked. "The Captain had been hit right across the bridge of his nose with a bullet and he was bleeding like a stuck hog."

Near their jeep, they encountered some American gun crews from A Company, 703rd Tank Destroyer Battalion, and told them to open fire on the center of town. The crewmen expertly sited their three-inch guns on the center of Brécy and blasted away at the Germans until they melted away, back into the night. Lieutenant Colonel Russell got on his radio and told all of his company commanders about the situation in Brécy and to make it through the town as best they could. Then he returned to the Sée River, where Doan's ford had been completed. The leading elements of the task force made it to the northern edges of Hill 242 by morning. There were still plenty of Germans around the area, but they were confused and vulnerable. The enemy did not yet realize it, but the U.S. 1st Army had just put itself in a position to threaten the flank of the whole German Army in Normandy.[1]

Eight miles to the west, in the vicinity of Avranches, the Americans were not just threatening the German flanks; they were on the cusp of breaking out of Normandy altogether. For several days now General Troy Middleton's VIII Corps had been advancing along the west coast of the Cotentin against crumbling resistance. At times, stalwart German units had fought brief skirmishes, but mostly Middleton's columns, led by the 4th Armored Division, had encountered carnage or defeated enemy soldiers who wanted only to surrender. "Many cows were killed and bloated," Eugene Luciano, a platoon sergeant in A Company, 10th Armored Infantry Battalion, 4th Armored Division, later wrote. "Houses and buildings were demolished. There was mud all over and the stench of dead animals and decaying flesh, rain soaked clothes, and shoes was an appalling, stinking sight. High in a tree, stuck between the branches, was a cow. There were many crater holes . . . from bombing." Elsewhere in the 4th Armored Division, Private First Class Orville Watkins, a .50-caliber gunner on a half-track in the 53rd Armored Infantry Battalion, watched as scores of German troops, hands held high, approached his convoy on the roads leading south. "As we moved up, we passed dozens of Germans coming out with their hands up. We didn't have time to take prisoners [so] we just kept going." The presence of joyful French civilians only added to the carnival atmosphere for the rapidly advancing 4th Armored Division. "The people were coming out to greet us with flowers, wine and kisses," Sergeant Luciano remembered, "happily shouting, clapping, applauding and very jubilant after four years of German occupation."[2]

Middleton was doing a good job as commander of VIII Corps, but there was a new command presence driving VIII Corps men more than they had ever been driven before. Lieutenant General George Patton was back in the war. For nearly a year now Eisenhower had suspended Patton in a kind of probationary limbo, as a result of Patton's bad temper and his big mouth. The previous summer, in Sicily, while serving as commander of the 7th

Army, General Patton had slapped two soldiers who were suffering from combat fatigue. The general did not recognize the existence of such a thing, and when he encountered these men in field hospitals that, in his view, should only cater to men with legitimate physical wounds he blew up. Weeks later, Drew Pearson broke this story in his *New York Times* column, provoking a public clamor for relieving Patton of his command.

Eisenhower weathered this public relations nightmare and stuck by Patton, but only in lukewarm fashion. When Ike assumed command of Overlord, he brought Patton to England to serve as the crown jewel in the Fortitude decoy. Since the Germans expected the Allies to land at Calais and since they expected Patton to command the invasion forces, why not use their own preconceptions against them? Ike installed Patton as the commander of the 1st U.S. Army Group (FUSAG), the notional army that, even at the end of July, the Germans believed would assault Calais. In fact, FUSAG was merely a fantasy force—it had no combat units, no weapons, no nothing, just radio signals and fake vehicles to fool German reconnaissance planes.

Patton got into more trouble in England. This time, while making an innocuous speech to a British ladies' club in Knutsford, he made an impertinent remark about postwar Anglo-American supremacy. This was not—to borrow a modern term—politically correct, in light of the major Soviet contribution to the Allied war effort. In 1942 and 1943, in the North African and Sicily campaigns, Patton had emerged as the leading American tactical commander, only to see the slapping incidents put his career in jeopardy. Now, after Knutsford, he was in real peril of being sent home in disgrace. The idea of sitting out the rest of the war was repugnant to him, almost impossible to imagine. When it came to subordinates, Patton was an ass kicker, but when it came to superiors he was an ass kisser, and he used the latter quality to its fullest extent to save his career and his opportunity to command. He ingratiated himself with Ike and Bradley, the latter of whom had once served under him in the Mediterranean.

Once again, Ike rode out the public relations nightmare that his old friend Patton had stirred up. He did this because, all along, he envisioned a new mission for Patton. Back in the spring, Ike had tabbed the flamboyant general to command the 3rd Army, an armor-dominated force that would exploit any breakthrough in Normandy. All of this was predicated, of course, on good behavior from Patton. In pursuit of the greater good, Eisenhower decided to look the other way at the Knutsford incident.

By the end of July, the American troop presence was so massive in Normandy—Americans comprised nearly two-thirds of all Allied strength—that there were enough divisions to build two armies: the 1st and the 3rd. Lieutenant General Courtney Hodges, who had served as Bradley's deputy at 1st Army, would now assume command of that force. Patton would take the 3rd. Bradley would move up to command both of them under the imprimatur of the 12th Army Group. All of this became official on August 1.

However, Patton was in Normandy by early July, and by July 28 he was with Middleton's VIII Corps (soon to be part of his 3rd Army), acting in a close supervisory capacity. It is fair to say that George Patton had waited his whole life for this opportunity. The man lived for war. Patton believed he had lived many lives and had fought in many wars of bygone eras. He had fought with Hannibal and marched with Napoléon, to name but a couple of his supposed past-life exploits. In his heart, Patton felt he was destined for martial greatness, and he had the feeling that this greatness would begin in Normandy. Years earlier, he had traveled here with his wife and studied the roads and terrain. He spoke French fluently. He knew the land well. True, he was a prima donna of the first order, a coarse loudmouth, a glory hound, and an insufferable Anglophobe, but he was, for the Allies, the right commander at the right place at the right time.[3]

As American soldiers advanced to Avranches in late July, Patton made his presence known. There was a sort of ants-in-the-pants urgency to Patton. His command jeep could be seen buzzing alongside American columns. The general would lean forward and shout at his soldiers to keep moving—always keep moving. If he thought the advance was not proceeding swiftly enough, sometimes he would stop his jeep, find the nearest officer, and tear into him. This happened to Captain Arnold Brown, commander of G Company, 358th Infantry. As Brown's company trudged south, single-file, on each side of a blacktop road, they saw a jeep approaching from the rear. Brown's first sergeant glanced at the jeep: "Do you know who that is?"

"No," Captain Brown replied.

"That's General Patton."

Brown had never seen General Patton before. He watched, in detached curiosity as the general ordered his driver to stop alongside G Company. Patton dismounted from his jeep. "Who's the %$^^#& commanding officer of this &%^$#@ outfit?" he asked in his usual profane manner.

All heads turned in Captain Brown's direction. Brown felt a sickening ambivalence. On the one hand, he felt he was doing a good job leading his unit. On the other hand, with the terrible experiences he had had in combat (including a fruitless assault on Seves Island on July 23), he almost hoped Patton would blow up and relieve him of command. Another part of him wanted the Germans to start lobbing artillery shells onto the road so that he could jump into the hole and avoid talking to Patton. But he had no such "luck." He stepped forward, saluted, and said, "I am, sir."

The general glowered at him for a moment but said little. "He looked me over a little bit and made a few comments. Then he got back in his jeep and drove on. It was just his way of letting everybody know that he's in charge of things and he's up there. So I'm one of those who could brag about being chewed out by General Patton."

Most of the time, during his travels, Patton sought to bolster morale or motivate the soldiers to keep going as fast as they could. Not far away from where Captain Brown encountered the general, another company commander, Captain James Strickland, H Company, 13th Infantry, 8th Division, heard a commotion as he and his men were marching south. "I turned around to see what the trouble was. It was General Patton striding in the middle of the road."

The general walked right over to Captain Strickland. "When did your men have a hot meal last?" he asked.

"This morning at breakfast, sir," Strickland replied.

"When did they have dry socks?"

"With their breakfast, sir."

"What's your mission?" Patton wondered.

The captain opened up his map case and showed General Patton. "My last orders were that we were going to move into reserve on this—"

"Reserve, hell! There is no such thing in my army. You will be on trucks and will move south." With that, Patton clambered into his jeep, reached over, tooted the horn, and drove away.

Farther along the column, Patton's driver slowed his jeep so the general could speak to some of Strickland's men. Private Gus Nicholas heard him "congratulating the men on what a fine job we were doing." An instant later, some stubborn Germans decided to resist the advance. They opened fire from somewhere on the flanks. "We all ducked into ditches on the side of the road. Patton just stood upright in his jeep, patted the driver on the shoulder to move along as if nothing were happening." In an instant he was gone.[4]

The 4th Armored Division's spearheads made it to Avranches with lightning quickness, by the declining hours of July 30. They spent the next day fighting in and around the town against scattered German counterattacks, but the enemy was more interested in escaping to the southeast than in recapturing Avranches. The town was damaged, but it still held much of its beauty. Avranches was sandwiched between two rivers, the Sée in the north and the Selune four miles to the south. The city was situated on a bluff 200 feet high, overlooking the bay of Mont-St-Michel. A person standing along the bluff could see the famous tourist attraction Mont-St-Michel, beautiful and stately, eight miles in the distance. Truly this was the gateway to the rest of France. If the Americans could get across the Selune River bridge at Pontaubalt, just south of Avranches, they could advance in whatever direction they pleased—west, past Mont-St-Michel and into Brittany, or east into the interior of France. Late in the day on July 31, Combat Command A of the 4th Armored Division crossed the Selune with shocking ease. Tanks, half-tracks, jeeps, and other vehicles under the CCA commander Colonel Bruce Clarke (who would one day become a general) crossed the bridge at Pontaubault, captured two dams, and seized a secondary bridge over the Selune.

Troops from the 6th Armored Division and the 8th Infantry Division poured over the bridges and sped west. In no time, they approached Pontorson, a town lying two miles south of Mont-St-Michel. In the back of a half-track belonging to B Company, 9th Armored Infantry Battalion, 6th Armored Division, Private Milton Moncrief and his buddies could sense that the Germans were in no shape to oppose this advance on Pontorson. In the front of the half-track, their .50-caliber gunner opened up at unseen targets, so Moncrief and the others raised their weapons and started blasting away, too. "We surprised the Germans as they were not set up to face a new force, being fully occupied fighting off troops of the 4th Armd Div. [south of Avranches]. It was like a wild west show. A P-47 flew over and straffed [*sic*] ahead of our column. All of our halftracks were firing to both sides of the road keeping the Germans pinned down. I had a close up view of an '88,' as our small arms fire kept the Germans off the gun. We advanced to a hill and took up a defensive position." As they did so, another company from their battalion took Pontorson.[5]

By August 1, Middleton's VIII Corps had captured over 8,500 enemy POWs and had gained more than fifty miles. The entire western flank of the German defensive position in Normandy had disintegrated. Once the Americans made it through Avranches and Pontabault and to Mont-St-Michel, they were, in football terms, in the open field. They could carry the ball in whichever direction they chose. The overarching question now was this: which way was the goal line, to the west in Brittany or to the east in the interior of France?

The capture of several Brittany ports had loomed large in pre-invasion planning. Allied planners earmarked the ports of St-Malo, Lorient, and Brest for capture following a breakout from Normandy. In addition, they conceived Plan Chastity, which called for the building of an improvised port at Quiberon Bay on Brittany's south coast near Lorient.

Each Allied division in combat needed 840 tons of supplies per day. Back in the spring, in England, the logisticians had calculated that, by D+90 the Allied armies would need roughly forty-five thousand tons of supplies each day. They hoped that Cherbourg, combined with small ports like Arromanches on the Calvados coast and the mulberries, would handle much of that tonnage. However, by August 1 Cherbourg was still not in full operation and one of the mulberries had been destroyed. As a result, the landing beaches themselves had been turned into impromptu unloading facilities (as related in a previous chapter). Even so, the combined facilities of Normandy were only handling 28,150 tons each day. Obviously, the math did not add up. The armies needed 45,000 tons each day (and they were only going to get bigger, thus necessitating more supplies), but they were only getting 28,000 tons. Brest, St-Malo, and Lorient could add 17,550 more tons per day. Quiberon Bay, at full capacity, could contribute 10,000 additional tons. Strictly from a logistician's point of view, the only sensible course of action for Patton's 3rd Army was to turn west, capture the Brittany ports, get resupplied, and then turn east to finish off the German Army.

The situation was not that cut-and-dried, though. For one thing, there were 50,000 German soldiers defending the Brittany ports. They could be expected to put up a serious fight, especially since Hitler had ordered them to fight to the death. Moreover, they would almost certainly destroy the port facilities, just as their comrades had done in late June at Cherbourg. Even if the Allies could seize the ports and get them in operation within a couple weeks, there was still the problem of moving supplies (especially fuel) over severely damaged French roads and railroads hundreds of miles from Brittany to advancing armies. More than any of that, though, there was the tactical situation. The Allies had just broken clear of Normandy. They were in a position to whip around the remnants of the western flank of the Germans and dash east, for Paris and the German border. In the process, they could envelop and annihilate a serious chunk of the German Army in France while seizing other ports in the east, at Calais. In fact, the situation was so favorable right now that there was a chance that the Allies could administer a war-winning knockout blow to the enemy. Did it really make sense to advance west (in the wrong direction, after all) for a few supply ports that might take many weeks to capture, repair, and put into operation? General Montgomery certainly did not think so. "The main business lies to the east," he wrote in early August.

General Bradley was slower to realize this. At first, when Middleton's VIII Corps broke through Avranches and the rest of Patton's 3rd Army followed (four divisions in seventy-two hours), Bradley stuck with the original Overlord plan that called for Patton to send his whole army into Brittany. By the time Bradley changed his mind, on the evening of August 2, some valuable time had been lost. The 4th and 6th Armored Divisions could have been slashing east, setting a trap for the Germans. Instead they were rolling into Brittany, advancing in the opposite direction of Germany. Patton's army consisted of three corps—Middleton's VIII, General Wade Haislip's XV, and General Walton Walker's XX. When Bradley ordered Patton to make his main push east, Patton decided to leave behind the VIII Corps to clear out Brittany while his other two corps headed east.

This meant that Patton's two most formidable mobile formations, the 4th and 6th Armored Divisions, were now devoted to a mission similar to what Cherbourg had been for Collins and his VII Corps in late June. Armored forces were ill suited to take heavily fortified port cities. They could only be taken by a planned, set-piece attack that coordinated artillery, air, engineers, and infantry. Tanks could provide fire support for advancing infantry in urban areas, but the more constricted the surroundings, the less armor could exploit its primary purpose—mobility.

Major General John Wood, commander of the 4th Armored, chafed at his unit's Brittany mission. To him, it made no sense to advance west when the war could only be won in the east. His unit had performed superbly to this point; he wanted his tanks to ramble through the open country that beckoned in eastern Normandy, Orleans, the Seine, Paris, and beyond. "I could have been there . . . in the enemy vitals, in two days," he later claimed, "I protested long, loud and violently, but no! We were forced to adhere to the original plan—with the only armor available, and ready to cut the enemy to pieces. It was one of the colossally stupid decisions of the war."

With the possible exception of Huebner, Ridgway, or Gavin, John Wood was the best division-level American commander in the European theater. One historian called Wood "the American Rommel." Wood was an athletic and fun-loving son of an Arkansas judge. As a young man he had attended the University of Arkansas on a football scholarship. At Arkansas he spent as much time playing pranks as football. But he was also a fine student who was planning to embark upon a career as a chemist. That changed when he found out he could attend West Point and play a couple more years of college football. At the Point, he developed a reputation as a sound leader who cared deeply for subordinates. He disdained the hazing that went on and did whatever he could to help plebes with academic problems (earning for himself the lifelong nickname Professor, or just P). He saw action at Château-Thierry in World War I and, like many other successful American generals of World War II, stayed in the Army during the rough interwar years.

Wood was the type of person who would speak his mind, regardless of the situation. He was confident, energetic, and a fine leader of troops. His men called him Tiger Jack. In early August, he could not understand why his superiors were not ordering him to advance east and he complained loudly to anyone who would listen. "They [Bradley and Patton] are winning this war the wrong way!" he sputtered at Middleton one day.

Privately, Patton agreed with him. He, too, thought Bradley's staunch adherence, for forty-eight crucial hours, to the original Overlord plan was foolish, but he was in no position to speak up. He had just emerged from a long probationary period. His impertinence and his big mouth had nearly torpedoed his lifelong dream of becoming a military legend. There was no way he was going to risk antagonizing Bradley at this crucial moment in his career. At times officers have to enforce plans or orders with which they do not agree, and Patton was in that position in Brittany. This was understandable. Patton did err, though, in assigning his two best armored divisions to port-clearing duty in Brittany. They would have been much better employed elsewhere, and that, more than anything, was what upset General Wood so deeply. The two men had enormous liking and respect for each other (partially because they were so alike), but now there was plenty of tension between them. In early August, Patton endured the complaints of his prickly subordinate, but he later mentioned to Wood that "you almost got tried" for insubordination for his diatribes and behavior in Brittany. Wood did not back down one bit: "Someone should have been tried, but it certainly was not I."

As Wood had predicted, Brittany turned into a dead end. Infantry units like the 8th, 83rd, and 29th Divisions fought bitter battles at such places as St-Malo and Brest. The two armored divisions sealed off the peninsula and gained plenty of ground, but only the infantry could take the ports. St-Malo did not fall until August 17. Brest held out until September 19. The enemy garrison at Lorient hung on until the end of the war. Plan Chastity never happened. The Brittany ports did not impact the Allied supply situation in any significant way. In short, the diversion of forces to Brittany was a waste of resources that impeded Allied total victory in the west in 1944, and most historians view it as such.

So who was to blame? Eisenhower should certainly have made it clear to his commanders that the breakout made the Overlord plan obsolete. Indeed, by August 2 he thought a major thrust into Brittany was useless. "I would consider it unnecessary to detach any large forces for the conquest of Brittany," he wrote General Marshall, "and would devote the great bulk of forces for the conquest of Brittany to the task of completing the destruction of the German Army, at least that portion west of the Orne, and exploiting beyond that as far as we possibly could." If he felt that way, he should have made sure his commanders carried out his vision. But Eisenhower tended to be hands-off when it came to tactical matters. At this point, he was a remote figure, back in England, detached from the fighting—a strategic commander making grand strategy decisions, not a tactical commander making battlefield decisions.

In the end, though, most of the blame should go to Bradley. He was a competent commander but mediocre in most respects. One of his greatest weaknesses was a lack of imagination. During the invasion planning he had failed to tap into the amphibious experience of Pacific vets like Corlett and Collins. In the hedgerows, Bradley had fought (for reasons not entirely his fault) a straight-ahead slugging battle reminiscent of the World War I trenches. Cobra was his most visionary moment in Normandy, and even it was marred by Bradley's lack of appreciation for the dangers of close air support. Now, after the breakout, his first inclination was to stick with an outdated plan that called for a major effort in Brittany. In culinary terms, he became fixated on a basket of bread on his table while a kitchen full of gourmet food awaited him. To be fair, Bradley did eventually junk the plan and adapt to the situation, but he wasted forty-eight crucial hours before doing so. By that time, Patton's best armored formations were already enmeshed in Brittany and valuable time had been lost.

After the war, Bradley was cognizant of the criticism of his Brittany decision, particularly the siege of Brest, and he sought to defend himself. In his first memoir, *A Soldier's Story*, published in 1951 when Bradley was serving as the first chairman of the Joint Chiefs of Staff, he addressed the issue: "Why . . . did we spend three divisions on Brest at a cost of almost 10,000 American dead and wounded?" Bradley's answer amounted to this: the enemy's crack 2nd Parachute Division, under the command of Major General Hermann Ramcke, one of Hitler's most dynamic commanders, was the real target. "The decision . . . was not dictated by any outdated OVERLORD plan of maneuver." Instead, Bradley claimed that Ramcke's division had to be cornered and eliminated; otherwise it would cause innumerable difficulties to his flanks and supply lines.

This contention, if sincere, is laughable and, if true, makes Bradley's move into Brittany even more flawed. He was claiming that he diverted substantial resources and tapered the momentum of a potential war-winning advance to deal with one isolated, albeit formidable, enemy division. The 2nd Parachute Division was comprised of good soldiers, but like most German troops, they were more dangerous on defense than offense. By August 1944, they were penned into Brest, cut off from their supply line to Germany, bereft of any hope of escape. Their only remaining option was to fight hard and kill off as many Americans as they could. By assaulting Brest, along with the rest of Brittany, Bradley played right into their hands. If, however, he had ignored Ramcke and continued his eastern advance, the German general could certainly have attempted to harass Bradley's flank along the eastern approaches to Brittany. Very simply, they would have been annihilated. Their journey across Brittany would have brought them into conflict with U.S. armored formations, French resistance fighters, and, most deadly of all, Allied fighter-bombers. Basically, by moving in the open they would have absorbed the full brunt of Allied firepower. Thus Bradley's 1951 explanation cannot be taken seriously.

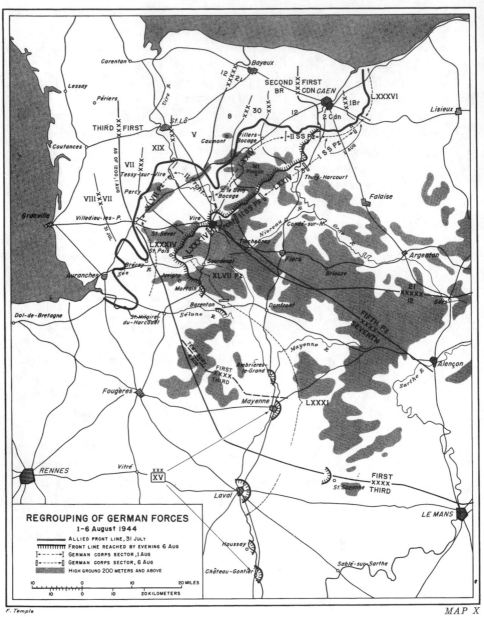

REGROUPING OF GERMAN FORCES
1–6 August 1944

▬▬▬▬ ALLIED FRONT LINE, 31 JULY
▭▭▭▭ FRONT LINE REACHED BY EVENING 6 AUG
⊢------⊣ GERMAN CORPS SECTOR, 1 AUG
⊟------⊟ GERMAN CORPS SECTOR, 6 AUG
▓▓▓▓ HIGH GROUND 200 METERS AND ABOVE

10   0   10   20 MILES
10   0   10   20 KILOMETERS

F. Temple

MAP X

GERMAN ORDER OF BATTLE ON NORMANDY FRONT
1 and 6 August 1944

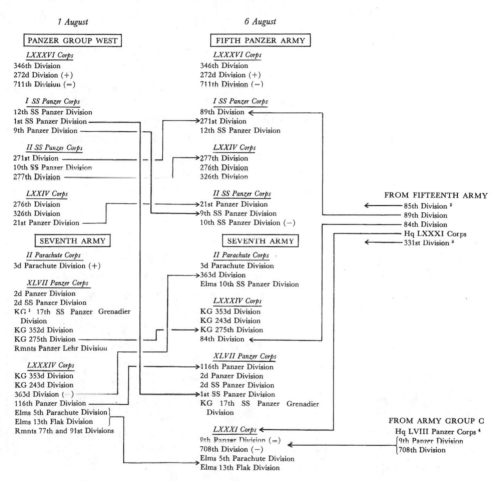

1 August

PANZER GROUP WEST

LXXXVI Corps
346th Division
272d Division (+)
711th Division (−)

I SS Panzer Corps
12th SS Panzer Division
1st SS Panzer Division
9th Panzer Division

II SS Panzer Corps
271st Division
10th SS Panzer Division
277th Division

LXXIV Corps
276th Division
326th Division
21st Panzer Division

SEVENTH ARMY

II Parachute Corps
3d Parachute Division (+)

XLVII Panzer Corps
2d Panzer Division
2d SS Panzer Division
KG[1] 17th SS Panzer Grenadier
   Division
KG 352d Division
KG 275th Division
Rmnts Panzer Lehr Division

LXXXIV Corps
KG 353d Division
KG 243d Division
363d Division (−)
116th Panzer Division
Elms 5th Parachute Division
Elms 13th Flak Division
Rmnts 77th and 91st Divisions

6 August

FIFTH PANZER ARMY

LXXXVI Corps
346th Division
272d Division (+)
711th Division (−)

I SS Panzer Corps
89th Division
271st Division
12th SS Panzer Division

LXXIV Corps
277th Division
276th Division
326th Division

II SS Panzer Corps
21st Panzer Division
9th SS Panzer Division
10th SS Panzer Division (−)

SEVENTH ARMY

II Parachute Corps
3d Parachute Division
363d Division
Elms 10th SS Panzer Division

LXXXIV Corps
KG 353d Division
KG 243d Division
KG 275th Division
84th Division

XLVII Panzer Corps
116th Panzer Division
2d Panzer Division
2d SS Panzer Division
1st SS Panzer Division
KG 17th SS Panzer Grenadier
   Division

LXXXI Corps
9th Panzer Division (−)
708th Division (−)
Elms 5th Parachute Division
Elms 13th Flak Division

FROM FIFTEENTH ARMY
85th Division [2]
89th Division
84th Division
Hq LXXXI Corps
331st Division [3]

FROM ARMY GROUP G
Hq LVIII Panzer Corps [4]
9th Panzer Division
708th Division

Note:
[1] Kampfgruppe
[2] En route to Fifth Panzer Army. Leading elements south of Rouen, 6 August.
[3] En route to Seventh Army. Leading elements near Briouze, 6 August.
[4] Hq LVIII Panzer Corps assumed command of 271st and 277th Divisions on Panzer Group West front, 2 August. It was reassigned to Seventh Army, 6 August.

Thirty years later, in his second memoir, *A General's Life*, he changed his story (perhaps realizing how fatuous his 2nd Parachute Division argument really was): "There was one overriding reason why I sent Patton and Middleton to Brittany: logistics. This is the dullest subject in the world, and no writer has ever succeeded in glamorizing it. The result is that logistics are usually downplayed or ignored altogether." In this version of his explanation, he emphasized the Allied supply difficulties and claimed that he thought Brittany would help alleviate them. He did mention Ramcke again, but only as an afterthought—logistics, Bradley wrote, were the main reason he sent Patton into Brittany. More than anything, the aging Bradley was challenging the idea that he had "inflexibly and stubbornly clung to the original Overlord plan merely because it was there." Maybe he had, maybe he had not, but it made no difference once he became fixated on Brittany. When he did so, he was relying on an outdated plan, whether because of inflexibility, stubbornness, or anything else. The damage was done and Bradley had made a bad mistake. That mistake stemmed from a lack of vision—an inability to analyze a rapidly changing situation and visualize the quickest, most effective way to total victory. That inability was the result of a mediocre mind ill suited to high command.[6]

Even as Middleton's VIII Corps fought and bled in a futile campaign in Brittany, the rest of the 3rd Army wheeled east throughout the early days of August. They were heading for a sixty-mile stretch of territory along the Mayenne River, which flowed from north to south. The primary objectives were the towns of Mayenne to the north and Laval, about ten miles to the south. General Haislip's XV Corps, screened by XX Corps' 5th Armored Division to the south, carried out the main advance on these two strategically located towns. The situation was so fluid, and so confused, that no one had any real idea what kind of resistance to expect. "Nobody knows anything about the enemy," one intelligence officer said, "because nothing can be found out about them." They were hard to find because, increasingly, they were melting away. Very few German soldiers stood between the 3rd Army and the Mayenne River. Haislip dispatched the 79th Division to Leval and the 90th Division to Mayenne.

Led by the 313th Infantry Regiment, the 79th Division on August 5 clambered aboard trucks and rolled east against little resistance. Still, there was some danger as the Americans approached small towns along the way. "The Frenchmen were so joyous to hear and see us coming," Private First Class Roger Campbell, a reconnaissance trooper, wrote, "someone would go to the church in town and ring the bell(s). This told the Germans how close we were to them. Then their artillery would target our positions and fire away. Getting rid of the church steeples in the small towns also eliminated an observation point for the enemy."

Campbell was a nineteen-year-old native of Louisville, Kentucky. He had been in the Army for less than a year, but he already had several weeks of combat experience. Like any good reconnaissance trooper, he could sense the presence of the enemy. During the advance, Campbell's unit got orders to search a wheat field that had just been harvested. The wheat was stacked in neat piles all over the field. As Campbell approached the field, he had the feeling that the enemy was close. "We started getting some small arms fire from the . . . stacks. We loaded our weapons with tracer bullets and proceeded to set each . . . stack on fire. When we started advancing, one of the . . . stacks wasn't burning. We started to give it another burst of fire when three Germans came [out] with their hands clasped over their [bare] heads."

Campbell's sergeant ordered him to march the prisoners back to a POW compound. When they were alone, the three Germans, still with their hands over their heads, knelt down, tried to kiss his boots, and begged, "No kaput! No kaput!" Private First Class Campbell did not know what they were talking about. He told them to get up and get moving. "*Macht schnell gehense!*" This happened three times before Campbell turned them over to the military police. When Campbell told the MPs what had happened, they explained why the Germans behaved the way they did: "They thought you were going to kill them [as] soon as you were out of sight of the rest of the men." The young soldier nodded his understanding. He knew there was no way he could ever do something like that. "I would never be able to look at myself in the mirror again."

The 79th made it to Laval by the evening of August 5. They found almost no Germans, but the enemy had blown the bridges over the Mayenne River. Luckily, they left the town's dam intact. French police opened up the sluice gates, and the Americans used the dam as an impromptu bridge. Later, on August 6, 79th Division engineers built several bridges. The Americans were across the Mayenne.[7]

The 90th Division's advance to the river, and the town of the same name, was similarly smooth. General McLain sent a fast-moving mechanized force under the command of his assistant division commander, Brigadier General William Weaver, to accomplish this mission. This Task Force Weaver was composed of armor from the 712th Tank Battalion and the better part of the 357th Infantry Regiment (on trucks), along with engineers, tank destroyers, self-propelled artillery, and medics.

Task Force Weaver had orders to move out at 0630 on the morning of August 5, but they experienced a three-hour delay while staff officers scrounged for a suitable number of trucks. Meanwhile, the soldiers lounged around and enjoyed the respite. "We sat around resting, napping and discussing past experiences, the war situation, and as usual ... women," one soldier recalled. Finally, at 0930, the trucks materialized and the column got going. They drove unopposed for more than two hours.

Colonel George Barth, the superb commander of the 357th, was riding in a jeep somewhere in the middle of the column. He could hardly believe the lack of opposition. "It seemed very strange to be rolling down the road at 20 miles an hour into enemy territory where before we marched and fought for every gain." It dawned on Barth that this mission was only one part of a bold American thrust that, if successful, could unhinge the whole German position in France. He sensed victory and detected that many of his soldiers had a similar mind-set. "[They] seemed to sense the fact that something big was in the wind—an undercurrent of excitement seemed to go down the column and you could almost see the men's spirits rise—morale was on the way up."

Morale got even better when French civilians clustered along the road and welcomed the Americans. "After they recovered from their astonishment at seeing Americans far behind what had been the German position, the people lined the streets of the little towns through which we passed. They pelted us with flowers and passed out wine to the men whenever we stopped. I tried to stop the latter practice but finally gave it up as a bad job."

On and on they rolled. The day was sunny, almost idyllic. By noon, they were on the outskirts of Mayenne. Here they halted while Weaver organized an assault on the town. The key objective was a bridge over the Mayenne River, right in the center of town. Weaver knew that the river bisected the town, so he decided to envelop Mayenne. He ordered the 3rd Battalion to attack north, cross the river, and cut the easterly roads that led out of town. The 2nd Battalion would do the same thing, but in the south. When this was accomplished, the 1st Battalion, under Major Edward Hamilton, would make the main assault on the bridge. All three prongs would have plenty of armored support and air cover. The attack began late in the afternoon.

Colonel Barth supervised the 3rd Battalion's assault. Moving from cover to cover, they worked their way down to the river. "Only sporadic fire came from the other side. As we watched the opposite hills, we saw three trucks of Germans who had probably spotted us and were pulling out. There didn't seem to be any more, so I ordered an immediate crossing using anything we could lay our hands on. We found a skiff and a larger, old boat—very leaky." As machine gunners covered them, they tore down a fence to make oars. "The men looked a little dubious, so I went over with them in the first boat." They made it safely to the eastern bank of the river. Colonel Barth turned around and came back for another load. Soon someone brought up rubber boats. Load by load, hundreds of Americans crossed the Mayenne River.

To the south, the 2nd Battalion also found some rubber boats and began rowing across the water. Resistance there was also sporadic and ineffective.

The whole thing was "a rather new experience for us," one G Company soldier wrote. "This was actually the first river we had ever crossed."

Not far away from where G Company was crossing, Lieutenant Max Kocour, who had started the Normandy campaign as a mortar forward observer, was now serving as the 2nd Battalion's operations officer. He believed that the most important aspect of his job was to know where the battalion's units were at all times. As a platoon of tanks backed him up, Kocour and two other soldiers hopped into a little wooden boat and rowed across the river about a mile south of the bridge. "The GI's stayed with the boat and I went up [a] wooded hillside. There was no sign of any activity." Kocour searched a farm and noticed a French farmer looking at him, with "his fingers to his lips in a sssh sign." The farmer pointed to the door of his house. "I cocked my grease gun and 45, and moved along the wall to the door." Kocour opened the door and saw three German soldiers, rifles stacked, sitting at a table eating dinner. "I stepped inside, between them and their guns, and said 'hand hock' . . . and they did it halfway." To remove any reluctance to surrender, Kocour told them in pidgin German that Patton's tanks were on the way. They stood up, hands held high. Kocour, the farmer, and several other Frenchmen marched the captive Germans down to the river. The whole way they sang "The Star Spangled Banner." At the river they met up with American soldiers who had just come across in rubber boats.

West of Mayenne, General Weaver knew that some of his men had crossed the river, but he was becoming impatient. The more time that passed, the better chance that the Germans would blow the bridge (they had wired it with eight 500-pound aerial bombs). His infantry could cross the river on boats but not his vehicles, and his vehicles were the key to any American lodgment east of the Mayenne River. The bottom line was this: no bridge, no vehicles. At last, Weaver could stand it no longer. He ordered Major Hamilton to commence with his assault.

Hamilton's people had been working their way through buildings on the western side of Mayenne. In the process, they had dealt with random Germans who seemed unaware of the presence of Americans in this area. "At various intervals, lone German vehicles continued to enter the western section of the city with the apparent intention of crossing the bridge, not knowing that we had occupied this part of the city," Major Hamilton later wrote. "These vehicles were taken under fire at point blank range by the battalion AT [antitank] guns, and the result was carnage."

Hamilton, by all accounts, was a brilliant commander—steady, tough, fair, and brave. In carrying out the bridge assault he had two worries. First, there was the possibility that the Germans could blow the bridge from under the feet of his men. Second, there were two 88mm guns, one 20mm, and a tank covering the bridge from the eastern section of Mayenne. Hamilton's mortar and artillery observers found a good vantage point on the roof of a house overlooking the western side of the river. From this OP they called down a ten-minute preparation of fire on the German guns while Hamilton's assault element, B Company, some engineers, plus a platoon of Shermans from the 712th Tank Battalion, huddled under cover. Hamilton ordered B Company's commander, First Lieutenant Burroughs Stevens, to attack when the barrage lifted at 1800.

Stevens planned to have his 2nd Platoon advance behind a tank and onto the bridge. As the barrage petered out, the tank rolled forward, but the lead squad of the 2nd Platoon froze in the face of enemy machine-gun and small-arms fire. Bullets ricocheted here and there off the concrete. The tank, under the command of Lieutenant Charley Lombardi, was all alone, vulnerable to *Panzerfaust* or 88 fire. Lieutenant Stevens, from the vantage point of a building near the bridge, watched this scene unfold for a few awful seconds. The soldiers of the lead squad were crouched in doorways. Their eyes were wide, their faces frozen with terror.

Stevens knew he had to do something. He did not feel fear, only urgency. Hamilton had told him to take this bridge, and he meant to do it. Lombardi and his crew were even now risking their lives to do so. Stevens could not idly sit by while his company failed to carry out its mission. Stevens sprang from the building and ran across the street and toward the bridge, urging his soldiers to follow him. "I realized no words could make them go, so I ran out behind the tank and the 1st squad (bless them) followed me." Two combat engineers also joined Stevens.

Major Hamilton was back in the street, trying to get the rest of the platoon moving. He hollered at them to fire their weapons. Close by a sergeant was also trying to rally the soldiers. "A bullet bounced off his helmet and a rifleman beside him . . . was killed." Hamilton and several other officers ran around organizing reinforcements and supporting fire for Stevens and his little group on the bridge.

At the bridge, Stevens's group was under intense fire. They took cover behind the tank and tried to trot forward as fast as they could. The enemy 20mm, in particular, was pouring devastating firepower onto the small expanse of the bridge. All at once, 20mm shells slammed into Private James McCracken, one of the engineers. McCracken "momentarily seemed to disappear," Major Hamilton remembered. The young engineer disintegrated in a shower of blood, marrow, and bone. Nearby, another 20mm shell blew half a leg off the other engineer. He fell to the bridge in a heap. "This did not deter this fine squad in its mission," Hamilton explained. "It proceeded to clear the bridge and the first tank rolled on across belching cannon fire."

On the bridge, Stevens and his brave men worked quickly. "We crossed and immediately cut all wires leading to the eight bombs mining the bridge. Looking back, I could see no more men coming across. I ordered the squad to clean out the buildings next to the bridge." Stevens took one man and made his way back across the bridge to retrieve the rest of his company. "I found the rest of my men crouching behind piles of dirt and the wall along the river. I assured them . . . the Germans had been cleared out next to the river."

Gradually, the Americans crossed the bridge and fanned out on the eastern section of Mayenne. Lombardi's tank blasted one of the 88mm guns. Major Hamilton told another platoon of tanks from the 712th to cross the bridge. "The second platoon of tanks wheeled to the north and south to protect the flanks, and AT guns were rushed across the bridge to cover the north and south entrances to the eastern section of the town."

By 2030, the Americans had effective control of Mayenne in addition to yet another secure bridgehead across the Mayenne River. That night, retreating groups of Germans repeatedly stumbled into American positions in and around the town. Major Hamilton watched as two enemy vehicles drove right up to his CP, totally unaware of the presence of the Americans. Several Germans got out and started walking toward them. The Americans opened fire, wounded one, and forced the surrender of three others. Two enemy officers took cover behind their vehicles and kept up a steady stream of fire. "At that moment a jeep with a 50-caliber came buzzing around the corner and pumped slugs into one of the vehicles at point-blank range, setting it on fire." Two of Hamilton's officers ran up to the vehicles and shot the two enemy officers point-blank with tommy guns, killing one and wounding the other. "The dead officer was so full of holes that he grotesquely resembled a sieve."

Just east of town, Lieutenant Jim Gifford's platoon of Sherman tanks, from C Company, 712th Tank Battalion, was in an overwatch position along a road that led out of Mayenne. In the darkness they heard a column of trucks approaching from the east. In the next moment, Gifford watched as an enemy column roared right past his platoon and went straight into Mayenne. "They crossed the [bridge] and reached the town square. Then they turned around, you could hear their transmissions shifting gears, and . . . they started coming back out. There were maybe four, five, six trucks. And as they went by us, we were waiting for them. We started to slam 'em with everything we've got, and blew them all up. We got them all. They were a mixture of infantry and air force men. We wiped them out. Whether anybody captured any of them I don't know."[8]

By morning the Germans were all gone. Haislip's XV Corps was decisively across the Mayenne River and Patton now ordered him to push for Le Mans, some thirty-five miles to the southeast. The 3rd Army advance continued.

If the 3rd Army was safely running in the open field, then the 1st Army, to the east, was busy blocking what defenders remained. By early August, while two of Patton's corps were racing to the east, Hodges and his whole 1st Army (not to mention the British and Canadians) were steadily advancing against the main German defensive line, south and east of St-Lô.

From Avranches all the way to Refuveille, there was a gaping hole in the German line. The 3rd Armored Division's seizure of Brécy exploited this by putting American soldiers right on the flank of the western end of the German line. General Collins ordered General Huebner to take his 1st Division and "envelop the enemy's left flank and exploit the breakthrough of his defenses" by capturing Mortain and its surrounding high ground. The division made it to Mortain and easily captured the high ground. The troops were under intermittent artillery fire, but the Germans did not put up anything remotely close to a coherent defense.

However, to the east, the Germans were dug into the usual hedgerow-strewn terrain. Their western flank was in serious jeopardy, but nonetheless they held fast. The U.S. advance depended on the capture of two key objectives: St-Pois and Vire. Starting on August 2, the 4th Division, along with CCB of the 3rd Armored Division, began a push for St-Pois. It took the Yanks three days to slug their way south and into St-Pois. The advance was steady but slow. General Barton's 4th Division soldiers made liberal use of their armored support. The tanks shot up anything in front of them. Units captured high ground around the town as quickly as possible. On the morning of August 5, they had St-Pois virtually surrounded and it was time to clear it out.

Lieutenant George Wilson, a platoon leader in E Company, 22nd Infantry, watched as American firepower blasted St-Pois and its outskirts. "Our artillery began to lay down a barrage on both the village of St. Pois and the ridge behind it. The infantry then started to move up." Wilson and his men were soon assaulting the stone buildings that comprised St-Pois. "Our company was ordered to go house-to-house. We took only a few prisoners, for most of the Germans had withdrawn."

With the enemy gone, Wilson and his soldiers relaxed and searched for loot. "Much to the delight of our men, we did find quite a bit of hard cider. After two weeks of steady fighting, our men were glad enough to have a taste of it." They filled their canteen cups from an assortment of numerous large cider barrels and drank to their hearts' content.

The 9th Division protected the eastern flank of the 4th during the push for St-Pois. Day after day, the Americans slowly advanced, averaging anywhere from three to five miles in a twenty-four-hour period. The 9th Division averaged about two hundred casualties per day between August 2 and August 6. The men had nothing but high esteem for the medics who treated these casualties. They saved innumerable lives during the push.

T/5 Roger Garland, a medic in A Company, 47th Infantry, saved several men. In the process, his hands became filthy with their blood. The blood was caked onto his fingers in rust brown streaks and smudges. One evening his platoon stopped for chow. They hardly had any water left. "About dark [we] 'dug in' near hedgerows in haystacks etc. We received word that hot chow was being sent to us. Unbeknownst to me, the platoon sergeant asked each fellow to [pour] a few drops of water from his canteen [into a helmet]. The last fellow brought the helmet to me and the sergeant said, 'This is for you, doc. We want you to wash the blood from your hands before you eat.'" Garland was stunned. He had become so inured to his surroundings and the carnage of war that he did not realize how filthy with blood his hands had become. He gratefully washed them and ate his hot chow with clean hands, a real luxury in combat.[9]

The most bitter fighting took place on the eastern flank of the 1st Army, in the drive to take Vire, an old fortress town whose history dated back to medieval times. Built on high ground, Vire had 8,000 inhabitants, and it was situated astride the river of like name, along with several converging roads. In an attempt to block the movement of German reinforcements, Allied planes had bombed Vire on D-Day. This partially destroyed the town, but now Vire's agony increased when the Americans decided that they had to have it. Hodges felt it was the key to any full-scale advance for his 1st Army.

Hard-core survivors from the enemy's 353rd Infantry Division, plus paratroopers and soldiers from miscellaneous units, defended Vire. They mined the roads that led into town from the north, and covered every mobile approach with antitank guns. Their artillery observers situated themselves on Vire's high ground and used this great vantage point to call down accurate artillery or mortar fire on the attacking Americans.

Throughout the first few days of August, American soldiers fought to secure the northern approaches to Vire. The fighting was similar to what had transpired in July—coordinated bloody assaults, hedgerow-to-hedgerow, against resolute defenders who often fought to the death. A new division, the 28th, had just been committed to combat. The 28th was a Pennsylvania National Guard unit, well trained but unprepared for hedgerow combat. The 28th, nicknamed the Keystone Division, fought northwest of Vire, steadily pushing through Percy and south to St-Sever-Calvados. Along the way, it seized a crucial piece of high ground called Hill 210. Enemy artillery devastated the Keystone soldiers at Hill 210. T/5 Wesley Reading, a medic in the 112th Infantry Regiment, frantically ran all over the hill, doing whatever he could for the numerous wounded. "We lost a number of men on that hill. One of the soldiers . . . near me was hit by a German 88 shell. It never exploded but it severed his head which then rolled down the hill. It almost made me vomit. We finally conquered the hill. That hill was crucial to the movement of our troops in having . . . high ground for observation." The 28th took its objectives, but, in one day alone, it lost 750 men.[10]

To the east, the veteran 2nd Division was also participating in the south-ward push. In exchange for five miles of territory, the outfit suffered 900 casualties. One of them was Private Melvin Bush, who remained unscathed for the first couple of days. Eventually, though, the grisly, unforgiving, front-line law of averages caught up with him. "Before we had moved 200 yards we had two men killed and one wounded in our squad. During the day we crawled out from under machine gun fire three times. By dark . . . there were sixty-two men and two officers left out of two hundred ten men and six officers. In the squad . . . there were five of us left of the original twelve."

On August 4, as his company was assaulting a nest of hedgerows two miles north of Vire, he got hit. "We had been in the fight about one hour when I was shot by a sniper and then machine gunned as I tried to, and did, crawl back to our lines . . . about 100 yards away. The Germans were firing an M.G. at me nearly all the way." A lieutenant blazed away at the enemy machine gunners, and that helped Bush escape. "I wasn't scared—there was no time for that, but I believe when I got into the ambulance about two hours later and could not hear guns firing was one of the happiest moments of my life."[11]

By August 4, thanks to the efforts of soldiers like Bush, the Americans were in a position for the final assault on Vire itself. The burden of taking the town fell to the 29th Division, an outfit that had already done so much hard fighting in Normandy. General Gerhardt had two regiments—the 115th and the 116th—in the lead, with his third, the 175th, in reserve. The 116th was about a mile north and west of Vire, advancing south against groups of Germans who were fighting a disciplined, planned rearguard action. The closer the Americans got to Vire, the stronger enemy resistance grew. This was especially true of artillery and mortar fire. German observers, perched all over Vire, called down withering, accurate fire.

Somewhere in the middle of the 116th Infantry's lead units, Rocco Russo, the intrepid F Company mortar man who had fought his way ashore on D-Day, was looking for a good spot to place his team's 60mm mortar. "We spent all morning crawling across fields and through mortar, machine gun fire and ar-tillery fire." They stopped at a hedgerow that they thought would make a good position, and started to dig a mortar pit. "We had been digging for about one hour when our squad leader, Sergeant Buddy Thaxton, who had been scouting for targets, joined us." Sergeant Thaxton told them to relocate to a different position. German observers on Hill 219, a scraggly mass of hedgerows just northwest of Vire, were looking straight down on them, and they needed to get moving.

Russo and the other men grabbed their mortar tube, baseplate, and am-munition and started to get moving. Seconds later, a German mortar shell zipped through the air and exploded right in their midst, "about three feet from where I was standing." Shrapnel ripped into everyone. One man was killed instantly; another got hit in the leg, another in the chest. Russo and his buddy dived into a hole. In the hole, Russo saw that the other soldier was hit badly in his arm. "I was helping him, not realizing that I had a serious wound to my lower abdomen. When I tried to stand up, my stomach was really hurting." He pulled down his trousers and found a small hole in his abdomen, but no blood was running from the hole. Eventually they made their way back two hedgerows to an aid station. The medics gave Russo a blood transfusion and evacuated him to a field hospital, where doctors removed much of his small intestine. For him, the Battle of Normandy was over.

The same could not be said for the rest of the men still on the line that night. As the sun rose on August 5, they resumed their inexorable advance on Vire. A mixture of infantry troops and tanks from the 2nd Armored Division's CCA rolled south on D-374, a road that led into the northern portion of Vire. They reached Martilly, a village located a mile north of Vire. From their towering OPs in Vire the Germans spotted them and fixed them. Just as the armor began to cross a stone bridge that spanned the Vire River, the Germans opened up on them with antitank and artillery fire. In just a few revolting minutes, the Germans destroyed fourteen American tanks. The burning, smoking, exploding hulks of the tanks littered the road and the fields that bordered Martilly. The stench of burned flesh and hair mixed uncomfortably with the boiling smell of burning fuel and steel. The advance was stymied.

To the west, the 115th Infantry was having an equally rough time. The soldiers of this unit secured Mesnil-Clinchamps by late morning and even cut the road that led west out of Vire, but then they ran into a deadly nest of resistance. Company I was in the lead as the regiment crossed the road. Private First Class Robert Grande was an assistant squad leader in I Company. The fighting of the last few days had whittled his platoon down to twenty-three men. This morning, after crossing the road, his squad cleared a farmhouse and resumed its advance. "We were ready to take off over the next hedgerow. We got about two feet beyond it when all hell broke loose. Foley [another assistant squad leader] got his—right between the eyes. I saw his knees buckle under him and that was the end."

The whole company was pinned down on either side of the hedgerow. "We realized that we were being picked off one by one. We shifted our fire from the direct front to the left flank." Grande glanced to his left and saw one of his comrades raise his rifle to shoot at something when the man flinched and slumped to the ground—dead. Fifteen yards away, one of the squad leaders was screaming for ammunition for his BAR. A sniper shot him right between the eyes, and he too collapsed in a heap. The squad leader's ammo bearer, a man named Young, was on the ground, crawling toward Grande, his eyes bulging in terror. "Everyone's dead except you and me!" he cried.

Grande knew he was right but was not sure how to respond. "I was about to tell him to lie down and play dead when a burst of machine-gun fire got him in his gut. He fell by my side, and I pulled him closer to the hedgerow and told him to be still. He called for a medic a couple times before he realized that it was impossible for a medic or anyone else to reach us. I told him to start praying—that's what I'd been doing since I hit that hedgerow. My legs began to get numb but I was scared as hell to move."

The minutes, and then the hours, ticked by. Young drifted in and out of consciousness. At one point he awoke and told Private First Class Grande that he was going to die. "I made believe that I was mad as hell at him and told him that a good Texan never dies. That brought a weak grin from him, and he went back into another state of unconsciousness." Grande lay still, thought of home, prayed, and waited. He could not get out of there until dusk, and by that time Young was dead. The 115th stopped and dug in.

Throughout the day, fighter-bombers tried to lend whatever support they could for the hard-pressed ground troops. The airmen ran into almost as much opposition. Lieutenant Quentin Aanenson, a twenty-two-year-old P-47 pilot in the 366th Fighter Group, flew into a vortex of hidden flak guns, hidden in ruined buildings, as he and his squadron strafed targets on the outskirts of Vire. "Suddenly . . . several 20mm explosive shells hit my plane—all about the same time. I had fire in the cockpit, and the entire rear of the plane was a mass of flames."

Lieutenant Aanenson could feel his heart racing. He had seen several of his fellow pilots die just like this, in flaming pyres plunging to earth. More than anything, he wanted to get out of his plane. "I tried to bail out, but my canopy was jammed from a flak hit. I wasn't going to let myself burn to death, so I put the plane into a steep dive, so I could crash into the ground as fast as possible. Doing that probably saved my life, because the flames were sucked out through the opening in the canopy—and the fire in the cockpit died out."

The fire was out, but smoke was still trailing from his engine. If Aanenson's base had been in England, as it had been two months before, he probably would not have made it. But, the 366th was now based in St-Pierre-du-Mont, not far away. In just a few minutes, Aanenson made it to his base, but now his main challenge was to land the plane. "I had no hydraulics, so I had no flaps or power brakes to help me in landing. Some of my instruments had been shot out. I landed at close to 170 miles per hour. When I hit the runway, the plane jerked left—only then did I know that I had a flat tire and a damaged left wheel. I fought to keep the plane on the runway, but the drag from the flat tire and damaged wheel was too great."

The plane crashed heavily onto its right wing and skidded to a stop.

Aanenson's right shoulder harness tore loose. "I was spun around, and the back of my head hit the gun sight. Two enlisted men . . . pulled me from the cockpit and dragged me away." The young Minnesotan was very lucky that his plane had not exploded. He was also fortunate that the gun sight did not crush his skull. "I ended up with a major concussion, and my ankles were blistered from the fire in the cockpit." The next morning, Aanenson went on a much-needed leave to London.

The only good news on August 5 was that the Americans succeeded in taking Hill 219. Gerhardt had originally planned to send a special task force into Vire (as he done at St-Lô), but he realized now that the best way to take the town was to infiltrate his infantry from Hill 219. The job went to the 116th Infantry, the battered, tried-and-true unit that—seemingly a lifetime ago—had assaulted Omaha beach at H-Hour on D-Day.

They waited for twilight on August 6 and began descending the steep eastern slope of Hill 219. Between the hill and the town of Vire was a deep ravine that was covered with thick underbrush and gray rock. The Vire River, at its most narrow, streamlike point, flowed at the bottom of the ravine. The ravine then gave way to another hill, on top of which was the town.

Major Charles Cawthon's 2nd Battalion was one of the lead units tonight. Since Omaha beach he had seen so many men die, so much suffering and tragedy. He was not ashamed to admit that it was all getting to him. Several days before, his commanding officer, Major Sidney Bingham, had been wounded, foisting the reluctant Cawthon into command of the battalion. To Cawthon, the fighting north of Vire seemed like a repeat of the St-Lô bloodbath. He was tired and jaded. A couple evenings before, as he reconnoitered the lines in solitude, he had experienced a strange hallucination—he thought he saw a German patrol wearing World War I uniforms. He, of course, told no one about this bizarre experience.

Tonight, when he got his attack orders, he was surprised. "I had not expected the attack order. The ravine and river, I thought, must be recognized as too formidable an obstacle for our depleted ranks." He had hoped that the 29th would envelop the town and attack from a less perilous direction, but it was not to be.

Now the 2nd Battalion quietly shuffled down the hill and into the ravine. Major Cawthon, in the twilight, stole a look at Vire. "[It] appeared in this light as a medieval town under siege, black smoke rising above it and artillery fire echoing along the defile. The two assault companies started in columns abreast down the steep hillside and were immediately lost to view in the underbrush and dark shadows. The battalion command group followed, slipping and sliding, holding onto brush and trees."

At the bottom of the ravine, the lead troops began taking 88 fire. "We forded the shallow river and started up the opposite slope toward a racket of gunfire beyond the wall of houses." A German tank, sitting in the middle of the D-374 road, opened fire. Cawthon watched as an artillery observer called down fire on the tank. A few moments later, a shell hit in front of the tank's turret, damaging its gun. The tank turned around and retreated into Vire.

The Americans ascended the hill under considerable small-arms fire. Machine-gun and rifle fire hit many soldiers as they tried to cross the road, but American artillery was pounding the enemy's rubble-strewn positions. Gradually, as the artillery grew in effectiveness and the infantry got closer to Vire, the enemy fire slackened.

Shortly before midnight, the Americans fought their way into Vire. Major Cawthon and his command group were trailing right behind the leading troops (his companies were hopelessly disorganized and depleted by now) and ran toward the protection that some nearby rubble afforded. "The night [was] lit by the undulating red glow of burning buildings, all overhung by a pall of smoke." The 116th Infantry soldiers roamed around in small groups, clearing out snipers and machine-gun nests in cellars, windows, and partially destroyed houses. "Two company commanders were casualties, as was the battalion executive officer. Parties of Germans were trying to surrender; tracer bullets crisscrossed and ricocheted off the rubble."

For the next few hours, until the sun rose, the Americans eliminated the remnants of enemy resistance in Vire. Cawthon's 2nd Battalion, along with the 3rd Battalion, spread out around the town and set up roadblocks at every entrance to Vire. The town was still under enemy mortar and artillery fire, but it belonged to the Americans. At dawn, Cawthon took a moment to study the nauseating remains of what had once been a beautiful little town. "Vire by daylight lost the dramatic appearance it had had by firelight the night before and became just another dismal place of gray, smoking rubble."[12]

The German situation in Normandy was now getting grimmer by the day. In the east, the British and Canadians were eating away at the right flank of the German Army. In the center, with Vire, St-Pois, Mortain, and Brécy in hand, Hodges had his pivot points to unhinge the whole German western flank. Farther to the west, Patton's army was in wide-open terrain, gaining real estate by the minute. To nearly every senior officer on either side, the Germans seemed to have no choice but to begin a general retreat to the east side of the Seine. But one powerful man on the German side did not see it that way. To Adolf Hitler, the situation called for bold action, an armored counteroffensive that could, if executed properly, reverse the whole course of the Battle of Normandy.

CHAPTER THIRTEEN

MORTAIN

At Barenton there were some indications of what was about to happen. Late in the afternoon on August 5, a task force from the 3rd Armored Division approached this little town that was situated on the N-807. The task force was made up of a company of half-tracks from the 36th Armored Infantry Regiment, a company of tanks, plus some tank destroyers, self-propelled artillery, and engineers. The mission of this force of nearly fifty vehicles, under the command of Lieutenant Colonel Carlton Russell, was to capture the town and open the way for other units to roll eastward to Domfront. Possession of Domfront would safeguard the flank of the 90th Division at Mayenne and continue the rout that was developing in Normandy. By and large, the Americans were not running into much opposition in this sector (right on the borderline between the 1st and 3rd Armies).

Still, Russell was not sure what to expect after the bizarre face-to-face encounter he had had with the Germans in Brécy a few days before. The truth was that intelligence was not really sure where the Germans were or what they were planning to do. They could very well be holed up in strength in Barenton, or they could be long gone. In spite of his ignorance of what lay ahead, Russell had to keep moving, as fast as his vehicles could go. All day long, the Mississippian had been getting pressure from his superiors, General Hickey and Colonel Doan, to take Barenton. Now Russell looked ahead and saw a bend in the road. If his maps were correct, Barenton was just around that bend. All at once, he heard the sickening *crack!* of an enemy antitank gun.

At the same moment, Lieutenant Ralph Balestrieri, a forward observer riding in one of the lead Shermans at the bend in the road, heard the enemy gun. A nanosecond later, a shell streaked by his head, close enough that it "nearly burned the paint off my steel pot [helmet]. The antitank gun was on the western side of the town and had a clear shot at the column but fortunately we were in a sunken road." The Americans could tell the gun was somewhere west of the town, but they could not see it.

Balestrieri's tank and several others quickly spread into fields on either side of the road. Some even found concealment behind hedgerows. In the meantime, one of the tank platoons cautiously moved forward, in an effort to find the enemy gun. Sergeant Alvin Beckmann, a tank commander in D Company, 32nd Armor, was perched in the turret of the lead tank of this platoon. "I inched my Sherman up to the curve in the road." Beckmann's driver had had a tank shot out from under him a few days before. "[He] was understandably nervous about having it happen again." Slowly the driver coaxed the tank around the bend. In an instant, Sergeant Beckmann heard the telltale *crack!* "An armor piercing shot zipped by the front of my tank. My driver backed up until we were out of sight of the German guns. I asked the other tanks if they had seen where the gun was and nobody had."

Beckmann was disappointed that no one had seen anything, because it meant that his tank would have to nose around the curve again. He ordered his driver "to move up." Reluctantly the driver threw the engine into gear and rolled forward. "Just as we rounded the curve for the second time, more German AP rounds went streaking past the front of my tank, seemingly inches from the armor. My driver slammed it into reverse quickly and hit the accelerator. I was thrown forward against the cupola and broke some ribs." Beckmann was in such pain that he had to be evacuated.

In the meantime, the column spread out and halted while Lieutenant Colonel Russell dismounted and conducted a personal reconnaissance. German antitank guns clearly had the bend in the road zeroed in. Russell estimated that, in addition to the antitank guns, there were at least 100 enemy soldiers and five armored cars in the town. The enemy had mined the road leading into Barenton, creating roadblocks, in addition to the kill zones of the antitank guns. The best thing to do, Russell decided, was wait until dark, clear the mines, call in artillery support, and then attack. The main avenue of attack would not be the bend in the road. Instead, Russell's men would force their way into Barenton from the south, across a mined bridge.

While Russell and his task force waited, the Germans started pouring 20mm fire into the hedgerow adjacent to Lieutenant Balestrieri's tank. Small pieces of shrapnel buzzed all over the place. The lieutenant managed to stay under cover, but one man, nearby, was not quick enough. "The medic went over and saw [a] big hole in the back of his helmet [*sic*] and what appeared to be an entry wound in the back of his head." The medic found no signs of life and pronounced the man dead, but he was wrong. Two hours later, the "corpse" stirred and asked what had happened. "One tanker almost fainted!"

As this went on, Lieutenant Colonel Russell reported his intentions to

General Hickey, who was miles away, at his CCA CP. Hickey did not like the idea of waiting to attack Barenton. He was under intense pressure from General Huebner—CCA was attached to the 1st Infantry Division—to keep his armored columns moving east, so that the flank north of Mayenne would be secure. As the first shadows of evening crawled along the road and the surrounding fields, Hickey repeatedly badgered Russell to attack.

At last, Russell could take no more. Exasperated, he launched his assault just as the sun was setting. "The pressure of Command on me from above . . . was so great, I just had to be all the way up front to get away from it." Russell was walking with the soldiers of his lead platoon, heading straight for the mined bridge. "We were checking for mines on the road prior to advancing into the town. So far as I know, no American was further forward." They had made it as far as the bridge when the Germans spotted them. Several guns opened up from the direction of the town or the hills beyond it; Russell was never sure which. "The rounds hit on the blacktop road in front of me and I could see sparks on the road. A shell fragment sliced off a part of the muscle of my right arm . . . and almost sheared off the barrel of my .45 automatic in its holster. Several other men who were near me were also hit."

A medic ran forward, sprinkled sulfa powder on Russell's wound, and bandaged his throbbing arm. Under his own power, Russell walked back to the column and briefed the next two officers in his chain of command, one of whom was Captain Thomas Tousey. "He was obviously in a lot of pain," Tousey said. An ambulance evacuated Russell and the other wounded soldiers to a field hospital. Tousey and the other officer decided to pull back, wait out the night, and send reconnaissance patrols into Barenton at dusk. By that time, the Germans were gone. Under cover of darkness they had pulled out and headed north, as if by design. The Americans deployed in and around Barenton and waited for orders to move east. Those orders were a long time coming. "Our communications section could not get anyone on the radio," Tousey recalled. He and his men could only glean this much—something big was happening to the north, in the same direction where the Germans had just "retreated."[1]

Hitler had an affinity for boldness. In the 1930s, as he rebuilt the German armed forces, flouted the Treaty of Versailles, and turned Germany into a great power again, he had repeatedly taken bold risks, often against the advice of his generals or his party cronies. Each time, events proved him correct, as Germany won a series of bloodless victories in remilitarizing the Rhineland and swallowing Austria and the Sudetenland and eventually the rest of Czechoslovakia. In the early years of the war, his aggressiveness translated into the conquest of most of Europe. Since then, the war had turned against this dictator, but he still trusted his instincts, and his instincts told him to remain aggressive. His fascist philosophy of life demanded it—the strong, the racially pure, in his view, could only thrive by relentlessly and ruthlessly attacking enemies. In such a life-and-death struggle as World War II, Hitler maintained that there was no time for sentimentality, circumspection, or defeatism. Only victory mattered.

So it was not surprising that in August 1944, at Normandy, when all signs pointed to defeat for Germany, Hitler thought only of victory. His generals believed that the situation in the west could only be saved by wholesale retreat. But Hitler neither trusted nor respected most of them, especially in the wake of a failed assassination attempt on July 20, for which many of his generals were responsible. Hitler's armies were crumbling under the hammer blows of the British and Canadians in the east and the Americans in the west, but perhaps he could turn the tables on the Allies. In early August, he ordered Field Marshal Günter von Kluge, to prepare an offensive with the aim of retaking Avranches and cutting off Patton's 3rd Army. Von Kluge had just recently taken over as commander in the west—Rommel was recuperating from his wounds, and Rundstedt had been sacked.

Von Kluge thought Hitler's idea was madness but knew he was in no position to disobey his Fuhrer (even now, hundreds of assassination plotters and their families were being summarily tried and executed). Von Kluge hoped the offensive might simply knock the Allies off-balance long enough for the German armies in Normandy to be withdrawn. Hitler saw the attack, code-named Operation Luttich, as an ideal way to compromise the entire Allied position in Normandy. "We must strike like lightning," he told his commanders, "when we reach the sea the American spearheads will be cut off. Obviously, they are trying all-out for a major decision here, because otherwise they wouldn't have sent in their best general, Patton. The more troops they squeeze through the gap, and the better they are, the better for us when we reach the sea and cut them off! We might even be able to eliminate their whole beachhead."

The plan called for the use of four armored divisions—the 2nd and 116th Panzer, along with the 1st and 2nd SS Panzer. These powerful armored formations, supported by well-armed infantry from units like the 17th SS Panzergrenadiers, would attack at Mortain under cover of darkness on the evening of August 6–7. Once the sun rose and burned off an anticipated morning fog, the Luftwaffe was supposed to support the offensive with more than 300 planes. The little town of Mortain (1,600 inhabitants) was nestled into a valley, nearly halfway between the Sée River to the north and the Selune River to the south. Mortain was about seven miles northwest of Barenton and 20 miles east of Avranches. Tiny Mortain was surrounded by hills, most notably Hill 314, just east of town, right at the edge of a wooded, rugged, hilly area of France known as La Suisse Normande (Norman Switzerland). If the Germans were going to make it to Avranches, they needed the westerly roads that spoked out of Mortain. Those roads would only be secure if the Germans could take Hill 314, a craggy, rocky tumor of high ground that so dominated the area that a man at its summit could see all the way to Brittany.

The Germans experienced all sorts of problems organizing their hasty offensive—for instance, the commander of the 116th Panzer was so disgusted with the attack order that he refused to participate, and his unit had no impact on the battle—but the attack was ready to go by the evening of August 6. The whole thing was, of course, very chancy. To the northeast, Montgomery's troops were steadily pushing toward Falaise as part of their Operation Totalize. To the southeast, American mechanized forces (led by the XV Corps) were streaking east, toward Le Mans. If Luttich failed, the bulk of the German Army in the west could be surrounded and annihilated. Hitler knew this and accepted it. In his view, great rewards only came from great risks.[2]

Throughout the day on August 6, even as three German armored divisions frantically positioned themselves for their attack, the 30th Division relieved the 1st Division at Mortain. Since taking Mortain a few days earlier, the 1st had dug itself into positions atop Hill 314 and in the surrounding area. Now the Big Red One was gone—speeding for Mayenne and points beyond. The soldiers of the 30th were tired and disoriented. After their bitter experiences during Operation Cobra, they were hoping for a rest. Instead, they had been trucked from Tessy-sur-Vire to Mortain. "The movement was executed so rapidly," Lieutenant Ralph Kerley, commander of E Company, 120th Infantry, later wrote, "it was impossible to secure maps of the area. The 2nd Battalion S-2 secured a few large-scale maps, scarcely enough for a company." They also used what 1st Division maps they could scrounge, but these were of limited value. "These had been in use for several days and were crumpled and badly marked." Kerley deployed his company at the southern edge of Hill 314 and, like every other small-unit commander in the division, tried to get situated as best he could.

Throughout the day on August 6, the 30th Division soldiers hunkered into the positions dug by the 1st Division, tried to get organized, and wondered who was on their flanks. The answer was almost no one. To the north, troops from the 9th and 4th Divisions were in place on either side of the Sée River. There were also tanks and half-tracks from the 3rd Armored Division. The southern flank, however, was wide open. There was one column heading for Captain Toussey's forlorn group at Barenton (and that column got bombed by the Luftwaffe on the evening of August 6) but little else.

As the clock ticked ever closer to midnight, German tanks, half-tracks, trucks, self-propelled guns, and infantry soldiers began moving west, toward

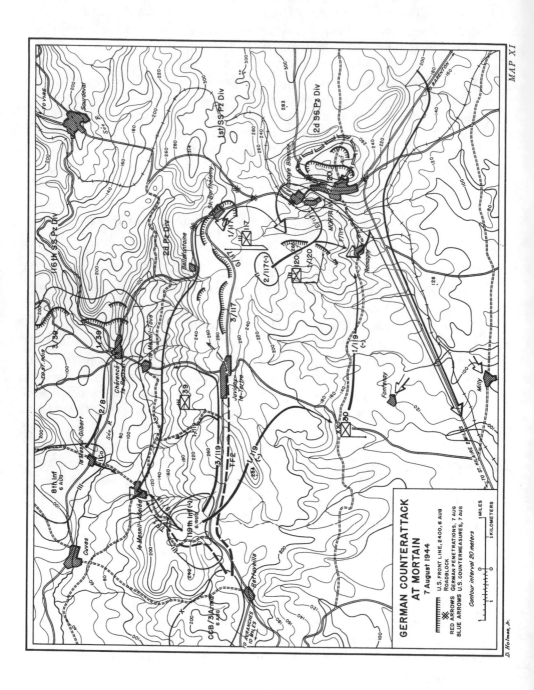

GERMAN COUNTERATTACK
AT MORTAIN
7 August 1944

U.S. FRONT LINE, 2400, 6 AUG
Roadblock
RED ARROWS   GERMAN PENETRATIONS, 7 AUG
BLUE ARROWS U.S. COUNTERMEASURES, 7 AUG

Contour interval 20 meters

1   0   1 MILES
1   0   1 KILOMETERS

MAP XI

D. Holman, Jr.

Mortain. These men were some of the best remaining soldiers Hitler had. Many of them were fanatical SS types who believed, to the very marrow of their bones, that they were the cream of humanity, Aryan supermen destined to dominate the world. These ruthless men neither asked nor gave any quarter. Other soldiers, moving steadily through the darkness, were hard-core Wehrmacht veterans with several years of combat experience. In their hearts they, too, believed in their superiority over their American adversaries.

The GIs had no idea the Germans were coming. Allied commanders understood that the Mortain area would be a logical place for any German counterattack, but they did not know of German intentions until the offensive was already under way. Ultra, of course, afforded senior Allied commanders the opportunity to read many German communications. But, in this instance, the Ultra cryptanalysts did not intercept and decode their first Mortain-related message until 1948 hours on August 6 (two others followed in the course of the evening). There is still no precise information as to when the analysts passed along this information to Bradley and the other high-level Allied leaders in Europe, but certainly not before 2000 hours. "Ultra was of little or no value. [It] alerted us to the attack only a few hours before it came," Bradley wrote, "and that was too late to make any major defensive preparations, as we had at Carentan."

If Bradley could not prepare for the offensive, he could certainly react to it. Upon receiving the Ultra transmissions on the evening of August 6, he called Patton and alerted him to put three divisions on standby, just in case they would be needed at Mortain. Bradley also sent an urgent message to General Collins, whose VII Corps was about to absorb the brunt of the enemy attack. "Enemy counterattack expected vicinity Mortain from East . . . or North within the next 12 hours." Collins took what precautions he could, but for the next twenty-four to forty-eight hours the job of defeating the German offensive fell to those young American soldiers who were, even now, strung out in foxholes, outpost positions, and roadblocks in and around Mortain. The time was 0038 on August 7.[3]

Private Thomas Street, a rifleman in F Company, 120th Infantry, was wedged into a slit trench, catnapping, when he heard the first indications of the German attack. His platoon was manning a roadblock at the northeastern foot of Hill 314, right in the path of the 2nd SS Panzer Division. In the darkness, Private Street was awakened by the sound of guttural voices screaming, "*Heil Hitler!*" A few seconds later, machine guns opened up and tracer bullets streaked through the area. Street did not know what to do. Having joined his unit shortly after Operation Cobra, he was relatively new to combat. "Everything was confused. We could hear the rumble of tanks on the road."

Private Street kept his eyes fixed on his squad leader. Surely he would know what to do. To the surprise of the young rifleman, the squad leader left his position and began moving up the hillside. "There seemed nothing to do but follow." Street sprang to his feet and took his place in a single file of soldiers ascending the hill. They could still hear the screaming and shooting behind them. They came to a barbed-wire fence. "As I followed the man ahead of me over the fence I got caught in it, took a few minutes to get untangled and then to my horror could see no one ahead of me."

Fear swept through Private Street. His heartbeat quickened and he took short, anxious breaths. For all he knew, German soldiers were right beside him, ready to cut his throat. The idea of being alone in the darkness, separated from his buddies, was terrifying. He strode purposefully in the direction where he thought his squad had gone and, to his great relief, eventually found them. As they kept moving, they noticed figures nearby. "We didn't know if they were Germans or Americans and held still trying to figure out who they were, when a grenade, fortunately the German concussion or 'potato masher,' rather than the fragmentation type, exploded a few yards from us. Then we knew."

A BAR man next to Street opened fire on the ghostly-looking figures. He glanced at Street and the others and said, "Let's go." They moved to a new position and waited for any further sign of the enemy. "We seemed to be alone with no idea where we were or where the rest of the squad was, or anybody else. There was nothing to do but wait, nerves taut, until we could see where we were."[4]

A couple miles to the west, on the other side of Hill 314, Lieutenant Ronal Woody, commander of G Company, was visiting his kitchen group, at the base of the hill, when he saw enemy troops and heard shooting. "When the firing started, I knew I had to get up to where my men were, up on top of the hill. They were shooting all around me as I climbed. Somehow I made it up there."

The Germans were seemingly everywhere. South of Hill 314, they overran roadblocks along with several antitank and machine-gun positions maintained by F and H Companies. Sergeant John Whitsett, who had served in the 120th—a national guard outfit—for several years, was sleeping in a foxhole near an antitank position when someone awakened him and told him to report to his brand-new platoon leader. "Everything was quiet. I started to walk up the road a little ways, smoking a cigarette. I could hear men moving." Whitsett thought the men were infantrymen who had been assigned to protect the guns, and he wondered where they were going. "I hopped up on a hedgerow so I could see better. I caught a glimpse of a German helmet. A guy saw me and started firing." Whitsett jumped down and ran back, warning the gun crews about the Germans.

The warning came too late. Already the infiltrating Germans had captured the guns and some of the crewmen. Whitsett figured this out and found a hiding place behind a hedgerow. "I laid there listening. Some Germans found our jeep and I could hear them messing with it. I figured I better get away from there, so when they drove the jeep past where I was hiding, I used the noise as cover." Whitsett caught the enemy by surprise. He ran right past them and they did not fire a shot.

North and south of Hill 314, enemy infantry and vehicles were on the move, speeding past U.S. roadblocks. By 0100, some of the Germans were in Mortain itself. Ever since the onset of darkness, Mortain had been under intermittent German shelling, causing many fires to rage throughout the town, bathing it in an eerie, unnatural light.

Lieutenant Colonel Eads Holloway, the commanding officer of the 2nd Battalion, 120th Infantry, had his headquarters at the western edge of town, in a stone farmhouse. His communications sergeant, Robert Bondurant, was stringing telephone wires along a nearby street when he saw movement in the flickering half-light that had been created by the fires. "There they were at the other end of the street—German soldiers. Maybe thirty or more. All with burp guns. The town was full of men." Bondurant, a former grocery clerk from Reidsville, North Carolina, was a six-year veteran of the 120th. He knew what to do. As unobtrusively as he could, he sidled away and, when he was out of sight of the Germans, ran as fast as he could to Lieutenant Colonel Hardaway's CP. "He called Regiment right away." The regimental commander, Colonel Hammond Birks, told them to "hold the town at all costs." With those cryptic words ringing in his head, Sergeant Bondurant went back to his switchboard and sat down. "We were told to stay, so I was going to stay."

T/5 Robert Bradley, the medic and Washington, D.C., native, was several doors down, working at the battalion aid station, treating the increasing number of wounded who were pouring in. "Sniper and automatic weapon fire was everywhere." He and the other medics resolved to move their aid station out of Mortain as soon as they could possibly do so.

Not far away, Holloway's headquarters group, augmented by C Company of the 120th Infantry, now found themselves in a bitter close-quarters fight. The Americans were outnumbered and outgunned. The commander of C Company got killed by concussion from an 88 shell that exploded near him. The U.S. troops were so hard pressed that they were soon fighting in isolated, desperate groups in clusters of buildings ranging from the center of Mortain to its western edges.

Corporal Dudley Wilkerson was fighting for his life with a small group from his C Company. "All hell was breaking loose with severe shelling, tanks moving in and German SS troops. A lieutenant asked me if I could load a bazooka. We went to the corner of a building and I put a shell in the bazooka. He fired and knocked out a German tank."

The officer turned to Corporal Wilkerson and hollered, "Run!" and the corporal soon saw why. "A shell from an 88 hit the corner of the building where we had been. It knocked me down. When I got up, I didn't see the lieutenant again. I don't know whether he was killed or not." Wilkerson regained his senses and started looking for his squad. "I heard a guy yell for help. He wanted somebody to cover him. He had a machine gun set up in a building that the front had been blown out of. He had a crossroad covered, and he was piling [enemy soldiers] up as they tried to cross the street. I stayed with him for some time, shooting at Germans who were throwing grenades from the windows of the building above us."

One of the grenades finally found its mark—it landed between Wilkerson's legs and exploded. When he came to, he saw that the machine gunner was dead. Wilkerson himself did not have any visible wounds, but he was terribly groggy from concussion. "A medic stopped by and helped me up. I could walk, but I kept passing out." He ended up in a basement, drifting in and out of consciousness. Mortain was steadily coming under the control of the 2nd SS.

To the northwest, the lead units of the 2nd Panzer Division were rapidly moving west in the shadow of the Sée River. They covered three miles before running into artillery units from the 9th Division's 39th Infantry Regiment. Lieutenant Anthony Ponticello, a forward observer for the 26th Field Artillery Battalion, heard the sound of tanks on the river road, but when he called to report the noises he was told that they came from friendly vehicles. They were anything but friendly. Within minutes, Ponticello got his authorization to fire. His batteries lobbed 500 shells at the enemy column's route of advance. The firing was blind, because of the darkness and a blanket of fog, but it briefly slowed the enemy down. When the Germans renewed their advance, they overran a 39th Infantry roadblock at Le Mesnil-Tove. The Americans disabled their vehicles and removed the breech blocks from their antitank guns before retreating to the south.

Some German infantry even crossed the Sée River. They pressed ahead until running into the lead units of the 4th Infantry Division at Lingeard. The surprised Americans scrambled to set up roadblocks. Lieutenant George Wilson of F Company, 22nd Infantry, was catching up on sleep when he got word from a staff officer to take his platoon and support an antitank unit that was in the path of the Germans. "[He] . . . told me very little. As we were in enemy territory, I thought I should know more about the road block, such as its exact location, how long we might be gone, and how much food and ammunition to take along. He refused to tell me anything except to get moving. I obeyed reluctantly. I could smell alcohol on the officer's breath, and I resented having to take orders from someone even slightly drunk."

As it was, American mortar fire devastated the advancing enemy infantry as they tried to take high ground near Lingeard. The mortar men rained more than 370 shells on the Germans, stopping them in their tracks. Their screams and moans echoed through the night. Later F Company riflemen captured sixty enemy soldiers and found the bodies of ninety more. The Germans made no further headway north of the Sée.

By the time the sun peeked over the eastern horizon, the Germans had achieved piecemeal penetrations of the American lines south of Mortain as far as Romagny, a town astride a main road that led to the sea, in Mortain itself, north of Mortain as far as Le Mesnil-Tove and Le Mesnil-Adelee near the Sée River, and immediately west of Mortain at the foot of a patch of high ground known as Hill 285. As bad as that seemed, it could have been much worse. The Germans had failed to grab the most important piece of terrain on the battlefield—Hill 314. There were elements of three American rifle companies, numbering about seven hundred men, atop Hill 314, and through the night they dealt mainly with patrol-sized German probes, not all-out attacks. This was a mistake on the part of the Germans, because their best hope of taking Hill 314 was in the confusion of the night, before American artillery and airpower could come into play and before the American ground soldiers could rally and realize that they were dealing with a major German attack.[5]

Lieutenant Murray Pulver's B Company, 120th Infantry, defended Hill 285. Pulver's CP was situated in the center of his defenses, near the top of the hill, about forty yards away from a small shed and house. Just before dawn, he awoke to the startling sound of gunfire emanating from the northern foot of the hill, where he had placed his 1st Platoon. Pulver was a steely, steady South Dakotan and former national guard sergeant who had worked his way up through the ranks. Just a couple weeks before he had been a platoon leader, but officer casualties in B Company had elevated him to command of the outfit.

Now he peered in the direction of the gunfire but could see nothing through foggy predawn mist. A few minutes went by and he heard the distinct ripping sound of a German machine gun. Shortly after this, he saw three figures approaching him through the mist. For the briefest of moments, he wondered if these men were enemy, but he soon saw that they were members of his 1st Platoon. One of the men, Private Harold Chocklett, slid into Pulver's foxhole and told him what had just happened.

He and the other 1st Platoon men at the roadblock had seen a pair of French civilians walking in front of a tank. When they challenged the civilians, they halted and told them, in broken English, that they were guiding a lost American tank back to their lines. Several Americans left their holes and walked over to inspect the tank. As they did so, the Germans crept behind them, set up a machine gun on a fence, and opened fire, killing three Americans instantly and scattering or capturing several more. Private Chocklett and his two companions had returned the fire (killing the two French people, one a girl, the other a man) and had then left. Lieutenant Pulver sent Chocklett to the mortar section with orders to lay down fire along the Germans' logical route of advance.

More contact reports were now pouring in to Pulver. All of his platoons, all of his roadblocks, were under pressure from German tanks and infantry, who were emerging from the mist like ghostly apparitions. Lieutenant Pulver grabbed his field phone, called battalion, and told them what was happening. The reply was simple and curt: "Hold at all costs." Pulver hung up and resolved to do his best to carry out this chilling order. "It was beginning to get light, but still very foggy. Suddenly I heard a tank come rumbling our way. It was coming down a lane in an orchard to our front."

One of Pulver's sergeants handed him a loaded bazooka. Pulver was actually pretty handy with these things. A couple weeks before, he had knocked out two enemy tanks during a B Company attack. Pulver shouldered the bazooka and took up a firing position behind a nearby stone wall that bordered the lane. Silently, as the seconds ticked by and his heart beat ever faster, he waited for the enemy tank to get within range. "That monster came out of the fog not more than ten yards away. I fired, hitting it right under the turret. The tank came to a stop." Lieutenant Pulver was so close to the tank that he swore that if he had been tall enough, he could have reached up and touched the muzzle of its main gun. He was close enough that several tiny fragments from the bazooka shell peppered his face, turning it into a bloody mess but doing no serious damage. "The concussion of the bazooka blast killed all of the occupants of the tanks, but the tank's motor continued to run and did so for most of the day."

Pulver's men admired what he had just done. Several of them crawled over to him and shook his hand. As they did so, a small group of German infantrymen ran right at them, through an adjacent field, shouting, *"Amerikaner! Kamerad!"* and firing their weapons. This was the enemy's way of demanding that the Americans surrender, but Pulver and his men had no intentions of obliging them. "The Jerries were in the open and we were behind [a] hedge. We got them all without any of . . . us getting a scratch."

Pulver was high on adrenaline now. He felt almost invulnerable. It occurred to him that a jeep loaded with ammunition, parked in a nearby barn, might fall into German hands. He told his sergeant to take over and crawled forty yards to the barn. Pulver planned to destroy the jeep with a rifle grenade. He fastened the grenade, peeked through a window, into the barn, and saw four Germans standing around the jeep. "I didn't dare break the window to shoot for fear of alerting them. I found a small door ajar next to the window. I eased it open carefully, stepped in, took aim, and pulled the trigger. The damn gun misfired! The Jerries heard the click and spotted me.

I dropped the gun and dove for the ditch as a hail of bullets ripped through the door." Pulver covered the forty yards back to his hole in seconds, but it seemed like hours, because bullets were spattering everywhere. Once he got there, enemy mortar fire began pouring in and his command group was pinned down. The fire also destroyed their phones and radios, severing their communication with battalion headquarters. Still they held on.

The Germans were trying hard to dislodge B Company from Hill 285, but the battle there had stalemated. In addition to Pulver, crews from the 823rd Tank Destroyer Battalion had knocked out several more enemy tanks and self-propelled guns along the tiny lanes that crisscrossed Hill 285. One of the tank destroyer men, Sergeant Ames Broussard, knocked out a Mark IV tank with a bazooka and got cut off from his buddies but still managed to make it back to them after dark.[6]

In order to have any chance of succeeding, the Germans needed to quickly seize—before the fog burned off, bringing Allied aircraft into play—every intersection and crossroads in the Mortain area. To do this, they needed to overwhelm the numerous American roadblocks that had been set up during the late afternoon hours of August 6. One of these intersection roadblocks was at L'Abbaye Blanche (named for a white abbey located near the road). This choke point, sandwiched between Hill 285 and Mortain, featured several bridges over the shallow Cance River and a railroad overpass. The Americans defended this intersection with four antitank guns from A Company, of the 823rd Tank Destroyer Battalion, one 57mm gun, mines, bazookas, and a scattered assortment of infantry with machine guns or rifles.

The night before, Lieutenant Tom Springfield, a platoon leader in A Company and the commander of this group, had made sure that his three-inch antitank guns were well dug in along the roads, covering every approach to L'Abbaye Blanche. All through the night, Springfield, a color-blind native of Wichita, Kansas, had heard shooting coming from Mortain and Hill 314 to their east. He and his men figured that soon enough whatever was going on there would affect them. "We listened, but we also stayed on our feet," Springfield recalled. He knew his platoon was good. Even back in the States, during training, they had consistently won every marksmanship award. What he did not know was that the whole Der Führer Regiment of the 2nd SS Panzer Division was headed straight for him.

The first indication came at 0500, after the sun had started to rise but while the fog still clung thickly to the ground. Somewhere out there was the sound of enemy vehicles, getting closer, but no one could see where they were coming from. All at once, a reconnaissance element from the Der Führer column crossed one of the Cance bridges. A motorcycle, with sidecar, an armored car, and an officer's limousine rolled right into the kill zone of the 57mm gun. Sergeant Jacob Rhyne, the gun crew's commander, gave the order to open fire. They got off two quick shots, destroying the armored car and the limousine. As flames consumed both of these vehicles, the Germans inside them tried to escape, only to be cut down by American .30-caliber machine-gun fire. The fires turned the cars into nothing but twisted, stinking junk. The enemy bodies lay sprawled around the bridge area. The whole mess effectively blocked this crossing for the Germans.

Several hundred yards away, the main portion of the enemy column tried crossing one of the Cance bridges (called Pont-de-la-Vacherie). Two of Springfield's guns were in perfect position to blast anything crossing this bridge. The lieutenant was at an OP, close to his guns, so that he could spot targets and control their fire. Springfield had trouble seeing through the fog, but he could tell that the Germans were walking right into the trap he had set for them. "The road was so steep, they had to shift into low gear to climb it. That's when we hit them."

With stunning swiftness, his crews unleashed a succession of shots, each of which scored a hit. An ammunition truck exploded in a breathtaking fireball. At the same time, the Americans heard the clanging sound of direct hits on three half-tracks and even a Mark IV tank. SS infantrymen tumbled out of their half-tracks and ran for cover, only to be scythed by American machine-gun fire. The commander of the Der Führer Regiment, along with his staff, fled from his vehicles and made it into a dairy barn just opposite the bridge, only to be pinned down there by the intensity of the American fire. Springfield had no idea they were there—he could hardly see anything through the fog. Only clangs and flashes, combined with the sight of scurrying figures, betrayed the fact that his crews were massacring the enemy. A few minutes later, the enemy tried attacking again, with a company of infantry, this time on one of Springfield's flanks, but they ran right into his other two guns. The American antitank crews picked off, at a distance of thirty meters, a self-propelled gun and a supporting vehicle, while the infantry poured withering fire into their enemy counterparts. The firefight lasted about fifteen minutes. German survivors were in ditches along the road, edging back from whence they came. Some of them tripped mines and blew themselves apart. The lucky ones escaped into the fog. They left without inflicting even one casualty on Springfield's men.[7]

Two miles to the north, at the vital crossroads village of St-Barthélmy, the situation was far more serious for the Americans. Lieutenant Colonel Robert Frankland's entire 1st Battalion, 117th Infantry, plus antitank guns from the 823rd Tank Destroyer Battalion, defended St-Barthélmy and its environs. The

Americans were dug into positions around the town, in a sort of concentric ring. The tank destroyer guns, of course, covered every likely roadside approach to St-Barthélmy. The town was a couple miles north of Mortain, immediately astride two major roads, D-5 and D-33, that led directly west to Avranches.

U.S. Army Regular officers in World War II often looked down upon the National Guard as a nest of inefficiency, amateurism, cronyism, and general foolhardiness. This was not an entirely inaccurate view. There were problems with the guard, but not quite as many as the regulars supposed. Robert Frankland represented everything that was right about the National Guard at mid–twentieth century. He was a product of one of the leading families of Jackson, Tennessee, and had been serving in this unit for nearly twenty years. He had risen from private to lieutenant colonel through sheer dedication and determination. He knew his men and they knew him. He displayed courage, toughness, and decency, sometimes all at once. "He was the finest soldier I ever served with," one of his sergeants said years later, "he just couldn't be beat."

All through the night, Frankland had received reports from French civilians that the enemy's 2nd Panzer Division was planning to attack St-Barthélmy, from the northeast, at dawn. In response to this, he placed two of his companies, A and B, in such a way that they covered the northern approaches to the town (in some cases individual squads manned roadblocks east of St-Barthélmy). Only C Company defended the southern flank of St-Barthélmy.

Frankland's intelligence information was only partially correct. The 2nd Panzer Division was on the way and it would attack from the north, but another major enemy unit also planned to attack St-Barthélmy. German plans called for the 2nd Panzer and the 1st SS Panzer (Liebstandarte Adolf Hitler), the most powerful unit in Operation Luttich, to converge on St-Barthélmy and then slash west. So even as Lieutenant Colonel Frankland prepared for the onslaught from the northeast, the 1st SS Panzer was approaching from the south, heading straight for C Company and its attached tank destroyer crews.

For nearly an hour on the morning of August 7, German artillery pounded the American defenders of St-Barthelmy. The GIs scrunched as low as they could get in their holes and prayed for the shelling to stop. When the fire finally ended, the leading columns of the 1st SS, including approximately fifty tanks, rolled steadily up the road that led to St-Barthélmy. In no time, these powerful enemy forces overran C Company's forward roadblock at La Sablonnière. These men were never heard from again. Onward the enemy came, through the fog.

Private First Class Alfred Overbeck, a C Company rifleman, was crouching in a foxhole near the road. Now he saw the enemy tanks through the morning mist. "They came out of a wall of fog. I don't know what kind they were. They were so big, they looked like battleships. They were bumper to bumper." Just ahead of the tanks Overbeck could see SS soldiers checking the road for mines. The sounds of tank engines and harsh German voices echoed through the air.

Nearby, Overbeck's squad leader cranked his field phone and asked his company commander what to do. The officer told him to remain in place. The rifleman were terrified. Against these tanks they had only their small arms and grenades. There was really only so much they could do. Overbeck fastened a grenade to the end of his rifle, took aim at the lead tank, and fired. "A rifle grenade won't stop a tank . . . not unless you drop it down the turret. But I got some foot soldiers, walking alongside the tanks. And I'm sure I hit a tank commander. He was standing up in his turret when my grenade went off right beside him." The tanks kept coming. Private First Class Overbeck and the others moved from foxhole to foxhole in an effort to dodge the rising volume of fire emanating from the German armor. "Artillery was falling all around, and tanks were everywhere. They would fire at anything."

A little farther up the road, behind Overbeck and the other infantrymen, were the only weapons that had any chance of stopping the German armor. Lieutenant George Greene's platoon of four antitank guns from B Company, 823rd Tank Destroyer Battalion, were dug into the ditches on either side of the road, just south of St-Barthélmy. Greene and his men were tired and edgy. Only a few hours before, they had finished digging their guns into what Greene considered to be proper positions.

Now, as they clustered around their guns and stared ahead into the fog, they could hear the German tanks but not see them. When the lead enemy tank closed to within fifty meters, its machine gun opened up on some C Company soldiers. Lieutenant Greene, with no other way of spotting targets, told his men to fire at the muzzle flashes of the machine gun. At the Number One gun position, east of the road, Corporal Walter Christianson pulled the lanyard of his three-inch gun. An armor-piercing projectile roared from the muzzle, leaving behind a sheet of flame, and scored a direct hit on the enemy tank's frontal armor. Immediately the tank, a Panther, as it turned out, caught fire. It ground to a halt, blocking the other German vehicles. The Americans could only see the flames flickering somewhere ahead in the fog. "A little while later," Lieutenant Greene said, "we heard a recovery vehicle come up to drag that one out of the way." He also heard German officers shouting instructions. Greene's men fired a couple more rounds at the noises, but with little effect.

At 0700, after a lull of about forty-five minutes and the apparent removal of the burning Panther, the Germans tried another attack. Clearly they were shocked by the resistance they were encountering south of St-Barthélmy. The 1st SS had expected that the 2nd Panzer would have already cleared out the town from the north. Instead, the latter unit had experienced traffic snarls (caused primarily by a downed British Typhoon fighter that crashed into a lead tank) and its attack was delayed. As a result, the German attack on St-Barthélmy was not well coordinated.

The SS tankers resumed their advance and closed this time to within thirty-five meters of Greene's guns. Once again, the lead Panther reconned by machine-gun fire. The crew of Gun Number One once more fired at the flashes. The armor-piercing round punched through the Panther's armor and exploded mightily. The Americans saw a fireball flash, and the Panther literally stopped in its tracks. The German armored column came to a halt while their infantry dealt with the scattered groups of C Company soldiers who were still in their holes along the road. For the time being, the enemy was again stymied (they also tried a flanking attack, a couple hundred yards to the west, and were stopped).

However, the situation soon got much worse for the Americans. Almost simultaneously, the 2nd Panzer attacked from the northeast of St-Barthelmy. These Wehrmacht soldiers combined with tanks and infantry from the 1st SS to put terrific pressure on Lieutenant Colonel Frankland's eastern defenses. They chewed Lieutenant Myrl MacArthur's A Company to pieces. His men had no bazookas to oppose the tanks that were attacking them at frighteningly close range. Within an hour, the Germans captured MacArthur, his command group, and dozens of other soldiers. The rest of the A Company men got killed or escaped in small groups into St-Barthélmy.

The Germans had the Americans greatly outnumbered. The equivalent of a whole German panzer division was now in action against one American battalion. All over the fringes of St-Barthélmy, desperate squad- or platoon-sized groups of Americans did the best they could against the enemy armor. Aside from the fog and Lieutenant Greene's guns, the Americans had little protection except for their rifles and machine guns. Alwyn Featherston, a historian of this battle, wrote that "Frankland's defenses should have disintegrated under the . . . assault. Instead, the outnumbered GI's fought back with incredible tenacity and resourcefulness."

The behavior of Lieutenant Colonel Frankland himself was perhaps the best example of this tenacity. Frankland was in a small house on the western edge of St-Barthélmy that served as his CP, shouting orders into his field phone, rallying stragglers, assessing the situation. At their roadblocks south of town, Greene's gunners were doing the best they could, but German tanks soon succeeded in slipping past them in the fog. All around St-Barthélmy, the enemy was infiltrating into the town. American bazooka teams hunted for German tanks, but they had trouble finding targets in the fog, much less getting close enough for a good shot.

At the CP, Frankland was on the phone. His operations officer, Captain David Easlik, was standing next to him. Easlik looked up and noticed something big outside a nearby window. He walked over to investigate and saw a German Panther parked right beside the CP. At nearly the same instant, Lieutenant Colonel Frankland heard noises coming from elsewhere in the house—probably the kitchen—and went to check them out. He got there just in time to see two Germans marching two of his radiomen out of the back door. Frankland drew his pistol, followed them, and shot both of the Germans as they exited.

Frankland now wasted no time. He gathered up his command group and supervised as they escaped out of a window, right under the nose of the Panther. As his men fled west, toward one of the company CPs, Frankland, a crack pistol shot, drew a bead on the Panther's tank commander as he stood in his turret. According to one of his men, Frankland "not only shot the tank commander, he jumped up on the tank and started blasting away down the hatch with his .45. He got the whole crew." There were two other German tanks in the street, but Frankland's little group escaped before they could do anything. In his after action report, Frankland never mentioned this incident. His men believed that if he had, he might have gotten the Medal of Honor.

They made it to B Company's CP, where Lieutenant Colonel Frankland called his regimental commander, Lieutenant Colonel Walter Johnson, and told him of the critical situation in St-Barthélmy. Johnson, whose command post 800 meters west of St-Barthélmy was under such intense artillery fire that he dubbed it "Chateau Nebelwerfer," wasted no time in responding. He ordered Lieutenant Lawson Neel to take his platoon of tank destroyer guns and go help Frankland's men in St-Barthélmy.

Neel was a thirty-two-year-old former department store clerk from Thomasville, Georgia. Today was his thirteenth wedding anniversary. His platoon, containing four guns, was dug into a roadblock position about a mile and a half west of St-Barthélmy. Neel collared his jeep driver, and the two men took off east, scouting for good locations to place their guns in St-Barthélmy. As they drove alone, into the fog, Neel kept thinking of his wife. "She's going to be a beautiful widow."

When they got to within sight of the town, Neel heard plenty of fire, all over the place. He was a veteran platoon leader, "a fantastic fighter," in the view of one of his officer colleagues. Neel knew there was no time to lose. He and his driver sped back to their original roadblock position and brought up a single gun, towed by a half-track. At the western entrance to St-Barthélmy, his crew stopped at a fork in the road, unlimbered the gun, and manhandled it into position in a muddy field. "It was like something you'd see in an old Civil War movie, where the gunners ride up, turn the gun around, and start firing. We had to park the half track across the road and carry the ammunition back to the gun. We hadn't been there three or four minutes before a German tank came down the road." Alongside the tank were dozens of enemy infantrymen.

The tank was so close, at most twenty meters away, that Neel and the others could hear a German officer shouting commands. Neel turned and shouted a command of his own: "Shoot, damn it!" The gun crew pointed their weapon at the Panther and opened fire. The armor-piercing round smashed right through the enemy tank's left sponson, destroying it immediately. The crew abandoned the tank and took cover in nearby buildings.

But the enemy infantry was right on top of Neel and his crew. "Like a stream of water from a hose, I could hear bullets bouncing off our gun shield. I took the firing pin, and we took off across the field."

As they fled, one of Neel's men turned to him and asked, "Sir, we're not running away, are we?"

Neel shook his head. "Hell, no. This is a strategic retreat."

It really was. Neel's group made it back to the rest of the platoon, and the lieutenant supervised the establishment of a new roadblock position. A bit later, when German armor came down the road, they knocked out two more enemy tanks and paralyzed the enemy column while Allied planes strafed them. The Germans made it no farther west on this road.

In St-Barthélmy, they were absorbed with clearing out the remnants of Frankland's 1st Battalion. South of town, Lieutenant Greene's antitank men fought bravely to the end. One by one, the Germans damaged, knocked out, or forced Greene's men to abandon their guns. Greene had resolved to defend the infantry here until the bitter end, and this was, alas, it. He had no more functioning guns. With German tanks and Panzer Grenadiers all around his positions, he tried to round up the remnants of his platoon and get them out of St-Barthélmy.

As he did so, he encountered an infantry sergeant who asked him for help. The man's machine gun was malfunctioning and his squad's position was about to be overrun. Greene led him to one of his platoon's half-tracks. The two men took a .30-caliber machine gun from the half-track and carried it forward to the sergeant's squad. Suddenly a round from a German tank exploded in an adjacent hedgerow. Shrapnel tore through the sergeant and he collapsed onto the ground. Greene was hit in the arm, but he ignored his wound. He sank to the ground and grabbed the sergeant, hoping he could save his life. "He died in my arms. It's pretty damn rough to have a guy blow up all over you. I must have lost my head for a moment. The guys claim I grabbed the machine gun and started firing. I don't really remember."

Greene was firing from the hip, like something out of a movie. He fired a long belt of ammo, allowing many of his soldiers to escape St-Barthélmy. Finally, his ammunition exhausted, he tossed the machine gun aside and turned to go, only to a see a German soldier right at his side, pointing a submachine gun right at his belly. Lieutenant Greene had no choice but to surrender.

It took the Germans six precious hours to secure St-Barthélmy. They inflicted 350 casualties on Frankland's intrepid 1st Battalion and destroyed Greene's platoon, but at horrendous cost. One historian estimated that the enemy lost forty out of seventy tanks at St-Barthélmy. Even more important, they lost time. The fog was burning off now, clearing the skies for Allied fighters. The Germans were still more than sixteen miles from Avranches, their timetable was completely blown, and their strength was ebbing as a result of staunch resistance from U.S. ground troops.[8]

Hill 285, L'Abbaye Blanche, and St-Barthélmy were bad enough, but the Germans' biggest problem was to the east, at Hill 314. By early morning, the Germans had effective control of Mortain itself (Hardaway and his headquarters men were holed up in a building, hiding), but that did not really matter. What mattered was that three isolated companies of stubborn Americans controlled the key piece of ground on which the outcome of the whole battle hinged.

Shortly after dawn, Private Street and the other wayward F Company, 120th Infantry, soldiers made contact with troops from E Company. Together they cautiously made their way to a ditch alongside a road at the eastern foot of Hill 314. "We crossed the road and continued single file, stopping often, as the sky got lighter." They got into several skirmishes with unseen enemy soldiers. At one point, Private Street thought that a machine gun was drawing a bead solely on him. Finally, he and the others made it to the relative safety of a stone wall that lined a road somewhere on the eastern edges of Hill 314.

A lieutenant whom Street did not know came along. "Are you new men or old men?" he asked Street and a couple of his comrades. They told him they were new. A disappointed look crossed the officer's face, but he beckoned them to follow him. "I need you up on the hill."

Street and two of his buddies reluctantly obeyed (they liked it behind the wall and did not want to move). They followed the lieutenant up the hill until he "pointed to a little promontory on the shoulder of the hill closest to the road. There was a low hedge of stones in a short arc on this promontory."

The lieutenant pointed to the promontory. "You set up there, and don't let anybody attack us from the road."

Street and the others were dumbfounded. "It looked like the most exposed spot possible, and it looked like we would be all alone out there. But we had no choice. We had to go. So we went, one at a time, crouching low." They made it uneventfully to the promontory. They did not know it, but the promontory was to be their home for the next several days.

As the fog lifted around Hill 314, the defenders began to see the true magnitude of the enemy attack, along with the seriousness of their situation. All during the night and in the foggy dawn, they had fought scattered enemy groups and had listened to the sound of vehicles or shooting. Now they had a breathtaking view of hundreds of German vehicles and thousands of German soldiers on the move. Lieutenant Ralph Kerley, E Company's commander, took one look and reported "columns of enemy armor and foot troops streaming [toward us] from the east and northeast."

The defenders of Hill 314 had almost nothing in the way of antitank weapons, but they did have a different kind of weapon that was even more potent. A serious, intelligent twenty-one-year-old second lieutenant from Valparaiso, Indiana, largely controlled the use of that weapon. Robert Weiss was a forward observer from the 230th Field Artillery Battalion. He and his observer team—four men in all—had been ensconced on Hill 314 since the previous day. Weiss's artillery was the security blanket the Americans on the hill desperately needed. Without it, they had no chance of survival. Even with it, their situation was grave.

Now, as the sun rose higher overhead, Weiss and his team were sitting around at Lieutenant Kerley's CP, located in a little draw below the eastern ridge of Hill 314. "Bit by bit, our understanding began to take shape in those early, hazy hours. Telephone lines to the rear, ours and that of the infantry, were gone, either deliberately cut by the enemy, chewed up by our tanks, or shot out in the fight back in the town. Tank and hostile infantry below our position on the Hill was increasing. Snipers banged away erratically at us from the rear."

Weiss had already called for a few fire missions, but in his words, they were "blind" shots. This meant that he himself did not observe the targets in the darkness or the fog. Now the situation was different. Runners brought him reports of enemy attacks against the hill. Weiss and his radioman scrambled up the rocky slope of the ridge to a nicely placed OP they had set up the previous day. "We crouched below the tops of bushes and grasses and I began searching" for targets through his BC (battery commander's) scope, essentially a raised pair of binoculars, mounted on a tripod. Soon Lieutenant Weiss spotted enemy half-tracks, loaded with infantry, heading toward the hill. Weiss relayed the necessary commands to his radioman. A few moments passed as the artillerymen of the 230th, at their positions a couple miles to the west, loaded and fired their 105mm guns. "Explosions of artillery shells reverberated across the picturesque farmland sloping away before us. The vehicles changed direction and ran off into trees and behind hedgerows." Weiss spotted German infantry and called down more fire. "Shells erupted in pairs, in fours and sixes, black clouds over the countryside. We had their range."

Within a few minutes, Weiss's little OP became a target. Withering accurate machine-gun fire buzzed uncomfortably close. "No one had to tell us what was happening." The enemy had spotted their OP. "The bullets carried a warning and sucked up my energy as they cut by. We dropped to the ground and listened to the snip-snip of the bullets just above our heads."

Weiss knew they had to get out of there. The enemy fire was way too close for comfort. He turned to his radioman. "Come on, let's go."

They found a new spot, not very far away, and went back to work as more enemy troops attacked the southern edges of Hill 314. They were only a mile away from Weiss and the other Yanks. "The troops and armor were not hard to spot as they came toward us. We took them under fire immediately using both time and ricochet fire. Concentration after concentration of shells exploded over and around the enemy. The advancing infantry took cover, and the tanks went into hiding for a time."

Weiss knew the terrain inside and out. He could see the enemy approach from every direction. He was good at his job. When he spotted targets, all he had to do was shout, "Fire mission!" to his radioman and relay the target information and the necessary coordinates. After that, it was simply a matter of adjusting fire, if need be. For the rest of the day Weiss, at various times, called down effective fire, devastating the Germans, inflicting casualties on them, keeping them at bay. The Americans on Hill 314 were holding steady— for now. The question was how long their food, water, and ammunition would hold out. Lieutenant Weiss was worried about something even more important. How long would his radio batteries last? Since his radio was his only means of communication with the outside world, his survival, and that of every other American on the hill, depended on those batteries. He and his men took to leaving the batteries out in the sun, in the hopes that the sunlight would warm the batteries and add to their capacity. It wasn't much, but it was all they could do.[9]

Besides Weiss's artillery and the courage of American ground troops, there was another weapon impeding the progress of the German offensive. Throughout the day on August 7, as the sun rose higher and higher, Allied aircraft began their familiar marauding. The best tank-killing plane in the Allied arsenal was the British Typhoon. The Typhoon could dive at 500 miles per hour and tear German armor apart with sixty-pound rockets or even sometimes 20mm shells.

General Quesada knew all about the Typhoon's effectiveness. He understood that it was the best weapon to destroy enemy armored columns on the roads south and north of Mortain. So he called Air Vice Marshal Sir Harry Broadhurst, who controlled ten Typhoon squadrons in Normandy, and asked for help. The American and the Briton crafted a plan. Broadhurst's Typhoons would shoot up German vehicles around Mortain while Quesada's Thunderbolts and Mustangs flew missions farther behind the German lines to impede the enemy's fighters flying from their bases near Paris. Quesada's fighter planes would hold them off while the British Typhoons provided close support for the hard-pressed American ground troops at Mortain.

Between 1230 and sunset, the Typhoon pilots flew nearly 300 sorties. At the controls of one of those Typhoons, Desmond Scott, a New Zealander, spotted German armor backed up on a road east of St-Barthelmy. He nosed his plane over and dived, and the rest of his wing followed. "The road was crammed with enemy vehicles—tanks, trucks, half-tracks, even horse-drawn wagons and ambulances, nose to tail, all in a frantic bid to reach cover. As I sped along to the head of this mile-long column, hundreds of German troops began spilling out into the road to sprint for the open fields and hedgerows. There was no escape. Typhoons were already attacking in deadly swoops at the other end of the column and within seconds the whole stretch of road was bursting and blazing under streams of rocket and cannon fire. Ammunition wagons exploded like multi-colored volcanoes. A large long-barreled tank standing in a field just off the road was hit by a rocket and overturned into a ditch. It was an awesome sight: flames, smoke, burning rockets and showers of colored tracer."

The British planes seemed to be all over the sky. They expended over 2,000 rockets and eighty bombs, along with countless 20mm rounds. One of their wing commanders called it the Day of the Typhoon. The British pilots claimed over eighty tanks destroyed. This was probably an exaggeration, but they certainly did tremendous, effective work on August 7. They basically shot up anything that moved and helped prevent the Germans from reinforcing their hard-pressed, stymied assault elements fighting at such places at St-Barthélmy, L'Abbaye Blance, Le Mesnil-Tove, and Hill 285.

Amid the chaotic, confused situation at Mortain—in some cases Germans and Americans were within yards of each other, and there was no definable, continuous front line—it was inevitable that the Typhoons would mistakenly strafe American troops. One of those Americans was Lieutenant Pulver, whose men were still holding out at Hill 285. Pulver was close to the spot where he had killed an enemy tank earlier that morning. The Germans were no more than 100 yards away, if that far. Pulver and his people could hear them shouting orders to one another. Pulver also heard the sound of an airplane overhead. "A British Typhoon buzzed us, circled around, and cut loose a rocket aimed at the knocked-out tanks just in front of me. My God, the heat from that thing almost singed my hair! We all grabbed our gear and ran back to the next hedgerow where there was a big hole. We all dove in as two more Typhoons dropped their loads, circled around, and came at us straight. The weapons carrier driver was killed as bullets broke through our cover. It's a puzzle why we weren't all killed." One of Pulver's sergeants, hoping to signal the British that they were shooting at friendly troops, threw a yellow flare into an open field. "The only effect it had was to bring a shower of mortar fire from the enemy."

In another instance, a Typhoon attacked four Shermans from the 743rd Tank Battalion, knocking one of them out. These were the exceptions, though. Considering the difficulty of identifying targets while buzzing along the deck at 500 miles per hour, the accuracy and skill of the British Typhoon pilots were superb. "I can still see those planes," Sergeant James Waldrop of the 117th Infantry admiringly said, "flying so low they were coming up with branches in their air scoops."

Quesada's fighter pilots also did a fine job on that crisis-ridden August 7. They flew 429 sorties and massacred the Luftwaffe fighter pilots before they could ever get to the skies over Mortain. They also strafed whatever German ground forces they spotted. "We found an entire German armored column that was fifteen miles long," Bill Dunn, the fighter pilot and Eagle Squadron veteran, recalled. "After hitting this column with our full group strength three times during the day, with bombs, rockets, and strafing, the road was jammed by burning, exploding and destroyed tanks, trucks, and armored personnel carriers."[10]

By nightfall, the German attack was at a standstill. Small units of Americans, aided by artillery and airpower, had fought so hard and so effectively throughout August 7 that the Germans had absorbed enormous casualties they could ill afford. They had gained no more than five miles of ground in any direction. Their timetable was completely shot. They were still more than fifteen miles from Avranches. Only the southern flank, along Route 177, held any promise for them. This was the weakest part of the American line, and the Germans had plunged right through it. But with Weiss and the other men of the "Lost Battalion" (really they were isolated, not lost) atop Hill 314, the road was under accurate, devastating U.S. artillery fire. Moreover, U.S. reinforcements were plugging the gap and surging toward Mortain in an effort to rescue the Yanks at Hill 314. So the Germans could not exploit even this small opening. Von Kluge recognized Operation Luttich for what it was—a failure—and was in favor of retreating, but Hitler would have none of this. He ordered a resumption of the offensive, all the way to the sea. For now, this was simply not possible, so von Kluge kept his forces in place while he prepared for another push. Hitler's original concept for Luttich was chancy but somewhat understandable; his order to resume the offensive after the failure of August 7 was unwise and foolish. By not letting von Kluge extract the remains of what had been excellent panzer divisions, Hitler all but guaranteed that these units would be decimated.[11]

Of course, none of these big-picture ruminations were so apparent to the embattled groups of Americans fighting for their lives around Mortain during the night on August 7–8. Most of the 2nd Battalion, 120th Infantry, was trapped on Hill 314, but the aid station medics seemed to have better luck. Sometime around dusk on August 7, they had packed up their equipment, boarded their jeeps, and driven west, all the way to a solid-looking stone house along a road at the foot of Hill 285. Across the road, a battery of artillerymen was firing in support of Hill 314. At the house the medics set up their equipment and made their patients as comfortable as possible. Outside, T/5 Robert Bradley and several other men improved slit trenches someone had previously dug. "We put extra logs and dirt over the parts of the slit trenches where our heads would lie to give us some extra protection against direct mortar hits." Exhausted, they finished digging and fell into a deep sleep for the rest of the night.

The next thing Bradley knew, someone was kicking him in the ankle. "*Raus! Raus! Raus!*" Bradley snapped awake, looked up, and saw a German soldier looming over him in the early-morning light. The muzzle of the German's rifle was in Bradley's face.

A few feet away, Jack Thacker, the regimental chaplain's driver, was also experiencing a rude awakening. "I was roughly awakened by a rifle barrel being jabbed into my side and hearing the word 'rouse' being said to me over and over. I immediately stood up and climbed out of my foxhole, and with the beginning of dawn, I was able to see other forms also complying to the orders of armed German soldiers. They had captured about ten of us: two or three doctors, some aid men, the chaplain, and myself."

With hands on heads, the small group of Americans started marching and kept going until they were somewhere east of Mortain. Their captors were from a six-man patrol that had been sent out to find some prisoners. Bradley did not want to lose his watch, so he wriggled it far enough up his wrist that his sleeve covered it. The chaplain, Gunnar Teilmann, surreptitiously tossed aside a German watch he had been wearing for several weeks, lest the enemy find it on him and exact some kind of reprisal. The Germans were more interested in medical supplies than anything else. "The Germans were particularly eager to get morphine and the water purification tablets," Bradley said.

Finally, the little group came to a halt and rested. One of the Germans spoke English, and a couple of the Americans spoke German. Thacker sat next to another GI and glanced around at the odd spectacle of the intermixed enemies. "As the six heavily armed German soldiers and the ten American GI's sat in a loose circle on the ground, we were rather casually interrogated. I recall no military information being asked for or given. Perhaps because they were field soldiers, their primary interest seemed to be about such things as where we lived, how old we were, and other personal data."

Later in the day, the German patrol handed the Americans over to intelligence officers who conducted a more thorough interrogation. From there they rode trucks east all the way to Germany. Thacker, Bradley, and the others spent the rest of the war in captivity.

Meanwhile, just moments after the enemy captured the aid station, they attacked the northern face of Hill 285. They got to the crest but no farther, as men from A Company, 120th Infantry, plus a tank destroyer unit under the command of Lieutenant Francis Connors, managed to keep them in check. Elsewhere on the hill, Lieutenant Pulver had no communication with higher headquarters. His radio batteries were dead, and his men were running low on food and water. "I decided to go back to battalion CP. I took a 1st platoon runner with me. On the way we were caught in a mortar barrage. I was hit in the face with a piece of shrapnel or stone, I didn't know which, but it shattered my lower front teeth and chipped my upper teeth. Outside of a fat lip, however, I was OK. My runner was also hit. He ran around in circles yelling. I had to tackle him to quiet him and dress a nasty wound behind his ear. All the while I was doing this, he kept apologizing for his crazy behavior."

Pulver and his runner made it back to the CP. When they got there, the battalion commander gave Pulver a strange look. He had thought all of B Company had been captured. Pulver told him the real situation, retrieved the necessary supplies, and returned to his unit (in spite of his shattered teeth).[12]

Throughout August 8, both sides grappled with each other, the Germans attacking halfheartedly westward, the Americans attacking east in an effort to rescue the defenders of Hill 314 and push the Germans back to their starting points east of Mortain. All along the six-mile front, from north to south, soldiers from several American divisions (the 4th, 9th, 2nd Armored, 3rd Armored, and, of course, 30th) fought a series of close-in, sharp, bloody skirmishes with the Germans. To the southwest, the 35th Division, a unit that General Bradley had diverted to deal with the German offensive, was pushing slowly toward Romagny and the southeastern edges of Mortain.

Allied planes were still making life (and death) miserable for the Germans. Just north of Barenton, where the small task force from the 3rd Armored Division had been joined by the 120th Infantry's 3rd Battalion and some tanks from the 2nd Armored Division, Joe Thompson, an American reconnaissance pilot, was flying low, right over a north–south road, looking for German vehicles. When he descended to an altitude of 100 feet, he found what he was looking for—"tanks with camouflaged netting moving slowly on this narrow route. I could see the German soldiers clamoring into their open jump seats." Thompson and his wingman roared right over the German column, so fast that the enemy did not even get off a shot. "I pulled up sharply, zigzagging furiously to avoid the flak I was sure would follow. Then I saw, perhaps a mile away, a flight of P-47 fighter bombers."

Thompson had no radio communication with the fighter pilots, but he soon got their attention by waggling his wings. When he was sure that they had seen him, he turned around and led them—like a scout dog—to the German column. Thompson watched, with great satisfaction, as the P-47s screamed in like birds of prey. "They dove with machine guns blazing—250 pound bombs under each wing." In their wake they left burning vehicles, death, and plumes of rising smoke.[13]

Several miles to the north, at Hill 314, the Germans were putting as much pressure as they could on the so-called Lost Battalion. The Americans had now been cut off for nearly three days. Medical supplies were running very low. Most of the wounded were packed together in the shadow of Lieutenant Kerley's CP. "We didn't have morphine, clean bandages, anything. We made the wounded as comfortable as possible. They were collected in each company and put in slit trenches."

As the morning unfolded, the enemy mounted a series of attacks against the hill. Lieutenant Weiss was in the same spot as yesterday. He and the others had spent a tense night hoping for reinforcements, wondering when the Germans would launch a massive attack. Neither came. "As the sun warmed the earth to receive a gorgeous summer day, enemy infantry, at least a platoon of those gray-green uniforms, assembled to the front for an attack."

Everything now depended on Weiss and the dwindling power of his team's radio batteries. The other observer on the hill, Lieutenant Charles Bartz, had no more communication with the outside. His radio batteries were dead. Nor was he even in touch with Weiss. "I suspect that as he sat there on the Hill, Bartz thought a great deal about death and dying. He seemed to me to be always looking over his shoulder, and I could already see the pale stamp of death on his face." The death Weiss saw on Bartz's face made him very uncomfortable. "I could not look him in the eyes or study his face for long."

In any event, even had Weiss wanted to, he had no time to look at his colleague. The Germans were attacking and it was time for another fire mission. Weiss relayed the necessary orders to his team. "A pall of exploding shells and smoke covered the German infantry, blackening the area around them. Dust and debris shot skyward." The artillery fire shattered this group of German infantry, but the enemy had plenty more to throw at the hill. "Then tanks. More infantry. Artillery fire brought all these intended onslaughts to a standstill. After an hour and a half, the enemy tried a new tactic. A single 88, the first of many to come that day, opened up on our position." The enemy shells tore at the rocky crags and promontories around the hill, bursting "into hundreds or thousands of jagged, body-severing chunks and slivers . . . [conveying] a brute power, unstoppable strength and deep malice. Big iron cut through the air, shattered boulders into sharp splinters, then bounced erratically over our heads. We crouched down behind the crags, on the face of the cliff to the rear, uncomfortably sheltered."

At one point, the enemy even lobbed in some white phosphorous shells. These were horrifying, terrifying weapons. They burst into thousands of white-hot burning particles, all of them descending malevolently, looking for skin to burn up. If even a small piece burrowed into a man's arm, it could burn through to the bone. "As suddenly as the blizzard had begun, it ceased. There had been only three or four, maybe five of the smoking demons." Immensely relieved that the enemy was apparently out of white phosphorous shells, Weiss and the other men exchanged sympathetic glances. "No one smiled, but we could breathe easily again."

Lieutenant Weiss spent the rest of the day matching wits with the enemy artillerymen, calling in counterbattery fire, keeping a lookout for more attacks. Kerley gave him a message to send to Colonel Hammond Birks and his 120th Infantry regimental headquarters: "Still holding original position. Elements of H are with me. In contact with G and K. Need batteries . . . medical supplies and food, basic load ammo for rifle company and 60 and 80mm [sic] mortars." Weiss added his own conclusion to the message: "Are we getting reinforcements?"

He received no answer.

Miles to the west, far behind the lines, General Omar Bradley was at his CP thinking about the situation at Mortain. By now he knew from Ultra intercepts that Hitler had personally ordered the attack on Mortain. Bradley knew the object of the attack—Avranches. He also knew that, in spite of the failure of their offensive, the Germans fully intended to renew their attack. Before Mortain, Bradley had been planning to unleash Patton all the way to Paris, to the Seine, in a long envelopment designed to gain as much ground as possible. But now his thinking was changing. Instead of this logistically challenging, time-consuming long envelopment, he wondered if the German gamble at Mortain now presented him with the ability to destroy their entire army in France. Perhaps he could effect a short envelopment. The Germans were trying to push west. As they did so, they plunged deeper and deeper into a trap, and he intended to spring that trap.

Bradley knew that Montgomery's men were on the move. The previous day his Canadian II Corps had launched Operation Totalize, an all-out southerly push for the towns of Falaise and Argentan. To the southeast, Haislip's U.S. XV Corps was about to capture Le Mans. What if, instead of pressing on to the Seine, he told Haislip to turn north and head for Argentan, with the intention of trapping the Germans west of the Seine? The more he thought about this, the more sense it made. In fact, it was such a great opportunity that he could hardly believe that the Germans were foolish enough to oblige him and persist in their suicidal offensive. He turned to Major Hansen, his ubiquitous aide. "Greatest tactical blunder I've heard of. Probably won't happen again in a thousand years."

All morning long, the general worked with his staff, preparing plans, assessing the feasibility of his exciting new idea. "This short envelopment was far preferable to my grander idea of a blitzkrieging long envelopment around Paris to Dieppe. Because the 'wheel' would be much smaller, we could go immediately, without waiting for a logistical buildup." That cinched it. Bradley would go with this short envelopment.

It was a fine idea, more practical and, in a curious way, more aggressive than the grander long envelopment. The long envelopment was, more than anything, about liberating terrain. The short envelopment was about destroying German combat power. Bradley understood that the latter was more important than the former. This was an unusual moment of vision and creativity for a man whose strengths were his even temper and his cool competence, rather than his flair or imagination. By the time the day was over, Bradley had spoken with Patton, Eisenhower, and Montgomery about the plan. Patton was lukewarm (he liked the dash and maneuver of the long envelopment), but Ike and Monty were amenable. Bradley outlined the plan to Eisenhower as the two generals ate a K-ration lunch somewhere near Coutances. From the start, Eisenhower loved the idea: "We must destroy the enemy rather than win territory. Now and not tomorrow." This was exactly what Bradley wanted to hear. Eisenhower immediately approved the short envelopment idea, and Bradley could not have been more pleased. "[Ike] was so enthusiastic about it that he returned to Twelfth Army Group with me to discuss the plan in greater detail with maps." Thus, by the end of the day on August 8, the Allies had a new primary objective—the complete and utter destruction of the German Army in Normandy.[14]

For Bradley's short envelopment plan to work, American forces at Mortain had to keep holding out. In a sense, Bradley was taking a calculated risk. Instead of throwing everything he had into Mortain, in reaction to the German attack, he was counting on the fact that the U.S. divisions at Mortain could hold the line while the rest of the Allied armies surrounded and annihilated the enemy in Normandy. This was a reasonable assumption. The Americans at Mortain had, after all, stymied the German attack within twenty-four hours; Avranches was now, in reality, just a pipe dream for the Germans. The best the enemy could now hope for at Mortain was to take Hill 314 and then somehow scrape together enough forces for another westward lunge.

At Hill 314, the Americans spent most of the night fending off a seemingly random series of German attacks. Lieutenant Weiss, fighting exhaustion, nearly lost track of how many fire missions he called in. "As each separate enemy onslaught crumbled, another took its place. They regrouped and returned, again and again." Each time, Lieutenant Weiss half-expected them to break through the American defenses and overrun the hill, but they didn't.

Still they kept coming. Elsewhere on Hill 314, Sergeant Luther Myers was sitting in a hole, perched over the trigger of a .30-caliber machine gun. For support, he had a rifle squad deployed in holes around him. Out of the inky blackness a German patrol attacked them with the suddenness of a lightning bolt. "The first thing we knew, they were throwing hand grenades at us. One of the grenades rolled under my gun before it went off."

The explosion jammed Myers's machine gun. As tracer rounds whizzed all over the place, he proceeded to fieldstrip the gun. As he did so, one of the riflemen, in a hole to the front, got hit in the elbow, yelped, and started to crawl back toward Myers and his foxhole. Myers repaired his gun and squeezed off several bursts, over the head of the wounded man, in the general vicinity of the Germans just beyond. "I could have got 'em all, but it wasn't worth it, not with my man crawling across my field of fire."

As the firing died down and the Americans tended to their wounded man, Sergeant Myers noticed a German soldier, roaming around, picking up weapons. "I shot him with an M1. I didn't even have to use the machine gun. I wasn't trying to stir up trouble. We weren't trying to win the battle so much as survive." Amazingly, the Americans held out. In the morning, they squinted at the quickly rising warm summer sun and prepared to deal with another day of isolation.

In Mortain, Lieutenant Colonel Hardaway and his command group—twenty-seven men in all—left their hiding place and tried to make it up Hill 314. The Germans cornered them and captured Hardaway and about twenty others. Only Lieutenant Guy Hagen and five other men escaped. These men rolled down an embankment and hid out in a ripe wheat field, right under the noses of the Germans. "They were digging all around us. We finally figured out it was an artillery area and they were digging in their guns between us and the hill." Hagen and his men had no choice but to stay put.

In the meantime, Lieutenant Pulver and the remnants of B Company tried to rescue the beleaguered, hungry defenders of Hill 314. The afternoon before, Colonel Birks had summoned Pulver and given him this mission: "I want you to pull your company out of line, fight your way through the enemy line . . . and deliver radio batteries and medicine."

Pulver was exhausted. He had not slept for forty-eight hours. As he listened to the colonel, he tried to focus, but he could not help but stagger a little. Another officer turned to Birks and said, "The man is exhausted, and so are all of his men. Their mission is just impossible."

Pulver felt the same way, but he said nothing. Colonel Birks just sighed and said, "We have to make a try. We can't lose half of the regiment."

Now Pulver and his people were even more exhausted, but they kept moving, nonetheless. They cautiously pressed east, hedgerow by hedgerow, all the way to Neufbourg, just west of Mortain. "On the way we ran into two large enemy patrols, but scattered both of them. In the process we lost three men. It took four hours to cover . . . 2.5 to 3 miles." At Neufbourg, they met up with a small reconnaissance group and some tankers. These men were happy to see B Company because they thought they had been sent to reinforce them, but Pulver quickly disabused them of that notion. "Are you kidding me?" their captain asked incredulously. "Come with me."

The two officers walked to an OP that offered a nice view of one of the roads that led to Hill 314. "My God, that road . . . was choked with German vehicles of all kinds! Through my binoculars I spotted at least 300 Germans. The place where Col. Birks had told me to break through was a sheer cliff. All other places that were accessible were crawling with enemy troops." Pulver knew his unit had no chance to break through to Kerley's isolated people on Hill 314. The B Company commander turned his company around. They went straight back to their original positions on Hill 285. The trek of not more than four miles took them all day and part of the night. The 2nd Battalion, 120th Infantry, was still very much isolated.

For these men, the battle was turning into a monotony of privation and terror. They had little idea of what was going on outside of the hill. They only knew that they were trapped and that they were not sure how much longer they could hold out. Lieutenant Weiss's radio batteries were still working. For that he was very thankful. By now, he had set up a new OP, gouged into a cliff, just behind the hill's eastern ridge. He and his men had scavenged small amounts of telephone wire and had strung the wire over small distances around the hill, setting up an impromptu network of OPs.

Weiss's day was just as busy as the previous two. All day long, he called down accurate artillery fire on the Germans as they tried to push their way onto or past Hill 314. Weiss would relay the necessary target information and coordinates to his radioman, who would then relay the information as briefly as he could and turn off the radio, so as to preserve the batteries. They shelled light tanks, bicycle troops, regular infantry, half-tracks, and even motorcycles. "The unending succession of fire missions squeezed a large dose of adrenaline into my system as I observed and adjusted shell bursts through the binoculars. The stream of activity, of shooting up enemy tanks, troops, guns, and vehicles . . . cut through the enveloping fatigue and masked it." As difficult as this situation was, Weiss felt good about his role. He knew he was making a major contribution to the survival of his comrades, and this filled him with a strange tinge of "excitement that buoyed my spirits."

Even so, he could not ignore his thirst or the pangs of hunger that emanated from his stomach. Three days before, Weiss and the others had gone up the hill with only two K-ration meals. The food supply was dwindling. "Five of us shared some bits of chocolate and one K ration, normally a single meal for one person."

Across the way, Private Street and the two other men in his position carefully divvied up a D-ration bar. These hard chocolate bars were designed to provide emergency nutrition in times of crisis, and this certainly qualified as a time of crisis. Soon they heard that there were raw vegetables in the fields of hillside farmers. Street and some other men went to investigate and found a cabbage field. "One of the soldiers kept watch while I gathered a cabbage, and then I kept watch while he did the same. That first bite of cabbage was about the most delicious taste I had ever experienced." Street also found a cistern from which he drew some "fairly greenish" water. They took turns going to the cistern, "running crouched low at full speed with bullets frequently snapping at our heels. The person whose turn it was would fill his and the others' canteens." They would then drop their purifying pills in their full canteens, "but this didn't help the taste."

Other soldiers were digging up raw carrots, radishes, or rutabagas. One infantryman, knowing Lieutenant Weiss's importance, gave him his prized rutabaga. "It was an act of special kindness for which I was grateful. I cut the thing into large chunks and slowly ate the moist, tasteless cellulose, filling some of the empty spots in my gut, but not relieving my hunger. I have never eaten another."

Brigadier General James Lewis, the division artillery commander, loaded up two of his spotting planes with radio batteries and medical supplies and told their pilots to drop their cargo over the hill. One of the Piper Cubs was shot down and the other nearly was. Neither of them got anywhere near the hill. Later the Air Force tried to drop supplies by C-47, but most of the cargo landed in German-controlled territory. Ingenious artillerymen even tried to fill large-caliber shells with medical supplies and batteries and fire the shells to Kerley's men, but this did not work, either. The impact of the shells landing on the ground destroyed almost all of the supplies. The desperate situation at Hill 314 continued.[15]

The only real way to relieve the suffering of the men on the hill was to get to them. Lieutenant Pulver's abortive attack had been little more than a failed supply run. It had no effect on the situation at Hill 314. Throughout the day on August 9, the Americans launched numerous attacks, all around the Mortain area, trying to regain some of the territory they had lost in the first hectic hours of Operation Luttich two days before and trying to fight their way to Hill 314.

Elements of the 2nd Armored Division were pushing north from Barenton toward Ger, a vital German supply point and crossroads, some three miles east of Hill 314. The 2nd Armored did not reach Ger. They were halted only a few miles away, but for the rest of the battle their leading tanks and half-tracks were like a dagger pointed at the German vitals. To the southwest of Mortain, the 35th Division had two regiments in action, slugging their way, slowly, bloodily and steadily up Route 177, but still several miles from Hill 314.

North of where the 35th was fighting, several task forces from the 3rd

Armored Division, in addition to infantrymen from the 30th and 4th Divisions, were doing their best to eliminate the deepest penetrations of the German advance, near such towns as le Mesnil-Tove, le Mesnil-Adelee, and Juvigny-le-Terte.

Slightly to the east of Le Mesnil-Tove, the 3rd Battalion, 119th Infantry, 30th Division, along with a 3rd Armored task force, was fighting the 2nd Panzer Division for patches of high ground. Whoever controlled this high ground controlled movement on the road that led east to St-Barthelmy and Mortain. The fighting here was similar to what had transpired in July—slow, costly fights for individual hedgerows or fields. The Germans had gone over to the defensive, something at which they excelled. Thus the American advance was slow and ponderous. The two sides battered each other with a constant stream of artillery shells.

Colonel William "Jug" Cornog, commander of the 3rd Armored Division's Task Force 2, was not pleased with the progress his unit was making. He was a huge man, massive in the shoulders and neck. Night and day, this West Point graduate lived with the constant worry that he and his task force would get the reputation of being "slow." He aimed to get his people moving, punch through the armored screen of the 2nd Panzer Division, and capture the high ground around Le Mesnil-Tove. Cornog's task force consisted of a battalion of armor, a battalion of armored infantry, some tank destroyers, and some engineers. He also had standard leg infantry from the 119th to support him.

Cornog summoned his commanders for an afternoon meeting, near the CP of Lieutenant Colonel Vincent Cockefair, commander of the task force's armored infantry battalion. The officers met in a shed that was nestled into an apple orchard. The shed was small, six feet by eight feet, with an open door and one window. It smelled and seemed like a chicken coop, but with artillery and small-arms fire buzzing everywhere Colonel Cornog figured it was an ideal meeting place. One by one, his officers showed up at the shed.

So did one of his platoon leaders, Sergeant Shelton Picard, of D Company, 33rd Armored Regiment. All Sergeant Picard knew was that Colonel Cornog wanted to see him. The tank sergeant had dismounted his Sherman and had run, through small-arms fire, several hundred yards to the shed. He reported to Cornog. "I was ordered by Col. Cornog to pull my tanks to the edge of a small community [probably le Mont Furgon] and to set everything on the site on fire, using white phosphorous ammo, and to destroy the church steeple, as we felt they were observing us from some high point." Indeed they were. The enemy artillery fire was not only copious; it was also accurate.

By the time Sergeant Picard left the shed, there were ten officers in and around the little building. One of them was Lieutenant Walter May, a mortar platoon leader in the 36th Armored Infantry Battalion. "We assembled just outside and alongside of the CP shed in a loose oval formation. I stood—and later hunched over—next to Colonel Cornog on his immediate left." Lieutenant Colonel Cockefair was to May's left, with two officers between them. "In general, things seemed normal considering the noise of combat around us."

Things were not normal. As May and the other officers conferred, a German artillery observer (possibly in the steeple that Sergeant Picard's tanks were about to destroy) spotted them. All at once, several enemy shells landed uncomfortably close to the shed. Lieutenant May noticed it immediately. "It seemed to shake the ground around us. All of us hunched down more under our helmets. There were no foxholes or anything else that could be called cover."

A round hit very close, no more than a dozen or so yards away. May thought the near miss called for a little levity: "If they come any closer, I'll think they are aiming at me!" Colonel Cornog, looking especially massive in this intimate setting, glared at him "with a humorless look that I've never forgotten." May felt like crawling under a rock.

On that note, Cornog dismissed them and began walking away. Then he turned around and came back, "as if to add something to the attack plan." The officers reassembled in and around the little shed. As they did so, an enemy artillery shell zoomed straight into the shed, right through the doorway, right through Lieutenant Colonel Cockefair, and exploded with a blinding red flash. In just that instant—a duration of no more than a snap of the finger—the shell brought death and dismemberment to much of the leadership of Task Force 2.

May, who was leaning against a wall, had the wind knocked out of him but was otherwise unhurt. Everyone else had been hit, and the shed was on fire. When May regained his senses, he opened his eyes and beheld a scene straight out of a slaughterhouse. "My first sight was of Lt. [James] Nixon as he just seemed to sit down and then lay back; what remained of his face and head turned ashen before my eyes." Most of the frontal bones of Nixon's head were gone, but somehow his brain was still functioning. Cockefair was obliterated, dismembered. "My attention then turned to Colonel Cornog. He was upright, left arm dangling half loping . . . in the direction of his CP. I ran after him, reaching him as he fell to the ground. I could see he was in very bad shape so I gave him a shot of morphine. As I did so, Colonel Cornog looked at me with a look that is so hard to describe but that I've never forgotten."

The colonel's eyes bored into May's. "Don't leave me," he said.

"I won't," May replied.

The lieutenant grabbed a pressure bandage from Colonel Cornog's first-aid kit and "stuffed it in the massive hole in his left shoulder. When that wasn't enough, I used mine also. That seemed to help. He also took a hit above his right hip and chest. By some miracle a jeep came by." May immediately commandeered it and ordered the frightened driver to help him put Cornog in the jeep.

With this accomplished, they took off for the aid station. When they got there, May and several medics managed to pick the big colonel up and put him on a stretcher. Captain William Cohen, the task force medical officer, was working on a wounded man but paused long enough to come over and see if he could save the colonel's life. Cohen knelt beside Cornog and went to work. "His right arm was off and the wound extended into the shoulder and right side and he was in shock." In spite of his grave condition, Cornog asked how Cockefair and the others were doing. "I told him that they were being taken care of. His axillary artery was pulsating, but severed and not bleeding and he was being given plasma."

There was little that Dr. Cohen could do. Cornog died in a matter of minutes. The medics turned to Lieutenant May and asked him if he was hit. "I said no. But I never figured out why (I've pondered this all my life)." May glanced at his hands. "[They] were covered with the Colonel's blood and there was much on my uniform. At the aide [*sic*] station they had me lay down on a stretcher for a time." The young lieutenant lay there and wept. Later, when he returned to his platoon, he tried to chase away the awful sights of the day by eating a K ration that consisted of pinkish-colored pimento cheese (typical for the lunch K ration). "I almost threw up. The color was not unlike my hands and uniform and what I had just survived."

Dr. Cohen visited the shed the next day. It had nearly burned to the ground, and the fire had consumed Cockefair's body. All he found of Cockefair was his pelvis, "and it was no larger than a child's. We identified him by his wallet, which escaped the fire." Lieutenant Nixon hung on for a short time but died, faceless, in a field hospital. Needless to say, Task Force 2, leaderless and battered, made no headway in its attack.[16]

Half a mile to the southeast, near St-Barthélmy, the Americans were pushing for an objective they called Road Junction 278 or, for short, RJ 278. The 3rd Armored Division's Task Force 3, under Lieutenant Colonel Samuel Hogan, was at the spearhead of this attack. Sergeant Emmett Tripp, a tank commander in G Company, 33rd Armored Regiment, had an extremely important job. "I had to lead the attack . . . because I commanded the only operational tank dozer in the battalion. We had learned that we should never attack down a road. The Germans always had them zeroed in or mined. Instead [we] would attack through the hedgerows."

On the afternoon of August 9, Tripp's dozer tank was in the lead. He and his crew were looking to punch through the hedgerow in front of them and create a pathway for the rest of G Company. "It seemed as if we initially surprised the Germans. We first came across some infantry in the hedgerows and sunken roads, eliminating them fairly quickly. Then we came up against

at least one Tiger tank, accompanied by Panthers and several Mark IV's."
Soon, he heard the booming sound of the main guns on the German tanks.
"They quickly knocked out four tanks in G Company. I think they were
from the 1st platoon. The platoon sergeant . . . had both of his legs blown
off." This man got captured by the Germans but later bled to death. During
the battle, Tripp was completely focused on his job. He had no idea that several German rounds barely missed his tank. "I didn't even know they were
shooting at me."

Not far away from Tripp and G Comany, First Lieutenant Harvey Patterson and his artillery observation team were crouched in a half-track, calling down shells on the German armor. Patterson was hollering orders to his
radioman, calling for fire from his own 391st Armored Field Artillery Battalion and any other artillery unit he could contact. "We fired continuously. I
could see the Germans and hear them talking. They were so close that once
I was denied permission to fire, which meant they were closer than 50 yards
from my location. Many times the tanks would move off of the roads and I
would go over to them on foot with a portable radio and an assistant. We
would get with the tank commanders, identify the targets they wanted and
call the halftrack, who forwarded our call for fire to the guns."

To the southeast, closer to St-Barthélmy, the 12th Infantry Regiment
(4th Division) was fighting for the same objective. All three of the regiment's
battalions were on the line, trying to push east, toward RJ 278 and St-
Barthelmy, but progressing very little. In the 3rd Battalion sector, Corporal
Alton Pearson's L Company squad was spread out in attack formation, trotting across a field. Around them they heard only eerie silence. The squad
made it safely to the cover of a hedgerow and paused. Pearson was eager to
keep going. Back in England, before the invasion, he had trained very hard
to assault Utah beach, only to break his ankle while running on an obstacle
course. He was devastated. He had wanted so badly to make the invasion
with his buddies. At first, he tried to hide the injury, but he couldn't put any
weight on the ankle. His company officers sent him to the medics and he
spent several weeks recuperating while his comrades went to France.

Now he was determined to lead his squad aggressively. In one motion,
he stood and scrambled over the hedgerow. "I went across . . . without being
fired on." He made it all the way to the next hedgerow. As he did so, he told
his men to come over to him. "Three of them started across and the Germans
opened up. Two of them were shot, but one of the wounded made it up to
the hedgerow along with the unwounded one. There we were, three of us
along on one side of the hedgerow and only God knows how many Germans
on the other. I had to figure out something fast."

Pearson looked around and saw that there was another hedgerow, "running 90 degrees from where we were, back to where the rest of our men

were." The only problem was that this hedgerow had a fifty-foot gap with no cover. He told the other two men that they would ease up to the gap, fire all their weapons to pin the Germans down, and then run fast back to their men. Pearson and the unwounded man made it, but the wounded soldier never even moved. Pearson was so full of adrenaline that he did not even notice this until he had made it to safety.

Someone had to get that wounded man. "I told the medics to go get him. As the first medic stepped across the hedgerow, he was shot in the leg and had to drag himself back to safety. I was really suffering, seeing that brave boy dying out there." In his heart, Corporal Pearson knew what he had to do. He glanced at one of his buddies, Sergeant Charlie Leech, "one of the bravest men I ever knew."

Leech looked at Pearson. "What are you going to do?"

Pearson sighed. "I wouldn't want my brother left out there. I'll go get him if someone will help me carry him."

"I will go with you," Sergeant Leech said.

Hoping to travel lighter (and be mistaken for medics), the two men discarded their ammunition and helmets. At last, they were ready to go. Neither of them knew if they would be alive in the next minute. They could only hope to survive. "God be with us," Pearson intoned.

With that, they shoved off. "All firing stopped until we got him back. [He] was shot several times through the chest and white as a sheet. I prayed for him and turned him over to the medics. I'll never know whether he lived or not. I don't know what came over me, but I didn't feel that I would be killed. If I had, I probably would not have gone. I wasn't brave. I just had trust in God." The fighting raged all day, but the 12th Infantry got almost nowhere.[17]

At Hill 314, the Germans were mounting yet another assault. Lieutenant Weiss saw a convoy of several trucks drive straight up the Bel Air Road—it went west to east, right over the hill, and was defended by a hard-pressed but stolid roadblock—and come to a stop several hundred yards from the American roadblock. All of this was happening in broad daylight, under a radiant sun. "Hordes of infantry in gray-green uniforms poured out of the vehicles and quickly formed a skirmish line stretching across the road and into the adjacent fields and behind hedgerows."

Weiss and his team knew exactly what to do. They cranked up their radio and called for a fire mission. "Infantry forming skirmish line," Weiss said, and relayed the proper coordinates. The officer at the fire direction center utilized every battery he could get. In mere moments, six batteries of 105mm howitzer and a battalion of 155s belched forth hundreds of shells.

"The powerful impact of all those guns firing together scattered the enemy infantry and bruised them badly."

The overwhelming barrage broke up the infantry assault, but the Germans responded with artillery fire of their own, "this time from a large gun someplace to the east. The frightful boom of its exploding shells was alien, full of evil and of such immensity that it shivered the rock and dirt beneath us." Luckily, the fire eventually slackened.

As the day wore on, the men on Hill 314 saw German vehicles, sometimes crammed with wounded, heading east. Things got quiet for a time, but then at 1800 the Germans tried a new tactic. From the vicinity of the German lines, west of Hill 314, two German soldiers, white flag in hand, strode toward the Americans. They spoke with Lieutenant Elmer Rohmiller, one of Lieutenant Kerley's platoon leaders. With great formality, and in good English, one told Rohmiller he was an SS officer who had come to offer honorable terms of surrender. The German officer said he personally admired the stand the Americans were making, but further resistance would be foolish, as the situation was clearly hopeless for the GIs. If the Americans listened to reason, he said, their wounded would be well cared for. If the Americans did not surrender, then as of 2000 hours the GIs would be "blown to bits."

Rohmiller wanted to tell the SS man to go to hell but figured he'd better let the German speak with someone in overall command. He blindfolded the Germans and led them to Lieutenants Kerley and Erichson (Erichson had seniority over Kerley, but it was hard for one man to exercise complete command and control on Hill 314). The SS officer looked at these two officers and saluted. "I have come to request your surrender . . . and to offer you and your men safe escort off this hill. You realize, of course, that your position here is hopeless."

There were still several wounded men lying around the CP and they could overhear what was being said. "Don't surrender!" many of them yelled.

"As you hear," Erichson said, "my men are prepared to argue that one."

The German was unruffled. "They are fools; you are not. As their commander it is your duty—"

"I'm aware of my duty," Erichson interrupted. "Do you have anything more to say?"

"Only this. If you do not surrender by 2000 hours today, your battalion will be annihilated."

Kerley broke in and, in unequivocal language, rejected the surrender ultimatum in language that was, in his words, "short, to the point, and very unprintable."

The Germans left. After darkness, the Americans braced themselves for an all-out enemy assault on Hill 314. At his little fire direction center,

Lieutenant Weiss arranged for a ring of artillery fire to plaster every possible avenue of attack. "In the darkness, we hunched down nervously below the crest, listened to the explosions of our own, unrelenting artillery. Nobody spoke. Nobody needed to. We all knew that in the black of the night we would make our stand."

Weiss gripped his carbine and waited for the onslaught of waves of infantry, but nothing happened. Tense moment after tense moment, then tense hour after tense hour passed, and still no attack. Finally, in the middle of the night, they heard something. A tank was coming, closer and closer, past the Bel Air roadblock, finally stopping just fifty yards away from the crest of the ridge under which Weiss and so many others were hiding. Terrified, they squirmed lower in their hiding places. The enemy tank fired a few rounds over their heads. Then the turret popped open; a helmeted German emerged and shouted, "Surrender or die!"

Curious to see what would happen next, Weiss stared over the ridge. "The tank commander hesitated. Rifles took aim, ready to fire. Then one man threw down his gun, ran up the slope and climbed onto the tank. The rest of us stood fast and held our breaths. No one else surrendered. And no one died, either. The turret slammed angrily shut like a hammer on an anvil. The tank backed and drove off. A lone prisoner clung to the side."

The rest of the Americans were still holding out at Hill 314.[18]

The next day, August 10, they continued to do so, as their comrades to the west fought hard to get to them. All along the front, the Americans were slowly pushing east, toward Mortain, toward St-Barthelmy, and toward Hill 314. Their progress was steady but unspectacular.

At RJ 278, Hogan's task force was once again on the attack. Hogan planned to assault the objective with a blend of four companies—two infantry (F and G of the 119th Infantry) and two armor (G and H of the 33rd Armor). Once again, Sergeant Tripp's dozer tank led the way. His tank inched down a small lane until Tripp found a suitable spot to punch through a hedgerow. He had no idea where the Germans were, but he knew they were dug in and camouflaged all over the area. For all he knew, when he rammed through this hedgerow he might be headed right into the muzzle of a *Panzerfaust*. He glanced back and saw a line of eight H Company tanks, packed together on the lane, behind his dozer tank. In the tank immediately behind Tripp's, Lieutenant Edmund Wray, H Company's commanding officer, looked nervous and apprehensive. Tripp had spoken with him before shoving off, and the lieutenant seemed to have little confidence in today's attack.

Now Tripp turned back to the task at hand. He ordered his driver to punch through the hedgerow. "I broke open a hole in the hedgerow and moved over to the right side, backing up against the hedges." Wray's tank crunched through the opening and kept going for about fifty yards, "when it was hit by a hidden German. For some reason the Germans did not shoot at me, perhaps their gun could not traverse to where my tank was parked." Actually, Wray's tank had been hit by a *Panzerfaust*. Tripp watched as the tank burned. He knew that if he did not act quickly, his Sherman might be next. He ordered his driver to back out of the field. They made it to safety, but Tripp's eighteen-year-old loader went berserk with combat fatigue. "I supposed that the sight of LT Wray's tank exploding unnerved him. He was evacuated and I never saw him again."

In the meantime, Lieutenant Wray and his crew were in deep trouble. Lieutenant Edward Arn, a platoon leader in F Company, 119th Infantry, was watching the whole ghastly scene unfold from the relative safety of the hedgerow. He and his men saw Wray roll out of the turret and drop "to his hands and knees beside the tank. [He] was terribly burned. He pulled himself to his feet and started back toward the hedgerow. It seemed as if he remembered something because he went back to the tank and tried to pull somebody else out. He helped get another man out and they both started to run, but the Jerries cut them down with a burst of machine-gun fire."

Enraged, Lieutenant Arn and his infantryman watched as a small group of SS soldiers emerged from cover and began to cluster around Wray's destroyed Sherman. The enemy soldiers foolishly began searching the Sherman for souvenirs, right under the muzzles of Arn's men. At the right moment, Arn ordered his people to open fire. In a few grim seconds, their bullets tore through the SS scavengers, killing or wounding almost all of them. "We let 'em have it. Mowed them down."

The American attack had barely started, but it was already headed for failure. After seeing what had happened to Wray's tanks, the other H Company Sherman crews stayed put. The little country lane, bordered on either side by hedgerows, was packed with U.S. tanks and half-tracks. In one of those half-tracks, Lieutenant Harvey Patterson's forward observer team was biding its time. "Our driver moved us back out of sight and parked the half-track behind a tall hedgerow," Corporal Charles Corbin, Patterson's radioman, recalled. By no means was this spot safe, because the lane was under enemy fire. "Some of the German AT rounds passed so close to our vehicle that I swear I could feel the heat generated by their passing."

One of the rounds scored a direct hit on a nearby tank. "[It] went up in flames and a tanker was having trouble getting out. Another tanker jumped on the tank and tried to help but was hit by a bullet. Then a shell beheaded the tanker. At this point we bailed out of the halftrack."

Close by, Lieutenant Patterson was crouching next to a Sherman, talking to the tank's commander, who was standing upright in his turret. The commander told Patterson that he had just graduated from West Point. "He . . . was saying that combat was just like what he had read about in books. He was pretty excited by the whole prospect. I was looking right at him when he was shot in the forehead by a sniper."

What Corbin and Patterson had just witnessed—besides the deaths of fellow Americans—was the first moments of an enemy counterattack. Three German tanks and dozens of SS infantrymen were trying to send Hogan's force into retreat. The Americans responded with machine-gun and artillery fire. Corbin was clutching a tommy gun, peeking over the hedgerow, trying to see something to shoot at. Standing next to him were a couple of F Company infantry soldiers. "An artillery shell landed behind me. I looked around and noticed that both of the infantrymen next to me had been severely wounded." Corbin's half-track driver, John Manual, had also been hit. Corbin helped him to his feet and took him to an aid station.

When Corbin returned, he saw Lieutenant Patterson crouched over the two wounded infantrymen. "I waved for him to come back but he waved for me to come to him." Patterson was doing everything he could to save the lives of these two men. It took him several moments to realize that he was in enemy gun sights. "I looked up and noticed several Germans looking over a hedgerow at me. I decided to pay no attention to the Germans and gave the wounded Americans some morphine." At this point, he saw Corbin waving to him. "I asked [him] to bring up our half track. Corbin did so and the two men, under fire, strapped the wounded men on either fender, and drove them to the safety of an aid station. As they did so, the enemy counterattack petered out and the situation at RJ 278, once again, settled into stalemate.[19]

In spite of the deadlock at RJ 278, the Americans had fought their way to within about a mile of Hill 314 by the end of the day on August 10. The 35th Division, augmented by armor from the 737th Tank Battalion, was closing in on the hill from the south. To the west, the Americans were close to recapturing St-Barthélmy; Springfield's group was still holding out at L'Abbaye Blanche; other units were inching their way east, toward Mortain itself. To make matters worse for the Germans, the 2nd Armored Division was still only a few miles south of Ger, threatening the underbelly of the whole enemy position around Hill 314 and in the Mortain area.

By the early-morning hours of August 11, even Hitler understood that it was time to withdraw. The Canadians were fighting a bitter, bloody battle north of Falaise, but their efforts threatened the whole northeast flank of the German armies in Normandy. Haislip's XV Corps had begun to carry out Bradley's vision of the short envelopment. Haislip had taken Le Mans and his formations were turning north for Alençon. Von Kluge knew that these two powerful pincers threatened to close on the Germans like a pair of steel jaws. If the Germans did not do something soon to forestall the closing of this trap, von Kluge knew they would suffer a devastating, irreparable defeat. How could the Germans renew a push for Avranches to the west when their supply lines in the east were nowhere near secure? Besides, there were nowhere near enough tanks to renew the attack (the Germans had already lost about 60 percent of their armor, and they could not begin to replace these losses with new tanks). So Hitler reluctantly acceded to von Kluge's wishes for an orderly withdrawal from Mortain.

The men atop Hill 314 had no idea that the Germans were about to withdraw, but they did notice, in the light of day on August 11, that German vehicles were now retreating eastward along the roads that flanked Hill 314. Rumors of relief swept through the ranks like wildfire, from thirsty mouth to thirsty mouth, all over the hill. "We're going to be relieved by noon," men told one another. They were wrong. The rumor had been sparked not just by the sight of retreating German vehicles but also by "hunger, raw indignation, visions of food and lunch," Lieutenant Weiss opined. "But no relief and no lunch came into our lives that day." Instead, the Germans continued to pound the hill with artillery, mortars, and even small-arms fire. Weiss called in more fire missions. He and the others had little choice but to hold on and hope for help. They had no idea that the battle had turned decisively in U.S. favor. "We could see no end. Our radio batteries had grown very weak. When they gave out, our principal means of defense would be lost."

The Germans were putting as much pressure on Hill 314 as they could, but they were being battered by American units from nearly every direction. Three miles to the north of Hill 314, atop a nameless hill that afforded a panoramic view of the German retreat, Corporal Robert Baldridge of the 9th Division's 34th Field Artillery was digging a slit trench for his artillery observation team. His leader, Lieutenant Donald Harrison, was peering into a BC scope while another man crouched near a radio, plotting enemy positions on a map.

After a few minutes, Lieutenant Harrison, a ROTC graduate of Ohio State University, turned to Corporal Baldridge and told him to get on the radio. Harrison had found a target. Baldridge stopped digging and turned the radio on. Harrison relayed the necessary information for a fire mission against German vehicles moving at an intersection just north of Hill 314. As Baldridge spoke into his radio, he kept his eyes on the target. "The first shot exploded only a hundred yards above the target. Harrison had me radio 'Down two hundred' in order to make sure he got a bracket, which is standard artillery procedure. The second round did come in somewhat below the intersection, so a bracket was obtained with only two shots which is good shooting." The shells pounded the enemy vehicles until they dropped out of sight in a cloud of smoke and dust.

At Hill 314, Lieutenant Kerley had a better view of the destruction caused by the proficiency of observers like Lieutenant Harrison. "The burning enemy columns could be seen for miles in all directions. The slaughter continued all day."[20]

Indeed it did. All over the Mortain area, the Americans attacked and took heavy losses and the Germans slowly retreated. Even so, the enemy was still holding in front of Hill 314. By nightfall, American troops had made it to the outskirts of Mortain, but it was clear to the American commanders that the men on the hill would not be relieved on this day. Could they keep holding out, or would the Germans—excruciating prospect though it may be— overwhelm them, kill them, capture them, destroy them, at this late stage, after more than five days of isolation?

That night, at 2150, Lieutenant Weiss's team turned on their radio long enough to send a carefully considered, sober message to the fire direction center: "Without reinforcements, can hold till tomorrow. Request message be sent to highest headquarters available." Within an hour, the message went all the way to General Hobbs, who knew that American forces were poised for a quick push to Hill 314 in the morning. "Reinforcements on the way. Hold out. Hobbs." Weiss never got the message. His radio, running dangerously low on battery power, could transmit but not receive.

In the darkness, the defenders of Hill 314 sank low in their holes and tried to remain resilient. They were past the point of exhaustion now, past the point of hunger, thirst, or desperation. They had absorbed 40 percent casualties. Some of the wounded had died for lack of proper care. Others were barely clinging to life. They would survive or they wouldn't—many could not even summon the energy to care which way things turned out. Most of the "unscathed" were as scared as they could be. The tension of the last several days had begun to take its toll.

At his rocky little OP, Lieutenant Weiss heard the awful sound of enemy tanks roaring up the Bel Air Road, straight at the American roadblock. With the incredible resolve that had carried them this far, the lieutenant and his men prepared yet another fire mission.

Not far away, Private Street and his two buddies were terrified at the sound of the tanks. One of Street's buddies, a man named Charlie, could no longer contain his fear: "They're coming to get us. They're gonna get us!"

Private Street was stunned that Charlie had come unhinged. "He was an ebullient, voluble person, much inclined to talk of his exploits and to put notches on his rifle for Germans he had shot, and a good man in a tight spot, as he had demonstrated, but he had come to the end."

Street was just as frightened by the sound of the tanks, but he did not know if Charlie was right about the Germans closing in for the kill. "So I just held him tightly in my arms until he calmed down. It began to sound as though the tanks were moving away from us, toward the east."

Street was right. The German tanks were retreating east. Lieutenant Weiss called down accurate artillery fire on them. "Exploding shells and jagged chunks of steel beat down mercilessly and destroyed German tanks, troops and vehicles, creating a junkyard collection of military iron along the way."

Weiss, Street, and the others hung on until the morning. As the sun rose, Lieutenant Weiss woke from a wispy, restless sleep in his little foxhole. He and his primary assistant, Sergeant John Corn, had shared this dusty, smelly hole for the last several days. Weiss summoned the energy to raise himself out of the foxhole, dust himself off, maneuver past Corn, and walk forty yards to the ridge. He peered through his binoculars and studied the Bel Air Road, looking for targets. As he did so, a shell landed back near his foxhole. Two of Weiss's men were shaken but unhurt. The same could not be said of Sergeant Corn. "I think I've been hit," he cried in a thin voice.

"Lieutenant, Corn's been hit," one of the men called to Weiss.

Weiss ran back to the foxhole that he and Corn had shared. "If I had been there, it would have taken my head off." Weiss bent over and examined his wounded sergeant. "Fragments of steel from the exploding shell had torn into Corn's right leg above the knee, almost severing it. His body was bleeding in many places. Unable to move, he lay calmly in the foxhole and seemed quite aware of what had happened to him. He exhibited no pain, no anguish."

They put a tourniquet on his leg and gave him some first aid. With the help of several riflemen, they moved Sergeant Corn several yards away, to a safer spot. He was bleeding badly and, without proper medical care, his prognosis was not good. Weiss knew he could do nothing more for his sergeant, so he returned to the task of calling in fire missions. As he did so, he sent several quick, desperate messages asking for medical care, but to no avail. "Corn's strength ebbed with each flying second, and death moved closer."

As the day grew ever warmer, Weiss took off his helmet and wiped sweat from his brow. His face was haggard, with several days' growth of moist, gritty beard. He was worn-out and frustrated. "Inside me, hate, rage and grief ran together in a stream of violence. I wanted a power that I did not have. I wanted to smash with a giant fist the tanks, trucks, troops that I saw now running away." The best he could do was call down more fire on them. None of that was any help to Sergeant Corn, though. By 0945, he was dead.

As Corn lived his final moments, American troops were closing in on Hill 314. The Germans had spent the night retreating, and now they offered only rearguard, sniper-type resistance to the American rescuers. Just before noon, a group of scouts, led by Lieutenant Homer Kurtz from G Company, 320th Infantry, 35th Division, made contact with Lieutenant Ronal Woody on Hill 314. "A guy came up to me and asked for our company commander," Woody remembered. "Hell, I had my insignia pinned inside my lapel and I looked like a ragamuffin." Woody told him that he was the company commander.

"We're relieving you, sir," the 35th Division scout said.

Woody smiled. "Allll-rrright!"

Elsewhere, Private Street and his two companions saw soldiers moving through the woods below their parapet position. At first they tensed and pointed their rifles, until they saw that the troops were Americans. "We got up from behind our parapet . . . and walked down the hill." They talked and shook hands with their rescuers and, for the first time, took in the devastation that was Hill 314. "We formed up and moved out onto [a] road, dirty exhausted; and incredibly on that road were cameramen, ambulances, where until a few moments before anything that moved would have [mct] only menace. We moved on down the road to an area where we got food and could wash and rest and finally relax a bit." Street and his two buddies were incredibly lucky. Their unit, F Company, 120th Infantry, suffered nearly 100 percent casualties. Only eight men escaped death, wounds, or captivity.

The 35th Division's quartermaster company loaded a truck full of food, water, and medical supplies and sent it up the hill. Ambulances followed closely behind the supply truck. Woody and his men loaded the wounded aboard the truck or the ambulances, and they were soon on their way to an aid station. The 35th Division soldiers shared their K rations with the survivors of Hill 314. Private First Class Leo Temkin was no fan of K rations, but after what he had been through, anything would have been welcome. "Funny thing. They tasted good."

Lieutenant Weiss's group did not get relieved until the early afternoon when soldiers from the 119th Infantry made contact with them. Weiss and his two surviving men were too weary to be overjoyed. They gathered up their radios and equipment and walked to the jeep they had parked several days before. "I flopped into my seat, exhausted, all strength and emotion wrung out. We drove somberly back to B Battery, each of us wrapped in his own thoughts. We had lost something, left it behind on the hill."

Weiss said it perfectly. Approximately seven hundred men served on Hill 314. Only 357 were able to walk off. The rest were killed, wounded, captured, or missing. In six days of fighting, the 30th Division suffered more than 1,800 casualties. The other American divisions that were involved in the battle suffered many thousands more. The Germans lost probably twice as many men and certainly many more tanks and vehicles than the Americans.[21]

The relief of Hill 314 ended the Battle of Mortain. The victory was not, in the final analysis, the result of airpower or Ultra intelligence. Nor was it even the result of firepower, even though U.S. artillery was, of course, vital. More than anything, the victory resulted from the stubborn resolve and fighting prowess of the American ground combat soldier. Time and again, these Americans fought ferociously when they were outgunned, outnumbered, and on the short end of the firepower equation—St-Barthelmy, L'Abbaye Blanche, Hill 285, and especially Hill 314 serve as evidence for that assertion. The incredible stand of the 30th Division, combined with the strong performance of the other major American units at Mortain, endures as overwhelming testimony to the myth of German tactical superiority at the small-unit level in World War II. The Americans were, in general, better soldiers, and they proved it time and again in Normandy. Mortain was just one more example. At Mortain, in the first forty-eight hours, the Germans had most every advantage, yet their offensive went almost nowhere, thanks to small groups of hard-pressed scared but courageous American soldiers. The Americans used plenty of firepower in this battle, but none of it would have mattered if the individual soldiers had not fought as well as they did.

In the wake of their failed offensive at Mortain, the Germans no longer had any chance for victory at Normandy (or, for that matter, on the Western Front). The question now was whether they could escape annihilation. The moment had finally come for Bradley to spring his trap, for the great steel jaws of the Allied beast to devour the enemy once and for all.

CHAPTER FOURTEEN

THE END AT NORMANDY

At the height of the Mortain battle, General Bradley hosted Henry Morgenthau, President Roosevelt's influential secretary of the treasury. More than twenty-four hours had passed since Bradley had devised his short envelopment plan. Now the general was in an excited, perhaps even giddy, mood as he briefed Morgenthau on the situation in Normandy. The two men stood in front of Bradley's elaborate situation map. As Morgenthau listened closely, Bradley gave him an extensive briefing. Bradley swept a hand over the map and pointed to the multicolored symbols that represented units of both sides. The Germans, he explained, were about to be encircled and crushed: "This is an opportunity that comes to a commander not more than once in a century. We're about to destroy an entire hostile army."

Morgenthau said nothing in response. The general glanced at the secretary and saw that he looked skeptical, so Bradley pointed to the German bulge at Mortain and said, "If the other fellow will only press his attack here at Mortain for another forty-eight hours, he'll give us time to close at Argentan and there completely destroy him. And when he loses his Seventh Army in this bag, he'll have nothing left with which to oppose us. We'll go all the way from here to the German border."

In the space of a few seconds of conversation General Bradley had just summed up his entire vision for the way he hoped to end the Battle of Normandy and maybe the war, too.[1]

By the afternoon hours of August 12, the situation was unfolding exactly as Bradley had envisioned. Instead of withdrawing east, the Germans had spent several days unsuccessfully pushing west at Mortain. Now they were in real

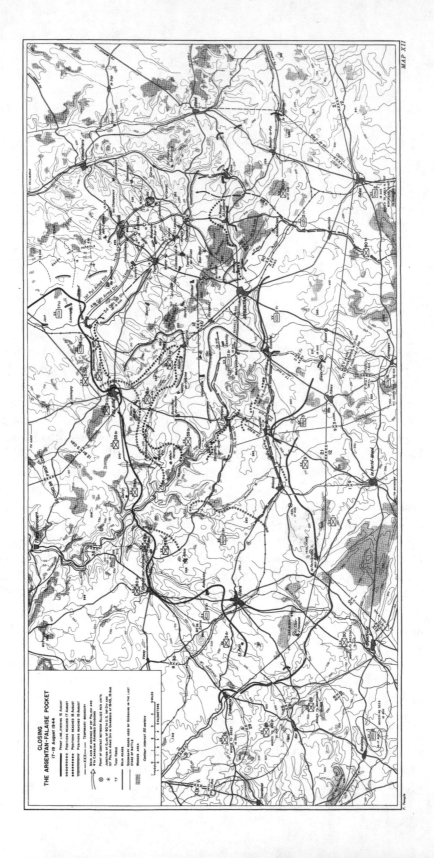

MAP XII

CLOSING

THE ARGENTAN-FALAISE POCKET

17-19 August 1944

peril of being trapped in a kind of terrestrial Bermuda triangle from Mortain in the west to Argentan due east and Falaise some fifteen miles to the north. For hundreds of miles around that triangle Allied units were attacking, putting pressure on the Germans inside their steadily shrinking pocket. The decisive blows—Bradley thought of them as steel jaws—were materializing in the east, of course. The Canadians, in their Operation Totalize, were pushing south for Falaise, in a slow, bloody, step-by-step battle that was reminiscent of the fighting around Caen in late June.

To the south, the other steel jaw was closing with much more alacrity. Even as the 30th Division fought its desperate battle around Mortain, General Haislip's XV Corps had dashed through Alençon and Sees. Now, on August 12, Haislip's corps was within a few miles of Argentan, the main American objective in this pincer operation.

In his corps, Haislip had the 79th Division (of Cherbourg fame), the 90th, the 5th Armored, and a unique formation, the French 2nd Armored Division. The French unit was equipped with American tanks, weapons, and uniforms. The division commander, Major General Jacques Leclerc, was a charismatic Gaullist leader who had led this same unit in North Africa. The name Leclerc was actually a pseudonym to protect his family during the years of German occupation. Predictably, Leclerc and his soldiers were burning with the fever of liberation. They badly wanted to throw the Germans out of Paris. They fought with élan but little regard for discipline or cooperation with the American units in the XV Corps.

For most of the day on August 12, the biggest obstacle in taking Argentan was not the Germans but the Forêt d'Ecouves, a wooded area about five miles south of Argentan. Haislip expected the Germans to defend the forest, so he decided to bypass on either side. The French were supposed to slide past it in the west, while the 5th Armored Division, commanded by Major General Lunsford Oliver, did the same thing in the east. But Leclerc, in his exuberance, disregarded this order. His division was split into three combat commands. He sent one of them west of the forest, another straight through it, and a third one to the east, on the roads that Haislip had reserved for the 5th Armored Division.

As it turned out, the Germans were not defending the Forêt d'Ecouves with any serious forces. The vehicles of Leclerc's easternmost combat command became enmeshed with fueling trucks from the 5th Armored Division, creating a monumental tense traffic jam that postponed the Argentan attack for roughly five hours. The American trucks were trying to move north to refuel Oliver's gas-thirsty armor. Not until well into the evening did military policemen finally unsnarl this avoidable traffic jam. By that time, retreating units from the enemy's 116th, 2nd, and 1st SS Panzer Divisions were in Argentan. They placed their artillery and tanks on high ground north of town and prevented the Allied units from taking Argentan (a French patrol did briefly enter the town, only to be thrown out by enemy tanks).[2]

Still, Haislip was confident that his men could take Argentan within the next twenty-four hours. He also believed his armor could make it to Falaise, the Canadian objective some eighteen miles to the north. When he reported this optimistic forecast to General Patton, his immediate superior, Patton told him to "push on slowly" in the direction of Falaise "until you contact our Allies."

Now, as the final moments of August 12 ticked away, Patton picked up the phone at his CP in Laval and called Bradley. He reported to Bradley what Haislip had told him and expressed his intention to keep going north (Haislip even had some patrols roaming around several miles to the northeast of Argentan).

But the Bradley of this evening was a very different man from the ebullient, swashbuckling soul who had briefed Morgenthau only a couple days before. Tonight Bradley was in a cautious, worried mood. His intelligence people were reporting that the Germans were preparing a counterattack against Haislip's left flank. Bradley had ordered General Collins and his VII Corps to swing east and plug the gap that existed to Haislip's left, but Collins had not yet completed this movement. The XV Corps, in that light, looked quite vulnerable. Bradley believed that nineteen potent enemy divisions were "stampeding east" toward Haislip's strung-out units. To the north, the Canadians were still six miles shy of Falaise. In all likelihood, they would need at least two or three more days to take Falaise. If Haislip took Argentan and kept going north, he would cross the inter-Allied army boundary, risking attacks from friendly fighters, artillery, or ground troops. Bradley wondered if it really made sense to keep Haislip's small units moving north, right into the guns of the British and Canadians. Even if the XV Corps made it to Falaise, Haislip had nowhere near enough troops to seal off the roads between Falaise and Argentan. The Germans would punch right through them, maybe even destroy Oliver's or Leclerc's armored divisions entirely. Even in a best-case scenario, if Haislip took and held Falaise, thus sealing the Germans in a trap, how would the British and Canadians view this audacious move? No doubt they would be deeply insulted; relations might be forever poisoned. To make matters worse, Bradley believed that Allied planes had dropped time-delay bombs all over the pocket, perhaps even within Haislip's route of advance. The envelopment plan seemed to be unraveling before his very eyes.

In Bradley's mind, all of these factors pointed to one inescapable course of action: Haislip must be halted at Argentan. As Bradley later put it, "I much preferred a solid shoulder at Argentan to the possibility of a broken neck at Falaise." Now, late in the evening on August 12, he clenched the phone in his hand and listened to the nasal, high-pitched voice of Patton as he lobbied for permission to keep advancing north. The more the exuberant Patton talked, the more irritated Bradley became. In truth, Bradley had never really liked Patton. He resented Patton in the detached way that mediocre, sensible types envy talented risk takers who always seem to find acclaim, no matter what chances they take and no matter what kind of impetuousness they display. Tonight Bradley was already angry at Patton for letting his troops venture across the inter-Allied boundary, thus risking attacks from British aircraft. In Bradley's view, Patton had "knowingly and willfully violated an Allied agreement."

Patton finished his report with a false claim: "We now have elements in Argentan. Shall we continue and drive the British into the sea for another Dunkirk?"

Of all the stupid things Bradley had heard Patton utter (and there were many), this might have topped the list. Bradley felt anger welling up inside of him. His voice was tight and cold: "Nothing doing. You're not to go beyond Argentan. Just stop where you are and build up on that shoulder." He closed with a warning about the impending German counterattack on Haislip. The British later found out about Patton's flippant remark and, understandably, were not pleased.

Now, at Laval, as Patton hung up the phone, he was stunned. He could not believe that Bradley had just ordered him to give up on the potential encirclement of an entire enemy army. For the next several hours he and his staff repeatedly lobbied Bradley to change the order, but to no avail (however, official historian Martin Blumenson believed that Bradley might have grudgingly agreed to a small advance to Argentan, only to change his mind). Omar Bradley had just made, in the view of George Patton and many historians, one of the most fateful, and foolish, decisions of the war.

Bradley's halt order has been heavily recounted and ruminated upon in the decades since the Battle of Normandy, so it need not be dwelt upon here. Indeed, the debate among historians over his decision has spawned countless books and articles. There are really only two major questions to consider: Was Bradley's basis for his decision sound? Did his decision cost the Allies a total victory in Normandy? The answer to both questions is a qualified no.

Bradley claimed, at various times, to have made the decision because of several considerations: the potential clash of friendly forces at Falaise, the possibility that American troops would run into the time bombs sown by Allied planes, inter-Allied relations, a lack of authority to send Haislip forward, and the very serious question of whether or not Haislip's thinly scattered forces, upon making it to Falaise, could actually hold the Germans in the pocket (recall that Bradley thought that the remnants of nineteen enemy divisions were "stampeding east").

Only the last consideration held any merit. Haislip's soldiers would have had a difficult time holding the Germans. Most likely they would have suffered heavy casualties and the Germans would have overwhelmed some, but not all, of their roadblocks.

None of Bradley's other justifications holds any weight. The time-delay bombs had twelve-hour fuses. Most had been dropped several days before. They would not have been a serious factor in any XV Corps advance on Falaise. Bradley had plenty of authority to go north; he was on a co-equal footing with Montgomery and could easily have consulted with him for some sort of mutual agreement. Failing that, Bradley could have taken his case to Eisenhower if he had felt strongly enough about closing the pocket.

Bradley's concern for a clash of friendly forces at Falaise revealed one of his greatest weaknesses—narrow-mindedness. After the war he wrote that "any head-on juncture becomes a dangerous and uncontrollable maneuver unless each of the advancing forces is halted by prearranged plan on a terrain objective. To have driven pell-mell into Montgomery's line of advance could easily have resulted in a disastrous error in recognition." Of course it could have. Bradley's deep concern for this friendly fire problem was laudable (although one wonders where this solicitude was the previous month during Cobra). But in carrying out his envelopment plan what did he expect? If the Germans were to be encircled and annihilated, then at some point Americans and Canadians had to join hands. One must ask why Bradley did not anticipate this or even plan for this. If he was worried about a clash of friendly forces, he should have planned for them to overlap—perhaps sent Haislip to a point east of Falaise while the Canadians fought for that town. It was as if Bradley, in theory, liked his envelopment plan but could not summon the will to carry it out in practice.

To his credit, he took full responsibility for the halt order amid the furious postwar debate, but to his discredit, he could not refrain from laying some of the blame on Montgomery, "for his failure to close [the] gap on time." Certainly Montgomery deserved some of the opprobrium. He had selected inexperienced Canadians and Poles for the attack on Falaise, and when they encountered problems he failed to reinforce them with seasoned British troops who might have helped capture the objective sooner. But that should not have mattered in the least. When it became clear that Monty was having trouble taking his objective and Bradley was not, Bradley could have kept his troops moving north; he could then have taken care of any friendly fire concerns, bruised egos, or command arrangements. The fact that he took none of these actions suggested that he did not truly believe in his bold encirclement plan.

In any case, the debate over his halt decision is a bit overblown. Even if Bradley had given the go-ahead to Haislip, it would not have meant, in some sort of magical way, a war-ending victory for the Allies in Normandy. Haislip, as previously mentioned, would have had a tough time keeping the Germans bottled up. Historian Carlo D'Este expressed this well when he wrote that "the ability of Haislip's XV Corps to keep the gap closed . . . was at best suspect. Despite crushing Allied superiority, the Germans in the pocket were still a dangerous fighting force." Beyond that, the Allies, when all was said and done, did end up winning a great victory at Normandy, in spite of (or because of, depending on one's point of view) Bradley's halt order. "The Argentan-Falaise gap was simply never the great tactical blunder that some armchair strategists claimed," D'Este cogently wrote.[3]

As Haislip's forces halted south of Argentan, other American troops, all over the expanse of the pocket, kept the pressure on the Germans between August 13 and 15. A few miles west of Tinchebray, Lieutenant Charles Curley and his platoon were in the middle of a pea soup fog. Curley and his men, from E Company, 38th Infantry, were part of the 2nd Division's push against the western edges of the pocket. Curley's orders were to secure a crossroads near La Paillot. He and his men, barely able to see one another, stumbled through the fog. Around them they heard only silence during an advance that took them through several empty fields. Soon three Sherman tanks joined them.

Curley, by now, had lost visual contact with the rest of his company. Still he kept going. "We moved on ahead, skirting the wet soil . . . and without meeting any enemy, reached a sunken road. We started through a gap in the hedge across the road and had moved out in the field when a burst of automatic fire made us hit the ground." The fog was finally starting to lift a bit. Curley looked around and saw a German aid station, complete with a Red Cross flag, in a field to the right. He and his men held their fire and tried to get their bearings. Curley pinpointed his platoon's location, radioed his company commander, and relayed the coordinates. His commanding officer told Curley he was not reading his map properly. According to the captain, the spot where Curley claimed to be was under German control. "As if I didn't know that," Curley said.

A command car, loaded with enemy wounded, drove toward them on the sunken road. Curley saw the wounded and told his platoon to hold fire. "I had to really yell at the bazooka team to keep them from firing." The car stopped next to the American position and Curley spoke to the German passengers. "After a short parley, I put two men in charge and headed the car back across the field to our rear."

Later another car, full of enemy soldiers with more hostile intent, appeared on the road. Curley watched as they hopped out and set up a mortar somewhere near a large tree. In seconds mortar shells started raining down on his platoon. One of the American tanks started firing at the tree, "hoping the burst would knock out the mortar. No such luck. The shells kept coming in. I saw Sergeant English, one of my squad leaders, who was standing beside one of the tanks, fall to the ground."

Curley leaped to his feet and ran to Sergeant English, only to find him dead, "with blood on his back." As Curley examined his dead sergeant, he realized someone from the rear was shooting at him. Spent bullets were chewing up the grass around him. Curley whirled around and saw a small cluster of buildings 300 yards to the rear. The firing must be coming from there. He picked up the EE-8 phone on the tank and asked the commander to pour some fire into the buildings. The tanks fired a few rounds until Curley received an angry call from his company commander, telling him the shells had nearly hit the rest of the company, which was engaged in a firefight somewhere near the buildings.

Curley put his field glasses to his eyes and studied the buildings. As he did so, the tank commander, a spectacularly unlucky man, unbuttoned his turret hatch "and stuck his head out just as a mortar shell hit on the rim of his turret. He was killed instantly and his body fell back into the tank. In seconds the tank roared into life, tracks started to turn, and the tank spun around, heading to the rear. The other two tanks followed immediately. I think that when the platoon commander fell into the tank, with a part of his head blown off, the crew panicked and took off."

Curley now had no more tank support, but his platoon was close to La Paillot crossroads. The captain called and told Curley that at 1400 artillery was going to lay a barrage on the crossroads. Because Curley's platoon was so close to La Paillot, he urged him to call off the fire mission. "He again said that I couldn't be where I was reporting to be because that position was behind the German lines." Frustrated and angry, Curley signed off and moved his men back to a sunken road and told them to dig in. He figured they were far enough from the objective that they would be safe from friendly artillery. He was wrong. "Right on schedule the artillery battalion let loose and the shells came over. I hit the ditch on our side of the road. One of my sergeants piled in on top of me. Explosions went off all around us." A hunk of shrapnel tore into the sergeant's back. Curley got on his radio and called the captain. "I was screaming . . . for them to cease fire."

The firing stopped. The sergeant and a few other men were wounded, but luckily, none of the wounds were serious. Even so, Lieutenant Curley was reaching the boiling point. "I was one hot and upset individual."

The platoon stayed in this spot until darkness, when the rest of the company joined them. The captain saw Curley, greeted him, and said, "Damn, you are where you said you were after all!" Curley wanted to explode. All day long, he had suffered needless casualties, partially because the command group had not believed his position reports. He stared at the captain a moment and then turned away. "I was so mad that I just sat down and broke out crying right in front of my men. I remember that my men crowded around me. A couple of them had their arms around my shoulder telling me to forget it, that everything was all right, and let's just show them the rest of the way to our objective."

They did so and spent the night in close proximity to the Germans, even capturing the remnants of an enemy company. The next day they headed for Tinchebray and met up with the British.[4]

To the south of the 2nd Division, four infantry divisions, plus elements of the 2nd Armored Division, were pushing north and east, through Ger, Domfront (defended by a ragged battalion of drunken Germans who were more than ready to surrender), and Flers. In general, the toughest enemy resistance was to the east of Domfront, where Collins's VII Corps was protecting the flank of the XV Corps and, at the same time, pushing north.

One of Collins's best units, the 9th Division, was trying to cut every east–west road that ran between Domfront and Argentan. Sergeant Max Dach's 47th Infantry Regiment was pushing for Beauvain. Dach, a squad leader by now, had been fighting since North Africa. "When we made an attack 2 scouts would go first. The Germans would let us come a few yards and then shoot at us. They had a big tank with them." All day long, they tried to flank the attack, but to no avail. "At dark the platoon Sgt. said we had to make a night attack." The sergeant asked his squad leaders to draw straws to see who would lead the attack. Much to his relief, Dach was lucky and drew a long straw. For several days now he had been suffering from a terrible case of dysentery. "I couldn't control my bowles [sic], had it in my pants, shorts stunk, no change of clothes, no bath for 3 days. It was bad."

Just as the attack was about to jump off, something fortunate happened. "C company by accident dropped a 60 millimeter mortar shell on the German tank. That was the end of the Germans. They withdrew, which was good for us." Dach and the other Americans advanced to the Domfront–Argentan road. "We set up a road block there, hoping to trap a lot of Germans, which we did." In spite of the dysentery, Dach stayed at the front. Several days went by before he felt better.[5]

Just east of the 9th Division, General Doyle Hickey's Combat Command A of the 3rd Armored Division rolled twenty miles north from Mayenne. "Crowds of cheering French civilians stood in the brilliant sunshine to throw flowers and offer cognac to dust-begrimed tankers," one officer recalled. "There was no artillery fire and the sky belonged to the veering Thunderbolts."

The joyride soon ended when Hickey's tanks, split up into separate task forces, ran into German defenses at Couptrain and Javron, on the southern shoulder of the pocket. The battle was really a struggle for a series of key crossroads and intersections between Couptrain in the south, Ranes in the center, and Fromental in the north. If the Americans could capture Fromental, they could deprive the Germans of a vital escape route along the Domfront–Argentan road (N-24).

The fighting was so intense that tanks sometimes battled one another at point-blank range. The roads were littered with burning Shermans and Panthers alike. The sickening smell of burning flesh, hair, and steel wafted through the air. At one point, Hickey's Task Force X was cut off in the vicinity of Ranes. They held out against tanks from the 1st and 9th SS Panzer Divisions. The enemy, though, was more interested in delaying the Americans than slaughtering them. Gradually, the SS divisions withdrew north, easing the encirclement of Task Force X. Even so, the Germans fought a stubborn delaying action. "Jerry assault guns and artillery contested every inch of the route," a 3rd Armored Division soldier remembered, "screaming meemies howled into division forward positions and the whiplash slam of 88's broke through a constant fabric of small arms." Not until August 17 did the Americans liberate Fromental, and by then it had lost much of its significance, since most of the German Army had retreated to the east.[6]

As all of this played out, the high command on both sides made important decisions. On the morning of August 13, Bradley listened to an intelligence briefing, based on Ultra, that convinced him that much of the German Army had escaped through the Falaise-Argentan gap. "This news was a shattering disappointment—one of my greatest of the war." The general believed that a golden opportunity had been lost, not because of his halt order but because of Montgomery's failure to take Falaise. Be that as it may, Bradley now had to decide what to do next. After some discussion with his staff, he decided on the following course of action: "We would continue to close the Falaise Gap, although this now seemed less important; and we would mount a second, larger, encirclement to the northeast, hoping to catch the bulk of the escaped German divisions before they reached the Seine."

Patton, who had chafed at the stop order the night before, loved this idea. Truthfully, he liked anything that meant swift, slashing advances over enormous swaths of terrain. He told Haislip to detach two divisions, the 79th and the 5th Armored, plus his corps headquarters, and dash east, to Dreux and Nogent-le-Roi on the Eure River, not far from the Seine. Three other units, the 80th Infantry Division, the 90th, and the French 2nd Armored, were to remain in place and keep up steady pressure on the southern edges of the German pocket near Argentan.

All of this meant, in essence, that Bradley was going back to his original concept of a long envelopment at the Seine. There was, of course, a fine line between flexibility and indecisiveness. Bradley felt he was demonstrating the former; he thought he was simply reacting to the developing situation. Unfortunately, the intelligence upon which he and Patton made these decisions was, as Bradley later put it, "egregiously wrong. We still had it within our power to close the trap, but we did not know it."

Unbelievably, the Germans, as of August 15, had not even made a final decision on whether to evacuate the pocket. Hitler for several days had been clinging to the vain hope that his army in Normandy could regroup, attack Haislip's left flank, and stagger the American advance. By August 15, with the remnants of Hitler's armies absorbing terrific punishment all over the pocket (both from the ground and the air), a counterattack was out of the question. To make matters worse, the Allies on that day successfully invaded southern France. Two giant pincers, one from the north, the other from the south, now threatened the continued existence of every German soldier in France. On this day ("the worst of my life," Hitler later called it), he finally had to authorize an all-out retreat from Normandy.

Von Kluge and Hitler's other generals in Normandy had already been moving their forces east, amid tremendous adversity. By August 16, when Hitler's order finally arrived, they began an all-out effort to escape east, out of the pocket, across the Orne and Dives Rivers (and eventually to the Seine). "Had we known this," Bradley wrote, "had we not been misled by intelligence . . . we would have held Haislip solidly in place on the Argentan shoulder and most likely would have sent Walker [commander of XX Corps] directly north on Haislip's right flank toward Chambois, to help close the gap. With Collins, Haislip and Walker forming a solid eleven-division east–west front along the southern edge of the pocket . . . we would probably have trapped most of the German force inside the pocket. But this falls into the nebulous and pointless 'what if' category of history."[7]

Le Bourg-St-Léonard was a little village located six miles east of Argentan and three miles southwest of Chambois. The village was nestled into the edge of a stand of woods and at the crest of a ridge that formed the watershed between the Orne and the Dives. The commanding terrain around Le Bourg-St-Léonard offered excellent observation of the Dives River valley, the very place where the German 7th Army, unbeknownst to Bradley, planned to escape Normandy. On the afternoon of August 16, at this previously anonymous burg, the Americans got their first indication that plenty of enemy troops still remained in the Falaise pocket. In a ferocious effort to escape the pocket, German armor and infantry attacked a 90th Division roadblock at Le Bourg-St-Léonard. "Tanks battled furiously throughout the encounter, tank destroyers waded into the fight with guns blazing . . . and the artillery blasted away with everything it had," the division historian wrote. The Americans initially retreated but returned in the evening to re-capture the village. The fighting in this area, though, was only beginning.

The concerted, organized way in which the Germans attacked at Le Bourg-St-Léonard set off alarm bells among the senior Allied commanders and their intelligence officers. Clearly the bulk of the enemy army was still in the pocket, desperately trying to find an avenue of escape. There might still be a chance to cut them off. General Montgomery was the first to recognize this. On the sixteenth, with the fighting still raging at Le Bourg-St-Léonard, he picked up the phone and called Bradley. Monty's forces had finally cap-tured Falaise that very day, but in terms of bringing off the encirclement, Falaise hardly mattered any more. Most of the Germans were now east of Falaise, fleeing through a six-mile gap that generally stretched from Trun in the north to Chambois in the south. So the British general proposed that the two Allied armies effect a linkup at Chambois.

As General Bradley listened to the proposal, he winced and clutched the phone, not because he disagreed with Montgomery's linkup plan but be-cause he knew that he himself had made a bad decision three days earlier when he sent much of Patton's XV Corps east to Dreux. "Monty's proposal could not have come at a more inopportune time. It was too late to turn Pat-ton around. Haislip, Walker, and Cook—in some of the most astonishing wide-open sweeps of the entire war—had already reached Dreux, Chartres, and Orleans." This was great, but it meant that Bradley did not have much left with which to close the pocket at Chambois. "The best I could promise was to disengage Gerow's provisional corps at Argentan and send it to Cham-bois." When Haislip took much of his corps to the east, he had left behind a provisional corps (80th, 90th Divisions and the French 2nd Armored). Bradley mentioned that Gerow was in command of this provisional corps, but in actuality, Major General Hugh Gaffey, Patton's chief of staff, thought he was in charge. It took nearly a day for the senior officers to sort out this con-fusing command melodrama, and that delayed the attack at Chambois.

Now, as Bradley stood and held the phone, he promised to do whatever he could to link up with Monty's forces and close the pocket. "I agree with you, sir," Bradley said, "we ought to go northeast" to Chambois and cut off the Germans. The two men bid good-bye to each other and hung up. For several hours thereafter Bradley was wracked with doubts about the deci-sions he had made over the course of the previous days. "I had privately sworn never to over-rely, tactically, on Ultra. And yet I had. Because of that mistake, I had imprudently sent Haislip, Walker and Cook [who commanded the newly activated XII Corps] far to the northeast. Had I not been so im-petuous, Haislip and Walker—and if necessary Cook—would have been available to close the jaws at Chambois and annihilate the Germans in the pocket. What I now had available—Gerow's makeshift corps—was not a proper response to the job I had been asked to do."

Bradley was correct that Gerow's three divisions were not enough to close the pocket, but he also knew that, in war, commanders rarely have all the resources they need. Adequate or not, Gerow's forces would have to do the job.[8]

As a preliminary to the operation, General Gerow wanted le-Bourg-St-Leonard. The town comprised an ideal jump-off point, and its location on a prominent ridge made it a perfect place for artillery observers. All day long on August 17, the Germans and Americans had struggled for control of the town. Around midnight on August 18, troops from the 90th Division infiltrated the village and secured the very positions Gerow craved. Under the able leadership of General Raymond McLain, the 90th had come a long way since its difficult days in June and July. At that time, the division was the most ineffective (and certainly the most poorly led) in the U.S. Army in Normandy. Now, in taking the lead role in closing the American side of the pocket, it was in the process of proving itself as one of the strongest U.S. units.

As the day dawned bright and sunny on August 18, the Tough 'Ombres (as the 90th Division men had nicknamed themselves) sought to ram the final nail in the coffin of the German Army in Normandy. All three of the 90th's infantry regiments, plus the attached 712th Tank Battalion, were in action between Le Bourg-St-Léonard and Chambois. They manned blocking positions, swarmed through fields, took prisoners, secured villages, and absorbed dozens of enemy attacks of varying strength and intensity.

Somewhere near Fougy, a tiny hamlet half a mile north of Le Bourg-St-Léonard, Private Jack Prince was leading his outfit, L Company, 359th Infantry. His job as first scout was to advance, along with another man (today it was his buddy Dugo, a Mexican-American man from Los Angeles), and find the enemy. Scouts were the eyes and ears of an infantry company. They were the most observant soldiers, sometimes the most independent. They were also expendable, because their job was so dangerous.

This morning, as Prince and Dugo led their company over the flat terrain near Fougy, they kept their eyes forward, trying to see the enemy before they saw them. All at once, they saw a man about forty yards ahead. Prince knew at once that the man was a German officer. Instead of opening fire, Prince and Dugo decided to make an attempt to capture the enemy officer. "*Hände hoch!*" they screamed, almost in unison. The man flinched and, in a swift motion, pointed his burp gun at the two American scouts. "He unloaded his machine pistol at us," Prince recalled. "I pulled Dugo down into a ditch and fired at the Nazi until he gave up."

The German officer dropped his burp gun, removed his helmet, and came forward with his hands on his head. As Private Prince took him to the rear, he tried to start a conversation. "Thinking I could open him up, I offered him a cigarette. Our officer called me a damned fool and said, 'Five minutes ago he was trying to kill you and now you buddy up to him.' Prince responded with a weak grin. "It was true."[9]

No more than two hundred yards away, the situation was far more tense. Sergeant Henry Williams—newly promoted—was behind the trigger of a .30-caliber machine-gun. The gun was resting on top of a small hedgerow, at the edge of a wheat field that some farmer had recently harvested. Williams had come to Normandy as a private, but now he was a sergeant, in charge of a machine-gun squad from M Company, 359th. He did not like this wheat-field position one bit, but some officer had told him to put his guns here and that was that. They had not even had time to dig in.

As Williams and the men watched in fascinated horror, a German tank—Williams claimed it was a Tiger, but it was probably a Panther—rolled into the wheat field and headed straight for them. The sound of the tank's engine was menacing, like the growl of an angry predator. Sergeant Williams turned and said to his men, "Don't shoot. Let him get through the hedgerow. Behind us is a tank destroyer and they will take care of it. Get as low as you can; cover yourselves as much as you can so you won't be seen."

The men eagerly complied. Williams looked around for a good place to take shelter. All he could find was a shallow depression to the side of the hedgerow, not far from the German tank. "I flattened out. The tank kept coming closer and closer. When the long barrel of the gun was over me I started shaking. When the front of the tank rose up on the bank of dirt I was like a snake; I slid out from under it. Then it stopped. I just knew I was dead. If I moved the tanker would kill me. If I stayed the tank destroyer would knock it out . . . and that would get me. I just didn't know what to do and yet I had to do something." Sergeant Williams started sliding on his back, away from the German tank. He wanted to jump up and run, but that was out of the question. When he had covered about twenty feet, he heard "something that sounded like thunder. I shook all over." The American tank destroyer had scored a direct hit on the German tank, setting it on fire. "I rolled over and on my knees was . . . trying to put as much distance between me and the tank as I possibly could. By this time, the ammo inside the tank was exploding. What a noise! The black smoke looked like a house on fire. None of our men were hurt. The ones in the tank never came out."[10]

A mile to the west, along a two-lane sunken country road, troops from the 2nd Battalion, 358th Infantry Regiment, were making a push for Bon Menil, a crossroads village located almost exactly halfway between Argentan and Chambois. Captain Arnold Brown, the self-made Kentuckian whose eighth-grade education had not prevented him from earning a commission and leading a rifle company, was urging his men forward. "A mortar round exploded nearby, and I felt something jerking my trousers below my knee. I jumped in a hole until the mortar barrage lifted." When the barrage ended and he left the hole, Captain Brown soon realized that he had been hit. "Uh-oh," he thought to himself. He looked at his leg and saw a piece of steel sticking out of it, just below the knee, right above his leggings. "It didn't hit the bone." He took out his first-aid kit and began to dress the wound. "The first thing I did was to sprinkle sulfa powder around the wounded area. I left [the fragment] in and put a bandage around it. Then I took my sulfa tablets and drank half a canteen of water."

Brown found his executive officer, briefed him, and headed back to the aid station. As he did so, he encountered a wounded man from his company who had a shredded hand. Brown and the other soldier started walking together. "We had to cross an open field to get back to the aid station, and whenever we got into the field, a German machine gun opened up on us. So we ducked down in this ditch." They lay there for a while and tried to get up. When they did, the German machine gun opened fire again. They settled down and waited longer. Eventually, G Company forced the German machine gunners to retreat, and the firing stopped. The two Americans made it safely to the aid station. Brown's Battle of Normandy was over.[11]

One of the most influential and inspirational figures that day for the 90th Division was General William Weaver, the man who had masterminded the brilliant seizure of Mayenne a little over a week ago. As the fighting raged, Weaver roamed around in his jeep, talking to his men, looking for ways to maximize pressure on the Germans, and sniffing around for action. Lieutenant Colonel Frank Norris, commander of the 345th Field Artillery Battalion, was at his unit's OP at Le Bourg-St-Léonard ridge when he noticed Weaver's jeep drive up and screech to a halt. "I greeted him happily and showed him what we were doing. You *had* to like, admire and respect Wild Bill as a fighting man, for that is what he was. Wild Bill was simply a personal example of combat leadership in action."

Norris led General Weaver on an impromptu tour of the 345th's positions. The guns boomed around them. "Suddenly, a loud, vigorous fire fight with lots of rifle, MG, and mortar fire broke out down the slope" about 1,000 yards away." Upon hearing the shooting, Weaver was no longer interested in having a conversation. He looked at Norris and said, "It sounds like they can use me down there."

With that, he took off down the hill. "My God, what a fighter!" Lieutenant Colonel Norris thought.

Just then, Weaver's radio operator sidled up to Norris, watched his general descend the hill, and said to Norris, "You know, Colonel, the only difference between me and that old bastard is that he intends to get himself killed in this war, and I don't."

General Weaver ended up in the middle of the firefight he had heard. He was soon in a house that was surrounded by German tanks on one side and Americans on the other. Weaver directed a successful defense of the house, and the American tanks repelled this German counterattack.

Meanwhile, Norris returned to the job of providing fire support for the infantry units that were pushing for Chambois. Norris's artillerymen were firing so many rounds that their tubes were on the verge of overheating. The ridge at Le Bourg-St-Léonard was an ideal observation point that yielded a perfect view of the whole valley through which the Germans were trying to escape. "Continuous artillery fire fell as the routed Germans tried first one road after another in full view of the OP. Most roads were blocked either by our own infantry or by knocked-out tanks, vehicles, and artillery. German columns out of touch with the situation would frequently drive right into our lines, and many sharp clashes resulted. Tank destroyers, adjusted by our own battalion observers . . . fired point blank at the bewildered Panzers."

Overhead, artillery liaison pilots in Piper Cubs had a panoramic view of the whole battlefield. The Allies had complete command of the air, so the little Cubs had nothing to fear from the enemy except for ground fire. These little planes flew over the whole valley and their pilots radioed precise, accurate target information to Norris's batteries, as well as those of many other artillery units in the area. "It is genuinely difficult to exaggerate the importance of these little Cub planes to our artillery. They provided unequaled capabilities in the discovery of worthy targets and the direct observation of the fire thereon. From a technical standpoint, these little planes permitted us to register fires accurately on all key points throughout the depth of the battlefield and then, by use of our excellent weather data, we could make the necessary adjustments to deliver precise, devastating fire, day or night, on any target within range." The Cub pilots today were logging fifteen hours in the air. Norris had nothing but admiration for them. He figured that they enhanced the effectiveness of his guns by as much as 40 percent.

The Germans were in the middle of a cauldron. One American officer, describing their predicament, said that they were in the equivalent of a "large funnel . . . about 40 miles high by about 16 miles wide at the top, [which now] came down to about a 2-mile opening at the bottom." Every inch of that opening was under Allied fire of every variety.

On a hill outside of Le Bourg-St-Léonard, Colonel Robert Bacon, commanding officer of the 359th, watched as swarms of Germans pressed east. He listened as his artillery observers called down fire from as many as fifteen separate batteries. "The Germans were so frantic and we had such a grip on the situation that the coordinates for the artillery remained unchanged. The

Germans kept blundering along the same routes; they began to disperse into the fields as we had hoped, and the artillery and air forces began to pour it into them with deadly effect. The boys . . . who were able to observe the damage just cheered and cheered as horses, cart trucks, German Volkswagens, soldiers, tanks, and weapons of all description went flying into the air, or disintegrated in flashes of smoke."

Several hundred yards east of Colonel Bacon, Sergeant Morse Johnson, a tank commander in A Company, 712th Tank Battalion, was guarding an easterly road. During a lull in the battle, he dismounted from his tank, sat against an apple tree, took out pen and paper, and jotted a short note to his mother: "The trapped Nazis have made several attempts to break out. There is the constant din of artillery, the drone of a reconnaissance plane, several trucks every five minutes going up with infantry or returning with prisoners, the ubiquitous jeeps, an occasional ambulance, some tank destroyers, a hot sun with thick, white clouds." A few minutes later, Johnson walked to the edge of a steep cliff that overlooked the valley where much of the fighting was going on. He put his binoculars to his eyes and took in an amazing scene. "There . . . unfolded perhaps as big a section of the trap the Germans were then in as could be seen at one time. [I] watched a convoy of Nazi trucks head down a road, come to the top of a rise and be utterly demolished."[12]

Some Germans were surrendering as quickly as they could; others were fighting savagely. Two miles west of where the 90th Division was pushing its way north into the southern belly of the German pocket, the 80th Division was encountering far too many Germans who wished to fight rather than surrender. The division's assignment was to flank Argentan on the right, capture the city, and cut off the roads leading out of that town. As French tankers provided fire support and protected the left flank, the 80th Division's 318th Infantry attacked on August 18.

About twenty-five hundred Germans, equipped with tanks, artillery, self-propelled guns, and automatic weapons, were dug in along high ground north of Argentan. Colonel Harry McHugh, the commander of the 318th, knew that this attack would be difficult for his green unit. "This was our first real fight." He had wanted to attack farther to the right, so as to outflank the German ridgeline defenses, but this movement would take him into the 90th Division's sector and he was forbidden to do so. "This annoyed me extremely as there was a gap of three miles between my unit and troops of the 90th Infantry Division."

So, instead, his regiment attacked through open terrain, right under the guns of the Germans. "The Germans . . . commanded a beautiful field of fire. I had difficulty in getting the men to move forward. I literally had to kick the men from the ground in order to get the attack started. To encourage the men I crossed the road without any cover and showed them a way across. I received no fire from the enemy, and it was a big boost to the men." They made it through Urou, an eastern suburb of Argentan, and kept going. "A tank, 400 yards to our front, started firing on us and I called up some bazookas to stalk him. However, the men opened fire at the tank from too great a range and the tank merely moved to another position. I walked up and down the road about three times, finding crossing for my troops. We advanced about 100 yards across the road, then the Germans opened up with what seemed like all the bullets and artillery in the world." McHugh brought his tanks up, but one by one, the Germans picked them off, setting them on fire, cooking the crewmen inside. The 318th's attack went no farther. McHugh pulled back and called in artillery on the Germans. Not until August 20 did the 80th Division pierce the German-held ridge and take Argentan.[13]

Meanwhile, as evening approached on August 18, the fighting to the east tapered off somewhat. The 90th Division had cut many roads, but it was still a mile short of Chambois. To the north, the Canadians had taken Trun and they were pushing south. The Poles, meanwhile, were advancing on Chambois from the north. A small gap, maybe a mile or two at the most, still existed between the two Allied armies. Some lucky Germans had escaped, but most were still trapped in the pocket, hoping to slip away during the night.

On the eastern flank of the 90th Division, crews from the 712th Tank Battalion set up roadblocks, along with their infantry brothers, and some tank destroyers. Periodically, during the night, German vehicles or troops bumped into the roadblocks, provoking sharp, brief engagements. At one of the roadblocks, Private Sam Cropanese, an A Company gunner, heard the sound of German tanks approaching. Over the radio, he heard officers ordering all the crews to wait until the enemy tanks got close enough to see. "[We] let the tanks get real close. The German tanks . . . were trying to break through our lines. All of a sudden all hell broke out." The air was full of the booming of main guns on American and German tanks. The flashes of the guns lit up the night like lightning. "[We] had every road covered, and . . . blasted the hell out of those tanks, caught 'em like crazy. What a beating they got. They were hit from all over. They didn't know where the firing was coming from. We took in a lot of prisoners there."

The shooting died down and, for the rest of the night, Cropanese and his crew heard the sound of a wounded cow moaning. They could also hear Germans moving somewhere out in the foliage. The driver, Eddie Pilz, spoke German, and he kept yelling at the Germans to surrender. Pilz and the loader, Private First Class Joe Bernardino, son of an Italian emigrant, were both very nervous. Their nervous tension soon degenerated into irritation with each other. Pilz bitched at Bernardino for biting his nails. Bernardino cussed him out. The two stopped speaking to each other. The more Private First Class Bernardino thought about this spat, the worse he felt about it. He resolved to apologize in the morning. He never got the chance.

In the morning, on August 19, the firefights grew more intense as the Germans became more desperate under the glare of daylight. During one attack on A Company's roadblock, a German armored vehicle (the crew was never sure what kind) scored a direct hit on the frontal armor of their Sherman. A hunk of shrapnel slashed through Pilz's throat, killing him instantly. Bernardino was right behind him. "I got shrapnel all over the whole left side of me, but I was all right. Sammy [Cropanese] got his jaw blown off." The tank commander got blown out of the turret, but he was OK. The shell continued right through the Sherman, went out the back, and killed two infantrymen who were making coffee behind the tank.

Cropanese hardly knew what had hit him. He spun around and fell to the ground. "I heard crying and moaning [from the mortally wounded infantrymen]. I'll tell you, I wouldn't want to hear that again. Medics got to me. The left side of my lip was hanging down. My nose was split open. A piece of my nose is still missing. A piece of shrapnel about an inch and a half hit me. It ripped me wide open, went in through the jaw, busted the jaw, and it stayed right in the bottom of the jaw, just missing the jugular vein." The medic sewed his lip back in place. Within a few hours, a jeep came up and evacuated Cropanese and the other wounded to a hospital in Le Mans.

Doctors operated on Cropanese and wired his jaw shut. After the operation, he was lying on a stretcher, half-conscious, struggling to live. His head was bandaged, his face was swollen, and it had a yellow pallor. All at once, he saw Joe Bernardino standing nearby and tried to call out to him. "Joe," he called weakly through his wired jaw.

Bernardino heard him, came over, looked down, and shuddered. Cropanese was such an awful, ghastly sight that at first he did not even recognize him. "Do you know me?" Bernardino asked. Before Cropanese could reply, Bernardino took a closer look. "Holy Jesus, is that you, Sam?"

"Yes, yes, it's me."

Bernardino felt absolutely terrible for not recognizing his friend. He had a lump in his throat. He stood there, not quite knowing what to say. "Ohhh, I knew that was you," he lied. "I just pretended I didn't recognize you."

The two wounded men settled in and talked about what had happened to their tank. More than anything, they were both just happy to be alive.[14]

In the meantime, the 90th Division was making an all-out push for Chambois and a linkup with the Poles. Lieutenant Jim Gifford, a platoon leader in C Company, 712th Tank Battalion, was preparing his platoon to move out.

He was standing on the top of a hill, somewhere on the eastern edge of the pocket, looking through binoculars at the valley below. "I'm looking down in the valley in the early sun and I see all these little sparkles . . . all over the valley." Gifford looked more intently at the sparkles, wondering just what they were. "It was thousands of bayonets flashing in the early morning sun. [German infantry] were walking toward us . . . about three miles away up that valley, and they're dispersed among . . . tanks moving along."

Stunned, Gifford lowered his binoculars and let out an involuntary gasp: "Holy shit!" He ran back to his tank, got on the radio, and told his superiors what he had just seen.

Many other pairs of American eyes were trained on the host of retreating Germans. Artillery observers, on the ground and in the air, saw them, as did forward air controllers. Within a few minutes, Lieutenant Gifford heard the humming of fighter engines. "Thunderbolts were flying in towards them, at treetop level, those guys were our saviors. They came flying in one group after another. They were knocking the shit out of them."

In one of those fighters, Captain Bill Dunn was in a steep dive, bearing down on a road that was choked with German troops, wagons, vehicles, and tanks. He waited until the right moment and opened up with everything in his plane's considerable arsenal. "It was like shooting fish in a barrel. The roads were absolutely jammed with enemy transport vehicles and tanks, all of which we methodically destroyed."

Dunn and the other pilots emptied their guns and flew away, leaving behind a funeral pyre of burning flesh, exploding ammunition, screaming horses, and screaming men.

On the ground, the 712th, in addition to artillery and tank destroyers, added to the nightmare for the Germans. Gifford's platoon pumped shell after shell into the valley. "They were catching bloody hell. We were firing at them from a mile or two away. We were blasting away at 'em. We were hitting everything." Still the enemy survivors kept moving inexorably along the roads, heading east, always to the east. Gifford and his men did the best they could to stop them. "You could fire at anything. You wanted to shoot a tank, you could shoot a tank. It was a slaughter, and most guys were shooting without even looking. There was so much equipment, for miles it was burning all over the place, and these guys were coming out waving flags and other papers." Hundreds of these surrendering enemy soldiers streamed past Gifford's tanks.

At St-Eugenie, where the 1st Battalion, 358th Infantry, was in blocking positions, several hundred Germans decided they had had enough of this horror. A German soldier on a motorcycle with a white flag surrendered to First Sergeant Rodney Cloutman of C Company. As he surrendered, he told Cloutman that the killing in the pocket was unbearable; hundreds of other

German soldiers wanted to surrender, but their NCOs and officers would not let them. Could Cloutman accompany him to his own lines and help him persuade all of the men in his unit to surrender? Cloutman knew this was a dangerous mission, but he went anyway. To his great relief, he found that most of the Germans did indeed want to surrender, so much so that they shot and killed two of their recalcitrant officers. First Sergeant Cloutman then "herded the Germans together like cattle, had them raise white flags . . . and marched them toward the British [probably Canadian] front line because it was closer than ours." Cloutman turned over 1,841 POWs to the Canadians. He earned a battlefield commission for this exploit.

For every group of Germans surrendering, though, there were many others who were fighting as hard as they could. Only 500 yards from where Cloutman accepted one German unit's mass surrender, several enemy tanks were trying to escape, past roadblocks manned by 358th Infantry Regiment bazooka teams. Privates First Class George Caldwell and Walter Giebelstein comprised one of those teams. Several enemy tanks tried to drive right past them. The two Americans had only five rounds of ammunition for their bazooka but put them to good use. Loading and aiming as carefully as they could, they destroyed four of the enemy tanks before exhausting their ammunition. For these deeds they both earned the Distinguished Service Cross.[15]

General Weaver assigned the lead role in taking Chambois to the 2nd Battalion of the 359th Infantry Regiment. Companies E and G advanced north up D-16, a road that led from le-Bourg-St-Leonard to Chambois. French tanks and a few U.S. tank destroyers were interspersed with the rifle companies. Company E, under Captain Edward Lienhart, was on the left, and G Company, commanded by Captain Laughlin Waters, was on the right. At 1300 on August 19, Waters and his men began their advance. "The terrain . . . was gently rolling, planted to summer crops and, after the initial rise, sloped down to Fel, which lay just south of Chambois and astride the Dives River."

Within an hour or two, they were within sight of Fel. Enemy mortar and artillery shells were exploding around the area, and small-arms fire could be heard in the distance. All of this fire was disquieting to the Americans, but it was ineffective. They made it into Fel with no problem, crossed the Dives, and kept going, minus the French tanks, which now "decided to leave us and go their own way," Waters politely said.

Chambois was at the top of a hill that was honeycombed with apple orchards. The French tank crews did not want to take any chance of getting bogged down in sloping terrain, with an unseen enemy no doubt lurking. So Waters and his infantrymen proceeded alone. "As we moved up the hill, the intensity of all kinds of fire increased." Captain Waters had orders to veer right, cut across the D-13 (a road that led east out of Chambois), enter the village from that direction, and hook up with E Company in the town. He was reluctant to do this until he knew what would be in his rear once he crossed the D-13. "To satisfy myself that my right flank (and later rear) was protected, I proceeded alone, along a line of trees perpendicular to D-13." He passed an orchard full of wrecked German equipment, "including trucks, automobiles, horse-drawn wagons, vehicles, weapons carriers etc. Many horses had been killed or wounded."

Waters found a good hiding spot in the grass along the road "and attempted to gauge the direction and volume of fire that was hitting Chambois, where many buildings were burning fiercely." After a few minutes, Waters saw a man, in British uniform, stride right into the middle of the road. The man just stood there, looking east and west, probably trying to ascertain the same information that Waters wanted to know. The firing continued uninterrupted. As the moments ticked by, Waters knew that he should get up and make contact with this brave man, but he was reluctant to leave the safety of his hiding place. "With great trepidation, I stood up and joined him." The two men shook hands and introduced themselves to each other. To his surprise, Waters found out that the man was not British. He was a Major Zgorzelski of the 10th Polish Dragoons, 1st Polish Armored Division. Zgorzelski spoke good English. He told Captain Waters that this was the first time Polish and American soldiers had ever met on a battlefield. "Neither of us appreciated at this time that this was another historic moment—the closing of the Falaise Gap." It was a great moment—the two mighty Allied armies had finally joined hands—but it hardly meant that the battle was over.

The Poles, Waters soon learned, were in the midst of a bitter fight at Mount Ormel, a ridge of dominating high ground about a mile north of here. Two armored regiments and three infantry battalions were cut off at Mount Ormel, holding out against repeated enemy attacks. As long as the Poles held Mount Ormel, they could rain down deadly accurate fire on anything and anyone moving along any easterly road out of Trun or Chambois. Knowing this, the Germans were doing everything they could to dislodge the valorous Poles, to no avail. The rest of the Polish Division, including the 10th Dragoons, had pushed on to Chambois to complete this linkup with the Americans. With this now a reality, Waters and Zgorzelski coordinated their plans to defend Chambois against the thousands of desperate Germans who were still trying to get through the town and escape east. The Poles would cover the northeastern side of Chambois, closest to their own hard-pressed forces at Mount Ormel. Waters and G Company would occupy eastern Chambois, even as they linked up with the rest of their battalion. With great warmth, the two officers signed each other's notebooks, exchanged formal salutes, and went about their respective missions.

Waters spread his company into a line of skirmishers, who swept through the orchard and into Chambois. They went house by house and street by street, against little resistance. "The streets were choked with all varieties of German transport. Ammunition carriers were burning; other carriers, tanks and equipment stood hub-to-hub in the street, disabled, with dead and wounded horses lying or standing in the traces."

At the western edge of Chambois, the soldiers of E Company were lying in ditches, behind walls or hedges, waiting for the word to enter the town itself. Staff Sergeant Clarence Adkins led a small patrol into the town, past an abandoned German motor pool, and encountered no resistance. As Adkins and his patrol headed back to the company, American artillery began exploding around them. Six men were wounded and one died.

While medics treated the wounded, Captain Lienhart ordered his men to remain in place while he straightened out the problem with the artillery. Two hours later, at 1700, when Lienhart was satisfied that the artillery would not fire again without direct orders to do so, E Company began its assault on Chambois. As tank destroyers fired into buildings, infantrymen advanced from block to block, pitching grenades through windows, kicking doors open, shooting anything that looked dangerous. In a matter of minutes the firing died down. Some forty Germans surrendered and the town belonged to the Americans.

Evidence of the enemy's imminent demise was everywhere. "On the main street just at the junction of [an] alley was an abandoned German troop carrier and beside it two Mark V Panther tanks, knocked out and burning," Technical Sergeant Wilton Barger recalled. "This street was littered with dead Germans, including SS and Panzer troopers. The gutters ran with blood, and the houses were in flames on either side of the road. In the space of two blocks from the edge of town to the main east–west street the French civilians, in a frenzy of excitement, cowered in one large house and its adjoining courtyard, but occasionally ran forth, young and old, to look at the dead Boche in their street." Everywhere Barger and the other Americans looked, there were burning vehicles, dead horses, and dead Germans. Discarded helmets, ammunition, and clothing were lying all over the place.

Lienhart's E Company soon linked up with Waters's G Company. The former established a CP in a stone building adjacent to D-13. Waters situated his headquarters on the eastern fringe of Chambois in a house belonging to the Buquet family. Soon F Company also entered Chambois. By now, the sun had set and the shooting died down. The Americans found about thirty abandoned badly wounded Germans whose comrades had put them in a damaged house and marked it with white sheets that hung from shattered, glassless windows. The Americans dispensed what medical care they could and evacuated several of the wounded enemy.

The next day, August 20, the fighting reached a climax for the Americans. During the night, the Germans had organized themselves into small but powerful groups, whose mission was to fight their way through the Polish/American cordon. They hit Mount Ormel with several ferocious counterattacks but never took it. The Poles received some supplies from the Americans, but for all intents and purposes they were cut off. Through sheer guts and guile they turned back every German attack.

The fighting at Chambois, the other exit point for the Germans, was almost as fierce. Technical Sergeant Barger watched as an enemy convoy tried to roll right past his company's positions in the town. An American machine-gun section opened fire. Barger crouched nearby and watched their tracers strike home. "The toll they took in those first minutes of daylight was two troop carriers with personnel and one self-propelled gun, all afire and abandoned. Interspersed with the carriers and guns were numerous foot troops who began to fire on our positions. During the first two hours of daylight our gunners expended 5000 rounds of ammunition, while our mortars fired the basic load of rounds at the vehicles and troops silhouetted on the skyline, hitting any target of opportunity."

At the eastern end of town, the situation was similar for Captain Waters and his people. "The Germans attacked with all of the fury they could bring to bear, fueled by their desperation to escape. Infantry, supported by tanks and self-propelled guns, plus artillery fire directed by the Germans from the Fôret de Gouffern, assaulted our positions. From my position in the Buquet home and around our portion of the perimeter defense, I could see German tanks maneuvering on the edge of the [forest] and could also see them shelling our positions. The fighting was so fluid that many times we were cut off from our lines of supply. The Poles were cut off from theirs even more than we were from ours."

Southwest of Chambois, on Le Bourg-St-Léonard ridge, American artillery observers could actually see the numerous frantic enemy columns pouring east, toward Chambois. The day was drizzly and that was a break for the Germans, because it negated the Allied fighter bombers. But the ubiquitous Piper Cubs were flying overhead, calling down withering accurate fire on the retreating Germans.

Corporal John Warner, a radioman for a 344th Field Artillery Battalion forward observation team, was staring at the whole spectacle, listening to chatter on his radio. "Right down below was all this mass of humanity and vehicles, they were trying to get out and they were trapped. Every kind of vehicle you could picture was coming up through there. And personnel. You could look over and see fifty, a hundred men."

Artillery shells were exploding all along the expanse of the enemy column, tearing apart men and machines. Warner listened as one of the Piper

Cub pilots, Lieutenant William Matthews, was calling for fire from a battery of 155mm Long Toms. When the fire did not come as quickly as Matthews would have wished, he radioed the battery: "What is holding up the Long Toms?"

"We are computing the data," the fire direction center responded.

"Stop computin' and start shootin'," Matthews replied.

Warner and the other men around him broke out laughing. For the rest of the war Matthews's clever phrase was an anthem of sorts for the 90th Division's artillery battalions.

The shooting did go on, all day long. For the Germans, the only way out of their ever-constricting kill sack was to put their heads down and keep going east. They repeatedly bumped into E Company's positions in Chambois. The U.S. infantrymen made liberal use of bazookas to repel enemy tanks, and machine guns against every other kind of enemy vehicle. In one instance, Sergeant John Hawk functioned as a one-man army, attacking enemy armor with bazookas, warding off enemy infantry with machine guns, directing the fire of two supporting M-10 Wolverine tank destroyers. In spite of a shrapnel wound in his right thigh, Hawk ran back and forth between the tank destroyers, shouting instructions. When Sergeant Hawk and the tank destroyers were finally finished, two enemy tanks were burning and 500 German soldiers came forward to surrender. The sergeant received the Medal of Honor for his courage.

During the day, hundreds of Germans, including many paratroopers, escaped, but many thousands more did not. As evening approached on August 20, more and more prisoners began pouring into the American lines at Chambois. The Germans were still fighting hard to the north, against the Poles, but resistance in the U.S. sector was petering out. Several hundred enemy, carrying white flags or wearing red cross–adorned clothing, warily trod into E Company's positions in western Chambois. Sergeant Barger was surprised to see that they brought with them forty American soldiers from the 80th Division whom they had captured several days earlier. "One German-speaking American had persuaded the whole lot of Germans to surrender, promising them fair treatment."

Captain Lienhart watched the defeated enemy soldiers shuffle dejectedly into Chambois. "The men of the S.S. and Panzer units were unhappy at finding themselves in this situation. They covered the uniforms of which they were so proud with raincoats and blankets. Among the prisoners were Mongolians, Russians, Poles, Czechs, and even Frenchmen. Faces of old and children. There were Heidelberg types, officers who asked for water to wash themselves and who refused to be parked in the same spot as their men."

Captain Waters had established a POW cage in a vacant space at the main intersection of Chambois, right in the middle of town, and it was close to being full. "Since we could not spare many soldiers for guard duty, all being otherwise occupied in perimeter defense, I had a machine gun mounted on top of the wall of the cage area. Each prisoner was told to lie face down, spread-eagled, and advised that any untoward movement would result in a burst of machine-gun fire. The instructions were apparently persuasive for there were no incidents."

The Poles were especially hard pressed to take care of any prisoners, so they kept turning them over to the Americans. Waters saw how the Poles treated their countrymen who were serving in Wehrmacht uniform. If the man was a private soldier, they gave him an Allied uniform and allowed him to join their unit. If he was an NCO or an officer, they shot him on the spot for collaborating with the Nazis.

That evening, a Polish captain and a sergeant, both of whom had been drinking generous quantities of calvados, came to Waters's command post with several hundred POWs in tow. Waters had heard that the Poles were coming in with 1,500 POWs tonight. These two men did not have anywhere near that many with them, but given the overcrowding problem in his own POW cage, Waters did not know how he was going to care for this new group. Waters saluted the Polish captain and greeted him.

"Captain, here are your prisoners," the Pole said.

"I don't want them," Waters replied.

"But I must leave them with you. Those are my orders," the Polish captain explained.

"I still don't want them. Get them out of here."

They argued for a moment until Waters asked, "You were supposed to have fifteen hundred prisoners. Where are they?"

"They are dead." The Pole said. "We shot them. These are all that are left."

"Then why don't you shoot these, too?" As soon as the words left his mouth, Captain Waters thought about what he had just said and corrected himself: "No, you can't do that."

"Oh, yes, we can. They shot my countrymen."

The Polish captain motioned for Waters to follow him and they walked until they were out of earshot of the prisoners. "Captain, we can't shoot them," he told Waters. "We are out of ammunition."

Waters took charge of them immediately. "That was the cincher. I . . . put them in the cage, and they were later moved to our rear echelons."[16]

For the Americans in Normandy, the fighting finally came to an end on August 21. Most all of the Germans in the American sector were dead, wounded, gone, or languishing in POW cages. There has never been a precise assessment of German casualties in the pocket (nor will there ever be). The Americans captured about 25,000 enemy soldiers, the Canadians and

Poles a like number. At least 10,000 Germans lost their lives. One of them was von Kluge, who was relieved of command and almost immediately thereafter committed suicide. Anywhere between 20,000 and 40,000 Germans escaped, but the majority of them were not combat troops. The average German division had no more than 300 men left. The *total* strength of the remnants of six panzer divisions that made it out was 2,000 men, sixty-two tanks, and twenty-six artillery pieces. In the main, the Germans lost almost all of their equipment. The typical German soldier who was lucky enough to survive and make it back to Germany took with him only his personal weapon and the clothes on his back. British investigators, searching between Argentan and Trun, counted 187 destroyed tanks or self-propelled guns, 157 armored cars, 1,778 trucks, 669 cars, and nearly 3,300 guns. The 90th Division alone took 13,000 prisoners and 1,000 horses while destroying 220 tanks, 160 self-propelled guns, 700 artillery pieces, 130 half-tracks, 2,000 wagons, and 5,000 motorized vehicles (trucks, cars, motorcycles, etc.). The Allies had won a great victory, roughly comparable with Tunisia or Stalingrad.[17]

All over the "Falaise pocket," American soldiers surveyed the hideous remains of what had once been a powerful enemy army. In the eastern outskirts of Chambois, Captain Waters walked the expanse of D-13. Parts of bodies were in trees, and entrails were on the road; wherever Waters looked, there were scenes of violent destruction. "The carnage was everywhere. Tanks had been shot out, dead Germans lay about, and one German self-propelled gun was burned out with corpses of the crew lying on the gun, so completely incinerated that there was nothing but charcoal in the forms of men. I saw, on the ground, portions of human spines that had been chewed, burned, and broken into bits by tank treads grinding on them until all that was left were pieces of vertebrae attended to by flies. The stench of raw, smokey, pervasive death lay everywhere, invading nostrils and bringing tears to one's eyes."

The putrid stench of death was so overwhelming that Major William Falvey, a staff officer in the 358th Infantry, could smell it in a Piper Cub, thousands of feet above the ground, during a mission to survey the battlefield damage. "One could hardly stand [the smell] in an airplane."

Back on the ground, an American senior officer who had served in World War I saw the carnage and knew that the horrors he had witnessed more than twenty-five years earlier did not compare to what was now before his eyes. "It was as if an avenging angel had swept the area bent on destroying all things German. I stood on a lane, surrounded by 20 or 30 dead horses or parts of horses, most of them still hitched to their wagons or carts. As far as my eye could reach . . . there were . . . vehicles, wagons, tanks, guns, prime movers, sedans, rolling kitchens, etc. in various stages of destruction. I stepped over hundreds of rifles in the mud and saw hundreds more stacked along sheds. I saw probably 300 field pieces and tanks, mounting large caliber guns, that were apparently undamaged. I left this area rather regretting I'd seen it."

Lieutenant Jim Gifford, the tank platoon leader, took several men and wandered around, putting wounded horses out of their misery. "Some of them were just laying down with their heads up. It killed me to see that. I remember one horse, he had a shell in his shoulder. It was sticking out, a big round shell, it was about ten inches long, and four or five inches of it were sticking out of his shoulder, and he's standing there, he had a shattered leg, and he's eating the grass. He's not even jumping around or anything . . . the poor sonofabitch."

Nearby, Corporal Warner, the artillery radioman, walked from his OP on Le Bourg-St-Léonard ridge into the valley where much of the destruction had taken place. "What I saw in the Falaise Gap was disgusting. Revolting. It was a mess. Everything, all kinds of vehicles, you can't believe it. I mean, of every description. People laying around, blown up. An arm over there, a leg over there. There was a communications half track, and it was blown up, just stopped there. And I was curious. I looked in the back of it to see what kind of instruments they had. And I'm standing on something . . . mushy. I looked . . . and it was a body. Burnt. It was just a mass of flesh, burned."

Warner moved away quickly and tried to forget what he had just seen, but he couldn't. He knew he was, at least in part, responsible for the gruesome scene around him, and it bothered him. In his heart, he knew that this destruction was necessary to rid the world of a monstrous tyranny. He also knew he had done his job well. But these charred lumps of hamburger around him had been, after all, human beings. "How in hell can you do something like that to another person? I don't give a damn who they are. Terrible. The smell is the most terrible [thing], that odor of burned flesh, you can't describe that, rotting flesh. And some of that I was responsible for." Warner returned to his unit, feeling awful. As he walked away from the battlefield, he kept thinking, "What the hell kind of a man am I?"

Miles to the west, Lieutenant George Wilson, whose unit had only briefly participated in this battle, nevertheless witnessed plenty of the carnage. "Dead Germans were literally stacked by the hundreds—in some places two and three feet deep. All of the roads for miles were strewn with German corpses and littered with hundreds of smoking or burning tanks, trucks and wagons." A mile or two to the east of Wilson, Corporal Robert Baldridge, the 9th Division artilleryman, was riding in a convoy that had trouble negotiating all the bodies and burned-out vehicles that were scattered all over the narrow Norman road. "[The roadsides were] littered with disabled tanks, vehicles, wagons and carts, dead horses, and dead bodies of German soldiers which sometimes were run over again and again due to the impracticality of moving them at the time. It was not a pretty sight. It was . . . sickening, unreal . . . as the roadside mess of Germans and their battered equipment were just pushed aside or run over."[18]

Shortly after the battle, another Allied soldier toured the killing ground, taking in the magnitude of what had happened there. Hands clasped tightly behind his back, General Dwight D. Eisenhower walked slowly through the fields and along the narrow lanes. More than five months had passed since Eisenhower had sat at his desk in London and read the Combined Chiefs of Staff directive that empowered him to wage war on Nazi Germany and defeat it. So much had happened since then. Now, in late August, as he walked the battlefield, he earnestly hoped that the destruction around him would lead to victory and a better world, for he knew he was seeing one of the greatest killing grounds in military history. Having never seen combat, he could only liken this chaotic mess to hellish scenes he had read about in Dante's *Inferno*. "Roads, highways, and fields were so choked with destroyed equipment and with dead men and animals that passage through the area was extremely difficult. It was literally possible to walk for hundreds of yards at a time, stepping on nothing but dead and decaying flesh."

At last, Ike had seen enough. He returned to his staff car. As he did so, he looked to the east. Somewhere over the horizon, far beyond a man's vision, Allied armies were pushing for the Seine. Soon they would liberate Paris. All over France, the Germans were in headlong retreat. On the Eastern Front, Soviet armies were deep into Poland and the Balkans. Optimists believed that the war in Europe would end before Christmas. Ike hoped they were right, but he was not sure they were. His armies, as ever, had logistical problems, and those problems were getting worse with every new mile gained. Would he have enough combat power to plunge into Germany and win this war before the Germans could recover from a summer of staggering defeats? The Battle of Normandy, Eisenhower understood now, had been a tremendous Allied victory, but would it be decisive? That was the question.[19]

Only history could answer that question. The Battle of Normandy did not end the war, but it decided the outcome. At Normandy, the Germans absorbed a defeat from which they never recovered. By the end of August, the enemy had lost 400,000 men, half of whom were in captivity. This was the functional equivalent of two field armies. They also lost over 22,000 combat vehicles of all types. At Normandy, the Allies suffered 209,703 casualties, of whom 125,847 were American. The victory was enormous, but the Allies were not able to capitalize on it well enough to end the war in 1944. Perhaps such a swift conclusion to the war was too much to expect. Historians still argue as to whether Eisenhower's broad front strategy was the best way to approach the conquest of Germany. Quite likely, the argument will continue unabated.[20]

What is not arguable is that, after Normandy, the Germans no longer had any real chance of ending the war on their terms. In the wake of this battle, one of history's greatest, the question was not whether Germany would lose the war but how long she could stave off the inevitable. Fought over the course of some eighty bloody days, the Battle of Normandy had been a bitter, tough clash of wills. Victory had required sacrifice, along with the endurance of terrible tragedy, horror, and waste.

It had also required the unity of the western Allies, something for which Eisenhower deserved much credit. Britons, Canadians, Frenchmen, Poles, and Americans had all fought together as an Allied team. But that team needed a leader, and the leader was the United States. Normandy was the harbinger of the postwar world, the one that saw a superpower United States lead the western world. Normandy was the beginning of American military supremacy. Normandy was not just the start of American leadership in the campaign to liberate Europe; it was the start of America's defense of Europe in the Cold War era (eventually through the NATO alliance). In the summer of 1944, the United States waged several major military campaigns: a strategic bombing effort in Europe, a submarine campaign to destroy Japanese sea-lanes around the Philippines and along the coast of China, an offensive in Italy, another one in the South Pacific, a major naval, air, and land effort in the Mariana Island chain, and, of course, the invasion of France. The latter effort was the most complicated, the most costly, and the most important of all. It was also the most pivotal and the most decisive. At Normandy, the U.S. Army took the lead in forging a new Europe that was free of the devastating imperial rivalries of the past. Out of the dust of this troubled past emerged a disunited Europe that nonetheless became economically prosperous and politically resilient. Normandy, in retrospect, was the dawning of a new era, not just in U.S. history but also in European history.

Just outside of the seaside town of St-Laurent, on a cliff side that overlooks a strip of beach that was once known as Easy Red, 9,387 Americans lie under a field of white crosses and Stars of David. Most of these Americans were killed in the Battle of Normandy. The cemetery is beautifully maintained and manicured. Those who are buried there deserve nothing less. On a typical day, a visitor can stroll among the graves, dignified row after dignified row, and smell the sea air, hear the whisper of the surf against the beach, and experience a peace and tranquillity that those 9,387 Americans did not enjoy in the summer of 1944. At this place of heroes, the past is somehow alive. The unseen faces of so many young Americans are there somehow—perhaps it is just their presence that one can sense.

They were sons, brothers, fathers, uncles, and friends. Nearly all of them were loved. Nearly all of them were important to someone in those days so long ago. Nearly all of them left behind a void in the lives of those they knew. Each and every one of them hoped for a long, full life, but for these dead men there would be no postwar world. They would never see their children grow to adulthood, nor would they bury their grandparents, parents, uncles, or aunts. For them, time stopped on the day they were killed. They are forever young. Year by year, they recede further and further into the anonymity of the past, known only to a dying few. To the generations that have followed them, and will follow them in the future, their graves are a living memorial to the past, to what Americans once did, in a place so far from home. For what, ultimately, did they give their lives? Very simply, they gave their collective future to ensure ours. In the final analysis, there was, for them, nothing more valuable, or more precious, that they could ever give. Such is the American legacy of the Battle of Normandy.

NOTES

Preface

1. The most prominent proponents of this point of view are Martin Van Creveld in his *Fighting Power: German and U.S. Army Performance, 1939–1945* (Westport, CT: Greenwood Press, 1982), Basil Liddell Hart in *The German Generals Talk* (New York: William Morrow, 1948), Max Hastings in *Overlord: D-Day and the Battle for Normandy* (New York: Simon and Schuster, 1984), and Trevor Dupuy, *A Genius for War: The German Army and General Staff, 1807–1945* (Englewood Cliffs, NJ: Prentice-Hall, 1977).

2. I am, by no means, alone in making the case that, contrary to earlier assumptions, American soldiers fought with great resilience and distinction at Normandy. Other books of varying scope have begun to shed light on this issue, such as Stephen Ambrose in *D-Day: The Climactic Battle of World War II* (New York: Simon and Schuster, 1994), Michael Doubler, *Closing with the Enemy* (Lawrence: University Press of Kansas, 1994), Joseph Balkoski, *Beyond the Beachhead: The 29th Infantry Division in Normandy* (Harrisburg, PA: Stackpole Books, 1989), and Peter Mansoor, *The G.I. Offensive in Europe: The Triumph of American Infantry Divisions* (Lawrence: University Press of Kansas, 1999).

3. Ambrose, *D-Day*, p. 25.

1. Inland from Omaha: The Week After D-Day

1. Gerald Astor, *June 6, 1944: The Voices of D-Day* (New York: Dell, 1994), pp. 343–344.

2. Stephen Ambrose in his *D-Day*, pp. 480–482, and Max Hastings in *Overlord*, pp. 77–78, discussed many of these same issues with similar, but not

identical, conclusions. For the German side of this issue, see Paul Carrell, *Invasion: They're Coming* (New York: Bantam Books, 1962), pp. 90–114; and Hans von Luck, *Panzer Commander* (New York: Dell, 1989), pp. 171–185.

3. Historical Division, Department of the Army, *Omaha Beachhead* (Washington, DC: Center of Military History, U.S. Army, 1945), pp. 120–121, Warren Coffman, *I Never Intended to Be a Soldier* (Greensboro, NC: Lifestyles Press, 1999), pp. 63–66.

4. Historical Division, Department of the Army, *Omaha Beachhead*, pp. 120–122; H. R. Knickerbocker et al., *Danger Forward: The Story of the First Division in World War II* (Nashville, TN: Battery Press, 2002; reprint of 1947 edition), pp. 193–195, James Lingg, unpublished memoir, pp. 20–21, personal Web site.

5. Historical Division, Department of the Army, *Omaha Beachhead*, p. 119; Franklyn Johnson, *One More Hill* (New York: Bantam Books, 1983), pp. 141–148.

6. Allen Towne, *Doctor Danger Forward* (Jefferson, NC: McFarland, 2000), pp. 103–104.

7. Richard Fahey, oral history, Dwight Eisenhower Center, University of New Orleans (hereafter referred to as EC). After the war, Fahey became an anesthesiologist.

8. Richard Willstatter, after action report, EC; Frank Feduik, Helen Pavlovsky Ramsey, oral histories, featured at www.history.navy.mil.com Web site. This is the Navy's official site.

9. Joanna McDonald, *The Liberation of Pointe du Hoc: The 2nd Rangers at Normandy, June 6–8, 1944* (Redondo Beach, CA: Rank and File Publications, 2000), pp. 129–132; Lou Lisko, oral history, EC; W. C. Heinz, "I Took My Son to Omaha Beach, *Collier's*, 6/11/56, p. 26.

10. Historical Division, Department of the Army, *Small Unit Actions* (Washington, DC: Center of Military History, United States Army, 1982), pp. 46–63; Patrick O'Donnell, *Beyond Valor: World War II's Ranger and Airborne Veterans Reveal the Heart of Combat* (New York: Free Press, 2001), p. 148; McDonald, *Liberation of Pointe du Hoc*, pp. 135–143; Historical Division, Department of the Army, *Omaha Beachhead*, p. 126; Salva Maimone, oral history, EC.

11. Robert Black, *Rangers in World War II* (New York: Ballantine Books, 1992), p. 217; Balkoski, *Beyond the Beachhead*, pp. 157–159; Francis Dawson, oral history, EC.

12. John Reville, Gerald Heaney, oral histories, EC.

13. Historical Division, Department of the Army, *Omaha Beachhead*, pp. 128–129; Black, *Rangers in World War II*, pp. 217–218; Balkoski, *Beyond the Beachhead*, p. 159; McDonald, *Liberation of Pointe du Hoc*, pp. 155–158; William Folkestad, *View from the Turret: The 743rd Tank Battalion During World War II* (Shippensburg, PA: Burd Street Press, 2000), pp. 19–20; Stan Askin,

"Immediate Action Needed," *World War II*, May 1987, p. 39; Heaney, James Eikner, oral histories, EC. Rocco Russo, unpublished memoir, p. 21, EC.

14. McDonald, *Liberation of Pointe du Hoc*, p. 158.

15. Historical Division, Department of the Army, *Omaha Beachhead*, pp. 129–130; Balkoski, *Beyond the Beachhead*, pp. 163–164; Joseph Ewing, *29 Let's Go: A History of the 29th Infantry Division in World War II* (Washington, DC: Infantry Journal Press, 1948), pp. 64–65; Folkestad, *View from the Turret*, p. 20; Astor, *June 6, 1944*, p. 362. Donald Nelson, Eikner, oral histories, EC.

16. Ewing, *29 Let's Go*, p. 62; Joseph Bria, oral history, EC.

17. Lester Zick, oral history, EC.

18. Robert Miller, oral history, EC; Harold Gordon, *One Man's War: A Memoir of World War II* (New York: Apex Press, 1999), p. 7. Gordon's daughter, Nancy, edited and published this work after her father's death.

19. Balkoski, *Beyond the Beachhead*, pp. 152–154; Bria, Robert Miller, oral histories, EC.

20. Balkoski, *Beyond the Beachhead*, p. 168; Gordon, *One Man's War*, pp. 10–12. Robert Miller, oral history, EC.

21. Historical Division, Department of the Army, *Omaha Beachhead*, p. 127, Balkoski, *Beyond the Beachhead*, p. 169; Ewing, *29 Let's Go*, p. 63; Gordon, *One Man's War*, p. 12. Robert Miller, oral history, EC.

22. Balkoski, *Beyond the Beachhead*, pp. 170–172; Historical Division, Department of the Army, *Omaha Beachhead*, p. 127; Ewing, *29 Let's Go*, p. 63.

23. Gordon, *One Man's War*, pp. 18–19.

24. Historical Division, Department of the Army, *Omaha Beachhead*, pp. 127–128; Balkoski, *Beyond the Beachhead*, pp. 172–173; Ewing, *29 Let's Go*, pp. 63–64; Forrest Pogue, *Pogue's War: Diaries of a WWII Combat Historian* (Lexington: University Press of Kentucky, 2001), pp. 162–166; Gordon, *One Man's War*, pp. 21–22; Zick, oral history, EC.

25. Historical Division, Department of the Army, *Omaha Beachhead*, p. 143; Balkoski, *Beyond the Beachhead*, p. 167; Ewing, *29 Let's Go*, pp. 65–66; Joseph Binkoski and Arthur Plaut, *The 115th Infantry Regiment in World War II* (Washington, DC: Infantry Journal Press, 1948), pp. 31–33. Lieutenant Miller received the Distinguished Service Cross for leading this patrol.

26. Colin McLaurin, "Normandy Diary," *Twenty-Niner Newsletter*, November 1995, pp. 12–13.

27. Binkoski and Plaut, *115th Infantry Regiment in World War II*, p. 35; Ewing, *29 Let's Go*, pp. 67–68; Maynard Marquis, oral history, EC.

28. Binkoski and Plaut, *115th Regiment in World War II*, pp. 36–37; William Boykin, James Hogan, Marquis, oral histories, EC.

29. Historical Division, Department of the Army, *Omaha Beachhead*, p. 145; Binkoski and Plaut, *115th Regiment in World War II*, pp. 38–40; Ewing, *29 Let's Go*, pp. 72–73; Glover Johns, *The Clay Pigeons of St. Lô* (Harrisburg, PA:

Stackpole Books, 2002; originally published in 1958), pp. 56–62; Balkoski, *Beyond the Beachhead*, pp. 186–188; Hogan, Marquis, Boykin, oral histories, EC.

30. Historical Division, Department of the Army, *Omaha Beachhead*, pp. 130–134; Samuel Eliot Morison, *History of the United States Naval Operations in World War II: The Invasion of France and Germany* (Boston: Little, Brown, 1957), pp. 155–176; Roscoe, *Destroyer Operations in World War II*, pp. 354–357; Steve Waddell, *United States Army Logistics: The Normandy Campaign, 1944* (Westport, CT: Greenwood Press, 1994), pp. 53–69; Roland Ruppenthal, *The United States Army in World War II: European Theater of Operations, Logistical Support of the Armies* (Washington, DC: Center of Military History, United States Army, 1995), vol. I, pp. 402–406; James Hudson, interview with Dr. Ron Marcello, 5/30/01, Oral History Collection, University of North Texas (hereafter referred to as UNT). For just one example of the pivotal role LSTs played in the supplying of the Normandy beaches, see Feduik, oral history, www.history.navy.mil Web site. Pharmacist Mate Feduik's LST-338 made, in his estimation, sixty separate trips to the beaches.

31. Historical Division, Department of the Army, *Omaha Beachhead*, pp. 139–141; *Combat History of the Second Infantry Division* (Nashville, TN: Battery Press, 1979), p. 24; Placido Patrick Munnia, oral history, EC.

32. Historical Division, Department of the Army, *Omaha Beachhead*, pp. 141–143; *Combat History of the Second Infantry Division*, pp. 24–26; Ralph Steele, oral history, EC.

33. Historical Division, Department of the Army, *Omaha Beachhead*, pp. 151–153; Knickerbocker et al., *Danger Forward*, pp. 199–201; Folkestad, *View from the Turret*, pp. 21–22; Coffman, *Never Intended to Be a Soldier*, pp. 67–69; Monfrey Wilson, oral history, featured at www.tankbooks.com. Charles Murphy, interview with Johnson, 4/13/93, SCUTK; Lingg, unpublished memoir, personal Web site.

34. The best discussion of Villers-Bocage is in Carlo D'Este, *Decision in Normandy* (Old Saybrook, CT: Konecky and Konecky, 1984), pp. 174–198. Also see Hastings, *Overlord*, pp. 129–137; and Robin Neillands, *The Battle of Normandy, 1944* (London: Cassell, 2002), pp. 101–104.

2. Inland from Utah: The Week After D-Day

1. Ed McCaul, "82nd Airborne Trooper at Normandy," interview with Bill Dunfee, *World War II*, circa 2000; Astor, *June 6, 1944*, pp. 288–289; Jerry Richlak, *Glide to Glory: Unedited Personal Stories from the Airborne Glidermen of World War II* (Chesterland, OH: Cedar House, 2002), pp. 119–120; Clay

Blair, *Ridgway's Paratroopers: The American Airborne in World War II* (Garden City, NY: Doubleday, 1985), pp. 255–256.

2. Gordon Harrison, *The United States Army in World War II: Cross Channel Attack* (Washington, DC: Office of the Chief of Military History, Department of the Army, 1951), pp. 343–344; DerykWills, *Put on Your Boots and Parachutes: Personal Stories of the Veterans of the United States 82nd Airborne Division* (Leicester: AB Printers, 1997), pp. 86–87; Stephen Ambrose, *Citizen Soldiers: The U.S. Army from the Beaches of Normandy to the Surrender of Germany* (New York: Simon and Schuster, 1997), pp. 17–21.

3. S. L. A. Marshall, *Night Drop: The American Airborne Invasion of Normandy* (Boston: Little, Brown, 1962), pp. 117–120; Charles Sammon to Cornelius Ryan, 3/21/59, EC.

4. Charles Miller, oral history, EC.

5. Blair, *Ridgway's Paratroopers*, p. 257.

6. William Jones, oral history, EC.

7. Historical Division, U.S. Army, *Utah Beach to Cherbourg: 6 June–27 June* (Washington, DC: Center of Military History, United States Army, 1984), pp. 61–63; Gerald Astor, *The Greatest War: Americans in Combat, 1941–1945* (Novato, CA: Presidio Press, 2000), pp. 573–575. John Pfister interview with Welch and Williams, 3/99, www.erieveterans.com.

8. J. Lawton Collins, *Lightning Joe: An Autobiography* (Baton Rouge: Louisiana State University Press, 1979), p. 203.

9. U.S. Army, *Utah Beach to Cherbourg*, pp. 63–65; Harrison, *Cross Channel Attack*, pp. 344–345; Marshall, *Night Drop*, pp. 124–125; W. J. Blanchard, *Our Liberators: The Combat History of the 746th Tank Battalion During World War II* (Tucson, AZ: Fenestra Books, 2003), pp. 10–13, "Unit History, 746th Tank Battalion," copy in author's possession.

10. Sammon to Ryan, EC.

11. U.S. Army, *Utah Beach to Cherbourg*, pp. 63–65, Harrison, *Cross Channel Attack*, pp. 344–345; Marshall, *Night Drop*, pp. 124–128; Ambrose, *Citizen Soldiers*, pp. 30–32; Astor, *Greatest War*, p. 576; Wills, *Put on Your Boots and Parachutes*, pp. 80–81; Forrest Dawson, editor, *Saga of the All American* (Nashville, TN: Battery Press; reprint of 1946 edition), n.p., Marvin Jensen, *Strike Swiftly: The 70th Tank Battalion from North Africa to Normandy to Germany* (Novato: Presidio Press, 1997), pp. 148–149. Earlier in the day on June 7, the 12th Infantry fought a bitter battle at Neuville, but was not able to control the entire town.

12. Astor, *June 6, 1944*, p. 376.

13. U.S. Army, *Utah Beach to Cherbourg*, pp. 65–71; Ambrose, *Citizen Soldiers*, p. 33; "4th Infantry Division History in World War II," 4th Infantry Division Web site.

14. U.S. Army, *Utah Beach to Cherbourg*, p. 103; Morison, *Invasion of France and Germany*, p. 157; Gerden Johnson, *History of the Twelfth Regiment in World War II* (Boston: Twelfth Infantry Regiment Association, 1947), pp. 67–71; "4th Division in World War II." Paul Massa, oral history, EC.

15. U.S. Army, *Utah Beach to Cherbourg*, pp. 106–107; Harrison, *Cross Channel Attack*, pp. 390–392; "4th Division in World War II."

16. U.S. Army, *Utah Beach to Cherbourg*, pp. 100–104, 108–115; Johnson, *History of the Twelfth Regiment in World War II*, pp. 70–84; Red Reeder, *Born at Reveille* (New York: Duell, Sloane, and Pearce, 1966), pp. 254–264; "4th Division in World War II" Red Reeder, *Assembly*, May 1994, p. 10.

17. Marshall, *Night Drop*, pp. 86–91. Owens's account is reproduced in Gavin, *On to Berlin*, pp. 124–126. Shultz's account is in O'Donnell, *Beyond Valor*, p. 136. Mark Alexander, *The Static Line*, November 2002, p. 33. John Dolan to Jim Gavin, 3/15/59 at www.dropzone.com. The D-Day fight at La Fière is described in the first volume of this series, *The Americans at D-Day*.

18. U.S. Army, *Utah Beach to Cherbourg*, p. 121; Marshall, *Night Drop*, pp. 129–132; Gerard Dillon, oral history, EC.

19. U.S. Army, *Utah Beach to Cherbourg*, p. 119; Marshall, *Night Drop*, pp. 138–141; Ralph DeWeese, unpublished diary, EC.

20. Ed Boccafogli interview with Aaron Elson, 2/19/94, www.tankbooks.com.

21. Tom Porcella, oral history, EC.

22. U.S. Army, *Utah Beach to Cherbourg*, p. 120; Marshall, *Night Drop*, pp. 141–150.

23. James Gavin, *On to Berlin* (New York: Bantam Books, 1978), p. 127; U.S. Army, *Utah Beach to Cherbourg*, p. 121; Marshall, *Night Drop*, pp. 131–137; O'Donnell, *Beyond Valor*, pp. 154–155; Richlak, *Glide to Glory*, pp. 168–174. Clinton Riddle, unpublished memoir, pp. 9–10, copy in author's possession. The 325th Glider Infantry had already lost about 10 percent of its strength during its violent glider landing around Ste-Mère-Eglise on the morning of June 7.

24. Marshall, *Night Drop*, pp. 153–154; Gavin, *On to Berlin*, p. 127; John Colby, *War from the Ground Up: The 90th Division in World War II* (Austin, TX: Nortex Press, 1991), pp. 20–22. In his memoirs, Gavin mistakenly wrote that he took General Devine to the forward position to point out artillery targets.

25. Colby, *War from the Ground Up*, pp. 22–23; Gavin, *On to Berlin*, p. 128; T. Michael Booth and Duncan Spencer, *Paratrooper: The Life of Gen. James M. Gavin* (New York: Simon and Schuster, 1994), pp. 193–195; Blair, *Ridgway's Paratroopers*, p. 273; Richlak, *Glide to Glory*, pp. 210–211, 221, 226. S. L. A. Marshall, Regimental Unit Study, Number 4, "The Forcing of the Merderet Causeway at La Fière, France: An Action by the Third Battalion, 325th Glider Infantry," Historical Manuscripts Collection, File Number 8–3.1, BB 4, pp. 1–3, CMH. Ridgway transferred Carrell out of the 82nd Airborne. Carrell ended up in the 90th Division, a unit he had

helped train. He commanded an infantry battalion, where he earned a combat infantryman's badge and a Purple Heart for severe wounds. In spite of this seeming redemption, the relief at La Fière ruined his career. He retired as a captain in 1947.

26. Marshall, *Night Drop*, pp. 154–156; O'Donnell, *Beyond Valor*, pp. 155–156; Dominique François, *507th Parachute Infantry Regiment, 1942–1945* (Bayeux, France: Heimdal, 2000), pp. 41–43; Marshall, "Forcing of the Merderet Causeway," pp. 4–6, CMH.

27. Marshall, "Forcing of the Merderet Causeway," p. 6, CMH; Richlak, *Glide to Glory*, pp. 213–215.

28. U.S. Army, *Utah Beach to Cherbourg*, pp. 120–125; Marshall, *Night Drop*, pp. 157–193; Gavin, *On to Berlin*, pp. 128–131; Booth and Spencer, *Paratrooper*, pp. 194–198; Harrison, *Cross Channel Attack*, pp. 397–401; O'Donnell, *Beyond Valor*, pp. 155–156; François, *507th Parachute Infantry Regiment*, p. 43; Blair, *Ridgway's Paratroopers*, pp. 273–277; Richlak, *Glide to Glory*, pp. 216–235; Marshall, "Forcing of the Merderet Causeway, pp. 7–70, CMH. Patrick O'Donnell, interview with Robert Rae, featured at www.thedropzone.com. For many years after the war, Rae and his 507th troopers believed that Gavin ordered them across the causeway because the attack of the 325th had completely failed. Such was the fog of battle. Gavin, Ridgway, and Jeziorski were all of the opinion that La Fière was their heaviest or "hottest" engagement. Ridgway wrote in *Soldier*, p. 13, that La Fière was "the hottest sector I saw throughout the war."

29. U.S. Army, *Utah Beach to Cherbourg*, pp. 125–126; Colby, *War from the Ground Up*, pp. 26–32; Oliver Wilbanks, unpublished diary, pp. 4–5, EC.

30. U.S. Army, *Utah Beach to Cherbourg*, p. 129; Colby, *War from the Ground Up*, pp. 36–40, 75–76; Ambrose, *Citizen Soldiers*, pp. 18–19; Michael Doubler, *Closing with the Enemy: How GI's Fought the War in Europe, 1944–1945* (Lawrence: University Press of Kansas, 1994), p. 36; Charles Cawthon, *Other Clay: A Remembrance of the World War II Infantry* (Boulder: University Press of Colorado, 1990), p. 76; Gavin, *On to Berlin*, p. 133; William McConahey, oral history, reproduced at www.military.com; Don Foye, interview with Aaron Elson, 9/7/00, reproduced at www.tankbooks.com. The photo-analysts also failed to determine the depth of the water in the inundated areas of Normandy. They saw grass poking through the water and assumed it was ankle depth when, in many areas, it was abdomen or even shoulder depth.

31. U.S. Army, *Utah Beach to Cherbourg*, p. 129; Colby, *War from the Ground Up*, pp. 29, 149–159, 475–491, 537–539; Collins, *Lightning Joe*, pp. 207–210; Omar Bradley, *Soldier's Story* (New York: Henry Holt, 1951), pp. 296–297. Max Kocour, unpublished memoir, p. 3, copy in author's possession. Colby's history of the 90th Division, unlike many divisional histories, is

brutally honest in its coverage and assessment of the division's problems. In my opinion, it is one of the best divisional histories of World War II.

3. Carentan

1. Bradley, *Soldier's Story*, pp. 285, 292; Bradley and Blair *A General's Life*, pp. 257–260; Leonard Rapport and Arthur Northwood, *Rendezvous with Destiny: A History of the 101st Airborne Division* (Nashville, TN: Battery Press, 2000; reprint of 1948 edition), p. 166.

2. Donald Burgett, *Currahee: A Screaming Eagle at Normandy* (Novato: Presidio Press, 1999), pp. 129–134; Mark Bando, *The Screaming Eagles at Normandy* (Osceola, WI: Motor Books International, 2001), pp. 98–99; *101st Airborne: Screaming Eagles at Normandy* (Osceola, WI: Motor Books International, 1994), pp. 95–99. Contrary to Burgett's account, some troopers believe the M5 Stuart was knocked out by German *panzerfaust* fire from a nearby ditch.

3. Marshall, *Night Drop*, p. 323; Rapport and Northwood, *Rendezvous with Destiny*, p. 156; S. L. A. Marshall, Regimental Unit Study Number 3, "506 Parachute Infantry Regiment in Normandy Drop," Historical Manuscripts Collection, File Number 8–3.1, BB 3, CMH, 56–57.

4. Rapport and Northwood, *Rendezvous with Destiny*, pp. 156–157; Robert Bowen and Chris Anderson, editor, *Fighting with the Screaming Eagles: With the 101st Airborne from Normandy to Bastogne* (London: Greenhill Books, 2001), pp. 62–67.

5. Marshall, *Night Drop*, pp. 323–326; Rapport and Northwood, *Rendezvous with Destiny*, pp. 156–157; Burgett, *Currahee*, pp. 134–137; Marshall, "506 Parachute Infantry Regiment in Normandy Drop," CMH.

6. U.S. Army, *Utah Beach to Cherbourg*, p. 78; Marshall, *Night Drop*, pp. 330–334; Rapport and Northwood, *Rendezvous with Destiny*, pp. 158–159; Bando, *Screaming Eagles at Normandy*, p. 99; *101st Airborne at Normandy*, pp. 98–99.

7. U.S. Army, *Utah Beach to Cherbourg*, pp. 78–79; Rapport and Northwood, *Rendezvous with Destiny*, pp. 166–171; Marshall, *Night Drop*, pp. 335–340.

8. Rapport and Northwood, *Rendezvous with Destiny*, pp. 170–171; Marshall, *Night Drop*, pp. 340–343.

9. Rapport and Northwood, *Rendezvous with Destiny*, pp. 173–180; Marshall, *Night Drop*, 347–354; Bando, *Screaming Eagles at Normandy*, pp. 102–104; *101st Airborne at Normandy*, p. 113.

10. U.S. Army, *Utah Beach to Cherbourg*, pp. 80–82; Rapport and Northwood, *Rendezvous with Destiny*, pp. 180–185; Bando, *101st Airborne at Normandy*, pp. 113–114.

11. Rapport and Northwood, *Rendezvous with Destiny*, pp. 183–196; Marshall, *Night Drop*, pp. 360–377; Bando, *101st Airborne at Normandy*, pp. 113–116.

Simmons stayed in the Army after the war and eventually rose to the rank of general.

12. U.S. Army, *Utah Beach to Cherbourg*, pp. 83–85; Rapport and Northwood, *Rendezvous with Destiny*, pp. 196–219; Marshall, *Night Drop*, pp. 376–412; Bando, *Screaming Eagles at Normandy*, pp. 118–119; *101st Airborne at Normandy*, 116–118. One of the soldiers who held off the Germans at the Cabbage Patch was none other than Staff Sergeant Harrison Summers, the D-Day hero of WXYZ. His story is recounted in McManus, *The Americans at D-Day*.

13. U.S. Army, *Utah Beach to Cherbourg*, pp. 87–90; Harrison, *Cross Channel Attack*, pp. 361–365; Rapport and Northwood, *Rendezvous with Destiny*, pp. 219–232; Ewing, *29 Let's Go*, pp. 78–83; Balkoski, *Beyond the Beachhead*, pp. 179–182, 196–203; John King, oral history, EC. King was the commander of K Company, 175th, the unit that established the initial contact with the 327th.

14. Burgett, *Currahee*, pp. 158–160.

15. Rapport and Northwood, *Rendezvous with Destiny*, pp. 230–232; Stephen Ambrose, *Band of Brothers* (New York: Simon and Schuster, 1992), pp. 94–98; Wayne Sisk, oral history, EC; Leo Boyle, Harry Welsh, interviews with Dr. Stephen Ambrose, n.d., EC.

16. Burgett, *Currahee*, pp. 169–179.

17. Len Goodgall, interview with Aaron Elson, 5/16/94, featured at www.tankbooks.com. Years later, at a reunion, Goodgall saw Bolles and apologized for shooting him. Bolles graciously accepted the apology.

18. Ambrose, *Band of Brothers*, pp. 98–101; Sisk, oral history, EC.

19. Rapport and Northwood, *Rendezvous with Destiny*, pp. 236–245; Bando, *101st Airborne at Normandy*, pp. 125–132; Bando, *Screaming Eagles at Normandy*, pp. 122–124; Ambrose, *Band of Brothers*, pp. 101–102; Donald Houston, *Hell on Wheels: The 2d Armored Division* (San Rafael, CA: Presidio Press, 1977), pp. 201–203; William True and Deryck Tufts True, *The Cow Spoke French: The Story of Sgt. William True, American Paratrooper in World War II* (Bennington, VT: Merriam Press, 2002), pp. 86–88.

20. Mervin Haugh, interview with Dr. Ronald Marcello, 5/31/99, Number 1298, UNT.

21. Bradley and Blair, *General's Life*, pp. 259–260; Ralph Bennett, *Ultra in the West: The Normandy Campaign* (New York: Charles Scribner's Sons, 1979), pp. 71–72. The official history ascribed the timely arrival of the 2nd Armored Division to a garbled message General Cota sent from Montmartin-en-Graignes. In the report, Cota related seeing "150 German soldiers," but a messenger believed he had said, "150 German tanks." In response, so the story went, Bradley diverted the 2nd Armored to the Carentan area, in order to secure the linkup of the Utah and Omaha beachheads. Cota's report was indeed garbled, but Ultra intelligence was the primary reason Bradley sent

the tanks to relieve the 101st at Carentan. See U.S. Army, *Utah Beach to Cherbourg*, p. 92; Ewing, *29 Let's Go*, pp. 81–83; Rapport and Northwood, *Rendezvous with Destiny*, pp. 242–245.

4. Stalled Before St-Lô

1. Harrison, *Cross Channel Attack*, pp. 379–381; *Combat History of the Second Division*, p. 27; Charles Curley, *How a Ninety-Day Wonder Survived the War: The Story of a Rifle Platoon Leader in the Second IndianHead Division During World War II* (Richmond and Petersburg, VA: Dietz Press, 1998), pp. 57–60.
2. Harrison, *Cross Channel Attack*, p. 381; Clement Turpin, personal Web site, www.angelfire.com.
3. *Combat History of the Second Division*, pp. 27–28; Henry Grady Spencer, *Nineteen Days in June 1944* (Kansas City, MO: Lowell Press, 1984), pp. 171–215. Spencer won the Silver Star for his leadership on June 19, 1944.
4. Cawthon, *Other Clay*, p. 83; Balkoski, *Beyond the Beachhead*, pp. 209–210.
5. Bob Slaughter, oral history, EC.
6. Harrison, *Cross Channel Attack*, 381–383; Balkoski, *Beyond the Beachhead*, pp. 211–212; Ewing, *29 Let's Go*, p. 84; Binkoski and Plaut, *115th Infantry Regiment in World War II*, pp. 54–59; Marquis, oral history, EC; Sidney Bingham to Thomas Francis Eagan, 1/11/47, EC.
7. Harrison, *Cross Channel Attack*, p. 383; Balkoski, *Beyond the Beachhead*, pp. 215–218; Ewing, *29 Let's Go*, pp. 85–88; Father Gerald "Rod" Taggart, unpublished diary, EC. Henry Hill, veteran's questionnaire, United States Army Military History Institute, Carlisle, PA (hereafter referred to as USAMHI).
8. Bradley, *Soldier's Story*, p. 295; Balkoski, *Beyond the Beachhead*, pp. 217–218.

5. The Struggle for Cherbourg

1. U.S. Army, *Utah Beach to Cherbourg*, pp. 133–135; Collins, *Lightning Joe*, pp. 210–211.
2. Richard Grondin, oral history, EC; Kocour, unpublished memoir, p. 4.
3. U.S. Army, *Utah Beach to Cherbourg*, pp. 134–135; Colby, *War from the Ground Up*, pp. 44–55, 485–486. Colby believed that the Fox and George Company soldiers panicked because they thought the friendly artillery was German. They were, in his opinion, so green that they did not know the difference. This is certainly a possibility, but it seems more likely that several days in battle would have taught them the difference between outgoing and incoming rounds. My feeling is that several friendly-fire episodes, including the one the night before, had made them quite wary of their

own artillery. The best way to escape American artillery fire was to run to the rear; the same could not be said for enemy fire.

4. U.S. Army, *Utah Beach to Cherbourg*, pp. 135–136; Joseph Mittelman, *Eight Stars to Victory: A History of the Veteran Ninth U.S. Infantry Division* (Nashville, TN: Battery Press, 1948), pp. 167–168; Robert Baldridge, *Victory Road*, (Bennington, VT: Merriam Press, 1999), pp. 52–54.

5. U.S. Army, *Utah Beach to Cherbourg*, pp. 135–136; David Waters, unpublished memoir, pp. 11–13, EC; Dillon, oral history, EC.

6. U.S. Army, *Utah Beach to Cherbourg*, pp. 137; Collins, *Lightning Joe*, pp. 211–212; Wills, *Put on Your Boots and Parachutes*, pp. 219–220; Tucker, *Thirty-five Days in Normandy*, pp. 35–36; Blanchard, *Our Liberators*, pp. 22–30; O'Donnell, *Beyond Valor*, pp. 167–168; Jack Isaacs, oral history, EC; McCaul, "82d Airborne Trooper at Normandy," interview with Dunfee, *World War II*.

7. Max Dach, unpublished memoir, p. 10, EC.

8. Baldridge, *Victory Road*, pp. 54–55.

9. U.S. Army, *Utah Beach to Cherbourg*, pp. 142–149; Collins, *Lightning Joe*, p. 215; Mittelman, *Eight Stars to Victory*, pp. 168–174; Harrison, *Cross Channel Attack*, pp. 408–416.

10. Morison, *Invasion of France and Germany*, pp. 176–179; Ruppenthal, *Logistical Support of the Armies*, pp. 406–415; Dwight Eisenhower, *Crusade in Europe* (New York: Doubleday, 1948), p. 261; Bradley, *Soldier's Story*, pp. 302–304; James Shonak to Dave Curry, 4/18/01, reproduced at Dave Curry's personal Web site. The British artificial harbor, Port Winston, survived the storm. Royal Navy officers who supervised the mulberry program estimated that, at best, the mulberries contributed only 15 percent of Allied supplies in Normandy. Rear Admiral John Hall, commander of Task Force O, thought the mulberries consumed more steel and more man-hours than they were worth. But Ike's chief of staff, General Bedell Smith, believed the mulberries were worth it. The 15 percent of supplies they contributed were, in Smith's view, critical. On balance, the mulberries were a great idea and an impressive engineering achievement, but Hall was correct. They did consume more resources than they were worth. Their contribution to the Allied supply effort was minimal.

11. Collins, *Lightning Joe*, pp. 215–216.

12. U.S. Army, *Utah Beach to Cherbourg*, pp. 153–156, 160–163; Mittelman, *Eight Stars to Victory*, p. 176; *The Cross of Lorraine: A Combat History of the 79th Infantry Division, June 1942–December 1945* (Nashville, TN: Battery Press 2000), p. 18

13. U.S. Army, *Utah Beach to Cherbourg*, pp. 152–165; Johnson, *History of the Twelfth Regiment in World War II*, pp. 86–92; Jensen, *Strike Swiftly!*,

pp. 158–161, 170; Coleman, unpublished memoir, EC; William Jones, oral history, EC; John Ausland, unpublished memoir, p. 7, EC; Sam Ricker, oral history, EC.

14. U.S. Army, *Utah Beach to Cherbourg*, p. 171; Collins, *Lightning Joe*, p. 218.
15. Harrison, *Cross Channel Attack*, pp. 378–379; Thomas Alexander Hughes, *Overlord: General Pete Quesada and the Triumph of Tactical Airpower in World War II* (New York: Free Press, 1995), pp. 145–151; Roger Freeman, *The Mighty Eighth: A History of the U.S. 8th Army Air Force* (Garden City, NY: Doubleday, 1970), pp. 155–157; Kenn Rust, *The 9th Air Force in World War II* (Fallbrook, CA: Aero Publishers, 1967), pp. 84–86.
16. Alvin Siegel, unpublished memoir, p. 114, EC.
17. William Hess, interview with Dr. Ronald Marcello, 2/19/99, UNT.
18. Leonard Schallehn, oral history, EC.
19. Hughes, *Overlord*, pp. 155–157; Bradley, *Soldier's Story*, p. 250. The argument over strategic versus tactical employment of air power continues to this day. Wars are seldom won without air power, but only rarely are they won *solely* with airpower. Like it or not, the Air Force is, in the end, a support branch for the ground troops. Thus its greatest responsibility should be tactical, not strategic.
20. William Dunn, *Fighter Pilot: The First American Ace of World War II* (Lexington: University Press of Kentucky, 1982), pp. 137–138.
21. Quentin Aanenson, "A Fighter Pilot's Story," unpublished memoir/documentary transcript, Record Group 403, Box 9, Folder 7, p. 5, Mighty Eighth Library; John Ashby Marshall to father, 7/1/44 and 9/18/44, MS1881, Box 16, Folder 15, SCUTK. Both of these quotes can also be found in John C. McManus, *Deadly Sky: The American Combat Airman in World War II* (Novato, CA: Presidio Press, 2000), pp. 155–156, 255–256.
22. Hughes, *Overlord*, pp. 159–163; Collins, *Lightning Joe*, p. 218.
23. Gabriel Greenwood, oral history, EC.
24. Hughes, *Overlord*, pp. 163–164.
25. Siegel, unpublished memoir, p. 115, EC.
26. U.S. Army, *Utah Beach to Cherbourg*, pp. 172–173; Hughes, *Overlord*, pp. 164–165; Rust, *9th Air Force in World War II*, p. 89; John Sullivan, *Overlord's Eagles: Operations of the United States Army Air Force in the Invasion of Normandy in World War II* (Jefferson, NC: McFarland, 1997), pp. 128–129; Wesley Craven and James Cate, editors, *The Army Air Forces in World War II: Argument to V-E Day: January 1944 to May 1945* (Washington, DC: Office of Air Force History, 1983; reprint of 1951 edition), pp. 199–201; Mittelman, *Eight Stars to Victory*, p. 177; Leroy McFarland, oral history, EC.
27. U.S. Army, *Utah Beach to Cherbourg*, pp. 179–182; Mittelman, *Eight Stars to Victory*, p. 177.

28. Dominic Dilberto, oral history, EC.

29. U.S. Army, *Utah Beach to Cherbourg*, pp. 179–182; Mittelman, *Eight Stars to Victory*, pp. 177–179; Lloyd Guerin, unpublished memoir, p. 1, EC.

30. U.S. Army, *Utah Beach to Cherbourg*, pp. 177–179; *Cross of Lorraine*, pp. 20–25; Byron Nelson, unpublished memoir, p. 13, EC.

31. U.S. Army, *Utah Beach to Cherbourg*, pp. 173–177; Harrison, *Cross Channel Attack*, pp. 430–432; Astor, *Greatest War*, pp. 612–613; Johnson, *History of the Twelfth Infantry Regiment in World War II*, pp. 92–103; Collins, *Lightning Joe*, pp. 219–220; Jensen, *Strike Swiftly!*, p. 176; Ausland, unpublished memoir, p. 9, EC; Ralph W. Hampton, unpublished memoir, p. 1, EC; Massa, oral history, EC.

32. U.S. Army, *Utah Beach to Cherbourg*, pp. 191–192; Mittelman, *Eight Stars to Victory*, pp. 179–181.

33. Johnson, *History of the Twelfth Infantry Regiment in World War II*, pp. 104–111; Hampton, unpublished memoir, p. 1, EC.

34. U.S. Army, *Utah Beach to Cherbourg*, pp. 190–192; Harrison, *Cross Channel Attack*, pp. 434–436; *Cross of Lorraine*, pp. 25–27; Edward Murphy, *Heroes of WWII* (New York: Ballantine Books, 1990), p. 210. Like so many Medal of Honor recipients, Kelly did not survive the war. He died of wounds in November 1944. Ogden was more fortunate. He lived through the war and later served as Governor Ronald Reagan's director of selective service in California.

35. Bradley, *Soldier's Story*, p. 312.

36. Morison, *Invasion of France and Germany*, pp. 198–202; Massa, oral history, EC.

37. Bernard Hydo, unpublished diary, EC.

38. Morison, *Invasion of France and Germany*, pp. 202–205; James Blackburn, Ross Olsen, oral histories, EC.

39. Morison, *Invasion of France and Germany*, pp. 205–212; Collins, *Lightning Joe*, p. 221. Martin Somers, "Right Hard Rudder! All Hands Below! The U.S. Battleship *Texas* in the Bombardment of Cherbourg," *Saturday Evening Post*, 9/16/44, pp. 18–19, 109–110.

40. U.S. Army, *Utah Beach to Cherbourg*, pp. 193–200, Harrison, *Cross Channel Attack*, pp. 438–441; Mittelman, *Eight Stars to Victory*, pp. 181–182.

41. Nelson, unpublished memoir, pp. 13–14, EC.

42. Hank Henderson, interview with Dr. Charles W. Johnson, 10/23/86, SCUTK.

43. Harrison, *Cross Channel Attack*, pp. 441–442; Waddell, *United States Army Logistics*, pp. 61–62.

44. Neillands, *Battle of Normandy, 1944*, p. 175.

6. The Hedgerow Maze

1. Foye, interview with Elson, www.tankbooks.com.
2. Martin Blumenson, *The United States Army in World War II: Breakout and Pursuit* (Washington, DC: Office of the Chief of Military History, Department of the Army, 1961), pp. 40–44, Doubler, *Closing with the Enemy*, pp. 36–38. Doubler's book is the best single study of how the U.S. Army improvised tactics to overcome the terrain and the formidable German resistance in Normandy.
3. Cawthon, *Other Clay*, pp. 87–88.
4. William Maher to parents, 7/1/44, Box 22, Folder 1853, Western Historical Manuscript Collection, University of Missouri–Columbia (hereafter referred to as WHMC).
5. John Aller, "I Saw It Through," self-published memoir (n.d.), p. 141, EC.
6. Ewing, *29 Let's Go!*, p. 89.
7. Lyle Groundwater, oral history, EC.
8. Colby, *War from the Ground Up*, pp. 56–58.
9. Cawthon, *Other Clay*, p. 87.
10. Brayton Danner, "A Bad Day near St.-Lô, and Other Remarkable Stories of World War II," self-published, 1999, pp. 83–88, copy in author's possession.
11. J. Q. Lynd, unpublished memoir, pp. 75–80, EC.
12. Johnson, *One More Hill*, pp. 154–156.
13. Doubler, *Closing with the Enemy*, pp. 42–58, Blumenson, *Breakout and Pursuit*, pp. 40–44, Peter Mansoor, *G.I. Offensive in Europe: The Triumph of American Infantry Divisions* (Lawrence: University Press of Kansas, 1999), pp. 149–156, Colby, *War from the Ground Up*, pp. 540–541. James Shonak to Dave Curry, 5/24/01, reproduced at Curry's personal Web site. O. T. Grimes, "Hedgerow Infantry Combat in WWII," EC. John A. Smith, "Chief of Staff Diary," 6/29/44, Box 2, 3rd Armored Division, University of Illinois Archives, (hereafter referred to as UI Archives).

7. La Haye-du-Puits

1. Blumenson, *Breakout and Pursuit*, pp. 53–61, Wills, *Put On Your Boots and Parachutes*, pp. 225–227, Tucker, *Thirty-five Days in Normandy*, pp. 40–45, Frank James Price, *Troy H. Middleton: A Biography* (Baton Rouge: Louisiana State University Press, 1974). Tucker did not see Caruso again until a reunion in 1986. Even then, Caruso "was as happy and jovial as he always was. He only had one leg, but he could still dance to anything better than I could."
2. John Delury, unpublished memoir pp. 34–36; Porcella, oral history, EC.
3. Robert Salander to parents, 7/10/45, Box 31, Folder 2591, WHMC.

4. Dwayne Burns, unpublished memoir, pp. 88–89, EC.

5. Mark Alexander, *The Static Line*, March 2003, p. 29.

6. Richard Mote, "My Combat Diary," EC.

7. Delury, unpublished memoir, p. 37; Porcella, oral history, EC.

8. O'Donnell, *Beyond Valor*, pp. 172–173; Booth and Spencer, *Paratrooper*, pp. 201–202; Blair, *Ridgway's Paratroopers*, pp. 292–294. Lieutenant Colonel Mendez was not the only officer who opposed this attack. In *Ridgway's Paratroopers*, Clay Blair revealed that several of Ridgway's senior commanders, including General Gavin, felt that the 82nd should not have been involved in this offensive at all. They were concerned that the division would be eliminated as an effective fighting unit. Ridgway listened to their concerns and rejected them, leading, in Blair's estimation, to a "great-and-lasting controversy . . . in the 82nd Division."

9. Blumenson, *Breakout and Pursuit*, pp. 61–63; O'Donnell, *Beyond Valor*, pp. 173–174. DeWeese, unpublished diary; Burns, unpublished memoir, p. 90, EC. The mother of the officer whom Mendez tried to carry to safety inexplicably blamed him for her son's death. This devastated Mendez, who already felt bad enough about the man's death. "It wounded me. I dreamt about it several times." Private Porcella enjoyed a special connection with Lieutenant Colonel Mendez. The two ate breakfast with each other shortly after the July 4 attack. Both of them were in a grief-stricken daze. For a time they talked about the men who had been killed or wounded. "Then in silence we sat there with our own thoughts. I don't know how much time went by." As Porcella finished his breakfast and left, he looked at Mendez, who had his head bowed. "I just stood there looking at him . . . and finally he looked up at me. There were tears running down his face. He watched as I wiped tears from my eyes. I gave him a weak salute, and turned around and left him to his own thoughts." Porcella, oral history, EC.

10. Blumenson, *Breakout and Pursuit*, pp. 72–76; *Cross of Lorraine*, pp. 32–35; Marc Griesbach, *Combat History of the Eighth Infantry Division in World War II* (Nashville, TN: Battery Press, 1988; reprint of 1945 edition), pp. 17–18; Gregory Canellis, "These Are My Credentials: An Oral History of the 13th Infantry Regiment in World War II," pp. 49–50, undergraduate thesis, Historical Studies Program, Richard Stockton College, 1999.

11. Colby, *War from the Ground Up*, pp. 98–102, 119–120.

12. Harvey Safford, oral history, EC.

13. Blumenson, *Breakout and Pursuit*, pp. 65–66.

14. Henry William, "Combat Boots," self-published memoir, reproduced at www.tankbooks.com Web site.

15. Blumenson, *Breakout and Pursuit*, pp. 66–67; Colby, *War from the Ground Up*, p. 103; Aaron Elson, *Tanks for the Memories: The 712th Tank Battalion During World War II* (Chi Chi Books, 2002), reproduced at www.tankbooks.com.

16. Blumenson, *Breakout and Pursuit*, pp. 68–69; Colby, *War from the Ground Up*, pp. 102–108, 119–120, 492–493; Elson, *Tanks for the Memories*.

17. Colby, *War from the Ground Up*, pp. 489, 511–512; Elson, *Tanks for the Memories*; Bob Levine, interview with Aaron Elson, 3/6/99, reproduced at www.tankbooks.com.

18. Colby, *War from the Ground Up*, pp. 78, 510–516; Elson, *Tanks for the Memories*; Levine interview with Elson, www.tankbooks.com. Dzienis's account is from a letter he wrote to Myron Kiballa, Gerald's brother, on 1/17/86. The letter is reproduced at www.tankbooks.com. Aaron Elson has written a book that covers the experiences of Flowers and his platoon in even more depth than *Tanks for the Memories*. The book is called *They Were All Young Kids: The Story of Lieutenant Jim Flowers and the First Platoon, Company C, 712 Tank Battalion, on Hill 122*, and it was published in 1997 by Chi Chi Press.

19. Blumenson, *Breakout and Pursuit*, pp. 69–72; Colby, *War from the Ground Up*, pp. 122–137, 495, 534–536; "Company G, 357th Infantry Diary," reproduced at www.tankbooks.com. Hamilton won the Distinguished Service Cross, a Silver Star, three Bronze Stars, and three Purple Hearts. On September 10, 1944, he was badly wounded at Hayange, France. He survived, but he lost an eye and his military career was over. He ended up working for the CIA after the war.

20. Blumenson, *Breakout and Pursuit*, pp. 78–82.

21. Collins, *Lightning Joe*, p. 228.

22. Benjamin Johnson, unpublished memoir, pp. 22–23, MS1881, Box 13, Folder 4, SCUTK.

23. Blumenson, *Breakout and Pursuit*, pp. 82–84; Collins, *Lightning Joe*, pp. 228–229; Blanchard, *Our Liberators*, pp. 53–54; Aller, "I Saw It Through," pp. 144–149, EC.

24. Johnson, unpublished memoir, p. 23, SCUTK.

25. Blumenson, *Breakout and Pursuit*, pp. 84–86; Collins, *Lightning Joe*, p. 229; Ernie Hayhow, *The Thunderbolt Across Europe: A History of the 83rd Infantry Division, 1942–1945* (Munich, Germany: F. Bruckmann, K.G., 1945), pp. 29–30; Aller, "I Saw It Through," p. 151, EC.

26. For a discussion of the prodigious turnover rate in front-line rifle companies, see McManus, *Deadly Brotherhood*, pp. 131–132.

27. Johnson, *History of the Twelfth Infantry Regiment in World War II*, pp. 122–123; Coleman, unpublished memoir, EC.

28. Blumenson, *Breakout and Pursuit*, pp. 86–90, 130–133; Johnson, *History of the Twelfth Infantry Regiment in World War II*, pp. 125–132; Hayhow, *Thunderbolt Across Europe*, pp. 32–33; Collins, *Lightning Joe*, pp. 229–230; Jensen, *Strike Swiftly!*, pp. 181–185. The 4th Division suffered 2,300 casualties in this VII Corps attack.

8. Prelude to St-Lô

1. Blumenson, *Breakout and Pursuit*, pp. 90–99; Historical Division, Department of the Army, *St-Lô: 7 July–19 July* (Washington, DC: Center of Military History, United States, 1946, and 1984 reprint), pp. 9–17; Folkestad, *View from the Turret*, pp. 41–42; Robert Hewitt, *Work Horse of the Western Front: The Story of the 30th Infantry Division* (Washington, DC: Infantry Journal Press, 1946), pp. 26–28.

2. Robert Bradley, *Aid Man!* (New York: Vantage Press, 1970), pp. 14–15, 58–59.

3. Blumenson, *Breakout and Pursuit*, pp. 104–110; Hewitt, *Work Horse of the Western Front*, p. 28; Haynes Dugan, "Third Armored Division History," manuscript copy, Box 59, UI Archives. Haynes Dugan to Travis Leon Ussery, 9/23/82, Box 1, UI Archives; Albert H. Bowman, unpublished diary, MS 2012, Box 3, Folder 13, SCUTK. Hewitt's 30th Division history is surprisingly restrained and understated in describing the traffic jam and Hobbs's displeasure. Corlett's illness got so bad that another corps commander, Major General Walton Walker, at times had to fill in for him during this battle.

4. Blumenson, *Breakout and Pursuit*, pp. 110–114; Folkestad, *View from the Turret*, pp. 42–44; Hewitt, *Work Horse of the Western Front*, pp. 29–30; Dugan, "Third Armored Division History," Box 59, UI. When Hobbs issued his ultimatum, he knew that Corlett was equally exasperated with Bohn.

5. Blumenson, *Breakout and Pursuit*, pp. 112–115; Charles Shrader, *Amicide: The Problem of Friendly Fire in Modern War* (Fort Leavenworth, KS: U.S. Army Command and General Staff College, 1982), pp. 79–84; Dugan, "Third Armored Division History," Box 59, UI. Incredibly, General Bohn was trying to establish radio contact with Redmond when the friendly-fire battle began. On an open radio at his CP, Bohn heard Redmond's cry of pain when his tank was hit and also his comment about being in "dreadful agony."

6. Blumenson, *Breakout and Pursuit*, pp. 115–116; Dugan, "Third Armored Division History," Box 59, UI Archives.

7. Blumenson, *Breakout and Pursuit*, pp. 116–117; Historical Division, Department of the Army, *St-Lô*, pp. 33–37, 42–45; Third Armored Division, *Spearhead in the West: The Third Armored Division*, self-published, 1945, pp. 67–68; Dugan, "Third Armored Division History," Box 59, UI Archives; Ralph Balestrieri, "Hauts Vents (Hill 91)—A Forward Observer's View," unpublished memoir, pp. 1–12, Box 59, UI Archives.

8. Blumenson, *Breakout and Pursuit*, pp. 117–118, 135–140; Historical Division, Department of the Army, *St-Lô*, pp. 37–42; Mittelman, *Eight Stars to Victory*, pp. 190–194; Hewitt, *Work Horse of the Western Front*, pp. 30–31; Thomas Kattar, oral history, EC. Companies A and C of the 899th Tank

Destroyer Battalion received Distinguished Unit Citations for their role in blunting the Panzer Lehr attack.

9. Agony and Bloodshed: St-Lô

1. Blumenson, *Breakout and Pursuit*, pp. 146–149; Balkoski, *Beyond the Beach-head*, pp. 233–235, 267–268.
2. Historical Division, Department of the Army, *St-Lô*, pp. 53–54; Ewing, *29 Let's Go*, pp. 93–94; Balkoski, *Beyond the Beachhead*, pp. 237–240; Binkoski and Plaut, *115th Infantry Regiment in World War II*, pp. 69–70; Johns, *Clay Pigeons of St-Lô*, pp. 93–95, 114–139.
3. Blumenson, *Breakout and Pursuit*, pp. 156–157; Historical Division, Department of the Army, *St-Lô*, pp. 54–58; Ewing, *29 Let's Go*, pp. 94–95; Balkoski, *Beyond the Beachhead*, pp. 240–246; Cawthon, *Other Clay*, pp. 92–96; Bingham to Eagan, EC; Russo, unpublished memoir, p. 25, EC.
4. Blumenson, *Breakout and Pursuit*, pp. 149–152; Historical Division, Department of the Army, *St-Lô*, pp. 58–61, 65–67; *Combat History of the Second Division*, pp. 29–33; Astor, *Greatest War*, pp. 620–621; Clem Turpin, unpublished memoir, personal Web site.
5. Blumenson, *Breakout and Pursuit*, pp. 149–153; Historical Division, Department of the Army, *St-Lô*, pp. 62–69; *Combat History of the Second Division*, p. 33; Curley, *How a Ninety-Day Wonder Survived the War*, pp. 79–93.
6. Balkoski, *Beyond the Beachhead*, pp. 245–248; Binkoski and Plaut, *115th Infantry Regiment in World War II*, p. 73; Johns, *Clay Pigeons of St-Lô*, pp. 151–157.
7. Historical Division, Department of the Army, *St-Lô*, pp. 76–77; Balkoski, *Beyond the Beachhead*, pp. 248–250; Binkoski and Plaut, *115th Infantry Regiment in World War II*, p. 71; Danner, "A Bad Day near St-Lô," pp. 170–175.
8. Historical Division, Department of the Army, *St-Lô*, p. 79; Ewing, *29 Let's Go*, p. 95; Balkoski, *Beyond the Beachhead*, pp. 249–254; Gordon, *One Man's War*, pp. 82–84; Taggart, unpublished diary, EC.
9. Blumenson, *Breakout and Pursuit*, pp. 162–163; Historical Division, Department of the Army, *St-Lô*, pp. 105–106; James Huston, *Biography of a Battalion: The Life and Times of an Infantry Battalion in Europe in World War II* (Mechanicsburg, PA: Stackpole Books, 2003; reprint of 1958 edition), pp. 14–38; Butler Miltonberger and James Huston, *All Hell Can't Stop Us: 134th Infantry Regiment Combat History of World War II*, transcribed onto 134th Infantry Regiment Web site by Roberta Russo; Bob Goldstein, unpublished journal, featured at 134th Infantry Regiment Web site; Lloyd Crumbling, interview with Dr. Ronald Marcello, 8/9/97, UNT. James Huston served in every capacity from rifle platoon leader to battalion operations officer. In the course of the war, he was the only officer in the 3rd Battalion, 134th Infantry, who never became a casualty.

10. Goldstein journal, 134th Infantry Regiment Web site. Goldstein was fortunate enough to survive his extensive wounds, but they eventually caught up with him. In 1999 he developed complications from those old wounds, and died from them a year later.

11. Blumenson, *Breakout and Pursuit*, pp. 162–163; Historical Division, Department of the Army, *St-Lô*, p. 107; Huston, *Biography of a Battalion*, pp. 34–39; Miltonberger and Huston, *134th Infantry Regiment; The 35th Infantry Division in World War II* (Atlanta, GA: Albert Love Enterprises, 1945) (there are no page numbers in this book). Crumbling interview with Marcello, UNT. Some 35th Division soldiers did press into St-Lô but Corlett ordered them back for fear that they would be cut off.

12. Binkoski and Plaut, *115th Infantry Regiment in World War II*, pp. 75–76; Balkoski, *Beyond the Beachhead*, pp. 255–257; Cawthon, *Other Clay*, pp. 96–97; Johns, *Clay Pigeons of St-Lô*, pp. 162–173.

13. Blumenson, *Breakout and Pursuit*, pp. 164–167; Historical Division, Department of the Army, *St-Lô*, pp. 108–113; Ewing, *29 Let's Go!*, pp. 97–99; Balkoski, *Beyond the Beachhead*, pp. 257–264; Bingham to Eagan, EC; Russo, unpublished memoir, pp. 26–28, EC, Danner, "A Bad Day near St-Lô," pp. 181–183. One reason Gerhardt was losing confidence in Ordway was because Ordway was suffering from combat fatigue.

14. Blumenson, *Breakout and Pursuit*, pp. 166–174; Historical Division, Department of the Army, *St-Lô*, pp. 108–122; Ewing, *29 Let's Go!*, pp. 96–104; Binkoski and Plaut, *115th Infantry Regiment in World War II*, pp. 77–82; Balkoski, *Beyond the Beachhead*, pp. 260–277; Johns, *Clay Pigeons of St-Lô*, pp. 200–221, 251; Cawthon, *Other Clay*, pp. 97–104; Danner, "A Bad Day near St-Lô," pp. 185–208; Jones, oral history, EC. Cawthon described Howie as "the finest gentleman I ever knew."

10. Cobra

1. Martin Blumenson, *The Battle of the Generals: The Untold Story of the Falaise Pocket—The Campaign That Should Have Won World War II* (New York: William Morrow, 1993), pp. 120–121; *Breakout and Pursuit*, pp. 175–176. For more information on the Argonne Forest and Grant's 1864 campaign, see John Whiteclay Chambers, *The Oxford Companion to American Military History* (New York: Oxford University Press, 1999), pp. 133, 431.

2. Blumenson, *Breakout and Pursuit*, pp. 195–198; *Battle of the Generals*, pp. 118–134; D'Este, *Decision in Normandy*, pp. 337–351, 370–390; Collins, *Lightning Joe*, pp. 232–237; Bradley, *Soldier's Story*, pp. 329–332; Ambrose, *Citizen Soldiers*, pp. 77–80; Neillands, *Battle of Normandy*, pp. 240–268; Russell Weigley, *Eisenhower's Lieutenants: The Campaign of France and Germany 1944–1945* (Bloomington: Indiana University Press, 1981), pp. 210–215; James Jay

Carafano, *After D-Day: Operation Cobra and the Normandy Breakout* (Boulder, CO: Lynne Rienner, 2000), pp. 71–74, 82–91.

3. Bradley, *Soldier's Story*, pp. 340–341; Carafano, *After D-Day*, pp. 101–109; Sullivan, *Overlord's Eagles*, pp. 136–138; Blumenson, *Battle of the Generals*, pp. 134–136; Hughes, *Overlord*, pp. 198–200; Richard Davis, *Carl A. Spaatz and the Air War in Europe* (Washington, DC: Center for Air Force History, 1993), pp. 458–466; Benjamin Franklin Cooling, editor, *Case Studies in the Development of Close Air Support* (Washington, DC: Office of Air Force History, United States Air Force, 1990), pp. 267–268; John Sullivan, "The Botched Air Support of Operation COBRA," *Parameters*, March 1988, pp. 106–108.

4. Blumenson, *Breakout and Pursuit*, pp. 198–202; Hayhow, *Thunderbolt Across Europe*, pp. 32–33.

5. Blumenson, *Breakout and Pursuit*, pp. 201–204; Colby, *War from the Ground Up*, pp. 137–145; Bradley, *Soldier's Story*, pp. 297–298; Chandler, *Papers of Dwight David Eisenhower*, volume 4, pp. 2080–2081; Foye, interview with Elson, www.tankbooks.com; Arnold Brown, interview with Mr. Aaron Elson, 9/8/97, www.tankbooks.com.

6. Bradley, *Soldier's Story*, p. 346; Ambrose, *Citizen Soldiers*, p. 81; *The Supreme Commander: The War Years of General Dwight D. Eisenhower* (Garden City, NY: Doubleday, 1970), p. 462; Butcher, *My Three Years with Eisenhower: The Personal Diary of Captain Harry C. Butcher* (New York: Simon and Schuster, 1946), pp. 618–619; Chandler, *Papers of Dwight David Eisenhower*, volume 5, p. 161; Blumenson, *Breakout and Pursuit*, pp. 215–223; Carafano, *After D-Day*, pp. 107–108; Craven and Cate, *Argument to V-E Day*, pp. 228–230; Sullivan, *Overlord's Eagles*, pp. 139–193; Hughes, *Overlord*, pp. 200–201.

7. Craven and Cate, *Argument to V-E Day*, pp. 228–230; Carafano, *After D-Day*, pp. 11–18; Hughes, *Overlord*, pp. 205–208; Blumenson, *Breakout and Pursuit*, pp. 228–231; *Battle of the Generals*, pp. 136–138; Sullivan, *Overlord's Eagles*, p. 139; Freeman, *Mighty Eighth*, p. 163.

8. Carafano, *After D-Day*, p. 16; Wilbanks, unpublished diary, p. 12, EC.

9. Eugene Fletcher, *Fletcher's Gang: A B-17 Crew in Europe, 1944–45* (Seattle and London: University of Washington Press, 1988), pp. 90–91.

10. Richard Baynes, unpublished memoir, p. 63, Record Group 403, Box 9.2, Folder 4, Mighty Eighth Library; John White, unpublished diary, copy in author's possession.

11. Blumenson, *Breakout and Pursuit*, pp. 228–231; Craven and Cate, *Argument to V-E Day*, p. 230; Hughes, *Overlord*, pp. 206–207; Freeman, *Mighty Eighth*, p. 163; Weigley, *Eisenhower's Lieutenants*, pp. 222–228; Hewitt, *Workhorse of the Western Front*, p. 36; Dale Smith, *Screaming Eagle: Memoirs of a B-17 Group Commander* (Chapel Hill, NC: Algonquin Books, 1990), pp. 176–177.

12. Craven and Cate, *Argument to V-E Day*, p. 230; Blumenson, *Breakout and Pursuit*, pp. 231–233; *Battle of the Generals*, p. 138; Sullivan, *Overlord's Eagles*, p. 139; Collins, *Lightning Joe*, pp. 238–239; Hughes, *Overlord*, p. 208; Bradley, *Soldier's Story*, pp. 346–348, Bradley and Blair, *General's Life*, p. 279; Carafano, *After D-Day*, pp. 109–111; Richard Hallion, *Air Power over the Normandy Beaches and Beyond*, pp. 16–20, www.aero-web.org/history Web site.

13. Ernie Pyle, *Brave Men* (New York: Grosset and Dunlap, 1944), pp. 295–297.

14. Hughes, *Overlord*, pp. 210–212; Pyle, *Brave Men*, pp. 297–298.

15. Raymond Conlin, unpublished memoir, pp. 1–2, reproduced at 357th Fighter Group Association Web site.

16. Pyle, *Brave Men*, p. 298; Chester Jordan, "Bull Sessions: World War II . . . from Normandy to Remagen," p. 42, copy in author's possession. I thank Mr. Jordan for sending me a copy of this well-written, descriptive memoir. Ray Reeder, unpublished memoir, reproduced at 3rd Armored Division Association Web site.

17. Hughes, *Overlord*, p. 212; Collins, *Lightning Joe*, pp. 239–240; Towne, *Doctor Danger Forward*, p. 117; Pyle, *Brave Men*, p. 298; Baynes, unpublished memoir, p. 64, Mighty Eighth Library.

18. Craven and Cate, *Argument to V-E Day*, p. 233; Ambrose, *Citizen Soldiers*, p. 84; Carafano, *After D-Day*, p. 112; John Crowe, "Days in the Wild Blue Yonder," unpublished memoir, pp. 98–99, MS1427, Box 1, Folder 9, SCUTK; John Symanski to Wanda & Friends, 6/6/94, copy of the letter in author's possession; Allen Knisley, "A View from a Grasshopper," unpublished memoir, p. 5, Box 59, UI Archives.

19. Craven and Cate, *Argument to V-E Day*, p. 234; Hughes, *Overlord*, p. 214; Freeman, *Mighty Eighth*, p. 164; Hallion, *Air Power over the Normandy Beaches and Beyond*, pp. 16–17, www.aero-web.org/history Web site; Astor, *Mighty Eighth*, p. 344; Knisley, unpublished memoir, p. 5, Box 59, UI Archives.

20. Pyle, *Brave Men*, pp. 299–300; Blumenson, *Breakout and Pursuit*, pp. 236–237.

21. Carafano, *After D-Day*, p. 114; Jensen, *Strike Swiftly!*, pp. 189–190.

22. Blumenson, *Breakout and Pursuit*, pp. 236–237; Mittelman, *Eight Stars to Victory*, p. 200; Jordan, "Bull Sessions," pp. 42–43. The 9th Division's rifle companies also lost communication with their supporting artillery battalions because the bombing obliterated telephone wires and a fire direction center. The casualty numbers do not take into account the hundreds of combat fatigue and concussion cases.

23. Carafano, *After D-Day*, pp. 114–116; Hughes, *Overlord*, pp. 214–215; Hastings, *Overlord*, pp. 254–255; Hewitt, *Workhorse of the Western Front*, pp. 36–37; Bradley, *Aid Man!*, pp. 65–66; Murray Pulver, *The Longest Year* (Freeman, SD: Pine Hill Press, 1986), pp. 21–22; Alwyn Featherston, *Saving the Breakout:*

The 30th Division's Heroic Stand at Mortain, August 7–12, 1944 (Novato, CA: Presidio Press, 1993), pp. 30–37.

24. Blumenson, *Breakout and Pursuit*, pp. 236–237; Hughes, *Overlord*, pp. 216–217; Bradley, *Soldier's Story*, pp. 348–349; Bradley and Blair *General's Life*, p. 280; Craven and Cate, *Argument to V-E Day*, pp. 233–234; Sullivan, *Overlord's Eagles*, p. 140; Carafano, *After D-Day*, pp. 116–120. On the afternoon of July 25, a contingent of officers found McNair's remains and quietly removed them. Under great secrecy they buried him in a brief funeral ceremony two days later. Bradley and Patton both served as pallbearers. The secrecy was not, as some have supposed, because of the embarrassment that McNair's friendly-fire death would have caused the Army. It was because McNair was supposed to replace Patton as the notional commander of the First U.S. Army Group, the Fortitude organization that continued to deceive the Germans about Allied plans in France.

11. Breakthrough

1. Blumenson, *Breakout and Pursuit*, pp. 238–241; Weigley, *Eisenhower's Lieutenants* pp. 228–232; D'Este, *Decision in Normandy*, pp. 401–403; Craven and Cate, *Argument to V-E Day*, pp. 234–236; Roger Steinway, "Armored Platoon Commander," *World War II*, circa 2000.

2. Blumenson, *Breakout and Pursuit*, pp. 241–243; Weigley, *Eisenhower's Lieutenants*, pp. 228–232; Carafano, *After D-Day*, pp. 175–181; Mittelman, *Eight Stars to Victory*, pp. 200–201; Blanchard, *Our Liberators*, p. 55; Murphy, *Heroes of World War II*, pp. 211–213; Steinway, "Armored Platoon Commander"; Jordan, "Bull Sessions," pp. 43–44. In 1980, after years of lobbying by his men, Urban received the Medal of Honor for his exploits on July 25.

3. Carafano, *After D-Day*, pp. 133–165; Weigley, *Eisenhower's Lieutenants*, pp. 228–232; Blumenson, *Breakout and Pursuit*, pp. 245–246; *Battle of the Generals*, pp. 143–144; Hastings, *Overlord*, pp. 255–256; D'Este, *Decision in Normandy*, pp. 403–404; Hewitt, *Workhorse of the Western Front*, pp. 37–41; Folkestad, *View from the Turret*, pp. 50–52; Bradley, *Soldier's Story*, pp. 348–349, 358; Collins, *Lightning Joe*, pp. 242–243; Henderson, interview with Johnson, SCUTK.

4. Mittelman, *Eight Stars to Victory*, pp. 200–201; Carafano, *After D-Day*, p. 195; Jordan, "Bull Sessions," pp. 44–45.

5. Blumenson, *Breakout and Pursuit*, pp. 252–253; Carafano, *After D-Day*, pp. 197–199; Knickerbocker, *Danger Forward*, pp. 229–230; *Spearhead in the West: The Third Armored Division*, self-published unit history, 1945, pp. 70–71; Christopher Cornazzani, oral history, EC; Robert Gravlin, "World War II as a Combat Engineer with the Third Armored Division," unpublished memoir, p. 5, Box 59, UI Archives.

6. Blumenson, *Breakout and Pursuit*, pp. 253–254; Carafano, *After D-Day*, pp. 200–207; Knickerbocker, *Danger Forward*, pp. 230–232; Collins, *Lightning Joe*, pp. 242–243; *Spearhead in the West*, pp. 70–71; Reeder, unpublished memoir, 3rd Armored Division Web site; John Kropilak, "The Members Write," *3rd Armored Division Newsletter*, December 1990; E. A. Struble to sister, 6/7/45, Box 34, Folder 2912, WHMC.

7. Blumenson, *Breakout and Pursuit*, pp. 254–255; Houston, *Hell on Wheels*, pp. 213–215; Hughes, *Overlord*, pp. 219–220; Doubler, *Closing with the Enemy*, pp. 63–70; Mark Bando, *Breakout at Normandy: The 2nd Armored Division in the Land of the Dead* (Osceola, WI: Motor Books International, 1999), pp. 41–42; George Wilson, *If You Survive* (New York: Ivy Books, 1987), pp. 17–21; Aanenson, "A Fighter Pilot's Story," p. 6, Mighty Eighth Library.

8. Blumenson, *Breakout and Pursuit*, pp. 255–256; Houston, *Hell on Wheels*, pp. 216–217; Bando, *Breakout at Normandy*, pp. 42–44; Wilson, *If You Survive*, pp. 21–36.

9. Graham Cosmas and Albert Cowdrey, *The United States Army in World War II: Medical Service in the European Theater of Operations* (Washington, DC: Center of Military History, United States Army, 1992), pp. 224–228, 239–278; Albert Cowdrey, *Fighting for Life: American Military Medicine in World War II* (New York: Free Press, 1994), pp. 251–259; *Medicine Under Canvas: A War Journal of the 77th Evacuation Hospital* (Kansas City, MO: Sosland Press, 1945), pp. 113–114; Mary I. Ferrell, "My Experiences in World War II as an Army Nurse," *Daughters of the American Revolution National Magazine*, March 1949, pp. 286–287; Fred Smith, "Company History Company 'C,' 45th Armored Medical Battalion" (Part I), *Third Armored Division Newsletter*, March 1988, pp. 2–5; Robert Kauffman, "The Normandy Ward," *Third Armored Division Newsletter*, March 2002, pp. 22–25.

10. Bradley and Blair, *General's Life*, p. 281; Hughes, *Overlord*, p. 222; *Spearhead in the West*, p. 70; "The Normandy Breakthrough," After Action Report of CCA, 3rd Armored Division, 7/27/44 through 7/31/44, Box 4, UI Archives. Map VII in Blumenson, *Breakout and Pursuit* contains an excellent portrayal of the progress of American forces by the evening of July 28–29.

11. *Spearhead in the West*, p. 72; Houston, *Hell on Wheels*, 219–221; Bando, *Breakout at Normandy*, pp. 47–66.

12. Houston, *Hell on Wheels*, pp. 230–233; Bando, *Breakout at Normandy*, p. 46; Wilson, *If You Survive*, pp. 43–50.

13. Blumenson, *Breakout and Pursuit*, pp. 277–279; Craven and Cate, *Argument to V-E Day*, pp. 242–243; Carafano, *After D-Day*, p. 240; Hughes, *Overlord*, p. 224; Bando, *Breakout at Normandy*, pp. 82–85; David Cane, Judy Barrett Litoff, and David Smith, editors, *Fighting Fascism in Europe: The World War*

II Letters of an American Veteran of the Spanish Civil War (New York: Fordham University Press, 2003), pp. xxvii, 111–112, 232–233; John Marshall to sister, 7/30/44, MS1881, Box 16, Folder 15, SCUTK; Aanenson, "Fighter Pilot's Story," p. 6, Mighty Eighth Library. Later, in the Roncey battle, Lieutenant Cane earned a Silver Star by leading a surrounded American convoy, including dozens of tanks, through an enemy cordon to safety.

14. This passage on the 2nd Armored Division's battle at the Land of the Dead is derived primarily from Blumenson, *Breakout and Pursuit*, pp. 279–281; *Battle of the Generals*, p. 148; Houston, *Hell on Wheels*, pp. 222–226; Carafano, *After D-Day*, pp. 238–246; Hastings, *Overlord*, pp. 260–261; and Bando, *Breakout at Normandy*, pp. 91–96, 113–136, 142–145. Sergeant Whittington earned a battlefield commission, stayed in the Army, served in Vietnam, and retired as a major in 1967. In January 1969, for reasons known only to himself, Whittington committed suicide with a .45-caliber revolver. Several other Land of the Dead survivors also took their own lives in the postwar years. I would like to thank Mark Bando for his outstanding work on this little-known but important battle in the Cobra/breakthrough struggle in Normandy.

12. Breakout and Chase

1. Blumenson, *Breakout and Pursuit*, pp. 306–309; *Spearhead in the West*, pp. 72–73; William Breuer, *Death of a Nazi Army: The Falaise Pocket* (Chelsea, MI: Scarborough House, 1990), pp. 126–128; "The Normandy Breakthrough," After Action Report of CCA, 3rd Armored Division, 7/30/44 through 8/1/44, Box 4, UI Archives; Carlton Russell, unpublished memoir, pp. 74–75, Box 62, UI Archives.

2. Eugene Luciano, "Our Blood and His Guts! Memoirs of One of General Patton's Combat Soldiers," self-published memoir, 1995, pp. 25–26; Orville Watkins, oral history, EC.

3. Martin Blumenson, *Patton: The Man Behind the Legend, 1885–1945* (New York: Berkley Books, 1985), pp. 216–231; *Patton Papers, 1940–1945* (Boston: Houghton-Mifflin, 1974), pp. 326–384, 439–453, 490–494; Carlo D'Este, *Patton: A Genius for War* (New York: HarperPerennial, 1995), pp. 538–627; *Eisenhower: A Soldier's Life* (New York: Henry Holt, 2002), pp. 438–442, 488–491, 506–509, 561–563; Butcher, *My Three Years with Eisenhower*, pp. 480–481, 490; Stanley P. Hirshson, *General Patton: A Soldier's Life* (New York: HarperCollins, 2002), pp. 466–503.

4. Brown, interview with Elson, www.tankbooks.com; Canellis, "These Are My Credentials," pp. 53–54. In his diary, Patton briefly discussed his visit to the 90th Division. He was unimpressed: "The division is bad, the discipline poor, the men filthy, and the officers apathetic." Patton had great

hopes that General McLain would improve the division and he was not disappointed. See Blumenson, *Patton Papers, 1940–1945*, p. 497.

5. Blumenson, *Breakout and Pursuit*, pp. 309–322; *Battle of the Generals*, pp. 148–151; Weigley, *Eisenhower's Lieutenants*, pp. 254–257; Kenneth Koyen, *The Fourth Armored Division: From the Beach to Bavaria* (Nashville, TN: Battery Press, 2000; reprint of 1946 edition), pp. 14–22; "4th Armored Division After Action Report," 7/28/44 through 8/1/44, reproduced at www.fourtharmored.com Web site. Milton Moncrief, unpublished memoir, pp. 2–3, 6th Armored Division Association, reproduced at 6th Armored Division Web site.

6. Hastings, *Overlord*, pp. 281–283; Ruppenthal, *Logistical Support of the Armies*, pp. 299, 306 307, 463–474; Waddell, *Normandy Campaign*, pp. 105–106; Weigley, *Eisenhower's Lieutenants*, pp. 257–275; Ambrose, *Citizen Soldiers*, pp. 89–90; Chandler, *Papers of Dwight David Eisenhower*, volume 4, pp. 2049–2050, volume 5, p. 162; Blumenson, *Battle of the Generals*, pp. 160–165; *Patton Papers, 1940–1945*, pp. 496–503; D'Este, *Decision in Normandy*, pp. 408–413; *Patton: A Genius for War*, pp. 629–631; *Eisenhower*, pp. 562–564; Bradley, *Soldier's Story*, pp. 362–367; Bradley and Blair, *General's Life*, pp. 285–286; Price, *Troy H. Middleton*, pp. 185–190; Caleb Carr, "The American Rommel," *Military History Quarterly*, Summer 1992, pp. 77–85. The best single place to start in any study of the Brittany decision is A. Harding Ganz, "Questionable Objective: The Brittany Ports, 1944," *Journal of Military History*, January 1995, pp. 77–95.

7. Blumenson, *Breakout and Pursuit*, pp. 426–427, 434–435; Weigley, *Eisenhower's Lieutenants*, pp. 278–279; *Cross of Lorraine*, pp. 38–39; Roger Campbell, *Teenage Soldier*, self-published memoir, 1999, pp. 61–63; *Paths of Armor: The Fifth Armored Division in World War II* (Nashville, TN: Battery Press, 1993; originally published in 1950), pp. 45–52; 5th Armored Division, after action report, 81/44 through 8/6/44, reproduced at 5th Armored Division Association Web site.

8. Blumenson, *Breakout and Pursuit*, pp. 434–435; Weigley, *Eisenhower's Lieutenants*, pp. 277–278; Colby, *War from the Ground Up*, pp. 173–188, 495; Elson, *Tanks for the Memories*; "G Company, 357th Infantry Diary," www.tankbooks.com.; Kocour, unpublished memoir, p. 10.

9. Blumenson, *Breakout and Pursuit*, pp. 444–449; Johnson, *History of the Twelfth Infantry Regiment in World War II*, pp. 140–150; Mittelman, *Eight Stars to Victory*, pp. 204–205; Wilson, *If You Survive*, pp. 55–56; Roger Garland to wife, circa August, 1944, MS 1314, Box 2, Folder 1, SCUTK. The VII Corps suffered 2,000 casualties between August 2 and August 7.

10. Blumenson, *Breakout and Pursuit*, pp. 449–450; *28th Infantry Division in World War II* (Nashville, TN: Battery Press, 2000; originally published in 1946); this book has no page numbers. Wesley Reading, "World War II:

My Personal Account," unpublished memoir, reproduced at www.memoriesofwar.com Web site.

11. Blumenson, *Breakout and Pursuit*, pp. 449–450; Melvin Bush to family, n.d, Box 4, Folder 390, WHMC.

12. Blumenson, *Breakout and Pursuit*, pp. 451–454; Ewing, *29 Let's Go!*, pp. 114–116; Binkoski and Plaut, *115th Infantry Regiment in World War II*, pp. 97–101; Cawthon, *Other Clay*, pp. 114–124; Russo, unpublished memoir, pp. 29–30, EC; Aanenson, "A Fighter Pilot's Story," pp. 6–7, Mighty Eighth Library.

13. Mortain

1. Mark Reardon, *Victory at Mortain: Stopping Hitler's Panzer Counteroffensive* (Lawrence: University Press of Kansas, 2002), pp. 75–76; Russell, unpublished memoir, p. 77; interview with Lt. Col. Mark Reardon, 1/14/93, Box 62, UI Archives; Ralph Balestrieri, unpublished memoir, pp. 1–5, Box 59, UI Archives; Alvin Beckmann, interview with Reardon, 2/2/93, Box 62, UI Archives; Thomas Tousey, interview with Reardon, 1/26/93, Box 62, UI Archives. Tousey and the other soldiers remained at Barenton for another four days.

2. Blumenson, *Breakout and Pursuit*, pp. 457–463; *Battle of the Generals*, pp. 173–176; Featherston, *Saving the Breakout*, pp. 47–56; Hastings, *Overlord*, pp. 283–285; David Irving, *Hitler's War* (New York: Avon Books, 1990), pp. 673–674.

3. Featherston, *Saving the Breakout*, pp. 69–73; Reardon, *Victory at Mortain*, pp. 178–179; Bennett, *Ultra in the West*, pp. 114–115; Bradley, *General's Life*, pp. 289–293.

4. Thomas Street, *How to Survive Combat as Point Man If You're Lucky . . . and Lose Friends If They're Not* (Bennington, VT: Merriam Press, 2002), pp. 20–23.

5. Blumenson, *Breakout and Pursuit*, pp. 468–470; Featherston, *Saving the Breakout*, pp. 74–82; Reardon, *Victory at Mortain*, pp. 80–83; Bradley, *Aid Man!*, pp. 69–70; Mittelman, *Eight Stars to Victory*, pp. 208–210; Hewitt, *Work Horse of the Western Front*, pp. 54–58; Wilson, *If You Survive*, pp. 56–57. The dominant hill mass east of Mortain has been alternately referred to as both Hill 314 and Hill 317 in accounts of the battle. I have elected to go with Hill 314 because that was what the Army called it in 1944.

6. Featherston, *Saving the Breakout*, pp. 86–89; Hewitt, *Work Horse of the Western Front*, pp. 61–62; Reardon, *Victory at Mortain*, pp. 99–100; Pulver, *Longest Year*, pp. 30–33.

7. Featherston, *Saving the Breakout*, pp. 64–65, 90–94; Reardon, *Victory at Mortain*, pp. 100–101; Allyn Vannoy and Jay Karamales, *Against the Panzers:*

United States Infantry versus German Tanks, 1944–1945 (Jefferson, NC: McFarland, 1996), pp. 37–42.

8. Blumenson, *Breakout and Pursuit*, pp. 470–475; Featherston, *Saving the Breakout*, pp. 95–107, 120–122; Hewitt, *Work Horse of the Western Front*, pp. 59–60; Reardon, *Victory at Mortain*, pp. 123–134; Vannoy and Karamales, *Against the Panzers*, pp. 22–36.

9. Featherston, *Saving the Breakout*, pp. 114–117; Reardon, *Victory at Mortain*, pp. 144–147; Hewitt, *Work Horse of the Western Front*, pp. 70–72; Street, *How to Survive Combat*, pp. 23–26; Robert Weiss, *Fire Mission! The Siege at Mortain, Normandy August 1944* (Shippensburg, PA: Burd Street Press, 2002), pp. 52–63. Also see Robert Weiss, "Experience of War: High Noon at Mortain," *Military History Quarterly*, Winter 1998, pp. 108–111.

10. Rust, *9th Air Force in World War II*, pp. 102–103; Craven and Cate, *Argument to V-E Day*, pp. 248–249; Featherston, *Saving the Breakout*, pp. 129–137; Hughes, *Overlord*, pp. 235–238; Hallion, *Airpower over the Normandy Beaches and Beyond*, pp. 21–22; Pulver, *Longest Year*, pp. 33–34; Dunn, *Fighter Pilot*, p. 146.

11. Blumenson, *Breakout and Pursuit*, pp. 464–465, 481–486; Featherston, *Saving the Breakout*, pp. 140–145.

12. Featherston, *Saving the Breakout*, pp. 146–148; Reardon, *Victory at Mortain*, pp. 148–149; Hewitt, *Work Horse of the Western Front*, pp. 64–65; Bradley, *Aid Man!*, pp. 70–72; Pulver, *Longest Year*, pp. 34–35; Jack Thacker, unpublished memoir, pp. 14–15, MS1764, Box 18, Folder 10, SCUTK.

13. Breast, editor, *Missions Remembered*, pp. 126–127.

14. Featherston, *Saving the Breakout*, pp. 163–170; Bradley, *Soldier's Story*, pp. 293–295, 370–375; D'Este, *Decision in Normandy*, pp. 422–428; Eisenhower, *Crusade in Europe*, pp. 274–276. After the war, Montgomery, whose memoirs were distressingly disingenuous, claimed that from the start he had misgivings about the short envelopment plan. If he had such misgivings, he never expressed them on August 8, when he would have been in a position to have some influence on Allied strategy.

15. Reardon, *Victory at Mortain*, pp. 159–161; Hewitt, *Work Horse of the Western Front*, pp. 73–74; Featherston, *Saving the Breakout*, pp. 150–151, 171–175, 200–201; Weiss, *Fire Mission!*, pp. 101–112; Pulver, *Longest Year*, pp. 35–36; Street, *How to Survive Combat*, pp. 26–27. Hewitt claims that each man got two K-ration meals from the first C-47 air drop. This is probably an exaggeration (some men do not recall getting anything), but Private Street does remember receiving two such meals from the air drop. In *Victory at Mortain*, p. 201, Mark Reardon wrote that many of the supply bundles landed in the vicinity of E Company (where Street was positioned).

16. Blumenson, *Breakout and Pursuit*, p. 487; Featherston, *Saving the Breakout*, p. 177; Breuer, *Death of a Nazi Army*, pp. 223–225; Reardon, *Victory at*

Mortain, pp. 196–197; Dugan, "3rd Armored Division History," Box 39, UI Archives; Walter May, "The Death of Colonel Cornog," *3rd Armored Division Newsletter*, June 1992, pp. 29–30.

17. Reardon, *Victory at Mortain*, pp. 194–196; Johnson, *History of the Twelfth Infantry Regiment in World War II*, pp. 157–159; Dugan, "3rd Armored Division History," Box 39, UI Archives; Alton Pearson, unpublished memoir, pp. 6–8, CSWS; Harvey Patterson, interview with Lt. Col. Mark Reardon, 12/19/92, and Emmett Tripp, interview with Reardon, 12/11/92 and 12/18/92, all interviews contained in Box 62, UI Archives.

18. Featherston, *Saving the Breakout*, pp. 181–183; Hewitt, *Work Horse of the Western Front*, pp. 72–73; Weiss, *Fire Mission!*, pp. 109–114.

19. Featherston, *Saving the Breakout*, pp. 186–187; Reardon, *Victory at Mortain*, pp. 204–206; Dugan, "3rd Armored Division History," Box 39, UI Archives; Charles Corbin, interview with Lt. Col. Mark Reardon, 1/20/93; Tripp, Patterson interviews, Box 62, UI Archives.

20. Featherston, *Saving the Breakout*, pp. 192–198; Hewitt, *Work Horse of the Western Front*, pp. 74–76; Huston, *Biography of a Battalion*, pp. 66–71; *35th Infantry Division in World War II*, Weiss, *Fire Mission!*, pp. 126–127, 135–137; Baldridge, *Victory Road*, pp. 69–70.

21. Blumenson, *Breakout and Pursuit*, pp. 489–492; Featherston, *Saving the Breakout*, pp. 204–208; Hastings, *Overlord*, pp. 286–288; Hewitt, *Work Horse of the Western Front*, pp. 76–77; Ambrose, *Citizen Soldiers*, pp. 96–100; *35th Infantry Division in World War II*; Street, *How to Survive Combat*, pp. 28–29; Weiss, *Fire Mission!*, pp. 145–154.

14. The End at Normandy

1. Bradley, *Soldier's Story*, pp. 375–376; *General's Life*, p. 296; Eddy Florentin, *The Battle of the Falaise Gap* (New York: Hawthorn Books, 1965), translated from French to English by Mervyn Savill, p. 78.

2. Blumenson, *Breakout and Pursuit*, *Battle of the Generals*, pp. 204–206, pp. 497–505; Featherston, *Saving the Breakout*, pp. 211–213; Neillands, *Battle of Normandy*, pp. 348–357; Weigley, *Eisenhower's Lieutenants*, pp. 296–298; Florentin, *Battle of the Falaise Gap*, pp. 118–129.

3. Blumenson, *Breakout and Pursuit*, pp. 506–509; *Battle of the Generals*, pp. 206–214; *Patton Papers, 1940–1945*, pp. 506–515; Bradley, *Soldier's Story*, pp. 376–378; Bradley and Blair, *General's Life*, pp. 298–299; Hastings, *Overlord*, pp. 314–315; Weigley, *Eisenhower's Lieutenants*, pp. 302–307; Neillands, *Battle of Normandy*, pp. 356–359, 385–387; D'Este, *Decision in Normandy*, pp. 442–455; *Patton: Genius for War*, p. 641; Chester Wilmot, *Struggle for Europe*, pp. 419–420; Carlo D'Este, "Falaise: The Trap Not Sprung," *Military History Quarterly*, Spring 1994, pp. 58–68. Bradley had doubts for

the rest of his life about his decision. Martin Blumenson, at a thirty-year commemoration of the Battle of Normandy in 1974, saw a young Frenchman sincerely congratulate Bradley on trapping the Germans in the Falaise pocket. Bradley took the young man's hand, held it for a long moment, and sputtered, "Thank you. Do you really think so? Yes, yes, of course, thank you." The argument over the closing of the pocket has sometimes degenerated into national chauvinism by British or American scholars. One American author, Richard Rohmer, was so eager to blame Montgomery for failure to close the pocket that he wrote a book claiming that the British general had deliberately allowed the Germans to escape "for the sake of face, for the sake of his job, and in order to deprive the Americans of the . . . credit and glory they would receive if it was they who completed the encirclement." There is no evidence to support Rohmer's absurd and malicious contention. Richard Rohmer, *Patton's Gap: An Account of the Battle of Normandy, 1944* (New York: Beaufort, 1981), pp. 225–227. Montgomery had many character flaws, but in my view there is no possibility that he, or any other Allied senior officer, would have prolonged the war and doomed thousands of Allied soldiers to death, for the sake of reputation or ego.

4. Blumenson, *Breakout and Pursuit*, p. 511; Curley, *How a Ninety-Day Wonder Survived the War*, pp. 119–132.
5. Blumenson, *Breakout and Pursuit*, pp. 510–511; Mittelman, *Eight Stars to Victory*, pp. 213–215; Dach, unpublished memoir, p. 12, EC.
6. Blumenson, *Breakout and Pursuit*, pp. 510–511; *Spearhead in the West*, pp. 75–80.
7. Blumenson, *Breakout and Pursuit*, pp. 515–524; *Battle of the Generals*, pp. 215–229; Bradley, *Soldier's Story*, pp. 378–379; Bradley and Blair, *General's Life*, pp. 299–302; Weigley, *Eisenhower's Lieutenants*, pp. 307–309; D'Este, *Decision in Normandy*, pp. 457–458; Bennett, *Ultra in the West*, pp. 121–124; *Cross of Lorraine*, pp. 43–46; *Paths of Armor*, pp. 56–71, 5th Armored Division, AAR, 5th Armored Division Web site; D'Este, "Falaise: The Trap Not Sprung," *Military History Quarterly*, pp. 64–66; Adolph Rosengarten, "With Ultra from Omaha Beach to Weimar, Germany A Personal View," *Military Affairs*, October 1978, pp. 127–129. The 79th Division and the 5th Armored made it to Dreux against almost no resistance. Other formations, like the 5th Infantry Division, the 4th and 7th Armored, were also on the advance, liberating such places as Chartres and Orleans.
8. Blumenson, *Breakout and Pursuit*, pp. 525–530; *Battle of the Generals*, pp. 229–230; D'Este, *Decision in Normandy*, p. 457; Weigley, *Eisenhower's Lieutenants*, pp. 309–311; Bradley, *Soldier's Story*, p. 379; Bradley and Blair, *General's Life*, pp. 303–304; Colby, *War from the Ground Up*, pp. 214–216; Florentin, *Battle of the Falaise Gap*, pp. 165–170.

9. Blumenson, *Breakout and Pursuit*, pp. 530–534; Colby, *War from the Ground Up*, pp. 221–223; Jack Prince, unpublished memoir, pp. 30–31, EC.

10. Williams, "Combat Boots," www.tankbooks.com.

11. Brown, interview with Elson, www.tankbooks.com.

12. Colby, *War from the Ground Up*, pp. 207–208, 220–223; Florentin, *Battle of the Falaise Gap*, pp. 201–203; Morse Johnson to mother, 8/18/44, reproduced at www.tankbooks.com Web site.

13. Florentin, *Battle of the Falaise Gap*, pp. 196–201.

14. Elson, *Tanks for the Memories*; Joe Bernardino, interview with Mr. Aaron Elson, 8/27/94, and Sam Cropanese, interview with Mr. Aaron Elson, 5/17/93, both interviews reproduced at www.tankbooks.com.

15. Blumenson, *Breakout and Pursuit*, p. 541; Colby, *War from the Ground Up*, pp. 223–225; Elson, *Tanks for the Memories*; Dunn, *Fighter Pilot*, p. 147; Hallion *Air Power over the Normandy Beaches and Beyond*. During the closing of the pocket, the British 2nd Tactical Air Force alone averaged 1,200 sorties per day.

16. Blumenson, *Breakout and Pursuit*, pp. 537–555; Keegan, *Six Armies in Normandy*, pp. 276–282; Colby, *War from the Ground Up*, pp. 228–242; Florentin, *Battle of the Falaise Gap*, pp. 303–304; John Warner, interview with Mr. Aaron Elson, circa 1995, www.tankbooks.com.

17. Blumenson, *Breakout and Pursuit*, pp. 555–558; Florentin, *Battle of the Falaise Gap*, p. 324.

18. Blumenson, *Breakout and Pursuit*, p. 558; Colby, *War from the Ground Up*, pp. 231, 240–241; Wilson, *If You Survive*, pp. 57–58; Baldridge, *Victory Road*, p. 71; Elson, *Tanks for the Memories*; Warner, interview with Elson, www.tankbooks.com.

19. Chandler, *The Papers of Dwight David Eisenhower*, volume 5, p. 164; Florentin, *Battle of the Falaise Gap*, pp. 320–322; D'Este, *Eisenhower*, pp. 571–572; Eisenhower, *Crusade in Europe*, pp. 279–280.

20. Blumenson, *Breakout and Pursuit*, pp. 700–701; Hastings, *Overlord*, p. 313; Neillands, *Battle of Normandy*, pp. 411–412.

SELECT BIBLIOGRAPHY

Archives and Manuscript Collections

Carlisle, PA. United States Army Military History Institute.

Champaign, IL. 3rd Armored Division Archives, University of Illinois.

Columbia, MO. Western Historical Manuscript Collection, University of Missouri–Columbia, World War II Letters.

Knoxville, TN. University of Tennessee Special Collections Library, World War II Collection (repository of the Center for the Study of War and Society).

New Orleans, LA. Dwight D. Eisenhower Center.

Savannah, GA. The Mighty Eighth Air Force Heritage Museum Archives.

Books

Ambrose, Stephen. *The Supreme Commander: The War Years of General Dwight D Eisenhower.* Garden City, NY: Doubleday, 1970.

———. *Band of Brothers.* New York: Simon and Schuster, 1992.

———. *D-Day: The Climactic Battle of World War II.* New York: Simon and Schuster, 1994.

———. *Citizen Soldiers: The U.S. Army from the Beaches of Normandy to the Surrender of Germany.* New York: Simon and Schuster, 1997.

Astor, Gerald. *June 6, 1944: The Voices of D-Day.* New York: Dell, 1994.

———. *The Mighty Eighth: The Air War in Europe As Told by the Men Who Fought it.* New York: Dell, 1997.

———. *The Greatest War: Americans in Combat, 1941–1945.* Novato, CA: Presidio Press, 2000. Baldridge, Robert. *Victory Road.* Bennington, VT: Merriam Press, 1999.

Balkoski, Joseph. *Beyond the Beachhead: The 29th Infantry Division in Normandy*. Harrisburg, PA: Stackpole Books, 1989.

Bando, Mark. *Breakout at Normandy: The 2nd Armored Division in the Land of the Dead*. Osceola, WI: Motor Books International, 1999.

——. *101st Airborne: The Screaming Eagles at Normandy*. Osceola, WI: Motor Books International, 2001.

——. *The 101st Airborne at Normandy*. Osceola, WI: Motor Books International, 1994.

Baxter, Colin. *The Normandy Campaign, 1944: A Selected Bibliography*. Westport, CT: Greenwood Press, 1992.

Bedell Smith, Walter. *Eisenhower's Six Great Decisions*. New York: Longmans, Green, 1956.

Bennett, Ralph. *Ultra in the West: The Normandy Campaign, 1944–1945*. New York: Charles Scribner's Sons, 1979.

Biggs, Bradley. *Gavin*. Hamden, CT: Archon Books, 1980.

Binkoski, Joseph, and Arthur Plaut. *The 115th Infantry Regiment in World War II*. Washington, DC: Infantry Journal Press, 1948.

Black, Robert, W. *Rangers in World War II*. New York: Ballantine Books, 1992.

Blair, Clay. *Ridgway's Paratroopers: The American Airborne in World War II*. Garden City, NY: Doubleday, 1985.

Blanchard, W. J. *Our Liberators: The Combat History of the 746th Tank Battalion During World War II*. Tucson, AZ: Fenestra Books, 2003.

Blumenson, Martin. *The United States Army in World War II: Breakout and Pursuit*. Washington, DC: Office of the Chief of Military History, Department of the Army, 1961.

——, editor. *The Patton Papers, 1940–1945*. Boston: Houghton Mifflin, 1974.

——. *The Battle of the Generals: The Untold Story of the Falaise Pocket—The Campaign That Should Have Won World War II*. New York: William Morrow, 1993.

——. *Patton: The Man Behind the Legend, 1885–1945*. New York: Berkley Books, 1985.

Booth, T. Michael, and Duncan Spencer. *Paratrooper: The Life of Gen. James M. Gavin*. New York: Simon and Schuster, 1994.

Bradley, Omar. *A Soldier's Story*. New York: Henry Holt, 1951.

—— and Clay Blair. *A General's Life: An Autobiography by General of the Army Omar Bradley*. New York: Simon and Schuster, 1983.

Bradley, Robert. *Aid Man!* New York: Vantage Press, 1970.

Brawley, John. *Anyway, We Won: Out of the Ozarks and into the Army in World War Two*. Marceline, MO. Walsworth, 1988.

Breast, John, editor. *Missions Remembered: Recollection of the WWII Air War*. Brentwood, TN: J.M. Productions, 1995.

Brereton, Louis. *The Brereton Diaries*. New York: William Morrow, 1946.

Breuer, William. *Death of a Nazi Army: The Falaise Pocket*. Chelsea, MI: Scarborough House, 1990.

Burgett, Donald. *Currahee! A Screaming Eagle at Normandy*. Novato, CA: Presidio Press, 1999.

Butcher, Harry, S. *My Three Years with Eisenhower: The Personal Diary of Captain Harry C. Butcher*. New York: Simon and Schuster, 1946.

Carafano, James Jay. *After D-Day: Operation Cobra and the Normandy Breakout*. Boulder, CO: Lynne Rienner, 2000.

Carrell, Paul. *Invasion: They're Coming*. New York: Bantam Books, 1962.

Carroll, Andrew, editor. *War Letters: Extraordinary Correspondence from American Wars*. New York: Scribner, 2001.

Carter, Kit, and Robert Mueller, editors. *The Army Air Forces in World War II: Combat Chronology, 1941–1945*. Washington, DC: Office of Air Force History, 1973.

Cawthon, Charles. *Other Clay: A Remembrance of the World War II Infantry*. Boulder: University Press of Colorado, 1990.

Chandler, Alfred, editor. *The Papers of Dwight David Eisenhower: The War Years*. Vols. 3, 4, and 5. Baltimore: Johns Hopkins Press, 1970.

Coffman, Warren. *I Never Intended to Be a Soldier*. Greensboro, NC: Lifestyles Press, 1999.

Colby, John. *War from the Ground Up. The 90th Division in World War II*. Austin, TX: Nortex Press, 1991.

Collins, J. Lawton. *Lightning Joe: An Autobiography*. Baton Rouge: Louisiana State University Press, 1979.

Cooling, Benjamin Franklin. *Case Studies in the Development of Close Air Support*. Washington, DC: Office of Air Force History, United States Air Force, 1990.

Cosmas, Graham, and Albert Cowdrey. *The United States Army in World War II: Medical Service in the European Theater of Operations*. Washington, DC: Center of Military History, United States Army, 1992.

Cowdrey, Albert. *Fighting for Life: American Military Medicine in World War II*. New York: Free Press, 1994.

Craven, Wesley, and James Lea Cate, editors. *The Army Air Forces in World War II: Europe: Argument to V-E Day, January 1944 to May 1945*. Washington, DC: Office of Air Force History, 1983; reprint of 1951 edition.

Curley, Charles. *How a Ninety-Day Wonder Survived the War: The Story of a Rifle Platoon Leader in the Second Indian Head Division During World War II*. Richmond and Petersburg, VA: Dietz Press, 1998.

Danner, Brayton. *A Bad Day near St. Lô, and Other Remarkable Stories of World War II*. Self published, 1999.

Daugherty, Leo. *The Battle of the Hedgerows: Bradley's First Army in Normandy, June–July 1944*. Hong Kong: MBI Publishing Company, 2001.

Davis, Richard. *Carl A. Spaatz and the Air War in Europe.* Washington, DC: Center for Air Force History, 1993.

Dawson, Forrest, editor. *Saga of the All American.* Nashville, TN: Battery Press; reprint of 1946 edition.

D'Este, Carlo. *Decision in Normandy.* Old Saybrook, CT: Konecky and Konecky, 1984.

———. *Patton: A Genius for War.* New York: HarperPerennial, 1995.

———. *Eisenhower: A Soldier's Life.* New York: Henry Holt, 2002.

Doubler, Michael. *Closing with the Enemy: How GIs Fought the War in Europe, 1944–1945.* Lawrence: University Press of Kansas, 1994.

Drez, Ronald, editor. *Voices of D-Day: The Story of the Allied Invasion Told by Those Who Were There.* Baton Rouge: Louisiana State University Press, 1994.

Dunn, William. *Fighter Pilot: The First American Ace of World War II.* Lexington: University Press of Kentucky, 1982.

Dupuy, Trevor. *A Genius for War: The German Army and General Staff, 1807–1945.* Englewood Cliffs, NJ: Prentice-Hall, 1977.

Eisenhower, David. *Eisenhower at War, 1943–1945.* New York: Vintage Books, 1986.

Eisenhower, Dwight, D. *Crusade in Europe.* New York: Doubleday, 1948.

Eisenhower Foundation. *D-Day: The Normandy Invasion in Retrospect.* Lawrence: University Press of Kansas, 1971.

Elson, Aaron. *Tanks for the Memories: The 712th Tank Battalion During World War II.* Chi Chi Books, 2002; reproduced at www.tankbooks.com.

Ewing, Joseph. *29 Let's Go! A History of the 29th Infantry Division in World War II.* Washington, DC: Infantry Journal Press, 1948.

Featherston, Alwyn. *Saving the Breakout: The 30th Division's Heroic Stand at Mortain, August 7–12, 1944.* Novato, CA: Presidio Press, 1993.

Fletcher, Eugene. *Fletcher's Gang: A B-17 Crew in Europe, 1944–1945.* Seattle and London: University of Washington Press, 1988.

Florentin, Eddy. *The Battle of the Falaise Gap.* Translated by Mervyn Savill. New York: Hawthorn Books, 1965.

Folkestad, William. *The View from the Turret: The 743rd Tank Battalion During World War II.* Shippensburg, PA: Burd Street Press, 2000.

Fortier, Norman "Bud." *An Ace of the Eighth: An American Fighter Pilot's Air War in Europe.* New York: Ballantine Books, Presidio Press, 2003.

Fowle, Barry, and Floyd Wright. *The 51st Again: An Engineer Combat Battalion in World War II.* Shippensburg, PA: White Mane Publishing, 1992.

François, Dominique. *507th Parachute Infantry Regiment, 1942–1945.* Bayeux, France: Heimdal, 2000.

Freeman, Roger. *The Mighty Eighth: A History of the U.S. 8th Army Air Force.* Garden City, NY: Doubleday, 1970.

Gabreski, Francis, *Gabby: A Fighter Pilot's Life as told to Carl Molesworth*. New York: Orion Books, 1991.

Gavin, James. *On to Berlin: A Fighting General's True Story of Airborne Combat in World War II*. New York: Bantam Books, 1978.

Giles, Janice. *The G.I. Journal of Sergeant Giles*. Boston: Houghton Mifflin, 1965.

Gordon, Harold. *One Man's War: A Memoir of World War II*. New York: Apex Press, 1999.

Greisbach, Marc. *Combat History of the Eighth Infantry Division in World War II*. Nashville, TN: Battery Press, 1988; reprint of 1945 edition.

Harrison, Gordon. *The United States Army in World War II: Cross Channel Attack*. Washington, DC: Office of the Chief of Military History, Department of the Army, 1951.

Hart, Basil Liddell. *The German Generals Talk*. New York: William Morrow, 1948.

Hastings, Max. *Overlord: D-Day and the Battle for Normandy*. New York: Simon and Schuster, 1984.

Hayhow, Ernie. *The Thunderbolt Across Europe: A History of the 83rd Infantry Division, 1942–1945*. Munich, Germany: F. Bruckmann, K.G., 1945.

Headquarters, First Army, U.S. Army. *Report of Operations, 20 October 1943–1 August 1944*. 7 vols. Carlisle Barracks, PA: United States Army Military History Institute, 1945.

Headquarters, First Army, U.S. Army. *Report of Operations, 1 August 1944–22 February 1945*. 4 vols. Carlisle Barracks, PA: United States Army Military History Institute, 1945.

Hesketh, Roger. *Fortitude: The D-Day Deception Campaign*. Woodstock, NY: Overlook Press, 2002.

Hewitt, Robert. *Work Horse of the Western Front: The Story of the 30th Infantry Division*. Washington, DC: Infantry Journal Press, 1946.

Hirshson, Stanley. *General Patton: A Soldier's Life*. New York: HarperCollins, 2002.

Historical Division, Department of the Army. *Utah Beach to Cherbourg, 6 June–27 June*. Washington, DC: Center of Military History, United States Army, 1984.

———. *Omaha Beachhead*. Washington, D.C.: Center of Military History, United States Army, 1945.

———. *Small Unit Actions: France, 2d Ranger Battalion at Pointe du Hoc, Saipan, 27th Division of Tanapag Plain, Italy, 351st Infantry at Santa Maria Infante, France, 4th Armored Division at Singling*. Washington, DC: Center of Military History, United States Army, 1982.

———. *St-Lô, 7 July–19 July*. Washington, DC: Center of Military History, United States Army, 1946 and 1984 reprint.

Houston, Donald. *Hell on Wheels: The 2nd Armored Division*. Novato, CA: Presidio Press, 1977.

Hughes, Thomas Alexander. *Overlord: General Pete Quesada and the Triumph of Tactical Air Power in World War II*. New York: Free Press, 1995.

Huston, James. *Biography of a Battalion: The Life and Times of an Infantry Battalion in Europe in World War II*. Mechanicsburg, PA: Stackpole Books, 2003, reprint of 1958 edition.

Irving, David. *Hitler's War*. New York: Avon Books, 1990.

Jeffers, H. Paul. *Theodore Roosevelt: The Life of a War Hero*. Novato, CA: Presidio Press, 2002.

Jensen, Marvin. *Strike Swiftly! The 70th Tank Battalion from North Africa to Normandy to Germany*. Novato, CA: Presidio Press, 1997.

Johns, Glover. *The Clay Pigeons of St. Lô*. Harrisburg, PA: Stackpole Books, 2002, originally published in 1958.

Johnson, Franklyn. *One More Hill*. New York: Bantam Books, 1983.

Johnson, Gerden. *History of the Twelfth Infantry Regiment in World War II*. Boston: 12th Infantry Regiment Association, 1947.

Karig, Walter, et al. *Battle Report: The Atlantic War*. New York: Rinehart, 1946.

Keegan, John. *Six Armies in Normandy*. New York: Penguin Books, 1982.

Kershaw, Alex. *The Bedford Boys: One American Town's Ultimate D-Day Sacrifice*. Cambridge, MA: DaCapo Press, 2003.

Knickerbocker, H. R., et al. *Danger Forward: The Story of the First Division in World War II*. Nashville, TN: Battery Press, 2002; reprint of 1947 edition.

Kohn, Richard, and Joseph Harahan, editors. *Condensed Analysis of the Ninth Air Force in the European Theater of Operations*. Washington, DC: Office of Air Force History, United States Air Force, 1984.

Koskimaki, George. *D-Day with the Screaming Eagles*. Medalia, MN: House of Print, 1970.

Koyen, Kenneth. *The Fourth Armored Division: From the Beach to Bavaria*. Nashville, TN: Battery Press, 2000; reprint of 1946 edition.

Lewis, Adrian. *Omaha Beach: A Flawed Victory*. Chapel Hill: University of North Carolina Press, 2001.

Litoff, Judy Barrett, and David Smith, editors. *Fighting Fascism in Europe: The World War II Letters of an American Veteran of the Spanish Civil War*. New York: Fordham University Press, 2003.

Mansoor, Peter. *The G.I. Offensive in Europe: The Triumph of American Infantry Divisions*. Lawrence: University Press of Kansas, 1999.

Marshall, S. L. A. *Night Drop: The American Airborne Invasion of Normandy*. Boston: Little, Brown, 1962.

Masters, Charles. *Glidermen of Neptune: The American D-Day Glider Attack*. Carbondale: Southern Illinois University Press, 1995.

Mauer, Mauer, editor. *Air Force Combat Units of World War II*. Washington, DC: Office of Air Force History, 1983.

McDonald, JoAnna. *The Liberation of Pointe du Hoc: The 2nd U.S. Rangers at Normandy, June 6–8, 1944*. Redondo Beach, CA: Rank and File Publications, 2000.

McManus, John C. *Deadly Brotherhood: The American Combat Soldier in World War II*. Novato, CA: Presidio Press, 1998.

———. *Deadly Sky: The American Combat Airman in World War II*. Novato, CA: Presidio Press, 2000.

Miller, Merle. *Ike the Soldier, As They Knew Him*. New York: G. P. Putnam's Sons, 1987.

Millett, Allan, and Williamson Murray. *A War to Be Won: Fighting the Second World War*. Cambridge, MA: Harvard University Press, 2000.

Mittelman, Joseph. *Eight Stars to Victory: A History of the Veteran Ninth U.S. Infantry Division*. Nashville, TN: Battery Press, 1948.

Morison, Samuel Eliot. *History of United States Naval Operations in World War II: The Invasion of France and Germany, 1944–1945*. Boston: Little, Brown, 1957.

Murphy, Edward. *Heroes of WWII*. New York: Ballantine Books, 1990.

Neillands, Robert. *The Battle of Normandy, 1944*. London: Cassell, 2002.

Neillands, Robin, and Roderick De Normann. *D-Day 1944: Voices from Normandy*. New York: Orion Books, 1993.

O'Donnell, Patrick. *Beyond Valor: World War II's Ranger and Airborne Veterans Reveal the Heart of Combat*. New York: Free Press, 2001.

Parillo, Mark, editor. *We Were in the Big One: Experiences of the World War II Generation*. Wilmington, DE: Scholarly Resources, 2002.

Perret, Geoffrey. *Eisenhower*. Holbrook, MA: Adams Media Corporation, 1999.

Pogue, Forrest. *The United States Army in World War II: The Supreme Command, the European Theater of Operations*. Washington, DC: Center of Military History, United States Army, 1996.

———. *Pogue's War: Diaries of a WWII Combat Historian*. Lexington: University Press of Kentucky, 2001.

Prados, Edward, editor. *Neptunus Rex: Naval Stories of the Normandy Invasion, June 6, 1944*. Novato, CA: Presidio Press, 1998.

Price, Frank James. *Troy H. Middleton: A Biography*. Baton Rouge: Louisiana State University Press, 1974.

Pulver, Murray. *The Longest Year*. Freeman, SD: Pine Hill Press, 1986.

Pyle, Ernie. *Brave Men*. New York: Grosset and Dunlap, 1944.

Rapport, Leonard, and Arthur Norwood. *Rendezvous with Destiny: A History of the 101st Airborne Division*. Nashville, TN: Battery Press, 2000; reprint of 1948 edition.

Reardon, Mark. *Victory at Mortain: Stopping Hitler's Panzer Counteroffensive.* Lawrence: University Press of Kansas, 2002.

Reeder, Red. *Born at Reveille.* New York: Duell, Sloane, and Pearce, 1966.

Richlak, Jerry. *Glide to Glory: Unedited Personal Stories from the Airborne Glidermen of World War II.* Chesterland, OH: Cedar House, 2002.

Ridgway, Matthew. *Soldier: The Memoirs of Matthew B. Ridgway.* New York: Harper and Brothers, 1956.

Rohmer, Richard. *Patton's Gap: An Account of the Battle of Normandy, 1944.* New York: Beaufort, 1981.

Roscoe, Theodore. *United States Destroyer Operations in World War II.* Annapolis, MD: Naval Institute Press, 1953.

Ruppenthal, Roland. *The United States Army in World War II: European Theater of Operations, Logistical Support of the Armies.* Washington, DC: Center of Military History, United States Army, 1995, vol. 1.

Rust, Kenn. *The 9th Air Force in World War II.* Fallbrook, CA: Aero Publishers, 1967.

Ryan, Cornelius. *The Longest Day.* New York: Simon and Schuster, 1959.

Shrader, Charles. *Amicide: The Problem of Friendly Fire in Modern War.* Fort Leavenworth, KS: U.S. Army Command and General Staff College, 1982.

Smith, Dale. *Screaming Eagle: Memoirs of a B-17 Group Commander.* Chapel Hill, NC: Algonquin Books, 1990.

Smith, Samuel E, editor. *The United States Navy in World War II.* New York: Quill/William Morrow, 1966.

Spencer, Henry Grady. *Nineteen Days in June 1944.* Kansas City, MO: Lowell Press, 1984.

Street, Thomas. *How to Survive Combat as Point Man If You're Lucky . . . and Lose Friends If They're Not.* Bennington, VT: Merriam Press, 2002.

Sullivan, John. *Overlord's Eagles: Operations of the United States Army Air Forces in the Invasion of Normandy in World War II.* Jefferson, NC: McFarland, 1997.

Tapert, Anette, editor. *Lines of Battle: Letters from American Servicemen, 1941–1945.* New York: Times Books, 1987.

Taylor, Barbara. *Miss You: The World War II Letters of Barbara Woodall Taylor and Charles E. Taylor.* Athens: University of Georgia Press, 1990.

Taylor, Maxwell. *Swords into Plowshares: A Memoir.* New York: DaCapo Press, 1972.

Towne, Allen. *Doctor Danger Forward: A World War II Memoir of a Combat Medical Aidman, First Infantry Division.* Jefferson, NC: McFarland, 2000.

True, William, and Deryck Tufts True. *The Cow Spoke French: The Story of Sgt. William True, American Paratrooper in World War II.* Bennington, VT: Merriam Press, 2002.

Tucker, William. *D-Day: Thirty-five Days in Normandy, Reflections of a Paratrooper.* Harwichport, MA: International Airborne Books, 2002.

Tute, Warren, John Costello, and Terry Hughes. *D-Day*. Sidgwick and Jackson, 1974.

United States Army Air Force. *Ultra and the History of the United States Strategic Air Force in Europe vs. the German Air Force*. Frederick, MD: University Publications of America, 1980.

United States Army Evacuation Hospital No. 77. *Medicine Under Canvas: A War Journal of the 77th Evacuation Hospital*. Kansas City, MO: Sosland Press, 1949.

Van Creveld, Martin. *Fighting Power: German and U.S. Army Performance, 1939–1945*. Westport, CT: Greenwood Press, 1982.

Vannoy, Allyn, and Jay Karamales. *Against the Panzers: United States Infantry Versus German Tanks, 1944–1945*. Jefferson, NC: McFarland, 1996.

von Luck, Hans. *Panzer Commander*. New York: Dell, 1989.

Waddell, Steve. *United States Army Logistics: The Normandy Campaign, 1944*. Westport, CT: Greenwood Press, 1994.

Webster, David. *Parachute Infantry: An American Paratrooper's Memoir of D-Day and the Fall of the Third Reich*. Baton Rouge: Louisiana State University Press, 1994.

Weigley, Russell. *Eisenhower's Lieutenants: The Campaign of France and Germany, 1944–1945*. Bloomington: Indiana University Press, 1981.

Weiss, Robert. *Enemy North, South, East, West: A Recollection of the "Lost Battalion" at Mortain, France*. Portland, OR: Strawberry Hill Press, 1998.

———. *Fire Mission! The Siege at Mortain, Normandy, August 1944*. Shippensburg, PA: Burd Street Press, 2002.

Wills, Deryk. *Put on Your Boots and Parachutes: Personal Stories of the Veterans of the United States 82nd Airborne Division*. Leicester: AB Printers, 1997.

Wilmot, Chester. *The Struggle for Europe*. New York: Harper and Brothers, 1952.

Wilson, George. *If You Survive*. New York: Ivy Books, 1987.

Wilson, Theodore, editor. *D-Day 1944*. Lawrence: University Press of Kansas, 1994.

Wolfe, Martin. *Green Light! A Troop Carrier Squadron's War from Normandy to the Rhine*. Washington, DC: Center for Air Force History, 1993.

Woodward, Ellis. *Flying School: Combat Hell*. Baltimore, MD: American Literary Press, 1998.

Zuckerman, Solly. *From Apes to Warlords*. London: Hamish Hamilton, 1978.

INDEX OF SUBJECTS AND PERSONS

Note: For military units, see the Index of Military Units.

INDEX OF MILITARY UNITS